Fichte

A thematic biography of the German philosopher Johann Gottlieb Fichte from birth to his resignation from his university position at Jena in 1799 due to the Atheism Conflict, this work explains how Fichte contributed to modern conceptions of selfhood; how he sought to make the moral agency of the self efficacious in a modern public culture; and the critical role he assigned philosophy in the construal and assertion of selfhood and in the creation of a new public sphere. Using the writings and private papers now available in the *Gesamtausgabe*, the study historicizes these themes by tracing their development within several contexts, including the German Lutheran tradition, the eighteenth-century culture of sensibility, the late Enlightenment, the Kantian philosophical revolution, the politics of the revolutionary era, and the emergence of modern German universities. It includes a reinterpretation of Fichte's political theory and philosophy of law, his antisemitism, and his controversial views on gender and marriage.

Anthony J. La Vopa is a professor of history at North Carolina State University.

FICHTE

The Self and the Calling of Philosophy, 1762–1799

ANTHONY J. LA VOPA

North Carolina State University

CAMBRIDGE
UNIVERSITY PRESS

PUBLISHED BY THE PRESS SYNDICATE OF THE UNIVERSITY OF CAMBR
The Pitt Building, Trumpington Street, Cambridge, United Kingdom

CAMBRIDGE UNIVERSITY PRESS
The Edinburgh Building, Cambridge CB2, 2RU, UK
40 West 20th Street, New York, NY 10011-4211, USA
10 Stamford Road, Oakleigh, VIC 3166, Australia
Ruiz de Alarcón 13, 28014 Madrid, Spain
Dock House, The Waterfront, Cape Town 8001, South Africa

http://www.cambridge.org

© Anthony J. La Vopa   2001

First published 2001

Printed in the United States of America

Typeface Bembo 11/12 pt.   *System* QuarkXPress [BTS]

A catalog record for this book is available from the British Library.

Library of Congress Cataloging in Publication data
La Vopa, Anthony J., 1945–
Fichte; the self and the calling of philosophy, 1762–1799 / Anthony J. La Vopa.
p.   cm.
Includes index.
ISBN 0-521-79145-6
1. Fichte, Johann Gottlieb, 1762–1814.   2. Philosophers – Germany – Biography.   I. Title.
B2847.L38   2001
193 – dc21
[B]   00-033698

ISBN   0 521 79145 6   hardback

For Gail

Contents

Foreword

I conceived this volume as a biography, the history of a man in his youth and the first two decades of his adulthood. A biography, I would insist, is what it has become. But since Johann Gottlieb Fichte was first and foremost a philosopher, and since I have taken pains to grasp and convey the meaning of his philosophy, the organization is as much thematic as it is chronological. And so the reader may find it useful to have a brief narrative map at the outset.

The volume covers the first thirty-seven years of Fichte's life, from his birth in 1762 to his resignation from his university position at Jena in 1799. By 1799 Fichte had spent five prodigiously productive years at Jena, lecturing to packed halls of students, and publishing the texts in which he constructed the philosophical system he called Transcendental Idealism. In lifestyle he was an eminently respectable bourgeois scholar; but there had been little of the ordinary about his route to an academic career, and, though he seemed to plunge philosophy into a new era of self-absorption, his thought also had alarmingly radical implications for the social and political order.

In 1770, at age eight or nine, Fichte had been suddenly removed from a village world of weaving and farming by a visiting nobleman who undertook to sponsor his education for the clergy. The nobleman had died by the time Fichte ended his university studies in the mid-1780s. For the next six years or so the young scholar had to earn his bread as a live-in tutor while seeking the new patron who might secure him a clerical appointment. It was a tutoring position that brought him to Zürich in 1788. There he became informally betrothed to Marie Johanne Rahn, known as Johanna, the daughter of a local patrician. Having failed to find a career opening in Leipzig in 1790, he returned to tutoring. His last tutoring stint was on a Baltic estate near Danzig. He did not return to Zürich to marry Johanna until the early summer of 1793. On July 18, 1796, Johanna gave birth to their only child, a son named Immanuel Hartmann.

The son's first name was a gesture of homage to Immanuel Kant. In the late summer and early fall of 1790, as he engaged Kant's *Critiques* for the first time, Fichte had found his calling as a philosopher. In the summer of 1791, in a hiatus between tutoring employments, he traveled to Königsberg to make Kant's acquaintance and, in an effort to impress him, wrote a Kantian critique of the concept of revelation. Published anonymously, the book was greeted with lavish praise as Kant's long-awaited contribution to the era's controversies about faith and reason. Once Kant revealed the real author, Fichte was virtually assured an academic career.

In May 1794 Fichte began his career at Jena, a university thriving under the enlightened rule of the ducal government at nearby Weimar. If he was a promising young celebrity, he was also a figure of some notoriety. His intemperate defense of the principles of the French Revolution, published in 1793, had made him suspect as an atheistic "Jacobin" in conservative circles. His first year at Jena was marked by bitter squabbles with the local clergy and indignant senior professors. To make matters worse, his efforts to mediate between the ducal government and secret student societies earned him the latter's wrath.

Fichte's next few years at Jena were fairly quiet, though his brutal polemicism caused concern even among philosophers sympathetic to his cause. He extended his system outward from its metaphysical core to the philosophy of law, ethics, and political economy. But his publication of an article on "the concept of religion" in November 1798 provoked the Atheism Conflict, which soon engaged the German intelligentsia in a controversy about the meaning of, and the appropriate limits to, academic freedom. Outmaneuvered by the ducal government and disillusioned by his failure to rally the "enlightened" public to his cause, he resigned his position and, in the opening months of the new century, moved his family to Berlin.

Acknowledgments

Though writing itself is a solitary act, this book – like the life of its subject – took shape in contexts rich in conversations, discussions, and unexpected encounters. Most of these occurred in institutions, both public and private, that make the study of the humanities a practical possibility in our era and that provide the settings for the collegial relationships and the friendships on which scholarship thrives.

In the spring of 1987, as I was committing myself, in very gingerly steps, to writing a biography with emphatically German themes, I was also commuting week after week to Washington, D.C., to attend J. G. A. Pocock's seminar at the Folger Library on eighteenth-century Anglo-Scottish and American political thought. My thanks to the Folger staff, and especially to John Pocock, who gave me, in his uniquely Anglophone way, precisely the set of comparative questions I needed.

I spent the academic year 1989–90 as a Fellow at the Woodrow Wilson International Center for Scholars, now housed in the Reagan Building but then (fortunately) still making do with a wing of the Smithsonian's Castle Building on the Mall. Charles Blitzer, the Center's director at the time, was a rare combination of scholarly cultivation, political savvy, and personal integrity. I take this occasion to mourn his passing. I would also like to acknowledge with gratitude his remarkable contribution to the survival of serious humanistic scholarship in the United States – a contribution that has been sadly disparaged in recent outbreaks of partisan savagery inside the Beltway.

Further progress on the book was made possible by a research grant from the American Philosophical Society in 1990; by a research fellowship from the National Endowment for the Humanities in 1994; and by a summer research stipend from the College of Humanities and Social Sciences at North Carolina State University/Raleigh in 1998.

Critical to the researching of the book were two visits to the Max-Planck-Institut für Geschichte in Göttingen, a unique and irreplaceable center for the study of eighteenth-century Germany. Thanks, once more, to my friends there – Hans Erich Bödeker, Inge Bödeker, Alf Lüdtke, Helga Lüdtke, Hans Medick, and Jürgen Schlumbohm – for their hospitality and their good company.

Chapters of the book were presented and critiqued at the Center for Seventeenth and Eighteenth Century Studies at the University of

California, Los Angeles; the Modern European History Colloquium at Louisiana State University; and the seminar of the Committee on the Conceptual Foundations of Science at the University of Chicago. Thanks especially to Peter Reill, director of the Center, and to Patrick Coleman, Jill Kowalik, Jayne Lewis, and Ellen Wilson (the exacting but tactful editor every scholar wishes for) in Los Angeles; to Suzanne Marchand, David Lindenfeld, and Jerri Becnel in Baton Rouge; and to Jan Goldstein and Constantin Fasolt in Chicago.

In ways I can hardly begin to fathom at this point, the book – and my professional life – have profited from my participation in the Triangle Intellectual History Seminar and Graduate Program. I am grateful to the group, which helped me revise three chapters in draft, and especially to the five other coordinators of the program, Charles Capper, Malachi Hacohen, Lloyd Kramer, Martin Miller, and K. Steven Vincent. Visitors will agree, I think, that we have created a badly needed national center for the study of intellectual history. I can confirm from the sessions on my own work that the Seminar combines, to an unusual degree, rigorous critique and reassuring collegiality.

Thanks in part to another fellowship from the National Endowment for the Humanities, I finished writing the book in 1998–99 as a Fellow – or, more precisely, a recidivist – at the National Humanities Center. Just in case there is anyone out there who hasn't heard yet, the Center is a wonderful place to work. The credit goes to Robert Connor, its director, to Kent Mullikin, its associate director, and to its entire dedicated staff. My thanks especially to Karen Carroll, without whose dauntless creativity in cyberspace the manuscript would never have been printed; to Patricia Schreiber, Sarah Woodard, and Lois Whittington, who guided me, very patiently, through my fledgling efforts as an academic administrator and kept me cheerful at harried moments; and to the Center's librarians, Alan Tuttle, Jean Houston, and Eliza Robertson.

My work also benefited immeasurably from the lively and convivial lunch sessions of the Biography Group at the National Humanities Center, which taught me so much about the craft of biographical writing and made my year at the Center all the more special. I extend my thanks and my warm greetings to Janet Beizer, Jon Bush, Ed Friedman, Rochelle Gurstein, R. W. B. Lewis, Elizabeth McHenry, Wilfrid Prest, Marilynn Richtarik, Ashraf Rushdy, Bert Wyatt-Brown, and Anne Wyatt-Brown.

Aside from many of the people mentioned above, the following read and commented on parts of the manuscript and offered needed encouragement: James Banker, Frederick Beiser, Holly Brewer, Erin Conroy, David Gilmartin, Gerald Izenberg, Owen Kalinga, Akram Khater, Mimi Kim, Lawrence Klein, Keith Luria, Nancy Mitchell, Catherine Peyroux, Fritz Ringer, John Röhl, Michael Sauter, Matthew Specter, Edith Sylla, Kenneth Vickery, Mack Walker, and Hugh West.

Thanks also to Joy Burke Raintree, whose meticulous assistance at the copyediting stage spared me many errors.

During my year at the National Humanities Center it was my great good fortune to have Suzanne Raitt as a colleague. Though busy completing a biography of her own, Suzanne managed to devote more time and thoughtful attention to my work than one can reasonably expect from a colleague, and particularly from one accustomed to engaging material far more rewarding to the literary imagination. She read and critiqued the entire manuscript, shared with me her own interest in philosophy, and strengthened me in my resolve to make the substance of philosophical thought an integral part of biography. She also gave me a model of elegantly seamless writing that I tried, with only limited success, to emulate.

In ways they may not realize, my mother Jane La Vopa and my stepdaughter Kelly O'Brien kept me from taking Fichte too seriously.

The book is dedicated to my spouse and colleague, Gail Williams O'Brien, a historian who worked on her own book, on a very different subject, as I worked on mine. It would be banal and, worse, inadequate to say that she gave me the support I needed to bring this project to completion. This is Gail's book as well as mine, though she has more sense than to devote years to an Idealist philosopher arrogant enough to think he had found the only way to Truth and mindfulness. She endured my obsessions and distractions, my moments (sometimes extended) of exasperation with the work, my writing blocks, my absences on research trips, my seemingly endless health problems, my prolonged crises of spirit. She kept me convinced that I could write the kind of book I wanted to write, even when the task seemed hopelessly beyond my reach. It is no fragile love that survives the long, hard writing of two books. I am profoundly grateful to her.

Abbreviations

FG   *J. G. Fichte im Gespräch. Berichte der Zeitgenossen*, ed. Erich Fuchs in collaboration with Reinhard Lauth and Walter Schieche, 6 vols. (Stuttgart/Bad Cannstatt, 1978–1992)

FR   *J. G. Fichte in zeitgenössischen Rezensionen*, ed. Erich Fuchs, Wilhelm G. Jacobs, and Walter Schieche, 4 vols. (Stuttgart/Bad Cannstatt, 1995)

F-S   *Fichte-Studien*

GA   *Johann Gottlieb Fichte. Gesamtausgabe der Bayerischen Akademie der Wissenschaften*, ed. Reinhard Lauth and Hans Gliwitzky (Stuttgart/Bad Cannstatt, 1962ff) (The roman numerals refer to the series within the edition: I. *Werke*; II. *Nachgelassene Schriften*; III. *Briefe*; IV. *Kollegnachschriften*)

GH   J. G. Fichte, *Der Geschlossene Handelsstaat. Ein philosophischer Entwurf als Anhang zur Rechtslehre zu liefernden Politik* (1800), in *Johann Gottlieb Fichte. Ausgewählte Politische Schriften*, ed. Zwi Batscha and Richard Saage (Frankfurt am Main, 1977)

NR   Johann Gottlieb Fichte, *Grundlage des Naturrechts nach Prinzipien der Wissenschaftslehre*, ed. and introd. Manfred Zahn (Hamburg, 1967)

PJ   *Philosophisches Journal einer Gesellschaft Teutscher Gelehrten*

SL   Johann Gottlieb Fichte, *Das System der Sittenlehre nach den Prinzipien der Wissenschaftslehre* (1798), ed. and introd. Manfred Zahn (Hamburg, 1969)

SSPK   Staatsbibliothek der Stiftung Preussischer Kulturbesitz, Berlin

Introduction

"The fate we share," Johann Gottlieb Fichte explained to the several hundred students who had packed into his lecture hall one evening in 1794, is that our "particular calling" entails precisely what "one's general calling as a human being" requires.[1] His own life bore witness to his conviction that the most human of callings, and the one to which Reason itself had assigned him, was philosophy. In his path to philosophy and in his practice of it, we find more than the usual share of startling turns and disillusioning struggles, all intimately connected with the cultural transformations and the political traumas of Germany and Europe in the age of the Enlightenment, the French Revolution, and the Napoleonic Wars.

In 1762, the year of Fichte's birth, the European Great Powers were limping to the end of the Seven Years War. In the same year Rousseau's *Émile* was burned by the public hangman in Paris, its author having fled the city to avoid arrest. Immanuel Kant was leading the quiet life of a bachelor and unsalaried university instructor in Könisgberg, his native city, on the far eastern edge of German-speaking Europe. Philosophically he was still in what he would later call his "dogmatic slumbers." In 1781, when Fichte was nineteeen, Kant published the first of the three *Critiques* that would leave western philosophy utterly transformed.

Like Kant and Rousseau, Fichte was of humble origins. If his ascent from plebeian obscurity to intellectual prominence was not unique, however, there was still something so stunning about it that one is tempted to share his belief that Reason had singled him out. In 1770, in the first of the seemingly miraculous turns in his destiny, he was plucked out of his family's village world of farming and weaving and set on the path to a clerical career. By 1792, when he made his debut in print, he was a fledgling philosopher with decidedly unorthodox and anticlerical views. His first major publication was originally taken to be a long-awaited work by Kant, with the result that he became, virtually overnight, the most celebrated of Kant's young disciples.

Fichte's next publications stigmatized him in many quarters as a German "Jacobin," one of that frightening new breed of intellectuals who threatened to inflict on German Europe the horrors that had befallen

[1] *Fichte. Early Philosophical Writings*, trans. and ed. Daniel Breazeale (Ithaca and London, 1988), p. 176.

revolutionary France. He would have to endure the stigma for the rest of his life. In 1794 he began a career in teaching and scholarship at the university of Jena, which was basking in the glory of Goethe's Weimar and earning more than a little glory on its own as the leading center for the study of Kant's Critical Philosophy. Fichte devoted the next five years to building, brick by brick, the philosophical "system" that he called Transcendental Idealism. To his philosophical opponents, including orthodox Kantians, his theory of the "self-positing I" seemed hopelessly solipsistic, if not megalomaniacal, and that impression was powerfully reinforced by the arrogant brutality of his public persona. In 1799 Kant himself finally issued a snarling public repudiation of Fichte's claim to have understood the "spirit" of the Critical Philosophy better than its progenitor had understood it.

Nonetheless, thanks in large part to Fichte's panache as an academic rebel and his commanding presence at the lectern, Jena remained the mecca of the German philosophical revolution through the 1790s. But the Jena moment proved to be a brief one, and for that, too, Fichte bears some responsibility. In 1798 he published the article that triggered the Atheism Conflict, one of the culminating moments in the controversies about faith and reason, religion and philosophy that had generated so much passion and had taken on such a heavy freight of political implications over the course of the eighteenth century. He tried but failed to use the Conflict to win recognition for a principle of academic freedom that we now take for granted, and his maneuverings cost him his university position.

The chief setting for the remainder of his career, not covered in this volume, was Berlin, where he moved in 1799 and where, under French occupation, he delivered the famous *Addresses to the German Nation* in 1807–08. Even his death from cholera in 1814 was bound up with the great public events of the day. He had contracted the disease from his wife, who was nursing soldiers wounded in the War of Liberation against Napoleon.

If Fichte's life was eventful and controversial, it was also, by any number of standards, of considerable intellectual significance. He does not, to be sure, enjoy the same stature as Kant or Hegel or Hume. If contemporary philosophers were asked to vote their choices for a Pantheon of Great Western Philosophers, and if they could reach anything like a consensus (a very dubious proposition), Fichte would almost certainly not be among the chosen few. And yet even scholars who find his philosophy thoroughly wrongheaded acknowledge its historical importance as the foundation stone of that immense edifice known as German Idealism and as a prime example of the "foundationalism" and "essentialism" that marked the western philosophical project until at least the late nineteenth century. Outside philosophy proper, Fichte's thought figures prominently in a wide variety of etiologies. His theory of the transcendental ego inspired the first generation of German Romantics.[2] A number of nineteenth-century socialists, including Ferdinand Lassalle and Jean Jaurès, looked to him as one of the first thinkers to question radically the concept of property underpinning modern capitalism.[3] Recent years have witnessed a new appreciation of his importance as a political theorist and of his pivotal role in reorienting the philosophy of law. That he was one of the founders of modern nationalism is obvious, though the nature of his contribution remains elusive. More than one scholar has seen lurking behind his "philosophy of freedom" a proto-vision of the modern totalitarian state.[4] His youthful antisemitism, undeniably virulent, has received renewed attention as the first expression of a "new kind of revolutionary Jew-hatred" that replaced Christian prejudice. In feminist historiography he figures as the "chief ideologue of bourgeois patriarchalism," the articulator par excellence of the "founding opinions" that still allow "liberal" civil societies, under cover of the usual rhetoric about rights and equality, to enforce gender inequalities.[5]

And so the biographer of Fichte is hardly lacking in themes, and he need not belabor the fact that his subject is worth a biography. And yet the only full-scale biography of Fichte in this century is Xavier Léon's *Fichte et son temps*, which was ready for printing in July of 1914 when the crisis that triggered the Great War intervened; it finally appeared in two volumes in 1922 and 1924. Léon had begun the project at the turn of the century. The very physical qualities of his volumes – their sheer thickness and weight, their leather bindings with gilt lettering, their covers of marbled paper – place them in the monumental tradition of nineteenth-century scholarship. A democratic "patriot" in the Jacobin tradition, fighting the good fight against the forces of authoritarian politics and religious obscurantism, he had been drawn to Fichte as a kindred spirit across the Rhine. By 1922, in a political atmosphere still echoing with the hate propaganda that the war had generated on both the German and the French sides, Léon's attitude toward his hero had necessarily

---

[2] Isaiah Berlin has called Fichte "the true father of romanticism"; "The Apotheosis of the Romantic Will. The Revolt against the Myth of an Ideal World," in Isaiah Berlin, *The Crooked Timber of Humanity. Chapters in the History of Ideas*, ed. Henry Hardy (New York, 1991), p. 225. For reinterpretations of Fichte's influence on early Romanticism, see Gerald N. Izenberg, *Impossible Individuality. Romanticism, Revolution, and the Origins of Modern Selfhood* (Princeton, N.J., 1992), esp. pp. 101–12; Mark Kippermann, *Beyond Enchantment: German Idealism and English Romantic Poetry* (University of Pennsylvania Press, 1986).

[3] Jean Jaurès, *Les Origines du Socialisme Allemand* (Paris, 1892?), pp. 55–68.

[4] See, e.g., Bernard Willms, *Die totale Freiheit. Fichtes politische Philosophie* (Munich, 1969); Leszek Kolakowski, *Main Currents of Marxism, 1. The Founders* (Oxford, 1978), pp. 50–6.

[5] Paul Lawrence Rose, *German Question/Jewish Question: Revolutionary Antisemitism from Kant to Wagner* (Princeton, N.J., 1992), pp. 117–32; Isabel V. Hull, *Sexuality, State, and Civil Society in Germany, 1700–1815* (Ithaca and London, 1996), pp. 314–23.

become more conflicted. He acknowledged that Fichte, in his German
messianic voice, had helped make possible the "satanic" machinery of
German aggression. But the philosopher had done so unwittingly. In the
end, Fichte was still the great philosophical missionary of the Revolution.
Unlike his contemporaries, he had envisioned for his nation "a democratic and liberating mission, a humanitarian mission."[6]

Today *Fichte et son temps* is of interest less as a study of Fichte than as
a French scholar's profession of faith and as a glimpse into the pathos of
Franco-German academic relations in the early part of this century. The
reader is likely to be struck by the immense distance that divides the
Fichte who fascinated Léon and his contemporaries, both French and
German, from the Fichte we now engage. It is not simply that Fichte's
relationship to the French Revolution and its Jacobin movement has
proved far more problematic than Léon wanted it to be. Whether we
admire Fichte or condemn him, we come at him with a whole new
agenda, reflecting the questions about knowledge, ethics, politics, and a
host of other subjects that now preoccupy us.

The nearly eight decades since the appearance of Léon's volumes
have not been lacking in brief biographies, intended largely to introduce
Fichte's thought, but no one has attempted a successor biography on
or even remotely near the scale of magnitude of Léon's.[7] The absence
of such a work points to one of the widest chasms in our modern
landscape of disciplinary knowledge. In an age when interdisciplinary
exchange has become a matter of course in the humanities and the
social sciences, intellectual history and the history of philosophy – and
by the latter I mean the study of past philosophy by philosophers –
have remained largely oblivious to each other, despite the considerable
overlap in their subject matters. To the intellectual historian a philosophical text may pose unique challenges, but the underlying assumption is
likely to be that this text, like any other, has an intended meaning that
can be recovered contextually, as the product of a particular time and
place. In the history of philosophy, on the other hand, the guiding question is whether the text contributes something to philosophy as it is
now practiced, perhaps as an anticipation of a current way of philosophizing or at least as a useful foil, a reminder of earlier misguided preoccupations or wrong turns in the discipline. These agendas are not, of
course, mutually exclusive, but there has been remarkably little effort to
bridge them.

---

[6] Xavier Léon, *Fichte et son temps*, 2 vols. (1922–24), 1:ix–xiii. The two German biographies from the
same period – Heinz Heimsoeth, *Fichte* (Munich, 1923), and Fritz Medicus, *Fichtes Leben* (2d ed.:
Munich, 1922) – were much less ambitious projects.

[7] See. e.g., Pierre-Philippe Druet, *Fichte* (Paris, 1977); Peter Rohs, *Johann Gottlieb Fichte* (Munich,
1991); Helmut Seidel, *Johann Gottlieb Fichte zur Einführung* (Hamburg, 1997).

In the case of Fichte, disciplinary segregation is heightened by the very nature of his thought. Since he claimed to have discovered universal truths, Fichte would have dismissed as perverse any effort to explain his transcendental idealism as the contingent product of a specific historical context. There are Fichte scholars who surely agree; to submit his thought to contextual interpretation is, in their view, to fail to take it seriously as philosophy. The historian may very well respond, of course, that a contextual approach *can* take Fichte's philosophy seriously and indeed that it must do so if it is to be credible. But that is easier said than done. Like Nietzsche, though for somewhat different reasons, Fichte is a "hard case."[8] He himself urged his readers not to take the "letter" of his philosophical texts too seriously. Their purpose was merely to prompt – to move the reader to undertake, in his own way, the journey into philosophical reflexivity that Fichte himself had taken and thus to grasp the vital "spirit" of transcendental idealism by his own effort. In a sense, then, the historian provokes the philosopher's defiant stare just by trying to find a stable set of meanings in the words on the page. When we add that some of Fichte's texts are forbiddingly opaque, it becomes understandable that, with rare exceptions, historians have been content to leave Fichte to the philosophers.[9]

In a particularly pointed way, then, Fichte challenges us to bridge the disciplines, even as he defies our efforts to do so. It will be obvious that in constructing my own bridge, I have kept both feet planted firmly on the historian's side. And yet it was two developments in the philosophical scholarship on Fichte that convinced me that a thorough biographical study had become possible. In 1959, in an office in the Bavarian Academy of Sciences in Munich, work began on a complete edition (*Gesamtausgabe*) of Fichte's writings, and three years later the first volume appeared. If the story of the origins and the progress of this mammoth project were told in full, it would take us deep into at least three generations of German historical experience, from the interwar years through the Cold War. Hans Jacob (b. 1898) began a Fichte edition in the 1930s, only to see the second of his edited volumes, already at the printer's shop, destroyed in an allied bombing attack. After the war Reinhard Lauth (b. 1919), a young academic philosopher at Munich, searched out Jacob and together they went about gaining access to material and winning financial support. In 1959, in an unusual agreement with the Prussian

[8] Allan Megill, "Historicizing Nietzsche? Paradoxes and Lessons of a Hard Case," *The Journal of Modern History* 68:1 (March, 1996): 114–52.
[9] The major exception, worth consulting on all aspects of Fichte's thought, is George Armstrong Kelly, *Idealism, Politics, and History. Sources of Hegelian Thought* (Cambridge, 1969), pp. 182–285. It is a measure of the disciplinary divide that Kelly's book has been largely ignored in recent Fichte scholarship.

State Library in East Berlin, they secured access to the main body of Fichte's papers (which had found their way, somehow, to Moscow). We can only imagine the "difficult negotiations" they had to weather, as the Cold War intensified and the German Democratic Republic moved toward the building of the Berlin Wall. Meanwhile, sometime in the mid-1950s, Manfred Zahn, then a student of Lauth, had discovered another substantial collection of Fichte's papers hidden in a chicken shed in a village in Upper Bavaria, where their owner Hans von Fichte, the last direct male descendent of the philosopher, had settled in the confusion of the postwar years. The Fichte family was persuaded to sell the collection to the Staatsbibliothek Preussischer Kulturbesitz in West Berlin, despite "a more lucrative offer from America." With these two library deposits as the core of their project, the editors and their students scoured both Germanies for additional material.[10]

Originally conceived as a roughly fifteen-volume project, the *Complete Edition* has reached twenty-nine volumes, with about eight more still to appear. It is an extraordinary example of what a well-conceived, thorough, and persistent enterprise in scholarly teamwork can accomplish, and for my purposes the editorial procedures make it all the more valuable. The editors have all, in the words of one of them, "felt bound to the ethos of transcendental philosophy, naturally to different degrees." This "existential interest" might have produced an apology for Fichte under cover of a scholarly edition. Instead it grounded a commitment to the greatest possible historical accuracy and thoroughness in presenting his writings, both published and unpublished, and surrounding them with relevant editorial information. To realize the latter goal the project proceeded chronologically, the editorial comment in each volume building on its predecessors. And, as if determined to spoil the historian-biographer by catering to his every need, the editors have supplemented the four series in the edition itself with a seven-volume collection of comments on Fichte by his contemporaries, gathered from a wide variety of published materials, correspondence, unpublished papers, and archival documents, and a four-volume series of reviews of Fichte's writings from the periodicals of the era.

No one scholar could have collected all this material and gathered all this editorial information in several lifetimes. It is, I think, appropriate that this volume appears as a nearly half-century project, conducted with all deliberate speed, nears completion. I have tried to do the project justice.

---

[10] The information on the history of the *Gesamtausgabe* has been generously supplied by Dr. Erich Fuchs, a long-time collaborator in the project and one of its editors since 1996. See also Wolfhart Henckmann, "Fichte-Schelling-Hegel," in *Buchstabe und Geist. Zur Überlieferung und Edition philosophischer Texte*, ed. Walter Jaeschke, Wilhelm G. Jacobs, Hermann Krings, and Heinrich Schepers (Hamburg, 1987), pp. 84–93.

The other development that convinced me of the feasibility of this project is the "mini-renaissance" in philosophical scholarship on Fichte since World War II.[11] In addition to the work of Lauth, his colleagues, and their students, there has been an impressive series of French contributions, building on, but also redirecting, a long-standing interest among French scholars in Fichte's political theory, his social and economic thought, and his philosophy of law. More recently, Anglophone scholars, especially in the United States, have weighed in heavily, particularly in the study of the epistemological foundations and ethical implications of Fichte's transcendentalism. The net effect of this multinational enterprise has been to rescue Fichte from two kinds of historical condescension. To Kantians, Fichte merited attention as the disciple who took a wrong turn, as Kant himself had so fiercely announced. In the Hegelian school, which set the agenda for a great deal of the work in the history of philosophy until quite recently, Fichte represented a pause in philosophy's Great March Forward. If the pause was fruitful in some ways, it served primarily to spotlight, by its shortcomings, the immensity of Hegel's achievement. What we have now is a substantial body of work demonstrating that Fichte was an important philosopher in his own right – that, as one American scholar has put it, he was "a major philosophical planet whose thought moves in its own orbit."[12]

No less condescending is the tendency in contemporary western philosophy to dismiss the pre-Nietzschean "canon" as a massive, centuries-long "metaphysical" delusion. New generations of Fichte scholars have not denied that his thought is a striking example, perhaps the example without rival, of the pre-Nietzschean search for an irreducible, or "foundationalist," truth on which all philosophy and indeed all knowledge could be built, and of the concomitant search for the "essential," or intrinsic, nature of the human being as a rational moral agent, discernible behind the vast array of historical, cultural, and even psychological differences in human experience. If Fichte's thought is foundationalist and essentialist, however, it turns out to be much less naïve, and certainly far more interesting, than the postmodernist critique would have it.

I began to engage the new Fichte scholarship with more than a little impatience. I was after Fichte the historical figure, and what I seemed to be getting was a purely philosophical mind. It was a mind connected only tangentially to the personality that had fascinated and troubled so many of Fichte's contemporaries. The historical context in which the mind operated appeared in this literature as a kind of backdrop canvas, a flattened allusion to the multifaceted and densely contoured world that had

---

[11] On the "mini-renaissance," see Tom Rockmore's introduction to Daniel Breazeale and Tom Rockmore, eds., *Fichte. Historical Contexts / Contemporary Controversies* (Atlantic Highlands, N.J., 1994), pp. 1–6.

[12] Ibid., p. 5.

formed and engaged Fichte. It will become apparent in these pages, however, that my debt to the philosophical scholarship on Fichte has been immense. At several junctures that scholarship has served as my indispensable guide through Fichte's texts, explicating their contributions to philosophy with a conceptual lucidity and logical rigor rarely found in intellectual history. Thanks to this literature, I have built into my own story of Fichte's intellectual development a diachronic tracking, sometimes footprint by footprint, of his perceptions of the critical issues in philosophy, his decisions to abandon what he concluded were wrong paths, and his breakthroughs in creating his own philosophical system. I do not, I should stress, see my use of the philosophical literature on Fichte as a matter of occasionally deviating from historical analysis or of providing historical analysis with a philosophical patina. We simply cannot historicize Fichte without recognizing that the field of philosophical argument in which he positioned himself – the field that the recent literature has remapped – is one of the salient historical contexts, and sometimes the crucial one.

What emerges from this literature is a new understanding of Fichte's distinctive contribution to modern conceptions of selfhood, and particularly to the construction of the self as an autonomous moral agent. Fichte's thought is a striking instance of what Charles Taylor has called the "radical reflexivity" of western philosophy since the late seventeenth century.[13] Like Kant, Fichte found the irreducible ground of moral agency in the transcendental realm of pure Reason, anterior to sense experience. But he also struck out into new territory by collapsing the distinction between cognition and will that Kant had striven to maintain; by developing his own theory of how the self, as a moral person, asserted itself in a relentless struggle against the resistance of things; and by making the very existence of the empirical self a function of its intersubjective relations with other selves. By 1799 his system, raying out in several directions from its reflexive premise, demonstrated how the self might be repositioned in a new world of public culture, of disciplinary knowledge, of social relations, of property and labor, of legal rights and constraints, of political power and authority.

The construal of selfhood, in these various sites and modalities, is the theme around which I have built this biography. To the extent, and it is a large extent, that I find that the new readings of Fichte's texts have clarified their meaning as contributions to philosophy (and to political theory), I take them as my point of departure. I also believe, however, that, if we are to achieve a historical understanding of the philosophical orbit Fichte created for himself, we need to position him in a dense cluster of contexts. "Internalist" revisionism is necessary but does not suffice; it

---

[13] Charles Taylor, *Sources of the Self. The Making of the Modern Identity* (Cambridge, Mass., 1989).

must be brought into interaction with a close study of extraphilosophi-
cal contexts.

The scholarly thoroughness and precision of the *Complete Edition* makes
this possible, since the scholars who produced it wisely included all sorts
of detail that is of marginal significance for their own work. In much of
the documentary and editorial detail we see Fichte as a social being, in
a society with its distinctive structures, norms, and tensions. In addition
to contextualizing his systematic contributions to social theory, we can
retrieve the less obvious social meanings that resonate through his thought
even at its most abstract. I do not mean to imply that despite recent skepticism about the social history of ideas in its cruder forms, Fichte's thought
should be read as a rationale for a social "interest." Even as he adopted
emphatically "bourgeois" values, he remained alienated from the groups
who constituted the eighteenth-century *Bürgertum.* The group with which
he identified was the new intellectual elite, not yet formed, that I have
called a modern clerisy. Despite his egalitarian impulses, his posture toward
"the People" – the uneducated and unpropertied masses who formed the
broad base of the social pyramid – was likewise profoundly ambivalent.
If Fichte defies old-style social reductionism, however, he also beckons us
to pursue the social history of ideas in other keys. The salient question is
not what group he represented but how he experienced the relational
terms of inequality and dependence – the enforced asymmetries of power
– in eighteenth-century German society. The surviving record of that
experience, particularly for the years when he was a would-be client in
search of patrons, is indispensable to understanding why his construal of
selfhood was so intimately connected with a vision of a new public
culture, where communication would be free of the distorting effects
of power.

Contextualizing Fichte's construal of selfhood is also a matter of understanding his thought from a rhetorical standpoint. Within the study of
philosophy itself, there is a new recognition that the effort to present
philosophical thought as purely demonstrative reasoning, distinguished
from the wily arts of the rhetorical tradition, is itself a rhetorical strategy,
a use of form to persuade. Likewise, there is a new willingness to include
in the study of philosophical meaning those more obviously figurative
devices of rhetoric that even the most purist texts – and some of Fichte's
are striking cases in point – exhibit.[14] While I share these views, I also
wish to use a rhetorical approach to push the historical contextualization
of Fichte's thought well beyond what philosophy's awareness of its own
rhetorical properties might license. I do not mean to imply that we can
gain a historical understanding of Fichte's philosophy by reconstructing

---

[14] See, e.g., Berel Lang, *Philosophy and the Art of Writing: Studies in Philosophical and Literary Style*
(Lewisburg, Penn., 1983).

its relationship to a specific rhetorical tradition, as, for example, Quentin Skinner has done to such effect in his study of Hobbes.[15] Instead I have pursued an admittedly eclectic strategy of rhetorical understanding, and at several levels. There is, first, the fact that for Fichte the quintessential outer-directed "activity" of the self, and the one that defined the philosopher's calling, was communicative action in the public sphere. That is to say that he conceived of selfhood as, in a broad sense, a rhetorical process. Not surprisingly, he aspired to give the presentation of philosophy a certain rhetorical efficacy, even as he spurned the rhetor's arts of manipulation. That ambivalence marks one of the recurrent tensions in Fichte's thought and is one of its distinguishing features in the context of German educated culture in the 1790s.

If we are attentive to the rhetoric Fichte actually employed, we see how figural and metaphoric language inflected his philosophical thinking through a variety of discourses – the Lutheran ethic, the language of mechanism in natural science, the eighteenth-century cult of sensibility, and so on – and in turn was inflected by it. We remain aware that we are encountering the author in a more or less mediate way, as a rhetorical persona or, perhaps better, as a voice, and we are alert to the significance of shifts in voice.

At still another level, I would contend, a great deal of what we do to understand texts contextually is a matter of placing them in what I will call, for want of a better phrase, their rhetorical circumstances. If a text, whether it be a published philosophical treatise or an intimate letter, is a rhetorical event, it is ipso facto a contextual event. One of its circumstantial features is that it is addressed to at least one specific audience, whether real or imagined (or both). We need to ask how the author envisioned his audience (or audiences) and sought to position himself in relation to it, and what sort of rhetorical community he wished to constitute. We also need to be attentive, of course, to the specific referents to which the text points us – because they tell us something about what occasioned it and perhaps something about what it in turn was meant to occasion. Fichte is a particularly appropriate subject for this kind of hermeneutic. His efforts to define philosophy as a kind of rhetoric were inseparable from his need to profess, and indeed to live, his convictions in several settings: the institution of preaching, which offered the most likely outlet for his youthful aspirations but also threatened to silence him; the expanding print market, to which he reacted first with vaulting optimism and then with growing disillusionment; the university at Jena, which gave him the forum he craved but also put him in a volatile relationship with colleagues and students; and the political establishment of his day, which he

---

[15] Quentin Skinner, *Reason and Rhetoric in the Philosophy of Hobbes* (Cambridge, 1996).

faced as a marginal figure until his university appointment in 1794 and from then until 1799 as an employee of the ducal government at Weimar, the dominant presence in university affairs.

★ ★ ★

To say that Fichte's thought is broadly rhetorical is also to say that he drew on the discursive resources of his culture. What resources? What use did he make of them? The questions may seem blatantly obvious, but in fact they have been occluded by much of the Fichte scholarship to date. To put the matter as simply as possible: if we are to understand Fichte's thought contextually (and rhetorically), we need to reverse the direction of approach. The great bulk of scholarship on Fichte looks back on him through the distorting lenses of modern ideologies. My strategy has been to remove these "isms," so far as a historian of the late twentieth century could do, and to come at Fichte through the eighteenth-century cultures – religious, political, and so on – in which he came of age, defined the dilemmas he and his generation of German intellectuals faced, and perceived his choices.

In the European-wide framework of eighteenth-century studies, and particularly in the history of political thought, this strategy might seem so obvious as to be hardly worth mentioning. The remapping of the century's political languages, particularly in the Anglo-Scottish and French worlds, is well advanced.[16] It has been so effective in removing the distorting lenses of modern "isms," in fact, that we are left wondering how to reconceive the lines of continuity that surely do run from early-modern political languages to modern political ideologies. In the study of eighteenth-century Germany, however, this kind of work has gotten a late start. Fichte poses a particularly daunting challenge. For one thing, he *did* become a founder of at least one "ism." With the *Addresses to the German Nation* he made himself one of the icons of modern German nationalism. In a great deal of Fichte scholarship the *Addresses* have formed a powerful magnetic field, pulling earlier texts toward them as so many anticipations of this culminating moment. In resisting that force, I have not meant to imply that the Fichte of the 1790s and the Fichte of the *Addresses* are unconnected. Again and again Fichte asked how intellectuals like himself could form a vanguard but at the same time bond with the great mass of the population in an inclusive public culture. The "nation," as it was imagined in the *Addresses*, was one of his answers. As late as 1799, however, I find no indications that he was moving toward

---

[16] See, e.g., J. G. A. Pocock, *Virtue, Commerce, and History. Essays on Political Thought and History, Chiefly in the Eighteenth Century* (Cambridge, 1985); Keith Michael Baker, *Inventing the French Revolution. Essays on French Political Culture in the Eighteenth Century* (Cambridge, 1990).

that answer. Fichte's nationalism was the product of a later phase of his intellectual career, in the very different context of the Berlin of early Romanticism and the Prussia of the Napoleonic Wars.

Nationalism has been only one of the distorting lenses. Liberalism, anarchism, democratic egalitarianism, socialism (or at least "state social-ism"), totalitarianism, racial (or at least proto-racial) antisemitism, bourgeois patriarchalism: all have exerted their teleological pull, with the result that the contextual recovery of Fichte's intended meaning has taken a backseat to the search for originary moments, or at least anticipatory moments, in the articulation of the modern spectrum of political ideologies.

If we change direction and come at Fichte through the eighteenth century, we have to contend seriously with the fact that Protestant culture, in distinctly German variations, played a major role in forming him. The point is not simply that Fichte's upbringing and formal education were typically Lutheran. Like other Germans of his generation, he experienced the Enlightenment as a distinctly Protestant phenomenon. The *Aufklärer* he admired as a young man had not joined French philosophes like Voltaire and Diderot, whose war against "the infamous" was directed at Christianity in all its forms. If we wish to know what drew him to phi-losophy and eventually to Kant, we need to see how, in his effort to find a calling and a kind of self-justification, he construed the broadly theo-logical issues at the center of controversy in the German Enlightenment.

This way of contextualizing Fichte promises to carry us beyond a long-standing truism: that the German philosophical revolution of the late eighteenth and early nineteenth century – first Kant's Critical Philoso-phy and then the various forms of Idealism – secularized Lutheran beliefs. The truism creates the illusion that we have resolved certain issues when in fact we have not really defined, much less engaged, them. Part of the problem is that the very concept of "secularization" begs so many ques-tions. Often enough, secularization pretends to explain a process for which it provides no more than a label. Or it offers a facile argument by analogy – implying that by identifying similarities between the sacred and the secular, we are demonstrating, and perhaps explaining, the underlying structural continuities in their intellectual content. More often the appeal to secularization as an explanation, though it might appear to be about intellectual subtance, boils down to a crude exercise in psychological reductionism. The secularization of religious ideas is seen to mark the displacement of a recurrent psychological urge, the rechanneling of a collective desire for absolute certainty, for example, or for absolute resolution of conflict.[17]

[17] See the critique of attempts to use "secularization"as an explanatory concept in Bernard Yack, *The Longing for Total Revolution. Philosophical Sources of Social Discontent from Rousseau to Marx and Nietz-sche* (Princeton, N.J., 1986), pp. 10–18, and the comments in Dale K.Van Kley, *The Religious Origins*

My own use of the term "secularization" is indebted to the work of M. H. Abrams. Nearly three decades ago, in his remarkable book on the Protestant roots of early Romanticism, Abrams used the term as a shorthand for a substantive understanding of an intellectual process. The process in question, Abrams argued, was not "the deletion and replacement of religious ideas but rather the assimilation and reinterpretation of religious ideas, as constitutive elements in a world view founded on secular premises."[18] Using this definition – we might call it the reformulation of the sacred within a desacralized discourse – Abrams traced the filiations between a cluster of ideas in the Protestant economy of salvation and early Romantic visions of rebirth, apocalyptic renewal, and the restoration of wholeness to individuals and communities. Following the same definition, I have sought to understand the development of Fichte's thought as a series of moments in the secularization of Lutheranism. Arguably the principle of *sola fide* in Luther's Reformation was a matter of *resacralizing* the Christian experience of God as the "wholly Other." Fichte's philosophy of selfhood and moral agency, far more radically than Kant's transcendentalism, was meant to replace this sacral core with a foundational premise that did not need, and indeed could not tolerate, a "wholly Other," and in that sense was emphatically secular.[19] All the more striking, then, that proceeding from that premise, Fichte did not purge his philosophy of the Lutheran tradition, but rather reformulated Lutheran themes. Some of the reformulations fell away as he matured as a philosopher. With others – the ones that remained basic to his philosophy through its many twists and turns – Fichte contributed to the strong element of continuity in the passage from a religious to a modern secular culture. His vision of selfhood recast the central paradox of the Protestant concept of calling: the process in which spontaneous inner freedom became, in its turn outward, a highly disciplined and indeed ascetic self-mastery. It was the practice of that self-mastery in work, conceived as a modern variation on the Lutheran ideal of calling, that would realize both a new kind of individual freedom and a new form of community. And it was in that sense, as self-mastery in its purest form, that philosophy was the calling above all others.[20]

of the French Revolution. From Calvin to the Civil Constitution, 1560–1791 (New Haven and London, 1996), pp. 10–11.

[18] M. H. Abrams, *Natural Supernaturalism. Tradition and Revolution in Romantic Literature* (New York and London, 1973), p. 13. See also Laurence Dickey, *Hegel. Religion, Economics, and the Politics of Spirit, 1770–1807* (Cambridge, 1987), which contextualizes the thought of the young Hegel within the Protestant religious culture of Old-Württemberg.

[19] On the distinction between "secularization" and "resacralization" as it applies to Luther, see John M. Headley, "Luther and the Problem of Secularization," *Journal of the American Academy of Religion* 55:1 (1987): 21–37.

[20] The search for a calling is one of the themes of Carl Pletsch, *The Young Nietzsche. Becoming a Genius* (New York, 1991).

My broadly rhetorical approach to Fichte's texts is designed in part to recover, within its formative contexts, this process of rupture (the rejection of Lutheran fideism) and continuity (the reaffirmation of the Lutheran ethic, albeit in a more secular mode). The process reaches a point of culmination, I argue, in Fichte's defense of his position in the Atheism Conflict. That defense in turn allows us to situate Fichte's contribution to the secularization of the Lutheran tradition within the larger framework of German educated culture in the late eighteenth century.

To claim that Fichte was also an outspoken voice of the Enlightenment, and indeed that in his behavior as well as his thought he personified that movement, may strike some readers as dubious. The more conventional view assigns him to the new generation of German thinkers in the 1790s who rejected the Enlightenment and hastened its demise. That makes a good deal of sense; Fichte pitted his philosophy against eighteenth-century rationalism in many forms, including German metaphysics, Anglo-Scottish empiricism and "common sense" philosophy, and French materialist psychology. And yet, Fichte's vision was, arguably, the ultimate articulation of a normative idea at the core of the Enlightenment's self-understanding and vision of a more rational order. I have in mind the discourse of publicity, with its commitment to public openness, to freedom of expression, to the scrutiny and criticism of authority in all its forms. In the last several decades we have learned a great deal about how this discourse emerged with the spread of print capitalism and concomitant changes in forms of social and intellectual exchange. We have come to realize that in the Enlightenment's visions of progress, the pivotal development was seen to be the formation and gradual expansion of an "enlightened" public. Such a public would be a collective conscience, formed somehow out of myriad private judgments; it would be the voice of criticism, the vehicle through which a society and a polity became self-critical; and in its exercise of critical scrutiny, it would be the tribunal to which even the state would be accountable.[21]

The Enlightenment was not simply a field of ideas but a process of communication that yielded, and to some degree reflected, a new ideal of public culture, with the exercise of communicative rationality as its constitutive element. The appeal of this ideal goes a long way toward explaining why and how Enlightenment thinkers combined a commit-

[21] The relevant literature is reviewed in Anthony J. La Vopa, "Conceiving a Public: Ideas and Society in Eighteenth-Century Europe," *The Journal of Modern History* 64:1 (March, 1992): 79–116. Particularly important for German studies is Hans Erich Bödeker and Ulrich Herrmann, eds., *Aufklärung als Politisierung-Politisierung als Aufklärung* (Hamburg, 1987). For examples of more recent work, see Dario Castiglione and Lesley Sharpe, *Shifting the Boundaries. Transformation of the Languages of Public and Private in the Eighteenth Century* (Exeter, 1995).

ment to profound changes with a refusal to countenance the possibility that revolution might be necessary. It gives us a new way to understand, from within eighteenth-century culture, a related and equally puzzling fact: that the Enlightenment was at once an emphatically political and a profoundly unpolitical and indeed even antipolitical movement.

In all this it has been obvious that Kant was a central figure – the thinker who, more than any other, made publicity central to the very authority of moral knowledge, and who tried to ground the discourse of publicity in a philosophically unassailable epistemology. Fichte's contribution to the discourse has remained largely unexplored, though he was surely Kant's most zealous legatee on this score. Publicity became for him the vital connection between the interiority of moral selfhood and the world without, the collective life of a self-critical society and polity. Once we realize the centrality of the discourse of publicity in Fichte's thought, aspects of his thinking about society, culture, and politics that might seem confusing, if not downright contradictory, by modern ideological standards become more understandable. Likewise we are in a position to understand the expectations with which he began his intellectual career; to mark the onset and trace the course of his disillusionment; and to explain contextually the controversy about his "character" by exploring the tensions between principle and practice in his rhetorical interventions in the public sphere. For all these themes as well, the Atheism Conflict is the appropriate endpoint for this volume.

One of the distinguishing features of the German discourse of publicity, and indeed of the actual German *Publikum* in the eighteenth century, was the central place of the universities. They are the site for our third discursive context, the reconceptualization and reconfiguration of *Wissenschaft*, the knowledge generated by the academic disciplines, as it evolved from its traditional corporate character in old-regime society to something recognizably modern. By the late eighteenth century, the German universities were pulled between, on the one hand, their public responsibilities as institutions of the dynastic states and their established churches and, on the other, their gathering commitment to a new kind of public openness as the creators and the vital souces of the "pure" knowledge that the term *Wissenschaft* was coming to evoke. Perhaps more than any other thinker of his generation, Fichte sought to resolve this tension. He did so not only by imagining a new mediating role for the university, between the state and society, but also by redefining the very meaning and purpose of *Wissenschaft*, as a form of knowledge and as a calling. Here again Fichte sought a way to ground knowledge in the interiority of selfhood and to give selfhood, through knowledge, a public voice – and here again the Atheism Conflict put his thought and his life to a severe test.

★ ★ ★

No amount of reassurance that a biographical reinterpretation of Fichte's life and thought is now possible, and no preliminary inventory of its themes, can dispel certain kinds of skepticism. After all, the prior question is, why biography? Is biography still a viable way of doing history, particularly when the biographical subject is a philosopher like Fichte? In a sense, the genre speaks for itself; in recent years biography has been making something of a comeback, often in innovative forms that bode well for its future, and philosophers have figured prominently among its subjects.[22] Even as the genre keeps reproducing itself, however, it is faced with objections about its advisability, its credibility, and even its right to exist. I have written the book with an eye toward those objections. Ultimately my answer to them is the book itself, my ways of practicing biography, chapter by chapter. I will suffice here with a few declarations of purpose, stated baldly but not, I hope, flippantly. They are no more than a précis, the summary statement yielded by my efforts to stake out a position on a terrain that has become exceedingly treacherous.

Fritz Ringer's skepticism is about intellectual biography, which he sees as a "species of methodological individualism." The prior task facing intellectual history, Ringer argues, is to produce systematic surveys of "intellectual fields" as "entities in their own right," each with a structure of "shared intellectual habits and collective meanings" that cannot be reduced to the "aggregates of individuals" who participate in them. Before we can understand the "peculiar relationship" of "outstanding thinkers" to their "world," we need to reconstruct that world. As Ringer's own work has demonstrated, the study of intellectual fields can reveal a great deal about the "tacit beliefs and cognitive dispositions" beneath "the surface of explicit thought."[23] I am left wondering, however, why Ringer draws such a rigid distinction in principle between his own approach and biography. Biography need not be as individualistic in method as he assumes it to be and as the term "intellectual biography" suggests. I proceeded from the premise that, conceived as a many-sided exercise in contextual history, the biography of an outstanding thinker can contribute significantly to the reconstruction of an intellectual field. The very commitment to a contextual recovery of meaning required that I reexamine, and to some extent remap, the diverse fields of argument to which Fichte's texts were meant to contribute. Admittedly, narrative, by its very particularity, may distract

---

[22] See, e.g., Elisabeth Young-Bruehl, *Hannah Arendt, for the Love of the World* (New Haven, 1982); Ray Monk, *Ludwig Wittgenstein. The Duty of Genius* (New York, 1990); Margaret Gullan-Whur, *Within Reason. A Life of Spinoza* (London, 1998); Steven Nadler, *Spinoza, A Life* (Cambridge, 1999).

[23] Fritz Ringer, *Fields of Knowledge. French Academic Culture in Comparative Perspective, 1890–1920* (Cambridge, 1992), pp. 10–12.

us from the kind of discursive structure Ringer has in mind; but a biographical narrative that is socially informed – one that takes us beyond
crude affinities between specific ideas and static social structures and
reaches beneath the surface of public argument to the play of ideas in the
normative terms of social relations – can help us understand how a field
forms, dissolves, or transmutes itself in a particular social setting and historical moment. This is one way, I would suggest, to keep the study of
an intellectual field from becoming the flattened survey of discursive patterns that Ringer himself has so adeptly avoided.

At another level of debate, the contextual biographer is likely to feel
that no matter what route he takes, he will be caught in the crossfire.
Traditionally the philosopher has peered into the interior of human consciousness and has claimed to find, in Michael Walzer's words, a "superagent," a "historically and morally departicularized self."[24] There is no more
striking case of the self as superagent than Fichte's transcendental concept
of the "I." What business does the historian-biographer have sniffing
around something that, by its very nature, eludes empirical demonstration? In postmodernist critiques, on the other hand, the notion of selfhood as, at bottom, a unitary identity, an essential capacity for autonomous
agency – the notion Fichte developed to the point of self-caricature – is
dismissed as a delusion of western philosophy. If the biographical subject
– the unitary and coherent self that biographical narrative, by its very
nature, posits – can no longer be meaningfully said to exist, where does
that leave the historian-biographer? What is the point of essaying a biography if the self, or the subject, is nothing more than a passive site of discursive conflicts, or just one more "position in language," or a centrifugal
swirl of fictive meanings?[25]

A historian-biographer of my persuasion – one reading empirical traces
in search of a historical self – necessarily rejects both of these positions
in practice, though both may also influence his or her practice. I approach
Fichte's transcendental concept of selfhood as a historical construct, formulated under specific conditions. To those who wish to engage the formulation of the concept as a purely philosophical move, this approach is
inevitably reductionist. I should stress, however, that the approach is not
meant to confirm recent attacks on the "logocentric" construal of selfhood. Quite the contrary; one of my purposes is to expose the historical shallowness of much of the postmodernist critique.

---

[24] Michael Walzer, "The Divided Self," in Walzer, *Thick and Thin. Moral Argument at Home and Abroad*
(Notre Dame and London, 1994), pp. 89–90.

[25] For current debates about selfhood, see, e.g., Richard Rorty, "The Contingency of Selfhood," in
Rorty, *Contingency, Irony, and Solidarity* (Cambridge, 1989), pp. 23–43; Seyla Benhabib, *Situating the
Self. Gender, Community and Postmodernism in Contemporary Ethics* (New York, 1992); Joan Wallach
Scott, *Only Paradoxes to Offer: French Feminists and the Rights of Man* (Cambridge, Mass., 1996), esp.
pp. 5–16.

Contextual biography cannot disprove "de-centered" views of selfhood and subjectivity. It can, however, demonstrate by example why it is still a historically viable practice to assume the existence of a discrete and integral self. The voice of Fichte in the early letters and unpublished writings, I contend, is the voice of a unitary, though tension-ridden, subject, and there is a real continuity between that subject and the university professor who lost his job in 1799. It is not simply that Fichte's texts reveal him developing a unitary sense of self by constructing a coherent life narrative. As we construct our own narrative of his life from the texts, we glimpse, if only obliquely, the continuity of the self as a personality, in its enduring attributes and in its recurrent inner tensions and perceptions of choice. In a sense, then, the "Fichte" of this book, like the hero of a nineteenth-century novel, is a character. Under the novelist's penetrating eye and guiding hand, he moves through a narrative that reflects the coherence of selfhood. I even presume to pass judgment on my character at critical junctures, though I try to avoid unhistorical judgment by applying to him his own ethical standards.

While I have not accepted the notion of de-centered selfhood, I have tried to take seriously the problematics of selfhood to which it points. If we define the empirical self as a structured core of psychological motives, then our access to Fichte's empirical self is quite limited and more or less opaque – and that despite the fact that the textual traces are in some ways unusually rich. Fichte's philosophical reflexivity was quite different from the psychological introspection of, say, Jean-Jacques Rousseau or Georg Christoph Lichtenberg. Intuiting the transcendental "I," in fact, left him with little incentive to examine the psychological "I," even when his behavior seemed to cry out for such an examination. What we have is a self mediated in several ways.[26] One mediation is Fichte's philosophical construct of selfhood. Then there are the social and cultural norms – the standards of honor, integrity, and human value – through which he sought to justify himself and his various forms of rhetorical and textual self-representation, from the published philosophical texts to private meditations, diaries, and intimate letters. I cannot emulate the novelist who, in conveying the interiority of his character, seems to roam at will behind mediated selves. Instead I am pulled outward to still another layer of mediation, the one evoked by the term "character" in the sense of public image. To some of his contemporaries, Fichte's public image – a product of his words and his actions but also of others' perceptions and misperceptions – posed difficult issues of judgment, issues of character. In the face of these issues,

---

[26] For illuminating comments on the psychological self and its textual mediations, see Gerald N. Izenberg, "Text, Context, and Psychology in Intellectual History," in H. Kozicki, ed., *Developments in Modern Historiography* (New York, 1993), pp. 40–62.

we may also have a conflicted reaction, though perhaps for different reasons.

Even if the philosophical student of Fichte does not reject contextual biography as reductionist, she may very well doubt that the genre is compatible with philosophy's way of engaging its own past. Richard Rorty's essay on "the historiography of philosophy" proposes a division of labor, one that he thinks will allow each side to continue happily cultivating its garden. Engaging "dead philosophers" philosophically, he argues, is an exercise in "rational reconstruction." If the dead are to be our partners in philosophically efficacious conversations – if they are to be of maximum adversarial value or of maximum value as thinkers who anticipated our own position – they have to be "re-educated," so to speak, rid of all the "outdated foolishness" that clutters their texts. Aside from its inherent interest, the "thick description" and the "nitty-gritty" of intellectual history is needed to keep rational reconstruction honest – honesty being defined here as "keeping in mind the possibility that our self-justifying conversation is with creatures of our own fantasy rather than with historical personages, even ideally re-educated historical personages."[27]

Rorty juggles two personas in the essay. There is the familiar proponent of unvarnished historical and cultural relativism, eager to knock philosophy off the disciplinary pedestal it has built for itself with the assumption that its province is timeless and universal Truth. He agrees with Quentin Skinner that if we are to remain self-aware about the historical contingency, or at least the possible contingency, of our own universe of discourse, we need to engage the "unre-educated" dead with the contextual historian's "ironic empathy." Hence the philosophical conversations made possible by rational reconstruction have to be "conducted in full knowledge of their anachronism." The conversation can be used for self-justification, but only if it is conducted in full awareness that it is an exercise in "brisk Whiggery."[28] Behind Rorty the brisk but self-conscious Whig, however, lies the Rorty whose presentmindness is not just a heuristic posture but an expression of profoundly condescending dismissiveness. The notion of rational reconstruction posits centuries of largely wasted effort in philosophy. It pivots on the assumption that contemporary philosophers, like contemporary natural scientists, stand on a

---

[27] Richard Rorty, "The Historiography of Philosophy: Four Genres," in Richard Rorty, J. B. Schneewind, and Quentin Skinner, eds., *Philosophy in History. Essays in the Historiography of Philosophy* (Cambridge, 1984), pp. 52–6, 70–1. For a critique of a parallel way of approaching political theory, see J. G. A. Pocock, "Political Ideas as Historical Events: Political Philosophers as Historical Actors," in Melvin Richter, ed., *Political Theory and Political Education* (Princeton, N.J., 1980), pp. 139–58. The issues are debated extensively in *Meaning and Context. Quentin Skinner and His Critics*, ed. and introd. James Tully (Princeton, N.J., 1988).

[28] Rorty, "The Historiography of Philosophy," pp. 51, 68.

peak far above their predecessors in the Dark Old (pre-Nietzschean?) Days, though in the relatively weak sense that they are more aware of what the real issues are, what is worth spending time on and what is not. That assumption – however self-consciously heuristic it may be, and however open in principle to the intellectual historian's reminders of its fictive status – functions to impoverish philosophy's engagement with its own past.

What rational reconstruction removes is the element of surprise, the need to come to terms with forms of thinking that are joltingly unfamiliar, that provoke self-doubt about one's own standards of rationality, or at least consternation that a past thinker, otherwise so rational by our standards, could be so apparently irrational on this or that subject. Rorty realizes that intellectual history, including contextual biography, does not reduce past philosophers to the status of antiquarian relics, beyond the pale of rational conversation. Nonetheless, he slights, even as he seems to acknowledge it, the capacity of contextual biography to make past philosophers more accessible, more likely to draw us into richer and more challenging conversations. The paradox of the genre, I would suggest, is that by returning a philosopher's thought to its contexts and thus restoring its contextual meaning, it enhances the power of his or her presence for us now. The possibilities for conversation, and for philosophical self-criticism through conversation, are widened.

That is the effect of surprise – an effect that Rorty's reconstruction precludes. It may be a matter of confronting strange but provocative ideas that make us wonder whether in our confidence that we have at last identified the "real" subject of philosophy we have arbitrarily constrained our vision. Fichte's concepts of intersubjectivity and of labor as property are cases in point; they suggest ways of rethinking, rather than simply dismissing, the role of essentialism in social theory. There is also, of course, the confrontation with strangeness in its uglier and more frightening manifestations, the ones that Rorty would prefer that the philosopher, as philosopher, excise. Were Fichte's antisemitism and hyperpatriarchalism intrinsic to his philosophy? It is an arguable question, and one that from a philosophical as well as a historical standpoint is *worth* arguing. At issue, philosophically as well as historically, is the potential for abuse in a philosophy like Fichte's. The philosopher has a responsibility to tackle the issue. To bracket it out on purpose – to knowingly turn a historical personage into a fictional voice for the sake of rational conversation – is to evade that responsibility.

Above all by calling our attention to the surprises that only contextual history can yield, the biographer-historian ought to keep philosophy honest. This book will, I hope, offer some surprises of this sort and may improve at least a few conversations.

PART 1
The Wanderjahre

Chapter 1

Alienation

On the night of July 24, 1788, Johann Gottlieb Fichte, age twenty-six, had trouble sleeping. Fichte found himself in a hiatus between employments as a private tutor and was taking the opportunity to make a rare visit to his family in Rammenau, the Saxon village of his birth. His insomnia yielded a plan for a literary satire, a substantial, though brief, document (eight pages in the printed edition) to which he must have devoted several hours. The product of a brooding mind, it is titled "Random Thoughts on a Sleepless Night."

Fichte planned to satirize what he called the "total moral corruption" of the age.[1] He began the "Random Thoughts" with a quick inventory: the decline of marriage and female virtue; rampant materialism; commercial greed; the "sultanism" of rulers and the "tyranny" of the "higher orders"; absurd contradictions in the laws; religious superstitions; clerical arrogance; the triviality of academic disciplines; salacious frivolity in the arts; depraved public entertainments; and so on. Under such conditions, the young intellectual observed, "a highly refined people" acquired a "twisted, internally contradictory character that places insights in eternal contradiction with the heart and with morals, so that the decrees of the understanding become in the end nothing but an empty shell of words."[2]

Fichte was en route from Leipzig to a new tutoring employment in Zürich. The position would take him out of the Electorate of Saxony, his native state, for the first time in his life. He was facing a kind of exile and had no idea when or how it would end. Perhaps for that reason he had decided on the visit to Rammenau, though the trip had to be made on foot for want of coach fare and took him still farther from Switzerland. Rammenau lies between Dresden, then the court residence of the Electorate, and the Neisse river, not far from the present border between the Federal Republic of Germany and the Republic of Poland. Traveling eastward from Leipzig across central Saxony, Fichte had reached his native

---

[1] "Zufällige Gedanken in einer schlaflosen Nacht," GA, II, 1: 103. The document is dated July 24, 1788, but at least part of it may have been written in the early morning of July 25. I agree with the editors that Fichte had been influenced by Christian Gotthilf Salzmann's *Carl von Carlsberg* and Christian Sintenis's *"Hallo" glücklicher Abend*, both mentioned in the text (p. 103). But the "Random Thoughts" also points to a much broader range of reading that had shaped Fichte's view of his age. [2] Ibid.

village by traversing the German heartland of the Reformation, where
Luther's evangelical church had entrenched itself nearly three centuries
earlier.

To the west, in Catholic France, 1788 was a year of ominous events.
Having dominated the international politics of continental Europe for
well over a century, the Bourbon Kingdom was entering the vortex that
would produce a revolutionary National Assembly, a Republic impelled
forward by popular violence, the trial and execution of Louis XVI, the
Committee of Public Safety, the Terror. By contrast Saxony and the other
Protestant states of North Germany entered the 1790s with a legacy of
prudent, well-ordered reform from above, sponsored by "enlightened"
rulers and their ministers. Over the previous several decades, to be sure,
advocates of rationalist policies had clashed with the guardians of Lutheran
Orthodoxy, and their disagreements were not without passion. But they
were not the stuff of revolution.

And yet German-speaking Europe did have its share of angry young
men, entertaining radical, if not revolutionary, visions, and Fichte was one
of them.

Fichte's anger was in part a reaction to his lack of career prospects. It
had been more than three years since he had ended his university studies
in the theology faculty at Leipzig. Since then he had sought but failed to
find a point of entry into the German academic and official elite, still
described in the corporate language of old-regime Europe as "the learned
estate" (*Gelehrtenstand*). Even more than most university graduates from
uneducated families, he was handicapped by the obscurity of his origins.
When Fichte told his younger brother in 1794 that even after leaving the
university he had still had "some peasant-like manners" (*einige bäuerische
Manieren*), he meant to evoke the rural world of his childhood and
particularly the coarseness associated with physical labor; he was not
referring to the specific position of his family.[3] In fact the term "peasant"
underestimates the lowliness of his birth. Rammenau was one of the
villages in Saxon Upper Lusatia (*Oberlausitz*) where the peasants, by virtue
of their landholdings and their traditional communal rights, still formed
the village elite. An increasing number of families, landless or with small
holdings, depended primarily on ribbon weaving for their livelihoods.
Fichte's father Christian belonged to this growing stratum in textile production. He worked in linen, and perhaps in wool as well; the production of silk ribbons, which were more elegant but also more subject to
the whims of fashion, was left to artisans in the towns.[4]

Born in Rammenau, Christian Fichte had left the village to appren-
tice with a linen manufacturer in the nearby town of Pulsnitz. He had

[3] GA, III, 2: 151.
[4] Bernd Schöne, *Kultur und Lebensweise Lausitzer Bandweber (1750–1850)* (Berlin, 1977), esp. pp. 24–7.

won his master's reluctant permission to marry his daughter Johanna Maria Dorothea, and the couple had returned to Rammenau to practice the weaving trade and farm the family plots. The list of godparents on the birth certificate for Johann Gottlieb, the first of their nine children, gives us a rough notion of the family's position in the village pecking order. By tradition, godparents were selected with an eye to forming ties with local families of wealth and influence. The only one of Johann Gottlieb's godparents who might have fit that description was Johann Georg Hanisch, a peasant (*Bauer*) from the village of Geissmannsdorf. The other two were George Fichte, listed as a wagoner (and bachelor), and Anna Rosina Fichte, the wife of a weaver and shoemaker.[5]

The Fichtes probably were not among the poorer weaving families in the area. The middle decades of the eighteenth century were a period of expansion in the weaving industry of Upper Lusatia. Christian Fichte had inherited land from his father and owned his own house, built in part with his wife's dowry. They had a large brood, but it was the steady supply of children that enabled weaving familes to operate their looms without hired help. At age five or six Johann Gottlieb was likely to have begun contributing his labor to the family trade – by winding lengths of yarn onto spools, for example, or by handling the connecting rod that set in motion the loom's cogged wheel.[6] Even as his father taught him to read in the evenings and as he received instruction from Johann Gottfried Dinndorf, the local pastor, he was preparing for the weaver's life.

On a Sunday in 1770, however, the nine-year-old's future had been recast, suddenly and irrevocably, by one of the most dramatic gestures of noblesse oblige in the eighteenth-century record. Passing through Rammenau on a visit to Count von Hoffmannsegg, his brother-in-law and the local estate lord, Baron Ernst Hauboldt von Miltitz had hoped to hear the Sunday sermon but arrived too late. Johann Gottlieb had already been singled out by Pastor Dinndorf as a potential recruit for the clergy. Now Dinndorf, perhaps sensing a momentous opportunity, brought him before the Baron and had him demonstrate his remarkable memory by reciting the sermon verbatim. Miltitz was suitably impressed; he decided then and there to sponsor the prodigy's education, and within a few hours he had won the parents' permission to take him away. The boy was brought first to Siebeneichen, the Miltitz estate on the Elbe river near Meissen. He would later recall that this sudden transferral to an ancient castle, surrounded by parks and great oak forests, left him intimidated and homesick. Perhaps realizing how disoriented the boy felt, Miltitz arranged for him to live in a nearby village with Pastor Gotthold Leberecht Krebel and his wife, a childless couple who provided something of the familial

[5] Fichte requested a copy of his birth certificate in 1806. It has been published in FG 1: 3.
[6] Schöne, *Kultur*, p. 44.

warmth he missed.[7] Roughly four years later, in 1774, Johann Gottlieb entered Schulpforta, one of the three ducal boarding schools (*Fürsten-schulen*) in Saxony, housed in a former Cistercian cloister on the bank of the Saale river near Naumburg. From there he went on to university studies in theology in 1780.

In the late eighteenth century a significant minority of German university students, particularly in the theology faculties, found themselves in circumstances similar to Fichte's. Stereotyped as "poor students" (*arme Studenten*), they were from families without substantial property and owed their survival to various forms of charity. A good number of these charity students were sons of village and small-town pastors. The parents of most of the others were artisans, shopkeepers, and petty officials in the towns.[8] Having spent his first nine years in a village and in a family that was inferior in status, and probably in wealth, to the local peasants, Fichte was a rare specimen indeed. By the time he returned to Rammenau in 1788 he had reason to wonder whether Miltitz's intervention – the miracle that had singled him out – had been the fateful wrong turn in his life. The Baron had died in 1774, just as his protegée was entering Schulpforta. The family's sponsorship had come to an abrupt end sometime during Fichte's university studies, when the Baroness had heard disturbing reports about her client's conduct at Leipzig. Fichte found himself cut off from the major source of his financial support and – a more ominous dilemma – from the family connection that would have insured him preferment in the Saxon clergy.[9]

Fichte had to resort to the same expedient that sustained so many other theology candidates during the search for an appointment. He earned his room and board as a live-in tutor in the homes of the affluent. In early 1788, after several years of tutoring on rural estates in Saxony, he returned to Leipzig in the hope of finding employment and "prospects" with a truly prominent family. He had to settle for a much less promising position with the family of a prosperous inkeeper in Zürich. When he left Zürich in the spring of 1790, he was informally betrothed to Johanna Rahn, a merchant's daughter, but he still lacked prospects and hence was in no position to marry.[10] Watching his friends from Schulpforta settling into pastorates and university posts, he was beginning to feel left out. His

[7] The details are from the account by Fichte's son Hermann, much of which he had probably received from his parents. Immanuel Hermann Fichte, *Johann Gottlieb Fichte's Leben und litterarischer Briefwechsel*, 2 vols. (Sulzbach, 1830–31), 1: 7–14 (FG 1: 5–10). On Miltitz and his intervention, see also Adolf Peters, *General Dietrich von Miltitz, sein Leben und sein Wohnsitz* (Meissen, 1863), pp. 1–3.

[8] For a profile of "poor students" and their careers, see Anthony J. La Vopa, *Grace, Talent, and Merit: Poor Students, Clerical Careers, and Professional Ideology in Eighteenth-Century Germany* (Cambridge, 1988), esp. pp. 19–57.

[9] See esp. Fichte's letter to Christoph Gottlob von Burgsdorff, July, 1790, in GA, III, 1: 149–51.

[10] The courtship and marriage will be discussed in Chapter 6.

Wanderjahre as a tutor would resume in June of 1791 and would not end until November 1792.

The detour to Rammenau in 1788 offered a dubious respite. Fichte was a virtual stranger to his brothers and sisters, whose horizons were limited to the world of farming and small-scale trade from which he been abruptly removed seventeen years earlier. His filial affection was markedly one-sided. The only surviving letter from Schulpforta is to his father, and it leaves no doubt of the tenderness Fichte still felt for him, despite the widening social distance between them. The thirteen-year-old proudly reported that he expected to receive one of the best grades in the annual examination. Unfortunately his success would cost him. A "fatal custom" required that he buy pastry for eleven of his fellow pupils. He needed some cash, though he knew it would be a heavy burden for his "dear father." He explained, very tactfully, that he could not give the pupils garters sent from home, as his father had apparently proposed; his fellow pupils preferred money to such things, and he would be "terribly hounded." He would be very pleased, though, if his father sent him a pair of garters, and not simply because he needed them badly; they would serve as "a very pleasant reminder" of him.[11]

Mother was another matter. Fichte would later confide to his fiancée that his mother had opposed her husband's tendency to favor the eldest at the expense of his siblings and that she "[had] never shown particular tenderness toward [him]."[12] That made all the more infuriating her disappointment that he was not doing the family proud by ascending the pulpit as a duly appointed pastor. In January of 1791, in defiance of his mother's disapproval of his decision to leave Zürich, Fichte would fire off a particularly bitter letter to his younger brother Samuel Gotthelf. "Let [the family] think I am dead," he snapped; "that is still farther [from them] than Switzerland." If they want to "make a show of me in their fashion," he wrote with his mother primarily in mind, "they can always say I am a village parson somewhere." As for "my good father," he added, tell him that I am sorry I cannot be there to sweeten his remaining days, and that I love him dearly – but tell him when you are "alone."[13]

The "Random Thoughts" conveys the sense of exclusion, deprivation, and moral outrage with which an impecunious young scholar confronted his society. By planning a literary project, Fichte sought to turn his dark mood to constructive purposes. "Would there not still be a book to be written," he asks, "that reveals the total corruption of our governments and our mores?" If the book was to have an impact on a "frivolous age," it would have to be a graphic satire, with "comical turns" conveying "the finest and most concealed irony." The narrator would be a French nobleman, a Marquis von St. He would report back to Paris on his visit to

[11] GA, III, 1: 6–7.   [12] GA, III, 1: 83.   [13] GA, III, 1: 207–10.

"the newly discovered south polar lands," which would differ from Europe only in being "a few steps farther advanced in misery and evil."[14] Like the Persian travelers in Montesquieu's *Persian Letters*, the Marquis would form judgments "only half correctly" about his hosts' government, their nobility, their judicial system, their economic life, their social mores, educational practices, and public entertainments. He would then come upon "a wise and happy people" and, like Diderot's French visitors to Tahiti, would attempt to "convert" and "subjugate" them.[15]

Fichte wisely abandoned this project; he lacked the gifts for irony and satire. To the extent that the "Random Thoughts" foreshadows his later career, it is in exhibiting the high seriousness with which he aspired to contribute to the regeneration of mankind. The document offers no more than oblique inklings of the upheavals in store for Europe from 1789 onward. In the Grub Street underworld of Paris, educated young men without prospects – young men excluded from the world of the salons and the academies – were nursing the "gutter Rousseauism" that would help drive the French Revolution toward the Terror.[16] Fichte's moral disdain was far removed from the politically charged pamphlet journalism of Grub Street. It owed far more, in fact, to the biblical jeremiad and the Lutheran sermon than to the increasing radicalism of French political invective in the 1780s. And as a variant on the jeremiad it was quite tame. As categorical as it was, Fichte's vision of corruption lacked the eschatological sense of urgency with which Luther had confronted a sinful people. The Lutheran economy of grace and redemption has acceded to the moralistic, utilitarian reformism that made the German Protestant Enlightenment so earnestly cautious. There is the usual concern with promoting population growth and agriculture; with turning scholarship in "useful" directions; with moral education. The moralists Fichte cites include Pestalozzi, the Swiss pedagogue, but there is no mention of Rousseau.[17]

And yet, in its distinctly German way, the "Random Thoughts" echoes Rousseau; there is the same mood of alienation from a thoroughly corrupt world, the same hatred of the abuses of power, wealth, and intellect in a "refined" society. The depth of Fichte's alienation can be measured by the sheer sweep of his resentments and frustrations. When this young

---

[14] "Zufällige Gedanken," p. 104.
[15] Ibid., p. 108. Diderot is mentioned in the text but in connection with a reform of the theater (p. 108).
[16] Robert Darnton, "The High Enlightenment and the Low-Life of Literature," in Darnton, *The Literary Underground of the Old Regime* (Cambridge, Mass., 1982), pp. 1–40. But cf. the corrective to Darnton's reading of the political significance of prerevolutionary *libelles* in Jeremy Popkin, "Pamphlet Journalism at the End of the Old Regime," *Eighteenth-Century Studies* 22:3 (Spring, 1989): 351–67.
[17] "Zufällige Gedanken," p. 104.

intellectual surveyed his age, the rot assumed many faces. His censure extended up and down the hierarchy of old-regime society, from the "dumb rearing" of children in rural families like his own to the greed of the princely courts. If the social specificity of Fichte's moralism was multivalent, however, it also had a certain dichotomous simplicity. He looked out on a world divided into exploiters and victims, and he could identify himself only negatively, as one of the victims.

★ ★ ★

Of all the species of corruption Fichte identified on that sleepless night in Rammenau, the nobility's "laughable pride of pedigree" was the most galling. A "wise" and "happy" people would be spared such arrogance; there would be no hereditary nobility, and indeed no hereditary ranks of any kind.[18]

By the 1780s it was neither unusual nor particularly radical to dismiss the pretensions of aristocratic lineage. Visions of a new, emphatically merito-cratic social order were in the air, and not just in France. They attested to educated commoners' need to validate themselves in the face of noble pedi-gree and to their confidence in the potentially universal extension of their own ethos. There seemed to be something irrational and obsolete about a social hierarchy in which the biological accident of "birth" normally deter-mined the status and the life chances of the individual, and the most obvious case in point was the continuing preeminence of the aristocracy. The ratio-nal alternative to this injustice and waste of human resources was a society that rewarded *Verdienst*, a word that connoted both "merit," in the sense of personal achievement, and the demonstration of merit in "usefulness" in service to the common good. What made people useful was relentless work discipline – the kind required in academic education and professional life as well as in commercial enterprise.

Though the German nobility was largely spared the virulent porno-graphic *libelles* that the French literary underground spewed forth, it drew its share of censure and resentment. German aristocratic life had a reputation for unbending exclusiveness that was probably well deserved. In the late eighteenth century *die Welt* – the high society of the German dynastic states, formed by dozens of court residences scattered across central Europe – was still segregated to a degree that *le monde* had ceased to be.[19] There was no German equivalent to the salon world that mixed blue-bloods, wealthy bourgeois, and celebrated and aspiring philosophes in France. Most of the German courts had pretensions to grandeur that soared far beyond their political significance, not to mention their tax

[18] Ibid., pp. 104, 108.
[19] Still rich in detail about the courts, though dated, is W. H. Bruford, *Germany in the Eighteenth Century: The Social Background of the Literary Revival* (Cambridge, 1965).

resources. Their apparently cosmopolitan attachment to French Classicism barely hid a smug provincialism. There were, of course, fabulously rich noble households, but in wealth many families attached to the courts could not compete with patrician families in great commercial centers like Hamburg and Frankfurt and Leipzig; and the courtier of shabby gentility was not uncommon. Aristocratic families of limited means found some consolation in ancient lineage, which was considered the sine qua non for admission into the charmed circles of court life. And the income derived from public employment could make up, at least to some degree, for lack of substantial landed property. Even rulers of the larger states – Frederick the Great of Prussia is the most striking example – gave exclusive preference to prominent aristocratic families at the highest levels of government and the judicial systems. Likewise most branches of the officer corps were aristocratic preserves, and in some states scions of noble families also enjoyed virtually hereditary rights to the most desirable ecclesiastical appointments.

Of the commoners who made up the great majority of German university students, most were sons of the educated *Bürgertum* in government service and the clergy. They had reason to complain about the privileges attached to "birth," since the aristocratic monopoly at the top of the administrative and judicial bureaucracies was an insuperable barrier to their career aspirations. And yet they were scions in their own right, privileged by their families' wealth, which afforded at least modest affluence, and by the fact that for them academic education was a patrimony, not something achieved by dint of individual effort. It was among the minority of "poor students," from families that were neither educated nor propertied, that the disjunction between achievement and available opportunities was most glaring. Lacking the inherited advantages and the family connections that usually launched careers, these young men had to vindicate themselves as exceptional cases – to win admission into the academic and official elite despite their plebeian origins – with sheer talent and hard work. While an aristocratic pedigree automatically opened doors at the highest echelons of church and state, the poor student was relegated to the shabby underside of public employment. If only for want of career alternatives, he studied theology in the hope of securing a clerical appointment. It was likely to be an obscure, poorly endowed pastorate or, worse, a teaching position in one of the many notoriously neglected Latin Schools scattered across Germany's small towns.

Poor students as a group were often stereotyped as "half-educated" interlopers, their boorish pedantry no substitute for the grace and wit expected in polite society. Fichte's unambiguously plebeian origins in a village weaving family threatened to magnify this stigma. For that very reason he was especially proud of his identity as a "scholar," particularly when he felt victimized by aristocratic arrogance. A case in point was his

run-in with a Capitaine von Bright, a guest at his employer's inn in
Zürich. Von Bright disdained to converse with a young tutor who "[ate]
the bread of Herr Ott," and made it clear that the tutor's very presence
violated "the laws of good manners." Fichte protested to Ott that he did
not have to endure "the boastings (*Pralereien*) of ignorant and conceited
people." Though he assured his employer that in his written retort to von
Bright he had moderated his tone, he had in fact used his pen to repay
the officer in kind for his "slashing contempt." Von Bright might dismiss
him as a mere hireling, but he was proud to be a man who lived "for
[his] work." Title aside, von Bright lived "for his money." Rather then
emulate the Capitaine's "cavalier" ignorance, Fichte would render him
"the respect due [his] station and his merits."[20]

Aside from its legal and de facto privileges, the aristocracy enjoyed preeminence by virtue of its glittering cultural presence. To be "worldly,"
in the positive sense of that term, was to meet the intricate and highly
formalized standards of politesse with which the courts and the great
households asserted their singular fusion of corporate status, aesthetic
sensibility, and public authority. In the late eighteenth century this etiquette still set the tone for politeness and taste, posing an intimidating
barrier to commoners.

It was in part a linguistic barrier, since the language of courtly politesse
was French. Herder was one of many educated commoners who lamented
the caste division that "a completely foreign language" had imposed.
French-speaking noblemen and German-speaking commoners were "split
apart . . . present[ing] themselves in a corrupt way," and were deprived of
"a *reliable communal organ of their innermost feelings.*" Hence "the *one* part
usually had to remain hanging on phrases, on words without content,
empty of inner cultivation (*innerer Bildung*), while the other, despite all
efforts at advancing, was always and forever confronted with a wall on
which empty sounds rebounded."[21] As Herder well knew, educated commoners might learn to read French, but that made the wall no less imposing; they were not likely to have acquired the inbred facility needed to
use the language in everyday sociability. Likewise few could feel confident about knowing the intricate calibrations of rank that courtly etiquette was designed to mark, and few had mastered the nuances of bodily
grace with which appropriate degrees of deference and condescension
were conveyed. The awkward gesture, the misuse of a *Kompliment*, the
intrusion of "pedantic" seriousness into "gallant" conversation: all were
telltale signs of boorishness.

[20] GA, III, 1: 26–9.
[21] Johann Gottfried Herder, "Haben wir noch das Publikum und Vaterland der Alten?" in *Herders
Werke in Fünf Bänden*, 5 (1978): 112–13. On the social and cultural significance of this language
divide, see also Anthony J. La Vopa, "Herder's *Publikum*: Language, Print, and Sociability in
Eighteenth-Century Germany," *Eighteenth-Century Studies* 29:1 (1995): 5–24.

32   *The* Wanderjahre

Though court society remained powerfully intimidating, it had become
a standard target for censorious moralizing in the course of the eighteenth
century. In the "moral weeklies" that proliferated in the middle decades
and in the imaginative literature as well as the journalism of ensuing years,
politesse was the foil against which a self-consciously bourgeois ethos
pitted its claims to moral superiority.[22] The claim found particularly ardent
expression in the new ideal of "friendship" – an ideal that the educated
German *Bürgertum* embraced with extraordinary enthusiasm. At issue were
irreconcilably different norms for sociability, each with its distinct mode
of communication and presentation of self. By the standards of the bourgeois alternative, politesse seemed rigidly artificial; the imperatives of rank
– the need to assert and acknowledge positions within a social pecking
order – always defined the terms for human exchange. Friendship was
so appealing because it was not social in this sense. It was a "natural"
bonding, a kind of intimacy in which purely "human" communication
transcended any social differences between the communicants.

Friendship had the same roots as "love," the poet Friedrich Klopstock
observed, though love had "a few more blooms."[23] While one of the
"cornerstones" of friendship was "the cultivated understanding," the other
was "the improved heart." It was the combination – this mutual nourishment of the intellectual and emotional – that made friendship vital
to the process of the self-cultivation that the word *Bildung* was coming
to evoke. Whereas the "art" of politesse lay in highly controlled, calculating formalism, friendship was warmly spontaneous and uninhibited. It
throve on the earnest discussion of weighty subjects that was taboo in
"gallant" conversation. Whereas intrigue and flattery were de rigeur in
courtly circles, the essence of friendship was a mutual openness and
frankness that did not stop short of mutual criticism. The courtier
was "a sealed letter," in Schiller's phrase, but there could be no secrets
between friends.[24]

---

[22] See esp. Wolfgang Martens, *Die Botschaft der Tugend. Die Aufklärung im Spiegel der deutschen Moralis-
chen Wochenschriften* (Stuttgart, 1968), pp. 342–70.
[23] Friedrich Klopstock, "Von der Freundschaft," in *Friedrich Gottlieb Klopstock. Ausgewählte Werke*, ed.
Karl August Schleiden (Munich, 1962), p. 936. On the cult of friendship, see, e.g., Wolfdietrich
Rasch, *Freundschaftskult und Freundschaftsdichtung im deutschen Schrifttum des 18. Jahrhunderts, vom
Ausgang des Barok bis zu Klopstock* (Halle, 1936), esp. pp. 88–111; Wolfram Mauser and Barbara
Becker-Cantarino, eds., *Frauenfreundschaft-Männerfreundschaft. Literarische Diskurse im 18. Jahrhundert*
(Tübingen, 1991); Michael Maurer, *Die Biographie des Bürgers. Lebensformen und Denkweisen in der
formativen Phase des deutschen Bürgertums (1680–1815)* (Göttingen, 1996), pp. 305–14.
[24] Dieter Borchmeyer, "'Der ganze Mensch ist wie ein versiegelter Brief' – Schillers Kritik und
Apologie der 'Hofkunst,'" in Achim Aurnhammer, Klaus Manger, and Friedrich Strack, eds., *Schiller
und die höfische Welt* (Tübingen, 1990), pp. 460–75. Quotation on p. 462. See also Martens, *Die
Botschaft der Tugend*, passim; Paul Mog, *Ratio und Gefühlskultur. Studien zur Psychogenese und Literatur
im 18. Jahrhundert* (Tübingen, 1976), esp. pp. 36–57; Maurer, *Die Biographie des Bürgers*; Nikolaus
Wegmann, *Diskurse der Empfindsamkeit. Zur Geschichte eines Gefühls in der Literatur des 18. Jahrhunderts* (Stuttgart, 1988), pp. 56–70.

In the shaping of Fichte's sense of self in youth and early adulthood, the dichotomy between courtly formalism (or at least the stereotype of such) and the "natural" intimacy of friendship played a critical role. Within this binary contrast he formulated the distinctions between human transparency and social opacity, free communication and forced dissimulation, that would preoccupy him for the rest of his life. He had absorbed the values of the friendship cult as a schoolboy and as a student. His homage to those values was conventional in its effusive sentimentality, but his commitment to being "open to friends" was sincere. Having a close friend was essential to his well-being; this was, in fact, the one area in which he was willing to acknowledge emotional need and dependence. In Leipzig in the late 1780s, the need was filled by Friedrich August Weisshuhn, one his former schoolmates at Schulpforta. Fichte would later recall their "sweet hours of soft warmth and of tender outpourings of the heart, with a glass of Medoc," in the winter of 1787–88.[25] Henrich Nikolaus Achelis, a fellow tutor, played the same role in Zürich, and he was one of the small circle of friends that figure in Fichte's diary from that period. When Fichte returned to Leipzig in 1790 he sorely missed old friends and was chagrined by the lack of new ones. During his stay in Königsberg in the winter of 1792 he found in Theodor von Schön still another intimate, a young man whom he could both "honor" and "love" despite his aristocratic lineage, and whose "heart" had responded to him in kind.[26]

In the bourgeois alternative to "worldly" culture, friendship was, as Klopstock's metaphor implied, the extra-familial complement to the joys of family life. While the new cult of domesticity gave patriarchal authority a new lease on life, it also made the home a haven for the emotional intimacy that seemed conspicuously absent from the aristocratic household. But Fichte had been abruptly removed from his family at an early age, and the resulting distance, at once physical and social, seems to have heightened resentments on both sides. His emotional investment in friendship was in part a compensation for his problematic, often frustrating relationship with his own family. He acknowledged as much to Weisshuhn in May of 1790, in a letter lamenting his lack of friends in Leipzig; "your heart is perhaps satisfied," he observed with more than a hint of self-pity, since "you have an excellent mother, excellent sister."[27]

Fichte's abiding fondness for his father made all the more painful his estrangement from his mother and the siblings who took her side. In May of 1791, when his travels brought him in the neighborhood of Rammenau, he let it be known that he was staying in a nearby inn, in the expectation – correct, as it turned out – that his brothers would come by and persuade him to visit home. The visit confirmed his feelings about

[25] GA, III, 1: 119. See also GA, III, 1: 23, 174–5. [26] GA, III, 1: 271, 277. [27] GA, III, 1: 120.

both parents. His father was still the good-hearted, upright soul he had always revered. His mother, for all her obvious efforts to please, was still coldly forbidding. He could "converse as [he] wanted to converse" with his younger brother Samuel Gotthelf, but their intimacy seemed so remarkable precisely because they were brothers. He saw their relationship as one of those rare cases in which "nature" – that is, consanguinity – had provided the harmony of hearts and minds on which friendship throve.

One of the ironies of Fichte's youth is that he felt deprived of the emotional comforts of family life in spite of, and in part because of, his extended employment as a live-in instructor of children. With brief interruptions he found himself on "the meandering track of the tutor's life," as one of his contemporaries called it, for most of his twenties – from sometime in the mid-1780s, when he had to end his university studies prematurely, until November of 1792.[28] As the advice in tutoring handbooks implied, and as the testimony of veteran tutors often confirmed, the household was a minefield, to be negotiated with extreme caution. Dealing with employers who had open-ended notions of his duties and who had their own ideas about how their children should be educated, the tutor had to maneuver to secure a measure of autonomy, both as an instructor and as a person with his own needs and interests. He could not find moral support among the other household employees; any hint of familiarity with the servants threatened to reduce him to their menial level. Under these circumstances freedom took the form of "open" communication with equals; and that could be found only in friendships with other educated young men, outside the household confines.[29]

In the Ott household in Zürich, Fichte's sense of isolation grew as his enlightened pedagogical strategy collided with the parents' conventional religiosity and expectations about discipline. His diary fragments recorded his fear that he would be trapped in "the most horrible situation" of "[having] no human being with whom one can speak thoughts of his heart."[30] He insisted that the Otts frankly acknowledge their disagreements with him and find a resolution (albeit on his terms). Standing on the same principle of openness, he categorically rejected their efforts to limit his free time to specific days and hours. For youth, he reminded the Otts, it was essential to be able to speak candidly with friends, and in his post he had "a double need for such strengthening."

---

[28] Frank Aschoff, "Zwischen äusserem Zwang und innerer Freiheit. Fichte's Hauslehrer-Erfahrungen und die Grundlegung seiner Philosophie," F-S 9: 27–45, is an informative account of Fichte's tutoring years.

[29] On the social significance of tutoring, see Ludwig Fertig, *Die Hofmeister. Ein Beitrag zur Geschichte des Lehrerstandes und der bürgerlichen Intelligenz* (Stuttgart, 1979); La Vopa, *Grace, Talent, and Merit*, pp. 111–33.

[30] "Tagebücher zur Erziehung der Ottschen Kinder," GA, II, 1: 153–4.

In relationships forced into specific time allotments, he protested, "no openness can be maintained"; "before I could say a word, I would have to think whether it is not subject to confiscation (*confiscabel*)."[31] To constrict his right to see friends was to deprive him of a vital free space, his only respite from the constrictions of the tutor's station.

Even as he chafed at his subordination in the Ott household, Fichte retained a sense of superiority over what he saw as the bourgeois philistinism of the family. All of his other tutoring employments were in aristocratic households, where he found himself in a much more vulnerable position. In petty but audible ways, the daily frictions and misunderstandings between parents and tutors registered the shocks of the collision between an aristocratic ethos and its self-consciously bourgeois antithesis. Though often aware of the new importance of academic learning for their sons' career prospects, aristocratic parents also expected the tutor to groom them in politesse; and it was precisely in this task that the typical tutor – the poor student, groomed in the scholastic learning that was still pedantic and boorish by aristocratic standards and lacking exposure to "the world" – was likely to be found wanting. The tutor, on the other hand, approached aristocratic elegance with the bourgeois moralist's distaste for its stiff artificiality and its corrupt "luxury." In principle, if not in practice, his mission was to administer a pedagogical antidote that would (somehow) promote the child's "natural" development while instilling in him the self-discipline of good work habits. This was clearly the task Fichte set himself. Against the "enervation of the higher orders from early youth onward" (his diagnosis in the "Random Thoughts"), the tutor had to wage relentless battle.[32]

The egalitarian mutuality of friendship was a respite from the grossly unequal terms of the battle. The tutor's credentials could not alter the fact that he was a live-in employee of more or less plebeian origins. The handbooks assured him that, even in aristocratic households, educational accomplishments and pedagogical expertise could more than compensate for these handicaps in winning the respect and perhaps even the "friendship" of his pupils' parents. But the reality was often quite different. Quartered in his pupil's bedroom, and expected to maintain a respectful silence at social gatherings, he was hardly distinguishable from the domestic servants. Under these circumstances the need for friends became all the more urgent. The intimacy of friendship was both a compensation for the tutor's social inferiority and his way of asserting the moral superiority of an alternative kind of sociability.

From the distance of Zürich, Fichte described his earlier employers among the Saxon rural nobility as "niggardly little *Krautjunkers*." "In this

---

[31] "Invective," GA, II, 1: 230–5.
[32] "Zufällige Gedanken," p. 106. See also La Vopa, *Grace, Talent, and Merit*, pp. 121–2.

region," he had lamented in the early fall of 1787, "I am . . . almost entirely without intelligent intercourse, without acquaintances and entirely unable to make an acquaintance." The provincial obscurity of such employers made their arrogance all the more intolerable. The Zürich stint was hardly an improvement; he found himself entrusted with "the tender plants" of "a petty bourgeois" in a thoroughly stodgy town. Resolved to avoid "beginnning again and again at the bottom and entering once again into thankless work," he now sought the opportunities and the connections that only a truly prominent house could offer.[33]

His next employment – with the von Plater household, on an estate near Warsaw – might have satisfied this aspiration but instead landed him in an embarrassing confrontation. Upon his arrival Countess Katharina von Plater did not hide her disappointment that he was not fluent in French. He protested – in a letter written in fastidious French and in a tone far more indignant than apologetic – that he would not have made the trip if he had been made aware that the assignment required "anything beyond Latin, history, geography, mathematics, and the mediocre knowledge of the French language that men of letters in [his] country possess" ("neither in Dresden nor in Leipzig," he assured her *en passant*, "will a tutor be found who knows the [language] better than I do").[34] Though the Countess appeared ready to work out an accommodation, either in her own household or with another employer in the area, he would have none of her "condescending tolerance."[35] In the first impressions recorded in his diary, she already epitomized the "woman of the great world," never "at home," always coming and going, speaking in "the tone of command" and "allowing her hand to be kissed by her obedient husband," and bejeweled to excess in red *camoisin*, always appearing "drunk" (*besoffen*).[36] "Since I have still seen few of her kind," the same diary entry notes, "it was unavoidable that she became insufferable to me." His communiqués to her were suitably defiant. Having seen "enough of the great world to know its dangers but not enough to have acquired its mores" and having learned some disciplines in depth rather than many superficially, he preferred "to depart for [his] fatherland or another land where thoroughness (*Gründlichkeit*) and German are still valued."[37]

This bravado display of reverse snobbery did not persuade the Countess to compensate him with a half-year's salary, as he had initially hoped, but it did secure him travel money to reach Königsberg. There he spent two intense weeks writing his first philosophical essay, a treatise on revelation, presented to Immanuel Kant and designed to demonstrate a young disciple's talents. Kant was suitably impressed, but Fichte soon faced des-

[33] GA, III, 1: 13, 45.   [34] GA, III, 1: 228.   [35] GA, III, 1: 232.
[36] "Tagebuch meiner Osterabreise aus Sachsen nach Pohlen, u. Preussen," GA, II, 1: 410.
[37] GA, III, 1: 228, 232.

titution. Since Kant demurred on his request for a loan to finance his return to Saxony, he had to abandon his resolve to be done with the tutor's miserable lot. His next (and final) employment took him to the Krokow estate, on the Baltic coast six miles west of Danzig. A hardened veteran with no illusions about "the world," he suddenly found himself in a great household that mocked his stereotypes and dismantled his defenses. "The entire house," he reported a few months after arriving, "is loveable to a degree I had not hoped to encounter under the moon." Indeed his situation was in a sense "too good"; he almost hoped for a "benevolent storm" to drive him away, since his ambitions were evaporating as he sank into a kind of "dream life."[38] As detached from his new contentment as he tried to remain, he found it irresistible.

The physical setting certainly had helped disarm him. With the Baltic surf in view, the Krokow estate was an oasis of civilized comfort (despite the occasional wolf preying on dogs in the courtyard). There were English and French gardens, complete with "kiosks and cascades, Chinese bridges and temples"; among the attractions of the household were "a friendly concert and a theater, fat sausage and good wine." But it was the presiding presence of Countess Luise, a forty-three-year-old mother of two children, that made all this so bewitching. To Fichte this "angel in human form" was precisely what the stereotypical grande dame was not. Accustomed to disdaining courtly superficiality, particularly in its female guises, he was now facing a female embodiment of genuine cultivation. All the more extraordinary, under the inspiration of this "benevolent goddess," the household exuded the familial nest warmth that "the world" disdained.[39] "If I should die today," he would write to a friend on November 12, 1792, just before leaving Krokow, "I could not say that I did not live happily for at least a year of my life, that I did not taste the joys of domestic life, the foretaste of peace of soul."[40]

Fichte was in the throes of an infatuation, though it could find no more than muted expression in filial reverence for a woman who was thirteen years his senior. The closest he came to admitting the passion of his attachment – to the Countess, and to himself – was to speak of "feelings" (*Empfindungen*) that "will endure no expression." What he could openly aspire to was the intimacy of friendship, despite the social chasm between them. The "outpourings of [his] heart" took the form of an effort to convert her to the Kantian philosophical principles that had transformed his own thinking. But he was given to moodiness, he admitted in his diary, and he got carried away in his arguments. She recoiled from his "passionate warmth in conversation"; his moodiness intensified; she took pains to put more distance between them.

---

[38] GA, III, 1: 277, 281.   [39] GA, III, 1: 276, 281, 300.   [40] GA, III, 1: 355.

As determined as he was to clarify the terms of their relationship, Fichte could not find what he called "the right tone" in his first attempt to resolve this crisis with a letter. On June 29, unable to endure his "ambiguous situation," he drafted and redrafted still another letter and added a list of "explanations," designed to avoid future "misunderstandings."[41] But he had not settled on a tone; the letter alternated indignation and self-laceration. It was intolerable to him that his openness might be perceived as a presumptuous violation of caste boundaries. It is "against my character," he protested in the "explanations," to "force myself on anyone." Since conventional social distinctions were irrelevant to his estimations of "the person" as "a moral being," he was all the more willing to observe them. The accompanying letter spelled out his grievance in tortured prose:

> I believe that the unusual situation of a tutor who on the one hand wishes to satisfy the wishes of the house in which he lives, but on the other hand has to maintain his personal honor, imposes on him these rules of prudence for his social behavior toward others: never to draw closer than he is drawn, always to remain at the distance in which he is left, and thus, e.g., to be as good as absent when he is not introduced, to mix in no conversation he is not drawn into, and so on, all the more so, the better one understands the art of attracting, and of making a claim when one wants to make a claim, in the house in which one lives. I believe further that no one, in whatever situation he is, is bound to respond with gratitude and subordination to mistrustful withdrawal following openness, disdainful coldness, misperception of our character and intentional avoidance of seeing it in the right light – no matter what the sex or the station of the other person.
> When possible I at least withdraw still farther when I am repulsed.[42]

This was the voice of the injured *Bürger*, seeking invulnerability in a combined retreat behind social protocol and assertion of moral superiority. But Fichte's other impulse was to crash through the rules, even at the cost of his dignity – to retrieve the intimacy of friendship by laying bare his vulnerability. In the first draft of his letter of June 29, he went so far as to admit to Countess Luise that having arrived with every intention of remaining "independent of people," he had "learned to revere [her] as [he] had never revered a person."[43] In the final version – the same letter in which he explained why, as matter of honor, the tutor had to keep his distance – he assured her that the warmth of his arguments flowed from his eagerness to persuade someone "dear" to him, and hence he was hardly in need of "forgiveness." And yet it was forgiveness he craved; he simply

[41] GA, III, 1: 311–16.
[42] GA, III, 1: 313–14. See also "– Nöthige Aufklärungen über gewisse Dinge. – um mögliche Misverständnisse zu heben.-," in GA, II, 2: 165–6.   [43] GA, III, 1: 312.

could not endure the thought that he had incurred "the contempt of the person whom [he] could not prevent [himself] from revering above everything in the world."[44]

Two days later Fichte noted in a letter to a friend that his occasional quarrels with the Countess only made them "better friends." But his confidence was premature; on July 12, after enduring another spell of the Countess's coldness, he concluded reluctantly in his diary that they would "never be friends again," since "her character is not what I first took it to be." He was resolved to "withdraw himself entirely," and the bitter irony was that she would "neither notice it nor feel it deeply"; "she is too self-sufficient to need anything outside herself."[45]

Did Countess Luise epitomize maternal benevolence or feminine duplicity, warm openness to friendship or frigid self-containment within a superior station? Our clashing images of her reflect Fichte's conflicting impulses and wildly fluctuating moods. She may simply have been annoyed by this young commoner's intellectual aggressiveness, or she may have sensed, and been frightened by, the passion behind it. And it is possible, of course, that she was alarmed by her own passion. Perhaps all that can be said is that Fichte's urgent need for intimacy threatened her self-possession. By the time he left Krockow in November of 1792, they seem to have worked out a modus vivendi. Perhaps because he admitted his moody impulsiveness, in fact, he may have succeeded in winning her sympathy for his philosophical convictions. But his reading of their crisis is striking. While he was disillusioned in a moral sense by the coldly self-contained side of her character, he was also – inseparably – vindicated in his social preconceptions. And in any case the Countess's friendship, like von Schön's, was precious precisely because it was exceptional. In the consciousness of this young *Bürger*, such exceptions left intact the contrast between the warm sustenance to be found among his own kind and the barrenness of aristocratic sociability. In July of 1792 – in the same letter in which he expressed his confidence that the Countess's friendship would survive an occasional quarrel – he complained of his "half life" at Krockow and the impossibility of making himself "understood" there. The Countess stood out from the other ladies of the household, for whom he had become "the vehicle of . . . passing the time" in a monotonous routine. He longed for the evenings he had spent in conversation with friends in Königsberg.[46]

★ ★ ★

Aristocratic hauteur brought out the *Bürger* in the young Fichte. It was a persona easily provoked to militant self-assertion, particularly when his

---

[44] GA, III, 1: 312, 315–16.   [45] GA, III, 1: 320; GA, II, 2: 173.
[46] GA, III, 1: 320, 324. See also Fichte's diary entries, in GA, II, 2: 171–3.

scholarly credentials or the dignity of his work was impugned. And yet
Fichte also regarded the *Bürgertum* with an outsider's distanced conviction
of superiority.

This is not to deny that Fichte's sense of personal integrity was bound
inextricably with his acquired identity as a "scholar" (*Gelehrter*). When he
turned to Kant for a loan in 1791, it was his precious "honor" as a scholar
that he offered as security.[47] But since the early eighteenth century the
corporate identity of the "learned estate" (*Gelehrtenstand*) had been under
attack, and indeed from within its own ranks. The ideal of piety and
eloquence – the hybrid agenda of Protestant humanism since the sixteenth century – seemed to have calcified beyond hope of recovery.
Critics descried the empty academic rituals; the tunnel-visioned preoccupation with confessional polemics; the antiquarian obsession with the
minutest details of the ancient world; the purely formalistic imitation of
classical models. The old-style scholar had become the "pedant" who, in
Johann Georg Schlosser's words, sought to prove "that you get a stomach
ache when you eat too much" by quoting Seneca. Such pedantry,
Schlosser observed, was a mark of "social incapacity (*gesellschaftliche Untu-
gend*)." Dusty and unkempt in appearance and boring in conversation, "the
Gelehrter in his study-room form" failed to please socially and hence was
an object of ridicule in polite circles.[48] Schlosser might have added that
to the extent that this social type was still to be found in the last decades
of the century, it was in the clergy and particularly among former poor
students from uneducated families. Incubated for years in the academic
ghetto and lacking opportunities to acquire the social polish that
might erase plebeian traits, they were least likely to combine learning with
"worldliness."

Like many other young scholars in the 1780s and 1790s, Fichte dismissed the old learning as a mere *Handwerk*, comparable to the mindless
routinism of a guild trade. When they took pride in being *Gelehrten*, it
was as members of a new breed, liberated from the stigmas and inhibitions of clerical corporatism. In the new elite they envisioned, scholars
would be qualified to mix comfortably with aristocrats as well as with
wealthy *Bürger* as the walls of their corporate ghetto disintegrated and as
they offered a new kind of scholarship, at once "useful" and cultivated,
to a broad educated public.

[47] GA, III, 1: 262–3.
[48] Johann Georg Schlosser, "Ueber Pedanterie und Pedanten," in Schlosser, *Kleine Schriften*, 6 vols.
(Basel, 1794), 5, pp. 257–9. See also R. Steven Turner, "University Professors and Professorial Scholarship in Germany 1760–1806," in Lawrence Stone, ed., *The University in Society*, vol. 2: *Europe,
Scotland and the United States from the Sixteenth to the Twentieth Century* (Princeton, N.J., 1974), pp.
495–531; La Vopa, *Grace, Talent, and Merit*. On continuity and change in the "learned estate," see
also the articles in Rudolf Vierhaus, ed., *Bürger und Bürgerlichkeit im Zeitalter der Aufklärung*
(Heidelberg, 1981), and Hans Erich Bödeker and Ulrich Herrmann, eds., *Ueber den Prozess der
Aufklärung in Deutschland im 18. Jahrhundert* (Göttingen, 1987).

By the time Fichte had attended Schulpforta the corporate walls already had large cracks, though in some ways the school was still a monument to old-regime privilege and hierarchy. As Fichte's friend Weisshuhn described it, Schulpforta was a despotism, with the older boys allowed to rule arbitrarily and sometimes brutally over the younger ones, but also a haven for the sweet joys of friendship. Parental wealth often compensated for lack of talent in the admission of pupils, but in its intensely competitive grading system the school was a strict meritocracy; individual performance was all that mattered. In its formal organization, the education was, from beginning to end, stubbornly traditional. In keeping with the Reformation ideal, the admission exam was limited to translating a Latin passage from the New Testament and answering a question from the Lutheran catechism. The valedictory addresses were meant to demonstrate graduating pupils' stylistic facility in Latin and their appreciation for the wisdom of the ancients. Under the guidance of open-minded younger teachers, however, the Enlightenment had breached the walls of this fortress of Protestant humanism and pupils of Fichte's generation had been allowed and indeed encouraged to sample contemporary literature. Weisshuhn recalled teachers reading, for example, Wieland, Pope, Swift, and Voltaire.[49] Fichte's own valedictory performance in 1780 was the work of a sophisticated, though unoriginal, eighteen-year-old. On "the correct use of the rules of rhetoric and the poetic art," the address drew on at least a passing acquaintance with – to name only some of the eighteenth-century authors cited – Voltaire, Rousseau, Gellert, Klopstock, Wieland, and Lessing.[50]

And yet there is a sense in which Fichte and his contemporaries were products of the corporate ghetto they disdained. The irony of their induction into academic culture was that it had been sufficiently open to give them a critical distance on its traditions but sufficiently closed to inculcate nonetheless an unmistakable pride of caste. As "useless" as formalistic classical learning might seem and as boorish as it might be by polite standards, they could not but be aware that it distinguished them, the tiny corps of initiates, from the great mass of the uninitiated. Perhaps more important than the formal substance of their education was its segregated setting in boarding schools that were still partially cloistered and in a student subculture that was still notoriously insulated from and antagonistic toward the "philistine" world of the local *Bürger*. Weisshuhn observed

---

[49] Friedrich August Weisshuhn, *Ueber die Schulpforte. Nebst einigen vorläufigen Betrachtungen über die Schulerziehung überhaupt* (Berlin, 1786), esp. pp. 89–97, 236–46, 272–7. Weisshuhn was contributing to a controversy about recent changes at Schulpforta, but in the course of doing so, he provided interesting detail about the intellectual climate and the pupils' corporate culture when he and Fichte had been there.

[50] The valedictory address, titled "De recto praeceptorum poeseos et rhethorices usu.," is in GA II, 1: 5–29.

that the school's "public divine service" would always remain "deficient" so long as the "rabble" (*Pöbel*) from local cottages and outlying settlements were allowed to attend.[51] That speaks volumes about the solidarity that the boys' academic induction produced and about the segregation it entailed. One need only consider the friends who figure in Fichte's correspondence and diary fragments from the late 1780s and early 1790s. Most of the old friends he wrote to and visited on his travels were former schoolmates from Schulpforta, and most of his new friends were, like him, theology students. With rare exceptions they became pastors, schoolteachers, professors.

At least on his mother's side Fichte's family had commercial roots, but his pride of caste included an inbred contempt for commercial life. If we define the *Bürgertum* as a commercial and propertied class, in fact, his social vision in the "Random Thoughts" was as antibourgeois as it was antiaristocratic. By the standards of true merit, the merchant's "money pride" (*Geldstolz*) seemed as laughable as the nobleman's "pride of pedigree."[52] In Fichte's order of values the intellectual integrity required in scholarship was something inherently superior to the mere "cleverness" needed to make money. He considered it a "weakness," he confessed to his fiancée in Zürich in March of 1790, that he was not entirely indifferent to the prestige that wealth commanded, though he had always "held [money] in contempt" as "on the whole a very trivial furnishing."[53] Remarks of this sort did not imply, of course, that he dissented from the growing chorus of complaints by schoolteachers, pastors, and even university professors about their incomes, which stood in such shabby contrast to the dignity they attributed to their professions. But to Fichte, as to many of his contemporaries, the scholar's enforced asceticism nonetheless had a moral advantage; it insulated him from the *Luxus* – the craving for material comforts and marks of prestige – that seemed to permeate an increasingly commercial society. It was in part the lack of such insulation, he observed when he returned to Leipzig in the summer of 1790, that explained the timidity and the outright hypocrisy of the scholarly community there. Even scholars were susceptible to the contagious mercenary spirit of a great commercial center.[54]

The scholar's pride of caste made simplicity of lifestyle and dedication to work the emblems of a kind of moral superiority, the righteous alternative to commercial wealth as well as to aristocratic pedigree. And yet academic education was also, like wealth and pedigree, a rare commodity. As a new image of the "scholar" as a cultivated man, at home in polite society, gained ascendancy, education was reconstrued as what Herder called "inner cultivation" (*Bildung*); but that made it, in social terms, no

[51] Weisshuhn, *Ueber die Schulpforte*, pp. 174–5.   [52] "Zufällige Gedanken," p. 105.
[53] GA, III, 1: 83.   [54] GA, III, 1: 162.

less precious than old-style learning had been. In 1780, the year Fichte began his university studies, there were roughly 3,700 university students in all of German-speaking Europe. Literacy rates rose in the course of the century, but by its close only about 25 percent of the adults in German-speaking Europe were literate.[55] In this steeply graded world, boys who ascended into academic culture from uneducated homes had to meet high expectations. If they were to sustain the honor of the scholarly estate, their plebeian traits – the crudities of their diction, their dress, their bodily carriage – had to be expunged. In Fichte's case this process of refinement may have been particularly thorough, since it had begun with an abrupt removal from his family and had continued despite the early termination of his university studies. From this angle, his years of tutoring take on a new significance. As humiliating as the terms of such employment might be, the exposure to polite society helped polish the rough edges off young men who had been cloistered within academic culture. At the same time, the widespread employment of tutors formed a safety net for young scholars without independent means and immediate career prospects. Unlike the Grub-Street literary underworld of Paris – the world in which many educated young Frenchmen had to eke out their survival – tutoring kept its recruits within the pale of eminently respectable society. The young men who had to resort to it might be alienated, as Fichte was, but they were not pariahs.[56]

Fichte's ascent into academic culture had not made him indifferent to the world he had left. In his affectionate image of his father as a simple, upright man there is more than a hint of nostalgia for the reassuring simplicities of popular life. In the "Random Thoughts" he ranged scholars like himself, who endured "extreme disdain" and "breadlessness," alongside the lower orders and especially the peasantry; they were all victims of the arrogance of the pedigreed and the greed of the propertied.[57] And yet, as heartfelt as his sympathy for the oppressed was, it could not erase the fact that an immense chasm divided the educated few from the uneducated mass in eighteenth-century society. His entire sense of self – his self-justification as a rare exception – rested on his awareness of having successfully crossed the chasm, as a letter to his brother Samuel Gotthelf in 1794 made abundantly clear. Now that Fichte was finally settling into an academic career at Jena, Samuel Gotthelf, though twenty-two years old and still living at home, hoped to follow in his footsteps. He was the only sibling with whom Fichte felt affinity, the brother whom "nature," rather than kinship, had made a "friend." Now, in his effort to counteract Samuel Gotthelf's naïve self-confidence, he emphasized the social distance that

[55] Horst Möller, *Vernunft und Kritik. Deutsche Aufklärung im 17. und 18. Jahrhundert* (Frankfurt am Main, 1986), p. 269.
[56] La Vopa, *Grace, Talent, and Merit*, pp. 70–82, 114–20.   [57] "Zufällige Gedanken," p. 105.

radically divergent life-courses had interposed between them. His brother
must have no illusions about the trial that awaited him. Before Samuel
Gotthelf could join him in Jena, Fichte insisted, he would have to
"develop [his] body and [his] manners," so that he "could appear in society
without offense."[58] And then there was the language barrier. Aside from
having to master the classical languages at a late age, Samuel Gotthelf
would have to rid himself of his "extremely corrupt" Upper Lusatian
dialect:

> I myself, though I left the region in early childhood, have had trouble puri-
> fying even my German speech so that my native land is no longer detected;
> you will never be able to do that. And I have never been able to learn to
> speak French well. . . . Another critical point is that the polite behavior of
> the great world is already necessary, and will become increasingly neces-
> sary, for the learned man who wants to belong to the higher class rather
> than remaining among the common learned *Handwerker*. . . . Such polished
> behavior is not learned in the later years, since the effects of early educa-
> tion are ineradicable. (Perhaps mine are no longer noticeable; but that is
> due to my very early life in the Miltitz house, my life in Schulpforta, among
> mostly better-raised children, my early learning of dancing, etc. And yet
> even after my departure from the university, I still had some peasant-like
> manners, which have only been eradicated by my many travels, by much
> tutoring in various lands and houses, and especially by my great attention
> to myself. And yet, do I know whether they are completely eradicated?)[59]

In the course of the previous year, thanks to his literary debut as Kant's
boldest disciple, Fichte had soared from obscurity as a "breadless *Gelehrter*"
to celebrity and a highly prized university appointment. In the letter to
his brother, however, he spoke simply as a man who had crossed the great
divide. His glance backward betrays the lingering insecurity of the inter-
loper, but there is nonetheless a sense of triumph. Fichte looked back on
his youth as an extended trial of purification, an ascent from the plebeian
to the refined that had required a complete remaking of the social
self. If he was to reconnect with the uneducated mass, it would require
a strenuous symbolic leap.

[58] GA, III, 2: 152.   [59] GA, III, 2: 151.

Chapter 2

The Road to Kant

In August of 1790, Fichte found himself at the first of several low ebbs in his fortunes. Two months earlier he had returned from Zürich to Leipzig in search of "prospects," but nothing had materialized. The friends he had expected to rejoin there had moved on. At age twenty-eight he considered himself too old to consort with students. He was too poor and obscure to mingle in the polite society of Leipzig, a commercial city described by another censorious young scholar – one looking up, like Fichte, from the bottom – as a mix of "money-pride, stinginess, extravagance, coarseness, and elegance."[1] Writing, he had discovered, was neither a financially rewarding nor a personally satisfying way to make a living. The periodical press was capricious, and concocting popular novels was not his forte.

Fichte's letters from this period convey a palpable sense of loneliness and self-pity. In early August, in the course of requesting a loan from Dietrich von Miltitz, his deceased patron's son, he reported that he had just pawned all his clothes except what he was wearing. He had needed the money, he explained, to stay alive and to maintain his "honor" by paying debts promptly. If he did not receive the loan within a few days, it would be too late to "save" him from "going under."[2]

In fact, Fichte was at the threshhold of the great turning point of his adult life. In the letter to Miltitz, he noted that he had at last found an opportunity to earn some cash by giving a student private lessons in Kant's philosophy. It was this "mere accident" occasioned by "need," he would soon recall, that led him to Kant's *Critique of Pure Reason*. Within a few days, as he advanced to the *Critique of Practical Reason*, he "threw [himself] entirely into Kantian philosophy . . . out of true taste."[3] On September 5, 1790, he wrote to his fiancée that his study of Kant had lifted him "above all earthly things."[4] A few weeks later he described

Chapter 2 was published in a slightly different form as "Fichte's Road to Kant," in Patrick Coleman, Jayne Lewis, and Jill Kowalik, eds., *Representations of the Self from the Renaissance to Romanticism* (New York: Cambridge University Press, 2000), pp. 200–229. Permission to appear in this volume is granted by the editors.

[1] Detlev Prasch, *Vertraute Briefe über den politischen und moralischen Zustand von Leipzig* (London, 1787), esp. pp. 140–3.
[2] GA, III, 1: 163–6.   [3] GA, III, 1: 167–8.   [4] GA, III, 1: 170–1.

to his friend Achelis his escape from bitter despondency to a "deep peace of soul":

> I came to Leipzig with a head that swarmed with great plans. Everything failed, and from so many soap bubbles all that was left over was the light foam from which they had formed. At first this disturbed my peace of mind a bit; and it was half in despair that I seized a *Partie* that I should have seized earlier. Since I could change nothing outside myself, I resolved to change what was inside me. I threw myself into philosophy, and indeed – and this is self-evident – into Kantianism. Here I found the antidote to the true source of my ill, and joy enough beyond that. The influence that this philosophy, and especially the moral part of it . . . has on the entire system of thought of a person, the revolution that has arisen through it especially in my own entire way of thinking, is inconceivable. . . . I now believe with all my heart in the freedom of the human being, and realize that only under this assumption is duty, virtue, and morality in general possible.[5]

It was above all the "principle of the necessity of all human actions," he continued, that was responsible for the corruption of the age.

In the late 1780s and the 1790s Kantian philosophy made a good number of converts among Germany's educated youth. It was not the first time that an eighteenth-century author had struck a chord in a generation coming of age. From the mid-1770s onward, a veritable youth cult had developed around Goethe's *Die Leiden des jungen Werthers*.[6] But even to today's readers Goethe's novel conveys an extraordinary sense of emotional immediacy. It is not hard to understand why the book overwhelmed young men, and indeed why, to the author's consternation, they found in Werther a hero to be emulated. Kant is quite another matter. Piece by piece, he was building an awesomely abstract and intricate philosophical system, and he did not pretend to be able to explain it in laypeople's language. The new philosophy was, in Fichte's apt description, "headbreaking."

And yet there is something quite familiar about the way Fichte construed and overcame his near despair – something not limited to Kantianism or indeed to German culture in the 1790s. He had entered a youthful crisis that was already fairly common throughout the West in the late eighteenth century and that would become still more common in the next century. At issue was whether selfhood as autonomous agency was an illusion and indeed whether the very notion of an integral self dissolved if the individual was merely one more object in a vast web of causes. We find an analogous case, all the more striking in view

---

[5] GA, III, 1: 193–4.
[6] See esp. Klaus R. Scherpe, *Werther und Wertherwirkung. Zum Syndrom bürgerlicher Gesellschaftsordnung im 18. Jahrhundert* (Bad Homburg, 1970).

of its obviously different setting, in the *Autobiography* of John Stuart
Mill. What brought the twenty-year-old Mill to the point of mental
and emotional paralysis in 1826 was the fear that he was merely a
"helpless slave of antecedent circumstances." For Mill, safeguarding the
integrity of the self meant finding a middle ground between "voluntaris-
tic euphoria" and "fatalistic dejection." He could accept neither the
"formalist" position, which "construe[d] persons as autonomous agents,
only intransitively related to the circumstances of their lives," nor the
"antiformalist" alternative, which "construe[d] persons transitively, as
products of a circumstantial setting that profoundly influences everything
they do."[7]

The same terms apply to Fichte's reading of his crisis, but there the
similarity ends. Mill has been aptly characterized as "one of the first
post-Christian theorists of human agency." Educated by a father with
militantly secularist convictions, he described himself in the *Autobiography*
as "one of the very few examples, in [his] country, of one who has,
not thrown off religious belief, but never had it."[8] By 1790 Fichte had
shed the orthodox Lutheranism of his childhood, but he was far from
being a post-Christian. In his ways of formulating his aspirations and
dilemmas, in fact, he was very much a German Lutheran, though of
the "enlightened" variety. For him, the need to resolve the conflicting
pulls of free will and determinism was also a need to reconcile faith and
reason.

In its dramatic structure, Fichte's inner "revolution," as he described it
to Achelis and others in the late summer and early fall of 1790, is reminiscent of the conversion experiences (*Bekehrungen*) that had figured centrally in Pietist preaching and autobiographical testimony since the late
seventeenth century. He did not, to be sure, experience his discovery of
Kant's "reason" as the infusion of a supernatural power, a reception of a
kind of grace; he was too much the eighteenth-century rationalist to make
that explicit analogy. But as a young Lutheran gripped by Kant's *Critiques*,
he needed a cultural precedent – a template which, with suitable adjustments, would give a recognizable structure to this transformative experience – and conversion was readily available. That he experienced
something like the emotional intensity of conversion is obvious. But there
is also conversion's typical dramatic sequence that begins with the pierc-
ing insight, occasioned by an apparent accident, but revealing the total
corruption of the person's life to date; that progresses to the experience
of rebirth, with its feeling of enormous relief from the burdens of

---

[7] Thomas L. Haskell, "Persons as Uncaused Causes: John Stuart Mill, the Spirit of Capitalism, and
the 'Invention' of Formalism," in Thomas L. Haskell and Richard F. Teichgraeber III, eds., *The
Culture of the Market. Historical Essays* (Cambridge, 1993), pp. 441–502, is an important reinterpretation of Mill's crisis. See esp. pp. 446–7.

[8] Ibid., pp. 449–50.

48 *The* Wanderjahre

self-delusion; that culminates in an eagerness to bear witness, to rescue others from the wrong path.[9]

Fichte's implicit construal of his crisis as a kind of conversion reminds us that he brought to Kant's *Critiques* an emphatically Protestant moral rigorism. That is why his assent to Kantianism was so much simpler than Wilhelm von Humboldt's or Friedrich Schiller's, though the three men were roughly contemporaries. Humboldt and Schiller grounded their aesthetic ideal of an unconditionally "free" *Individualität* in Kant's ethics, but they also infused it with a neo-pagan reverence for sensual expression. The latter they derived from the new Hellenism, which was hard to reconcile with Kant's eminently Lutheran tendency to equate fulfillment of duty with the repression, not the channeling, of sensuality. They had to detach the emancipatory thrust of Kant's individualism from the iron constraints of his asceticism.[10] Fichte had no such ambivalence. Kant allowed him to reaffirm the commitment to duty – or, perhaps better, to a kind of ascetic freedom exercised in and through moral rigorism – with which he had entered adulthood.

The other reason that Fichte's crisis differed from Mill's, both in its origins and in the way he construed it, is that it occurred in a quite different setting. By 1826 Britain had the most advanced market economy in the world. What makes Mill's resolution of his crisis especially relevant to the modern condition is his understanding that on the great issue he confronted, the implications of the market were double-edged. Market culture seemed at once to open new possibilities for exercising free agency and to multiply circumstantial constraints on agency. In 1790 Fichte was only beginning to become aware of a similar duality, as he tried intermittently to eke out a living in the still modest but expanding market of German print capitalism. Far more relevant to his crisis is the fact that German societies in the late eighteenth century were still, in the tradition of old-regime Europe, corporate hierarchies. Though their university-educated intelligentsias were beginning to take on recognizably modern features, they remained, on the whole, corporate enclaves, over-

---

[9] On the Pietist conversion experience, see, e.g., Wolf Oschlies, *Die Arbeits- und Berufspädagogik A. H. Franckes (1663–1727)*, Arbeiten zur Geschichte des Pietismus, vol. 6 (Witten, 1969), pp. 184–92; Erhard Peschke, *Bekehrung und Reform: Ansatz und Wurzeln der Theologie August Hermann Franckes*, Arbeiten zur Geschichte des Pietismus, vol. 15 (Bielefeld, 1977), pp. 111–14; Anthony J. La Vopa, *Grace, Talent, and Merit: Poor Students, Clerical Careers, and Professional Ideology in Eighteenth-Century Germany* (Cambridge, 1988), pp. 145–64.

[10] On Humboldt's reception of Kant, see esp. Christina M. Sauter, *Wilhelm von Humboldt und die deutsche Aufklärung* (Berlin, 1989), pp. 294–309. On Schiller see Josef Chytry, *The Aesthetic State. A Quest in Modern German Thought* (Berkeley, Calif., 1989), pp. 77–90. Friedrich Schleiermacher was another young German intellectual who had to come to terms with Kant in the early 1790s as he negotiated the choice between freedom and determinism, though from a quite different religious background. Schleiermacher's engagement with Kant is lucidly explained in Albert L. Blackwell, *Schleiermacher's Early Philosophy of Life. Determinism, Freedom, and Phantasy* (Chico, Calif., 1982).

shadowed by commercial wealth and aristocratic display, but perched at a safe distance above what they saw as the vulgarity of uneducated culture. Their intricate networks of patronage typified the ways of old-regime societies, sponsoring, as they had for centuries, limited movement across the well-guarded boundaries of social distinction. In this world the young Fichte faced two dilemmas: how to justify his exceptionality, his virtually miraculous ascent from unusually plebeian origins into an educated elite; and how to advance from the precarious outer edge of the elite to a secure and visible place within it. He lived with recurrent tensions between his search for a new kind of public voice – a voice that would break through corporate barriers – and his likely confinement to a conventional clerical role; between his need for personal autonomy and public openness and his chronic dependence on patrons; between his self-construction as a modern scholar, at home only in a rigorously secular world of "speculation," and his impulse to remain connected somehow to the popular religious culture he had left, the emotionally vibrant and comforting world of his father's piety.

It was this field of tensions that Fichte tried to negotiate, albeit indirectly, with the intellectual resources of enlightened Lutheranism, and that Kantianism empowered him to cut through.

★ ★ ★

Honor, duty, struggle: within this triad the young Fichte sought to fashion an identity and define a purpose. Put simply, the road to honor (*Ehre*) lay through fulfillment of duty (*Pflicht*); and meeting the imperatives of duty required a relentless struggle (*Kampf*) against both inner demons and external obstacles.

Fichte's commitment to struggle lay at the center of his efforts to construct a viable sense of selfhood. It was not simply that he accepted conflict as a harsh fact of life; he liked to think of himself as someone who throve on conflict and the test of wills it entailed. This combative posture already marks Fichte's way of confronting the world and of confronting himself when he enters the historical record as a private tutor in the mid-1780s, several years before discovering Kant. Tutors of Fichte's background were more often censured for their servile compliance than for the stubborn defiance he exhibited. He took very seriously the enlightened tutor's responsibility to undo the damage done by misguided and indulgent parents. Looking back on his tutoring employment in Zürich, he recalled a "ceaseless war" against "a host of prejudices, obstructions, and insolences of all sorts" – a war he "wanted to win" while guaranteeing himself "an honorable retreat."[11]

---

[11] Fichte to Weisshuhn, May 20, 1790, GA, III, 1: 120. See also Frank Aschoff, "Zwischen äusserem Zwang und innerer Freiheit. Fichtes Hauslehrer-Erfahrungen und die Grundlagen seiner

Fichte's description of his parents – the loving, indulgent father and the cold, unbending mother – suggests the source of his combativeness. His father's favoritism gave him an acute sense of his exceptionality, but that self-image collided with his mother's resistance to privileging him at the expense of his siblings. One of his first struggles, we can imagine, was in the face of that maternal obstacle. For the most part, however, we are left wondering about the specific strains this familial tug-of-war occasioned and how it combined with other childhood experiences to begin shaping Fichte's personality. There simply is not enough evidence to build a credible etiology.

What *can* be explained historically are the forms Fichte's impulse to struggle assumed, the idioms it employed, the outlets it sought. In a homiletic exercise from the mid-1780s, Fichte evoked the Christian's relentless "struggle (*Kampf*) against sinful desires." He confided to his fiancée from Leipzig in late December 1790 that rather than attend church services, he devoted his Sundays to the "sacred duty" of "self-examination" (*Selbstpüfung*) and prayer.[12] "The voice of duty is worthy of honor to you above all else" began his précis of the "rules for self-examination" for 1791; and a "main examination" every evening would make that voice still "louder." This was followed by a litany of mea culpas, attributing an impressive list of faults – his "vanity," his "inflexibility," his "hardness," his "reckless openness and talkativeness" – to the "pride" that was "a sure sign of any neglected side of [his] heart." The first failure to conduct this "impartially strict" examination, he warned himself in conclusion, "will throw you back into your previous total corruption" and "will make you forever unimprovable."[13]

For Fichte's generation, as for earlier generations of German Lutherans, duty and honor were inconceivable without an internal struggle, a willed mastery over the "nature" within. However secular their idealism might become, it was still driven by the ethic of self-denial that had inspired Lutheranism from its inception and that, since the late seventeenth century, had received a powerful new stimulus from the Pietist revival. Fichte's education had imbued him with the eighteenth-century rationalist's skepticism toward the "enthusiasm" (*Schwärmerei*) – the unbridled emotionalism and the mystical pretensions – of Pietist religiosity. Likewise he had come of age with a rationalist's distaste for Lutheran Orthodoxy. By the time he drafted his "Rules," his asceticism no longer

Philosophie," in Wolfgang H. Schrader, ed., *Anfänge und Ursprünge. Zur Vorgeschichte der Jenaer Wissenschaftslehre* (F-S 9) (Amsterdam/Atlanta, Ga., 1997), pp. 27–45, which emphasizes the importance of Fichte's experience of "dependence" as a tutor for his formulation of his concept of freedom. On tutoring, see esp. the introductory essay in Ludwig Fertig, *Die Hofmeister. Ein Beitrag zur Geschichte des Lehrerstandes und der bürgerlichen Intelligenz* (Stuttgart, 1979); La Vopa, *Grace, Talent, and Merit*, pp. 111–33.

[12] GA, III, 1: 203.   [13] "Regeln der Selbstprüfung für das Jahr 1791," GA, II, 1: 379–80.

operated within the economy of salvation that Luther's *sola fide* had evoked. The exercise in self-discipline was not in preparation for the supernatural intervention – the infusion of grace – that justified the Christian despite his natural corruption. And yet, there was still the assumption of a fundamental human corruption, inherent in sensual gratifications, passionate impulses, and social vanities. Moral development was still a victory of the spirit over the flesh, a self-denying advance toward purely spiritual transcendence. In the absence of grace, the only antidote to corruption was a rational act of the will within the natural man, an exercise in self-discipline that achieved self-mastery.

Rooted deep in Fichte's early upbringing in a pious Lutheran family and village, this ascetic ethos found confirmation in his Kantianism and survived all subsequent mutations in his thought. In keeping with the Lutheran legacy and particularly with its recent reaffirmation in Lutheran Pietism, introspection did not mean withdrawal from the world. Quite the contrary; like so many other *Gelehrten* of his generation, Fichte was driven by an inner-worldly asceticism, an ethos that made inner self-mastery the means to efficacious service *in* the world. Though the world was not to be resanctified in the Pietist sense, within a traditional Christian eschatology, reform still aimed at a thoroughgoing moral regeneration. It was this outer-directed struggle – the self-sacrificing devotion to service – that the self-discipline achieved in inner-directed struggle made possible.

Even in the young Fichte's immediate surroundings, among friends and employers, the relationship between inner and external struggle sometimes became problematic. As Fichte's rules for self-examination suggest, he was well aware that it was a short step from "honor" to "pride." The insistence on self-mastery became pride when it prevented him from admitting need even to his friends, for fear that they would offer him help merely "*out of pity for need*" rather than out of respect for his person.[14] One of his reactions in conflicts with employers – one way he sought to assert a self-disciplined will – was to force others to be as open as he liked to think he was. Struggle here meant breaking through the inhibitions imposed by the tutor's inferior rank and financial dependence. By forcing a confrontation with the Otts in Zürich, and later with Countess Luise at Krockow, he could *will* a mutual frankness that would in effect negate the reality of his employers' power and his own vulnerability. But as these conflicts escalated, Fichte sought invulnerability in a tactic that was anything but frank. Bent on victory in a battle of wills, he resorted to a calculated, self-contained withdrawal – and thus made self-discipline a weapon in a power struggle.

---

[14] Fichte to Johanne Rahn, March 15–16, 1790, GA, III, 1: 83.

In the long run, of course, these were the petty skirmishes of a transitional phase. The road to duty and honor lay through the lifelong practice of a calling (*Beruf*) in the world. It was above all in his struggle to find a calling and, in secular terms, to launch a career that Fichte's commitment to openness collided with the realities of his situation. "I do not want merely *to think*," he wrote to his fiancée in March of 1790, "I want *to act* (*handeln*)." At the close of the letter he expanded on this aspiration; "I have only one passion, only one need, only a fullness of feeling of myself; to have an effect outside myself (*ausser mir zu würken*)."[15] Fichte was *not* voicing an intellectual's frustration with a life devoted to words and theory to the exclusion of practical deeds. What he rejected was the self-enclosed world of scholarship in its traditional conception, as the exclusive property of a corporate culture. The alternative – the life of action he sought – was the communicative action in which words had a real impact on a larger audience. For his generation the determination to escape the corporate ghetto of the learned estate was, in positive terms, an aspiration to affect the larger society and polity by asserting a truly public voice. Ultimately it was in this capacity, as intellectuals addressing a public audience, that they sought to break through the walls and inhibitions of the old-regime hierarchy with "purely human" forms of communication.[16]

Fichte's very choice of verb (*würken*) recalls Goethe's famous diagnosis of the educated commoner's dilemma in *Wilhelm Meisters Lehrjahre*. What makes a life in the theater so alluring to Wilhelm is the impossibility of breaking through, the lack of a viable public outlet for the commoner's aspiration to "have an effect." "A *Bürger* can achieve merit and even develop his spirit in extreme necessity," Goethe has Wilhelm lament in a much-quoted passage, "but his personality gets lost (*geht verloren*), however he may present himself." Unlike the nobleman, who "gives everything through the presentation of personality," the *Bürger* "gives nothing." Whereas the essence of the nobleman is "to perform and have an effect (*tun und wirken*)," the function of the *Bürger* is merely "to achieve and produce (*leisten und schaffen*)."[17]

The bourgeois moralists among Goethe's readers were being asked to admit that the courtly tradition could not be dismissed out of hand as corrupt (and corrupting) formalism. In his person, as in his physical setting, the ideal nobleman embodied the "representative publicness" with which his order exhibited its unique fusion of social preeminence and

---

[15] GA, III, 1: 72–3.

[16] On efforts to break through the corporate shell of the *Gelehrtenstand*, see esp. Rudolf Vierhaus, ed., *Bürger und Bürgerlichkeit im Zeitalter der Aufklärung*, Wolfenbütteler Studien zur Aufklärung, vol. 7 (Heidelberg, 1981).

[17] *Goethes Werke*, vol. 7, ed. E. Trunz (Munich, 1973), pp. 290–2; Dieter Borchmeyer, *Höfische Gesellschaft und französische Revolution bei Goethe* (Kronberg/Ts., 1977), pp. 30–53.

public authority.[18] When the exhibition took a rhetorical form, it had a public effect not by communicating information but by giving verbal expression to the ceremonial elegance that gave this world its distinctive aura. The very formalism of language bore public witness to the kind of freedom peculiar to lineage and inherited landed property. In his language, as in everything else, the nobleman could be expected to present himself elegantly because he had been free to develop a complete "personality," to cultivate the many facets of his person. Performing the conventions of rank with inbred ease, he conveyed a public presence on all occasions and in all situations.

For the commoner, the implication of this ideal was that no matter how educated he might be, he was condemned to a truncated private existence. By the very fact that he had to become something and enter a functional occupational role, he could have neither a "personality" nor a public voice. In a sense, though, this dilemma was more acute for the protagonist in Goethe's novel than for young intellectuals of Fichte's plebeian background. Wilhelm, like Goethe himself, is a prosperous merchant's son. For him, the conventional path is represented by his cousin, who champions a utilitarian work ethic, a life single-mindedly devoted to the commercial calling, at the opposite pole from aristocratic personality and publicness. Most poor students, on the other hand, grew up with the expectation that they would enter the clergy, perhaps as schoolmen but preferably as pastors. It was because they *were* disadvantaged and lacked alternatives, of course, that they had to accept the shabby financial rewards that most pastorates offered. But the office nonetheless exercised a strong appeal, and that was because it represented the only public platform accessible to young men of their background.

The appeal of the pastorate had its focal point in the sermon. Particularly in villages and small towns, the Sunday sermon in the local church was likely to be the only regular public event witnessed by boys from uneducated families. It was public not simply because it embodied the institutional authority of church and state but also because – and this dimension of public status was much more rare in a corporate society – its audience was drawn from all levels of the social hierarchy. What enthralled the audience was a rhetorical performance; the eloquent sermon represented a supreme display of the same verbal prowess with which the exceptional poor boy excelled in school and won his teachers' approval. It was the lure of the pulpit in all these senses that Karl Philipp Moritz – a contemporary of Fichte and, like him, a former poor student from an uneducated family – recalled in his autobiographical

---

[18] The term "representative publicness" is from Jürgen Habermas, *The Structural Transformation of the Public Sphere. An Inquiry into a Category of Bourgeois Society*, trans. Thomas Burger with the assistance of Frederick Lawrence (Cambridge, Mass., 1989), pp. 5–14.

novel *Anton Reiser*. As a young boy, Anton was mesmerized by a local preacher who "carr[ied] away" his audience "irresistibly." This "public orator," with "ceremonial seriousness in his expression," chastised the leading citizens for their opulence and their indifference to "injustice and oppression." He even called to account individual families "by name."[19]

This exalted vision of the pulpit retained a hold on Fichte well beyond his university years. What had prompted a visiting baron to sponsor his education for the clergy in 1770, after all, was his ability to recite the Sunday sermon verbatim. Preaching had figured centrally in the turning point of his life. To Fichte, as to Moritz, the heroism of the pastorate lay not in the daily rounds of pastoral care but in feats of pulpit oratory. He grew up with the expectation that the pulpit would offer him a platform from which to assert a public voice. It is a measure of the tenacity of this expectation that in the late 1780s and early 1790s, as he became increasingly reluctant to stoop to the "hypocrisy" that a pastoral appointment would probably require, Fichte's hopes remained fastened on securing one.

His "goal," Fichte reported to his friend Weisshuhn from Leipzig in May 1790, was still to become "a preacher not without renown."[20] A few weeks later, in search of a pastorate in Saxony, he traveled to Dresden to win the sponsorship of Christoph Gottlob von Burgsdorff, the president of the High Consistory. When Burgsdorff tried to steer him into an academic career in classical studies, Fichte protested that the subject was "too unimportant to fill a human life" and would not allow him "to effect (*würken*) as much as he could effect." He dared inform his potential patron that he would be a mediocrity at the lectern but could "excel" in the pulpit. Determined to develop his natural vocation for preaching, he continued his study of the rhetorical arts, already evident in his valedictory address at Schulpforta. In Leipzig in the summer of 1790, despite his chronic lack of money, he took private lessons with a *Gelehrter* who trained actors in "declamation." The instructor "sits in darkness and unknown," he wrote to his fiancée, because he lacks "a spirit of initiative" and in any case "is no preacher." He himself aspired to be "the first in the art"; that is how he would "make [his] reputation, or there would no longer be any justice in the world."[21]

But could this ambition really be satisfied in a pastorate? In what sense would the office confer a public persona on its occupant? The clerical

[19] Karl Philipp Moritz, *Anton Reiser. Ein psychologischer Roman* (1785–90: Insel, 1979), pp. 66–76. See also La Vopa, *Grace, Talent, and Merit*, pp. 70–1.
[20] GA, III, 1: 120.
[21] GA, III, 1: 130. In Zürich in the summer of 1789, Fichte hoped to pursue this interest and at the same time to find a means of support by launching a school for training in public speaking. Nothing came of the plan. GA, II, 1: 128–34, 210.

journals of the late eighteenth century were filled with complaints about the stultifying remoteness and obscurity that so many young theology candidates had to endure in rural parishes and about their grim prospects for ever escaping this form of intellectual exile. What did it matter that you commanded the attention of an entire community every Sunday, if your audience was limited to the village locals? As young men became aware of this reality – as they came to realize that most pulpits were public platforms only in the most limited sense – the heroic visions of boyhood gave way to a sense of frustration.[22] Even as he looked to the pulpit for a public platform, Fichte was aware of this dilemma. He could not "slink in the usual way," he informed his parents in June 1790, merely to "place [himself] in a village pastorate."[23] For the moment, at least, he was captivated by the vague possibility that he could find employment at a court, as a preacher, or as the tutor to a young prince. There was a large element of fantasy in this ambition and more than a little waffling in his efforts to justify it. When he imagined himself at court, he alternated between two personas: the self-confident *Bürger*, eager to test his antidote to worldly corruption, and the young innocent hoping to acquire a measure of worldly "cleverness." What mattered was that court society – the same world that epitomized the frivolity and dissimulation of aristocratic culture – was the center of public power for the larger society and polity. Fichte was entranced by the prospect of "effect[ing] something greater" in "a larger theater."[24]

In the late 1780s and early 1790s, Fichte confronted the real threats to his integrity in his efforts to secure a pastorate. The very conditions for clerical preferment were bound to frustrate his aspiration to assert a voice that would be truly human in substance and truly public in scope and impact. The pastorate was one of the many offices distributed through the multitiered patronage networks of old-regime society. In Saxony, the highest tier was formed by the great noble households – the preeminent families, which had virtually hereditary rights to the highest ecclesiastical offices and which controlled many pastoral appointments directly or through relatives and clients. Well-positioned patrons were especially important for theology candidates of Fichte's obscure background, who lacked the family connections that oiled the careers of young men from clerical dynasties and educated bourgeois families.

By the late 1780s Fichte was in danger of becoming a client manqué, condemned to watch his former schoolmates advance while he languished, perhaps interminably, on the tutoring circuit. The patronage that

---

[22] La Vopa, *Grace, Talent, and Merit*, pp. 326–35.   [23] GA, III, 1: 139.
[24] GA, III, 1: 69–73, 81–7. On bourgeois perceptions of court life, see esp. Borchmeyer, *Höfische Gesellschaft*; Paul Mog, *Ratio und Gefühlskultur. Studien zur Psychogenese und Literatur im 18. Jahrhundert* (Tübingen, 1976), pp. 36–46; Nikolaus Wegmann, *Diskurse der Empfindsamkeit. Zur Geschichte eines Gefühls in der Literatur des 18. Jahrhunderts* (Stuttgart, 1988), pp. 56–70.

promoted poor students – with the charity that made possible their education and with the preferment that launched and advanced their careers – formed a chain. The client climbed from link to link on the strength of each sponsor's testimony about his promise and his "character."[25] For Fichte, the key link had been the Miltitz household; but the Baron had died in 1774, and roughly a decade later the Baroness, reacting against disturbing reports about his conduct as a student, had washed her hands of him. The patronage chain had snapped at its key link, and it could not be repaired.

In the summer of 1790, when he traveled to Dresden to win the support of Burgsdorff, Fichte received a painful reminder of his predicament. To this potentially powerful sponsor there was something suspect about a young man who had forfeited the approval of the Baroness von Miltitz and had been unable to retrieve it. At Burgsdorff's insistence, Fichte wrote to the Baroness, begging her "complete forgiveness" – but to no avail. The irony, he informed Burgsdorff in a fruitless effort to coax him over this hurdle, was that the Baroness had written him off as a good-for-nothing without ever bothering to tell him exactly what had displeased her.[26]

The rumors that had displeased the Baroness may very well have been about Fichte's religious heterodoxy. He thought of himself as "a Christian" rather than as a Lutheran in the confessional sense, and if he had a choice, he would settle in the parish where "one thinks most freely and lives most tolerantly."[27] A decade earlier, when the Saxon government and clerical establishment were still sponsoring enlightened reform from above, patronage might have been flexible enough to place a candidate with such views. But in 1788, a government-sponsored crackdown on the clerical enlightenment had begun to radiate out from Prussia to the other North German states, including Saxony. From 1789 onward, the French Revolution gave a powerful new impetus to this reversal of course. In the new wisdom, "enlightenment" was to blame for the popular unrest in France; and to spare Germany similar horrors, church and state had to ensure the orthodoxy of the clergy and above all of local pastors.[28]

In March of 1790 Fichte still hoped to become a preacher in Saxony if an "*honest* opportunity" arose.[29] But that was the issue; in the very effort

---

[25] La Vopa, *Grace, Talent, and Merit*, pp. 83–110.

[26] GA, III, 1: 140–3, 145–7, 149–51. To judge by her letter to her son Dietrich on April 28, 1792, urging him not to join the French revolutionary army, Baroness von Miltitz was pious but not dogmatic, and socially conservative but not politically reactionary. The letter is quoted at length in Adolf Peters, *General Dietrich von Miltitz, sein Leben und sein Wohnsitz* (Meissen, 1863), pp. 12–14.

[27] GA, III, 1: 131.

[28] Details on the crackdown in Prussia and its spinoffs in Klaus Epstein, *The Genesis of German Conservatism* (Princeton, N.J., 1966), esp. pp. 142–53, 352–69, 441–67.

[29] Fichte to Johanne Rahn, March 17, 1790, GA, III, 1: 89.

to secure an appointment, he might have to compromise the openness and hence the integrity he hoped to bring to the pulpit. In his combative posture Fichte prided himself on defying this temptation. He observed in June 1790 that the younger clergymen in Saxony adopted a "slavish, light-shy, hypocritical way of thinking" in the face of "a more than Spanish Inquisition," and that that was in part because they lacked inner "power" to resist.[30] He himself was stimulated by the prospect of "battl[ing] through all the entrenchments and still mak[ing] a [clerical] career."[31]

But could he wage the battle at all without a camouflage? If he would not stoop to blatant falsification to win a new patron, he stopped well short of the openness on which he prided himself. He reported to his fiancée that although Burgsdorff suspected him of being "heretical," "I showed myself to him completely" with an essay in theology. The essay has been lost, but to judge by the letter with which Fichte followed up his visit, he had been quite circumspect. Rather than defend his heterodoxy, he emphasized his eagerness to serve his "fatherland" (the same fatherland he was deriding for its benighted religious policy in other contexts). If Burgsdorff "were to find [him] on the wrong path," he could be assured that "the goodness of God . . . would not leave [him] on it forever."[32]

It was not simply the test of his religious convictions, however, that made Fichte's experience as a client so formative. That test was part of a larger conflict between the imperative to conform and the need to be open – a conflict that pitted his determination to *form himself* against the social norms and arrangements that were designed to form him. As personal, informal, and scattered as the eighteenth-century workings of patronage were by modern bureaucratic standards, they were not random. The overall effect was a controlled selection of recruits for the clergy. Control was exercised not simply by weeding out the openly heterodox but also by requiring outsiders – that is, recruits from uneducated families – to exhibit the deference they were expected to have absorbed. By the late eighteenth century, to be sure, the Orthodox Lutheran view of the patron as a mediating instrument of the Lord, marking the guiding hand of Providence in the client's life, had lost much of its substance. But even when personal sponsorship was removed from this theological framework, it continued to be validated by the paternalistic norms that sanctioned hierarchy throughout old-regime society. Unlike the cult of friendship, which made intimacy a function of unconditional equality, paternalism found its normative model in the parent-child relationship. Thanks to the power that rank and wealth conferred, even the women who sometimes dispensed patronage, particularly in aristocratic circles,

[30] GA, III, 1: 131. [31] GA, III, 1: 155. [32] GA, III, 1: 149–51, 157–61.

could be endowed with a measure of the patriarchal authority of the ideal pater familias. There were, of course, resentful clients – young men who felt victimized by patrons abusing their authority. It is a measure of the resilience of paternalistic norms, however, that resentment rarely took the form of a critique of patronage as a social and institutional structure. Paternalism, by its very logic, focused grievances on individual abuses, with the result that the larger issue of injustice in the distribution of life chances was occluded. The individual sponsor was expected to treat his (or her) client with the same combination of justice and benevolence, sternness and affection, that a parent owed his children. The conventional terms of intimacy in such relationships required the client to assume the openly deferential posture appropriate to filial dependency. He confided in his patron as a novice in search of the mentor's advice; as a supplicant in need of a sponsor; and perhaps as a penitent seeking the forgiveness needed to retain or to regain sponsorship.[33]

This was the posture Fichte had to assume if he was to have any hope of preferment in the Saxon clergy. On one level, he blamed himself for failing to master the rules of the game. There was an element of genuine self-reproach in his admission to potential sponsors that as a student he had failed to learn how to make himself "agreeable" and "accommodating." But at a deeper level the imperatives of clientage cut against the grain of Fichte's self-construction, and his efforts to comply with them make painful reading. He was not above sounding the religious chord, and indeed he pounded it when the occasion demanded. So long as he was disdained by someone he revered, he wrote Baroness von Miltitz in the effort to secure her pardon, he could not regain "confidence in [himself] and others" and approach God once again "with joy." All the more devastating, he added, was the disdain of those "who were for him in place of God on the earth."[34]

Even in his more obsequious moments, Fichte's omissions hedged his self-degradation. In refusing to make excuses for the "final sad events" that had provoked the Countess, he also avoided a specific admission of fault. More often, though, he took pains to offset the client's conventional language of reverential gratitude with the moralistic idiom of merit and service that came so much more naturally to him. If Burgsdorff passed him over for an appointment, he would accept his fate in all humility; he had no doubt that the president considered only "merits" and the "capacities" to acquire them.[35] In a letter to Count von Callenberg, another potential patron among the Saxon nobility, he recalled their earlier meeting with the requisite awe; but "I make bold," he concluded,

---

[33] La Vopa, *Grace, Talent, and Merit*, pp. 85–97. On paternalist ideology, see also Bengt Algot Sørensen, *Herrschaft und Zärtlichkeit. Der Patriarchalismus und das Drama im 18. Jahrhundert* (Munich, 1984).
[34] GA, III, 1: 145–7.   [35] GA, III, 1: 150.

"to separate the station, which would imprint on me mute reverence, from those characteristics of the spririt and the heart that invite me to lively admiration and, if I may say so, to trust and love."[36]

Fichte tried the same mix of idioms in his correspondence in the summer of 1790 with Marie Christiane von Koppenfels, the *grande dame* through whom he hoped to secure an appointment at the Weimar court. In the initial version of his first letter he praised her "kind condescension" and her "friendliness" (*Freundschaftlichkeit*). The latter term did not survive a second draft, probably because it was deemed too bold. But Fichte did assure the lady that he did not revere in her the providentially assigned "rank" she "[had] in common with many," since "that would only fill [him] with mute respect and recall [to him] the duty to withdraw." It was reverence for "the woman of spirit, of taste, of heart, of broad knowledge" that "expand[ed] [his] heart" and spurred him to "everything noble and good."[37] With this kind of pseudo-intimacy, Fichte, even as he acknowledged the legitimacy of his potential sponsor's vastly superior rank, tried to spare himself the conventional forms of obsequiousness. But he was also playing the game, and doing so in a way that put the language of merit in the service of flattery.

It was above all in the imperatives of clientage that the young Fichte experienced the contingency and the vulnerability of the socially powerless. The manipulation of language offered a kind of protective shield, but he still had to contend with the voice of duty within. It told him that true honor lay not in social calculation but in the honest assertion of an inner self. As he moved toward his initial formulations of a new ideal of "public" communication, the false self-presentations, and indeed the false intimacies, exacted from the client were his negative referents. As he rendered, grudgingly, the requisite deference, he learned how arbitrary power – the power that flowed through the hierarchical structure of old-regime society and that still found effective camouflage in reigning social norms – precluded "human" openness. He would soon imagine a kind of communicative action that promised to extrude power entirely.

★ ★ ★

While Fichte was searching for a place, he was also confronting the issues that preoccupied intellectuals of his generation and made so many of them receptive to Kant's philosophy. Two draft sermons written sometime in the mid-1780s, when he was still a tutor in rural Saxony and was preparing to make his reputation in the pulpit, provide our first glimpse of his struggle on this front. The surviving record then leaps across several years

---

[36] Fichte to Graf Georg Alexander Heinrich Hermann von Callenberg, Dec., 27, 1789, GA, III, 1: 41–2.
[37] Fichte to Marie Christiane von Koppenfels, June 11, 1790, GA, III, 1: 137.

to a highly condensed meditation entitled "Some Aphorisms on Religion and Deism," written in Leipzig toward the end of that depressing summer of 1790, sometime after he had read the *Critique of Pure Reason* but before he had moved on to the *Critique of Practical Reason*.[38]

In Fichte's passage from the beliefs and doubts of his boyhood to his Kantian resolution of a spiritual crisis, the draft sermons and the aphorisms are brief and scattered moments. And yet they form the two parts of a whole; they record the opposed voices in a young man's internal argument. While one voice insisted on the freedom of the will, the other dismissed our subjective experience of freedom as the illusion we need to endure the iron constraints of our condition. It was this argument that Fichte thought he had resolved, albeit reluctantly and painfully, in the summer of 1790, just as he was beginning to engage Kant's *Critiques*.

The fact that an opportunity to earn urgently needed tutoring fees, and not an overpowering curiosity about the new philosophy, occasioned Fichte's initial plunge into the *Critique of Pure Reason* is in itself significant. It reminds us that Fichte's path to Kant did not lead him through a canon of philosophical literature. This is precisely where he differed from Karl Leonhard Reinhold, the first of the celebrated figures among Kant's young disciples and the one who made the forbidding architectonic of the master's system accessible to the educated public in the late 1780s. Raised a Catholic in Vienna, Reinhold had migrated to Protestantism and to Weimar, where he became Wieland's son-in-law and his editorial assistant for the widely read *Der Teutsche Merkur*. When he turned to Kant in 1785, he recalled four years later, it was in search of a way to recover the "peace" in his "heart" that "speculative philosophy" had destroyed. Over the previous ten years he had worked through all four "main systems" of philosophy, including the contributions of Leibniz (on whom he had lectured) and Locke (whose thought he claimed to know "firsthand"). "Metaphysics" had offered "more than one plan to resign himself now with his head, now with his heart, but no single plan capable of satisfying the earnest demands of both at once." In an "entirely unexpected way," the *Critique of Pure Reason* had resolved "all his philosophical doubts . . . for both head and heart."[39]

---

[38] The two sermon drafts – "An Mariä Verkündung" (d. March 25, 1786), and "Über die Absichten des Todes Jesu" (probably also written in 1786) – are in GA, II, 1: 53–66 and 75–98. "Einige Aphorismen über Religion und Deismus" is in GA, II, 1: 287–97. My analysis of these texts has been greatly aided by Reiner Preul, *Reflexion und Gefühl. Die Theologie Fichtes in seiner vorkantischen Zeit* (Berlin, 1969).

[39] Karl Leonhard Reinhold, *Versuch einer neuen Theorie des menschlichen Vorstellungsvermögen* (Prague, 1789), pp. 51–6. On Reinhold, see Reinhard Lauth, *Philosophie aus einem Prinzip: Karl Leonhard Reinhold* (Bonn, 1974); Frederick C. Beiser, *The Fate of Reason. German Philosophy from Kant to Fichte* (Cambridge, Mass., 1987), pp. 226–65; Gerhard W. Fuchs, *Karl Leonhard Reinhold – Illuminat und Philosoph* (Frankfurt am Main, 1994).

In Fichte's spiritual crisis, as in Reinhold's, the language of "head" and "heart" was a serviceable shorthand for the choice between critical rationality and emotional spontaneity. Unlike Reinhold, however, Fichte approached Kant's *Critiques* as a philosophical neophyte of markedly parochial background. In the years immediately following his university studies, his tutoring employments in rural Saxony kept him far removed from intellectual entrepôts like Weimar. Until 1788, when he took the employment in Zürich, he had never left his native Saxony. His interests, of course, extended well beyond his immediate experience. If we can believe his self-advertisement to a potential patroness, his "favorite authors" included Montaigne and Rousseau as well as Lessing, Wieland, Goethe, and Schiller. In Zürich, in his evening translation exercises, he had made himself familiar with at least part of Montesquieu's *De l'esprit des lois*. By 1790 he had read Rousseau's *La nouvelle Héloïse*, and probably *Émile* as well.[40] But on Fichte's route to Kant there is no equivalent of Reinhold's systematic exploration of the philosophical terrain. It is safe to asssume that when he and his friends argued philosophy, they drew on an eclectic fund of largely secondhand knowledge.

Fichte was, in his way, an eighteenth-century rationalist, but he was largely a product of the religious culture of German Lutheranism. In Germany, it was Lutheran clergymen, including professors in the theology faculties of the many universities, who had set the tone for the Enlightenment since the middle decades of the century. By the 1780s they were presiding over a broad movement for renewal of the established churches. Eager to learn from the English and French varieties of rationalism, they had also been adept at weakening the corrosive impact of imported thought as it was absorbed into a native religious tradition.[41] For all the breadth of his aesthetic and philosophical interests, Lessing's career was emblematic of this emphatically Protestant and theological orientation of the German Enlightenment. The son of a Lutheran pastor with impressive scholarly interests, Lessing was contemptuous of academic "theologians." But he remained, in his own words, "a lover of theology," and in his final years he found ways to satisfy a veritable addiction to religious polemics. In 1777, when Lessing published the *Fragmenten* from Hermann Samuel Reimarus's relentless attack on

[40] Fichte to Marie Christiane von Koppenfels, Nov. 11, 1790, GA, III, 1: 134; "Tagebuch Zürich," GA, II, 1: 212.
[41] See Walter Sparn, "Vernünftiges Christentum. Über die geschichtliche Aufgabe der theologischen Aufklärung im 18. Jahrhundert in Deutschland," in Rudolf Vierhaus, ed., *Wissenschaften im Zeitalter der Aufklärung* (Göttingen, 1985), pp. 18–58; Hans Erich Bödeker, "Die Religiosität der Gebildeten," in *Religionskritik und Religiosität in der deutschen Aufklärung*, Wolfenbütteler Studien zur Aufklärung, vol. 11 (Wolfenbüttel), pp. 145–95. Still useful for biographical detail and succinct expositions of theological issues is Karl Aner, *Die Theologie der Lessingzeit* (Halle/Salle, 1929).

biblical Christianity, Fichte was a fifteen-year-old schoolboy. As he followed the ensuing controversy and got his first taste of the excitement
of intellectual combat, he began to define the issues he faced.[42]

In the course of the *Fragmenten* controversy, it had become apparent
that in his often devious but always provocative style, Lessing was conducting a campaign on two fronts. Lutheran Orthodoxy was "foul water,"
he had confided to his brother in 1774, but the "new-fashioned theology" wanted to replace it with "liquid manure." "Under the pretext of
making us rational Christians," a new breed of "bunglers and half-philosophers" was "mak[ing] us extreme irrational philosophers."[43] Lessing was
taking aim at the generation of Lutheran theologians and preachers who
had given the German Enlightenment such a moderate, not to say timid,
profile in comparison with its French and English counterparts. Known
collectively as the Neologists, they included Friedrich Wilhelm Jerusalem,
the court preacher at Braunschweig; Johann Salomo Semler, the presiding theologian and biblical scholar at Halle; and Johann Joachim Spalding, the Probst of the Nikolaikirche in Berlin and one of the most widely
read authors of his generation. Fichte would later recall that Spalding's
Die Bestimmung des Menschen, a highly popular example of the Neologists'
cautious syncretism, had "thrown into [his] youthful soul the first seed of
higher speculation."[44]

In a sense, Lessing's derision was undeserved. In his insistence on "faith"
rather than "merit," Luther had anchored his church in the Augustinian
doctrine of original sin. Since the legacy of the Fall was an inherent and
radical corruption of human nature, man could not hope to earn "merit"
in the eyes of God. Sanctification could come only through the "faith"
that God, in an entirely free exercise of his mercy (*Gnade*), instilled with
His grace. If there was a single stance that defined the Neologists as a
group, it was their rejection of this categorically pessimistic view of human
nature, with its refusal to concede any efficacy to human agency. They
regarded Christian virtue, to be sure, as a triumph over sensuality, and to
that extent they remained faithful to the ascetic impulse in Lutheranism.
But they also insisted that the triumph did not require a supernatural
intervention, a wrenching turn effected by grace, since the moral nature
of the natural man had inherently good impulses. Human nature was
"incomplete," not corrupt to the core; with the proper training and guidance, it was "perfectible."

The Neologists were, in fact, redefining the very grounding of Christian truth. Once the Orthodox belief in an inherited natural corruption

---

[42] FG 1: 16–17. Epstein, *Genesis*, pp. 128–41, is a succinct account of the *Fragmenten* controversy.
[43] Quoted in Epstein, *Genesis*, p. 134. On Lessing's theology, see Leonard P. Wessel, *G.E. Lessing's
Theology. A Reinterpretation* (The Hague, 1977).
[44] GA, I, 5: 447. See also Bödeker, "Die Religiosität der Gebildeten"; Aner, *Die Theologie der
Lessingzeit*.

was discarded, the view of Christ's suffering and death as a redemptive sacrifice – a vicarious atonement for a corrupted humanity, unable to atone for itself – became superfluous. Christ's mission might remain a divine one, but it would have to be in another sense. Even the meaning of the Redemption could be reinterpreted in the light of the new confidence in man's inherent capacity for ethical perfectibility. To Orthodox Lutherans, dogmatic tradition had unimpeachable authority because it rested on the transcendent objectivity of Revelation, proven by the Gospel miracles. What emerges from the Neologists' writings is an emphatically subjective criterion for the truth-value of the Christian tradition. The uniqueness of Revelation lay in its capacity to awaken the inner impulses and fulfill the inner needs of the human personality, not in the disclosure of a supernatural objectivity otherwise beyond human grasp. In keeping with this new subjectivism, the Neologists' biblical scholarship interpreted much in the Gospel narratives as the historically contingent expressions of a specific culture.

And yet the Neologists might be said to have deserved Lessing's scorn. They are perhaps best described as rational theists – which is to say that if a truly philosophical position required a thoroughgoing skepticism, they were indeed only "half-philosophers." While the French *philosophes* were waging a war *à outrance* against Christianity as such, the Neologists were quietly trying to rationalize Protestantism from within. Though they were more than willing to acknowledge that the legacy of the Reformation had been corrupted by irrational accretions, they did not share the radical skeptic's view that all religions, including Protestantism, were variations on mankind's penchant for superstition. In its essence, Protestantism was distinguished from other religions by its unique rationality; it represented the most advanced stage that mankind's understanding of its relationship with God had reached. The Gospels were not literally inspired in their every word, but in their distilled core they were the depository of a Revelation. They recorded the eminently rational moral truths that God had sent Christ to teach. Not all biblical miracles were to be explained as cultural metaphor; some were historical facts, needed to reinforce the moral authority of Christ's teaching by demonstrating the divine source of his mandate. Chief among the latter, of course, was the Resurrection.[45]

By the 1780s, the Neologists were the reigning elders of an Enlightenment establishment. As illusory as it soon proved to be, their confidence in the inevitable demise of Orthodoxy made sense in Prussia and several other North German states where they enjoyed the sponsorship of

---

[45] Typically Jerusalem, who had openly rejected the doctrine of original sin as early as the 1740s, defended the historical facticity of the Resurrection in his *Considerations on the Most Prominent Truths of Religion*, published in 1778. Aner, *Die Theologie der Lessingzeit*, pp. 302–3.

"enlightened" governments. But new threats were gaining momentum, and in the face of them the Neologists felt compelled to defend a middle ground – a rationally defensible but emotionally grounded religious belief, holding "head" and "heart" in a delicate balance. Since the *Sturm und Drang* movement of the early 1770s, educated youth had shown a marked susceptibility to the allure of irrationalism, whether it took the form of a Wertherian cult of inspired genius or a Rousseauian reverence for the "truth" of authentic feeling. To the Neologists, all this was suspiciously reminiscent of the Pietist enthusiasm they had rejected as young men. There was the same unbridled emotionalism and the same tendency to mistake emotional abnormality for privileged lucidity about spiritual truths, if not for direct inspiration. In this direction, the Neologists emphasized that there was no substitute for rational understanding, no matter how emotive religious experience might legitimately be.

From the other direction, the threat was posed by advocates of a purely "natural" religion – the modern variety of deism, with God reduced to an objective principle of pure rationality, manifested to the human intellect in the harmonious regularity of natural laws. There was no room here at all for imaginative feeling; religion, if the word still applied, became purely a matter of cold deliberation and judicious consent. Though disdainful of the excesses and self-delusions of Pietist fervor, the Neologists were not rationalists in this exclusive sense. They could not repudiate the feelings of awe and solace that had suffused their own childhoods in pious Lutheran homes. They knew from experience that religion, if it was to have existential depth, had to offer consolation and hope, and that on both counts, it had to address quintessentially human emotional needs. As Spalding put it in 1784, the human being deprived of "stirrings" (*Rührungen*) of the heart "feel[s] the most painful loss"; human beings have an inherent need "not merely *to understand but also to feel; not merely to be enlightened, but also to be warmed.*"[46]

Fichte's exercises in homiletics from the mid-1780s record a young man's efforts to find his bearings within this field of multivalent tensions. For all their philosophical resonances, Fichte's questions and answers were still firmly embedded in Lutheran theology and biblical exegesis. Both sermon drafts are replete with scriptural citations, and the more complete one ends with a prayer. Even as Fichte followed the conventions of pulpit oratory and imagined himself addressing the spiritual needs of a hypothetical flock, however, he used the occasion of the drafts to explore ways of constructing a personal identity, with space for the autonomous exercise of will within a larger framework of constraints.

---

[46] Johann Joachim Spalding, *Vertraute Briefe die Religion betreffend* (2nd rev. ed.: Breslau, 1785), p. 219. See also Spalding, *Gedanken über den Werth der Gefühle in dem Christentum* (5th ed.: Leipzig, 1784).

It had been roughly seven years since Lessing had conducted his *Fragmenten* controversy, but in "On the Intentions of Jesus's Death," the longer but more fragmentary sermon draft, Fichte was still taking up the gauntlet Reimarus (via Lessing) had thrown down. In addition to pointing out inconsistencies in the Gospel narratives, Reimarus had appealed to commonsense logic to expose the Resurrection as a hoax.[47] Christ could have proved his divinity, after all, simply by not dying. Better still, the Resurrection could have been arranged as a public demonstration before the Jewish nation. In Fichte's counterargument, it was precisely its reliance on "demonstrations . . . wrapped in a certain dark light" that made Christianity (by which he meant Protestantism) "unique" among religions. If Jesus had simply disappeared, the resulting confusion would have destroyed his work. On the other hand, a public demonstration would have produced a "coerced" certainty about the Resurrection, a "persuasion" limited to the "understanding" and hence "too strong, too forceful." While Christian "proofs" were *"correct* and *satisfying* to the sharpest spirit of research," they did not "impose themselves" because they were not merely a matter of "sharpening our understanding." By "activat[ing] inner feeling of the true and the good" – by satisfying the emotional needs of a "pure heart" – Christian belief "warm[ed]" and "correct[ed] our understanding" and thereby "perfect[ed] our entire nature."[48]

The belief in the uniqueness of Christianity; the grounding of the truth of Christian revelation in human subjectivity; the explanation of Jesus's divine mission in terms of his moral teaching and example rather than his redemptive sacrifice: all this places the Resurrection sermon on the Neologists' middle ground. On closer inspection, though, Fichte's version of the "friendship" between reason and emotion in Christian belief has different terms of reciprocity. To the Neologists it was the exercise of critical judgment that grounded the autonomy of the enlightened Christian. Emotion, though vital, had to remain subordinate to the governing power of reason. Unbridled emotion produced self-deluded "enthusiasts," and by manipulating this pathological irrationality, fanatics won the swarm of blind followers conjured by the term *Schwärmerei.* Fichte's emphasis reversed the dynamic; it was emotion that grounded autonomy and purely rational persuasion that threatened it. His language is often borrowed from the eighteenth-century aesthetic and literary cult of "sensibility" (*Empfindsamkeit*), but in its deepest resonances it points to an antecedent impulse in Lutheranism.

Fichte's conception of human autonomy was still structured by the set of oppositions – between the faith of the reborn Christian and the

---

[47] See esp. "Uber die Auferstehungsgeschichte" (Fünftes Fragment) and Lessing's commentary, in G. E. Lessing, *Gesammelte Werke*, vol. 7 (1956), pp. 778–816.
[48] GA, II, 1: 79–80.

"fleshly" reason of the Old Adam, and between the "inner" depth of true spirituality and the externality of mere legalism – that Luther had made central to Protestantism from its inception. To be gripped by faith meant, of course, to discard the illusion of human freedom; receptivity to the supernatural gift came with the realization of total helplessness. But faith penetrated through the "heart," and that was to say that the force of its grip lay in activating emotional predispositions and satisfying emotional needs at the irreducible core of the human personality. Hence the Christian paradox of freedom in slavery: faith, even as it made the believer a passive instrument in the hands of the Lord, was experienced as an act of spontaneity, an immediate, self-generated grasp of truth. Lutheran belief was a "living knowledge" (*Erkenntnis*) that had its vital source in, and derived its impelling force from, the affective seat of the personality. Without nourishment from that source, the reliance on logic and on the evidence of the senses in the process of "persuasion" (*Uberzeugung*) as well as the rational comprehension achieved by the "understanding" (*Verstand*), were merely vehicles of external coercion. Like the passions, they were "fleshly" in the sense that they remained merely human modes of inter-subjectivity. To be "convinced" in this purely rational sense was to submit to an intrusion of human power rather than to grasp the gift of faith in an act of inner freedom. The result was the external conformity to the letter of the law that the false Christian mistook for righteousness.

It was this opposition between an external coercion, exercised in and through rational argument, and an inner freedom grounded in emotion that Fichte applied to his defense of the Resurrection. In a sense, he remained entirely within the conventions of his chosen idiom. He did not confront, much less explain, the constraints imposed by his origins, his poverty, his precarious dependence on patronage. Focusing on how Revelation mediated the relationship between the individual believer and his God, he acknowledged social factors only as instruments of, or as obstacles to, that mediation. In his economy of salvation, the collective middle term was a spiritual community of believers, not a society with a discernible structure and a causal role in its own right. And yet, in an oblique but important sense, Fichte's personal agenda had a social dimension. As a "scholar" of plebeian origins, on the margin of the educated elite and facing the possibility of remaining there, he had two insepara-ble concerns: to justify himself as an exceptional case and to remain inte-grated into a socially inclusive Christian community despite his critical distance on the world he had left. If he thought of himself as in some sense deserving of privilege, he also sought bonds with a larger public – with the audience on which he aspired to have an effect. In his projec-tion of a rhetorical community and in the way he envisioned freedom *in* community, Fichte asked how a society dichotomized into an educated elite and an uneducated mass could also form an integrated public.

At issue in the Resurrection sermon was the nature of religious community and the place Fichte ought to assume within it. If Christianity had relied solely on "sharp, deeply thought considerations and strict proofs," it would have been a "mere scholarly discipline (*Wissenschaft*)" for "*a few good heads*," exercising "less influence on practical life" and contributing less to "the happiness of its individual members and the whole." Or it would have been merely a political movement, a mass blindly following a head (*Haupt*), like the "monarchy" with which Mohammed welded "fantastic, unimproved men" into a "revolutionary" movement.[49] Again Fichte reversed the usual associations; it was an exclusive reliance on reason and not an excess of emotion that made for mass manipulation.

Fichte did not bother to explain how a one-sided reliance on rationality could result in *both* scholarly exclusiveness and a revolutionary mobilization of the masses. What is striking is that both images were foils, marking the appeal of an emotionally grounded community of belief to a young scholar of his background and aspirations. Such a community promised a kind of subjective autonomy that allowed and indeed required participation in a socially inclusive religious culture; and in that sense it reconciled the private and the public, inner freedom and membership in a collective body. Christianity as Fichte conceived it was a genuinely popular religion, in that its foundation was in the universal needs and impulses of the human heart. It did not necessarily exclude "sharp" scholars like himself, but it required them to keep their rationalism "warmed" and thereby continually revitalized by a "living" knowledge shared with their less intelligent, or at least less educated, brethren. The "few good heads" could experience the inner freedom of Christian belief, but only if they remained bonded with the larger community as "good hearts."

In the other draft sermon, the immediate subject – the Annunciation – occasioned an exploration of the meaning of Christian election. Fichte reminded his hypothetical audience that ultimately it was not Mary's "outstanding merits" and "purity of heart" that explained her selection as the mother of Jesus. Rather, God, in the completely free exercise of his "mercy," gave her "the most advantageous opportunity to become one of the most excellent people on the earth." The implication was not that most people were beyond the pale of God's mercy; every human being, even among the pagans and the Jews, was given "some opportunity *to become good*."[50] But just as God singled out Christianity to achieve a higher degree of moral perfection than other religions, so too, within the larger community of Christians, he guided a select few to greater heights.

---

[49] GA, II, 1: 87–90.   [50] GA, II, 1: 55–7.

Fichte's personal stake in this view of providential election became obvious as he elaborated:

> He [God] gives some a *better natural* understanding to recognize the truth and a *better, softer, more pliant* heart to succeed in loving it and obeying it. He gives them *better education (Erziehung), better instruction in youth*. . . . he surrounds them *with more virtuous society.* The world that surrounds us, especially in youth, does much to give our soul its direction. . . . *He unites all circumstances of their life, all the earthly destinies they encounter in the world, for the purpose of improving their souls.* . . . Fortunate is he who the Divinity educates with a loving strictness, who is reminded of His existence through sufferings and pain at every stupidity, every thoughtlessness, every neglect of his duty, every forgetting of the God watching over its exercise.[51]

Fichte went on to explain that the "unfortunate" and the "fortunate" waged their "struggles" against corruption with very different prospects for victory. The unfortunate – the people whose "poor understanding" and "*unfeeling* heart" were reinforced by a corrupt upbringing – could emerge victorious if they wanted to "win through the power of religion," but the odds were against them. Providence arranged the life of the fortunate – through natural gifts of head and heart, through an advantageous education and intercourse with "the most virtuous people" – to make the struggle "easier" and allow them to "climb higher" in virtue. But this was a privilege that had to be justified, and indeed by fulfilling a very strict rule of accountability. The fortunate had to fulfill their potential in their innermost subjectivity, in the interior realm of motives visible only to God.[52]

We are reminded that Fichte's religiosity, for all its roots in the Lutheran subsoil, no longer operated within the Orthodox economy of salvation. Conspicuously absent is any dichotomy between an Old Adam mired in human corruption and a reborn Christian in the grip of God's saving grace. Instead, following the route the Neologists had taken, Fichte found the structuring principle of spiritual biography in an ideal of self-development (*Bildung*). God did not intervene in the individual life by wreaking a sudden and dramatic "turn" (*Bekehrung*) from nature to grace. Sanctification was now an inner, organic process in which the individual, under the guiding hand of providence, developed his innate natural capacity for moral perfectibility. By the 1780s the Neologists were using this concept of the individual's biography – what Semler called "the moral history" of the "more capable human beings" – to recast the Lutheran distinction between an elect and a visible church and to give it a social dimension Luther had not intended. The elect were those Christians who, by virtue of their natural capacities, were more "morally alert" and

---

[51] GA, II, 1: 59–60.   [52] GA, II, 1: 60–2.

"capable" than the mass of "external Christians." In its essential content, their profession of faith was no different from that of the mass, and in that sense they remained integrated into a larger public community of belief. But whereas the mass passively accepted a public dogma, the "thinking Christians" came at truth in their own ways and grasped it in a process of active comprehension. The underlying implication was clear enough; if the educated elite were to remain within a Christian public community, they had to be granted the inner freedom, the right to pursue a "moral private religion" that their privileged insight warranted.[53]

The life-history was now conceived as a providentially guided advance in *Bildung*. It was this conception that Fichte applied in the Annunciation sermon. If he was clearly indebted to the Neologists, he also brought his own sense of urgency to their concern to justify the privileged freedom of an educated elite. The Neologists had resolved the tension between Free Will and providential necessity more or less implicitly; the external life plot – its formative events and circumstances – at once made the "elected" Christian an instrument of providence and promoted a process of inner self-determination. Fichte was more self-conscious about this resolution and more explicit about reconciling the imperatives of duty with a felt need for willed "action." He remained too securely anchored in the Lutheran ethical tradition, of course, to entertain the possibility of moral relativism. The elected Christian was not free to decide what his duty was; he could simply seize or neglect opportunities to fulfill a higher standard of duty. But in this latter sense – in the assertion of will in the face of God-given opportunities – the elected Christian enjoyed a kind of privileged freedom, the corollary to his active grasp of religious truth.

Most of the Neologists were sons of educated officials – most notably of pastors. They regarded their membership in the learned estate as a birthright. It was Fichte's very different social experience that underlay his insistence that the elect meet a higher standard of perfectibility. By the very rigor of that standard, he sought to justify his exceptional social ascent. At the same time, though, the Neologists' confident assumption that this higher "perfectability" could be achieved *within* a larger public community of belief had special importance for Fichte. It addressed his countervailing aspiration to membership in an inclusive collectivity,

[53] See, e.g., Johann Salomo Semler, *Über historische, gesellschaftliche und moralische Religion der Christen* (Leipzig, 1786), esp. pp. 226–47, and Semler, *Abhandlungen von freier Untersuchung des Canon*, ed. Heinz Scheible (Gütersloh, 1971). See also Bödeker, "Religiosität," pp. 151–3, 175–6, 180–1; Peter Hanns Reill, *The German Enlightenment and the Rise of Historicism* (Berkeley, Calif., 1975); Gottfried Hornig, "Die Freiheit der christlichen Privatreligion. Semlers Begründung des religiösem Individualismus in der protestantischen Aufklärungstheologie," *Neue Zeitschrift für systematische Theologie und Religionsphilosophie* 21 (1979): 198–211; Trutz Rendtorff, *Kirche und Theologie. Die systematische Funktion des Kirchenbegriffs in der neuen Theologie* (Gütersloh, 1966), pp. 36–56.

preserving some kind of connection between elite and mass. In the providential economy of life chances, the elect, in this new image, were not
a breed apart, the chosen few in a predestined dichotomy; they occupied
a higher level of spirituality in a hierarchical continuum.

The draft sermons may have been meant to impress potential patrons,
but they were not exercises in hypocrisy. Tentatively and with highly selective exegeses, Fichte made the sermon format serve his need for self-
definition and self-justification. And yet, even as he was developing these
personal variations on the themes of rational theism, Fichte was playing
devil's advocate for a radical alternative. As early as 1784, a year or two
before the sermon drafts, he argued the case for uncompromising determinism in discussions with friends; and in 1788 and 1789 he tried to persuade friends in Zürich to the same position.[54] At the same time that he
saw himself shaping a self and a life in some sense, he confronted the possibility that he was merely another object passively being shaped. As he
sought a way to assign himself a mission, a calling that would give his life
moral meaning, he faced the possibility that within the seemingly infinite webs of causation, his life was morally meaningless.

In its eighteenth-century version, determinism applied to human
behavior the mechanistic principle of causation with which modern
science, inspired by Newton's explanation of motion, was constructing a
physical universe of regular, predictable laws. Its operating assumption was
that the processes of human subjectivity, like the workings of the physical universe, were reducible to actions and reactions within a chain of
sufficient causes. The result was an uncompromising environmentalism,
applied to ideas as well as to actions, that reduced rationality to an
"epiphenomenon of natural causality."[55] Thought was the product of sense
experience, which was itself caused by external stimuli. All this was the
standard fare of French materialist psychology, but Fichte had probably
first encountered the full-blown case for determinism in a version that
was rather crude by the philosophical standards of the era, the 1772
edition of a book by Carl Ferdinand Hommel, a professor of natural
law and criminal law at Leipzig. Hommel, to be sure, had taken pains to
give his argument reassuringly Protestant, and German, twists. Modern
scientific determinism struck him as entirely compatible with the
Lutheran doctrine of predestination and indeed was simply another way
of stating it. Conveniently, the "feeling" (*Empfindung*) of being free – a
feeling inherent in human nature – was also testimony to the higher
wisdom of providence; without that feeling, individuals could not be held

[54] See esp. Preul, *Reflexion*, pp. 94–130.
[55] The phrase is from Armin G. Wildfeuer, "Vernunft als Epiphänomenon der Naturalkausalität. Zu
Herkunft und Bedeutung des ursprünglichen Determinismus J. G. Fichtes," Schrader, ed., *Anfänge
und Ursprünge*, pp. 61–82, which demonstrates Fichte's reliance on Hommel for his conception of
mechanistic determinism.

accountable for their actions, and hence the state would have no moral ground for using the threat of punishment and the prospect of reward to maintain order. This was to say that from a rigorously philosophical standpoint, freedom of the will was no more than a "fiction," though in an eminently utilitarian corollary, the fiction was socially and politically indispensable.[56]

The specter of this mechanistic reductionism and fatalism haunted the German debate about Spinoza and "pantheism" in the 1780s. As in the earlier controversy about Reimarus, Lessing was at center stage, though this time as the contested icon rather than as the instigator. In 1785, Friedrich Jacobi's published version of a conversation with Lessing – a conversation in which Lessing was alleged to have admitted that he had always been a "Spinozist" – sent shudders through the Enlightenment establishment.[57] This was precisely the effect Jacobi had intended. He was wielding the revered figure of Lessing in an assault on the Neologists' compromise between head and heart. If Lessing had indeed been a Spinozist, as Jacobi defined that persuasion, then "rational" theologians were deluding themselves and misleading the public. Lessing's secret was dramatic proof that rationalism inevitably led to materialist determinism and thence, to atheism. The only escape from this inherently nihilistic momentum was the blind "leap of faith" with which the Christian admitted the impotence of reason in the face of religious mystery.

Fichte certainly was aware of this controversy, but he neither accepted Jacobi's ad-ultra implication about rationalism nor embraced his alternative. Instead he made determinism the ground for what he called a "pure deistic system," with God retained as "the eternal and necessary being," the "first cause" in the chain of sufficient causes. To put it another way, he stopped short of atheism, but only by stripping away all traces of theistic anthropomorphism and reducing the concept of a Divinity to a purely logical necessity.

It was with a commitment to this "deistic" (i.e., determinist) alternative that Fichte thought he had resolved his internal argument – the argument that seemed to demand a choice between the iron constraints of necessity and a freedom grounded in spontaneity, between head and heart, between reason as power and faith as a very different kind of empowerment – in the summer of 1790. His eighteen "aphorisms" on "religion" and "deism" record his abandonment of the Neologists' middle ground. The aphorisms have none of the tentative repetitiveness of the sermon

---

[56] Carl Ferdinand Hommel, *Ueber Belohnung und Strafen nach Türkischen Gesetzen* (2nd ed., 1772: Berlin, 1970). Hommel's book was first published in 1770 under the pseudonym Alexander von Joch.

[57] F. H. Jacobi, "Ueber seine Gespräche mit Lessing," in Gotthold Ephraim Lessing, ed., *Gesammelte Werke*, ed. Paul Rilla, vol. 8 (Berlin, 1956), pp. 616–34. On the Spinoza controversy, see esp. Beiser, *The Fate of Reason*, pp. 44–108; Hermann Timm, *Gott und die Freiheit. Studien zur Religionsphilosophie der Goethezeit*, vol. 1: *Die Spinozarenaissance* (Frankfurt am Main, 1974).

drafts. A series of concisely formulated definitions and conclusions, advanced in strict logical sequence, they record Fichte's resolve to settle matters, to justify his own acceptance of determinism in a way that would make the choice irrevocable. In a sense, they return us to our point of departure. Fichte was still arguing that a public Resurrection would have been too "forceful" for a religion "grounded more on feelings (*Empfindungen*) than on convictions (*Ueberzeugungen*)." But, on one level, he had finally applied the lesson that Lessing's two-front polemic had been designed to drive home. "Religion" could and should be an internally self-sufficient system of beliefs proceeding from emotionally self-evident principles. The effort to purify religion with philosophical rationality, "to unite as far as possible speculation with the claims of religion," resulted in "a deism that [did] not even work as deism" and that made its advocates "suspect of not going to work very honorably." The advantage of his own, consequential deism was that it left the Christian religion "its entire subjective validity," since "it never [came] into collision with it."[58]

Through most of the aphorisms, the very impersonality of the format conveys a sense of relief and even of liberation. The young "speculator" had used rigorous logic to purge himself of his elders' need to unite head and heart in a workable marriage. Using the distinction between "religion" and "speculation," he opted for an epistemological division of labor between cleanly different kinds of knowledge. But he also assigned himself to one side of that division, and in the last two aphorisms, this self-definition turned an impersonal exercise in logic into a personal lament. The speculator faced "moments when the heart takes revenge on speculation," when "the entire [deterministic] system" is thrown into "disorder," when "a pressing desire (*Sehnsucht*) for reconciliation arises." But there was no "means of escape," since it was too late to "cut himself off from those speculations beyond the boundary." A compulsion for rational "speculation" that "proceeds straight ahead," without regard for consequences, had become "natural to him"; it was "interwoven with the entire turn of his spirit."[59]

In the light of Fichte's theological preoccupations, it is not hard to understand the sense of loss and embitterment that surfaces in the aphorisms. In the very act of repudiating his earlier vision of Christian freedom, Fichte magnified what he had lost. The believing Christian not only aspired to seize God-given opportunities; "his heart demands a God who lets Himself be entreated, who feels sympathy, friendship . . . [and] with whom [he can] enter a relationship of mutual modification." In his intensely personal relation with his God, in other words, the Christian asserted his will in the hope of changing his assigned life course, even as

[58] GA, II, 1: 288. [59] GA, II, 1: 291.

he allowed himself to be changed by it. But if the rational theist had found ways to ground freedom in an inner reality of human experience, the pure deist had concluded that freedom was an illusion. "Speculation" revealed "a Being that has no point of contact whatsoever" with any human being. Since "any change in this world [was] necessarily determined by a sufficient cause," Fichte reasoned in the fifteenth aphorism, both the "activity" and the "suffering" of "each thinking and feeling being" was what it must be. What believers called "sin" was simply a product of this necessity; and it in turn produced results that were "just as necessary as the existence of the Divinity" and hence were "ineradicable."[60]

The deistic alternative was emphatically secular and in that sense modern, but it too lacked an explanation of justice and injustice in terms of the social structure. Society was still subsumed under an extrasocial abstraction. The difference is that providence has been replaced by a mechanistic law of causation – a law that in contrast to the believer's imagined relationship with his God, was forbiddingly impersonal as well as inflexible. In the absence of freedom and hence of responsibility, the individual could neither justify himself morally nor identify injustice in the constraints that faced him.

The pain of disillusionment was reinforced by another realization: in facing up to his impotence, Fichte had acquired a new sense of his social isolation. With the epistemological division of labor to which Fichte committed himself in the aphorisms, an aspiration to community acceded to resigned acceptance of cultural and social segregation. Whereas in the draft sermons the "few good heads" had remained bonded to the mass in a larger community of belief, there was now a watertight dichotomy between the "speculators" and "non-speculating mankind." Christianity was "the best popular religion (*Volksreligion*)" – which was to say that belief in Christ's mediation had a unique power to satisfy human "need," transcending historical and cultural differences, but also that such belief was limited to "good and simple souls."[61] The latter phrase was ambivalent; it evoked emotional spontaneity and innocence, but it also connoted ignorance and weakness. The "speculator" could recommend such a religion "with the innermost warmth" to "those who need it"; but his own deism effected "a certain inflexibility," which "prevent[ed] participation in the pleasant feelings (*Empfindungen*) that flow from religion."[62]

There was something intensely personal about Fichte's commitment to an impersonal determinism. It was not simply that he had sacrificed his moral self-justification, his God-given right to rise above the social world of his origins. He had also lost his conviction of a bonding with that world through emotive symbols and metaphors. Reluctantly, but with the

[60] GA, II, 1: 287–90.   [61] GA, II, 1: 287–90.   [62] GA, II, 1: 290.

iron grip of logic, Fichte accepted the conclusion the draft sermons had avoided: that the zone of privileged insight – the zone occupied by intellectuals like himself – had no common ground of subjectivity with the religious culture of the masses. If the voice of speculation had public resonance, it was within that caste-like zone. The same critical distance that allowed its occupants to "proceed straight ahead" also prevented them from participating in and having a direct impact on a public community of belief.

The final irony is that in taking this painful step, Fichte did *not* commit himself unreservedly to critical rationality over emotional belief. As the distancing effect of logical rigor acceded to introspective regret, the aphorisms conveyed a heightened ambivalence about *both* head and heart. In a sense, as the antipode to the rationalist's submission to "persuasion," the spontaneity of the believer's emotional commitment was still a kind of freedom. But to satisfy emotional "need" was also to admit dependence, to succumb to human weakness; in that sense Christian belief was not for "the strong" but for "the sick, who need the doctor."[63] Speculators, of course, were free precisely because they had transcended need. They had the intellectual fortitude required to "proceeed straight ahead," without flinching in the face of personal loss. But the exercise of this kind of privileged freedom exacted a high price. Whereas in the sermon drafts the elect had been endowed with "softer" and "more pliant" hearts as well as with superior natural intelligence, the new intellectual elite was burdened with a certain "inflexibility," an inability to respond to the inner stirrings of the heart. Fichte had confronted a kind of coercion inherent in rational autonomy, the inverse of the Christian paradox of freedom in slavery. The person who seemed "invincible in the field of speculation" experienced his intellectual freedom as a grim but irreversible fate, and he could not release himself from its grip even when he felt the "pressing desire" to escape back into an eminently human satisfaction. If his rationality was his strength, it was also an inhuman compulsion. Its freedom had to be endured.

★ ★ ★

We are now in a position to understand why Fichte seized on Kantianism in his search for self-justification, and why the order in which he read Kant's *Critiques* had such a powerful effect.

When Fichte's tutoring responsibilities led him to the *Critique of Pure Reason* in the late summer of 1790, he confronted the text as a reluctant but unflinching determinist. Not surprisingly, he focused on Kant's third Antinomy and gave it a markedly one-sided reading. In this exercise in "transcendental dialectic," the thesis demonstrated the necessity of assum-

[63] GA, II, 1: 289

ing transcendental freedom. The antithesis demonstrated, with equally rigorous logic, that everything in the world takes place solely in accordance with the laws of nature and hence was subject to the law of causality. It was the thesis that clinched the issue for Fichte. He concluded from it that even "the most sharp-witted defender of freedom who ever was" (i.e., the voice of the thesis) had been unable to provide a rational proof. The concept of freedom had simply been inserted from "somewhere else," and probably from "feeling" (*Empfindung*).[64] Fichte was still echoing Hommel.

Taken by itself, Kant's thesis might be said to yield this interpretation; but in his search for confirmation of his pure deism, Fichte had wrenched the Antinomy out of the larger context of Kant's argument. Kant's aim was not to prove or disprove either position but to demonstrate that in their claims to knowledge beyond sense experience, both could be true *or* false. What he claimed to have identified were the ordering structures inherent in our "theoretical" understanding of the natural world – the innate concepts which, by imposing order on the "sensible manifold of intuitions," constituted the condition of any knowledge of nature, including human psychology. This kind of knowledge applied only to phenomena or to things as they appeared in sense experience. Since noumenal being, the reality of things-in-themselves, was beyond sense experience, we could not understand it.

Fichte had concluded from his selective reading of the *Critique of Pure Reason* that his deterministic system was unassailable. Hence it was all the more wrenching to find his conviction being demolished as he read the next treatise, the *Critique of Practical Reason*. To his amazement, he reported to his friend Weisshuhn, "the concept of absolute freedom" had been "proven" to him. It was this discovery that transported him into "a new world," elevated "above all earthly things." Suddenly and quite unexpectedly, he had a compelling justification for the conviction of moral meaning and responsibility he had recently abandoned.

To Kant, eighteenth-century moral philosophy had fostered two pernicious illusions: that the will unavoidably sought to satisfy material, emotional, or social "interests," and that "happiness" in any of these senses could be the object of morality. In making itself the instrument of these "interests," as in responding to the dictates of external authority, the will *allowed itself* to be determined – or, in Kant's terms, it sacrificed autonomy for heteronomy. It failed to be what it could and should be, the cause without cause, the locus of unconditional moral freedom. By limiting "theoretical" knowledge to the phenomenal world of sense experience, Kant had opened the way to a radically new moral theory, premised on the claim that "practical" (i.e., moral) knowledge was grounded in the

[64] GA, II, 1, 290.

noumenal self, the "I" as pure rational "intelligence." When the rational intellect turned inward – when it reflected on itself – it became aware of the Moral Law, the law of its unconditional autonomy. This idea of transcendental freedom could not be "understood" (in the way that physical causation, for example, was understood), but it was nonetheless an unavoidable "fact of reason," self-evident in our inner awareness of our spontaneity.

Fichte was exhilarated by the sheer cogency of Kant's argument, which liberated him from the compulsion of his own logic. The self-styled determinist now felt justified in abandoning conclusions he had come to reluctantly with a deep sense of loss and in embracing the conviction of freedom that his combative personality craved. Rather than choosing between mutually exclusive alternatives, as he had felt compelled to do in the aphorisms, he could now resolve his internal argument within a Kantian set of dualisms. In the second *Critique*, Kant had "proven" the possibility he had raised toward the close of the first one: that the human being was morally free in his "intelligible character" *at the same time* that he was determined by natural causation in his "empirical" (or phenomenal) character.

If Kant's logical cogency gripped Fichte with unusual force, that was because it resolved his internal argument between head and heart. The personal wholeness Fichte had sought as a Protestant believer and had despaired of as a determinist now seemed within reach. This is not to imply that, via Kant, Fichte returned to the Neologists' "half-philosophy." Instead he found a purely philosophical way to reconstitute the Neologists' middle ground. To Kant, moral autonomy was a "fact," evident in the ordinary exercise of rational intelligence, and not an emotionally grounded intuition. He took pains to distinguish knowledge of the Moral Law from the emotional embrace of supernatural truth that grace was said to induce and from the innate emotional preference for the good that some eighteenth-century moral theorists (including some Neologists) had attributed to human nature. Whenever emotional need (or any other need) was deemed a legitimate motive for moral action, the will responded to "external" sense objects rather than to its intrinsic imperatives; it abandoned autonomy for heteronomy. But Kant also acknowledged that in the sense world a moral intention, like any other, must be impelled by a desire and an "interest" in satisfying it. A "good will," he argued, was a "higher faculty of desire." While other interests subjected the will to heteronomy, the paradox of the "interest" that motivated moral action was that it was disinterested. That was because the moral law induced a feeling of reverence for itself, as an imperative that overrode all empirical desires. The feeling resulted from a prior recognition of an objective and absolutely binding law, but it also affected the will by reinforcing that recognition. The impulses of the heart, in this sense, had an essential role in Kant's moral theory.[65]

There was another reason that Fichte found Kant's argument for "absolute moral freedom" so compelling: it made inner spontaneity the source of a fundamentally Protestant ethos. While "nature" was consigned to the realm of appearance, it was also the resistant substance against which the will had to struggle as it sought to realize its moral potential. Only on the assumption of "the freedom of the human being," Fichte wrote to his friend Achelis in November 1790, "[were] duty, virtue and in general morality possible."[66] A morally free will did not do what it wanted to do, but what it ought to do. Its freedom lay in fullfilling its duty, despite the constraints of the natural self. The exercise of freedom required a relentless "strengthening for further effort" and hence the same ascetic self-mastery – the same struggle within – with which the Protestant believer sought to suppress natural corruption. This was, in fact, the first way in which Fichte's conversion changed his daily life in the late summer and fall of 1790. In early September he reported to his fiancée that although he had previously been "too unsteady to follow a fixed course," he was now observing a strict regimen. Accustomed to rising late, he was getting up at five every morning to "force [himself] to self-overcoming." His tutoring responsibilities were sandwiched between mornings and evenings devoted to study. In a parallel effort to "become completely master over [himself]," he had taken to depriving himself of "something [he] would have liked to have." The point was to "declare war on every emerging passion as soon as it reveal[ed] itself."[67]

When Fichte spoke of the new "peace" his conversion had brought him, he was not referring simply to his restored sense of personal wholeness. He had learned to "concern [himself] more with [himself]," he assured his fiancée, and not to bother with "things outside [himself]."[68] He did not retreat into monastic seclusion, but his ascetic turn inward at least brought a temporary respite from ambition and the attendant threats to his "honor." Having fretted for months about his penury, Fichte now faced his "shaky external situation" with equanimity. Having risked his precious integrity in the quest for new patrons, he was now determined to preserve his "independence" and indeed to shun worldly power by refusing to be either "lord" or "servant." For this marginal intellectual, it would seem that Kant's epistemological dualism – his distinction between noumenon and phenomenon – had an immediately relevant social corollary. It clarified the choice between self-contained integrity and

---

[65] This aspect of Kant's thought is emphasized in Roger J. Sullivan, *Immanuel Kant's Moral Theory* (Cambridge, 1989).
[66] GA, III, 1: 193–4.   [67] GA, III, 1: 172–3.   [68] GA, III, 1: 186–7.

dissimulation in the pursuit of "prospects." Indifferent to "all brilliance of the World," Fichte now strove "not to appear, but to be."[69]

But what would this Kantian convert actually *do*? His immediate project (left uncompleted) was to provide his fellow scholars with a clear synopsis of the master's *Critique of Judgment*, which had just appeared. For the long term, however, his sights were still fastened on the pulpit; the aspiring preacher now had "a far more uplifting material" for developing and exercising his "capacity for eloquence." Here again Fichte had found a new route to self-justification in the *Critiques*. He saw the Kantian reorientation of his calling as an alternative to dishonorable place-seeking, though he had no practical strategy for securing a pastorate without forfeiting his independence. What mattered was that, in principle, Kantianism offered him a way to "have an effect," to justify himself as an intellectual by asserting a truly public voice. Fichte had drawn intensely personal inferences from Kant's moral theory, but his reading had not been willful. Kant insisted repeatedly that as abstract as the several formulations of the Categorical Imperative were, neither extraordinary intelligence nor formal education was needed to grasp their essential moral truth. This was because the formal criterion of universality (or noncontradiction) was rationally self-evident and because its self-evident rationality induced an emotional response, the feeling of reverence, that powerfully reinforced it. For Fichte, this conception of moral knowledge had two momentous implications. Unlike the "speculator" of his pre-Kantian thinking, the Kantian rationalist did not exercise coercive "persuasion" and hence did not violate the Lutheran ideal of inner freedom to which Fichte, at bottom, remained attached. Clarification of the moral law activated the listeners' latent capacity for moral insight and hence induced them to *emancipate themselves* from the illusions of heteronomy. And in this kind of communication, the communion of hearts had a perfectly legitimate and indeed necessary role. For this latter reason, Fichte counseled his fiancée that it was only misguided "reasoners" (*Vernünftler*) like himself who needed Kant's "head-breaking" antidote. She should "believe only in [her] own feeling," since she was one of the "honorable people" who had always "felt" (but had not "thought") the truth of Kant's message.[70]

All this is to say that Kant's moral theory offered Fichte a symbolic route out of his social isolation. Having numbered himself among the coldly logical "speculators," cut off from the emotionally satisfying beliefs of the masses, he had found a way to reconnect. The Categorical Imperative promised to be the grounding for the inclusive public community, at once cognitive and emotional, that he had originally sought in his elders' half-philosophical Lutheranism. If the Kantian turn inward were to regenerate an age "rotten to its roots," it required a new mode of

[69] GA, III, 1: 194.   [70] GA, III, 1: 171.

communicative action. The uprooted intellectual had found a rhetorical mission and with it a moral justification. As a Kantian preacher he would make philosophy "popular" (*populär*) and "effective in the human heart through eloquence."[71] His vocation was to "imprint [Kant's] moral principles on the heart of the public with energy and fire, in a popular form of presentation."[72]

Fichte would soon try to achieve such a rhetoric – to give the public voice of the philosopher a truly popular form – in his Kantian defense of the principles of the French Revolution.

[71] GA, III, 1: 170–2   [72] GA, III, 1: 195.

Chapter 3

The German Machine

Fichte did not meet Kant until July 1791, nearly a year after reading the *Critiques*. Having made the trek from Saxony to Poland only to discover that his admittedly limited facility in French fell well short of his employer's expectations, he had found himself, once again, unemployed and without prospects. He might have returned to Leipzig, the scene of his Kantian rebirth nearly a year earlier. Instead he traveled east from Warsaw to Königsberg, "the nearest entrepôt of learning," and more to the point, the home of Kant himself. He hoped to make himself known somehow to the Sage of Königsberg as "a good head" and thereby to win his patronage in the seemingly endless search for a position.[1]

On July 4 the young stranger visited the sixty-seven-year-old philosopher for the first time. His diary records his disappointment; Kant seemed "drowsy" and received him "without special attention." Fichte resolved to win the support of this "great spirit" in a "tired" body with a written performance.[2] On July 14, having holed up in his room for nearly two weeks, he sent Kant the first draft of the substantial manuscript that would be entitled *An Attempt at a Critique of All Revelation*. He was submitting it, he explained in an accompanying letter, in lieu of the usual letters of recommendation, though its content might very well amount to "nothing."[3]

By early September, with the philosopher's reaction still pending, Fichte was once more on the edge of complete penury. He confided to his diary that, if he was going to reveal his dilemma to anyone, it would be to Kant; but he could not screw up the courage to make a face-to-face request for a loan. Instead he sent Kant a letter, rewritten several times to achieve the proper mix of self-assertion and self-criticism. He needed the money, he explained, to return to his native Saxony to find a village pastorate.[4]

Kant demurred on the loan, but he had taken an interest in the young man and in ways Fichte could not have foreseen, changed the course of his life. Thanks to Kant's intervention, Fichte secured the tutoring employment that brought him into Countess Luise's enchanting circle on the Krockow estate. Though he had read through only part of Fichte's

---

[1] "Vorbereitung auf die Kantische Visite," GA, II, 2: 11.
[2] GA, III, 1: 243; GA, II, 1: 415.   [3] GA, III, 1: 252.   [4] GA, III, 1: 256–64.

manuscript, Kant brushed aside the author's doubts about its quality, and shortly after Fichte's departure from Könisgberg, Kant arranged for its publication with the Hartung firm.[5]

What followed was, as Fichte later recalled it, "a favorable, unforeseen, uncalculated incident [that] raised [him] up."[6] The book appeared without an author's name on the title page. The omission may have been inadvertent, or Hartung may have calculated that the *Attempt at a Critique* would be mistaken for Kant's long-awaited treatise on religion and its publisher would profit accordingly. In any event, a publishing quirk suddenly lifted Fichte's veil of obscurity. In the first review to appear, Gottlieb Hufeland, a well-known professor of law at Jena and the editor of the *Jenaer Allgemeine-Literaturzeitung*, assured readers that Kant's authorship of this "highly important book" would be obvious to "anyone who has read even the smallest of his writings." The reviewer for another learned journal made the same mistake, with similar praise for the latest achievement of the "great thinker."[7] Unwilling to take credit for someone else's work, and perhaps concerned to avoid an imbroglio with the Prussian censorship, Kant himself intervened with a public notice on August 14, 1792. The real author was "the theology candidate Hr. Fichte," Kant informed the reading public, and he himself had not played "the slightest part, either in writing or orally, in the work of the skilled man."[8]

Fichte's triumph was not without a sour note. In the *Allgemeine deutsche Bibliothek*, before Kant's notice appeared, an acquaintance of Fichte from Königsberg had also identified him as the author, but only to demonstrate that "a very insignificant book" had received so much praise simply because Kant was assumed to have written it.[9] Understandably infuriated, Fichte failed to realize that this attack would probably mean that subsequent reviewers would be stung into welcoming him as a prodigious new talent. If they panned the *Attempt at a Critique*, after all, would they not be proving the snide implication that scholars judged each other by reputation (or lack of it) rather than by the merit of their work?

Having been plucked out of his native village as a young boy, Fichte was now catapulted into public renown as a thirty-year-old. He wrote his fiancée that unlike many other writers with no less talent, he would not be "buried under the great flood" and would not have to "struggle through half a life just to be noticed."[10] The "incident" left him grateful but also reconfirmed his sense of having been singled out for a special

[5] *Versuch einer Critik aller Offenbarung* (Königsberg, 1792), reprinted in GA, I, 1: 15–123. My quotations are from *Attempt at a Critique of All Revelation*, trans. Garrett Green (Cambridge, 1978).
[6] GA, III, 1: 403–4.
[7] FR 1: 1–22. See also Karl Leonhard Reinhold's appraisal of the *Attempt at a Critique*, in FG 1: 35–6.
[8] *Intelligenzblatt der Allgemeine Literatur-Zeitung*, Nr. 102 (August 22, 1792), in FR 1: 23.
[9] FR 1: 22. [10] GA, III, 1: 403.

mission. He planned a sequel to the *Attempt at a Critique* that would examine the concepts of providence and miracles. As he settled into the "dreamy comfort" of Krockow, the project fizzled. His other plan was to write a book on "the fair sex," but that too came to nothing. Alternately exulting and brooding over his "friendship" with Countess Luise, he was in no condition to enlighten the public on the female of the species.

When he finally shook off his lethargy, he began clearing a path through a thicket of political, social, and economic issues. The first result was the *Reclamation of the Freedom of Thought from the Princes of Europe, Who Have Oppressed It until Now.*[11] Published in the spring of 1793, this brief pamphlet, cast as a fiery "oration" (*Rede*) to the European rulers, denounced government secrecy and censorship and appealed for unconditional freedom of public expression. In a fitting irony, it appeared anonymously, with its place of publication given as "Heliopolis, in the last year of the old darkness."

Meanwhile Fichte had set to work on a more substantial essay, and he returned to it in the summer of 1793. It appeared in two installments, both anonymous, under the no-nonsense title *A Contribution toward Correcting the Judgment of the Public about the French Revolution.* Though left unfinished, the *Contribution* amounts to over two hundred dense pages in its modern edition. In it Fichte posed two questions: whether the Revolution's objectives had been "legitimate," and whether the Revolution had shown "wisdom" in its choice of "means." The first question he answered affirmatively and exhaustively, though not without some rough passages; the second he left in abeyance.[12]

Our focus will be on the *Reclamation* and the *Contribution*, and particularly on the latter. The *Attempt at a Critique* was, to be sure, an impressive exercise for a fledgling philosopher. The reader who concluded that Kant was "at least the author of the author, just as the sun is the mother of moonlight," missed the fact that in its emphases the book bore Fichte's signature.[13] In the main countours of its argument, however, *The Attempt at a Critique* was the entirely predictable work of a disciple. With the *Contribution* the disciple began to strike out on his own. Whereas in the first book Fichte had rarely abandoned the abstract, impersonal language of

---

[11] *Zurückforderung der Denkfreiheit von den Fürsten Europens, die sie bisher unterdrückten,* in GA, I, 1: 167–92. There is a modern edition in *Johann Gottlieb Fichte, Schriften zur Revolution,* ed. Bernard Willms (Cologne, 1967), pp. 167–92. My quotations are from the English translation ("Reclamation") by Thomas E. Wartenberg in James Schmidt, ed., *What Is Enlightenment? Eighteenth-Century Answers and Twentieth-Century Questions* (Berkeley, Calif., 1996), pp. 119–41.

[12] The full text is in GA, I, 1: 203–404 and in *Fichte, Schriften zur Revolution,* pp. 35–215. My citations are to the latter edition. For a French translation of the *Contribution* see *J. G. Fichte. Considérations destinées à rectifier les jugements du public sur la Révolution française,* ed. Marc Richir (Paris, 1974).

[13] The comment was by Jens Immanuel Baggessen, in a letter to Schiller. FG 1: 46.

Kant's system, the *Contribution* is a rhetorical experiment abounding in unexpected turns and evocative metaphors. More flawed as a philosophical enterprise, it is far richer as a record of Fichte's expanding horizons and his renewed efforts to resolve the conflicting aspirations of his youth.[14]

The *Attempt at a Critique* made Fichte something of a celebrity in educated circles, but the *Contribution* burdened him with a notoriety he could not shake. His authorship was soon known, and the timing could not have been worse. When Fichte began writing the *Contribution*, Paris was in the violent grip of the sans-culottes movement; the National Assembly had acceded to a democratically elected Convention; Louis XVI had been tried and executed. In the summer of 1793, as Fichte was writing the second part, the Committee of Public Safety came to power. By the very fact that he dared defend the Revolution at this juncture, whatever his grounds for doing so, Fichte made himself an exposed target. That he was not a German Jacobin should now be obvious, despite the persistent tendency among French scholars to hail him as a kind of fellow-traveler in a positive sense.[15] It makes some sense to characterize as German Jacobins those radicals (Georg Forster, for example, or Friedrich Cotta) who openly threw their support to revolutionary France and worked to join parts of the Holy Roman Empire to the French Republic – though the label suggests that they had far more in common with the Jacobins

---

[14] Particularly helpful on Fichte's political thought is Alexis Philonenko, *Théorie et praxis dans la pensée morale et politique de Kant et de Fichte en 1793* (1968: Paris, 1976). Unlike most other students of Fichte's thought, Philonenko focused on the *Contribution* as the base line for understanding Fichte's subsequent development of a "system." His interpretation is also distinguished by its close textual reading. See also Hans Siegbert Reiss, "Fichte als Politischer Denker," *Archiv für Rechts- und Sozialgeschichte* 48 (1962); Georges Vlachos, "Le droit, la morale et l'expérience dans les écrits révolutionnaires de Fichte," *Cahiers de philosophie du droit*, Nouv. Série 7 (1962): 211–45; Zwi Batscha, *Gesellschaft und Staat in der politischen Philosophie Fichtes* (Frankfurt, 1970); Bernard Willms, *Die totale Freiheit. Fichtes politische Philosophie* (Cologne and Opladen, 1967). The philosophical context of the *Contribution* is also emphasized in Luc Ferry, "Fichte," in François Furet and Mona Ozouf, eds., *Dictionnaire Critique de la Révolution Française* (Cambridge, Mass., 1989), pp. 933–7.

[15] For modern readings of the young Fichte as a "Jacobin" in one sense or another, see Martial Guéroult, "Fichte et la Révolution Française," in Ernest Barker, ed., *La révolution de 1789 et la pensée moderne* (Paris, 1940), p. 171; Xavier Léon, *Fichte et son temps*, 2 vols. (Paris, 1922–24), I, pp. 180–203. But cf. Pierre-Philippe Druet, *Fichte* (Paris, 1977), p. 56, where Fichte is said to have espoused "the ideology of 89" in 1792 and 1793.

Historians in the former German Democratic Republic also tended to emphasize Fichte's affinities with Jacobinism, though from a different standpoint. See, e.g., Claus Träger, "Fichte als Agitator der Revolution. Über Aufklärung und Jakobinismus in Deutschland," in Manfred Buhr, ed., *Wissen und Gewissen. Beiträge zum 200. Geburtstag Johann Gottlieb Fichtes, 1762–1814* (Berlin, 1962), pp. 158–204, and Manfred Buhr, *Revolution und Philosophie. Die ursprüngliche Philosophie Johann Gottlieb Fichtes und die Französische Revolution* (Berlin, 1965), pp. 42–71. For Buhr, Fichte's similarity with the Jacobins lay in his justification of "the use of revolutionary force" against counter-revolutionaries, even to the point of their physical destruction. Against the backdrop of the East Bloc purges of the 1950s, this was a chilling misreading.

of the Parisian Clubs and the Committee of Public Safety than was actually the case. For Fichte the label is quite misleading. He was not at all involved in revolutionary politics; more important, he had little interest in the Jacobins' political agenda. The *Contribution* is completely lacking in references to the radical politics of the early 1790s, and indeed to the personalities who figured in them. The actual revolutionary changes Fichte defended were the abolition of legal privileges, and especially of aristocratic privileges, and the national appropriation of church properties. To judge by this agenda, the *Contribution*, far from being a brief for Jacobinism, was a defense of the moderate revolution of 1789. And it was only a partial defense; uninterested in forms of government, Fichte was as indifferent to the constitutional monarchy of 1789 as he was to the democratic republic of 1793.

A more salient context for gauging the radicalism of the *Contribution* is German natural law theory. In the German tradition, in sharp contrast to the Lockean tradition, the interpretation of an original "social contract" served to justify absolutism. The contract had been necessary not to secure natural liberties but to guarantee order by sacrificing those liberties to an absolute authority that could not be defied. Society had a legitimate existence only as the construction of an order-imposing state. From the 1770s onward, however, with the importation of physiocratic thought and, more dramatically, under the impact of Kant's *Critiques*, German natural law theory underwent a sharp change of course. Society was granted a new independence vis-à-vis the state, and state authority was deemed legitimate only to the extent that it protected natural rights that were inalienable.[16] Fichte, like several other Kantian natural law theorists in the 1790s, carried this shift to radical conclusions. In the *Contribution* he maintained that society had not needed the state to constitute itself and establish the institution of private property, and that the survival of both property and the larger social order was not contingent on state authority. Human beings had an inalienable right to reject any government that prevented the satisfaction of their human needs. It was their moral duty as well as their right to reject any government that obstructed their moral development. Indeed anyone was free to exit any contract unilaterally until its promises were actually fulfilled. This latter contention was alarming even to the more radical Kantian revisionists, and modern interpreters have characterized it, not without justification, as anarchistic individualism.

---

[16] See, e.g., Diethelm Klippel, *Politische Freiheit und Freiheitsrechte im deutschen Naturrecht des 18. Jahrhunderts* (Paderborn, 1976); Klippel, "The True Concept of Liberty. Political Theory in Germany in the Second Half of the Eighteenth Century," in Eckhart Hellmuth, ed., *The Transformation of Political Culture. England and Germany in the Late Eighteenth Century* (New York, 1990), pp. 447–56; Keith Tribe, *Governing Economy. The Reformation of German Economic Discourse 1750–1840* (Cambridge, 1988), esp. pp. 19–34, 119–48.

If we reduce the *Contribution* to this natural law argument, however, we at once overestimate it and skim over its layered meanings. The work is not a thoroughgoing, internally consistent reformulation of natural law theory but a young intellectual's initial, groping, unfinished effort to confront a broad range of issues with an uncompromising moral vision. Though the vision was intended to be universal in application, it was inspired or – perhaps better – provoked by a distinctly German set of political and religious circumstances. The voice of the philosopher, building his argument on Kantian a priori principles, is clear enough; but in the way he applied a priori principles and in the way he embedded them in other meanings, Fichte was already diverging from the master. His Kantianism is inflected by several other eighteenth-century languages, some emphatically secular, others still religious in their resonances, and the inflections are critical to the meaning of the text.

★ ★ ★

A theology candidate from a family as plebeian as Fichte's, and one whose conversion to Kantianism had been as wrenching, can hardly be considered typical of the younger generation of German intellectuals. And yet, in their perspective on the German scene, Fichte's writings in 1792–93 formed one of several markers of a generational shift. In 1786, when the nearly half-century reign of Frederick the Great in Prussia finally ended, Fichte was twenty-four. The men who formed his generation were still in their twenties when the French Revolution burst on the scene. They had been raised on the rationalist ethos of a Protestant Enlightenment, and they owed a considerable intellectual debt to the elders of an Enlightenment establishment that had entrenched itself in government and in the clergy in Prussia and several other North German states. But in the late 1780s and early 1790s, when the German intelligentsia was confronted with a rapid succession of crises at home and abroad, it became apparent that some of the younger men were a new breed.

In this German Protestant world, with the Enlightenment acceding to new impulses and something like a modern ideological arena beginning to take shape, Fichte sighted his targets for a Kantian critique of the old regime in the *Reclamation* and the *Contribution*. The crisis that came to overshadow all others, of course, was the Revolution itself. In the early 1790s, as constitutional monarchy succumbed to the democracy of the clubs and the streets, France confronted the rest of Europe with an unprecedented spectacle of political upheaval. With the collapse of royal authority the country seemed to have regressed to the fanaticism of the sixteenth-century Religious Wars, except that now confessional zealotry had its militantly secular rivals. The new wars pitted the devout against the rabidly anti-Christian, the defenders of monarchy against enthusiasts of the democratic republic, people recoiling with horror from popular violence against others eager to ride its crests. All this was a far cry from the Enlightenment's *Publikum* of reasonable men, committed to gradual reform within a framework of stability and confident that the public airing of disagreements would eventually yield a consensus.

In the Protestant states of North Germany, the cataclysm of the Revolution had been preceded by an internal shock. Its tremors radiated out from Berlin, where the *Berlinische Monatsschrift* had established itself as the central organ of the North German Enlightenment. Thanks to the unstinting patronage of Baron Karl Abraham von Zedlitz, the Prussian Minister of Ecclesiatical Affairs under Frederick the Great, rationalist clergymen had gained entry to university professorships and prestigious pastorates in the major towns and had come to dominate many of the governing consistories of the Lutheran state churches. In July 1788, two years after Frederick William II ascended the throne, Zedlitz was replaced by Johann Christoph Wöllner, a favorite of the new king and one of his brethren in the notoriously obscurantist Rosicrucian Order. Within a matter of days Wöllner, acting in the King's name, issued the Edict Concerning Religion that would make him the bête noire of Germany's enlightened public.

The royal preamble to the edict threw down the gauntlet to the clerical establishment of the German Enlightenment. Leaping over Frederick the Great, it explicitly identified with the example of his pious father Frederick William I. Its measures were aimed at "unbridled" propagators of "miserable, long refuted errors," and these included "deists" and "naturalists" as well as Socinians and "other sectarians." Preachers who "spread [such errors] among the people with impertinent impudence under the much abused banner of *Aufklärung*" now faced a choice: henceforth they could either adhere strictly to orthodox dogma or vacate their offices. New appointments to pastoral vacancies and to teaching positions in the universities and the schools would be limited to "subjects who provide no ground for questioning their internal adherence to the creed they are employed to teach."[17] In December 1788, as the protests against this drastic shift in course mounted, Wöllner issued a new Edict of Censorship, designed to stop the flow of irreligious writings. Over the next few years several North German governments, including Electoral Saxony, followed the Prussian example.

In the early 1790s Prusssia and its neighbors faced the challenge of containing a Revolution that claimed a universal mission. They acted with the momentum provided by the religious crackdown. Governments already committed to protecting the populace from unbridled rationalism were poised to prevent "Jacobinism" from finding a German audience. When popular violence became endemic in revolutionary France and

---

[17] Quoted in Klaus Epstein, *The Genesis of German Conservatism* (Princeton, N.J., 1966), pp. 142–4.

began to spill across its borders, it became all the more urgent to prevent "licentiousness in morals" (Frederick William II's phrase) by enforcing confessional orthodoxy. As might be expected, the distinction between Jacobin radicalism and homegrown reform sentiment soon blurred.

The religious crackdown was the great internal trauma of the German Enlightenment, and that was because it shattered complacent assumptions and deeply cherished expectations. There was a cruel irony to the fact that the crackdown had been launched in Prussia. When Kant equated "the age of enlightenment" with "the century of Frederick" in 1784, he was not simply rendering homage to his sovereign. Inside and outside Prussia, educated Germans took pride in the fact that the Hohenzollern Monarchy under Old Fritz was one of the most enlightened states, if not the most enlightened, in Europe. Prussia had acquired this reputation chiefly because of the unusual degree of religious toleration within its borders. Kant was only slightly exaggerating when he claimed that Frederick "considers it his duty, in religious matters, not to prescribe anything to his people, but to allow them complete freedom."[18] Himself an avowed atheist, subscribing to the materialist philosophy of his French philosophes in residence, the King had extended freedom of public expression to deists and proponents of "natural religion" as well as to dissenting Protestant sects. With Zedlitz presiding over ecclesiastical affairs, the Sparta of the North had become a refuge for mavericks hounded out of other German states.

In 1769 Lessing, always ready to puncture complacent optimism, had taken a jaundiced view of this so-called "Berlin freedom." "Scurrilous anti-religious pamphlets" might be "[brought] to market to one's heart's content," he had chided Friedrich Nicolai, the Berlin publisher, but Prussia would prove to have "the worst slavery" in Europe if "someone should appear at Berlin to raise his voice for the rights of subjects and against exploitation and despotism."[19] Lessing was probably right, but most of his contemporaries saw Prussian freedom in a different light. They were confident that religious toleration was the first step in the creation of a new order. As freedom of expression granted to religious opinion expanded gradually to encompass political issues, government would make itself accountable, morally if not constitutionally, to a critical *Publikum*. Did not the public discussion surrounding the drafting of a new General Legal Code demonstrate that this process was already underway? A king who sponsored religious toleration, Kant observed, could also "allow his subjects . . . to put before the public their thoughts on better ways of drawing up laws, even if this entails forthright criticism of the current

---

[18] *Kant. Political Writings*, ed. Hans Reiss and trans. H. B. Nisbet (2d, enl. ed.: Cambridge, 1991), p. 58.

[19] Quoted in Martin Schmidt, "Der Beitrag der evangelischen Kirchengeschichte zum Aufstieg Berlin," *Jahrbuch für die Geschichte Mittel-und Ostdeutschlands* 20 (1971), p. 84.

legislation." In 1786 Friedrich Gedike, the co-editor of the *Berlinische Monatsschrift*, celebrated the same partnership between religious and political freedom in a series of "letters" on the Prussian capital.[20]

Two years later the boom fell and Prussia suddenly stood for a very different relationship between religion and politics. If Frederick's open market on religious issues had promised to be the core of an open political order, the new enforcement of confessional orthodoxy – reinforced as it soon was by the need to insulate German subjects from French revolutionary contagion – seemed to impose a tight lid on political debate. The Prussian monarchy now set an example not as a pathbreaker in toleration and rational reform but as the sponsor of a hopelessly obscurantist reaction.

It was a measure of the strength of Germany's clerical enlightenment that its reigning elders stubbornly protested the reaction and obstructed efforts to enforce it at every turn. Their younger disciples, still trying to launch careers in the Lutheran church, had to tread softly; but they had been too deeply influenced by rationalist theology to make peace with Orthodoxy, and hence, at least on the theological front, their sympathies lay with the embattled *Aufklärer*.

And yet the crackdown drove a wedge between veteran *Aufklärer* and some of the bright young men coming of age in its shadow. Since the late seventeenth century, *Kameralistik*, the science of state administration, had played a vital role in shaping the priorities of the German Enlightenment. Mainstream reform thought had been suffused with cameralism's utilitarian ethos and had sustained its emphatically statist orientation. Reformers looked to the state as the engine of progress, advancing and when necessary impelling the transformation of the traditional corporate hierarchy into a more rational and productive order. The road to virtue lay not through Christian other-worldliness, but through work-discipline in this life and through the "usefulness" it insured. The exemplary *Bürger* would be the embodiment of an inner-worldly work ethic, devoting himself to the role that the state, in the interest of the common welfare, assigned him in a modernized but still hierarchical division of labor.[21]

Statist utilitarianism undermined some of the critical supports of the old-regime corporate order, and it implied far-reaching changes. In a rational division of labor and distribution of rewards, talent and merit would replace "birth" as the constitutive principles of hierarchy. At the

[20] *Kant. Political Writings*, p. 59; Anthony J. La Vopa, "The Politics of Enlightenment: Friedrich Gedike and German Professional Ideology," in *The Journal of Modern History* 62: 1 (March, 1990): 34–56.
[21] See, e.g., Tribe, *Governing Economy*; Marc Raeff, *The Well-Ordered Police State* (New Haven, 1983); Anthony J. La Vopa, *Grace, Talent, and Merit. Poor Students, Clerical Careers, and Professional Ideology in Eighteenth-Century Germany* (Cambridge, 1988), esp. pp. 165–96.

top – in the higher offices of governnment, and in the educated elite that
staffed them – inherited privilege would accede to individual achievement. But even the defenders of the utilitarian ethos had to acknowledge
that there was something grimly constraining about it. In the interest of
the common welfare – or more precisely, in the interest of state-defined
priorities – the full intellectual and emotional potential of the "human
being" (*Mensch*) had to be sacrificed to the functional requirements of
"usefulness" in occupational life. University graduates were no exception; however sharp-witted and creative they might be, they would
have to accept the subordination and the routinism that bureaucratic work
unavoidably entailed. It would be the task of a new system of public education to shape the expectations as well as the capacities of each *Bürger*
to his future occupation and to scrupulously avoid the "overeducation"
or "miseducation" that would burden society and the state with "useless"
malcontents.

From this perspective Wöllner's crusade was an aberration – a tragic
reversal of the state's rationalizing and enlightening mission, but surely
only a temporary one. In a rational order, state and church would work
hand in glove – the state guiding reform from above, the church (along
with the schools) advancing it from below by inculcating a new civic
ethic. To many young men of Fichte's generation, however, state and
church seemed to have formed a different pairing. If they shared the rationalist distaste for Orthodoxy, they also chafed under the iron imperatives
and the calculated restrictions of statist utilitarianism. Rationalism in this
guise struck them as hyperfunctional, dessicated, oppressive. Ironically the
Wöllner crackdown jolted them to fuse the two strains of their discontent – their rationalist hostility to Orthodoxy and their vaguer frustration
with the imperatives of the rationalist ethic – into a single vision. Where
their elders saw a sharp break between enlightenment and reaction, they
tended to see variations on the same theme of abusive power camouflaging itself as benevolent paternal authority.

It was above all a transvaluation of metaphor that conveyed this vision.
The utilitarian state and the obscurantist church fused into a single image
of a coercive, dehumanizing machine. The image was far from exercising
universal appeal among the upcoming generation, but for some it gave
concentrated expression to a sense of alienation from both governmental
and confessional authority. It had that value for young men as different
as Wilhelm von Humboldt, the aristocratic scion who disdained to pursue
a career in the Prussian judicial bureaucracy, and Fichte, the village
weaver's son still relegated to the outer edge of the intelligentsia.[22] The

---

[22] See, e.g., Paul R. Sweet, *Wilhelm von Humboldt. A Biography*, 2 vols. (Columbus, Ohio, 1978–80),
1, pp. 83–9.

new meaning they imparted to the metaphor of the machine is the most striking index of their shared frustrations and their shared distance from their elders.

In Enlightenment rationalism, the machine had often been employed as a normative image within the framework of the Newtonian universe. The machine was an artifice, but it was not unnatural in the negative sense; the wonder of its art lay in imitating the order and the predictability of physical motion. To make a society and polity machinelike in this positive sense was to bring them into closer alignment with the harmony and the intricate balance of the natural order. German reform thought was distinguished by the uninhibited enthusiasm with which it applied this logic to justify statist utilitarianism. With a centralized state acting as the omnicompetent mechanic, society, with its increasingly complex division of labor, would form into a dynamic system of interacting parts. The machine metaphor evoked dynamism within order, progress within a framework of stability.[23]

In the last decade of the century alienated young men, well aware of this metaphoric tradition, seized on the image of the machine and made it central to their new idiom of moral condemnation. What struck them about the interaction of mechanical parts was that motion was always in response to external force. The machine was a system of *Macht*, a word that connoted "power" in the sense of coercive force, pressure from outside. The alternative – the ideal they pitted against the oppressive machinery of German life – was "inner" spontaneity, the self-generated "energy" or "force" (*Kraft*) of the self-determining personality.[24]

The dichotomy between "external" coercion and "inner" spontaneity had deep roots in German Lutheran culture. One thinks of the Lutheran distinction between external conformity to the law and inner faith – the faith that God's grace infused but that the believer experienced as a spontaneous impulse of the heart. By reemphasizing the inner experience, the

---

[23] See David F. Lindenfeld, *The Practical Imagination: The German Sciences of State in the Nineteenth Century* (Chicago, 1997); Otto Mayr, *Authority, Liberty and Automatic Machinery in Early Modern Europe* (Baltimore and London, 1986), pp. 102–21. Mayr emphasizes the "liberal" implications that the machine metaphor acquired in the course of the early modern era but also notes the authoritarian tradition infusing the metaphor in the German states. For interesting comments on the relationship of mechanical to organic metaphors in European political thought, see Ahlrich Meyer, "Mechanische und organische Metaphorik politischer Philosophie," in *Archiv für Begriffsgeschichte* 13 (1969): 128–99.

[24] Particularly important on this shift is Peter Hanns Reill, "Anti-Mechanism, Vitalism and their Political Implications in Late Enlightened Scientific Thought," in *Francia-Forschungen zur westeuropäischen Geschichte* 16: 2 (1989): 195–212. Reill is correct, I think, in tracing the shift to the rise of "vitalist" science as an alternative to "mechanical" philosophy. In that sense, Fichte was an exception; his view of physical nature remained mechanical. Whereas others placed the "mechanical" state in opposition to the vital spontaneity of physical nature, Fichte made the state an integral part of a nature governed by mechanical laws.

intense "stirrings" of genuine piety, the Pietists had sought to breathe new vitality into a church atrophied in external conformity. In a language often echoing Pietist religiosity, the *Sturm und Drang* movement of the 1770s had celebrated the creative spontaneity of "genius" and had demanded its exemption from the mechanical conformity that aesthetic rules, social conventions, and the practical, everday work-world required.

For Fichte's generation, however, Kant's *Critiques* and essays, published from 1781 to 1790, formed the crucible. If the metaphor of the machine became a shorthand for oppression in all its guises, that was because Kant's writings had endowed it with new intellectual authority. Kant's episte-mology reduced everything in the physical world – the world ordered by the theoretical categories of the understanding – to a means, an instru-ment of something else; and "law" meant iron necessity in the blind (i.e., amoral) transmission of power. At the same time, however, Kant took great pains throughout his writings to prevent any erosion of the principle of unconditional autonomy and hence of unavoidable responsibility in the moral realm. To entertain any notion that moral decisions could be made in response to an external stimulus – even if the stimulus took the form of an expected "good" result – was to license the reduction of the human being to a machinelike animal. And this conceptual perversion of the Moral Law had its mechanical counterpart in the workings of human laws and institutions. "In some affairs which affect the interests of the com-monwealth," Kant observed in 1784 with reference to government offi-cials and clergymen, "we require a certain mechanism whereby some members . . . must behave purely passively"; but with the advance of enlightenment, he concluded, governments "find that they can themselves profit by treating man, who is *more than a machine*, in a manner appro-priate to his dignity."[25]

In the hands of alienated young intellectuals, Kant's dichotomy between moral self-determination and mechanical coercion was bound to acquire a radical coloration. If the inner core of human nature was moral in Kant's sense, then external nature in all its manifestations was artificial, indifferent to human values if not brutally dehumanizing. In this revalu-ation of the "natural," the ideal of inner spontaneity acquired a new polit-ical thrust – indeed, a thrust that drew its force paradoxically from a rejection of "politics." Assigned to the realm of external nature, politics meant a chain of human actions and reactions in the application of power. In a sense, the fondness for mechanical metaphors in the language of enlightened absolutism and its advocates among the *Aufklärer* acknowl-edged this brutal reality. But the same language also obscured the reality by blending mechanism into a pervasive paternalist discourse, thereby sanctifying power as benevolent authority. Appealing to the ideal of the

---

[25] *Kant. Political Writings*, pp. 59–60.

benevolent father, state and church represented themselves as the natural embodiments of moral authority. Now paternalism had to be stripped of its bevolent mask and exposed for what it was – the machine's self-serving camouflage.

When Fichte embraced Kant's philosophy in the late summer of 1790, it was in eager apostasy from the bleak conclusion that mechanical determinism governed the moral as well as the physical universe. Kant's uncompromising dualism – his insistence on a purely rational Moral Law, completely independent of mechanical coercion – not only gave him a new "inner" peace. Now Fichte had a new conceptual apparatus and a renewed sense of mission with which to confront the poverty of German public life. As a clerical candidate he experienced firsthand the meshing of political and confessional gears in the German machine. In early August of 1790, as he was reading Kant for the first time, he watched "the frightening *Politik* speading out from political economy (*Staatsöconomie*) to the religious [sphere]" in his native Saxony.[26] A "more than Spanish inquisition," he had lamented to his fiancée, was reducing an unusually "enlightened" younger clergy to a "slavish, light-shy, hypocritical way of thinking."[27] When his tutoring employments brought him into Prussian territory, he collided head-on with Wöllner's crusade. The new censorship blocked the publication in Prussia of his *Attempt at a Critique*, as it did the second part of Kant's own essay on religion. By February of 1792 Fichte was extending his contempt from the Saxon to the Prussian "Inquisition."[28]

It was not until a month or two later, however, that Fichte's alienation found a radical voice. Until then his Kantian conversion, for all its power to effect a "revolution" in his inner life, left intact assumptions about public life that were anything but revolutionary. The *Reclamation* became an impassioned call for unlimited freedom of expression, but it began as a defense of Wöllner's policy. The first draft was occasioned by Ernst Christian Trapp's protest against Wöllner's establishment of an examination commision to cleanse the Prussian clergy of rationalists. Trapp was a hard-bitten veteran of the rationalist camp, but he had taken pains to couch his protest within an encomium to German Protestantism. He sought to persuade Frederick William II that as a Protestant ruler, his proper responsibility lay in guaranteeing the freedom of the "republic of letters." The modern "kingdom of truth and scholarship" was a natural product of the Protestant tradition. In it rulers and government ministers, like everyone else, had only as much "rank" as their "wisdom" merited; and "external coercion" and "political force" had no place. The tragedy was that a well-intentioned, just King had been misled into a policy that

---

[26] Fichte to Johannes Tobler (Aug. 1) 1790, in GA, III, 1: 162.   [27] GA, III, 1: 131.
[28] Fichte to Theodor von Schön, Feb. 16, 1792, in GA, III, 1: 291.

contradicted the very essence of Luther's legacy. As a result, a state that had been "the model and pride of Europe" for a half-century, especially "with regard to freedom of conscience," was in danger of regressing to the "spiritual slavery" of papism. Accomplished writers and scholars – men who ought to be free to express their thoughts as responsible adults – were being treated like "naughty boys."[29]

In the first draft Fichte rejected Trapp's view of the King's responsibility. He did so reluctantly, in full awareness that he was arguing against the *Aufklärer* who had "developed [his] spirit through their writings" and whom he "revered" (and for that reason, he noted, he hoped to remain anonymous). As a "scholar" and a "theologian," however, he could not deny that Prussian scholars had abused their freedom. Principles appropriate only for the "brighter, more knowledgeable head" were being popularized, with the result that "the People" (*das Volk*) would be "led astray into dry, barren sand deserts." Echoing the language of Wöllner's edict, Fichte argued that the King, as the "father of his people," had to protect the populace from such confusion. The new censorship was the proper expression of his paternal benevolence.[30]

This first draft, it should be noted, was written shortly *after* Fichte's *Attempt at a Critique* ran afoul of the Prussian censorship. What he hoped to accomplish is hard to know. He may have wanted to demonstrate a sane via media between the self-righteous alarms sounded by affronted *Aufklärer* and the intemperate outbursts by Wöllner's partisans. In any case, having drafted an ardent defense of Prussian censorship (one that belied his claim to be a disinterested mediator), Fichte seems to have become outraged by his own logic – and he proceeded to shake himself violently from the grip of official ideology. The defense of royal policy acceded to the *Reclamation*, an exercise in radical demystification of the notion that the ruler's paternal "vocation" was "to care for our *happiness*." In the preface to the *Reclamation*, Fichte called on the public to declare unlimited war on governmental paternalism, to root out this all-pervasive "prejudice" from "all the recesses of the entire system of our knowledge." The responsibility of government, he went on to argue, was to administer justice, not to "watch over our happiness." Freedom to communicate and thereby to learn was an inalienable human right that a just government would guarantee unconditionally. Instead, governments sought to deprive their subjects of vital knowledge, as though they were "children" who had

---

[29] Ernst Christian Trapp, *Freimüthige Betrachtungen und ehrerbietige Vorstellungen über die neuen Preussischen Anordnungen in geistlichen Sachen* (Brunswick, 1791).

[30] Fichte, "Zeruf an die Bewohner der preussischen Staaten," in GA, II, 2: 189–94. See also GA, III, 1: 120, 130–1, 150. Cf. Druet, *Fichte*, pp. 55–6, which suggests that the Parisian popular uprising of Aug. 10, 1792, induced Fichte to abandon his position in the "*Zeruf*" for the egalitarian vision of the *Reclamation* and the *Contribution*. I find this explanation unnecessary and without documentary justification.

to be kept from "a harmful toy." Behind the posture of paternal benevolence was the brutal mechanics of power. When human beings were
excluded from the so-called mysteries of state administration or when
they were commanded to think through their confessor or through
religious edicts, they became "completely the machine that [the state]
desire[s] to have."[31]

Within the more elaborate structure of the later *Contribution*, this condemnation of the dehumanizing machine was grounded explicitly in a
Kantian reworking of natural law theory. In Fichte's Kantian reading of
Rousseau's *Du Contrat Social*, the "state of nature" was to be understood
as a normative concept, not as a description of a historical actuality. It
depicted the intellectual and moral interaction of human beings under
the law of their own nature (i.e., under the Moral Law), exercising an
inalienable natural right to moral self-determination that the state neither
created nor had the authority to limit. The only legitimate role for the
state was to administer alienable rights that did not conflict with moral
duty. Existing states, however, were anything but legitimate, since they had
been created to enforce "the right of the stronger" and their insatiable
appetite for power – for exclusive domination of their subjects' wills –
led them to more and more outrageous violations of inalienable human
rights. Fichte attributed their "constitutions" to a mere "throw of chance,"
a blind configuration of power in physical nature – which was to say that
from the standpoint of man's moral nature, they were fundamentally and
perversely unnatural.[32]

The machine metaphor acquires its full rhetorical force in Fichte's
indictment of a blatant violation of nature. In his hands this rhetorical
strategy, common enough among Kantians, shapes an all-encompassing
and categorical vision. In the "Idea for a Universal History with a Cosmopolitan Purpose," Kant had speculated that modern states were becoming inadvertent instruments of "enlightenment." This was in part because,
by the very nature of the international competition for power, no state
could afford to "neglect its internal culture," and in part because commercial prosperity required more and more "civil freedom."[33] But that was
in 1784, before Wöllner's crackdown and before the Revolution had given
the crackdown a new impetus. Nine years later, it struck Fichte as a contradiction in terms to see the existing state-system as a vehicle for moral
progress, however unintentional its role might be considered. In pursuit
of unlimited expansion "outward," every government sought an unlimited monopoly of rule within its borders. It "developed" its subjects'
capacities only to make them more "useful" cogs, and it harnessed knowl-

---

[31] Fichte, *Reclamation*, pp. 123, 131–3.　　[32] Fichte, *Beitrag*, pp. 72–7.
[33] *Kant. Political Writings*, pp. 50–1.

edge, whether in the form of an officially enforced religious dogma or of secular scholarship, to that purpose.[34]

What became apparent in the *Contribution*, of course, was the larger political agenda that Fichte's demystification of paternalism was meant to serve. He was battling the tendency in counterrevolutionary ideology to regard the institutions of the old regime, for all their failings, as reasonable alternatives to the new French "barbarism." He denied that revolutionary France had suddenly posed a threat to a rational international order. The phrase "balance of power" had thrown up a smokescreen of apparent rationality, obscuring the tendency of every existing state, by its very nature, to seek "universal monarchy." Likewise Fichte denied the familiar claim that old-regime corporate bodies served as barriers against despotism by preserving traditional "liberties." Where others saw a rationalizing state threatening to level the corporate hierarchy, Fichte saw the meshing of gears. Within the larger machine of international competition and under the pretext of keepings its parts in balance, each state interlocked with its society in an intricate machinery:

> Through the marvelous artifice of the subordination of the estates, the sovereign has pressed on what was closest to him; this in turn on what was right under it; and so on down to the slaves who worked the field. Each of these forces resisted the impact, and pressed upward in turn, and thus was maintained, through the manifold play of the machine, and through the elasticity of the human spirit that animated it, this curious artifice that sinned against nature in its construction, and produced, even where it started from one point, the most varied products, in Germany a federative republic, in France an unlimited monarchy.[35]

In this inversion of conventional imagery, the extremes of the European spectrum – the centralized monarchy of the Bourbon Kingdom and the baroquely decentralized constitutionalism of the Holy Roman Empire of the German Nation – became variations on the same phenomenon: the corporate state (*Ständesstaat*), the old-regime fusion of bureaucratic power and corporate privilege. Whatever its formal structure, the meshing of state and society formed a pyramidal force field. Fichte's counter to the defense of corporatism was that corporate solidarity and privilege, far from being bulwarks against despotism, were deeply implicated in it. Even as corporate bodies exerted counterpressure, they transmitted power from the top. In their very resistance, in fact, these "states within the state" isolated themselves and thus made it easier for the state to enlist them in the repression of "everything that does not want to recognize [its] will as its law."[36]

---

[34] Fichte, *Beitrag*, pp. 76–7.   [35] Ibid., p. 76.   [36] Ibid., pp. 76, 116–17.

★ ★ ★

Apart from the state, the other gear in the German machine, and the one that seemed to be acquiring inexorable force, was the Lutheran church. In the sixth chapter of the *Contribution* (the last chapter he wrote), Fichte sought, without much success, to bring his attack on the new church-state alliance to a head. Often advancing only by way of contorted logic, this chapter is a fitting end to a project that had run out of steam. It is nonetheless a striking marker for Fichte's radical turn. The chapter demonstrates how sharply Fichte's application of a priori theory was diverging from Kant's roughly simultaneous efforts, and how far removed it left him from the Enlightenment elders he had revered.

In April 1792, a few months before he announced Fichte's authorship of the *Attempt at a Critique*, Kant had published the first in his own series of essays on religion. Roughly a year later, as Fichte was entering the road to the *Contribution*, the entire series appeared under the title *Religion within the Limits of Reason Alone.* The book brought Kant a stinging rebuke from his sovereign for misusing philosophy to undermine Christian doctrine. Precisely on that score, however, Kant's approach seems remarkably restrained from this distance. His purpose was not to demonstrate an irreconcilable conflict between religious belief and critical rationality but "to discover in Scripture that sense which harmonizes with the most holy teachings of reason."

Using his Critical Philosophy as a sharp but supple tool, Kant had reformulated the attempt at a reconciliation of faith and reason, head and heart, that had characterized the Lutheran Enlightenment. In its effort to win over the Jewish nation "without directly offending the people's prejudices," Christianity had violated its "original intention . . . to introduce a pure religious faith."[37] But Kant demonstrated how the "mystical veil" could be lifted to reveal the pure lode. In his dexterous reworkings, most of the central scriptural doctrines – original sin, Christ as the Son of God, the immaculate conception, the trinity, the redemption, justification by faith – became "narrative" or "figurative" representations of moral truth, accommodated to man's receptivity as a sensual being under specific historical conditions.

Kant's approach to doctrinal tradition was paralleled by his view of the historical role of confessional religion. His a priori ideal – the archetype against which to judge any existing church – was the "ethical commonwealth," a purely spiritual communion in which the moral personality prescribed the law for itself without any "external law." If this "invisible church" were approximated as far as was humanly possible in a "visible church," it would take the form of a universal institution with no need

---

[37] Immanuel Kant, *Religion within the Limits of Reason Alone*, trans. and introd. Theodore M. Greene and Hoyt H. Hudson (New York, 1960), pp. 116–18.

for the power configurations of a "political constitution." In historical fact, though, there were particular "visible churches," each with a "statutory ecclesiastical faith" constructed from scriptural revelation. Kant described how easily such a faith atrophied into a rigid orthodoxy and a mere "religion of divine worship," its clergy exercising "domination" under the cloak of "service" and commanding "drudging" and "mercenary" displays of external piety by exploiting its flock's terrors and misguided hopes. In these cases, he observed with an eye squarely on the recent crackdown, "the church in the end rules the state."[38]

Again, though, Kant's censure of obscurantism was counterbalanced by his brief for an enlightened Protestantism. So long as the statutory church remained conscious that it would one day become "dispensable" and hence remained open to change, it could be an efficacious "vehicle" for the advance of the species toward the ethical commonwealth. To insure this openness, it was essential that clerical guardianship of scriptural interpretation within the church be offset by "public freedom of thought" and the critical scrutiny it made possible. Though the clerical "leading string" would one day fall away, it had been and still remained indispensable. "The authority of Scripture," Kant wrote, "cannot be neglected, because no doctrine based on reason alone seems to the people qualified to serve as an unchangeable norm." To be sure, belief could not be forced on "any man," and the "few" must be allowed to continue sowing "the seed of the true religious faith." Assuming that this freedom was secured, however, "the most intelligent and most reasonable thing to do from now on is to use the book already at hand as the basis for ecclesiastical instruction and not to lessen its value through useless or mischievous attacks."[39]

Fichte's *Attempt at a Critique* had begun with an elaborate explication of Kant's ethical theory and had anticipated his mentor's basic line of argument. Mentor and disciple shared a concern to secure a place for belief in revelation within a rational ethics while at the same time demolishing, once and for all, the assumptions that had licensed so much abuse. And yet Fichte's exercise differed in scope and in emphases, and the differences already suggested a less conciliatory approach. His agenda was limited to proving, as a deduction from a priori principles, that the concept of divine revelation was possible, and to establishing the criteria under which belief in any particular revelation would be "permissible" (though certainly not necessary). Conspicuously absent from this doggedly abstract procedure was the kind of reappropriation of the substance of Christian doctrine that Kant had offered.

Here again Fichte saw the workings of the machine. He agreed with Kant in principle that revelation could be a vehicle of moral progress, but his preoccupation was with avoiding any concession that might license

[38] Ibid., pp. 87–114.   [39] Ibid., pp. 103, 112, 122–3.

"mechanical" coercion. The concept of revelation was a regrettable but unavoidable necessity for "human beings, and whole races of human beings . . . who through dominant sensibility have been deprived of the sense of morality either wholly, or to so great a degree that one could not influence them at all in this way." In such cases only a concept of God as "moral lawgiver," commanding obedience "directly through the senses," could "establish moral feeling." But therein lay the danger; this "alienation" of "the moral law within us" – this "translation of something subjective into a being outside us" – all too easily made our faith the instrument of our oppression.[40] Fichte ended with a warning that "coercion of conscience" was "infinitely harder" than "physical coercion," since "the soul is brought to an anxious fear and torments itself until it finally brings itself to lie to itself and to feign faith within itself."[41]

Fichte was beginning to explore the psychological dynamics of what he called "alienation." In the *Contribution*, this religious psychology became only one element in a critique of ideology in all its guises (of which more later), but it remained an element with uniquely insidious power, the thoroughgoing self-delusion that took hold through the believer's deepest anxieties. In this ultimate intrusion of mechanical power, the inner voice of conscience was silenced by a completely internalized domination.

In the sixth chapter of the *Contribution* this theme emerged, to be sure, in the service of a more conventional eighteenth-century argument. Fichte simply wanted to limit the jurisdiction of any "visible church" to the inner realm of belief, and hence to ban it from the "political" world of external action and coercion. As a contractual society, the church could require a public profession of belief by its members (and could exclude those who refused); but it could not bring the power of the state to its aid in this enforcement of confessional conformity. But the sixth chapter was not simply an argument for separation of church and state. Aiming to circumscribe confessional authority, Fichte attempted an a priori deduction of "the necessary system of the visible church." The apparent rigor of this precedure was meant to demonstrate how the emotional weakness of most believers became the point of departure for ideological coercion with a vengeance. The believer's anxiety – his need for confirmation of his belief – could be assuaged only with a collective profession of faith. Since belief, by definition, had to remain within the realm of conscience, it had to be demonstrated voluntarily. Hence, confessional conformity represented alienation at its most paradoxical, in the form of a sincere (though self-deluding) conviction that confessional dogma was "the single and pure truth." This subjugation was effected through "the alienation of the inner office of judgment," its displacement onto God as an external moral judge.[42] If a church was "consequential,"

[40] Fichte, *Attempt at a Critique*, pp. 73, 105–8.   [41] Ibid., p. 171.   [42] Fichte, *Beitrag*, p. 180.

it made itself the judge of "purity of heart," in place of God. Its very inner logic, in other words, drove a visible church to become the total negation of the free consensus in an "invisible church"; inevitably it became, to recall Kant's terms, an "orthodoxy" and a "religion of divine worship," at the opposite pole from an ethical commonwealth.

The shadow of the religious crackdown looms over this argument. When Fichte warned of a "party" trying to establish "a great system of obscurantism (*Verfinsterung*)," his readers knew very well that he had Wöllner and his partisans in mind.[43] But Fichte's logic was likely to outrage Lutheran *Aufklärer* at least as much as the Orthodox. His tone became heavy with sarcasm when he explained the two ways in which German Lutheranism might become "consequential." One was to emulate Catholicism and make the articles of belief as "incredible" as possible, thereby drawing the believer into a "labyrinth" from which he would seek escape by "giv[ing] himself blindly into the hand of his leader." The other "consequential" route was a return to the intentions of the "enlightened free spirits (*Freigeister*)" who had founded Protestantism and for whom "[their] own reason" was the only authority. In that case, of course, there would be no need for confessional churches. Fichte warned that there was no middle ground; any attempt to purify dogma inevitably led to questioning of the entire "system."[44]

The sixth chapter was not a succesful exercise. Fichte insisted on its a priori rigor, but in fact at critical junctures the argument turned on psychological (and historical) analysis. He was pulled between his determination to strike at the roots of Protestant obscurantism and his residual conviction that in its essence, Protestantism represented a progressive historical moment. As flawed as it was, however, the chapter was an appropriate endpoint for Fichte's youthful radicalism. It was not simply an attack on the new breed of clerical "bullies," but an uncompromising rejection of institutional religion as such.

If Fichte had departed from Kant, he had also put distance between himself and his pre-Kantian mentors. A few years earlier the young theology candidate had struggled to reconcile tension-ridden aspirations, and the elders of the Lutheran *Aufklärung* – the men who had sought to purify the Lutheran faith without sacrificing its emotional grounding – had pointed the way. Now the young philosopher, the avowed "free spirit," mocked their lack of nerve. His vision of revolution was, on the face of it, no less provocative.

[43] Ibid., p. 201.   [44] Ibid., pp. 190–5.

Revolution: The Popular Tribune

In the *Contribution*, Fichte's alienation from the old regime was palpable and his opposition to the counterrevolutionary policies of the German states and state churches could not have been more outspoken. And yet the text is likely to strike the modern reader as confused, not to say baffling – chiefly because its author's position on "revolution" is hard to pin down. Was revolution a legitimate recourse by a people dissatisfied with its government or was it a plunge into chaos to be avoided at all costs? Was Fichte drawing salient distinctions between legitimate and illegitimate revolutions or was he waffling on the moral issues that revolution poses?

When we bring these questions to the *Contribution*, we begin to realize just how multivocal and fraught with tensions it is. The text has at least four features that complicate the Kantian logic of its argument. First: Fichte was adding his voice to an international debate about the French Revolution and revolution in general, though his access to the debate was mediated by distinctly German political idioms. Second: his vision of revolution drew on and gave new meaning to a Lutheran discourse of individual and collective rebirth, even as his a priori argument rejected Lutheran confessional authority. Third: he spoke not simply as a philosopher but also as a marginal intellectual assuming the role of popular tribune. He conceived the *Contribution* as an experiment in the rhetoric of print communication – one that would break through ideological barriers to reach "the People" and that would constitute its audience as a new kind of egalitarian community. And fourth: Fichte's identification with the People – what we might call his philosophical populism – was at once reinforced and constrained by his economic thinking. He saw the material deprivation of the masses as the most flagrant injustice of the existing order. And yet he did not, and indeed could not, recognize need as a legitimate motive for collective action.

These features give the *Contribution* an unsual density of meanings, but they also threaten to make it incoherent. It is perhaps best described as a failed experiment. Fichte was at least dimly aware of the failure, though

Chapter 4 was published in a slightly different form as "The Revelatory Moment: Fichte and the French Revolution," *Central European History* 22:2 (June, 1989): 130–159. Permission to appear in this volume is granted by Emory University.

he was not entirely sure how to account for it. He did not abandon the project simply because his interests changed or because his marriage intruded. Having begun the essay with an intense conviction of his own critical empowerment, he watched it succumb to internal strains.

★ ★ ★

As late as the fall of 1792, when the Revolution was entering its most radical and violent stage, Fichte's correspondence reveals no more than a casual interest in it. The Krockow estate, that island of civilized domesticity in the Baltic wilds, was worlds removed from the tumult of Paris. Fichte's distance from the great political crisis of the era can be gauged by his writing plans. No longer interested in writing about "the fair sex," he now planned to follow up his *Attempt at a Critique* with an essay on providence and miracles.

It was a book, and not another episode in the Parisian spectacle, that prodded Fichte to shift his attention to the Revolution and the controversies surrounding it. Sometime in the spring of 1793 he read August Wilhelm Rehberg's recently published *Investigations on the French Revolution*, a two-volume collection of reviews that had begun to appear in the *Jenaische Allgemeine Literatur-Zeitung* in 1789.[1] Rehberg had used the review form to develop a trenchant critique of the course of events in France, from the fiscal crisis of the mid-1780s and the failures of royal policy in the face of it to the increasingly violent factionalism of the Parisian clubs and their popular followings. To call Rehberg a German disciple of Edmund Burke would be to slight his own acumen as a political observer. But Burke's *Reflections*, published in November 1790, had reinforced Rehberg's own judgments and enriched his arguments; and in that limited but important sense, the pieces collected in his *Investigations* introduced the German public to Burkean conservatism well before Friedrich Gentz's translation of the *Reflections* appeared in 1793.

The *Contribution* was intended to deliver a knockout blow to Rehberg's critique, but its author had more in common with his opponent than he was willing to admit. What divided Fichte and Rehberg was not a generational conflict; separated by only five years, they both confronted the Revolution as young men. Striking at first glance, in fact, is their shared pattern of religious crisis and underlying stability. Rehberg had anticipated Fichte in his youthful fascination with Kantian philosophy, though his enthusiasm for the master's "metaphysical" abstractions had been more qualified than Fichte's. The protagonists had in common both a personal skepticism about religious doctrine and a deep streak of Lutheran moralism.

---

[1] August Wilhelm Rehberg, *Untersuchungen über die französische Revolution*, 2 vols. (Hanover, 1793).

In other ways, though, it would be hard to imagine two more different protagonists. Rehberg had been born into the Hanoverian state patriciate, a university-educated, affluent officialdom, operating in the shadow
of the governing aristocracy but forming a bourgeois elite perched far
above the social milieu of a village weaving family like Fichte's. Whereas
Fichte, the classic "poor student," eked his way through the "bread-
and-butter curriculum" (Brotstudium) in theology at Saxon universities,
Rehberg had attended the University of Göttingen, famous for its aristocratic elegance, where he had been free to cultivate his interests in
classical languages and philosophy. Fichte's disappointments as a clerical
candidate extinguished any loyalty he might have had to his native Saxony,
but Rehberg's Hanoverian patriotism was the bedrock of his life. Fichte,
one might say, was rootless but provincial, while Rehberg was rooted but
cosmopolitan, at least in his familiarity with foreign and especially English
political conditions. In 1783, at age twenty-six, Rehberg had found
employment in Hanover as secretary to the Bishop of Osnabrück (who
was also the Duke of York); and five years later this powerful connection
had gained him access to the inner workings of German and European
politics as secretary in the Geheime Ratskollegium, one of the executive
organs of the Hanoverian government.[2] The twenty-six-year-old Fichte
had just begun his long and fruitless search for patrons and a career opportunity, probably in the obscure ranks of the clergy.

The essays in the Investigations amounted to a contemporary history of
the Revolution that may be unrivaled. Rehberg read the Revolution's
flood of pamphlet literature as a seasoned man of affairs, following the
course of events in detail, assessing decisions and sizing up personalities
with a keen eye for turning points and unintended consequences. He
offered judicious observations about the intricacies of the monarchy's
fiscal crisis, the fateful decisions that produced an Estates General and
wrenched events out of the King's control, the issues surrounding the
abolition of "feudalism" and the nationalization of church properties, the
futile efforts to fashion a flawless constitution. Even if he had wanted to,
Fichte was in no position to engage Rehberg on this terrain. He simply
lacked the requisite fiscal and legal expertise, not to mention the political savvy. Instead his attacks alternated between flights into transcendental theory and below-the-belt vilification. The latter took the form of
contemptuous dismissals of Rehberg as a typical sycophantic bureaucrat,
the dimwitted, self-serving mouthpiece for a corrupt establishment. The

---

[2] Klaus Epstein, The Genesis of German Conservatism (Princeton, N.J., 1966), pp. 547–94. Ursula Vogel,
Konservative Kritik an der bürgerlichen Revolution. August Wilhelm Rehberg (Darmstadt and Neuwied,
1972), is an insightful analysis of Rehberg's social and political thought. On the Hanoverian state
patriciate, see Joachim Lampe, Aristokratie, Hofadel, und Staatspatriziat in Kurhannover (Göttingen,
1963). For a portrait of a similar elite of law graduates in Osnabrück, see Jonathan B. Knudsen,
Justus Möser and the German Enlightenment (Cambridge, 1986), pp. 31–52.

gnawing envy of the outsider and the arrogance of the philosophical neophyte fed on each other. And the result was, surprisingly, something significant. Fichte's assault on Rehberg (and, through Rehberg, on Burke) became a critical moment in his intellectual career and a noteworthy episode in the emergence of modern political argument.

The overarching issue was how to conceive the relationship between the French Revolution and eighteenth-century philosophy. It was an issue that the revolutionaries themselves had provoked as early as the summer of 1789, in the very way they imagined their project. Whereas "revolutions" had referred to specific, unintended ruptures with the past, the Revolution was celebrated as a planned act of transformation with universal significance.[3] It was in the latter sense that Friedrich Gentz welcomed the Revolution in December 1790 as "the first practical triumph of philosophy, the first example in the history of the world of the construction of government upon the principles of an orderly, rationally constructed system." Several months earlier, in his *Reflections*, Burke had reached the oppposite conclusion: the tragedy of the Revolution lay precisely in the fact that it was a "philosophic" enterprise, driven to excess by the "frenzy" of Rousseau's disciples.[4]

Burke soon had his German followers (including converts like Gentz), but in Germany the debate about the relationship between the Revolution and philosophy assumed a distinctive complexity as Kant's Critical Philosophy won converts among the educated. Some Kantians were convinced that their philosophical breakthrough would inspire a moral rebirth and hence spare Germany the descent into barbarism that France was enduring. It fell to Fichte to champion the alternative view: that Kant had brought Rousseau's moral ideal to conceptual maturity and that the Revolution was an extraordinary step forward in its realization.

Rehberg charged the "metaphysical" revolutionaries in France with having misunderstood Rousseau, particularly by ignoring the import of his distinction between the General Will and "the will of all." If they *had* understood him, they would have realized that his political theories were pure fantasies, completely irrelevant to the mundane realities of political life. It was this patronizing dismissal that infuriated Fichte; he challenged it with one of the most defiant passages in the *Contribution*:

> Not long ago a man appealed to you who went our way, and whose only mistake was that he did not pursue it far enough. . . . Rousseau, whom you

---

[3] Keith Michael Baker, "'Revolution,'" in Colin Lucas, ed., *The French Revolution and the Creation of Modern Political Culture*, vol. 2: *The Political Culture of the French Revolution* (Oxford, 1988), pp. 41–62; Reinhart Koselleck, "Historical Criteria of the Modern Concept of Revolution," in Koselleck, *Futures Past. On the Semantics of Historical Time*, trans. Keith Tribe (Cambridge, Mass., 1985), pp. 39–54.

[4] Edmund Burke, *Reflections on the Revolution in France*, ed. Conor Cruise O'Brien (New York, 1986), esp. pp. 237 and 284. Gentz quoted in Epstein, *Genesis*, p. 436.

called a dreamer time and time again, behaved too kindly toward you, the empiricists, since his dreams are being realized under your eyes; that was his mistake. . . . Under your eyes, I can add to your shame, if you do not already know it: awakened by Rousseau, the human spirit has completed a work you would have declared the most impossible of all impossibilities . . . perhaps in quiet the spirit [of its author] is nourishing young, powerful men who foresee his influence in the system of human knowledge through all its parts, who foresee the entirely new mode of human thinking that that work must effect.[5]

Like many other intellectuals of his generation, Fichte identified with Jean-Jacques as the virtuous outsider, the moral critic who preferred to keep his distance from a corrupt Establishment. But there was a distinctly German slant to his Rousseauian pedigree; Rousseau became John the Baptist to Kant's redemptive mission. Not surprisingly Fichte went on to insist that Rousseau's "state of nature" and "social contract" were normative models of a priori reason, not actual historical conditions. He made Jean-Jacques, with some cause, a proto-Idealist.[6]

Why did this young outsider assume the task of correcting the prevailing judgment of the Revolution? Confronted with Rehberg's variant on Burke's polemic, Fichte became acutely aware of two implications of his own philosophical commitment. One was that a new empowerment was inherent in his own powerlessness; by the very fact of his marginality, he was in a privileged position to wield the critical power of Kantian philosophy. The other was that as a Kantian he had a revolutionary political mission. His task was to expose ideology before the Tribune of Reason, to confront the privileged and the powerful with their ideological self-delusions.

In Fichte's argument with Rehberg and Burke, philosophy became, on one side, the specter of ideology at its most frightening and on the other, the knife that cut through ideology's mystifications. Neither side used the term "ideology"; it was not coined until 1796. This is a case in which the concept had begun to crystallize well before there was a single word for it. Three of its key elements had emerged from the rationalist critique of religious belief since the seventeenth century: that ideology is knowledge distorted by collective social interests; that the distortion entails self-deception (what Marxists would later call "false

---

[5] Fichte, *Beitrag*, pp. 57–8, from the edition in *Johann Gottlieb Fichte, Schriften zur Revolution*, ed. Bernard Willms (Cologne, 1967).

[6] Ibid., pp. 64–5. On the identification with Rousseau as uncorrupted outsider, see esp. Robert Darnton, "The High Enlightenment and the Low-Life of Literature," in Darnton, *The Literary Underground of the Old Regime* (Cambridge, Mass., 1982), pp. 1–40, and Carol Blum, *Rousseau and the Republic of Virtue. The Language of Politics in the French Revolution* (Ithaca, N.Y., 1986), pp. 151–68.

consciousness"); and that the interests and resulting distortions are transparent to the critical eye.[7]

Against this backdrop, Burke's *Reflections* had the effect of turning the weapon of rational criticism on its inventors. The real ideologues, he charged, were the rationalist critics themselves. Reform was sometimes necessary, Burke conceded in the *Reflections*, but it had to aim at preserving the broad contours of a "natural" order. To revere nature meant to bow before the wisdom of history. For Burke the past patterned into the organic evolution of historically specific communities. The crux of this evolution was the unbroken transmission of traditions – of what he called "prejudices" – through the family and the "little platoons" of a corporate hierarchy. Government was the business of the propertied and leisured few, the small elite whose center of gravity rested in the permanence of landed property and whose respect for the specificity of the nation's evolution, and hence for the intricacies of its traditions, arose from direct involvement in the variegated details of statecraft.

Hence Burke's famous defense of "prejudice," which in Enlightenment discourse had been the code word for the host of habitual, unexamined beliefs that could not withstand the acid criticism of reason. Now Burke was arguing that such beliefs ought to be "cherished" precisely "because they [were] prejudices." Having endured in concrete communities over many generations, they offered the statesman a far more reliable compass than the abstractions of "the whole clan of the enlightened among us." Burke unloaded on the clan an arsenal of metaphor. The legacy of Enlightenment philosophy was the "ranting speculations" of "political theologians" and "theological politicians," the "political gospel" of "warm and inexperienced enthusiasts."[8]

Among other things, the *Reflections* was an extended indictment of political radicalism as "enthusiasm," and it was that indictment that conveyed Burke's implicit concept of ideology. To Burke, French men of letters were dangerous not only because they had organized themselves into an artificial "interest," with ambitions that could not be satisfied in a natural hierarchy, but also because they formed a kind of sect. To call

---

[7] The term "ideology" was introduced by the French philosopher Destutt de Tracy in 1796 to describe his "science of ideas." "Ideologues" (its derivative) was given currency by Napoleon as a dismissive term for impractical intellectuals who presumed to mix in politics. On the early history of the concept of ideology, see George Lichtheim, "The Concept of Ideology," in Lichtheim, *The Concept of Ideology and Other Essays* (New York, 1967), pp. 3–11; Hans Barth, *Truth and Ideology*, trans. Frederic Lilge (Berkeley, Calif., 1976), esp. pp. 20–37; Ulrich Dierse, "Ideologie," in Otto Brunner, Werner Conze, and Reinhart Koselleck, eds., *Geschichtliche Grundbegriffe*, vol. 3 (Stuttgart, 1982), pp. 131–69. For a particularly rich contribution to the conceptual history of the concept of "ideology," see Paul Ricoeur, *Lectures on Ideology and Utopia*, ed. George H. Taylor (New York, 1986).

[8] Burke, *Reflections*, pp. 93–100, 183.

them "enthusiasts" was to evoke the militant sectarianism of the Münster Anabaptists, the French Catholic League, and the more alarming varieties of English Non-Conformist Protestantism. The vital link between religious and secular enthuasiasm was epistemological; in both cases fanaticism was powered by the self-deceptions of overheated imaginations. In the grip of his own chimeras, the religious enthusiast could not be shaken from the conviction that he had been singled out for a divine inspiration, or at least that he enjoyed privileged access to supernatural truth. Likewise the political radical was a self-deluded rationalist, transfixed by his "metaphysical" vision of "nature." Mistaking this internally generated fantasy for privileged insight into the essence of things, he drew up blueprints for creating a perfect social and political order. He was too self-righteous to confront his own lust for power.[9]

It was this attack on metaphysical enthusiasm that Fichte sought to meet. That he had encountered it in Rehberg rather than in Burke made some difference. To Burke, the substance of the new "metaphysical" radicalism merited little attention, since its real significance lay in camouflaging ruthless ambition. Rehberg, on the other hand, had begun his writing career as a defender of Kantianism and had taken the trouble to read Rousseau. He knew firsthand the seductive power of the new philosophy, and hence he regarded the idealism of the new breed of radical intellectuals as all too sincere. It was precisely because they were in thrall to chimerical abstractions, and hence were blinded to their own motives, that they were so ruthless. His language echoed Burke's in evoking the specter of religious fanaticism; but the specter had a German shape, as his frequent characterization of the radicals as metaphysical *Schwärmer* (rather than as *Enthusiasten*) reminds us. *Schwärmerei* was the indigenous German term for "enthusiasts," and it was preferred by many German authors reacting against the Revolution, perhaps because in its original usage in religious polemics it already had a broader range of politically charged connotations than its English counterpart. From the verb "to swarm," as in a swarm of bees, *Schwärmerei* evoked the image of a blind mob or, to shift to a more neutral phrase, a mass mobilization.[10] Resonating with this

[9] On the discourse of "enthusiasm" and its polemical and political uses, see Michael Heyd, *"Be Sober and Reasonable": The Critique of Enthusiasm in the Seventeenth and Early Eighteenth Centuries* (Leiden, 1995); Lawrence E. Klein and Anthony J. La Vopa, eds., *Enthusiasm and Enlightenment in Europe, 1650–1850* (San Marino, Calif., 1998). On Burke's image of the *gens de lettres* as "enthusiasts," see esp. J. G. A. Pocock, "The political economy of Burke's analysis of the French Revolution," in Pocock, *Virtue, Commerce, and History. Essays on Political Thought and History, Chiefly in the Eighteenth Century* (Cambridge, 1985), pp. 193–212. In Pocock's apt phrase, Burke saw the *gens de lettres* as "organized without being adequately patronized." See also Michael Freeman, *Edmund Burke and the Critique of Political Radicalism* (Chicago, 1980), esp. pp. 74–9, 240–1.

[10] Lessing, "Ueber eine zeitige Aufgabe," *Gotthold Ephraim Lessings sämtliche Schriften*, ed. Karl Lachmann (1880–1924; reprint, Berlin, 1968), vol. 16: 293–302, is a particularly interesting meditation on the meaning of *Schwärmerei*. For examples of the polemical use of "enthusiasm" by

analogy, Rehberg's image of radicalism reinforced the imputation that philosophy had become a tool of demagoguery. He dismissed the principle of popular sovereignty as an absurdity, since it allowed political *Schwärmer* to prey on the "passions" of an ignorant populace. There were other reasons that Rehberg offered a young German the fixed target that Burke could not have been. Having begun his publishing career with a strong interest in the new German philosophy, he imposed schematic clarity on the epistemological choices that often lay half-buried in Burke's rhetorical flights and organic metaphors. On one side was philosophical "theory," which he equated with "metaphysical" generalization; on the other stood the empirical particularism of "experience" (*Erfahrung*), in the historical evolution of a specific community, in corporate and religious traditions, and in the statesman's direct involvement in "practical" affairs. Rehberg's social dichotomies were as neat as his philosophical distinctions. Despite the note of envy in his description of Burke's rhetorical feats in the House of Commons, he had reason to feel that his own career in the Hanoverian government – like Burke's career as a Foxite Whig – exemplified the ascent of bourgeois talent under aristocratic patronage. He too was convinced that a governing aristocracy must be based on heredity but should remain porous. If the French revolutionaries had had the wisdom to establish a hereditary "senate," he argued, public-spirited "parties" (as opposed to "factions" or "cabales") might have emerged, with educated commoners pursuing political careers under aristocratic patronage. Such career outlets would be limited, of course, to truly exceptional "men of affairs," who were not to be confused with the swarm of "philosophical" and literary intellectuals. In his review of the *Reflections*, Rehberg spelled out the implication for Germany: that "scholars" (*Gelehrten*) like Fichte belonged outside the political nation. Aside from being propertyless, their lack of "practical" experience disqualified them from public decision making.[11]

All this outraged Fichte's philosophical convictions at the same time that it heightened his sense of alienation.[12] In Fichte's hands, Kant's justification of theory became a purist commitment. Taking his cue from Kant's defense of Plato's Republic in the *Critique of Pure Reason*, the young "philosopher" refused to grant moral authority to empirical practice.[13]

German observers of the Revolution, see Bernd Weyergraf, *Der skeptische Bürger. Wielands Schriften zur französischen Revolution* (Stuttgart, 1972), esp. pp. 20, 40; Klaus L. Berghahn, "Volkstümlichkeit ohne Volk? Kritische Überlegungen zu einem Kulturkonzept Schillers," in Reinhold Grimm and Jost Hermand, eds., *Popularität und Trivialität* (Frankfurt, 1974), p. 65; Anthony J. La Vopa, "The Philosopher and the *Schwärmer*: On the Career of a German Epithet from Luther to Kant," in Klein and Lavopa, eds., *Enthusiasm*, esp. pp. 103–12.

[11] Rehberg, *Untersuchungen*, vol. 2, pp. 372–81. On Rehberg's agreements with and divergences from Burke, see esp. Vogel, *Konservative Kritik*, pp. 98–106; Epstein, *Genesis*, pp. 547–94. See also the discussion of the German debate about "theory" and "practice" in Knudsen, *Justus Möser*, pp. 164–86.
[12] Fichte, *Beitrag*, pp. 39, 66–8.   [13] Fichte to Kant, April 2, 1793, in GA, III, 1: 389–90.

The "is" had to be confronted with the "ought," and only Kant's a priori ethical knowledge, completely independent of sense experience, could supply the requisite normative standard. There was no other way to escape the circularity of deriving norms for judgment from the experience to be judged. When "empiricists" objected that "philosophical principles, however undeniable, are not realizable," they really meant (but left unsaid) that "we do not want to realize them." To accept their appeal to "experience" was to preclude all possibility of changing the status quo. "History" was the story of the strong devouring the weak. If we relied on it for guidance, we would become trapped in complete relativism as we came to realize that all norms, including our own, were historically contingent. In fact, though, Rehberg and others abused the appeal to history; their historical "proofs" were really applications of unexamined assumptions, perpetuated in the upbringing of successive generations.[14]

By making "prejudice" the locus of "latent wisdom," Burke and Rehberg had thrown down the gauntlet to the Enlightenment's ideal of critical rationality. Now Fichte responded to their challenge by subjecting prejudice to a new, emphatically Kantian critique. The result was a counterconcept of ideology, developed in binary opposition to Burke's. Ultimately the argument turned on the relationship between moral knowledge and social knowledge. For Burke, moral knowledge was inherently social since it was "refracted" through the layered density of a historically constituted social hierarchy. Claiming to speak from within this density, Burke exposed the artificial and hence dangerous interest of intellectuals who stood outside it. To sum up the lesson of "enthusiasm": when consciousness ceased to be socially imbedded, it became solipsistic.

In Fichte's logic, the achievement of moral self-awareness required a willed act of social disembodiment. It was in that sense that the individual "[made] himself in agreement with himself" as he came to honor the moral law. As he "separate[d] out all foreign additions from his development (*Bildung*)," he heard the "inner voice" of the conscience, the "pure, original form" of the self.[15] To put it another way: the voice of conscience became clear to the measure that self-awareness was extracted from the social density of experience. This was an introspective turn, but not a solipsistic one. In the very process of achieving self-awareness, the individual was empowered with a new lucidity about the social world, an ability to see through its veils. Having gained self-knowledge, he was in a position to understand why others – those still enclosed within society's distorting lenses – lacked it.

It was with this claim to privileged insight that Fichte developed a strikingly modern concept of ideology. The *Contribution* differed markedly

---

[14] Fichte, *Beitrag*, pp. 42–59. [15] Ibid., pp. 48–9.

in that regard from the more famous response to Burke, Thomas Paine's *The Rights of Man*. Behind the flow of events Paine saw conspiratorial malevolence, which in turn implied a willed effort to deceive. What struck Fichte was how self-interest was justified in a process of collective self-deception. This explained why ideology had such a tight hold on those who lacked Kantian self-awareness, despite the fact that its distortions were transparent to the Kantian critic. Ideology established its grip in a social process that began with the child's upbringing in a particular milieu. With every step in that upbringing, unexamined "principles" became more closely "interwoven" with the "I," so that in the end "they are not uprooted without it being uprooted at the same time." In this way "the dark feeling of our interest" influenced our will and our judgment as well as our understanding. Hence it was not surprising that selfish aristocratic interests were pressed as rightful claims; "we ourselves believe in complete earnestness in the legitimacy of our claims; we are not making an effort to lie to you; long before you, we have lied to ourselves."[16]

Arguably Fichte's concept of ideology, like his adversaries', was open to the charge of itself being ideological. Students of the concept have asked whether it is self-devouring – whether, in Paul Ricoeur's apt phrase, it is "absorbed into its own referent." It may be that any claim to stand above "interest" can be dismissed as a camouflaged vehicle for interest; and protestations to the contrary may be the surest sign of self-deception. Did not Fichte's interest lie in proving that intellectuals like himself should be the moral arbiters of their society? In that case his argument with Rehberg and Burke was a precocious demonstration of our modern entrapment within an all-inclusive arena of contestation, an endless process of mutual unmasking that denies credibility to any claim to objectivity.[17] At least for the moment, though, we may suspend this philosophical issue. The relevant historical point – the crucial one for understanding Fichte's point of departure in the *Contribution* – is that he did claim exemption from the unmasking process. What intoxicated him about his newfound identity as a Kantian "philosopher" was the conviction of having found a transcendent vantage point, a position outside – and above – the ideological arena. The intoxication became palpable when the young outsider confronted the insiders. The official establishment, he argued, was no more qualified to judge the French Revolution than was "the common *Bürger* sighing under harsh burdens" or "the shackled countryman." In the defense of privilege, as in efforts to destroy it, "interest" shaped

---

[16] Ibid., pp. 42–6.

[17] See Ricoeur, *Lectures*, esp. pp. 1–18, 159–80, 216–31, and the discussion of Fichte in Jürgen Habermas, *Knowledge and Human Interests*, trans. Jeremy J. Shapiro (Boston, 1972), esp. pp. 191–213. On the conceptual paradox see also Dierse, "Ideologie," pp. 166–7; Peter Christian Ludz, *Ideologiebegriff und marxistische Theorie. Ansätze zu einer immanenten Kritik* (Opladen, 1976), esp. pp. xiii–7, 39–49, 123–34.

perception and judgment. The only legitimate "judge" was the "speculative thinker," the theorist who was "neither oppressor nor oppressed."[18]
He was beyond the pull of interest, since he was not implicated in the
force field, the dynamics of power, that structured the social hierarchy.
Social marginality, in other words, was the ultimate moral advantage;
powerlessness became the new grounding for moral authority.

★ ★ ★

Fichte had found a way to deny the relevance of historical empiricism to
the issues posed by the Revolution, but that is not to say that he lacked
a historical framework. In his eyes Kant stood in a direct line of descent
from Luther as well as from Rousseau. This awareness of a German lineage
gave him a sweeping historical vision. We are introduced to it in the
opening paragraphs of the *Contribution*:

> The French Revolution appears to me to be important for all mankind. I
> am not speaking of the political results which it has had for that land as
> well as for neighboring states, and which it probably would not have had
> without the unrequested meddling and the reckless self-confidence of these
> states. . . . So long as human beings do not become wiser and more just,
> all their efforts to become happy are in vain. Released from the prison of
> despotism, they will murder each other with the remnants of their broken
> shackles. . . . All occurrences in the world appear to me to be instructive
> signs which the great Educator of Mankind provides so that (mankind)
> learns from them what it needs to know. Not that [mankind] learns it *out*
> of them; we will never find anything in all of world history that we our-
> selves have not first put into it; rather, [mankind], through its judgment of
> real occurrences, has an easier way to develop out of itself what lies in
> itself: and so the French Revolution appears to me to be a rich painting
> about the great text: the right and value of human beings.[19]

To judge by his brief but suggestive comment on "political results,"
Fichte blamed the excesses of the Revolution on foreign intervention.
More striking, though, is the looming presence of Lessing, the heroic
figure of Fichte's youth. The leitmotif of Lessing's *The Education of the
Human Race*, published in 1780, was that "revelation" was to "the whole
human race" what "education" was to "the individual person." Like a
schoolmaster developing his pupils' innate potential, God used revelation
to promote an educational process that mankind would in any case have
undergone "on its own." This divine pedagogy had unfolded in a historical economy of metaphors, each a more or less partial truth, appropriate
to a particular stage in mankind's development, but pointing in the right
direction. Only recently had mankind begun to outgrow its need for

[18] Fichte, *Beitrag*, p. 45.   [19] Ibid., p. 34.

truths wrapped in, and partially obscured by, the narrative imagery of Scripture, so that it could grasp truth in its pure rationality.[20] It was this vision of providential history that framed Fichte's "judgment" of the French Revolution. If we take it seriously, his indifference to the actual course of events becomes more understandable. The Revolution's internal narrative faded to insignificance in view of its place in the larger narrative Providence had designed for mankind. Even if the participants took a wrong turn, the event remained an immensely instructive symbolic representation, a "rich painting" for observers in Germany and elsewhere. Kant had "secured" the "substance" (*Stoff*), and the revolutionary canvas provided the "direction" and the "colors" for "weak eyes." Like Lessing's revelation, the Revolution was a revelatory moment. It inspired observers to take the Kantian turn inward, to realize their latent capacity for moral insight.

Fichte did not simply conceive of the Revolution as metaphor. He also tried to capture its revelatory significance with a metaphoric language linking history to biography, the advance of human culture to the moral development of the individual. Like Lessing, Fichte was drawing on a rich tradition of biographical metaphor in Protestant culture. But there was a fault line in this tradition, and in German Lutheranism the line cut very deep. Since the early eighteenth century the German Lutheran Church had been suffused with the fervor of the Pietist revival, which sought to purify Protestant religiosity by returning it to its evangelical roots. At the same time, though, Lutheran clergymen had proved remarkably open to the secular humanism of the Enlightenment, and particularly to its pedagogical concerns. While this duality allowed creative bondings of the sacred and the secular, it also made for persistent tensions in German thinking about reform and revolution. The tensions reverberate through Fichte's *Contribution*, and they make it understandable that his effort to sustain a coherent argument about the Revolution was not entirely successful.[21]

In the biographical metaphor that Fichte shared with Lessing, the controlling idea was natural entelechy. It points us to the German Enlightenment and its characteristic preoccupation, one might say obsession, with educational reform and the pedagogical "art" (*Kunst*). Pedagogy insured realization of the pupil's inborn entelechy by promoting his natural

---

[20] Lessing, "Die Erziehung des Menschengeschlechts," *Gesammelte Werke*, ed. Paul Rilla, vol. 8 (Berlin, 1956), pp. 590–615. On Lessing's historiosophy, see esp. Hermann Timm, *Gott und die Freiheit. Studien zur Religionsphilosophie der Goethezeit*, vol. 1: *Die Spinozarenaissance* (Frankfurt, 1974).

[21] The metaphors were not limited to German Protestantism; see the discussion of German and English early Romanticism in M. H. Abrams, *Natural Supernaturalism. Tradition and Revolution in Romantic Literature* (New York, 1971). But cf. Bernard Yack, *The Longing for Total Revolution. Philosophical Sources of Social Discontent from Rousseau to Marx and Nietzsche* (Princeton, N.J., 1986), pp. 11–18.

maturation. The art lay in guiding and enhancing the growth process without forcing nature's schedule. In its metaphorical extension to a society, or to the species, this pedagogical ideal was eminently suited to justify the moderate reform agenda of the German Protestant Enlightenment. The optimistic premise was that progress was a historical inevitability, but the cautionary lesson was that progress must not be forced. When the removal of traditional restraints outstripped the pace of moral improvement, progressive change degenerated into disorder. The via media – the alternative to both immobilism and chaos – was seen to lie in the formation of an "enlightened" public. This *Publikum* would constitute a collective conscience, a high court of appeal on public issues, and reform would advance as governments became increasingly accountable to it. For the present the enlightened public was necessarily limited to the educated few; only gradually, with the diffusion of "enlightenment" over generations, would it expand out – and down – to encompass the masses.[22]

There was a certain smugness about this optimism, evident even in the positive German reactions to the French constitutional and legal reforms of 1789. The conventional assumption was that in the German states several decades of well-ordered reform from above had obviated the need for such drastic changes. In the early 1790s the German defense of gradualism became an incantation against revolution in any form. Reacting against those who blamed events in France on the excesses of the Enlightenment, reformers insisted that only the gradual dissemination of the Enlightenment's ethic of rational self-discipline could protect the masses from radical "enthusiasts."

As a child of the Enlightenment and as a veteran tutor, Fichte was thoroughly imbued with the premises and implications of gradualism. By 1793, to be sure, he was adding provocative twists. Readers of the *Reclamation* were surely shocked to learn, as France approached the Terror, that "state upheavals" like the Revolution could effect a great leap forward in human progress. And to Fichte, "enlightenment" was not a trickle-down process; "worthiness for freedom," he argued, "must rise up from below." But the great leaps forward were at the cost of terrible suffering and at the risk of a retrogression to barbarism. Popular initiative must remain limited to moral self-improvement, since "emancipation without disorder can only come down from above." Though obviously "unjust," the existing governments could not be openly rejected, much less actively resisted;

---

[22] On pedagogy and natural entelechy see Anthony J. La Vopa, *Grace, Talent, and Merit. Poor Students, Clerical Careers, and Professional Ideology in Eighteenth-Century Germany* (Cambridge, 1988), esp. pp. 165–96. The vast eighteenth-century German literature on "enlightenment" is surveyed in Werner Schneiders, *Die wahre Aufklärung. Zum Selbstverständnis der deutschen Aufklärung* (Freiburg and Munich, 1974). For samplings of the literature see Zwi Batscha, ed., *Aufklärung und Gedankenfreiheit. Funfzehn Anregungen, aus der Geschichte zu lernen* (Frankfurt am Main, 1977); James Schmidt, ed., *What Is Enlightenment? Eighteenth-Century Answers and Twentieth-Century Questions* (Berkeley, Calif., 1996).

they could only be shamed into reform as they found themselves in moral isolation.[23]

The corollary to Fichte's rejection of "violent revolution," one might plausibly conclude, was a commitment to gradualism. In this version of the revolution-as-revelation, new ideals opened new horizons of expectation and thus kept the gradual advance of mankind pointed in the right direction. And yet the *Contribution* can also be read as a justification for a dramatic rupture with the past or perhaps better, a radical breakthrough. Here the guiding metaphor was spiritual rebirth, a theme rooted in Paul's Epistles and central to evangelical Protestantism from its inception. To be "reborn" was to transcend the corrupt natural self, the Old Adam, and become the receptacle of God's saving grace. Within German Lutheranism, the Pietist movement had sought to revive this experience of sanctification since the late seventeenth century. Like the English Calvinists, the Pietists had conceived of rebirth as a wrenching conversion experience (*Bekehrung*). The dramatic turning point – the "breakthrough" (*Durchbruch*) – came when the Christian finally realized his utter helplessness as a corrupt natural creature, and thereby achieved the passivity needed to receive God's mercy.[24]

That revolution aims at the "rebirth" of a society, or at least of a polity, is now one of the clichés of secular political discourse. When a Lutheran of Fichte's generation used the metaphor of rebirth, it was with full awareness of its sacred resonances. The implication was that in the history of a community, as in the spiritual biography of a Christian, the revelatory moment opened the way to an experience of transcendence. But Fichte can also be said to have secularized the metaphor – by harnessing it to his Kantian argument and by making it an idiom for his own grievances and aspirations. In the *Contribution* there is no call to enter a state of helpless passivity, no expectation of an infusion of a supernatural power; the revelatory moment is a willed turn inward, a Kantian awakening of latent moral insight. When Fichte exposed the corruption of his era, he did so as an outsider with a transcendent vantage point. Corruption meant ideological self-deception; it was embodied in the defense of unjust corporate privileges and in the dehumanizing paternalism of machinelike governments. The antidote was not a gradual, trickle-down process of enlightenment but the wrenching breakthrough to a radically inclusive and egalitarian *Publikum*. Here revolution meant a collective act of transcendence, and it was so appealing to Fichte because it promised to bond the "philosopher" to the uneducated mass.

---

[23] Fichte, *Beitrag*, pp. 11–13, 35–9.

[24] This tradition of "psycho-historical parallelism" is emphasized in Abrams, *Natural Supernaturalism*. On conversion in German Lutheran Pietism, see La Vopa, *Grace, Talent, and Merit*, pp. 137–64.

Kant, it should be stressed, shared the conventional assumption that enlightenment must be a tutelary process, a gradual and cautious diffusion from above. And yet there was also a latent potential for egalitarian radicalism in Kant's conviction that the common person, however uneducated he or she might be, *felt* moral imperatives as intuitively self-evident truths.[25] In the *Contribution*, Fichte drew consequences from this egalitarian implication that Kant stopped well short of. Participation in Fichte's *Publikum* was not contingent on the possession of education or wealth or any other social quality. It was an inalienable human right, following necessarily from the human duty to develop a moral personality. Exercising freedom in this sense entailed the unrestricted right to know; in the open society Fichte advocated, no one could be excluded from the public exchange of ideas or from participating in the public scrutiny of government.

What some contemporaries found especially shocking about the *Contribution* was Fichte's corollary argument: any human being had the right to abrogate unilaterally his contract with the state, as he could abrogate any other contract, if it no longer fulfilled his legitimate needs. Indeed he had the duty to do so if it obstructed his moral self-development.[26] No less emblematic of Fichte's radicalism, however, was the rhetorical form of the *Contribution*. The Revolution became an opportunity to constitute an egalitarian rhetorical community, premised on a radically new relationship between speaker and interlocutor. In the absence of indigenous precedents, this was a leap in the dark for a German intellectual. In eighteenth-century England a democratic rhetoric of opposition to the Whig Oligarchy had emerged, but there was no equivalent in the German states. Nor did Germany have anything comparable to the increasingly democratic idiom with which French trial lawyers had taken to speaking for "the nation" and flailing the Establishment.[27] The German discourse of "popular enlightenment" was infused with a blatantly paternalistic concern to insure the survival of the moral restraints that underlay social order, and to prevent the rise of popular expectations that could not be satisfied. It seemed obvious that enlightenment had to be administered in carefully controlled dosages. Likewise a clean distinction had to be main-

---

[25] See, for example, Immanuel Kant, *Fundamental Principles of the Metaphysics of Morals*, trans. T. K. Abbott (1785: Buffalo, 1987), pp. 26–31. These aspects of Kant's moral theory are emphasized in Roger J. Sullivan, *Immanuel Kant's Moral Theory* (Cambridge, 1989), pp. 4–6, 131–7. See also the discussion of Kant's concept of "interest" in Ernst Wolfgang Orth, "Interesse," *Geschichtliche Grundbegriffe*, 3: 333–5.

[26] Fichte, *Beitrag*, pp. 68–74; Pierre-Philippe Druet, *Fichte* (Paris, 1977), p. 61.

[27] See, for example, Jean Starobinski, "La chaire, la tribune, le barreau," in Pierre Nora, ed., *Les Lieux de Mémoire*, vol. 2: *La Nation* (Paris, 1986): 449–58; Sara Maza, "Le tribunal de la nation: les mémoires judiciaires et l'opinion publique à la fin de l'Ancien Régime," *Annales* 42 (1987): 73–90. On German rhetorical traditions, see Irmgard Weithase, *Zur Geschichte der gesprochenen deutschen Sprache*, 2 vols. (Tübingen), 1961.

tained between the exchange of ideas within the "republic of letters" (or the republic of the learned) and the dissemination of ideas to the uninitiated. In the republic, strict equality must prevail; it was the sheer cogency of ideas and not the status of persons that ought to command respect. A tutelary enlightenment, on the other hand, was one in which the authority of reason was reinforced by the educational credentials and official status of those who purveyed it. There is no better example of this emphasis on control from above than the extensive literature on the pastorate (and especially the rural pastorate) as a beacon of popular enlightenment. Pastors were enjoined to make their sermons more accessible to the uneducated, and in that sense to be "popular"; but they also were expected to speak in the authoritative voice of men of superior education and rank.[28]

These were the pedagogical and rhetorical assumptions with which Fichte was familiar. In the initial draft of the essay that would become the *Reclamation*, it was in the spirit of these assumptions that he had defended the recent reimposition of censorship in Prussia. But Fichte's image of himself as a conventional popularizer had not been without its tensions. In a remarkable passage toward the end of the *Attempt at a Critique*, he had asked how someone like himself, who did not "feel [a] need" for a faith grounded in revelation, could nonetheless fulfill his duty to "have an effect on the hearts of others." His answer was, to be kind, improvised; the preacher-skeptic experienced his audience's faith as a "passing faith," an emotional commitment that could not be feigned, though it "cooled down" once he left the pulpit.

In the *Contribution* Fichte sought to have an effect on the masses in a radically different way, through a new form of public communication. His change of mind may have been occasioned by a specific event, but the more likely explanation is that he had had to confront a contradiction between his defense of censorship and his radicalized Kantianism. As he pursued the egalitarian implication of Kant's moral theory, his youthful ideal of a Protestant community of belief – a community in which the few "good heads" would remain bonded to the uneducated mass in a shared spontaneity of "the heart," even as they distanced themselves from the masses' naïve faith – was at once confirmed and recast.[29] The *Contribution* was inspired by his conviction that the intuitive grasp of moral truth – a grasp that was both cognitive and emotional – could ground an egalitarian rhetorical community. In this sense, as he justified the Revolution as a breakthrough, Fichte broke through the conventions of his culture and his milieu. Having thought of himself as a "popular enlightener" in the pulpit, he now aspired to the radically unconventional role of philosopher-tribune. Now was the time for knowledge of human

---

[28] See La Vopa, *Grace, Talent, and Merit*, pp. 335–41.   [29] See Chapter 2.

"duties, rights, and prospects" to burst through the walls of the academic ghetto, where it had been guarded jealously by "a few elect," and to become "a common property of mankind . . . like air and light."[30]

Since he "would like to be read . . . [and] to find an access into the soul of the reader," Fichte explained, he had "attempt[ed] to unite [himself] in some way with the great crowd (*grossen Haufen*)." He lacked rhetorical precedents in his own culture, but he was impelled by the implications of the Kantian turn inward. In the most striking implication, one of the axiomatic assumptions of Enlightenment reform thought was completely inverted. The masses were not less open to enlightenment – that is, to true enlightenment – than the educated. Quite the contrary; like Rousseau, but with a Kantian rationale, Fichte argued that moral truth was more accessible to the masses, and indeed by virtue of their formal ignorance. The most cunning kind of self-deception was academic sophistry. Only academe ("the school") could obscure what was "clear to the natural, uneducated human understanding": that "doing one's duty is something entirely different from seeking one's advantage in a rational way."[31] To put it another way, the grip of ideology was much tighter at the peak of the social pyramid than at its base.

Again, Fichte, the outsider, claimed to occupy a uniquely privileged vantage point. He was a "philosopher," not a "scholar." Having brought his own moral insight to full consciousness, and having extricated himself from the ideological rationales of the educated elite, he could bond with "the great crowd" in a direct and pure form of communication. This was a rhetorical posture that explicitly extruded tutelage and deference from public communication. Instead, Fichte aspired to be a "friend" to "the person who needed such a friend and had no better one in his proximity." He was drawing on the eighteenth-century cult of friendship, and he was well aware that "friend" evoked intimacy on terms of strict equality and mutual respect. Hence his role was to "think before his readers, not for them." Thinking "for" them was an ideological exercise, perpetuating "opinion, illusion, prejuduce," but thinking "before" them activated latent moral insight by inducing "reflection."[32] The philosopher made himself an instrument of the revelatory moment.

In the *Reclamation*, as he had assumed a new rhetorical posture in the face of censorship, Fichte had imagined giving an "oration" on behalf of "the People." In the *Contribution* he abandoned this fiction of an orator-

---

[30] Fichte, *Beitrag*, pp. 34–5, 62–3. Fichte's egalitarian rhetoric may have been unique in its philosophical ambitions, but he was not alone in developing such a rhetoric. For other examples, see Hans-Wolf Jäger, *Politische Kategorien in Poetik und Rhetorik der zweiten Hälfte des 18. Jahrhunderts* (Stuttgart, 1970), and Inge Stephan, *Literarischer Jakobinismus in Deutschland (1789–1806)* (Stuttgart, 1976). For the more typical perspective, see the analysis of Schiller's view of "popularity" in Berghahn, "Volkstümlichkeit."

[31] Fichte, *Beitrag*, pp. 40–7.   [32] Ibid.

ical performance, and with good reason. He aspired to be read, not heard, by a mass audience, and he was in fact intoxicated by the communicative potential of print. Unlike the face-to-face communication of an oration, print communication seemed to make for a kind of *impersonal* intimacy. In Kantian terms, of course, the creation of an egalitarian *Publikum* through print involved a communion of moral personalities; it bonded people through their purely human essences, rather than through the empirical accidents of their social identities. It was in this sense that Fichte celebrated the communication of truth as "the most intimate means of uniting spirits with spirits."[33] But this was also to say that in another sense, print communication was so appealing because it could be impersonal. As a vehicle of Kantian moral insight, it had no respect for persons, or more precisely, for personal differences in status and power. Its dizzying potential as revelation lay in effecting symbolic leaps across social chasms and through social shells.

It was this paradox – the impersonality of intimacy through print – that allowed Fichte to commit himself to a strategy of anonymity in the *Contribution* as well as the *Reclamation*. The essays, in fact, were to begin an entire series on law and politics, all to appear anonymously. Only after he had won sufficient "respect" would he "acknowledge [himself] voluntarily."[34] In an era of government censorship it was standard practice for authors to protect themselves with anonymity. The practice seemed all the more necessary in the early 1790s, as the German governments sought to dispel the specter of revolutionary upheaval with stricter censorship restrictions and harsher enforcement. And yet there were authors who questioned, in print, whether anonymity was an honorable expedient. If censorship was an abuse of authority, Herder argued, anonymity was an abuse of freedom.[35] Did not an author forfeit credibility if he claimed to speak to (and perhaps for) an open "public" but refused to make public his own identity? Fichte was clearly troubled by such objections, though he risked being permanently shut out of a career if he attached his name to his writings. It is a measure of his ambivalence that in both the *Reclamation* and the *Contribution* he took pains to defend his resort to anonymity and that the defense alternated between bravado and embarrassment.[36]

If Fichte's qualms were assuaged, at least to a degree, that was because he saw his use of print as constituting a new kind of rhetorical community. The author who achieved an impersonal intimacy with his readers

[33] Ibid., p. 62.
[34] Fichte to Kant (Sept. 20, 1793), in GA, III, 1: 431–2; Fichte to Theodor von Schön (Sept. 20, 1793), GA, III, 1: 433–5.
[35] Johann Gottfried Herder, "Haben wir noch das Publikum und Vaterland der Alten?", in *Herders Werke in fünf Bänden*, vol. 4 (Berlin and Weimar, 1978): 130–3
[36] Fichte, *Beitrag*, pp. 11, 39.

– a relationship in which social impersonality was a condition of moral equality – had neither the need nor the obligation to reveal his personal identity. He was committed to a higher order of public openness.

★ ★ ★

In the *Contribution*, "the People" figured largely as an imagined aggregate of readers, but they assumed a social profile when Fichte confronted the issue of mass poverty. To that issue, in fact, the philosopher-tribune brought an unusual depth of sympathy. It found expression above all in his discussion of the elimination of the compulsory labor services the peasants owed their estate lords. When he addressed the objection that estate lords deprived of compulsory labor without compensation and unprepared for this sudden change would suffer unjustly from a drastic collapse in their standard of living, he shifted his rhetorical posture. Now he spoke as one of the "advantaged." He used this change of voice, however, to explode the self-serving assumptions of the advantaged from the inside. He drew a distinction between, on the one hand, the spiral of "imaginary" needs that the addiction to "luxury" generated among the affluent and, on the other, "natural necessities" like food and shelter. Ironically "we," the advantaged, could easily empathize with someone deprived of his fine wine or his coffee with milk, since we knew from personal experience how easily "dispensable" items become "indispensable" through habit; but the hunger of the truly poor, which we have never known, left us cold.[37]

Here was a striking example of the cunning with which self-interest fashioned an ideological justification. Was not happiness or suffering, after all, relative to expectations, and could not expectations be lowered? This view of the psychology of deprivation implied that rich and poor were really in the same boat – and that the solution to the plight of the hungry was to keep their expectations suitably circumscribed, rather than to provide for the satisfaction of their basic needs. Perhaps drawing on his own experience, Fichte asked his readers to make the leap of imagination that this facile logic allowed them to avoid. His point was that hunger differed from frustrated *Luxus* absolutely, not by degree. Whereas a socially acquired consumer habit could be changed, an imperative of "nature" was inescapable. Ultimately it was the difference between self-inflicted suffering and victimization. Whereas we could deprive ourselves of superfluous items "with a kind of voluntary action," there was "not a trace of free will" in the deprivations of the hungry.[38]

A society that left people in sheer physical want, Fichte seemed to be saying, was guilty of an intolerable injustice. But if that were the case, why limit the remedy to the removal of compulsory labor services? Did

---

[37] Ibid., pp. 134–42.   [38] Ibid., p. 139.

not the poor have the right to demand, and if necessary to force, a redistribution of wealth? Why did Fichte's insight into the plight of the poor not lead him to advocate a social revolution from below? The answer is not simply that like most of his contemporaries, he had an instinctive fear of the mob violence that social revolution might entail. His fear of social disorder went hand in hand with his confidence in his economic prognosis. In the fourth chapter, on "the favored classes in general," his elaboration of Kantian natural law theory became a diagnosis of the economic crisis "in almost all the monarchical states," along with a simple prescription for economic recovery. It is a brief moment in the text, and the structure of its logic is not always apparent. But these few pages merit close scrutiny, since they mark Fichte's first effort to translate his philosophical critique of the old regime into a vision of an alternative economic and social order – one that would make revolution superfluous.

An oversupply of currency and an accompanying inflation, Fichte observed, were widening the abysss in most dynastic states between the wealthy few and the "armies of people who have nothing." This situation he attributed in turn to the states' "reigning mania for enriching themselves by way of commerce and factories, at the cost of everything else"; to "the rampant trade of our era," which "threatens everyone who participates in it, even in the most distant way, with the complete ruin of their property circumstances"; to "the unlimited credit, which the printed money of Europe increases more than tenfold." Fichte went on to describe a crisis that threatened to end in total collapse. Unable to control their hunger for luxury, landed proprietors drove up the prices of agricultural necessities – and the price of land was inflated accordingly. While the urban merchant profited by supplying this consumer demand, the artisan was "driven into a corner" and the peasant "[had] nothing and will never have anything but bare subsistence." Eventually the estate lord would become "the exclusive owner of all the wealth of the nation" – either because he would learn how to control his consumer appetite, or because the current system of trade would "[suffer] an upheaval, as it surely will."[39]

The key to avoiding this scenario was to emancipate agricultural labor by removing compulsory service:

Liberate the trade with the natural inheritance of the human being, with his powers; you will witness the remarkable drama *that the productivity of landed property, and of all property, stands in inverse proportion to its size*, and that the land will gradually be distributed among many without coercive agrarian laws, which are always unjust – and your problem will be solved.[40]

[39] Ibid., p. 136.   [40] Ibid., pp. 136–7.

The passage includes one of Fichte's rare classical allusions, and perhaps the only indication in the text that he was familiar with the factional controversies of the Revolution. The "agrarian law" – the Gracchi's plan for an equitable redistribution of land under the Roman Republic – had been the subject of heated debate in Paris since late 1790, when the Abbé Claude Fauchet had advocated a version of it in a lecture series. Fauchet's practical proposals were moderate enough; there would be a progressive tax on land, for example, and new marriage and inheritance laws would prevent the formation of overly large estates. His defense of these reforms, however, rested on the radical principles that everyone who labored on the land had a "right" to it, and that in a "well-ordered society . . . everybody has something, and nobody has too much."[41]

In 1791, as an advocate of the agrarian law, Gracchus Babeuf began to form the vision of agrarian communism to which his "Conspiracy for Equality" would commit itself five years later. Fichte obviously disagreed; like the orators of the Jacobin Club, he found the repudiation of the principle of private property wrongheaded and alarming. His point was not that "a more equal distribution of holdings" was undesirable, but that it did not require a coercive "intrusion into the rights of property." The key was to eliminate compulsory labor services, which were a patrimonial entitlement rather than a basic right of property. "Hired at a fair wage," Fichte predicted, "a third" of the former compulsory laborers would do more work than all of them did under present conditions.[42]

One is tempted to conclude that far from being a proto-communist (or indeed a proto-socialist), Fichte drew his economic principles from Adam Smith and other founders of modern "liberal" economic thought. In fact, though, the twenthieth-century reader who imposes a Smithian grid on Fichte's economic diagnosis will find its logic hopelessly contradictory. A virtually utopian faith in the potential of a free market in land and labor stands side by side with the conviction that the new ascendancy of "commerce" and "factories" will have disastrous consequences. For all his enthusiasm for market contracts, Fichte obviously did not share Adam Smith's conviction that commercial expansion would lift the entire society, including its laboring classes, to new levels of affluence. Quite the contrary; a commercial and industrial expansion feeding on *Luxus* threatened to concentrate all wealth in the hands of a rural elite.

To appreciate the difference between Smith and Fichte, one need only juxtapose their views on "luxury" consumption. In *The Wealth of Nations*, Smith relished ironic twists of history, and a case in point was the shift from huge households of retainers and servants to "durable consumption" in "frivolous objects" (the famous "trinkets" and "gewgaws"). Inadver-

---

[41] R. B. Rose, *Gracchus Babeuf. The First Revolutionary Communist* (Stanford, Calif., 1978), pp. 101–2.
[42] Fichte, *Beitrag*, pp. 172–3.

tently and indeed out of pure selfishness, the wealthy had contributed to the welcomed transition from feudalism, with its scarcities and personal dependencies, to the widespread "opulence" and contractual independence of modern commercial society.[43] To Fichte the new luxury consumption was the engine of the current crisis, not an agent of long-term progress. He blamed the estate owners' addiction to *Luxus* for widening the gap between rich and poor and bringing societies ever closer to economic collapse.

It is hardly surprising that Fichte's perspective was not Smithian. He almost certainly had not read Adam Smith by the time he turned his sights on economic issues in the *Contribution*. To that point he had shown little interest in economic literature of any variety; and in any case *The Wealth of Nations*, though available in German translation since the late 1770s, had hardly begun to win a reputation in Germany as a pathbreaking work when Christian Garve's new translation appeared in 1794. The eighteenth-century pedigree for Fichte's analysis – a vague pedigree, to be sure, but discernable – begins in mid-century France with the "physiocratic" doctrines of Quesnay and his disciples. In the 1770s several German authors had taken up Physiocracy as an alternative to the mercantilist and cameralist orthodoxies that guided economic policy in the German states. Fichte may have had some familiarity with this literature, but more likely he was introduced to physiocratic theory through more recent German reworkings of natural law theory.[44] In any case, the debt to Physiocracy is unmistakable in his assumption that agriculture was the proper foundation for a healthy economic order; in his corollary disapproval of the mercantilist preference for commerce and industry; in his combined faith in the free market and respect for private property.

It is equally striking, though, that Ficht's rational order had a different social shape and political framework. Whereas Quesnay looked to the formation of large-scale capitalist enterprises to revolutionize agricultural productivity, Fichte welcomed the prospect that a landed elite would accede to a multitude of small proprietors. From his standpoint, in fact, the route to greater productivity in all sectors of the economy lay through smallness, and not through "economies of scale." Nor did Fichte share the French physiocrats' tendency to look to a centralized monarchy – an "enlightened" absolutism – to push through reforms against the resistance of entrenched corporate interests. He saw the centralized state and corporate enclaves as gears in the same oppressive machine, and he expected his rational economic order to emerge as both fell away.

[43] Adam Smith, *The Wealth of Nations, Books I–III* (London, 1986), pp. 479–520.
[44] Diethelm Klippel, *Politische Freiheit und Freiheitsrechte im deutschen Naturrecht des 18. Jahrhunderts* (Paderborn, 1976); Klippel, "Der Einfluss der Physiokraten auf die Entwicklung der liberalen politischen Theorie in Deutschland," *Der Staat* 23 (1984): 205–26.

What is striking is that Fichte's logic prevented him from considering the possible dangers of his own prescriptions. Arguably the effect of eliminating the landlord's patrimonial jurisidiction would not be simply to free peasant-tenants of onerous labor services; it would also unburden the landlords of traditional "paternal" obligations that went well beyond the letter of the law. The smallholding peasant's freedom to dispose of his labor in market contracts – and thus, in Fichte's expectation, to work to full capacity for his own and others' benefit – might do more harm than good if he found himself helpless in the face of market forces. And in an era of rapid population growth, was it not grossly unrealistic to expect small-scale agriculture to eliminate mass poverty? Would the alleviation of mass poverty not come precisely where Fichte saw disaster looming, in the growing preponderance of commerce and industry in modern economies?

Fichte could ignore these possibilities because he assumed that the contractual freedom of the market – in the use of private property and in the disposal of labor – would revolutionize agricultural productivity and insure general prosperity. It was an assumption he shared with many contemporaries, including most of the progeny of the French Enlightenment who were sucked into the maelstrom of the Revolution, from the bourgeois deputies of 1789 to the Jacobins of 1793. To men who equated corruption and injustice with an ossified corporate order, the culprit was legally inherited privilege. Capitalism was the solution, not the problem; within a framework of legal equality, the market freedom to exploit private property and make contracts promised to unleash all the productive energies that privilege had kept repressed.

Precisely because he conceived of the old regime as a vast web of privilege, Fichte could leap over the obvious differences in his own circumstances and identify with the rural poor as a fellow victim. In the interminable search for a career opening, his aspirations had collided more than once with the prerogatives of "birth" in public life. The same aristocracy that used its seigneurial privileges to exploit the peasantry had kept educated commoners like himself at a safe distance from the more desirable government offices. Hence in the fifth chapter of the *Contribution* it made perfect sense to follow an evocation of a free-labor market in agriculture, unleashing at last vast productive energies, with a call for "careers open to talent" in state employment. Freed from the labor services owed to their patrimonial lords (not to landed proprietors as such), the peasants would sell their labor to their best advantage and, at least in some cases, prosper as independent farmers. Likewise, as "birth" acceded to talent and merit in a competitive market, public employment would experience a freeing up of human resources. In both scenarios it was the free agent – the man whose aspirations were limited only by obligations and restrictions he himself had contracted to accept – who worked and achieved to capacity.

Hence Fichte's economic thought was, from one angle, simply an extension of his defense of the Revolution's principle of legal equality. Within the metaphoric structure of the *Contribution*, however, the free market and private property also bonded with a priori principles as elements of a larger moral vision. Following Kant's lead, but again driving Kantian logic to new extremes, Fichte brought the languages of economics and philosophy, of commercial exchange and intellectual communion, into a symbiosis in which each acquired heightened legitimacy by analogy with the other. The symbiosis was not without its ambiguities. In Fichte's thought, as in Kant's, contracts and property figured on both sides of the dichotomy between *Willkühr* and the Moral Law. *Willkühr* – the arbitrary exercise of will – operated in the world of empirical (or "sensual") desires and instrumental power relationships, where the individual pursued his "advantage" and his "happiness" as he defined them. This was the world of "alienable" rights, as opposed to the moral realm where duty was categorical and hence rights (which empowered the individual to perform his duty) were "inalienable." In a contract – one, for example, in which real property was acquired or exchanged, or in which labor was employed for a wage – each side gave up some alienable rights for others. While the crux of morality was purity of intention, all that mattered in this contractual universe was external behavior – and, in the event that such behavior failed to honor a contractual promise, justice (as opposed to virtue) was insured by "external" legal compulsion.

To Fichte, as to Kant, there was a wide range of such contracts that did not interfere with the performance of moral duty and hence were perfectly legitimate. This was to say, however, that they were legitimate by default; they were permissible only because, in Fichte's terms, the "pure I" (the noumenal self) could realize itself in the phenomenal world only within the embodied form of a "changeable I," an empirical flux of needs, emotions, and mental processes – and only so long as moral personality remained free to determine itself. And yet there was also a sense in which property and contracts acquired legitimacy by virtue of their vital role in moral self-determination, and it was primarily in that capacity that they figured in the *Contribution*. "Culture for freedom" was the final purpose of the human being in the state of nature (i.e., in the moral state), and hence it should also be the goal of the state. To acquire *Kultur* in this sense meant to achieve "complete independence . . . from everything that is not our pure self." Wrapping his asceticism in a Kantian idiom, Fichte described a relentless struggle in which the "pure I" not only "subjected" the "changeable I," but also harnessed its "powers" to moral self-discipline. In the process the pure I – the moral personality – became a property-holder *within* the self; it made instincts, emotional impulses, and intellectual capacities the "instruments" of its struggle against a resistant world of external things. And in investing in those things the form of its inner mastery, it established a "right of dedication" (*Zueignungsrecht*) over them, an exclusive right to use portions of mankind's common property (*Eigentum*).[45]

All this is reminiscent of a Lockean grounding of the right to property in an investment of the self through labor. What is striking about Fichte's German (and Kantian) variation, however, is the expansive use of the term *Eigentum* to encompass both things and ideas, so that they borrowed from each other's sanctity as they folded into each other. An idea was a kind of *Eigentum*, in the basic moral sense that it was an integral part of a unique personality, an emanation of a discreet self. To exchange ideas freely was to make "free use of [one's] property" in the moral realm. It was a matter of mutual right, as in contracts regulating physical property. The only difference – a crucial one, to be sure – was that rights to communicate ideas and to receive them were inalienable, since both acts were indispensable to moral self-development.

As a vehicle of the "culture for freedom," property-as-external thing could acquire the same moral value as ideas. It was in the establishment of an exclusive right to use things – land, for example – that the moral personality acquired mastery over the inner powers of the "changeable I," pitted itself against a resistant externality, and thereby advanced in freedom. In this realm the contractual acquisition and exchange of property were not merely external actions, and they were not permissible only because they were irrelevant to the Moral Law. Through them the pure self advanced toward "independence" from the blind laws of physical nature by engaging it and appropriating it. Like the exchange of ideas, albeit in the murky flux of experience rather than in the translucent realm of conscience, contractual exchanges provided the Moral Law with its substance, its vehicles for self-realization. Fichte's point was not simply that *Eigentum*-as-thing could be morally analogous to *Eigentum*-as-idea. Often implicitly, but with a language rich in metaphoric affinities, he extended his ideal of pure communication from the exchange of ideas to the free-market exchanges of property, including the wage earner's property in his own labor. Ironically, this was the basis for his disturbing argument that contracts could be broken unilaterally. A contract, to be sure, was about mutual advantage, not moral duty; but ultimately its binding authority, like the moral authority of an idea made public, lay in "truthfulness" or "purity of the heart." Precisely because one party could not be sure of the other's truthfulness until it was manifested in action, he was not bound to that point by the other's "right."[46]

Though grounded morally in purity of intention, contracts did not allow the direct and immediate intimacy – the mutual transparency – that print communication could effect. Indeed, as arrangements about the dis-

[45] Fichte, *Beitrag*, pp. 68–77, 88–98, 108–9.   [46] Ibid., pp. 86–8.

tribution of power, they contrasted starkly with the power-free communication of moral knowledge. On both counts market contracts were opaque and amoral, if not immoral. And yet in Fichte's vision they nonetheless shared – or ought to share – something of the virtue of egalitarian impersonality that made print communication so appealing. Free-market contracts, purely instrumental and strictly bounded, promised liberation from the intricate couplings of "liberties" with privileges and from the pervasive deferences and exclusions that made the old regime so oppressive. To grant noblemen an exclusive right to purchase noble estates, Fichte argued, was to "[give] to the universal symbols of the value of things a particular value, derived from the person of the possessor."[47] Money was to things in a free market what print was to ideas in a wide-open *Publikum* – a universal and socially neutral medium of exchange, and hence no respecter of status. Here again impersonality seemed to be the necessary condition of egalitarian reciprocity.

What we find in Fichte's economic vision, then, is a highly complex fusion of eighteenth-century economic discourses with Kantian principles. It becomes apparent that in his parallel ways of thinking about property exchange and the communication of ideas, Fichte shared with liberal discourse a tendency to subsume economic agency under an ideal of *moral individualism.* The result was a marked ambivalence about the poor, which helps explain why his sympathetic identification with their plight did not produce a brief for social revolution. As much as he thought of old-regime societies as machinelike structures of inequality, he could not call for a popular revolution against structural injustice. Fichte's resolution of the issues surrounding compulsory agricultural labor is especially instructive. He argued that ownership of property was heritable, but no one could inherit a contractual advantage. Hence the disadvantaged – the laborers – would be freed from an onerous obligation, though minimal compensation to the landlords might be justified. On the other side of the same ledger, however, the laborers could not claim compensation for past exploitation. It had been their own fault, after all, that they had remained in an exploitative contract. The sufferings of poverty might be involuntary, but there was a sense in which everyone, even the poorest laborer, brought suffering upon himself in the free world of market contracts.

It would take Fichte several years to confront the possibility that the very structure of property relations, its inherent arrangement of power, made the freedom of the market a serviceable fiction for the advantaged and a cruel joke for the disadvantaged.

★ ★ ★

---

[47] Ibid., pp. 170–1.

Fichte wrote the second installment of the *Contribution* in Zürich, where he had returned in the summer of 1793 to prepare for his wedding. A few months later his *Wanderjahre* finally ended; he was appointed to succeed Karl Leonhard Reinhold as the resident Kantian philosopher at Jena. Even if he had not been distracted by his marriage and his professorial responsibilities, however, his second question – whether the Revolution showed "wisdom" in its choice of "means" – would probably have remained unanswered. In the postscript he admitted that he had produced the second installment more to keep his promise to someone who had recommended it to a journal than in the expectation that "the public would honor [it] with its attention."[48] He might have added that in its form as well as its substance, the *Contribution* had entered a cul-de-sac.

Inherent in Fichte's mix of biographical metaphors was an ambivalence about the Revolution and about revolutions as historical phenomena that he could not resolve. If we define revolution as a radical rupture with the past (or, in positive terms, as a radical breakthrough to a new order), then Fichte occupied the same standpoint as most other German observers. He appealed to natural entelechy as the alternative to revolution. And yet the *Contribution* was also intended to effect a revolutionary breakthrough – the one evoked by its metaphor of rebirth and implied in its vision of an unconditionally egalitarian public.

The point is not simply that Fichte's language conveyed his ambivalence. The received languages – the dual legacy of German Lutheran culture – shaped his perceptions of the Revolution and defined his choices. If he could not make a choice, that was because his own biography pulled him in conflicting directions. The embittered outsider assumed a Rousseauian posture toward a corrupt Establishment. His alienation found expression in the expectation that in the impending moment of transcendence, "philosophers" like himself would bond with the uneducated mass in a community that canceled out the power of education and property. But this was merely a symbolic bonding, projected across an immense social chasm. In the more than two decades since his removal from his family, the village weaver's son had been thoroughly inducted into educated culture.

As intoxicated as Fichte was with his own power to unmask, he was not entirely removed from the dense medium of ideology. If revolution meant an upheaval driven by the basic needs of the poor, then Fichte, like most of his contemporaries in the German intelligentsia, found it both unnecessary and illegitimate. It was unnecessary because orderly legal reform would make possible a kind of free moral agency that by its sheer release of human energy would overcome poverty. It was illegitimate

---

[48] Ibid., p. 212.

because need, however severe and however widespread, could not be the ground of moral action. Fichte shared with his fellow members of the educated elite an image of popular violence as the unleashing of selfish, bestial "passions" that threatened to destroy civilization, and hence an instinctive horror of "upheaval" from below. At this level of his thinking, Kantian moral theory, far from being the instrument of rational criticism, reinforced conventional antirevolutionary wisdom. To Fichte, as to Kant, the human will became truly free as it subordinated the motive force of material and psychological need to the imperatives of self-discipline and not as it acquired the capacity to satisfy need.

This did not, of course, prevent Fichte from defending the Revolution. Its popular violence, he suggested, had been provoked from outside; in any case it was irrelevant to the Revolution's revelatory significance. But the underlying issue that Rehberg (and Burke) had posed was whether violent "means" were the inevitable consequence of the Revolution's philosophical agenda. In the *Contribution* Fichte largely side-stepped the issue; he could neither justify violent means nor explain how, in the face of entrenched interests and their ideological defenses, the Revolution's philosophical agenda could be realized without violence. This dilemma provided another reason for anonymity, as he acknowledged to Kant in September, 1793. In the *Contribution* he had "denounced many injustices with complete frankness and zeal"; but he was "not yet so far as to have proposed means for correcting them without disorder."[49]

Even if we bracket out the issues of poverty and violence and focus on Fichte's vision of revolution as rebirth, the *Contribution* can be said to have reached an impasse. The purpose of the essay was, in his own words, to fuse "Kantian thoroughness" with "socratic popularity."[50] Radicalizing the conventional notion of popularity, Fichte aspired to break through the social inhibitions in eighteenth-century concepts of a *Publikum*. He would do so by denying privileged authority to educational credentials as well as to "birth" and wealth, so that the educated and propertied elite would be absorbed into a socially inclusive and emphatically egalitarian sphere of public communication. As the *Contribution* grew, however, this rhetorical experiment proved to be largely a commitment in principle, not a sustained practice. Appeals to the common man gave way to an elaborate exercise in deductive reasoning from Kant's a priori principles. The reader has to keep his bearings through a painstaking reconstruction of the progression from the state of nature to a social contract, and thence to the creation of a state. He then finds himself on an ambitious excursion into the historical origins of the nobility's manorial rights. Logical intricacy borders on convolution in the last chapter; the a priori analysis of

---

[49] GA, III, I: 431–2   [50] Fichte, *Beitrag*, p. 43.

the confessional churches as contractual communities occasions still
another historical detour, this time on ecclesiastical endowments. Having
begun as an experiment in egalitarian transparency, designed to bypass the
educated elite, the *Contribution* ended by exhausting the patience of most
of its educated readers. The voice of the philosopher-tribune had been
smothered by philosophical (and historical) thoroughness.

Fichte's parting gestures acknowledged this rhetorical breakdown,
though he considered his readers at least as much to blame as he was. He
would continue the essay, he announced at the end of the first installment, only if "the public disproves in fact the usual objection that for a
long time it will not be mature enough for such investigations."[51] Having
presented his inner self to the judgment of his readers, he was now putting
his readers on trial. By the time he wrote the postscript to the second
installment, they seemed to have failed the test. Responding to the "many
complaints about the obscurity of the first volume," he upbraided readers
for their "flightiness and distractedness." "Philosophical investigations"
aspiring to "thoroughness" could not be "read through as easily as a
modish novel, or travel accounts, or even philosophical investigations built
on the conventional system of opinion." While he would "take care to
write more intelligibly," the public might likewise "take care to read more
attentively."[52] He had assumed the antagonistic posture toward the reading
public that he would retain for the rest of his career.

In another sense, though, the *Contribution* reached an impasse because
it carried eighteenth-century thinking about a *Publikum* to its extreme
but logical conclusion. The "public" would constitute itself as a collective
conscience with unimpeachable moral authority. Its objectivity derived
from the fact that – and here is one of the central paradoxes of eighteenth-century rationalism – each of its members contributed to it from
the inner sanctum of his (or her?) conscience. Hence print was assigned
the awesome role of effecting a purely human exchange, at once intimate
and public. The ideal print relationship suspended all social distinctions
and removed all socially distorted lenses, so that each participant in the
public forum could contribute his judgments from a position of unconditional cognitive and moral autonomy. This ideal had taken shape in
reaction against the old-regime corporate hierarchy, with its intricate
gradations of status and public authority and its myriad vertical ties of
patronage and deference, paternalism and dependence. *Das Publikum*
evoked a normative standard for the free circulation of rational criticism,
a utopia pointing to the human possibilities that ideology dismissed as
impossible.[53]

---

[51] Ibid., p. 118.   [52] Ibid., p. 213.

[53] Charles Taylor aptly describes this imagined public as "a kind of metatopical space," allowing "a discourse of reason outside power, which nevertheless is normative for power"; "Liberal Politics and
the Public Sphere," in Charles Taylor, *Philosophical Arguments* (Cambridge, Mass., 1995): 264–6. See

In Burke's indictment, of course, the ideal was utopian in the pejorative sense; it was a mere fantasy, irrelevant to the real world of politics. For Burke politics was and always would be about interests and power. The issue was not "liberty" in the abstract, but how power was used. What was "natural" about the British social hierarchy and political constitution was the capacity to produce "harmony" out of the "opposition of interests," the "reciprocal struggle of discordant powers."[54] "A certain quantum of power," Burke observed, "must always exist in the community, in some hands, and under some appellation."[55] Burke was open to the charge of whitewashing vested interests, but his polemic against radicalism was well aimed. Was rationalist criticism not a kind of ideological self-deception? Did it not excuse itself from acknowledging its own aspiration to power? And did it not deprive itself of any way of coming to terms with power in any form?[56]

To Fichte "politics" was indeed about interests and the power needed to satisfy them, and that was precisely why it was morally repugnant. Revolution as collective moral rebirth would eliminate interests and power from human relationships. Once governments turned to promoting "culture for freedom," the machine would become "more and more simple," until it had nearly disappeared. As society approached "the highest unanimity of attitudes," there would be less and less contestation about rights.[57] It was not simply that Fichte imagined a post-breakthrough world in which contestation – the "play" of power – would be reduced to the point of near extinction. His vision allowed no room for the play of power in the breakthrough itself – and hence no way to think of revolution as a social process. Ideology, after all, is not simply distortion. It produces the symbolic representations – the justifications of "interest" – that bind individuals into social collectivities and effect change through contestation.[58] It was precisely this kind of social bonding and political mobilization that

also Jürgen Habermas, *The Structural Transformation of the Public Sphere. An Inquiry into a Category of Bourgeois Society*, trans. Thomas Burger (1962: Cambridge, Mass., 1989), esp. pp. 89–117, 159–75, and Terry Eagleton, *The Function of Criticism. From 'The Spectator' to Post-Structuralism* (London, 1984), pp. 9–27. Also relevant are Lucian Hölscher, "Öffentlichkeit," in *Geschichtliche Grundbegriffe*, vol. 4: 433–53; Keith Michael Baker, "Public Opinion as Political Invention," in Baker, *Inventing the French Revolution. Essays on French Political Culture in the Eighteenth Century* (Cambridge, 1990), pp. 167–99; Mona Ozouf, "L'opinion publique," in Keith Michael Baker, ed., *The French Revolution and the Creation of Modern Political Culture*, vol. 1: *The Political Culture of the Old Regime* (Oxford, 1987), pp. 419–34.

[54] Burke, *Reflections*, pp. 91, 122.   [55] Ibid., p. 248.

[56] The classic statement of these issues is Reinhart Koselleck, *Critique and Crisis. Enlightenment and the Pathogenesis of Modern Society* (1959: Cambridge, Mass., 1988). See also Alexis Philonenko, *Théorie et praxis dans la penseé morale et politique de Kant et de Fichte en 1793* (1968: Paris, 1976), p. 116. Philonenko blames the failure of the *Contribution* on Fichte's radically individualistic and anti-empirical moral theory, which prevented him from using Rousseau's theory of the General Will to construct a "positive principle" for political community.

[57] Fichte, *Beitrag*, pp. 76–80.

[58] Ricoeur, *Ideology and Utopia*, pp. 1–18, 254–66.

Fichte's appropriation of Kantianism *à outrance*, with its intensely personal expectation of power-free intellectual exchange and emotional communion, did not allow.

If Fichte's vision of a "public" was defiantly egalitarian, it was also radically individualistic. Committed to a purist version of an eighteenth-century ideal, he could not emulate the French Jacobin leadership and apotheosize the collective power of the masses as the unitary Will of "the People" (or "the Nation"), pitted against selfish "interests." At the same time, though, he could not regard the straightforward assertion of "interest" by particular social collectivities as a positive force for change. Hence his third way – a scenario of one-by-one withdrawal, as each individual, in the privacy of his conscience, decided to abrogate his contract with the state. If and when those who had seceded entered a contract to form a new state, "the revolution, at the time encompassing only a part, (was) completed." The revolution was not a collective seizure of political power but an individual withrawal from it.[59]

It was above all in the *form* of the *Contribution* that this self-constriction became manifest. Fichte was entranced by the power of revelation, of pure reason operating through the "colors" of the French Revolution and the metaphors of the philosopher-tribune. In his vision of an egalitarian public, revelatory power pierced through ideological encrustations and prompted the transcendent turn inward. But the power that dissolved existing solidarities could not forge new ones. If the new rhetoric was to constitute a Heliopolis of moral freedom and equality, it had to be pure. Even as the socratic philosopher sought to reconnect with the masses, he implicitly condemned the kind of rhetorical ascendancy that impels collective action. The revelatory power of the Revolution – its refraction of pure reason through a historical moment – could not legitimately become the symbolic power of ideology.

"If the times and circumstances summoned him," Lessing once observed, the philosopher was tempted to join those who "swarm[ed] for the rights of mankind."[60] Fichte bore witness to the temptation in the *Contribution*, but resisted it. He was no *Schwärmer*, since he could not, in good conscience, aspire to "make a swarm."

---

[59] Fichte, *Beitrag*, pp. 113, 118. Other Kantians had other ways out of the same dilemma. Johann Benjamin Erhard, for example, held out the theoretical possibility that a popular "insurrection" could achieve a "moral" revolution, but only if it embodied the "unanimity" that "proceed[ed] from universally valid principles." Johann Benjamin Erhard, *Ueber das Recht des Volks zu einer Revolution, und andere Schriften*, ed. Hellmut G. Haasis (1795: Munich, 1970), pp. 59, 90–7.

[60] Lessing, "Ueber eine zeitige Aufgabe," pp. 299–300.

Chapter 5

Jews, Christians, and Freethinkers

Fichte's *Contribution* did not join Burke's *Reflections* and Paine's *The Rights of Man* among the classics of western political thought. He had taken a clumsy and ill-timed plunge into the debate about the Revolution, and it landed him in a thicket of issues he could not resolve. If the essay as a whole did not make a lasting impression, however, it included one small patch of writing – a single substantial paragraph, with a footnote of roughly equal length – that has become justly notorious. The paragraph was occasioned by Fichte's need to counter a possible objection to his radical version of contract theory. If individuals were free to abrogate unilaterally their contract with the state, would the result not be a proliferation of "states within the state"?

The phrase "state within a state" carried a heavy freight of alarmist stereotypes. It brought to mind the French Huguenots and other sectarian minorities, whose refusal to accept state sovereignty was seen to have occasioned bloody civil wars. In the eighteenth century, freemasonry and its occultist offsprings were also vulnerable to the charge of forming states within the state. Their cult of secrecy, and indeed their very existence outside the corporate hierarchy and seemingly beyond the reach of absolutist authority, provoked fear of potential civil disorder. Redeploying the phrase to serve his radical critique of the old regime, Fichte in effect turned the tables on defenders of the status quo. He reminded his readers that the corporate hierarchies of old-regime Europe already accommodated numerous states within the state, all busily abusing their privileges to exploit outsiders. Cases in point were army officers, the nobility, the Protestant and Catholic clergies, and the craft guilds.[1]

It is Fichte's discussion of his first example, the "powerful hostile-minded state" formed by international "Jewry" (*Judentum*), that is likely to send a shudder through the modern reader. In the midst of an impassioned Kantian appeal for a new order of human rights, legal equality, and individual freedom, Fichte denounced the Jews as an inveterately depraved people who would "tread . . . other *Bürger* entirely under foot"

---

[1] Johann Gottlieb Fichte, *Beitrag zur Berichtigung des Publikums über die französische Revolution*, in Fichte, *Schriften zur Revolution*, ed. Bernard Willms (Cologne and Opladen, 1967), pp. 113–17. On the background to Fichte's use of the phrase "state within a state," see Jacob Katz, "A State within a State. The History of an Anti-Semitic Slogan," in Katz, *Emancipation and Assimilation: Studies in Modern Jewish History* (Farnborough, Hamps. England, 1972), pp. 47–76.

if they were granted civil rights. Far from seeing Jews as victims of discrimination, Fichte castigated them for choosing to remain in arrogant segregation from Christian society. Committed by the very nature of their religion to "hatred of the entire human species" and engaged in "petty trade" that was "deadening for any noble feeling," Jews could not be expected to stop plundering their Christian neighbors. Granting them civil rights would only make Christians more vulnerable to their spoliations. The only guarantor against that danger – and here Fichte penned his most notorious comment – was "to cut off all their heads in one night and replace them with others in which there is not a single Jewish idea."[2] It was a sledgehammer attempt at humor, meant to punctuate his conviction that Jewish depravity was virtually ineradicable. Written in 1793, as heads were rolling under the guillotine in revolutionary France, the remark exhibited Fichte's penchant for verbal brutality.

Fichte's diatribe is regarded, with good reason, as a particularly ominous marker of the transition from old-style Christian "Jew-hatred" to the more secular but no less pernicious antisemitism of the modern era. This pivotal significance was flagged as early as 1794 in *Eisenmenger der Zweite*, a pamphlet devoted to refuting Fichte's (and, to some degree, Kant's) characterizations of Judaism. The fact that Fichte's antagonist was Saul Ascher, a twenty-seven-year-old book dealer and publicist in Berlin, is not without its ironies. From a well-established and fairly affluent family in the Jewish community of the Prussian capital, Ascher had acquired a secular education in German as well as in French and English. He was one of the younger members of the generation of intellectuals who gave the Jewish Enlightenment of Berlin (the *Haskala*) a more radical coloration in the late 1780s and early 1790s.[3] Seeking a way to retain his Jewish identity while participating in a secular public culture, Ascher called for a thorough reform of his religious community, one that would pull Judaism out of what he regarded as its ghettoized backwardness, into the mainstream of a progressive German learned culture. He shared with Fichte a great admiration for Kant and a conviction that "superstition" would disappear as religion returned to its essence, the purely rational morality distilled in Kant's philosophy. In 1788, in a pamphlet on the "civic improvement of the Jews," Ascher had argued that the corruption of

[2] Fichte, *Beitrag*, pp. 113–17.
[3] Saul Ascher, *Eisenmenger der Zweite: Nebst einer vorgesetzten Sendschreiben an den Herrn Professor Fichte in Jena* (Berlin, 1794). On Ascher see esp. Ellen Littmann, "Saul Ascher, First Theorist of Progressive Judaism," *Leo Baeck Institute Year Book* 5 (1960): 107–13; Walter Grab, "Saul Ascher. Ein Jüdisch-Deutscher Spätaufklärer zwischen Revolution und Restauration," *Jahrbuch des Instituts für Deutsche Geschichte* 6 (1977): 131–78. See also Steven M. Lowenstein, *The Berlin Jewish Community. Enlightenment, Family, and Crisis, 1770–1830* (New York and Oxford, 1994), pp. 35, 207. Lowenstein describes Ascher's father as "just rich enough to fit into the upper tax bracket of Berlin Jewry" (p. 35).

Judaism was not attributable to nature or to tendencies inherent in the Jewish religion, but to centuries of discrimination. Four years later, in his *Leviathan*, he had called for a moral purification of Judaism, a repudiation of the "machinelike" legal and ritual formalism of rabbinical Orthodoxy under the guidance of Kantian principles.[4]

Fichte and Ascher had something else in common: they were relegated to the fringes of German public life, and they blamed the orthodox obscurantism of their respective religions for keeping them marginalized. In *Leviathan* Ascher conveyed his frustration with an exercise in historical sociology – grossly oversimplified, to be sure, but indicative of his awareness of larger debates in the late eighteenth century about the role of an increasingly complex division of labor in forming modern economic and civic life. Preoccupied with obeying the Law in all its Talmudic and rabbinical intricacy, Judaism had not been able to develop a civil society based on a specialized division of labor. The Law had made it impossible to give priority to socially legitimated work over the detail of ritual observance. As a result, Ascher argued, Judaism, unlike other religious cultures, had required a choice between "religion" and the pursuit of a "calling" as a *Bürger*. Men like himself – the "reformed" or "so-called freethinkers" – found themselves in a painful dilemma. If they failed to honor the Law when it interfered with their professional obligations, they would be "despised" by their coreligionists; if they oberved the Law to the letter, they could not practice a profession. The solution – the only hope for Ascher and like-minded men, who wished to be both Jews and *Bürger* – was to shed the "old constitution" of the Law and reduce Judaism to its core beliefs.[5]

And so in 1793, when the *Contribution* appeared, these two young freethinkers found themselves in similarly ambivalent positions; they were both alienated from the religious communities with which they still identified. When Ascher challenged Fichte a year later, however, he did not speak as one outsider to another. By then Fichte had received his appointment to a university position at Jena. Ascher began his pamphlet by profiling himself as an "autodidact" who was daring to upbraid the "Professor of Philosophy" for his "eccentric" thinking. Having opened with an outsider's mock gesture of humility, he proceeded to critique Fichte's diatribe sentence by sentence; and then, after taking on Kant as well, albeit more cautiously, he charged Fichte with introducing a "Jew-hatred from principles."[6]

It was this reformulation of an ancient prejudice that Ascher wanted to convey by dubbing Fichte a second Eisenmenger. The reference was

[4] Saul Ascher, *Bermerkungen über die bürgerliche Verbesserung der Juden, veranlasst bei der Frage: soll der Jude Soldat werden?* (Frankfurt/Oder, 1788); Ascher, *Leviathan, oder Ueber Religion in Rücksicht des Judenthums* (Berlin, 1792).

[5] Ascher, *Leviathan*, pp. 128–9, 219–27. [6] Ascher, *Eisenmenger*, pp. xviii–ix, 92.

to Johann Andreas Eisenmenger's *Judaism Uncovered* (*Entdecktes Judentum*), a work published nearly a century earlier in 2,100 quarto pages. Eisenmenger had devoted his seemingly inexhaustible scholarly energy to the traditional Christian obsession with converting Jews; his onslaught of quotations from Hebrew, Aramaic, and Arabic sources was meant to effect conversions by proving that Judaism abounded in absurd superstitions and licensed and indeed commanded grossly immoral behavior toward Christians (including ritual murder).[7] While Ascher meant his title to recall this legacy of religious prejudice and persecution, his more urgent purpose was to expose the new kind of victimization Jews were facing in a secularizing age. He wrote from a deep sense of disappointment. Having expected Kantianism to purify his own religion, as it was purifying Protestantism, he now saw it becoming a vehicle for excluding Judaism from the Enlightenment's ideal of "humanity." "There is evolving before our eyes," he warned, "an entirely new species of opponents, who are armed with more fearful weapons than their predecessors."[8] Kant himself had launched a secular logic of antisemitism, grounded in philosophical principles of morality rather than in religious beliefs or political considerations; and now one of his young disciples was spinning out its implications in a "consequential system of intolerance." Once Judaism was identified as "the antinomy of [the Kantian] critical principle of religion," "the rightness of the idea of Jew-hatred [could] be deduced a priori." Precisely because the new Jew-hater was so confident that he was operating within a "rational system," he did not have to ask himself whether his image of Judaism as "evil" perpetuated an irrational bias. Thus he could avoid feeling guilty. He had a new and eminently philosophical reason for convicting Judaism of perversely blind stubbornness. The crime of the Jews lay not in rejecting Christianity but in remaining indifferent and indeed hostile to the Kantian moral ideal of rational autonomy. From this standpoint Judaism was the example par excellence of misanthropic and "slavish" prejudice, so deeply rooted as to be virtually ineradicable, and hence undeserving of the toleration to which an enlightened age was committed in principle.[9]

Ascher's pamphlet exposed an ominous but seductive logic, already apparent in Kant's thought but far more pronounced in Fichte's, that passed off irrational bigotry as the legitimate and indeed necessary corollary to a commitment to moral universalism. Largely ignored in its own era, the pamphlet has a prominent place in a recent reinterpretation of German antisemitism. The interpretation proceeds from the assump-

[7] On Eisenmenger's book, see Jacob Katz, *From Prejudice to Destruction: Anti-Semitism, 1700–1933* (Cambridge, Mass., 1980), pp. 13–22; David Charles Smith, "Protestant Anti-Judaism in the German Emancipation Era," *Jewish Social Studies* 36 (1974): 205–07.
[8] Ascher, *Eisenmenger*, pp. 34–35.   [9] Ibid., pp. 78–81.

tion that the "inner psychological structure" of antisemitism, though basically the same everywhere, has manifested itself in different national cultures in different ways. The modern German variation – a uniquely virulent one – has been the ideology of "revolutionism," which has been hard to identify because it defies the usual political labeling from "left" to "right." Revolutionism has its roots in the eschatology of the Lutheran Reformation, with its vision of the Jews as a perversely "blind" people whose sufferings were the just punishment for their sin of deicide and with its conviction that mankind could not be fully redeemed until the Jews were converted. It was above all German "philosophical" revolutionism that gave these themes a new lease on life and indeed made them central to a rapidly secularizing culture. Ascher's pamphlet points us to the key figures in this development: Kant, whose hostility to Judaism was integral to a new vision of secular redemption, and Fichte, whose diatribe in the *Contribution* articulates for the first time "a new kind of revolutionary Jew-hatred" with a political bite. It is also in Fichte's text that we see the beginnings of the "anticapitalist" impulse in modern antisemitism, which became central to revolutionist agendas for the redemption of humanity through the regeneration of Jewry. The very brutality of Fichte's language – one thinks of his remark about cutting off heads – points to the long-term implication of this ideology. One way or another, Judaism had to cease to exist. Regeneration meant extinction.[10]

There is something salutary about singling out Fichte's anti-Jewish outburst and about insisting on its significance in the long-term history of continuity and change in antisemitic ideology. In political theory and the history of philosophy, virtually all the literature on Fichte's *Contribution*, including the best recent scholarship, simply ignores the diatribe as irrelevant to Fichte's contribution as a philosopher. The fact that the Jew-hatred of the *Contribution* is largely absent from Fichte's later writings does not justify this neglect.[11] Even if he later shed or at least

---

[10] Paul Lawrence Rose, *German Question/Jewish Question: Revolutionary Antisemitism from Kant to Wagner* (Princeton, N.J., 1992), esp. pp. 18–19, 117–32. For correctives to Rose's interpretation of Fichte's antisemitism, cf. Katz, *From Prejudice to Destruction*, pp. 54–6, Karl Menges, "Another Concept in the 'Sonderweg'-Debate? P. L. Rose's 'Revolutionary Antisemitism' and the Prehistory of the Holocaust," *German Studies Review* 28: 2 (May, 1995): 291–314, and Paul R. Sweet, "Fichte and the Jews: A Case of Tension between Civil Rights and Human Rights," *German Studies Review* 16 (1993): 37–48, which focuses on Fichte's role in a controversy about a Jewish student in the newly founded University of Berlin in 1811–12. See also Erich Fuchs, "Fichte's Stellung zum Judentum," F-S 2 (1990): 160–77. Anthony J. La Vopa, "Jews and Germans: Old Quarrels, New Departures," *Journal of the History of Ideas* (1993): 677–82, includes a critique of Rose's book.

[11] The major exception is an unpublished manuscript from 1807. See Richard Schottky, "Fichtes Nationalstaatsgedanke auf der Grundlage unveröffentlichter Manuskripte von 1807," F-S 2 (1990): 116.

moderated the prejudice, it was an integral part of his thought in 1793. Though it was not a view peculiar to him, it cannot be neatly detached from the philosophical core of his text as a merely borrowed and therefore historically incidental element. Saul Ascher's warning was on the mark. In Fichte's hands, the anti-Jewish logic of Kantian ethics did acquire a new momentum – and that means that his diatribe, as anomalous as it proved to be within his own corpus, *is* an especially regrettable signpost in the modern secularization of a religious prejudice.

To explain the diatribe as an expression of German philosophical "revolutionism," however, is to grossly oversimplify and in some ways to distort its historical meaning. The characterization of Fichte as a German "revolutionist" does, to be sure, require us to think about his pivotal role in the evolution of a discourse; but it also detaches the diatribe from the intellectual substance and the rhetorical properties of the *Contribution*. We lose sight of the historically specific meanings Fichte gave to the concept of philosophical redemption in 1793 and we ignore the dense field of other eighteenth-century discourses through which he plotted his philosophical argument. Indeed, if we accept the notion that Fichte's Jew-hatred marks the deep structure of a national psyche, we abandon specific historical contexts for a flight into a kind of psychocultural metahistory. We cannot grasp the contextual meaning of Fichte's words by thinking of him simply as a German, or even as a typical German intellectual. Like Ascher's rebuttal, Fichte's argument reflects an intellectual's marginal status and conflicted relationship to both his religious community of origin and the secular world of Enlightenment culture.

What grievances fueled Fichte's outburst? What ambivalences does it betray? If we bring these questions to Fichte's antisemitism, the diatribe becomes a coda on the themes of the *Contribution*, albeit an unintentional one, remarkable more for its dissonances than for its harmonic resolutions. Fichte's indictment of the Jews is revealing on two scores: as a locus for the central dichotomies that structured his larger argument, and as a particularly sensitive register of the tensions he could not resolve.

★ ★ ★

To a degree this moment in the *Contribution* marks a larger set of tensions in the German Enlightenment.

If Fichte's anti-Jewish rhetoric was categorical, it nonetheless had an unmistakably apologetic and faintly paranoid undertone. Having spewed forth his venom in the text, he tried to assume the posture of detached observer in the footnote. He felt compelled to insist that he had every right to speak his mind on the Jewish issue, however much he might displease "certain learned tribunals" that had taken up the cause of Jewish emancipation. Those who "[spoke] sugar-sweet words of tolerance and human rights and civil rights" could rest assured that "the poisonous breath of intolerance [was] as far removed from these pages as it [was] from [his] heart."[12]

Fichte's mix of outspoken conviction and thinly veiled defensiveness is understandable against the backdrop of the previous several decades. During Fichte's boyhood and youth, centuries-old hostilities and barriers between Jews and Germans had begun to erode, only to open new channels for prejudice. In the middle decades of the eighteenth century, the scattered Jewish communities of the German lands were still an alien presence, corporatelike in their extensive self-governance but relegated to an anomalous status outside the webs of mutual obligation and the calibrations of "honor" in a Christian corporate hierarchy. Jews were segregated from the majority culture by their religion and its sacred languages; by the exegetic intricacies of Talmudic law and ritual; by their use of Yiddish as a daily language; by their relegation to ghettos (and by the special taxes they still had to pay for the "privilege" of residing in them). There was a thin upper crust of court bankers and affluent merchants, but the great majority of Jews occupied a shadowy world of peddling, used-clothes dealing, and small-time money-lending – the world whose reputation for "haggling" and cheating was evoked with the term "petty trade" (*Kleinhandel*).

And yet in 1762, the year of Fichte's birth, the Berlin Academy of Sciences had awarded first prize in its essay contest on "evidence in metaphysics" to the young Jewish scholar and philosopher Moses Mendelssohn. Such an act would have been unthinkable nineteen years earlier, when Mendelssohn, the fourteen-year-old son of a scribe, had entered Berlin steeped in Talmudic scholarship but penniless and largely unversed in German. Over the next two decades, as Mendelssohn had mastered the serene abstractions of German philosophical discourse and had won acceptance among the luminaries of the Berlin Enlightenment, he had become something of a celebrity in educated Germany. He was living proof that a Jew, and indeed a Jew committed to the ritual observances of Jewish law, could also be a full-fledged citizen of the German republic of letters. His friendship with Lessing, the intellectual hero of Fichte's youth, seemed to herald a new era of enlightened tolerance in Jewish-Gentile relations. By the time Mendelssohn died in 1786, a Jewish Enlightenment was well under way in Berlin and several other German cities. Its younger generation of teachers, scholars, and publicists, Ascher among them, were questioning whether the faithfulness to the Mosaic Law that Mendelssohn had so strenuously defended was in fact compatible with their goal of integrating Judaism into a new German public culture.[13]

---

[12] Fichte, *Beitrag*, p. 115.
[13] See esp. Jonathan I. Israel, *European Jewry in the Age of Mercantilism, 1550–1750* (rev. ed.: Oxford, 1989), pp. 237–62; David Sorkin, *The Transformation of German Jewry, 1780–1840* (New York, 1987),

Mendelssohn had remained acutely aware that Jews like himself, strad-
dling two worlds that were still largely walled off from each other, had
put themselves in a highly vulnerable position. To a degree, in fact, he
had anticipated Ascher's warning. The rationale for oppressing Jews was
changing, he had observed in 1782, as religious superstition acceded to
"philosophical prejudices." Once charged with desecrating crucifixes and
knifing Christian children, Jews were now shut out of useful crafts, trades,
and scholarly disciplines on the grounds that they lacked "moral feeling"
and "culture." Fichte's diatribe offered a particularly alarming confirmation that the logic of intolerance was indeed undergoing this mutation.[14]
It is a measure of his compulsion to antagonize that he came very close
to smearing the icon of Mendelssohn that Lessing had done so much to
fashion and that the older generation of *Aufklärer* cherished. When Fichte
expressed doubt that any Jew could "[push] through *to general love of justice,
humanity, and truth,* through the fixed, one might say, insurmountable
entrenchments that lie before him," Mendelssohn inevitably came to
mind.[15]

Fichte's direct though unnamed target was Christian Wilhelm Dohm,
a young diplomat in the Prussian service and a gifted writer in the
cause of enlightened reform. In 1781, partly as a gesture of friendship
to Mendelssohn, Dohm had published *On the Civic Improvement of the
Jews,* the first extensive brief for Jewish emancipation. He built his case
on the very premise that Fichte flatly rejected: that Jewish corruption
was the product of environmental conditions, and that therefore a reform
of those conditions – the emancipation of Jews from their pariah status
– would result in their regeneration. The emancipation of the Jews, he
contended, would multiply state resources by creating a new class of
productive *Bürger.*[16] Dohm's book crystallized a growing sense in the

pp. 61–78. Sorkin emphasizes that the *Haskala* was not simply a response to the German Enlightenment but also the product of reform sentiment generated within the Jewish community, and
that emancipation created a subculture rather than an "assimilated" group. He has summarized his
very persuasive revisionism in "Emancipation and Assimilation. Two Concepts and Their Application to German-Jewish History," *Leo Baeck Institute Year Book* 35 (1990): 17–39, and "The Impact
of Emancipation on German Jewry: A Reconsideration," in Jonathan Frankel and Steven J. Zip-
perstein, eds., *Assimilation and Community. The Jews in Nineteenth-Century Europe* (Cambridge, 1992),
pp. 177–98. On Mendelssohn, see Alan Arkush, *Moses Mendelssohn and the Enlightenment* (Albany,
N.Y., 1994), and for a fresh view of Mendelssohn as a Jewish scholar and reformer, David Sorkin,
Moses Mendelssohn and the Religious Enlightenment (Berkeley, Calif., 1996).

[14] Mendelssohn's introduction (1782) to Menasseh Ben Israel's *Rettung der Juden,* in *Moses Mendelssohn's
gesammelte Schriften,* ed. Georg Benjamin Mendelssohn, 7 vols. (Leipzig, 1843–45), 3, pp. 182–3.
[15] Fichte, *Beitrag,* p. 115.
[16] Christian Konrad Wilhelm von Dohm, *Über die bürgerliche Verbesserung der Juden* (1781: Hildesheim
and New York, 1973). On Dohm, see Klaus Epstein, *The Genesis of German Conservatism*
(Princeton, N.J., 1966), pp. 220–9; Horst Möller, "Aufklärung, Judenemanzipation und Staat:
Ursprung und Wirkung von Dohms Schrift . . . ," Walter Grab, ed., *Deutsche Aufklärung und Judenemanzipation, Jahrbuch des Instituts für Deutsche Geschichte,* Beiheft 3 (Tel Aviv, 1979), pp. 119–53.

ranks of German academe and officialdom that the pariah status of Jews had become an anachronism and that legal reform was overdue. Just a few months after the book had appeared, Joseph II had decreed a partial emancipation of Jews under Habsburg rule. In 1792 the Prussian government would grant Jews complete freedom of worship and extend full rights of citizenship to selected families. In this area, as in so many others, revolutionary France followed the lead of the "enlightened" governments of old-regime Europe, though it acted far more consequentially. On September 27, 1791, the Constituent Assembly declared all French Jews to be full-fledged citizens of the newly constituted nation.[17]

Fichte was more than a little uncomfortable about flying in the face of a trend that epitomized enlightened progress to many of his elders and contemporaries. By rejecting "enlightened" arguments for Jewish emancipation, however, he was not defying the Enlightenment as a whole. Eighteenth-century rationalism produced its own species of intolerance, and the Jews were especially vulnerable targets. If a religion was "superstitious" to the extent that it preserved its traditional rituals and prescriptions, then Judaism, in its stereoptypical image, was hopelessly benighted. Since the late seventeenth century, in fact, English and French Deists had commonly blamed Jewish influence for the corruption of Christ's pure and eminently rational moral teaching. Squarely in this tradition was the response to Mendelssohn in 1784 by Johann Heinrich Schulz, a Lutheran pastor in East Prussia who published atheistic works anonymously. Schulz argued that if the Jews continued to observe the Law, as Mendelssohn had urged them to do, they would remain deeply hostile to and segregated from "humanity." It was in Judaism that "actual fanaticism [was] most at home." Other religions had become fanatical to the extent that they were "infected by the poison of the Mosaic religion." If Jews did not accept the "brotherly hands" that Christians were now extending to them, they would remain hated as "a particular state within the state."[18]

[17] See esp. Gary Kates, "Jews into Frenchmen: Nationality and Representation in Revolutionary France," in Ferenc Fehér, ed., *The French Revolution and the Birth of Modernity* (Berkeley, Calif., 1990), pp. 103–16.

[18] Johann Heinrich Schulz, *Philosophische Betrachtung über Theologie und Religion überhaupt und über die Juden insonderheit* (Frankfurt am Main, 1784), esp. pp. 210–15. On Schulz and the controversy surrounding him, see Epstein, *Genesis* pp. 147, 152, 364. Somewhat dated but still indispensable on Enlightenment antisemitism is Arthur Hertzberg, *The French Enlightenment and the Jews: The Origins of Modern Anti-Semitism* (New York, 1968). See also Frank E. Manuel, *The Broken Staff. Judaism through Christian Eyes* (Cambridge, Mass., 1992), pp. 175–221, 249–92; David Sorkin, "Jews, the Enlightenment, and Religious Toleration – Some Reflections," *Leo Baeck Institute Year Book* 37 (1992): 12–16; Peter Erspamer, *The Elusiveness of Tolerance: The "Jewish Question" from Lessing to the Napoleonic Wars* (Chapel Hill, N.C., 1997).

It may have been in Schulz's book that Fichte had first seen the phrase "state within a state" applied to the Jews. Though Schulz's language was unusually heated, he offered a stereotype of Judaism that echoed through the Enlightenment, from early philosophes like Voltaire to philosophers like Kant. The issue was whether Jews could or could not be "improved"; that they were in need of improvement, and indeed of thorough regeneration, seemed obvious to virtually all observers. Judaism seemed to embody corruption to an extreme, whether the corruption was to be explained as inherent to it or as the effect of discrimination. The anthropomorphic image of a misanthropic God; the tyrannical rabbinate; the empty formalism of Talmudic laws and rituals: all these stereotypical attributes made Judaism a particularly regrettable atavism. As an implication of their religious beliefs, or as an ironic result of their oppression, Jews were misanthropic. In either case, their misanthropy took the form of an ethical double standard in commercial relations; they treated Christians with a ruthlessness and mendacity they spared each other.

To the extent that Fichte broke with an "enlightened" consensus on Judaism, it was by taking sides in an argument *within* the Enlightenment. He joined a small chorus of rationalists who had found Dohm's brief for Jewish emancipation wrongheaded. The most prominent of them was Johann David Michaelis, a renowned professor of "oriental" studies at Göttingen and a pioneer of the new biblical criticism. In 1783 – ten years before Fichte protested that if Jews were granted legal equality, Christians would be all the more vulnerable to their commercial exploitation – Michaelis had issued the same warning in an extensive critique of Dohm's book. He had also anticipated Fichte in observing that by persisting in their dietary proscriptions, Jews excluded themselves from a critical mode of participation in human fellowship.[19]

In a sense, then, Fichte's observations about the Jews were unexceptional. His image of their religion was typical of the Enlightenment, and even in his rejection of emancipation he was simply committing himself to one side of an argument. And yet, in a debate abounding in shared prejudices, Fichte's contribution remains a particularly ugly performance. If Michaelis's tone was often supercilious and sarcastic, Fichte's was strident. Others opposed Jewish emancipation, but Fichte distinguished himself by the vehemence with which he blamed the Jews' own arrogance and misanthropy for their pariah status and pressed his conviction that they were irredeemable. Insisting that he was not motivated by "private animosity" and indeed that he had often protected Jews from

[19] Michaelis's review of Dohm's book has been reprinted in Dohm, *Über die bürgerliche Verbesserung*, Zweyter Theil, pp. 31–71. On Michaelis, see also Manuel, *The Broken Staff*, pp. 252–62; Anna-Ruth Löwenbrück, *Judenfeindschaft im Zeitalter der Aufklärung. Eine Studie zur Vorgeschichte des modernen Antisemitismus am Beispiel des Göttinger Theologen und Orientalisten Johann David Michaelis (1717–1791)* (Frankfurt am Main, 1995).

"teasing," he left no doubt that he was personally outraged by the prospect of Jews enjoying the rights of *Bürger*.[20] If we are to trace that outrage to its sources, we need to subject his indictment to closer scrutiny.

★ ★ ★

It is a truism that in its passage from the old regime to modernity, anti-semitism distilled and focused hostility to a rapidly expanding capitalist order and to the revolution in values capitalism seemed to require. Fichte's *Contribution* has been regarded as pivotal in part because it adumbrated a "new anti-capitalist Jew-hatred."[21] At first glance, the passages in question seem to confirm this view: Fichte's wrath is focused on dishonorable, exploitative Jewish "petty trade," and his warning is that emancipation will make Jewish exploitation all the worse.

But this reading obscures as much as it clarifies. It lifts Fichte's diatribe out of the overall argument of the *Contribution* and, as important, detaches it from the terms of the late-eighteenth-century controversy about the Jews. What it means to be anticapitalist depends on the definition of capitalism. If the defining characteristic is a free market in property and labor, then Fichte's vision of a new agrarian order was virtually utopian in its commitment *to* capitalism. If "capitalism" evokes a modern commercial society and its consumer culture, Fichte was emphatically anti-capitalist. His attack on the Jews was a point of intersection for these sentiments, and a highly revealing one. In 1793 there was nothing obviously contradictory about combining enthusiasm for capitalism in one guise with antipathy to it in another. Within Fichte's stock of values and ideas, the combination made eminent sense. This is not to deny that in the eyes of some observers, particularly in the Anglo-Scottish world, the free market, urban-based commercialism, and a new scale of consumerism were coming to seem inextricably linked. But Fichte would not begin to come to terms with this vision of the future until the turn of the century.

To appreciate the meaning of Fichte's pro-capitalist sentiments in 1793, one need only compare the *Contribution* to Dohm's *On the Civic Improvement of the Jews*. Dohm wrote as a government official as well as an *Aufklärer*. While he occasionally appealed to the principle of natural rights, his book was essentially an application of the paternalistic utilitarianism of the German Enlightenment, with its combination of "statist" and neocorporate logic. The way to tap the dormant human energies and resources of old-regime societies was not to tear down their corporate orders, but to modernize them – to create an adjusted hierarchy of corporations, each assigned its place by virtue of its relative "usefulness" (i.e., its functional contribution to the whole) rather than in recognition of

---

[20] Fichte, *Beitrag*, p. 115.   [21] Rose, *German Question/Jewish Question*, p. 18.

inherited legal privileges. It was the responsibility of the rationalizing state bureaucracy to effect this transformation and to maintain a dynamic equilibrium among the corporate parts. Dohm saw no reason that the Jews should not be allowed to remain a religious subculture with a large measure of communal self-government, so long as state-sponsored reforms curbed their penchant for usury and fraud, channeled many of them into the crafts and perhaps even into agriculture, and countered rabbinical influence with a new, "enlightened" education. "Improved" in these ways, an unusually industrious, quick-witted population would impart new energy to a dynamic order:

> The great and noble task of government consists of mitigating the principles of exclusivity of all these different societies in such a way that they do not become disadvantageous to the great social union (*Verbindung*) that comprises them; that each of these divisions serves only to stimulate rivalry and activity without producing aversion and separation; and that they all merge themselves into the great harmony of the state. Government allows to each of these particular societies its pride, and indeed its prejudices that are not harmful; but it strives to inculcate in every part more love for the state; and it will have attained its great objective when the nobleman, the peasant, the scholar, the Christian, and the Jew is, still more than all this, a *Bürger*.[22]

Dohm's achievement was to incorporate the cause of Jewish emancipation into the larger reform agenda of German rationalism. It was indicative of his allegiance to reform in this key that he made straightforward use of the machine metaphor to conceptualize the relationship between a rationalizing state and a modernized corporate hierarchy. One need only recall Fichte's image of the ruthless competition among the old-regime's dynastic states, each satisfying its greed for power *through* "the marvelous artifice of the subordination of the estates," to appreciate the intellectual chasm that separated him from Dohm. Dohm's fine-tuned machine was, in the eyes of this young Kantian, ·a monstrous juggernaut. Far from preventing excesses, state interest licensed and indeed dictated abuse of privilege and mutual exploitation from the top to the bottom of the corporate hierarchy. To Dohm, Jewish emancipation would enhance the machine's productive energy by adding a "useful" part; to Fichte, it would make the machine all the more oppressive.

There was something curiously ambivalent about Fichte's view of the Jews' special legal status. He believed that the state had in effect carried its manipulation of corporate solidarity to an extreme by harnessing Jewish commercial ruthlessness to its purposes; but it had also provided

---

[22] Dohm, *Über die bürgerliche Verbesserung*, p. 26. .

Christians a modicum of protection that they would lose if Jews were granted full rights as *Bürger*. More striking, though, is that in Fichte's eyes the essential problem posed by corporatism was cultural (or perhaps better, ideological), not legal. What the argument about the Jews threw into bold relief was the question whether corporate subcultures and a free-market economy were compatible. Dohm's vision of progress turned on the premise that they *were* compatible. To him it was in the interest of the state to encourage free-market competition and acquisitiveness to a degree. The state could do so safely because the individual energies released in free-market exchanges would flow through and remain socially constrained by a multitiered channel of corporate solidarities. In this perspective, modernized corporate subcultures – each prevented from degenerating into caste-like selfishness but otherwise perpetuating its unique ethos – were natural intermediate bodies, magnets pulling the energies of myriad individuals into the dynamic of the whole. Properly cleansed and reoriented, the Jewish commercial ethos would exert a powerful magnetic force.

To Fichte, on the other hand, that same Jewish ethos was a lethal force, and emancipation would make it all the more potent. His logic was, on one level, physiocratic. He expected the natural laws of the free market, and not the guiding hand of the state, to produce a dynamic equilibrium. Fichte was not alone, of course, in conceiving of the Jews as a commercial caste and hence as a threat to the free play of market forces. What was new and alarming was his philosophical variation on this theme. Precisely because this alien caste threatened to obstruct the market, it offended his Kantian vision of a new moral order. It was in the labor performed by free-market agents that Fichte had found the vehicle for moral self-realization, the way to achieve willed self-mastery in the struggle against physical and sensual nature. Seen in that light, free-market exchange promised an escape from the moral straightjackets of corporate privilege. It was also, like the free communication of ideas, the antidote to the ideologies that justified privilege in the political and social machines of the old regime. Where Dohm credited corporate subcultures (properly regulated) with generating social cohesion and insuring social order, Fichte blamed them for keeping ideological blinders on potentially free individuals. Hence it is not surprising that Fichte launched his attack on the Jews as part of a larger assault on "states within the state" and on the principle of corporate solidarity they embodied. Nor is it surprising that at this juncture his harshest words were reserved for the Jews. Like many of his contemporaries, he took it as fact that Jewish commerce operated on a double standard – that because of their conviction of enjoying a special relationship with God and because of the "hatred of the entire human race" their pariah status induced, Jews felt free to work in consort to exploit Christians. For Fichte there could be no more dramatic example of the power of ideology to rationalize the ruthless pursuit of corporate self-interest.

From one angle, then, Fichte saw Jewish commercial activity as the antithesis of free-market exchange and of the human liberation it seemed to promise. If *Judentum* was incompatible with capitalism in this sense, however, it represented the rampant spread of corruptive capitalism in another. As a village boy in Rammenau and as a denizen of the world of student poverty, Fichte had probably absorbed the animus against Jewish peddling and moneylending that pervaded his surroundings. By the time he wrote the *Contribution*, that animus had been incorporated into his economic diagnosis of the crisis gripping the old order. Encouraged by greedy states and fed by a hunger for "luxury" among landed proprietors, "the rampant trade of our era" was polarizing societies into the wealthy few and the great mass of poor.[23] In this vision, Jewish "petty trade" was not simply a vehicle for Jewish avarice; it formed one of the arteries through which urban-based commerce was poisoning rural society by satisfying its addiction to "luxury."

Here again Fichte was not entirely at odds with rationalist reformers like Dohm, though he rejected their larger conception of the proper relationship between society and the state. In Dohm's well-ordered machine, the craving for "luxury" – or, in modern economic terms, the spreading demand for consumer goods – would have to be kept in check; otherwise self-indulgence would sap the ethic of work discipline that drove the machine forward. Likewise the ethos of commerce, like any other corporate ethos, had tendencies that had to be curbed. Merchant capitalism, Dohm reminded his readers, was worlds removed from the simple life of the artisan. Relatively insulated from market fluctuations and content to uphold the "honor" of his modest station, the artisan had no reason to violate the boundaries of his limited expectations. The merchant, on the other hand, operated in a world of incessant risk and ruthless competition – a world in which the commercial ethos, left to itself, tended to degenerate into a calculating, small-minded obsession with profit, manifested in tasteless display. Trappped in the dark corners of commerce generation after generation, the Jews exhibited this tendency to an exaggerated degree.[24]

Dohm had juxtaposed a shop-worn stereotype of the parvenu merchant with a no less hackneyed idyll of the contented craftsman. He certainly meant well; his point was that Jewish greed and fraud were a matter of degree, an extreme case of a tendency inherent in commercial culture, and not a case of unique depravity. The ambivalence implicit to this position is in marked contrast to Mendelssohn's radically positive valuation of commerce in general and Jewish commerce in particular in his published

---

[23] See Chapter 3.   [24] Dohm, *Über die bürgerliche Verbesserung*, pp. 99–110.

comment on Dohm's book. One need only observe the vitality and the affluence of a city like Amsterdam, Mendelssohn observed, to realize that the "middlemen" in modern economic life had no need to apologize for their existence. Far from being "useless" parasites, as was often claimed, they were remarkably useful to both producers and consumers. Their productivity lay in facilitating the distribution of raw materials and in "spread[ing] the products of industry into all corners." Seen in this light, "the most insignificant Jewish trader (*Handelsjude*) is . . . no mere consumer (*Verzehrer*), but rather a useful resident (I dare not say *Bürger*) of the state, a true producer." If the state wanted to prevent middlemen from exploiting producers, it should stop licensing monopolies and instead create a completely free market that would automatically produce "equilibrium."[25]

Mendelssohn's apologia for middlemen merits more attention than it has received, and not just because it goes so far in challenging the age-old stereotype of Jewish petty trade as parasitical and dishonorable. Mendelssohn had mounted a spirited defense of the intricate division of labor and the pervasive consumerism in modern commercial societies and of the role of the free market in producing such societies. While Dohm had reservations about this vision of a capitalist world-in-the-making, Fichte could not accept it at all. That was in part because he subscribed to the physiocratic belief that in a healthy economy, urban-based commerce would remain secondary to agriculture. But again his Kantianism heightened his animus. In his version of the Kantian ideal, labor had ethical value to the extent that it advanced the individual's moral self-realization in a battle against the natural world and the natural self. This was an ideal that gave the farmer and the artisan a new ethical dignity; in so doing, it gave a new ethical force to the condemnation of parasitical commerce, particularly in its Jewish form, as a threat to their existence.

Even when Fichte thought of himself as a popular tribune, breaking through the figurative walls of the academic ghetto, he looked out on the economic world through the lens of his own caste and found something inherently dishonorable about the commercial pursuit of profit. It seemed obvious to him that Jewish petty trade was "deadening for any noble feeling," and hence that the walls of the real ghettos ought to remain standing. Kantianism – or, more precisely, the meaning Fichte found in Kantianism – reinforced this view. Fichte's ideal of freedom in work, rooted as it was in a Lutheran ethic, was a call to self-denial. It breathed a spirit of inner-worldly asceticism, radically at odds with Mendelssohn's affirmation of a world of commercial affluence and its spreading comforts.

★ ★ ★

[25] *Moses Mendelssohn's gesammelte Schriften*, vol. 3, pp. 188–93.

It was standard procedure in anti-Jewish discourse to ground a condemnation of the Jews' commercial ruthlessness in hostile stereotypes of their religious beliefs and practices. For Fichte, however, the religious issues posed by the Jews had intensely personal significance. They forced to the surface both the ambivalence and the outrage that marked his efforts to claim a place in German society.

When Fichte condemned the Jews' self-segregation, it was in the voice of a Christian addressing his coreligionists; and yet, when he protested the new toleration being extended to Jews in Christian states, he spoke as a persecuted "free thinker" (*Selbstdenker*). The shift in voice is revealing at several levels. Six years after drafting sermons that were barely muted self-justifications and a full three years after embracing Kantianism, Fichte remained deeply ambivalent about his relationship to his Lutheran heritage. The ambivalence was in part a matter of historical perspective. In the short term, Fichte counted himself among the victims of the new onslaught of Lutheran obscurantism that Woellner had launched. And yet he retained the virtually instinctive tendency of the eighteenth-century "enlightened" Lutheran to look back on the foundation of his church as a great leap forward in rational freedom. Even as he rejected the very principle of confessional religion, he continued to trace his intellectual lineage, via Kant, to Luther himself.

This double image reflected the dualities that ran through Fichte's new-found identity as a Kantian philosopher. His a priori critique of the status quo had an emphatically secular, and indeed in some senses anti-Christian, thrust; but the ethic that inspired that critique had tenacious Lutheran roots and vibrant Lutheran resonances. His aspiration to assert a public voice pulled him in two directions at once. He imagined himself a popular tribune, using print to effect the metasocial communion among morally autonomous individuals that confessional religion, by its very nature, precluded. At the same time, though, he shrunk back from the prospect of being excluded from the social solidarity and the collective belief of a concrete religious community. If his voice could not resonate through the emotionally charged symbols of such a community, would it not be a voice in the wilderness?

Fichte's yearning for inclusion in a Christian community of belief surfaces in his condemnation of the Jews' arrogant self-segregation. Here the use of "we" and "us" bonds him with his audience as a fellow Christian. Jewry is "separated by the most binding thing that humanity has – by its religion – from our meals, from our cups of joy (*Freudenbecher*), and from the sweet exchange with us from heart to heart."[26] The language virtually equates the human with the Christian. In the face of the Jewish presence, Fichte's Kantian reverence for "humanity" provides a new sanc-

---

[26] Fichte, *Beitrag*, p. 114.

tion for his ethnocentrism. The Jews, he implies, have no one but themselves to blame for their pariah status; they have placed themselves beyond
the pale of human love. That implication stands oddly juxtaposed to his
acknowledgment that the Jews, though undeserving of "civil rights,"
cannot be deprived of "human rights."

It struck Fichte as absurd that "loving tolerance" was extended toward
"those who do not believe in Jesus Christ," while "those who believe in
him" were "publicly curs[ed] and deprived" of "civil honor and bread
earned with dignity."[27] On one level, this reaction bore witness to Fichte's
residual Lutheranism. If he was a maverick, he could nonetheless identify
with his heritage by castigating the Jew as the Other, the alien in "our"
midst. But Fichte also spoke as a "freethinker," and he was outraged that
men like himself were being treated as pariahs while Jews were being
lifted out of their pariah status. The reference to victims of intolerance –
to those deprived of "civil honor" and "dignity" – was probably meant
to evoke the fate of Johann Heinrich Schulz, the controversial Lutheran
pastor and anonymous atheist who had publicly attacked Jewish "fanaticism" in 1784. Until 1786 clerical efforts to take disciplinary action against
Schulz had been blocked by Frederick the Great's unusually tolerant
Minister of Ecclesiastical Afairs. But in May 1792, Schulz had finally been
removed from office as the first clerical casualty of Woellner's crackdown.
It was a symptomatic and depressing turn of events to young men like
Fichte, who aspired to "have an effect" in the pulpit but were much
farther removed from confessional orthodoxy than their "enlightened"
elders.

Like Fichte's outburst nearly ten years later, Schulz's attack on Jewish
fanaticism in 1784 had marked his frustration as an outsider. Schulz had
been provoked not only by Mendelssohn's appeal to Jews to continue
their observance of the Law, but also by his argument that atheists, unlike
Jews, should not be given civic rights. He had found it outrageous that
a "philosopher" advocating toleration for his coreligionists, even as he
urged them to remain fanatics, could be so intolerant toward a humane
and open-minded freethinker like himself.[28] Fichte clearly identified
with Schulz; when he questioned his "enlightened" elders' image of
Mendelssohn as a living proof that Jews were redeemable, it was with a
similar sense of grievance. Where he differed from Schulz was in
the philosophical grounding of his animus toward Judaism. Schulz was a
rationalist of the old school – an outspoken advocate of materialist
determinism, intent on subjecting all received truths, including revelation,
to the "test of reason" and regarding Christ as a philosopher of pure moral
reason. Fichte's intolerance was grounded in Kant's a priori principle of
ethical freedom.

[27] Ibid., pp. 114–15. [28] Schulz, *Philosophische Betrachtung*, esp. pp. 208–24.

It was this connection that forced Saul Ascher to face up to the dark side of Kantianism. In *Eisenmenger der Zweite* Ascher could not bring himself to blame Kant for Fichte. But he did argue, out of a painful sense of disillusionment, that Kant's philosophy, for all its univeralist claims, had a deep Christian bias – and he was right.[29] Kant's dichotomy between autonomy and heteronomy reformulated Luther's distinction between "inner" freedom and "external" coercion; and in so doing it gave a new lease on life to the Lutheran stereotype of Judaism as a kind of anti-religion, negating the evangelical ideal of freedom by enforcing blind conformity to the Law. That implication was made abundantly clear in Kant's own *Religion within the Limits of Reason Alone*. Kant was intent on demonstrating that Christ's ethical teaching – his message that pure moral-ity was an inner act of ethical freedom – marked a radical departure from Jewish tradition. In fact Judaism was "not a religion at all" but rather a "political" theocracy, enforcing the "external compulsion" of a misan-thropic God and offering materialistic incentives to induce conformity to its "burdensome ceremonies and observances." Kant speculated that if Judaism nonetheless had become "ripe" for the Christian ethical "revolu-tion," that may have been because it had been penetrated by "the ethical doctrines of freedom of the Greek sages." To gain a foothold, however, Christianity had had to adapt itself to the "prejudices" of "men whose heads, filled with statutory dogmas, have been almost entirely unfitted for the religion of reason."[30]

In Kant's image, Judaism represented heteronomy with a vengeance. In Fichte's *Contribution*, the same image took its place in a justification of revolution as a revelatory moment. Fichte's God – the God whose "instructive signs" became visible in historical events like the French Revolution – was the Divine Pedagogue gradually guiding all of mankind to an awareness of "human right and human value." Stereotypes of Jews cringing before a misanthropic God and claiming an exclusive revelation as the Chosen People took on a new though still familiar eschatological meaning. Judaism in those guises was a direct affront to Fichte's secular-ized vision of a divine economy of revelation.

When Kant characterized Judaism as a "political" institution, he meant to evoke a world of arbitrary and coercive power, at the opposite pole from his ideal of an "ethical commonwealth" of morally pure intentions and power-free communion. Fichte's antisemitism turned on the same dichotomy; but in the eyes of this isolated freethinker, the dichotomy had a pointed immediacy. The new tolerance for Jews was not an expres-sion of true enlightenment; it was another case of the machine-state

[29] Ascher, *Eisenmenger*, pp. 66–80.
[30] Immanuel Kant, *Religion within the Limits of Reason Alone*, trans. and introd. Theodore M. Greene and Hoyt H. Hudson (New York, 1960), pp. 74, 116–18.

extending its arbitrary power through the ideological camouflage of paternalism. To a ruling elite fusing authoritarian statism and Lutheran obscurantism, it made sense to tolerate Judaism precisely because it *was* a "political" theocracy:

> Prevailing tolerance of Jews in states where there is no tolerance for free thinkers shows with crystal clarity what is actually intended. – The upholding of your belief is so dear to your paternal heart. Look at these Jews; they do not believe at all in Jesus Christ; that you must not allow; and yet I see that you overload them with kindness. – "Oh, they have superstitions, and that suffices for me. Believe in Zoroaster or Confucious, in Moses or Mohammed, in the Pope, Luther, or Calvin, it makes no difference to me; so long as you believe in an alien Reason (*fremde Vernunft*). But you want to have reason *yourself*, and that I will not allow. Be immature, or else you will grow to the level of my head."[31]

Here was, in Fichte's eyes, the bitter paradox of toleration. By its very willingness to extend toleration to Jews, the paternalism of the German states and their churches betrayed its despotic political agenda.

In the animus toward political power in Fichte's antisemitism, we see the two impulses that made it so difficult for him to settle into an identity and come to terms with his cultural patrimony. He claimed the privileged insight of the outsider, but he wanted somehow to remain an insider. His Lutheran heritage offered him the social solidarity and the symbolic density through which a public voice might resonate and "have an effect." But he wanted his voice to resonate on its own terms – as the voice of the distanced freethinker, dissenting from the community of belief that secured him against isolation.

---

[31] Fichte, *Beitrag*, p. 115.

Chapter 6

Love and Marriage

Johanna Fichte, née Rahn, has appeared frequently in this profile of the young Fichte, but only as one of several people to whom he confided his frustrations and ambitions.[1] Their courtship and the early years of their marriage merit more attention, and not simply, as so often happens in biographies, to complement the study of a public career with occasional glimpses into the private and the intimate. Fichte's relationship with Johanna was integral to the process in which he formed a public persona. In the terms of their intimacy we hear, more audibly than anywhere else, the mix of self-doubt and assertive self-justification that a young German scholar brought to his search for a public mission.

Once again the language of head and heart figures large in Fichte's thinking, and once again it is deeply rooted in Lutheran piety and in the literary idioms it spawned. Now, however, Fichte's use of such language to assert a social identity is inseparable from his need to posit and enforce gender distinctions. When their courtship began, Fichte was an impecunious tutor, on the margins of respectable society. His marriage to Johanna was soon followed by his appointment to a teaching position at Jena. In the ways he valued Johanna and in the ways he found fault with her, we see the anxious efforts of a man of plebeian origins to win acceptance in the educated *Bürgertum*, even as he became known as a philosophical and political radical intent on maintaining a critical distance from the academic establishment.

Though Fichte's relationship with Johanna confirms to a degree the current historical wisdom about "gendering," it also yields a cautionary tale. The commitment to "duty" and "honor" that Fichte held so sacred and that drew him so powerfully to Kantianism, did, to be sure, reflect

---

[1] Karen Kenkel, "The Personal and the Philosophical in Fichte's Theory of Sexual Difference," in W. Daniel Wilson and Robert C. Holub, eds., *Impure Reason. Dialectic of the Enlightenment in Germany* (Detroit, 1993), pp. 278–97, relates the early correspondence between Fichte and Johanna to Fichte's later "theory of sexual difference." The article marks a badly needed start in exploring the connections between Fichte's marriage and his philosophy, but it is lacking in social and cultural context. The other important exception to the general neglect of Fichte's relationship with Johanna is Ilse Kammerlander, *Johanna Fichte; ein Frauenschicksal der deutschen Klassiker* (Stuttgart, 1969). Kammerlander used unpublished material in the Fichte Nachlass, including a few items not included in the *Gesamtausgabe*. Her study lacks a critical framework but is factually precise and informative.

a cultural process of redefining the male and the female in the late eighteenth century; but that process had more twists than one might expect.

★ ★ ★

When Fichte met Johanna he was a twenty-eight-year-old tutor, surviving from position to position on the edges of the educated *Bürgertum* and searching in vain for the patron who would launch his career. He had spent part of the spring and summer of 1788 in Leipzig – unemployed and still without prospects. Under better circumstances he would not have considered taking the position that would keep him in Zürich for the next twenty months. The several years he had spent instructing the children of boorish "Krautjunker" in rural Saxony had left him with "a certain resistance . . . to beginning again and again at the bottom and entering once again into thankless work."[2] He had hoped to find a position in a great noble household or perhaps even at a court. Instead he faced complete penury and had no choice but to accept employment in the household of Antonius and Anna Dorothea Ott, the proprietors of one of Zürich's more stylish inns. He found himself instructing the two pampered children of a commercial bourgeois family, in a city known for its rigid conventionality and offering little in the way of intellectual stimulation.

The one bright spot in this disheartening situation was the modest salon that Johann Hartmann Rahn, a textile manufacturer and city official, hosted on Saturday evenings. There Fichte found entrée to the local educated elite, which included clergymen, professors at the Gymnasium, merchants, and tutors. Herr Rahn developed a fatherly affection for Fichte; the intense young man reawakened fond memories of his own youth. Through the father Fichte came to know his thirty-five-year old daughter Marie Johanne, known as Johanna, who ran the household. By February, 1790, Fichte's friendship with Johanna was entering a new stage of intimacy. There were intense conversations, letters exchanged furtively in a city with a sharp eye for scandal, brief but precious meetings outside church and on promenades. By the time Fichte left for Leipzig in early May 1790, they were informally betrothed. Fichte had promised to write as often as possible.

As a window onto this first stage of their courtship, the surviving correspondence has obvious limitations. From Johanna we have only a fragment, probably a P.S. to a missing letter she sent Fichte at the end of March 1790, just before he left Zürich.[3] Hence we see the relationship, and Johanna, almost entirely through Fichte's eyes. His letters, though numerous, yield only a few scattered traces of an intimacy that formed

---

[2] Fichte to Karl Christian Palmer, Dec. 27, 1789, in GA, III, 1: 43.   [3] GA, III, 1: 94–5.

in many hours of conversation. And yet the letters are quite revealing. Several of them were attempts to continue conversations and clear up possible misunderstandings; they give us some sense of what Fichte and Johanna talked about and of the emotional tenor of their communication. To a degree, letter writing seems to have loosened their inhibitions. In a letter of March 20, 1790, about a week before he left Zürich, Fichte agreed with Johanna that "unfortunately [their] oral speech has not been as open and heartfelt as [their] written [speech]."[4] Apparently Fichte found it hard to be open under the scrutiny of Zürich society, even in the relatively congenial setting of the salon.

This is not to say that Fichte's commitment to epistolary openness is to be taken at face value. His reverence for their "friendship"; his wonderment that "at the first look, the first conversation, [his] entire heart was so open for [her]"; his pledge of the "complete openness" that her "beautiful open soul" deserved; his awe at entering "an entirely new mode of being": such language had pervaded the culture of sensibility, or *Empfindsamkeit*, in German-speaking Europe since the middle decades of the century.[5] Fichte and Johanna were engaged in a recognizable rhetorical exercise, the highly stylized opening of the inner self to the other in epistolary exchange. The paradox of the exercise was that the spontaneous revelation of self – the embrace of intimacy as a "natural" relationship of mutual transparency – had become a highly self-conscious art. Fichte was still trying to master the art. Fortunately, he assured Johanna at the outset of their correspondence, he had already formed his style "a little" in "frequent correspondence with a young woman"; that was why it was not "even stiffer."[6]

As Fichte in effect admitted to Johanna, he did not take naturally to the mutual transparency that the culture of *Empfindsamkeit* required. For that very reason, he was especially reliant on a language that might have struck many of his contemporaries as outdated or at least banal in its conventionality. And yet this early correspondence with Johanna is not merely a stereotypical instance of a declining fashion. If the language was famil-

[4] GA, III, 1: 91.
[5] GA, III, 1: 52, 56–7, 115. There is a massive literature on *Empfindsamkeit*, both as a literary discourse and as a broader cultural phenomenon. Particularly useful for my purposes were Georg Jäger, *Empfindsamkeit und Roman. Wortgeschichte, Theorie und Kritik im 18. und frühen 19. Jahrhundert* (Stuttgart, 1969); Michael Maurer, *Die Biographie des Bürgers. Lebensformen und Denkweisen in der formativen Phase des deutschen Bürgertums (1680–1815)* (Göttingen, 1996), esp. pp. 267–78, 305–23; Wolfram Mauser and Barbara Becker-Cantarino, eds., *Frauenfreundschaft-Männerfreundschaft. Literarische Diskurse im 18. Jahrhundert* (Tübingen, 1991); Lothar Pikulik, *Leistungsethos contra Gefühlskult. Über das Verhältnis von Bürgerlichkeit und Empfindsamkeit in Deutschland* (Göttingen, 1984); Anne-Charlott Trepp, *Sanfte Männlichkeit und selbständige Weiblichkeit: Frauen und Männer im Hamburger Bürgertum zwischen 1770 und 1840* (Göttingen, 1996), esp. pp. 125–71; Nikolaus Wegmann, *Diskurse der Empfindsamkeit. Zur Geschichte eines Gefühls in der Literatur des 18. Jahrhunderts* (Stuttgart), 1988.
[6] GA, III, 1: 51.

iar and indeed trite, it was also shaped to the formative experiences, the needs, and the expectations of two individualized personalities in specific circumstances. While to some degree the language substituted rhetorical artifice for the complete transparency it claimed to effect, it also provided the resources for an intellectual and emotional bonding across considerable distance.

The distance was in part social. For generations the Rahn family had been firmly ensconced in Zürich's patriciate of property, education, and public office, albeit on one of the lower rungs.[7] From that height Fichte's family was obviously plebeian; and there was, of course, the added problem that he was a mere private tutor with no property and no apparent career prospects. In a sense, then, their common "bourgeois" identity was tenuous at best. What the culture of *Empfindsamkeit* gave them was an intensely moralistic disapproval of aristocratic culture. In that negative sense, pitting their *Bürgerlichkeit* against the privileged legal status, the parasitic idleness and the social glitter of the group at the pinnacle of the corporate order, they had a shared identity. This bond would find overt political expression in their sympathetic, though not uncritical, view of the French Revolution. Johanna, like her father, was a Swiss republican who had no use for aristocratic pretensions. But the Revolution reinforced a dichotomy that already framed their mental map of the social order. Echoing Klopstock, Rousseau, and many others, they assumed that an unbridgeable chasm separated the hyperhierarchical formalism of court life from the more egalitarian naturalness and openness of their own social ethos. It was the difference between the code of "gallantry," with its meaningless flattery in the service of seduction, and the honest (and chaste) communion that courtship ought to entail; between worldly, superficial, and capricious *grandes dames* and women who held sacred their duties as wives and mothers; between a relentlessly manipulative and dissimulating world of masks and a world that aspired to validate itself, to embody an ideal of pure "humanity," through its relationships of mutual transparency. With this contrast uppermost in her thoughts, Johanna tried to dissuade Fichte from seeking a tutoring position at the Danish court. Fichte defended his pursuit of this prospect, but in a way that confirmed their shared stereotype. The challenge of being at a court would be "to accommodate [himself] sometimes to others, to deal with false persons, or with persons entirely contrary to [his] character." That was something he had to learn if he was to "have an effect" on the world. Johanna doubted that he was constitutionally able to acquire this skill.[8] Her underlying fear, one

---

[7] On the patriciate and the Rahn family, see Rolf Graber, *Bürgerliche Öffentlichkeit und Spätabsolutistischer Sozietätenbewegung und Konfliktkonjunktur in Zürich 1746–1780* (Zürich, 1993), esp. pp. 246–55.

[8] GA, III, 1: 71–2.

suspects, was that he could acquire it – and the honest, upright man she loved would become a mere courtly persona.

One form their mutual openness took – the one that the modern reader is most likely to find familiar – was a kind of psychological self-assessment. Each explained the attraction to the other as a result of family experience, though Johanna was more explicit on the subject. In a later letter to Fichte's brother, whom she would soon meet in person, she warned him to picture her "as comically" as she "really" was. She described herself as small, with prematurely wrinkled skin, "an unpleasantly long chin," and no upper teeth.[9] This self-portrait may have been partly in jest, but it leaves no doubt that Johanna regarded herself as anything but a beauty. She contrasted herself with her younger sister Juliana Frederika, who had been "very beautiful as a young girl" and, "always flattered," had become a "cold soul," quite "vain," with "a comfortable complacency [*ein behagliche Genügsamkeit*]."[10] Johanna seems to have accepted a kind of trade-off; if she herself could offer little in the way of physical attributes, she had been amply endowed with warmth and receptivity to others. The turning point in Johanna's life had been her mother's death in 1780, when she was twenty-five. In his grief her father turned to her, and she in turn found her mission in providing the domestic warmth and comfort he needed. By the time Fichte came along she was thirty-five and her father was sixty-nine. She saw herself as having gladly remained unmarried for her father's sake, but now she faced the likelihood that she would soon be alone. She found it quite natural to follow her father's lead in developing an affection for Fichte. The father's approval confirmed her own conviction: Fichte was a man to whom she could transfer her devotion without compromising her moral standards.

If Johanna found a surrogate father in Fichte, she also filled an emotional void in Fichte's upbringing. He confided to her that his father had been "too tender" toward him, to the point of neglecting his obligations to his other children. In contrast, his mother had "never" shown him "particular tenderness" and had turned some of his siblings against him – and that despite the fact that mother and son were strikingly similar in "spirit" and "body."[11] Though he tried to regard this maternal coldness with a certain ironic distance, as an inexplicable oddity of his life, the sense of deprivation and the resentment cut very deep. He found something reassuringly maternal in the warmth of Rahn's devoted daughter, seven years his senior.

If we limit our view to these obviously psychological dimensions of their relationship, however, we miss the historically specific cultural idioms with which Fichte and Johanna drew together and set the terms of their intimacy. At the center of the story is the figure of Friedrich Klopstock,

---

[9] GA, III, 2: 243.   [10] GA, III, 2: 105.   [11] GA, III, 1: 83.

who was Johanna's maternal uncle. In the late 1740s Klopstock had burst
onto the literary scene with the first songs of *Der Messiah*, his epic of the
life of Christ. Lionized by his German readership and honored with a
lifelong pension by the King of Denmark, he had become the poetic
Titan of *Empfindsamkeit*. His odes to his betrothed and later wife Meta
(Johanna's aunt) were emblematic of the ideal of love and marriage in
this febrile literary discourse. In one of the most famous scenes in
Goethe's *Die Leiden des jungen Werthers*, it is the recollection of Klopstock's
ode "Celebration of Sping" ("Die Frühlingsfeier") – a recollection occasioned by a terrifying thunderstorm and the gentle, fragrant rain in its
aftermath – that moves Werther to kiss Lotte's hand in a "flood of emotions." Hoping to promote Fichte's efforts to launch a literary career,
Johanna encouraged him to write an essay on this typically hymnic
example of Klopstock's poetic inspiration. At the end of March, just before
he left Zürich, she reminded him that he had promised her a portrait
for her armband. She would keep it next to the portrait of her father.
That place had been reserved for Klopstock, but now Fichte had replaced
him.[12] She could not have found a more dramatic way to convey her
devotion to him.

Klopstock was a distinctly German and Protestant figure, and even in
that world he had become something of a distant icon by 1790. Young
devotees of *Empfindsamkeit* were more likely to be reading Rousseau's *La
nouvelle Héloïse*, or Goethe's *Werther* (1774), or Johann Martin Miller's
Siegwart. Eine Klostergeschichte (1776). Among the literary cognoscenti,
Klopstock himself was still revered for his heroic role in the German literary renaissance, but his work was coming to be regarded as somewhat
vaporous in its visionary pretensions, and indeed as dangerously mystical.
In the growing intimacy between Fichte and Johanna, however, Klopstock
was a much more immediate and welcomed presence. By cultivating a
special attachment to the poet, they could in effect ground their union
of hearts in a shared experience of youth. What mattered to Fichte was
not current literary trends but personal memories. In June of 1793, in a
letter to Klopstock, he would hail the poet, quite sincerely, as "the only
person who loosened from [his] eyes in earliest boyhood the first tears of
emotion [*Rührung*]."[13] His experience had been typical; it was above all
Klopstock who had introduced educated young men of his generation to
the new literary expressions of Protestant religiosity.

For Johanna, devotion to Klopstock was a matter of family loyalty. It
was not simply that she was the poet's niece; he was the centerpiece of

---

[12] GA, III, 1: 94–5.
[13] GA, III, 1: 418. See also the example of C. F. D. Schubart's recollection of his first reading of Klopstock, quoted in Maurer, *Die Biographie des Bürgers*, p. 271. On the filiations between *Empfindsamkeit*
and various strands of eighteenth-century German Protestantism, see esp. Gerhard Kaiser, *Klopstock. Religion und Dichtung* (Gütersloh, 1963).

her family's legend of itself. In 1795, when he was close to death, Herr Rahn would enshrine the legend in a brief autobiography, recorded by his daughter in cramped penmanship, with no margins, on seven large pages (her reputation for thrift was well merited). Until he had inherited his father's municipal office in Zürich, Rahn had struggled as a manufacturer in the precarious world of textiles. Though proud of his work ethic and his technical skills, he remembered himself as a "fiery" young man, unrivaled in his enthusiasm for Klopstock's poetry. When the poet visited Zürich in 1750, he stayed in Rahn's home for several months and they became virtual "brothers." The force of Klopstock's *Empfindsamkeit* gave his friend's life a new direction. He decided against marrying one of the local daughters, in defiance of the expectations of the Zürich "public." The most likely choice was a woman he admired but for whom he did not feel an "exclusive" love. And so he accompanied Klopstock back to Hamburg with the single-minded purpose of marrying the poet's favorite sister, Johanna Viktoria, to whom he had read the sections of *Messiah* he had just completed. Rahn felt the highest "love" and "respect" for her "at first sight." Sixteen years after her death, he remembered his wife as "the best, most noble soul" he had ever known.[14]

Johanna had grown up in a household in which marital affection and reverence for Germany's most celebrated bard had been tightly interwoven. It was through Klopstock – or, more precisely, through the broadly literary and devotional culture that Klopstock represented – that she and Fichte formed a bond of religious sensibility, despite their differences in belief. Johanna may not have been an orthodox Lutheran, but she was devout. She feared that from their talks about religion he would conclude that she was too pious for him. He assured her that her truly Christian "capacity" had nothing to do with the "pitiful empty-headedness" and "the most tragic falseness of the heart" that characterized the woman of excessive piety (*Frömlerinn*). Where the *Frömlerinn* worshipped God "mechanically," as though performing a "compulsory labor," Johanna did so out of simple wisdom. Her faith was an authentic expression of her "character," not an effort to placate God and impress others.[15]

Their shared religiosity found expression above all in a highly spiritualized ideal of love between a man and a woman and in their accompanying confidence that the emotion they evoked in each other, however

---

[14] The dictated autobiography, in what appears to be its first draft, is in the Fichte Nachlass, C. 17, SSPK. There is no mention of the document in the *Gesamtausgabe*, probably because it was not considered directly relevant to Fichte's writings. Parts of the account of Rahn's friendship with Klopstock and his marriage are quoted in Kammerlander, *Johanna Fichte*, pp. 13–14. On the young Klopstock in Zürich, see Paul Grosser, *Der junge Klopstock im Urteil seiner Zeit. Ein Beitrag zur Geschichte des deutschen Geistes im 18. Jahrhundert* (Würzburg-Aumühle, 1937), pp. 14–15, 44–61; Albert Köster, ed., *Klopstock und die Schweiz* (Leipzig, 1923).
[15] GA, III, 1: 61.

intense it might become, was clearly different from erotic passion. To be sure, Fichte wrote Johanna, Rousseau had demonstrated in the *Confessions* that there were many different kinds of love; but the only lasting kind – and the only kind that did not corrupt – was based on mutual "inner esteem" (*Wertschätzung*).[16] It was not the prospect of physical union but the uniting of two souls, each finding the ideal of virtue inscribed in the other, that explained their powerful stirrings of the heart. In a sense, this sentiment was the most telling symptom of the conventionality of their courtship. In the cult of reciprocal "tenderness" (*Zärtlickkeit*) we hear a Lutheran emphasis on the spontaneity of the heart, fused with an equally Lutheran insistence on rigorous self-control (which in turn had strong affinities with the ethic of rational self-discipline). The effect was to legitimate the emotional intensity, and indeed the volatility, of mutual attraction but without unleashing the passions or licensing the pursuit of carnal pleasure.

The letters do not offer any strikingly new variations on these themes. But Fichte and Johanna were not simply echoing an ideal; they made it serve their mutual needs. Johanna thought of herself as an unattractive older woman. Was it not likely that this young foreigner had been drawn to her merely out of lack of experience with women or for want of other amusements, and that he would put her behind him once he left Zürich? Fichte assured her that, precisely because they were not in the grip of physical desire, they need have no doubt about the spiritual purity of their "respect" for each other.[17] If his response disappointed her, it also eased her insecurity. Fichte may also have found something reassuring in the ideal of a disembodied longing – of desire soaring above physical attraction. Here was a woman who shared his ideal of spiritual union and hence did not have to be courted with the "flattery" of the "gallant" lover – a ritual he found silly and in which he knew himself to be inept. At a deeper level, he had found a "sister soul" who did not threaten the ascetic impulse that was such a marked feature of his temperament. He could love without abandoning his moral rigorism – indeed, without exposing it to doubt.

For Fichte, Johanna's Christian – and Klopstockian – wisdom lay above all in her simple belief in Providence. It was a belief he urgently wanted to share, though he could not help subjecting it to skeptical scrutiny. When they met he was still trying, without success, to find a way around the "deistic" determinism that he found so compelling on logical grounds. Even as he continued to entertain that position in arguments with friends, including Johanna's father, he addressed Johanna in her own language. In early March of 1790 he was trying to find her a volume of sermons by Christian Bastholm, the royal Danish court preacher. The ninth sermon

---

[16] GA, III, 1: 61.   [17] GA, III, 1: 56.

in that collection was meant to demonstrate that the belief in Providence, far from encouraging "sloth" or "indifference," ought to obligate people to develop and use to the fullest the natural "powers" God had given them. Revelation and rational proofs aside, this was the "necessary" and "salutary" (*heilsam*) view. The only alternative, after all, was to explain even the smallest circumstances of life as the results of a "blind divinity," a "ball of chance (*Ball des Ungefehrs*) . . . without rule, without wisdom."[18]

Fichte approved of Bastholm's sermon because, to a degree, it expressed his own conviction – the other voice in the internal argument he was still conducting. That Providence had brought him and Johanna together meant that their mutual attraction was not a mere "blind" force of Nature, ultimately generated by animal instincts and appetites. Likewise Providence would now guide him through the choices he had to make about their future. Its guiding hand was discernible not simply in the apparent coincidences of their external lives but also in their "inner" biographies, the formations of personality and character that had made them soul mates. The inner workings of Providence lay in the *Bildung* of a personality, which assumed its individualized form in the very way it became virtuous. What connected this inner process with the external life course was the social setting, the relationships with family members and others that developed the individual's inborn "powers" and gave them a particular social direction.

This was the view of Providence working through *Bildung* that Fichte had already applied to himself in his sermon drafts.[19] It made people the instruments of God's Will, but in a way that left room for the conviction that individual moral agency mattered, and hence, that beneath the apparently meaningless workings of mechanical causation, human life had moral meaning. In the sermon drafts, Fichte used this concept of providential *Bildung* to explain why rare cases like himself had been lifted out of obscurity into the ranks of an educated elite with privileged moral insight. He sought to justify his own life course. Now he applied the same logic to Johanna and their union. Apparently Johanna, in the typically confessional mode of *Empfindsamkeit*, had confided to him her earlier ambitions. "I can very well imagine," he responded,

> That you have not always been so comprehending, so steady, as you are now; that you have acquired your present rational way of thinking and deep knowledge of the human heart only through experience; that you have gone through the liveliness of the first years of youth. One does not receive a way of thinking like yours in the stillness of all passions. And then has the demand for a larger world excited you? – Quite naturally, since

---

[18] Christian Bastholm, *Geistliche Reden über wichtige Wahrheiten der Religion Jesu*, 2 vols. (Copenhagen, 1781), 2, pp. 219–44.
[19] See Chapter 1.

you must have felt in yourself strong working powers, striving for development. Domestic life could have no attraction for you, since you still did not have the full power to have an effect in it. You were loved by your blessed mother; but that was already habitual for you, you were accustomed to nothing else from childhood onward, you regarded that as something owed you. – Now your heart was pierced, crushed, and at the same time, for a while, deadened by the death of this excellent woman; and now the love of your father was directed to you, as a new appearance, an unexpected good fortune, and hence it became all the more precious to you. You could serve him, you could manage a house, and manage it to make things easier for such a beloved father; and so a new heart arose in you; it was as though you had been re-created [*umgeschaffen*]. See here a plan, a wisely laid plan of Providence to make you what you should become, what you are now, and what for you was the best mode of existence according to the wisdom of Providence. So, I believe, Providence proceeds with all human beings (*Menschen*).[20]

In sum: Providence had directed Johanna to her proper role, the management of a household. At the same time that it had destined her to be a "friend" to her husband, it had prepared her to serve him at home, as she was serving her father. In the culture of *Empfindsamkeit*, this dual assignment for women was essential to a new ideal of marital bliss. For Fichte and, one can surmise, for many other males of his generation, the understanding of intimacy with a woman as friendship had the advantage of keeping deeply rooted scruples and fears about sexual pleasure at bay. It was another way of idealizing the relationship as a moral communion, a symbiosis in virtue, soaring above the mere satisfaction of animal needs. There was a tension at the core of this sacral view of love and mariage. The equality considered essential to friendship – the equality without which mutual openness was unthinkable – had to operate within the obvious hierarchy of authority in a patriarchal household.[21] Fichte and Johanna saw no need to contend with this latent contradiction. They were not aware of it. To them friendship in courtship and marriage was analogous to, and yet different from, friendship between males – and that meant that the relationship was in a sense more equal, even as it rested on emphatically gendered terms of inequality.

Fichte could reveal himself to Johanna in a way that he could not reveal himself to his male friends. That was the mark of their special equality, the one he found so exhilarating and that made their intimacy such a relief. He was well aware that for all his commitment to openness, he had

---

[20] GA, III, 1: 75–6.
[21] See esp. Heidi Rosenbaum, *Formen der Familie: Untersuchungen zum Zusammenhang von Familienverhältnissen, Sozialstruktur und sozialem Wandel in der deutschen Gesellschaft des 19. Jahrhunderts* (Frankfurt am Main, 1982), pp. 285–309.

a tendency to icy withdrawal. What occasioned this reaction, he knew, was the "pride" he had acquired as a poor schoolboy and student, embarrassed by his circumstances and terrified of becoming an object of his friends' pity. Two days after arriving in Leipzig he wrote to Johanna's father that his "prospects" were still rather confused. Herr Rahn must keep that information to himself, Fichte stressed; to "elicit [sympathy]" was to him "worse than death."[22] Enslaved by pride, he could not admit need, particularly when the admission might invoke pity for his always straitened financial circumstances.

In Johanna he found someone to whom he could reveal his money difficulties without shame, and indeed admit the pettiness to which his pride drove him in the very act of speaking frankly of its power over him. In the privacy of their intimacy he could strip off his thick protective coating of "honor." That was a tremendous relief, though it was not easy. The two drafts of the letter he wrote Johanna from Leipzig in mid-May 1789 reveal a man torn between his impulse to withdraw into "silence" and his desperate need for help. The costs of the trip had left him with virtually no cash, and so now he faced "unpleasantness, prostitutions, ruin" if she did not mail him money right away. He would "reveal [himself] in this way" to "no other mortal," including her father. Only she could "know about these things without thinking less of [him]"; and, he added in the second draft, that was because he "felt deeply" that "in the eyes of God" they were "only one person."[23] This was to say that the very completeness of their union – and of the equality it entailed – made the defense of honor unnecessary. It was under the gaze of another person that one felt shame; and in the unique intimacy with Johanna, the distinction between self and other seemed to evaporate.

There is another way of explaining why the relationship exempted Fichte from pride and shame. Precisely because Johanna was female and their relationship was so intensely private, the rules of honor in the more public world of male friendships did not apply. Theirs was a kind of moral equality, in other words, that operated within a larger world of unquestioned inequality between the sexes. And that social inequality in turn rested on a way of gendering intellectual and moral powers that was central to the culture of *Empfindsamkeit*. Though Fichte did not think of the simple wisdom he found in Johanna as irrational, he did see it as an essentially emotional capacity, a receptivity more of the "heart" than of the "head."

The implication is not that serious intellectual exchange was absent from Fichte's intimacy with Johanna. In the journal he kept for his employers in Zürich, Fichte wrote that "it [could] not occur to any reasonable man to want to make a young woman actually learned." He was

[22] GA, III, 1: 106.   [23] GA, III, 1: 110–16.

simply stating a reigning assumption of the era, at least among educated males: scholarly learning seemed obviously incompatible with the duties of a wife and mother. Fichte went on to insist, however, that it was essential to a woman's happiness that she be made "rational in [her] sphere." "Thinking and judging for oneself" was "an entitlement of the human being, not of the sex," and it required knowledge from several scholarly disciplines, including natural science, history, and the study of "civic institutions" (*bürgerliche Verfassung*). To judge by her reading notes, this ideal had guided Johanna's education. In the excerpts she copied from a pedagogical treatise, education was defined as empowering the human being to become "a rational and self-active being." Such an education could not be accomplished with "drilling," or by inculcating religious dogma.[24] Clearly Herr Rahn had subscribed to the pedagogical reform movement of the late eighteenth century, and he seems to have been unusually open-minded about its implications for women. It was not uncommon for men to forbid the reading of Rousseau to young women under their authority. Johanna *had* read Jean-Jacques (including his particularly scandalous *Confessions*), though she seems to have approached him with special caution. Another excerpt from her readings describes Rousseau as an author whose "free play of the power of imagination" had ended in "self-deification." Most of his writings required "a cultivated (*gebildete*) reader," who must "*examine sharply.*"[25]

The culture of *Empfindsamkeit*, precisely because it was a literary culture, gave Fichte and Johanna a shared universe of reading and conversation in which ideas as well as emotions were exchanged. The ideal was mutual cultivation for moral ennoblement, albeit with men playing the guiding role. What did not belong there was a communicative rationality that was "scholarly" in nature, broadly "philosophical" in its analytical rigor, and "public" in its import and scope – and in all three capacities, exclusively male. In Fichte's eyes Johanna's emotionally grounded belief made her, like his father, a good and simple soul. Educated men and their "sister souls" differed in the relative power of "head" and "heart," just as "free-thinking" intellectuals and the believing masses differed. There was, however, a significant distinction between the way Fichte regarded class divisions and the assumptions he brought to issues of gender. Fichte

---

[24] "Einen Menschen erziehen heisst . . . ," Fichte Nachlass, C. 2, SSPK. The excerpts from Johanna's reading are not dated. I have assumed that they predate her meeting Fichte.

[25] "Auszüge aus Büchern von Johanna Fichte," Fichte Nachlass, C. 11, SSPK. On German-speaking women's reading habits in the eighteenth century and on efforts to keep them from reading Rousseau, see Ursula A. J. Becher, "Lektürpräferenzen und Lesepraktikem von Frauen im 18. Jahrhundert," in Hans Erich Bödeker, ed., *Lesekulturen im 18. Jahrhundert* (*Aufklärung* 6, Heft 1 (1991), pp. 27–42). On the distinction between a "learned" (or "scholarly") woman and a "cultivated" woman, see esp. Maurer, *Die Biographie des Bürgers*, pp. 539–48; Trepp, *Sanfte Männlichkeit*, pp. 139–60.

regretted that his "speculation" cut him off from the masses; in his more utopian moments, he hoped that Kantianism would bond him with the masses in a single community. In contrast, he took the cognitive and emotional division of labor between himself and Johanna to be perfectly natural and indeed sacrosanct. The point is not that the ideal of marriage as a union in virtue was mere cant; it carried a new emphasis on freedom of moral choice for women as well as men. But the emphasis was powerfully qualified by the assumption that when it came to intellectual matters, their relationship was self-evidently tutorial. It speaks volumes that one of Fichte's projects in Leipzig – one he mentioned to Johanna without any inhibition – was to found a new journal, intended especially for women, to guide them to proper reading material and steer them away from both the frivolous and the inappropriately learned.[26]

Fichte brought this view of the male and the female, the rational and the emotional, to his reading of Kant's *Critiques* in the late summer and early fall of 1790. On August 12, 1790, he wrote to Johanna that he was "throwing [himself] head over heels" into Kantianism and that "head and heart [were] gaining by it."[27] On September 5 he asked her to report his momentous discovery of a philosophical justification for human freedom to her father, so that Herr Rahn would know that their efforts to refute determinism in their discussions in Zürich had proceeded from "a false principle." He regretted that in listening to the discussions, Johanna had been "so often misled." He saw no reason to explain to her in philosophical terms what Kant had actually accomplished. Instead he reassured her that in Kant's ethics the moral wisdom of her heart had been confirmed beyond any doubt. "From now on," he wrote, "believe only in your own feeling (*Gefühl*), even if you cannot contradict the reasoners (*Vernünftler*); they will also be contradicted, and already are."[28]

Kant's ethics confirmed to Fichte that unlike the "speculators," good and simple souls intuited moral truths. They did not have to grasp the truth in a process of rational persuasion; their emotional dispositions made it experientially self-evident. In that sense, Fichte's appreciation of Johanna as a moral person had received a new philosophical justification. But so had his conviction that his calling, as a male, assigned him to a separate sphere of reasoning, grounded in but distinct from Johanna's world of the heart. As a woman, she need not, and should not, bother with philosophical arguments. Refuting "the reasoners" was men's work.

★ ★ ★

On December 6, 1790, Fichte wrote to Johanna that "no change in [his] circumstances" would prevent him from returning to Zürich in April to

[26] GA, III, 1: 114–15. [27] GA, III, 1: 166. [28] GA, III, 1: 171.

marry her. His letter had a special note of earnestness; in parts, in fact, it reads more like a prayer, or a sermon, than a love letter. He was awed by the realization that he must "provide [her] in the future – God make it late – with a replacement for [her] most noble father." In its wisdom, Providence had prevented him from settling for a "dolled-up creature of [her] sex" (*Zierpuppe Deines Geschlechts*), and had led him, despite his "deep unworthiness," to a life companion in whom "manly sublimity of spirit united with female tenderness." He saw a future in which each would communicate "power" (*Kraft*) to the other, so that when they looked back at the end of their lives, they would see the same providential wisdom they marveled at now.[29]

In a long letter written nearly two months later, on March 1, 1791, Fichte informed Johanna that rather than waiting until April, he would return to Zürich at the end of the month. He could scarcely believe that "the sweetest happiness of [his] life" was so near; that "the most splendid soul, the one selected for [him] among all others" would soon be his. He was sick of watching his "hopes" collapse in Leipzig, and could not continue being "driven" here and there "like a wave." Only their union could dispel a sense of "emptiness" that even his engagement with Kant's philosophy did not relieve.[30]

Just four days later, on March 5, Fichte sent his younger brother Samuel Gotthelf a letter that reads as though a totally different person had taken up his pen. He describes Johanna with a certain generic detachment, as Rahn's "single daughter," and he recounts their relationship as an episode he must now put behind him. The father had developed a paternal affection for him, and "entirely without [Fichte's] doing," the "darling" [*Liebling*] of the father had become the darling of the daughter. Fichte's "heart" had been "empty"; an earlier involvement had long since been eradicated. And so he had "allowed [himself] to be loved, even without desiring it too much." He and Johanna had made each other "indefinite promises" before his departure from Zürich. Recently she had urged him to return to Zürich, and in his "mood at that time" – it was the "period of [his] philosophy, [his] high peace of soul and [his] entire indifference toward all brilliance [*Glanz*] of the world" – he had consented without a moment's reflection.[31] Obviously his mood had changed – or, as he put it, a "change [had] occurred in [his] soul." In the very way he recounted how the bond with Johanna had formed, he was constructing a rationale for breaking it. And that was precisely what he did. The relevant letter has not survived, but we know (from one of her later letters) that he advised her to find someone "more worthy." He did not tell her where he was going. When he left Leipzig in the spring of 1791 to take up a tutoring position in Warsaw, it was not simply for

[29] GA, III, 1: 201.   [30] GA, III, 1: 217–29.   [31] GA, III, 1: 222–3.

want of other prospects. He needed to place himself beyond Johanna's epistolary reach.

We can only imagine Johanna's reaction to this turn of events. She must have been shocked, though she may also have had her suspicions confirmed. His letters had become more and more infrequent, and the excuse that he was very busy may not have been convincing. At any rate, with the benefit of hindsight, we can see the implicit reservations, the gropings for possible ways out, that accompanied the apparent solidification of Fichte's commitment to marriage. In the early months in Leipzig he had continued to insist that a "prospect" would turn up there, well after his efforts to secure patrons and to launch a literary career had failed. When he first told Johanna of his decision to return to Zürich, it was with the dubious qualification that his responsibilities toward his current pupils would keep him in Leipzig for some months. Even in the letter of March 1 – the one informing her that he would be in Zürich by the end of the month – he hedged. There was the possibility of a legal suit against him (for exposing someone's fraud in print), and so he might, of course, have to stay in Leipzig to defend his "honor."[32] Fichte was a lover trying to keep escape routes open, in the very act of proclaiming his solemn commitment to the marriage for which Providence had destined them both.

In the diary he kept en route to Warsaw, Fichte confessed to himself that he had left Leipzig not only to evade "[his] *Zürcherinn*," but also "to flee [his] conscience." He would speak later of his return to Johanna as the fulfillment of a "sacred duty." Conscience and duty were not words he used lightly. And yet his words are obviously at odds with the content and, more striking, with the tone of the letter to Samuel Gotthelf. There is something cynical, even callous, about his depiction of his own passivity; it is not far from a blatant admission that he had let the relationship happen merely out of convenience, to keep himself amused in difficult circumstances. One is tempted to conclude that behind the rhetorical masks of *Empfindsamkeit*, he was simply a cad.

Had Fichte been as wracked by guilt as his later comments suggest? Did he find it as easy to fake love as his words to his brother might lead us to believe? Are we in a position to understand his behavior at all? However we interpret his behavior, we should be careful not to apply to it an anachronistic standard. If *Empfindsamkeit* is taken to be a German variant on the modern ethos of authenticity, it is wrenched out of its historical context. To strive to be "authentic," in the meaning that term acquired in Romanticism and its offshoots, is to commit oneself to an ethos of "intransigent subjectivity." The emblematic figure is the creative artist who asserts his individuality unconditionally, in defiance of social

---

[32] GA, III, 1: 186–7, 218.

norms and expectations. *Empfindsamkeit* may have pointed in that direction in some ways, but its reverence for individual spontaneity went hand in hand with a broad acceptance of social conventions. The duality helps explain two otherwise curious features of its discourse of love. To Fichte, as to so many other men and women in the late eighteenth century, love in the key of *Empfindsamkeit* was a highly self-conscious emotional and mental state.[33] This is not to imply that professions of love were false – at least not if falseness means the opposite of authenticity in the modern sense. Fichte's epistolary commitment to Johanna was not an "authentic" expression of his true self, but it also was not a calculated exercise in role-playing. In its eighteenth-century context, the role itself was an assertion of moral principle; to educated and propertied *Bürger* seeking moral self-validation, *Empfindsamkeit* filled a social need as a code of reciprocal honesty, an alternative to the relentlessly calculating role-playing they attributed to aristocratic sociability. Its language could, to be sure, serve as an instrument of manipulation; but it could also communicate, in however stylized a manner, inner impulses. Indeed, the language can be said to have effected intimacy precisely because it had a certain agency of its own; it could intensify the feeling it was meant to reveal, and perhaps even generate it.

But there *was* something stylized or, perhaps better, formulaic about the language of *Empfindsamkeit*. Particularly striking – and here again Fichte's letters are exemplary – is that the love relationship was idealized as an exclusive pairing, the providential union of one unique personality with another, but at the same time, in the language of "virtue," the individualizing traits of personality were subsumed under a generic set of moral attributes. The result was a celebration of uniqueness and exclusiveness that is likely to strike the modern reader as curiously lacking in specificity. It is not simply that lovers steered clear of the physical details that made for sexual attraction. Conspicuously absent from their professions of love were references to the particularities of the beloved's appearance, manner, and sensibility.

In this stylized rhetoric of emotion, one hears the voice of self-consciousness – the detached observation of self, even in the throes of an apparently spontaneous self-release. The inadvertent effect of remaining self-conscious about one's raptures was that a space was reserved for withdrawal from them if circumstances required. The circumstances might very well be social. It was a principle of *Empfindsamkeit* that rigid social distinctions ought not to be a barrier to "love"; but it was also an assumption, often left unspoken, that the imperatives of love could not ride roughshod over considerations of respectability and honor. *Empfindsamkeit*

[33] This analysis is especially indebted to Wegmann, *Diskurse der Empfindsamkeit*, pp. 71–80. See also Pikulik, *Leistungsethik*, pp. 239–57.

had simply narrowed the parameters within which such considerations were deemed legitimate. Fichte's decision to break with Johanna was, from one angle, entirely in keeping with this delicate balance between the individual and the social, inner spontaneity and the exercise of social discipline. He had left Zürich determined to earn the right to marry Johanna in the eyes of her family and friends in Zürich. To them he was still a student in search of prospects. He had to achieve recognition as an adult male, and that meant making his mark as a "scholar," whether by finding a clerical appointment or by establishing a reputation as a writer. He had failed on both counts, and the decision to return to Zürich was an admission of failure. To Johanna this was not a problem; she had her own money (presumably her inheritance), and she was confident that they could live comfortably enough in Zürich. If he was inclined to earn a bit from writing, that would help, but it was not necessary. Precisely because Fichte found this route out of his financial straits so tempting, he was loath to take it. It was one thing to confess to Johanna the pettiness of his pride, but quite another to overcome it. In this case, in fact, he saw nothing petty about his sensitivity; a fundamental issue of male honor was at stake. If he married her without having launched a career, would he not be regarded as a fortune seeker? He had feared this from the very start of their relationship. In a sense he feared himself, and that is why he found her eagerness to apprise him of her financial situation so unsettling. There are some things, he wrote her, of which the mere appearance is degrading, and he was "secure against no weakness" if it "offer[ed] itself . . . in the shape of honor." He might flee the relationship, in other words, precisely because the very existence of her "property" would make his motives seem dishonorable to others, and perhaps to himself. Her friends and countrymen would consider him "unworthy" of her, he wrote from Leipzig in May 1790, if he returned without "office" or "reputation." When he did decide to return, it was with the hope that this humiliation could still be avoided. Could they not pretend that he was coming back to lodge for a year with his dear friend Herr Rahn? Then he might have time to launch a career before people learned of their plans to marry.[34]

While Fichte acted out of respect for (or fear of) conventional social expectations, however, he also acted in defiance of them. In his complaints about Zürich we see how easily he shifted from one posture to the other. Bourgeois Zürich seemed obsessed with social appearances, with reputation, and ultimately with money – that was why his lack of prospects was so embarrassing. There is reason to doubt, of course, that he would have been significantly less anxious if Johanna had lived somewhere else. It was a fact of bourgeois life that men were expected to put off marriage until

[34] GA, III, 1: 83–4.

their professional circumstances allowed them to support a family at an appropriate level of comfort, and Fichte simply was not in that position. But Zürich also posed a problem in another sense. Herr Rahn's salon had been a godsend, but it had not changed Fichte's view of Zürich as stuffy and intellectually barren. When he described to Johanna the advantages of a large city like Leipzig, where one could live and study "unnoticed" and "undisturbed," and where "each lives as he can; dresses as it pleases him . . . and does what strikes him as good," the contrast with her own city was obvious and pointed. The stifling conformity of Zürich society was emblematic of the fact that the city was a provincial backwater, far from the centers of German educated culture. To return to marriage in Zürich, he feared, would be to settle into a life of provincial obscurity. As he plunged deeper and deeper into Kantianism, this prospect seemed all the more likely and all the more intolerable. No one had ever heard of Kant in Zürich. A young scholar who wanted to spread the word about Kant would find no audience there or anywhere else in Switzerland.

All in all, Fichte's engagement with Kant's philosophy had a complicated impact on his relationship with Johanna. It confirmed his moral estimation of her, but it also intensified his resistance to her entreaties. The problem was not simply that marriage would require his return to Zürich; it threatened to deprive him of the new sense of personal freedom he experienced as he turned Kant's moral principles into a posture toward life and a definition of his public mission. In his early days in Leipzig he had complained bitterly about his loneliness, but in November of 1790 he confided to a friend what he could not admit to Johanna: that for the last four or five months – his first months as a Kantian – he had led "the happiest life that [he could] recall in all the days of [his] life."[35] What he prized above all was his newfound sense of "independence" and "peace." Blanketed by his Kantian vision of moral freedom, he had lost interest in the battle to launch a career. His desperate search for patrons had acceded to a quiet withdrawal, an indifference to how he might be impressing others. The initial loneliness had become a state of happiness in self-sufficient solitude. This new mode of spirituality had not displaced his union with his "sister soul," but it made acting on that union all the more problematic. Marriage in Zürich, he knew, would return him to the struggles he was now so content to avoid.

Fichte was, of course, postponing his public ambitions, not discarding them – and at some level he knew that. Ironically, the form his ambition now assumed also pulled him away from Johanna. If he was to make his mark as a Kantian, he needed time to experiment, to master the art of popularizing a "head-breaking" philosophy; and he feared that family

---

[35] Fichte to Henrich Nikolaus Achelis, Nov. 1790, in GA, III, 1: 193.

obligations would prevent him from doing so. Again, the prospect of life in Zürich magnified a more fundamental problem. In Fichte's case the conversion to Kantianism had reinforced a young man's desire to keep his options open, to pursue aspirations that transcended conventional expectations. As he put it in the letter to his brother, he felt "too much power and drive in [himself] to have [his] wings cut off right away by a marriage, to chain [himself] to a yoke from which [he could] never free himself, and to decide now so willingly to spend [his] life entirely as an everyday human being (*Alltags Mensch*)."[36] He may have hoped that when he was finally ready to settle down, Johanna would still be waiting. But if his decision meant that he would lose her, so be it.

The point of all this is not that Fichte acted honorably by his own standards. To call his behavior inauthentic would be unhistorical, but it was, even by his own standards, dishonest. What is striking, and disturbing, is that the element of self-consciousness in Fichte's *Empfindsamkeit* served to silence, or at least to muffle, conscience. In Fichte's letter to his brother, the distancing effect of self-consciousness was not simply to reserve a space for withdrawal in the face of legitimate social obstacles; it became the route of escape from a conventional life in marriage, though it was precisely to such a life that he had committed himself. Indeed, Fichte came very close to denying – to his brother and to himself – that he had ever entered a commitment. If the voice of conscience was to be kept at bay, self-consciousness – an integral part of his feelings for Johanna even at their most intense – had to be transformed into something like a posture of indifference. More important, a man who defined character, and indeed manliness, in terms of active effort now had to portray himself as the passive one, the one who had allowed himself to be pulled, willy-nilly, into a vague sort of commitment. The retrospective narrative of his behavior in Zürich implied that, in a sense, he was not violating the sacred ethic of reciprocal feeling to which *Empfindamkeit* bound its devotees. His point to his brother (and presumably to himself) was that he was simply correcting a mistake – slipping out of something he had carelessly, and irresponsibly, allowed himself to be pulled into. In the very act of regretting his mistake, he implied that in the final analysis, he was not morally responsible for committing it. This same mix of self-incrimination and self-exoneration would characterize his reactions to later crises.

Having fled marriage in March of 1791, Fichte was eager to embrace it nearly two years later. Sometime in late November or early December 1792, he renewed contact with Johanna from Danzig and begged her forgiveness. Once again a critical letter has not survived. We are left wondering how he explained his disappearance; on what grounds he expected to be forgiven; how he described the intervening changes in his circum-

---

[36] GA, III, 1: 223.

stances and his state of mind. Friends had warned him that Johanna's response was likely to be a "cold letter," but he had been confident that if any woman could forgive him, it was his "chosen one" (*Auserwählte*). He was right; Johanna's response was anything but cold. She did not, to be sure, neglect the opportunity to fuel his remorse. His absence had caused her to suffer "unspeakably," particularly during the twenty-three weeks when she had had to nurse her father through a nearly fatal illness without a comforting word from the other man she loved. But in the end she exonerated him and assured him of her lifelong devotion. She attributed his disappearance to "adverse accidents" that Providence had set in their path and assured him that "the demand of [her] conscience" was to remain steadfast in her commitment to him. Clearly the fault had lain with external circumstances and not with his character. In her "heart" he was still "the good, honest, upright Ficht." It was precisely what he needed to hear.[37]

Why did he now embrace the prospect of a marriage he had fled two years earlier? It was probably no accident that he renewed contact with Johanna just a few weeks after he decided to leave his last tutoring position, the one on the Krockow estate outside Danzig. Under the maternal guidance of "the benevolent goddess" Countess Luise von Krockow, a noble household on a grand scale – the kind he was prone to censure on principle – had allowed him to experience at last "the joys of domestic life." And yet the Countess had also disappointed him by withdrawing periodically into what he considered a typically aristocratic posture of cold self-sufficiency, designed to keep a worshipful young commoner at the proper emotional distance.[38] Hence his infatuation with her had had a double effect: reawakening his yearning for familial nest warmth and at the same time confirming his conviction that genuine feminine warmth and openness were to be found only in the homes of the *Bürgertum*. The experience is likely to have renewed his appreciation for the simple goodheartedness, and indeed for the undisguised emotional neediness, of his *Bürgerin* in Zürich.

More important than his need for domesticity, however, was his confidence that he could now marry without throwing his honor into question or sacrificing his ambitions. The pivotal event had been Kant's public notice of August 14, 1792, informing the public that Fichte was the author of the much-celebrated *Attempt at a Critique of All Revelation*. The mistaken authorship had made him a literary celebrity. He admitted to Johanna that he could regard himself as "no longer unworthy of [her] in the eyes of the world" only because he been suddenly "raised . . . up" by this "uncalculated accident."[39] With his dramatic appearance in print he had come of age as a man. Though he still lacked a position with an

[37] GA, III, 1: 368–70.   [38] See Chapter 1.   [39] GA, III, 1: 403–4.

income, he had earned the right to full-fledged membership in the republic of scholars – and he felt confident that the prospects opened by that
public identity would suffice to dispel any suspicion that he was after
Johanna's money. If he still needed reassurance on that score, Johanna
knew how to provide it. She reported to him while he was en route back
to her that scholars in Zürich who had read the *Attempt at a Critique
of All Revelation*, were now "do[ing] him justice" and acknowledging
that he was "a full man" (*ein ganzer Mann*). He would know best what
scholars meant by that phrase.[40]

Returning to Zürich to marry Johanna was no longer a retreat into
provincial obscurity or a commitment that would severely limit his career
options. Now that he had established a reputation, Fichte saw the marriage as offering him a precious moment of freedom as an author. He
still found Zürich "unendurable," and he assumed that at some point he
would find a suitable employment, probably as a pastor, somewhere in
North Germany. But in the meanwhile he would be in a position to
avoid fixed professional responsibilities and be "nothing but Fichte." Being
Fichte meant being a man of letters, devoting himself to making Kant's
revolutionary ideas accessible to the reading public. In that task Johanna
would be his companion, his helpmate, and his indispensable inspiration.
Her act of forgiveness had made her the embodiment of his audience,
the representative of the "humanity" he aspired to form. It had "given
new flight to [his] plans for [humanity's] ennoblement." While Johanna's
simple virtues would sustain his philosophical respect for "humanity as a
whole," her domestic presence would humanize the philosophical zealot
in him. She was no longer the obstacle to his ambitions but the only
person who could temper his "stormy" heart with her "softness" and
"mildness." They would improve each other – he by inducing her to
worry less, particularly about himself, and she by helping him to balance
"work that grips" with healthy relaxations.[41]

And so Fichte returned to Zürich to wed. Johanna begged him to
hurry, but his trip lasted several months. As eager as he was to be with
her, he needed to establish contacts with circles of scholars in the cities
en route – and, one must add, he was enjoying his new celebrity. The
delay in their reunion became an opportunity to bring the epistolary
rhetoric of *Empfindsamkeit* to a fever pitch. The lovers' correspondence
peaked where the language of *Empfindsamkeit* was wont to peak – in the
admission that feelings had become so intense as to transcend the capacities of language, with the unspoken (or obliquely spoken) implication
that physical union was now the only source of relief. "My soul is torn
by the demand to possess *you*," Johanna wrote to him in Leipzig at the
beginning of May, "and my body suffers much from the storms in my

[40] GA, III, 1: 399.   [41] GA, III, 1: 387–8, 412, 417.

heart." My heart is so "full of feelings," she added, "that I cannot bring them to words, entrust them to this paper."[42] Fichte was not to be outdone. "Emotion (*die Empfindung*) presses into my heart," he wrote back from Stuttgart on June 9; "my blood stops flowing (*stockt*), and boils more violently; my pen shakes. I cannot write what I feel; I will be as little able to speak of it."[43] He abandoned himself at last to what he called his "sweet ecstasy (*Schwärmerei*)" – and watched himself doing so. The intensity of *Empfindsamkeit* did not remove the self-consciousness essential to its rhetorical flights.

He hoped that they could marry immediately upon his arrival, but Johanna explained, very tactfully, that Zürich etiquette would not allow anything so rash. They would have to wait "some weeks," and in the meantime he could not stay in the Rahn household. She did, however, arrange for them to reunite alone in a village inn outside the city, so that they could fall into each other's arms without embarrassment or scandal.[44]

There were delays in getting the needed documentation, and so the wedding did not take place until October 22, 1793, more than four months after Fichte's arrival in Zürich. He had already recorded the historical lineage of the event in his reverential letter to Klopstock, written from Zürich on June 22. The poet had not seen his niece since her childhood. If he knew Johanna, Fichte assured him, he would "bless" her "out of the fullness of [his] deep, all-encompassing heart," as he had perhaps blessed no one since his Meta. And he would bless the man she had chosen.[45]

★ ★ ★

Having failed us at two critical junctures in the courtship, the surviving correspondence now offers a rare view into the early years of a marriage. For his first three months in Jena, from mid-May to mid-August 1794, Fichte was without Johanna. She had had to remain behind in Zürich to tie up loose ends in her own and her father's finances. In early May 1795, at the height of his conflict with the student societies in Jena, he retreated to a rented castle in the village of Osmannstädt near Weimar – and he stayed there, with only occasional visits from Johanna, for the next five months. Their extant correspondence from these periods of separation is much less one-sided than the letters from the early phase of their courtship. We hear much more from Johanna, who now becomes a personality in her own right. The rhetoric of *Empfindsamkeit* is muted and indeed accedes at times to a quite audible testiness, particularly on Fichte's part. Much of the discussion is about mundane matters – money,

---

[42] GA, III, 1: 397–8.   [43] GA, III, 1: 415.   [44] GA, III: 1, 407.   [45] GA, III, 1: 418.

household details, social circles in Jena. That is precisely what makes it unusually revealing. We watch a couple settling into a new life of work and domesticity, in a world very different from Zürich. It was a bumpy and occasionally bruising process.

The terms of the process were probably less typically bourgeois than would at first appear to be the case. By the mid-1790s the formation of a recognizably modern, and emphatically bourgeois, familial culture was well under way in the middle ranks of German society, particularly in its urban settings. To judge by recent research, however, we have been too quick to assume that the ideological articulations of that culture – its normative self-definitions in public discourse – provide accurate descriptions of lived experience. At the ideological level we do find the binary dichotomies that would become standard in the new patriarchalism of nineteenth-century bourgeois societies. It is a deliberately gendered ideology that takes the "natural" order of things to be one in which husbands compete in the professional arenas of the public sphere while their wives manage households, nurture children, and provide their menfolk with needed emotional refuge. Men are devoted to their work, or at least are preoccupied with it – and they can be so because their wives see to their happiness and comfort at home. In this sexual division of labor, temperaments are distinguished accordingly. Men are by nature active, even aggressive, and rigorously, even ruthlessly, rational; their wives complement them with self-sacrificing passivity and emotional warmth. The preferred groom is mature and judicious; the preferred bride is childlike, waiting to be molded.[46]

In the intimate testimony to be found in letters and diaries, however, there is considerably more overlap and flexibility in male and female subjectivity than these strictly gendered territorial divisions would seem to allow. To take the most imposing example: in a study of the commercial and professional *Bürgertum* of Hamburg in the late eighteenth and early nineteenth centuries, men (as suitors, husbands, and fathers) turn out to be far less rigidly patriarchal, more emotionally oriented, more resentful of the demands of work, less attracted to childlike femininity, and less concerned to monopolize the "public" sphere and keep their wives relegated to "private" domesticity than the reigning ideological stereotypes have suggested.[47]

If these educated and propertied *Bürger* of Hamburg are typical, then Fichte's marriage is atypical by virtue of its very faithfulness to an emerging ideological model. Fichte would make his distinct contribution to the

---

[46] The classic analysis of this ideology is Karin Hausen, "Die Polarisierung der 'Geschlechtscharaktere' – Eine Spiegelung der Dissoziation von Erwerbs- und Familienleben," in Werner Conze, ed., *Sozialgeschichte der Familie in der Neuzeit Europas* (Stuttgart, 1976), pp. 363–93.

[47] Trepp, *Sanftige Männlichkeit*, passim.

ideology in 1796, when he included in his treatise on Natural Law an extreme justification for bourgeois patriarchy – a position that struck many of his contemporaries as absurd and that serves as a prime exhibit in recent feminist critiques of the gender ideology that has undergirded apparently egalitarian philosophical visions. What is striking, however, is that in the years prior to 1796 Fichte had already spelled out and begun to enforce the rules of the new patriarchy in his own marriage. At times, in fact, he enforced them with a verbal harshness not unlike the public language that made him a notoriously brutal polemicist. There are two particularly explicit moments. In the early summer of 1794, Fichte grew exasperated with Johanna's resistance to his plans for establishing a house-hold and with her repeated complaints that he was overworking and not writing her often enough. He decided to punish her with a "head-washing" (*Kopfwaschen*), as a parent would punish a child. "I am now tired of your weaknesses," he informed her in a particularly angry letter; she must "leave *them* in Zürich, where they belong," and "not bring them with [her] to Jena."[48] Johanna refused to take his harshness seriously. "You have become a quite cross Fichte," she wrote in a bemused tone, at once conciliatory and pointedly reproving: "Let us be good children, my dear! It is better for the heart, and certainly does no disgrace to the under-standing." She wanted to "get over" his "pitiless" disciplining, though she could not help worrying about his excessive work.[49] Responding nine days later, Fichte concluded, with audible self-satisfaction, that the head-washing had worked; now she knew how to behave to keep his love and respect. He had used the opening of the same letter to correct any mis-conceptions Johanna might have had about the relative importance of his work and their private life. "Tired" by a day spent in philosophical "spec-ulation," he could now turn to her and "chatter" (*plaudern*) a bit. She shouldn't count on him writing at any other time; "my daily work, the business of my life, in which I work with happiness, is to me the first." She should be grateful that unlike other scholars who had little time to spend with their wives, he at least would not be "vexing" and "ill-humored" in her presence.[50]

Fichte was quick to follow his head-washings with reassurances of his affection, but the days of ineffable joy were clearly over. Johanna would have to learn not only that the space allotted to their domestic happi-ness, as precious as it was, had to be quite confined, but also that she could not presume to intrude into her husband's public affairs. In July of 1795 she advised him not to publish a defense of his involvement in the crisis over student societies at Jena. His response is a locus classicus in gendered distinctions between the public and the private:

[48] GA, III, 2: 160.   [49] GA, III, 2: 173.   [50] GA, III, 2: 176.

As I have often requested of you orally, so I now ask you in writing, so that you can overcome it – from now on let this be; since you receive nothing further thereby, except that another time I will not tell you what I wish to do, and *that the openheartedness (Herzlichkeit) in our communication (Umgange) will receive a jolt.* . . . So let me hear nothing further from you about this matter, and let that be the case in general, if you can change it – indeed thoughts about *expenses, economy (Oekonomie)* – or about *my ethical behavior (sittliches Betragen) in the world* – or about the *uprightness of my character:* this let me hear from you, since you are my wife (*Weib*), and an honest, upright wife – but about my *public* activities, about my *relationship to the public*, to the *university*, to *German literature*, let me hear nothing from you; since you are no man, and thus has God commanded.[51]

Arguably there is a direct continuity from the courtship to Fichte's view of a proper marriage. Before leaving Zürich for Leipzig, after all, Fichte had made it quite clear to Johanna that the domestic sphere, and not the "great world," was her God-ordained destiny; and she had seen no reason to question that assignment. It was an assignment entirely in keeping with the terms of intimacy in the culture of *Empfindsamkeit*. In its gendered distribution of reason and feeling, in its apotheosis of the devoted wife and mother, and in its critique of aristocratic marital arrangements, that culture had already begun to demarcate the new boundaries between male and female, public and private. But courtships in the idioms of *Empfindsamkeit* ended in a variety of marriages, including the much less rigidly bifurcated kind to be found among the bourgeois families of Hamburg. What the case of Fichte and Johanna demonstrates is the specific circumstances that might position a marriage at one extreme of a fairly wide spectrum.

Most obvious is that the terms of gender were conditioned by the factor of age. In the North German *Bürgertum* of Fichte's generation, husbands were on average ten years older than their wives.[52] Men put off marriage until they had entered careers and thus could afford to support families respectably – and then chose spouses among the younger women still available. Seven years younger than Johanna, Fichte had inverted the conventional age difference. While he had been anxious about appearing to act dishonorably, he had also found a certain attraction in the devotion of an older woman. This helps explain why in his courtship letters the lines of gender were far more fluid than his later pronouncements would lead one to expect. There were, of course, the usual dichotomies: his speculative prowess versus her simple feeling; his "restless urge to expand" (*unruhigen Ausbreitungstrieb*) versus her "mildness" and "softness"; his hunger to "act" publicly versus her contentment with a life of domes-

[51] GA, III, 2: 390.   [52] Rosenbaum, *Formen der Familie*, pp. 331–2; Trepp, *Sanfte Männlichkeit*, p. 145.

tic virtue.[53] But in the early days in Zürich, Fichte confided to Johanna that he "rejoice[d] in being a child" in their relationship.[54] He meant not only that he felt innocent in her presence but also that he found in her a reassuring strength of character. That strength was maternal, but it had a certain "male" quality as well. In the letter from Jena on December 6, 1790 – the one in which he asked for money and at the same time announced his intention to return to Zürich to marry her – he stood in awe of her "childlike" love and innocence; but it was her combination of "manly sublimity" (*männliche Erhabenheit*) and "female tenderness" that distinguished her from the typical "dolled-up creature." In the letter of March 1, 1791 – the one he would contradict three months later in the letter to his brother – he bemoaned his lack of "steadfastness" of character, his weakness in allowing himself to be "driven" here and there "like a wave." In her he had found a "more virile soul" (*männlichere Seele*) who could "fix this inconstancy."[55]

With such language Fichte turned his urge to expand – the restless male ambition on which he usually prided himself – into a weakness of character that had resulted in scattered and futile efforts to launch a career. He was trying to come to terms with his own failure. The underlying fact of those early years was that for all his horror of personal dependence, he was dependent on Johanna. It was not simply that he needed her emotional strength and her sober practicality. During his stay in Zürich, her contacts in Switzerland and North Germany (and her father's) had opened the possibility of at last finding a patron and a position. When he faced complete penury in Leipzig, she was his benefactress. Their marriage and his university appointment did not end his practical dependence; they simply made it less urgent. While she remained in Zürich, he could live, modestly, in Jena on his paltry salary and his teaching fees; but as large as his student audiences became, and as much as he hoped to earn from his publications, he could not manage the expenses of setting up a household for the two of them and her father. For that he needed money over which she retained legal control and perhaps money she could borrow from her father. If it had been difficult, and indeed mortifying, to ask her for money earlier, he now found his financial dependence intolerable. When he proposed to buy a house, she resisted; surely land was a safer investment. He responded petulantly. He would buy a house only when he could do it with his own money – and that would take "some time."[56]

This is not to imply that Fichte's purpose in working so hard at teaching and writing was to end his financial dependence on his spouse. He worked hard because he was a driven man, a scholar with an increasingly ambitious sense of mission. In this regard he differed markedly from some

[53] See esp. GA, III, 1: 170–1.   [54] GA, III, 1: 92.   [55] GA, III, 1: 201, 219.   [56] GA, III, 2: 177.

of the men in bourgeois Hamburg. In 1820 the Hamburg jurist Martin
Hieronymous Hudtwalcker noted with relief in his diary that thanks to
his upcoming civic duties, he would be liberated for a while from a profession he found "exhausting, consuming, and treacherous." Two decades
earlier Ferdinand Beneke had written of the irreconcilable conflict
between trade, that "eternally mindless game of chance," and his yearning to "live only for his nobler destiny."[57] There was no such conflict in
Fichte's view of his life. In becoming a philosopher he had at last found
his true calling. The rigors and blessings of that calling were the subject
of his first public lecture series at Jena. He saw it as the singular good
fortune of the new breed of philosophers he represented that in the very
practice of their profession, they were ennobling themselves – realizing
the full potential of their humanity – in the most efficacious way possible. Though Fichte was far from being a typical academic professional of
his generation, something like this kind of rationale for relentless work
may have been common among his fellow scholars – and that in turn
suggests that the professor was more inclined, by the very nature of his
self-estimation, to give unquestioned priority to the demands of work
than was the businessman or the lawyer. In any case, it is hardly surprising that Fichte expected his wife to give priority to his work; far from
questioning it, he himself held it sacred.

We return to a core impulse in Fichte's personality: the quest for self-
validation through work. The needed validation was both moral and
social; the moralist's devotion to duty was inseparable from the plebeian's
anxious determination to justify his ascent into the educated and scholarly *Bürgertum*. Bourgeois respectability required a strict separation
between the public world of male work and the private realm of female
domesticity, but that is not the whole story. There was also a sense in
which the requirements of respectability tended to blur the public/private
distinction. Fichte had inadvertently acknowledged this blurring in his
lecture to Johanna on their respective spheres; she was entitled to admon-
ish him not only for spending habits harmful to the household budget
but also for "ethical behavior in the world" that might embarrass her.
When it came to embarrassment, the line between ethics and social convention and the one between "inner" character and the external trappings
of the social persona were very blurry indeed. Fichte's social anxiety found
expression in his efforts to adapt Johanna to an academic society very different from her world of family and friends in Zürich. Jena was no longer
the provincial backwater it had been a few decades earlier. Thanks to its
new renown as a progressive academic entrepôt and thanks to its ties to
the ducal court at nearby Weimar, it had become a place where style –
in conversation, in dress, in entertainment – mattered. When Johanna

[57] Quoted in Trepp, *Sanfte Männlichkeit*, pp. 215–16.

mixed in "society" or appeared on the street, or indeed when she received visitors at home, her private status took on a public dimension. She was being judged – and so was her husband.

This was another kind of dependence; and as Fichte sought to avoid being stigmatized as a parvenu, he was acutely aware of it. The more controversial he made himself in his lectures and publications, in fact, the more intent he was that neither he nor his wife give Jena society any cause for questioning their credentials as a respectable bourgeois couple. At one level, to be sure, he took it as proof of Johanna's moral superiority that she could not meet Jena's expectations for elegance and wit in a professor's wife. In August 1795 he sent a remarkably candid letter from his village retreat to Marie Christiane von Koppenfels, one of his acquaintances at the Weimar court. His enemies in Jena had spread the rumor that he was unhappily married, and it was premised, he knew, on the perception that his wife was unsuitable. If Frau von Koppenfels held that opinion, he wrote, that was understandable; his wife was "not made to shine on a prominent stage here, and with her presuppositions she may very well commit improprieties, and so one must know her for a long time, and in domestic life, to estimate her in terms of her very high value."[58] Even as he reacted defensively to criticism of his spouse, he took a certain pride in her lack of "worldly" qualities.

But he *was* defensive, even before Johanna moved to Jena. He informed her on May 26, 1794, that he had described her to people in Jena so that they would "know in advance what to expect and what not to expect." And he intended to "sharply investigate" all the wives – not, to be sure, to choose her friends for her, but to be in a position to "advise [her] with understanding." The best prospect was a Frau Anna Henriette Schütz, the wife of a Hofrath, who had shown him special kindnesses. Of all the wives in Jena, she was "by far the most educated for the great world." He did not want Johanna to "copy" her; she should, from a certain distance, learn from her "without notice" about the "*good* tone" that "eases and enlivens social intercourse and impresses others." For "intimate intercourse" (and as a counterpoint to Schütz's worldliness), there was Friedrich Schiller's wife Charlotte. Unlike the worldly Schütz, Frau Schiller had the virtue of entering friendship out of true "*need*"; and she was known as "a very good person, natural, good-humored, of blameless reputation, etc."[59] Johanna did become a friend of Charlotte Schiller, but she put her foot down when it came to Schütz. There may have been a twinge of jealousy in her response, but she was also taking the opportunity to give Fichte a bit of his own medicine. Schütz struck her as the kind of person who presumed to make plans before she got to know the people concerned – and when the plans did not work out, good night! And there

[58] GA, III, 2: 370.   [59] GA, III, 2: 116–17.

was something unseemly, even scandalous, about her efforts to marry off her thirteen-year-old daughter. The woman had "a restless, intriguing head, which would be better placed at a court, where there would be more latitude for it." If he decided that contact with Schütz was "basically not honorable" (as she clearly wanted him to decide), he should make the break before her arrival. Johanna obviously could "never have the slightest trust in her."[60]

In her lettters from Zürich Johanna made clear her reluctance to leave her home, though she would make the sacrifice as his loyal and obedient spouse. She read his reports on the sophistication of Jena society with a certain moralistic skepticism. Fichte found this attitude obtuse. Looking back from the academic heights of his new world, he was confirmed in his opinion of Zürich as stiff, narrow-minded, petty, at once arrogant and cringing. It was not simply a question of place; to Fichte, Zürich was a caricature of everything "bourgeois" in the negative sense. When he lashed out at the city, he was striking at her – asking her to expunge the petty bourgeois in her makeup. And yet he also wanted her to be bourgeois in the positive sense, without the pretensions and the guile of aristocratic women and bourgeois women with aristocratic airs. As we trace the fine line he wanted her to walk, we see the fine line he had chosen for himself. He needed a private center of domesticity, where virtue could be nourished but without bourgeois smallness, provincialism, philistinism. He needed a wife who could acompany him into a "polite" academic (and even courtly) world while providing the domesticity that would help keep him beyond the corrupting grasp of polite society.

It was Johanna's public blunders that heightened his insecurity. Her thriftiness was essential in view of their financial circumstances, but it was, in another way, a handicap. It led her to commit "improprieties" that reflected back on him and raised questions about their marriage. In mid-August 1795, Johanna joined a group on a visit to him in Osmannstädt, apparently to save the cost of renting a coach (or a wagon?) by herself. He was horrified; she would be seen as paying her husband a merely "ceremonial" visit, where they could not talk alone. It was a faux pas, he wrote in high dudgeon, that she alone was unable to see and that brought shame on both of them. Again she needed a head-washing in writing; "as much as I love and respect you, I always shudder as soon as I do not have you under my eyes, thinking of the improprieties to which you are led merely by your tasteless frugality."[61]

Johanna was probably able to shrug off these fits over small matters. More serious was the conflict between her need for close relations with kin – a need heightened by her sense of isolation in Jena – and his fear that such contacts would damage his reputation. While still in Zürich she

[60] GA, III, 2: 169.   [61] GA, III, 2: 379.

had been delighted to learn that a Frau Schmidt, the wife of a law professor in Jena, was one of her mother's sisters. The news had stirred up a host of memories of her beloved mother, about matters she had not understood as a child. If only out of respect for her mother's memory, she hoped to get to know her aunt. In this case, however, the Klopstock connection posed a threat to Fichte; he had heard disturbing rumors about Frau Schmidt's marital situation. Johanna could do as she pleased, he wrote; in such matters she was "her own master." He simply wanted to spare her the "unpleasantnesses" that "relations" with "such a character . . . must necessarily entail." He himself "now [took] no notice of her [Frau Schmidt's] existence" and did not intend to take any notice beyond what "respectability" required.[62]

Whether Johanna heeded this warning is not clear. On another family matter, this time on Fichte's side, her husband had his way despite her best efforts. In the late summer of 1794, Fichte decided to sponsor his younger brother Samuel Gotthelf in his efforts to acquire an academic education, though only after issuing a detailed warning about the formidable difficulties he would face in overcoming a late start and shedding his "peasant" manners. Johanna was delighted at the prospect of a young brother-in-law joining her household. Though he claimed a special affection for this brother, Fichte would not have him in his home, a constant reminder to new friends and colleagues of just how plebeian his origins really were. The boorish villager would have to be prepared elsewhere to "appear in society without offense." Fichte insisted that Samuel Gotthelf come to Jena incognito and then sent him off immediately to a boarding school in Meissen. Johanna appended a note to one of Fichte's grim responses to his brother's complaints about life as a schoolboy. In Jena, she assured him, "each person can soon find his way." She saw no reason why he should not at least visit them occasionally. "You and I," she wrote, "we would soon convert our Fichte; I always think that he takes the matter much too seriously."[63] Fichte finally had his brother join him in Osmannstädt, but the experiment was not a success. He was disappointed by the young man's lack of progress. Looking back on that summer, Samuel Gotthelf realized that it had been a fatal mistake to leave school to join his brother. If he had waited, he mused, "perhaps [Fichte] would have formed a better opinion of [him] from the beginning, would not have treated [him] so coldly, and [Samuel Gotthelf] would not have been required to be so inhibited toward him."[64] Samuel Gotthelf left to pursue a military career and then returned to his native village, where he died in 1800.

Johanna had had to contend with a guest of a different sort: Friedrich August Weisshuhn, one of Fichte's close friends from his schooldays and

[62] GA, III, 2: 140–1, 160.   [63] GA, III, 2: 265.   [64] GA, III, 2: 295–6.

an aspiring philosopher himself. When Weisshuhn came to lodge with the Fichtes he was in the last stages of an illness. Johanna nursed him as best she could, though she could not help complaining to her husband that this "strange person" showed her "little respect," was a "terrible hypochondriac," and babbled endlessly about his impending death out of sheer "roguery." He will "always be very sick for a long time," Johanna predicted in early April 1795, and "will make our life sour."[65] She had miscalculated; Weisshuhn died in the Fichte home on April 21.

And so Fichte and Johanna settled into a world that she found abundant in "exterior politeness" but morally shallow. She had some friends, including Frau Schiller and a few students from her husband's coterie. Her father died on September 30, 1795, just before Fichte returned from Osmannstädt to resume his academic duties. Fichte wrote her a tender letter, assuring her that he would have come if he had known the end was near, and "in the name of reason" insisting that she had not neglected her father and should not feel guilty.[66] On July 18, 1796, Johanna gave birth to their first and only child, a son named Immanuel Hartmann after Kant and Herr Rahn.

To Jena society, the Fichtes were something of a puzzle; it was not clear whether they were hopelessly mismatched or oddly suited. He the "Napoleon of philosophy," an intimidating public figure, combative, compensating for his lack of "charm" and conventional "dignity" with the sheer force, and indeed the brutality, of his intellectual performance; she the goodhearted Swiss housewife, not without cleverness and even a certain nobility of character, but beyond help when it came to the social graces and particularly to fashion.[67] At home, the philosopher and the housewife seem to have settled fairly comfortably into the domestic routine they both needed. Their marriage provided warmth, affection, and even a kind of day-to-day intimacy, though at some cost to both of them.

[65] GA, III, 2: 286–7.   [66] GA, III, 2: 410–11.   [67] See, e.g., the descriptions in FG 1: 139–40, 336.

PART 2
The Jena Years

Chapter 7

The Self and the Mission of Philosophy

As early as February of 1793, when he was still in Danzig, a conversation with an "independent thinker" had shaken Fichte's Kantian convictions. Over the next several months he began to confront the need to make Kantian philosophy a truly systematic *Wissenschaft* by establishing it on an unassailable "first principle." His first, tentative effort in that direction was a lecture series on the Critical Philosophy, given in Zürich to a small circle that gathered in the home of J. K. Lavater in the spring of 1794.[1]

Like other young Kantians, Fichte found himself in a problematic relationship to the Sage of Königsberg. The complex architectonic of the three *Critiques* was at once intimidating and highly vulnerable to attack. Its critics included skeptics who remained unconvinced by Kant's refutation of David Hume; proponents of metaphysics in the tradition of Leibnizian-Wolffian rationalism; "popular" philosophers who preferred "healthy common sense" to Kant's transcendental deductions. Having to fend off assaults on all sides, Kantians were coming to realize that for all his thoroughness, Kant had stopped short of realizing his own agenda. It was left to his disciples to plunge into territory he had sighted but had left largely unexplored. They could not repudiate the master, and that was not simply because they remained in awe of him. They knew very well that their own legitimacy derived from their Kantian lineage. To repudiate Kant was to abandon the protective shelter of his architectonic, to enter the philosophical battles of the 1790s as isolated renegades. It was not much of a step, however, from defending Kant to revisionism. Kantians were careful to protect themselves by claiming to be making manifest the master's latent insights and implications.

Fichte's system was a startling new departure, and for that very reason he took pains to avoid being stigmatized as a heretic and declared anathema by his Kantian "comrades in belief." He insisted that he was the only one who had truly understood Kant. He might seem to be deviating from the *Critiques*, but that was because he had penetrated behind their mere "letter" to their "spirit." Whereas others were content with a literal understanding of the founding texts, he was their creative, though still faithful, interpreter. Fichte offered several justifications for assuming this role, all

---

[1] The last lecture in the Zürich series, and the only surviving one, has been translated in *Fichte. Early Philosophical Writings*, trans. and ed. Daniel Breazeale (Ithaca and London, 1988), pp. 82–6.

emphasizing that he was merely completing Kant's work. In early December 1793, he wrote to a friend that Kant was an "amazing, unique man" who had "a capacity for divining the truth without being himself aware of its grounds." It was also possible, though, that Kant had "not estimated his era highly enough to communicate [the ground of truth]"; or that he had shied away from the "superhuman reverence" that would have been accorded him. In any case, the problem lay with his self-appointed disciples, who were now appealing to the "fact" of a "substratum" of consciousness as an act of faith, requiring neither "proof" nor "explanation." They did not stop to think that they were encouraging their "opponents" to indulge in equally arbitrary procedures and that the result would be a chaos of subjectivities.[2]

It was in this state of apprehension about the Kantian philosophical revolution that Fichte received the offer of a university appointment at Jena. The opportunity to replace Reinhold, Kant's best-known and most effective interpreter to date, was too attractive to pass up. But Fichte nonetheless had reason to regard the Jena appointment as an unwanted intrusion. He had hoped that with the modest financial independence his marriage had brought him, he could devote the next few years entirely to realizing his ambition to construct the system that would put the house of philosophy in order. He knew that the demands of teaching would scatter his efforts. His proposed compromise was to postpone the move for a year, but the Weimar authorities feared that if Reinhold were not replaced immediately, Jena would forfeit its central role in the Kantian movement.

The burdens of academic office did scatter Fichte's efforts; as a result, his first year at Jena was often frustrating. The other effect, however, was that the many dimensions of Fichte's quest for "system" became apparent much sooner than otherwise would have been the case. Though he knew he needed more time, Fichte felt compelled to give himself a distinct profile by unveiling the system in his private lectures. In 1794 and 1795 he published the lectures as the *Foundations of the Entire Doctrine of Knowledge*, the text known in contemporary scholarship simply as the *Wissenschaftslehre*. In the spring of 1794, before arriving in Jena, he had published a brief "invitational work" for prospective students. Entitled *Concerning the Concept of the Doctrine of Knowledge*, it stated the basic insights of the system and laid out their implications for a reconfiguration of the entire field of academic knowledge. In an effort to secure a large clientele for his private lectures, he also offered a series of "public" (i.e., free) lectures on "the duties of scholars." The surviving public lectures, five of which he also published in 1794, record Fichte's rethinking

---

[2] Fichte to Friedrich Niethammer, Dec. 6, 1793, in GA, III, 2: 20–1.

of philosophy's central role in the construction of a rational social order and the regeneration of public culture.[3]

By virtue of their shared context and their intimately related contents, these three texts form a whole, though they have rarely been considered as such. They were the joint products of a remarkably ambitious and unusually controversial academic debut. Fichte had two objectives: to reconceive the self as a moral agent; to position philosophy at the center of a new configuration of knowledge so that it could validate its claim to be the moral arbiter for a modern public culture. Linking the two was his concept of *Wissenschaft*, a term usually translated as "science" but often used to refer to kinds of disciplinary knowledge quite different from, and in some cases defined in juxtaposition to, the contents and procedures of the natural sciences. *Wissenschaft* would ground the public voice of philosophy in the inner sanctum of selfhood, and would form the channel through which the inner self entered a life of public "activity."

If we are to appreciate the historical significance of Fichte's debut, we need to place it in the context of the larger intellectual field of German educated culture in the 1790s. To judge by the scarcity of external referents in his texts, he aspired to the splendid isolation of a philosophical loner. In fact, though, Fichte was engaged in a multivalent strategy of positioning – a relational strategy that involved both drawing on and distancing from several discourses at once.[4] He had to come to terms with the Critical Philosophy, as Kant had formulated it and as others were elaborating it. Like Kant, but with a more radical sense of purpose, he sought to reassert the moral rigorism of a Lutheran ethos, even as he removed that ethos from the transcendent truth claims of Lutheran fideism. If he was to win acceptance for his system as *the* source of moral authority, he had to banish from the realm of legitimate philosophizing the antisystematic latitudinarianism that some of his contemporaries practiced under the banner of "popular philosophy." He was also aware that alternative concepts of *Wissenschaft*, with their own claims to public authority, were emerging outside philosophy. At one extreme, he faced the increasingly

---

[3] J. G. Fichte, *The Science of Knowledge, with the First and Second Introductions*, ed. and trans. Peter Heath and John Lachs (Cambridge, 1982). Unless otherwise indicated, quotations are from this translation. I have used Breazeale's excellent translations of *Über den Begriff der Wissenschaftslehre oder der sogenannten Philosophie* and the Lectures in *Fichte. Early Philosophical Writings*, pp. 94–135, 144–215. The first five lectures were published in September 1794 as *Einige Vorlesungen über die Bestimmung des Gelehrten*. Breazeale notes that there were twelve lectures altogether, delivered from May 23 to the end of August 1794. Aside from the five published in *Einige Vorlesungen*, three others, entitled "Concerning the Difference between the Spirit and the Letter within Philosophy," have survived. Ibid., pp. 185–7.

[4] On "the positional or relational attributes of ideas" within an "intellectual field," see Fritz Ringer, *Fields of Knowledge. French Academic Culture in Comparative Perspective, 1890–1920* (Cambridge, 1992), pp. 4–12.

confident knowledge claims of the natural sciences; at the other, the ideal of selfhood and disciplinary knowledge that was taking shape in a new historical hermeneutics.

Hence Transcendental Idealism had to define its mission – and the mission of the philosophically constructed self – in relation to several rivals at once. Fichte's aim was to establish the moral ascendancy of his Doctrine of Knowledge over them all. He set to work with the ruthless confidence of the dialectician and with the fervor of the visionary.

I. THE SELF AS ACT

The Critical Philosophy and its Idealist offshoots at the end of the century are not known for their accessibility, but even in this company Fichte's *Wissenschaftslehre* is a notoriously impenetrable text.[5] Its opacity is due in part to the circumstances in which it was written. Having decided to construct his own philosophical system, Fichte soon realized that the *Wissenschaftslehre* was only the first, groping effort in a project that was likely to occupy him for the rest of his life. The work was necessarily hurried;

---

[5] The scholarship on the *Wissenschaftslehre* is now immense. Among the older contributions, see, e.g., Dieter Henrich, *Fichtes ursprüngliche Einsicht* (Frankfurt, 1967); Peter Baumanns, *Fichtes Wissenschaftslehre: Probleme ihres Anfangs* (Bonn, 1974). Recent approaches are well represented in Erich Fuchs and Ives Radrizzani, eds., *Der Grundsatz der ersten Wissenschaftslehre Fichte* (Tagung des Internationalen Kooperationsorgans der Fichte Forschung in Neapal, April 1995) (Neuried, 1996); Wolfgang H. Schrader, ed., *Die Grundlage der gesamten Wissenschaftslehre von 1794/95 und der transcendentale Standpunkt* (Tagung der Internationalen J. G.-Fichte-Gesellschaft, 1994) (Amsterdam/Atlanta, Ga., 1997). My reading of the *Wissenschaftslehre* is heavily indebted to recent Anglophone contributions. Especially useful were Frederick Neuhouser, *Fichte's Theory of Subjectivity* (Cambridge, 1990); Rudolf A. Makkreel, "Fichte's Dialetical Imagination," in Daniel Breazeale and Tom Rockmore, eds., *Fichte. Historical Contexts/Contemporary Controversies* (Atlantic Highlands, N.J., 1994); Daniel Breazeale, "How to Make an Idealist: Fichte's 'Refutation of Dogmatism' and the Problem of the Starting Point of the *Wissenschaftslehre*," *Philosophical Forum* 19 (1988): 97–123; Breazeale, "Fichte's *Aenesidemus* Review and the Transformation of German Idealism," *Review of Metaphysics* 34 (1981): 545–68; Breazeale, "Philosophy and the Divided Self: On the 'Existential' and 'Scientific' Tasks of the Jena *Wissenschaftslehre*," F-S 6 (1994): 117–47; Breazeale, "Certainty, Universal Validity, and Conviction: The Methodological Primacy of Practical Reason within the Jena *Wissenschaftslehre*," in Daniel Breazeale and Tom Rockmore, eds., *New Perspectives on Fichte* (Atlantic Highlands, N.J., 1996), pp. 35–59; Breazeale, "The Theory of Practice and the Practice of Theory: Fichte and the 'Primacy of Practical Reason,'" *International Philosophical Quarterly* 36:1, Issue No. 141 (March, 1996): 47–64; Wayne M. Martin, "'Without a Striving, No Object Is Possible': Fichte's Striving Doctrine and the Primacy of Practice," in Breazeale and Rockmore, eds., *New Perspectives*, pp. 19–33; Martin, *Idealism and Objectivity. Understanding Fichte's Jena Project* (Stanford, Calif., 1997); A. J. Mandt, "Fichte's Idealism in Theory and Practice," *Idealistic Studies* 14:2 (May, 1984): 127–47; Günter Zöller, *Fichte's Transcendental Philosophy. The Original Duplicity of Intelligence and Will* (Cambridge, 1998). There are useful descriptions of Fichte's theory of selfhood in Mark Kipperman, *Beyond Enchantment: German Idealism and English Romantic Poetry* (University of Pennsylvania Press, 1986); Frederick C. Beiser, *Enlightenment, Revolution, and Romanticism. The Genesis of Modern German Political Thought 1790–1800* (Cambridge, Mass., 1992), pp. 63–74.

he was writing from lecture to lecture, in a frantic effort to present the rudiments of the system in the first philosophy course he had taught. Fichte readily admitted in the preface to the first edition that the result was "most imperfect and defective." As he paced before his students in seminar, he could compensate for the defects with oral clarifications (though one wonders how much they helped). Readers of the published version had to decipher what was there. The author could only hope that they would withhold judgment until "future expositions of the system . . . finally presented [it] in full."[6]

These complications of its birth aside, the *Wissenschaftslehre* was bound to be an exceptionally difficult exercise in philosophical argument. Extending the "transcendental deduction" that Kant had developed in the *Critique of Pure Reason*, Fichte sought to establish a "transcendental idealism" on the first principle that the self (his term is the "Ich" or "I") "originally and unconditionally posits its own existence." The argument proceeds regressively; or, as he put it, its "course is an unbroken progression from conditioned to condition."[7] The reader follows a dialectical chain of propositions about "theoretical knowledge," Kant's term for our understanding of the natural world. Each synthesis yields an internal contradiction, which can only be resolved in a new synthesis. In a spiraling process of abstraction, proposition B becomes the necessary condition for the possibility of proposition A, and so on. The procedure seems more appropriate to geometry than to an exploration of the inner space of consciousness, and that is no accident. Fichte was intent on endowing his first principle with the self-evident certainty of a geometric theorem.

In the larger structure of the argument, theoretical knowledge turns out to harbor a fundamental contradiction, one that can be resolved only by demonstrating that the very possibility of theoretical reason is contingent on its subordination to the moral knowledge that Kant called "practical" reasoning. In the transition from the theoretical to the practical, the deduction reverses direction; a dialectical spiral out from the first principle becomes a plunge back into it. Having entered the text as its point of departure, the self-positing "I" becomes its point of culmination.

Following the intricacies of the dialectic from step to step without losing sight of the overarching structure of the argument is a challenging task. It is not made easier by Fichte's terminology. Like the philosophical system builders who preceded him, Fichte sought to avoid the messy ambiguities and overlappings of meaning in everyday speech by using a technical language of abstraction. Much of this language he inherited from Kant; but in his effort to probe the transcendental depths that Kant had

---

[6] Fichte, *Science*, pp. 3–5.
[7] Ibid, p. 25. On the difference between Descartes's progressive deduction and Fichte's regressive procedure, see Tom Rockmore, "Antifoundationalism, Circularity, and the Spirit of Fichte," in Breazeale and Rockmore, eds., *Fichte*, p. 101.

only glimpsed, he also developed his own set of philosophical neologisms. There is an "absolute" as well as a finite self-positing "I," and opposed to both is the "Not-I (*Nicht-Ich*)." Self-positing is not a "fact" (*Tatsache*), but an "act as fact" (*Thathandlung*). The philosopher becomes aware of this a priori act in an "intellectual intuition" (a notion that made more conventional Kantians very uneasy).

How do we get a fix on this text? We will begin with a wide-angle lens and then narrow our focus. One of the sources of modern western conceptions of the self, Charles Taylor has argued, lies in the philosophical turn to "radical reflexivity" from the late seventeenth century onward. The turn involved a rejection of ancient views of the cosmos as a normative order of being, defining the good for the human subject. Now the subject defined the good *from within*. Subjectivity was conceived as a cognitive and moral capacity to disengage from the "external" world, including one's own sense experience as an embodied self. The inner subject grasped the external world in a cognitive process of objectification. In that process Nature was reduced to an aggregate of things in "mechanical" relationships of time and space and, as such, was subject to instrumental control, as a means to moral agency.[8]

There is a sense in which this philosophical turn, at least in the variations it assumed in the eighteenth century, endangered the very concept of selfhood it was meant to secure. The dilemma can be formulated this way: does not radical reflexivity, even as it posits an inviolable self, threaten to obliterate it? How do we objectify the world, including our own sense being, without objectifying our selves and thereby subjecting our selves to the same mechanical laws that govern objects? Can we maintain a viable distinction between the self, as a moral person, and things? Clearly such a distinction requires that disengaged reason have a unique moral dignity by virtue of the fact that it is grounded in a true human nature, deeper than, and perhaps qualitatively different from, the nature that is the object of instrumental reason. But what is this human nature?

By the 1790s this issue and related ones had produced, in Taylor's phrase, "two 'frontiers' of moral exploration," one represented by Rousseau, the other by Kant. If the differences between them are not immediately apparent, that is because they occupied a great deal of common ground. Though Rousseau and Kant both rejected the Augustianian doctrine of original sin, they echoed Augustine in conceiving of morality in terms of the transformation of the will. In opposition to a kind of ethical thinking widespread in the Enlightenment, both thinkers adamantly denied that the calculation of "interest," however "enlightened," could be the ground of moral behavior. Both located virtue in the

---

[8] Charles Taylor, *Sources of the Self. The Making of the Modern Identity* (Cambridge, Mass., 1989), esp. pp. 143–76.

autonomous self, able to follow the voice of conscience, to grasp universal law within itself, depite various forces – material, social, political, and so on – impinging on it from without. And both were, in a limited but important sense, moral egalitarians. They believed that they were articulating the moral intuitions that ordinary people experienced as self-evident, and hence that the capacity for virtue was not a function of superior education, or wealth, or any other social distinction. It was in this sense that Kant noted to himself in 1765 that having read Rousseau, he no longer "despised the common man who knows nothing." Rousseau had taught him to "respect human nature."[9]

Where Rousseau and Kant differed in their respect for human nature was in the way they conceived the inner moral agent. To Rousseau it was the grids of unequal power relationships in society that threatened selfhood understood as moral personhood. The moral self was an inner core of impulses and emotions that were naturally good and that had to be liberated from socially generated needs and socially imposed conventions. Moral agency was in some sense an act of self-expression, the freedom to honor an ethic of authenticity that defied social artificiality by heeding the voice of Nature within. When Kant took his "critical" turn to transcendentalism, it did not take the form of a reflexive embrace of Rousseauian authenticity. That would have been, in Kant's view, a surrender to heteronomy, a submission to natural forces external to the moral self. Moral truth could not be found in impulses of nature within the person; it could only be defined by "the nature of reasoning." Selfhood was grounded in a kind of certainty that was qualitatively distinct from the objectification of nature, including our psychological and emotional makeups as natural beings. The inner self was a "practical" will, conforming to a conception of moral law that was inherent in its rationality.[10]

In the *Contribution*, Fichte hailed Rousseau as a misunderstood seer and identified with him personally as a fellow victim of a corrupt age. In the public lectures, Fichte, though still empathetic, offered a more critical image of Rousseau. Jean-Jacques had become a tragically flawed figure, good but weak, acutely sensitive to the corruption all around him but unable to find the right path out of it. The shift in estimation is not as radical as it might at first appear to be. In the *Contribution* Fichte had placed Rousseau in a line of heroic spirits that began with Luther and ended with Kant. That is to say, he already viewed Rousseau through two distinctly German lenses. He was still doing so in 1794, and that is

---

[9] Quoted in Ernst Cassirer, *Rousseau, Kant, Goethe. Two Essays*, trans. James Gutmann, Paul Oskar Kristeller, and John Herman Randall, Jr. (Princeton, N.J., 1970), pp. 1–2. See also the comparison of Rousseau and Kant in Robert C. Solomon, *Continental Philosophy since 1750. The Rise and Fall of the Self* (Oxford, 1988), pp. 16–43.

[10] Taylor, *Sources of the Self*, esp. pp. 314, 355–67.

critical to understanding what he sought to accomplish in the *Wissenschaftslehre* and how he went about doing it. There was the immediate philosophical context formed by Kantianism or, more precisely, by the field of argument that had formed around Kant's *Critiques*. And then there was the larger religious culture. Precisely because the philosophical field of argument was itself suffused with a religious tradition, it could not be purely philosophical. Fichte's *Wissenschaftslehre* is a case in point. Even a cursory reading of the text reveals Fichte's reliance at key points on a richly metaphorical rhetoric, marking his indebtedness to the Lutheran tradition and testifying to his efforts to recast that tradition within a more secular conceptual framework.

In this German context, at once technically philosophical and broadly religious, we can trace in some detail Fichte's intellectual crisis and his way of resolving it, despite the opacity of the *Wissenschaftslehre*. In a wealth of sources – correspondence, the writings that formed the path to the *Wissenschaftslehre*, the public lectures that accompanied it, the two "Introductions" published in 1797 – Fichte himself identified the source of the doubt that began to erode his sense of mission as a Kantian; the intellectual jolts that made him resolve to develop his own Doctrine of Knowledge; the moral issues he was addressing, and what his resolution of them was meant to accomplish.

Most of the *Wissenschaftslehre* was, on the face of it, a doggedly impersonal exercise in dialectical reasoning, but Fichte made no secret of his personal stake in the outcome. In his first "Introduction" to the *Wissenschaftslehre*, he observed that "[the] sort of philosophy one chooses depends . . . on [the] sort of man one is; for a philosophical system is not a dead piece of furniture that we can reject or accept as we wish; it is rather a thing animated by the soul of the person who holds it."[11] Taken out of context, the remark would seem to carry the puzzling implication that for all his apparent commitment to Truth, Fichte was a modern relativist, and indeed that his relativism rested on a crudely psychological reductionism. But Fichte was not suggesting that a person's philosophical convictions were merely a function of his psychological makeup. His point was that his epistemology both rested on and sustained his moral estimation of himself and others. "One reaches idealism," he noted, "if not through dogmatism itself, at least through the inclination thereto." The Idealist and the Dogmatist represented "two levels of humanity":

> The desire not to lose, but to maintain and assert himself in the rational process, is the interest which invisibly governs all [the philosopher's] thought. . . . Some, who have not yet raised themselves to full consciousness of their freedom and absolute independence, find themselves only in the presentation of things; they have only that dispersed self-consciousness

---

[11] Fichte, *Science*, p. 16.

which attaches itself to objects, and has to be gleaned from their multiplicity. Their image is reflected back at them only by things, as by a mirror;
if these were taken from them, their self would be lost as well . . . The man
who becomes conscious of his self-sufficiency and independence of everything that is outside himself . . . does not need things for the support of
himself . . . The self which he possesses, and which is the subject of his
interest, annuls this belief in things; he believes in his independence out of
inclination, he embraces it with feeling. His belief in himself is direct.[12]

The passage echoes with the conviction of the reborn Christian,
looking back on the Old Adam he has shed. Fichte is recalling his own
pre-Kantian "inclination" to delude himself into a precarious and ultimately false sense of self – a self that would have been "lost" for want of
supporting illusions if it had somehow fallen through the multiple causal
webs of "things." He had been rescued from this inclination by his reading
of Kant's *Critiques* in the summer of 1790. As late as the spring of 1793,
when he wrote the first part of his essay on the French Revolution, his
rhetoric conveyed a seemingly unshakeable conviction about the implications of the Kantian conversion. Fichte assured his readers that if we
look inward, we can discern "the pure, original form" of the self, as it
"would be without any experience." In discovering this self we become
aware of the "fact" of the Moral Law within us, which issues its commands through the "inner voice" of conscience.[13]

But by the fall of 1793, and perhaps earlier, Fichte was coming to
realize that the equation of the Moral Law and "pure" selfhood had more
pitfalls than his rhetoric had allowed. The underlying question was
whether the Critical Philosophy had really purged itself of the inclination to see the self as a reflection of things. When he set about constructing his system in 1794, it was with the realization that he now had
to confront an implication of Kant's transcendentalism that he (following
Kant) had left largely implicit. If his belief in his moral autonomy was to
endure, it had to be grounded in a new sense of selfhood – a holistic
view of the pure self, in no way dependent on anything "outside" itself
– as the irreducible source of free agency.

Any effort to reconceive selfhood in this way had to contend with the
implications of Kant's famous dualisms. Kant's epistemological point about
our "theoretical" understanding of the natural world, including our own
psychology, was double-edged. On the one hand, experience would
simply be impossible if the mind did not impose its universal categories
on the "manifold" of sense data. What constituted experience, Kant
insisted, was the interchange between the categories and the content

[12] Ibid., pp. 15–16. See also Breazeale, "How to Make an Idealist."
[13] Johann Gottlieb Fichte, *Schriften zur Revolution*, ed. Bernard Willms (Cologne and Opladen, 1967), pp. 48–9.

supplied to them by the intuitions of sensibility. If intuitions without categories were blind, categories without intuitions were empty. Kant was equally insistent, however, that the understanding and sensibility were completely heterogeneous faculties. The a priori concepts of the understanding were purely intellectual forms, existing beyond time and space; the stuff of intuition was empirical data within time and space. If they were so cleanly different, it was hard to see how interchange between them was possible. And if the possibility of interchange could not be demonstrated, Kant's transcendental deduction about the necessary conditions of all possible experience suffered a serious loss of credibility. Kantians might be confronted with an unbridgeable dualism between the universality of the purely intellectual and the particularity of the empirical.

In the early 1790s, Kant's most trenchant critic on this issue, as on several others, was Salomon Maimon, a former rabbi who, after years of wandering in Poland and Germany, had settled in Berlin. Given Fichte's antisemitic outburst of 1793, and given his contempt for people of dissolute habits, it is perhaps just as well that he and Maimon never met. But Maimon's *Attempt at a Transcendental Philosophy* (*Versuch einer Transcendentalphilosophie*), published in 1789, and his writings over the next several years contributed powerfully to Fichte's rethinking of his own Kantianism. Fichte found a cogent elaboration of his doubts in Maimon's attack on the Transcendental Deduction, and particularly in his radical questioning of the Kantian dualism between the understanding and sensibility. Today "people look down on [Maimon] from their heights," Fichte wrote to Reinhold in the spring of 1795, but in future centuries it will be recognized that "through him the entire Kantian philosophy as it has currently been understood, even by you, has been overthrown from the foundation."[14]

This was a stinging observation to make to Reinhold, who had become a target of Maimon's critical acumen and was conducting a bitter debate with him. Fichte did not hesitate to acknowledge, however, that it was Reinhold who had led the way in the search for a "first principle" that would systematize philosophy. Maimon saw little point to Reinhold's effort (his own question was whether principles were true and not whether they systematized knowledge). Fichte shared Reinhold's conviction that the discovery of a first principle would realize the possibility that Kant himself had raised. He was intent on succeeding where his predecessor at Jena seemed to be faltering.

[14] GA, III, 2: 282. On Maimon, see esp. Frederick C. Beiser, *The Fate of Reason. German Philosophy from Kant to Fichte* (Cambridge, Mass., 1987), pp. 285–323; Felix Krämer, "Parallelen zwischen Maimon und dem frühen Fichte," F-S 9 (1997): 275–90.

One requirement for a first principle was that it bridge the chasm between understanding and sensibility in our theoretical knowledge of the natural world. Ultimately at issue, however, was whether the larger, overarching Kantian dualism between the theoretical and practical realms could be overcome. In the first *Critique*, Kant had looked forward to the day when philosophy might form a complete system grounded in a single idea. In the second *Critique* he had gone so far as to entertain the possibility of "bringing some day into one view the unity of the entire pure rational faculty (both theoretical and practical) and of being able to derive everything from one principle."[15] He had suggested the direction such an inquiry might take by positing a "transcendental unity of apperception" – the original self-awareness of the thinking "I," without which the unity of consciousness was inconceivable. But these were scattered speculations; they offered little guidance as to how Kant's sprawling philosophical universe could be given systematic unity.

With the a priori, universal categories of theoretical understanding, Kant had brought the laws of Newtonian physics within consciousness and had made them its organizing principles. To attribute causal efficacy to an object was not to know it as a thing-in-itself, in its actual state of being outside consciousness. Instead, the law of causation governed relations between phenomena. Causation was conceived in thoroughly mechanistic terms; objects received and in turn transmitted force, which is to say that in the series of natural causation, no object could be an active cause without also being a passive effect. But if "practical" or moral reason was also assumed to be governed by natural causation, Kant argued, there could be no moral freedom and hence no morally good will. In the practical realm noumenal (or supersensible) subjects were free to conceive and choose what ought to be, rather than conforming to natural necessity. To the extent that the subject realized its potential for pure rationality, it was a self-legislating agent, an uncaused cause.

It was above all this concept of the self-legislating moral agent that made Kantianism so appealing to young men in the late 1780s and the 1790s. In the face of the implacable laws of natural science and the crude reductionism of materialist psychology, they were being told that moral freedom was in fact unconditional. But had Kant demonstrated or simply asserted this freedom? Could it be demonstrated in Kantian terms? Here again the issue was whether an interchange between two fundamentally heterogeneous realms was conceivable. The dualism between theoretical and practical reason seemed to create a double bind. One might argue that if a moral act was to have an effect on the phenomenal world, it had to break into the chain of causally governed events. But in that case, it

---

[15] Immanuel Kant, *Critique of Practical Reason*, trans. Lewis White Beck (New York, 1985), p. 94.

would seem, the act itself became causally determined. The alternative was to concede that moral agency could not be efficacious in the natural order. But then moral freedom was more illusory than real; freedom would seem to be confined to an "inner" space, and to be impotent in the face of "external" constraints.

To Reinhold, the discovery of a first principle promised to resolve these issues once and for all. Without such a principle, he observed in 1790, "the bases for our ethical duties and rights and hence these duties and rights themelves, must remain forever undecided."[16] Reinhold envisioned a truly "elementary" philosophy, rigorously restricted to describing consciousness itself. Where Kant had regarded the "unity of apperception" as a logically necessary postulate, Reinhold wanted to describe that unity as a substantive fact of consciousness. For the fact to be universally accepted, it had to be completely self-evident; if it needed proof of any sort (even logical proof), it could not be the irreducible foundation that philosophy needed.

In a sense, Reinhold argued, Kant had neglected the obvious. He had used the term "representation" (*Vorstellung*) liberally to describe objects in consciousness, but without defining it. No one could deny that the I had representations. From this elementary fact Reinhold derived his first principle, which stated that "in consciousness, the representation is distinguished from, and related to, the subject and object, by the subject."[17] As banal as it sounded, the principle was designed to convey two critical points: that consciousness was grounded in self-consciousness, and that both theoretical and practical reason were rooted in a single faculty of representation.

Sometime in 1793 Fichte began writing his "personal meditations" on Reinhold's Elementary Philosophy. The meditations record his struggle to articulate his growing conviction that Reinhold's principle of consciousness could not serve as the first principle, and his initial groping for a way to pursue his alternative, an exploration of what he called the "unconditionedness of the I."[18] In the course of pondering Reinhold's

---

[16] Karl Leonhard Reinhold, "Ueber die Möglichkeit der Philosophie als strenge Wissenschaft," in Reinhold, *Über das Fundament des Philosophischen Wissens. Über die Moglichkeit der Philosophie als strenge Wissenschaft (1790)*, ed. Wolfgang H. Schrader (Hamburg, 1978), p. 367. Gerhard W. Fuchs, *Karl Leonhard Reinhold – Illuminat und Philosoph* (Frankfurt am Main, 1994), is a good introduction to Reinhold's life and thought. My synopsis of Reinhold's contribution is heavily indebted to Beiser, *The Fate of Reason*, pp. 226–65. On the difference between Reinhold's and Fichte's view of philosophy as transcendental *Wissenschaft*, see esp. Martin, *Idealism and Objectivity*, pp. 81–9; Alexander von Schönborn, "Fichte und Reinhold über die Begrenzung der Philosophie," F-S 9 (1997): 241–55.

[17] Quoted in Beiser, *The Fate of Reason*, pp. 252–3.

[18] "Eigne Meditationen über ElementarPhilosophie/Practische Philosophie," GA, II, 3: 48. Indispensable on this text is Reinhard Lauth, "Genèse du 'Fondement de toute la doctrine de la science'

work, he received the jolt that finally committed him to developing his own system and made him think out, in rough terms, the concepts and the structure of argument the effort would entail. He had undertaken a review of a treatise titled *Aenesidemus*, published anonymously by Gottlob Ernst Schulze, a professor of philosophy at Helmstedt, in 1792. The treatise took the form of a series of letters in which Aenesidemus, a self-styled "Humean" skeptic who represented the author's position, conducted an argument with an enthusiastic but obviously outmatched defender of the Critical Philosophy. Schulze fired a battery of specific criticisms at Reinhold, but his ultimate aim was to demonstrate that the Critical Philosophy itself was guilty of the "dogmatism" it claimed to reject. "In philosophy," Schulze-Aenesidemus contends, "nothing can be decided on the basis of incontestably certain and universally valid first principles concerning the existence or nonexistence of things in themselves and their properties nor concerning the limits of man's capacity for knowledge."[19]

Fichte agreed to review *Aenesidemus* in early 1793, but it took him nearly a year to complete the task. The book "confounded me for a long time," he wrote to a friend in mid-December 1793. *Aenesidemus* had "overthrown" Reinhold in his eyes and had made him suspicious of Kant. Since he could not live "under an open sky," he had resolved to rebuild "from the ground up." And he was doing just that; he had "discovered a new *Fundament* from which all of philosophy can be developed very easily," so that "in a few years we will have a philosophy that proceeds like geometry with respect to evidence (*Evidenz*)."[20] In the review Fichte took pains to demonstrate his continuing solidarity with Reinhold and Kant, but it was a tortuous and not altogether convincing performance. The review had become the occasion for unveiling his own system; and he left no doubt that what had compelled him to do so was the skeptical attack on the Critical Philosophy, which had effectively exposed its tendencies to violate its own principles. He remained unpersuaded, to be sure, by the skeptic's argument that the search for a first principle was futile. What had nonetheless "confounded" him was the realization that for all its claims to the contrary, the Critical Philosophy was vulnerable to the charge of being another "dogmatism," claiming transcendent knowledge, and especially of being another determinist species of

de Fichte à partir de ses 'Méditations personnelles sur l'Élementarphilosophie,'" *Archives der Philosophie* 34 (1971): 51–79. See also Neuhouser, *Fichte's Theory of Subjectivity*, pp. 38–41.

[19] *Aenesidemus oder über die Fundamente der von dem Herrn Professor Reinhold in Jena gelieferten Elementar-philosophie* (1792), published anonymously and without place of publication. On the significance of this text, see esp. Beiser, *The Fate of Reason*, pp. 266–84. On Fichte's review, see Breazeale, "Fichte's Aenesidemus Review," and Breazeale's preface to the translation in *Fichte. Early Philosophical Writings*, pp. 53–8.

[20] Fichte to Heinrich Stephani, mid-Dec., 1793, GA, III, 2: 28.

dogmatism. Kant had failed to shut the door tight against such charges, and with the best of intentions Reinhold was encouraging others to open the door wide. Fichte was intent on refuting the charge once and for all – or, in positive terms, on demonstrating the transcendental freedom of the self as a moral agent.

Fichte faulted both Kant and Reinhold for not declaring themselves "loudly and strongly enough" against "that old mischief . . . perpetrated with the thing in itself."[21] His point about Kant was well taken. To Kant, the thing-in-itself was unknowable as a noumenal reality, but its existence independent of consciousness had to be "thought" as a necessary condition for our representations. As for Reinhold, Fichte was being unusually kind. As Reinhold elaborated and defended his theory, he tended to fall into the very pitfalls he had originally intended to avoid. Determined not to resort to illegitimate "metaphysical" claims to transcendent knowledge, he followed Kant in arguing that the noumenal reality of the thing-in-itself – whether of the subject as a nonempirical entity, or of an extra-conscious object – was simply unknowable. But what, then, did it mean to say that the representation, though "distinguished from" the object, was also "related to" it? In the face of complaints about the vagueness of this language, Reinhold argued that the "content" (as opposed to the "form") of a representation "relates" to the object in the sense that it "represents" it or "corresponds" to it. Did this not make consciousness in some sense contingent on things-in-themselves? And what did that imply about the freedom of the subject vis-à-vis its representations?[22]

Encouraged by the apparent implications of Reinhold's move, Schulze/Aenesidemus concluded that the Critical Philosophy did violate its own transcendental restrictions by claiming to deduce the reality of things in themselves. Fichte's response was to insist on a radical excision of the very thought of a thing-in-itself. For the mind, everything – even the thought of something outside it – is posited within itself. Hence it is the task of the Critical Philosophy to show that there is no need for "a passage from the external to the internal or vice versa." By demonstrating that "everything which occurs in our mind can be completely explained and comprehended on the basis of the mind itself," the Critical Philosophy "points out to us that circle from which we cannot escape" (though the compensation is that within the circle, we are furnished with "the greatest coherence in all of our knowledge").[23] As usual in Fichte's reasoning, the epistemological point serves to dispel an alarming moral implication. If the thing-in-itself is admitted into philosophy, then consciousness becomes the reflection of an ontologically prior reality

---

[21] Fichte. Early Philosophical Writings, p. 72.
[22] Beiser, The Fate of Reason, esp. pp. 252–65.   [23] Fichte. Early Philosophical Writings, p. 69.

– of something "more real" outside itself. The very notion of an irreducible moral self begins to dissolve.

Even if the thing-in-itself were banished, however, there was another sense in which Reinhold was unwittingly exposing a vulnerability in the Critical Philosophy. If Reinhold was "consequential" about his generic principle of representation, Fichte observed in mid-December 1793, he knew nothing of the "practical imperative" and "must become an empirical fatalist."[24] Kant's dualism had left unclear why the "practical imperative" – that is, the Moral Law – could be efficacious in the phenomenal world of causality. Reinhold's concept of the faculty of representation threatened to resolve this dualism in precisely the wrong way. He claimed to have identified the generic faculty at the root of both theoretical and practical reason. What he had actually done in Fichte's view was merely to describe the faculty basic to theoretical reason. If Reinhold's claim were accepted, the practical imperative would lose its autonomy (not to mention its efficacy) as it was subsumed under theoretical laws.

Here again Fichte found an alarming implication spelled out in *Aenesidemus*. Schulze was not persuaded by Kant's moral theology, which reasoned that a Moral Law that required us to strive toward what is impossible would be irrational, and hence that we must have a "practical" faith in the two objective realities, the existence of God and the immortality of the human soul, that make it possible to achieve the highest good. In Schulze's inversion of this inference, we cannot judge whether an action is commanded or forbidden until we decide whether it is possible to do it or to refrain from doing it, and only theoretical principles can guide that decision. One of Fichte's implicit grievances against Reinhold's first principle was that it threatened to confirm this inversion, since it unwittingly grounded everything, including practical reason, in our understanding of the phenomenal world. The catastrophic implication – the one that Schulze had spelled out in his refutation of Kant's moral theology – was that moral duty (and freedom) only extended as far as the constraints of causality allowed. Morality became a matter of adapting to natural determinants rather than striving to overcome them.

It was in response to this assault on the "primacy" of practical reason that Fichte sketched out his alternative system at the end of the *Aenesidemus* review. "Far from practical reason having to recognize the superiority of theoretical reason," he concluded, "practical reason is founded on the conflict between the self-determining element within us and the theoretical-knowing element."[25] The dialectical progression from

---

[24] Fichte to Heinrich Stephani (mid-December, 1793), in GA, III, 2: 28.
[25] *Fichte. Early Philosophical Writings*, pp. 74–7.

theoretical to practical knowledge in the *Wissenschaftslehre* was designed to reveal the dynamic of this conflict. The moral self – "the self-determining element within us" – emerges as the active and creative agent, the primordial "I" without which there could not be a thinking self. Ultimately, then, one becomes a transcendental idealist by an act of the will, not an act of intellect. The self is an "ought," not a metaphysical or ontological "is."[26]

What does it mean to define the self in this way, and how does the individual become self-aware in the transcendental sense? Fichte came to these questions with an acute awareness of how they could not be answered if the self was to be the irreducible grounding of consciousness. Obviously any concept of the self that might imply its reduction to an object or thing with phenomenal status was unacceptable; even if causal force was attributed to such an entity, how could it break out of the causal series of the natural order – the series to which the "ought" of moral freedom, as a supersensible mode of action, was not subject? In Reinhold's alternative, on the other hand, the subject related to the representation by actively imposing a "form" on it. Here again, as in his argument that the object supplied the content of representation, Reinhold seemed to imply that a thing-in-itself – in this case, a noumenal subject – was the source or cause of a part of consciousness. As both Maimon and Schulze were quick to point out, this implication strayed illicitly beyond the transcendental circle, both by claiming knowledge of noumenal reality and by extending to that reality a concept of causation that applied only to relationships between phenomena in theoretical understanding.

What Fichte announced in the *Aenesidemus* review and sought to demonstrate in the *Wissenschaftslehre* was that the irreducible self could be understood neither as a thing qua phenomenon nor as a thing-in-itself, a preexisting noumenal ground for consciousness. Consciousness is grounded in a primordial act of self-consciousness – an act that cannot be directly grasped in consciousness – in which the self "posits itself absolutely." To think of self-positing exclusively as an act is to deny that the primordial "I" exists in itself or for objects in a causal series. The self is unique in that it "comes to exist for itself" in an act of unconditionally spontaneous self-awareness. In that sense, the I is self-grounding; there is no kind of "being" prior to the act. Fichte's point was not simply that the self is not an object in relation to external objects. It cannot make itself an object vis-à-vis itself, even when it reflects on itself. When the "I" thinks about itself, as opposed to thinking about anything else, it does not create a representation that is in some sense independent of it. Its self-reflection is its being, since thought and object, agent and product,

---

[26] See esp. Mandt, "Fichte's Idealism"; Breazeale, "The Theory of Practice and the Practice of Theory."

are one. To put it another way, the self has no kind of being apart from the act of self-positing that is self-consciousness.[27]

By identifying the primordial and irreducible self as a pure act, Fichte sought to break through several epistemological impasses. Toward the end of his discussion of theoretical knowledge, however, the reader is faced with an impasse that seems to make it impossible to speak of a coherent self in any meaningful sense. If consciousness is said to be grounded in the act of self-consciousness, have we not created another unbridgeable dualism? The primordial act of self-consciousness – the act of self-positing – is "absolute" in the sense that it is infinite and unbounded. But the "intelligent" self – the self as consciousness – cannot exist without positing a Not-Self, completely opposed to it, and thereby restricting itself. Can there be a unitary self in which the infinite and unbounded and the finite and restricted somehow coexist? If the absolute self enters a finite existence, does it not forfeit its unconditional freedom? If it retains its freedom, will it not annihilate the Not-Self and thereby eliminate the necessary condition for its finite existence?[28]

Only a transition to practical knowledge, Fichte argues, can remove this barrier from the transcendental deduction. In effecting the transition, Fichte complements his dialectical procedure with strikingly emotive language, rich in distinctly German resonances. Most of this language, it should be noted, is conspicuously absent from Fichte's renewed efforts to explain the Doctrine of Knowledge in the lecture series he gave from 1796 to 1799. By then the demonstration of the primacy of practical reason, which had preoccupied him in 1794, had been subsumed under an insistence on the reciprocal interplay of the theoretical and the practical, and indeed on their "equiprimacy," within every moment of consciousness. Hence Fichte could abandon his earlier effort in the *Wissenschaftslehre* to construct a dialectical "progression from the conditioned to the condition," and instead follow "a much more natural path" from the self as practical "act" to the self as theoretical "fact." That in turn meant that in explaining a priori self-consciousness as a purely philosophical form of reflexivity, he no longer had to treat as "a series of actions" what was "really only one action." He could avoid, or largely avoid, the "many misunderstandings" that arose from the "arbitrary" use of "sensible expressions," evoking experience in time and space, to "talk about anything mental or spiritual."[29]

---

[27] The point is made especially lucidly in Zöller, *Fichte's Transcendental Philosophy*, pp. 37–47.

[28] Fichte, *Science*, pp. 190–217.

[29] Fichte. *Foundations of Transcendental Philosophy (Wissenschaftslehre) Nova Methodo (1796/99)*, trans. and ed. Daniel Breazeale (Ithaca and London, 1992), esp. pp. 86, 100–4. On the emphasis on "equiprimacy" in this reformulation of the Doctrine of Knowledge, see esp. Breazeale, "The Theory of Practice and the Practice of Theory."

In the *Wissenschaftslehre*, Fichte clearly had been reluctant to resort to "sensible expressions." In the second half of the text the argument continues to advance dialectically through a schema of abstract concepts. Infinitude and finitude; subject and object; intuitant and intuited; active and passive: each pair forms a binary opposition. To capture the dynamics of binary relationships, Fichte constructs a triangular field of forces and counterforces, its points labeled A, B, and C. In the movement back to a first principle, however, these strategies did not suffice to demonstrate the supremacy of the moral self in its struggle with the embodied self. Fichte conveys the struggle by having dialectical reasoning act as though it were both temporal and spatial. It becomes the vehicle for a dramatic narrative, an extended metaphor centered on the image of ceaseless "striving" (*Streben*) against the "resistance" (*Anstoss*) posed by the Not-I. The metaphor evokes powerful but multivalent images of vitalistic energy, of dynamic forces in conflict, of conquest and subjugation.[30]

The vital link in this drama – its mediator, so to speak – is the "productive imagination," whose "active power" Fichte calls "the state of intuition." If the move to a self-positing "I" did not signal a decisive break with Kant, this move surely did. Kant had always been careful to locate "transcendental spontaneity" within the epistemological confines of the understanding. Fichte finds that spontaneity in imaginative intuition. Only in that source, he now concludes, can we ground "the possibility of our consciousness, our life, our existence for ourselves, that is, our existence as selves." In imaginative intuition Fichte found the prerepresentational force he had been seeking. "The power of *imagination*," Fichte wrote, is

> the interplay of the self, in and with itself, whereby it posits itself at once as finite and infinite – an interplay that consists, as it were, in self-conflict, and is self-reproducing, in that the self endeavors to unite the irreconcilable, now attempting to receive the infinite in the form of the finite, now, baffled, positing it again outside the latter, and in that very moment seeking once more to entertain it under the form of finitude.[31]

The inner power of synthesis lies not in resolving or dissolving contradictions, but in "lay[ing] hold" of both [opposites] at once by "waver[ing]" between the "demand" to unite them and "the impossibil-

[30] M. H. Abrams's description is especially suggestive; "Throughout Fichte's system . . . the relation of the ego to the non-ego is couched in metaphors of *Machtpolitik* – a power language of challenge, conflict, and the struggle for mastery between two hostile forces – in which the ego cannot rest content short of achieving absolute freedom, in the conquest and annihilation of the adversary which it has itself set up." *Natural Supernaturalism. Tradition and Revolution in Romantic Literature* (New York, 1973), p. 358
[31] Fichte, *Science*, p. 193.

ity of carrying it out."[32] As this drama unfolds, the wavering of the imagination becomes the dynamic of the striving self. Fichte defines the pure activity of self-positing as a "boundless striving, carried to infinity."[33] The self cannot exist as a finite intelligence without also positing a Not-Self, the world of objects in consciousness, which constitute an opposition within the self and make possible empirical self-consciousness. The striving self encounters this Not-I as a "check" or "resistance" (*Anstoss*) to its capacity for infinite expansion. In reaction the self turns back into itself, but only to reassert its aspiration to infinity. It reasserts itself not by expanding its theoretical knowledge but by generating moral ideals beyond the restrictions posed by the Not-Self. Though the self can be said to be "dependent" on the Not-Self "in respect of its existence," it remains "absolutely independent" in "the determinations of this its existence.[34] Its striving is a ceaseless effort to conceive what ought to be and to make the resistant Not-Self conform to this alternative moral vision. It is a process in which the "absolute" self, using the not-self as its medium, seeks to absorb the finite intelligent self into its pure, infinite act. If the process were to be completed, pure self-consciousness and empirical self-consciousness would be one. This teleological resolution cannot, of course, be fully achieved in finite existence. But we exercise our freedom, our capacity for unconditional self-determination, by striving to approach it.[35]

It is not hard to understand why this transcendental drama was so appealing to Fichte's philosophical imagination. The mix of abstract deduction and metaphoric evocation served to demonstrate what he had asserted rather facilely in the *Contribution*. To intuit the "pure, original form" of the self was to become aware of our self-legislating capacity, our freedom to generate the Moral Law, the "ought" of practical reason, spontaneously from within. The identity of subject and object in "absolute" self-positing is a paradigm for the practical activity of making nature – or, in Fichte's terms, the Not-Self – conform to our ends. By the end of the *Wissenschaftslehre*, Fichte has not simply transformed the first principle from a "fact" to an "act"; the act has become a regulative idea, a categorical demand that the self makes upon itself and the world. Practical reason, as Fichte now defines it, is the "demand that everything should conform to the self, that all reality should be posited absolutely through

---

[32] Ibid., p. 201. My analysis of the role of the imagination in Fichte's dialectic is especially indebted to Makkreel, "Fichte's Dialectical Imagination."
[33] Fichte, *Science*, p. 201.　　[34] Ibid., p. 246.
[35] Ibid., pp. 218–61. Neuhouser, *Fichte's Theory of Subjectivity*, offers an especially lucid critique of the concept of striving. Also helpful is Mandt, "Fichte's Idealism." The concept of striving was introduced at the end of the *Aenesidemus* review; *Fichte: Early Philosophical Writings*, pp. 75–6.

the self." What is irreducible in the self is the unconditional freedom to reason practically.

In the *Wissenschaftslehre* Fichte reconfirmed his sense of selfhood by returning his system to its point of departure. Along the way he had had to offer solutions to two especially recalcitrant issues. Intent on avoiding Reinhold's illicit intrusion of the phenomenal into the noumenal realm, Fichte explained why striving was a unique kind of causal force. If the self is not caused by the Not-Self, it is also not a cause in the theoretical sense. Striving is "a cause that is not a cause": it "strives to be a cause" without "possessing causality." Fichte's meaning is in part that since there cannot be a finite self without resistance to it, striving cannot be causal in the theoretical sense; its moral efficacy cannot be contingent on its effecting, or resulting in, a canceling of the Not-Self. Indeed the efficacy of the Moral Law does not lie in producing any effect in the natural order. It generates practical acts guided by its purely rational ideals, and those acts may or may not break into the causal series in which objects are related.[36]

No less paradoxical was Fichte's way of accounting for the fact that our "representations" are "accompanied by a feeling of necessity."[37] Why is it that the self *feels* determined by objects outside itself? This was the question with which Fichte had introduced the *Wissenschaftslehre*. He knew from his own experience that the Idealist had to resist the "inclination" to succumb to this feeling – or, as he put it in 1797, to "find [oneself] only in the presentation of things." He located the source of the feeling within his dramatic narrative; it arose when the self encountered the "resistance" of the Not-Self, or what one scholar has called "the resisting surface of things."[38] In the larger dynamic of striving, the feeling of being determined is a necessary illusion; by turning the self back on itself, it reinforces the drive to spontaneous activity. The Not-Self is the field of action that the self creates to assert itself, the receptivity that the mind gives to itself. In the very process of demonstrating its capacity to be receptive, the self asserts its unconditional freedom. The "feeling of necessity" is an experience of passivity; without it, the empirical "I" could not be an active moral agent. The very relentlessness of the resistance makes the self continually aware of its own self-generated moral force.

★ ★ ★

There is an illusion of universality, Charles Taylor observes, in modern western concepts of the self. Purporting to identify the essence of the human being as such, such concepts in fact are "historically local" self-interpretations. In part their historical specificity reflects the fact that in

---

[36] Fichte, *Science*, pp. 224–52; Neuhouser, *Fichte's Theory of Subjectivity*, pp. 102–16.
[37] Fichte, *Science*, pp. 6–7.   [38] Makkreel, "Fichte's Dialectical Imagination," p. 15.

early modern Europe philosophical reflexivity fused in multiple ways with the Protestant ethos that Max Weber called "innerworldy asceticism" and that Taylor sums up with the term "the punctual self." Taylor has in mind the moral agent who, defining his own ends from within, seeks to shape and master his embodied self and his world accordingly. Following Weber, Taylor emphasizes the contribution of the Calvinist ideal of calling to this "punctual" ethos.[39] Fichte's resort to a dramatic narrative of striving makes explicit what the *Wissenschaftslehre* would otherwise have left implicit: that in his fusion of philosophy and religious tradition Lutheranism played a similar role. *Streben* was an eminently Lutheran term evoking the "inner" struggle for spiritual perfection, and it is not surprising that Fichte turned to it to evoke the dynamics of selfhood. He was not rejecting the model of spirituality in which the term had long been central, but recasting it.[40]

At the center of this recasting was the ethos of the calling. In Lutheranism, as in Calvinism, it was in the calling that the mystery of Christian freedom played itself out. Freedom meant inner spontaneity, the experience of faith as a self-generated impulse; but somehow, in the inner-worldly asceticism of the calling, spontaneity became an outer-directed imperative to control oneself and, through self-mastery, to have an effect on the world. In 1790 Fichte had embraced Kantianism because it seemed to resolve this mystery in philosophically persuasive terms. Now, as he pushed forward where Kant seemed to have stopped short, he had to reconcile spontaneity and control in his own terms. In its implications, to be sure, his system was more secular and indeed more threatening to Christian belief than Kant's Critical Philosophy. There was no room in it for the anthropomorphically represented God of theism, much less for evangelical fideism. And yet, even as Fichte sought to preclude all forms of belief in the transcendent, he conceived a new philosophical justification for the ethos that Protestant fideism entailed.

That he turned to the imagination is, at least at first glance, a measure of his daring, not to say his recklessness. He was fully aware that he risked opening himself to the charge of *Schwärmerei*, the German term for religious "enthusiasm," evoking the "swarming" excess and violence of radical sects since Luther had applied it to Anabaptism in the 1520s. To the established churches, *Schwärmerei* was a frightening mirror opposite of the paradox of Christian freedom; a false sense of spontaneity resulted in ravings, mass frenzies, anarchy. From the late seventeenth century onward, as explanations of this phenomenon in medical terms gained the

---

[39] Taylor, *Sources of the Self*, esp. pp. 113, 211–33.
[40] On the Lutheran roots of *Streben* and on its eighteenth-century usages, see esp. Fania Oz-Salzberger, *Translating the Enlightenment. Scottish Civic Discourse in Eighteenth-Century Germany* (Oxford, 1995), pp. 159–64.

ascendancy, it had become a truism that the vulnerable faculty was the imagination. The imagination was easily overheated – in which case it fed off the emotional drives called the passions, and it gave form to those drives in chimerical but compelling images. In the *Schwärmer* the passions and their imagistic products ran riot, and the self, in thrall to its own self-indulgent fantasies of direct revelation, lost control. In the Protestant *Aufklärung* this diagnosis had been extended to a broad range of alarming divergences from the standard of rational self-discipline, from the genius cult of the *Sturm und Drang* to the radical politics of the French Revolution.[41]

Against this backdrop, Fichte's grounding of selfhood in the dialectical play of the "productive imagination" was a startling move. In an effort to inspire his student audience, he elaborated this theme in the lectures; but he did so in a way that cleanly dissociated his philosophical spirituality from what he called the "wild, misshapen monstrosities" of "overheated imagination" in "enthusiasm and fanaticism."[42] Emotion was indeed the key to the power of the imagination. In our theoretical knowledge, in fact, the imagination only shaped into representations the raw materials that "feeling" provided. There was a critical distinction, however, between this kind of feeling and the "spiritual feelings" that "lie in a deeper region of our spirit, in its most secret sanctuary." When the imagination drew on the latter, it became the "intellectual spontaneity" peculiar to the philosopher.[43]

Imagination in this sense was really the transcendental philosopher's *counter* to the *Schwärmer*'s imaginative excesses. Rather than generating volatile images, it constructed moral "ideals." It did so by abstracting from representations to the process of representing, so that what remained "after one has abstracted from everything possible" would be "the pure I," "the abstracting subject."[44] It was a process in which "one's sensibility must wither away." Radical reflexivity in this key echoed with the Lutheran battle of the "spirit" against the "flesh." It was not, of course, a matter of hair shirts and fastings. Quite the contrary; Fichte counseled his listeners to see to their bodily health. The point, though, was not to enjoy the body, but to prevent it from "remind[ing] us of its existence." If the body was kept healthy, it would not get in the way of the effort to ignore it.[45]

<hr/>

[41] On enthusiasm and *Schwärmerei*, see Hans-Jürgen Schings, *Melancholie und Aufklärung. Melancholiker and ihre Kritiker in Erfahrungsseelenkunde und Literatur des 18. Jahrhunderts* (Stuttgart, 1977); Michael Heyd, *"Be Sober and Reasonable": The Critique of Enthusiasm in the Seventeenth and Early Eighteenth Centuries* (Leiden, 1995); Anthony J. La Vopa, "The Philosopher and the *Schwärmer*: On the Career of a German Epithet from Luther to Kant," in Lawrence E. Klein and Anthony J. La Vopa, eds., *Enthusiasm and Enlightenment in Europe, 1650–1850* (San Marino, Calif., 1998), pp. 85–115.
[42] *Fichte. Early Philosophical Writings*, p. 200.
[43] Ibid., pp. 193–200.   [44] Ibid., p. 204.
[45] This lecture was first published in Karl Hase, ed., *Jenaisches Fichte-Büchlein* (Leipzig, 1856).

All forms of outer-directed striving were grounded in the inner striving, the struggle that Fichte called "disciplined, strict abstraction."[46] Rigorous abstraction was the key to Fichte's secular reformulation of the paradox of Christian freedom. It was a process that began with intimations of an impenetrable inner spontaneity and that ended in rational control over the natural self and, through that self-control, in the appropriation of the natural world for moral ends. The self achieved a willed self-mastery that was at once constraining and empowering – that channeled moral energy from its inviolable source in inner spontaneity into the outer-directed struggle to subjugate the natural world to the imperatives of a rational order. The vehicle of this self-mastery was transcendental philosophy, the highest form of *Wissenschaft*. It represented in its purest form the inner-worldly asceticism of the punctual self, the moral person at work in the calling. The rebirth of the Old Adam, one might say, now lay in the act of reflexivity and not in the reception of grace. But this transcendental turn inward, like the experience of conversion, empowered the moral person to engage in an intense struggle to regenerate a corrupt world. To commit oneself to this kind of philosophical "speculation" was to enter a "thorny" path, an ascent to "a higher, spiritual order of things" through "care, effort, and labor."[47] Exercising freedom in relentless self-discipline, the masters of *Wissenschaft* would guide mankind toward the "golden age."

Committed to this ethos, Fichte could still empathize with, and indeed identify with, Rousseau's alienation from a corrupt society. He could not, however, follow Rousseau in yearning for a lost golden age, a primitive state of innocence. In the fifth public lecture Fichte warned his students that rather than struggling to give progress a moral purpose, Rousseau had succumbed to self-indulgent passivity; and that was because, confusing human nature with "mere, undeveloped feeling," he "never penetrated by any path to the foundation of all human knowledge." "Do not allow yourself to be overcome by [the] pain" of human relationships, Fichte urged his audience at the close of the lecture. "Act! Act! That is what we are here for."[48]

2. THE AUTHORITY OF SYSTEM

By itself the *Wissenschaftslehre* might be taken to signal a radical involution of Fichte's thought. Having used Kantian ethics to seize social and political issues by the throat in the *Contribution*, he now seemed to be retreating into a purely philosophical privatism. In fact, though, Fichte did not consider his turn inward to a pure self – the turn he mapped in the

---

[46] Fichte. *Early Philosophical Writings*, p. 205.   [47] Ibid., pp. 205–7.   [48] Ibid., pp. 179, 184.

Wissenschaftslehre – as a withdrawal into private subjectivity. The turn had become his new route to the assertion of an authoritative voice in German public life. Through an act of philosophical imagination – an act in which the dynamic of striving was experienced as an emotional need – the mind became aware of the grounding of consciousness in an originary act of self-consciousness. Fichte's search for his God-given mission as a young Lutheran had culminated in his philosophical view of himself as an instrument of "speculation."

Fichte saw himself reasserting philosophy's claim to a unique objectivity as a form of public knowledge. His claim rested not on the capacity to explain how the mind represents objects external to itself but on an intensely reflexive grasp of the "inner" truth. This was radical reflexivity at its most paradoxical. The ground of objective moral truth could only be intuited, in a plunge into the interior of consciousness, and that interior could only be imperfectly figured, not grasped, in language. The paradox was open to abuse, as was painfully evident in Fichte's efforts to browbeat rivals like Reinhold into acknowledging his ascendancy. While they were misled by personal interests and "passions," his self-exploration had given him a lofty detachment – a disinterested objectivity – as the impersonal instrument of Truth.[49] It was a logic that tended to blind Fichte to his own egotism. But it also had the effect of renewing his commitment to a philosophical radicalism with a political bite. Having shed personal motives and needs to plumb the self as such, he was in a position to submit the world around him to a fundamental critique.

As he struggled with the dialectical abstractions on which his system was to be built, Fichte began spinning out his new critique. Taken together, the prospectus entitled *Concerning the Concept of the Doctrine of Knowledge* and the public lectures represent a remarkably sweeping effort to project a social order and a public culture on the basis of Fichte's reformulation of Kantian a priori principles. What had shifted was the philosopher's angle of vision and, with it, his public persona. Fichte no longer spoke as an alienated outsider who, by virtue of his very marginality, felt empowered to censure his era, and who sought to bypass "the schools" in a direct bonding with the common man. However alienated he might still be, he was now a participant in an academic and official culture. It was central to his concerns that philosophy achieve recognition as a genuine *Wissenschaft* and that it assume its rightful place in the new public culture that seemed to be taking shape. He no longer expected Kant's philosophy to effect a sudden breakthrough to an ethical community through its popularization in the print market. Instead, the regeneration of the society and the culture would emanate from the universities, where the transcendental principles of the Doctrine of Knowledge would con-

---

[49] See esp. Fichte to Reinhold (end of March–April, 1795), in GA, III, 2: 279.

stitute the foundation for all academic knowledge and would form the normative core of a new public order.

The effort to make philosophy the foundational mode of inquiry, the source of "indefeasible claims for knowledge," extended back at least to Descartes, but German circumstances explain why a renewal of that effort seemed both timely and urgent to Fichte's generation of Kantians.[50] By the 1790s the term *Wissenschaft* had become a kind of talisman in German academic discourse. The shift in its meaning over the previous several decades marked the disintegration of the traditional culture of the German Protestant universities and the beginning of their modern reconstitution. Since the Reformation the universities had had a dual mission. As credentialing centers filling the needs of church and state, they prepared young men for careers in the clergy, in law and government service, and in medicine. Their broader cultural assignment was to transmit a distinctly Protestant humanism by instilling "piety" through study of the Word of God while inculcating "eloquence" through mastery of classical rhetorical and literary forms. In this world, "learned" status grew out of and remained rooted in the broad basis of humanistic knowledge, though it also implied mastery of a professional expertise. So long as it did not conflict with Orthodoxy, humanistic study was assumed to build character; and through mastery of the forms of eloquence – in writing, in public speaking, and in conversation – character presented itself publicly.[51]

The philosophy faculty was the successor to the medieval arts faculties. Housing a wide array of humanistic studies, including philosophy proper, it represented the breadth of knowledge and the mastery of form that conferred "learned" status. Nonetheless the philosophy faculty formed the bottom rung on the universities' hierarchy of institutional prestige and rewards. This was in part because in principle, if not always in practice, it was subordinate to theological authority, and in part because, in contrast to the credentialing faculties of theology, law, and medicine, it was considered propadeutic and often remedial. Its poor-cousin status was reflected in academic career patterns. With rare exceptions, scholars used the philosophy faculty as the antechamber to careers in the "higher"

---

[50] See esp. Tom Rockmore, "Antifoundationalism, Circularity, and the Spirit of Fichte," in Breazeale and Rockmore, eds., *Fichte*, pp. 96–112, and Rockmore, "Fichte's Antifoundationalism, Intellectual Intuition, and Who One Is," in Breazeale and Rockmore, eds., *New Perspectives*, pp. 79–94. Also interesting on this issue is John Sallis, "Fichte and the Problem of System," *Man and World. An International Philosophical Review* 9:1 (Feb., 1976): 75–90.

[51] On the early modern German universities, see Friedrich Paulsen, *Geschichte des gelehrten Unterrichts auf den deutschen Schulen und Universitäten vom Ausgang des Mittelalters bis zur Gegenwart*, vol. 1 (3rd. enl. ed.: Berlin and Leipzig, 1919); Wilhelm Roessler, *Die Entstehung des modernen Erziehungswesens in Deutschland* (Stuttgart, 1961); R. Steven Turner, "The 'Bildungsbürgertum' and the Learned Professions in Prussia, 1770–1830," *Histoire sociale-Social History* 13:25 (May, 1980): 105–35; Charles E. McClelland, *State, Society, and University in Germany 1700–1914* (Cambridge, 1980).

faculties, where the endowments and the teaching fees were significantly more generous.

As late as the 1790s much of this culture and its institutional hierarchy were still in place; but in the course of the century they had come to seem increasingly obsolete, particularly to succeeding generations of the academically educated, and their legitimacy had waned. Academic knowledge had broken out of its traditional Protestant and humanistic molds. As cautious as it was, the rationalism of the *Aufklärung* had undermined the authority of the theology faculties as guardians of scriptural Orthodoxy. Taking Newtonian physics as its model, the study of science had, in Kant's words, undergone "a single and sudden revolution" that had launched it onto "the secure path of a science (*Wissenschaft*)."[52] The renaissance of classical studies, particularly under Christian Gottlob Heyne at Göttingen and Friedrich August Wolf at Halle, had made the Latinity of the old dispensation seem pedantic and aridly formalistic. As their traditional authorities and standards lost credibility, the universities had to accommodate a veritable flood of new knowledge about physical nature, the ancient world, the historical context of Scripture, the variety of human cultures, the stages of social and economic development, human psychology and social behavior, and a host of other subjects.[53]

We see forming here, at least in vague outline, our modern spectrum of disciplinary communities in the natural sciences, the social sciences, and the humanities – the spectrum that the philosophy faculties, in their renewed form, would encompass in the nineteenth century. In the traditional academic culture, *Wissenschaft* had been a personal credential that came with breadth of learning. Now the term evoked the impersonal standards that a field of inquiry had to meet to count as a "science" or, to introduce a phrase that does more justice to the inclusiveness of the German term, as a "scholarly discipline." As Protestant humanism lost its capacity to keep learning morally centered, and as the traditional hierarchy of faculties came under question, the new standards of *Wissenschaft* were used to validate new territorial claims and to reformulate old ones, in a remapping of knowledge. If a field of study was to put itself (or keep itself) on the map – if it was to validate its claim to be a rigorous *Wissenschaft* with an autonomous jurisdiction – it had to constitute itself as a system. A system was a clearly bounded, self-contained whole; it had

---

[52] *Immanuel Kant's Critique of Pure Reason*, trans. Norman Kemp Smith (New York, 1965), pp. 17–26.
[53] See, e.g., Peter Hanns Reill, *The German Enlightenment and the Rise of Historicism* (Berkeley, Calif., 1975); Anthony J. La Vopa, "Specialists against Specialization: Hellenism as Professional Ideology in German Classical Studies," in Geoffrey Cocks and Konrad H. Jarausch, eds., *German Professions, 1800–1950* (Oxford, 1990), esp. pp. 29–30.

its distinctive methods and normative premises, from which it derived its own criteria for truth value and a certain internal coherence.[54]

In the ideal, a reconstituted field of *Wissenschaften* would form an integral whole. In his inaugural lecture before the Prussian *Akademie der Wissenschaften* in 1790, Friedrich Gedike, the coeditor of Berlin's leading Enlightenment journal, contrasted the "pedantic one-sidedness" of old-style learning with the harmonious cooperation of various specialized branches of *Wissenschaft* in the Academy, "as in a single moral person."[55] Gedike was indulging in wishful thinking; as specialization advanced, the prospect of a new moral unity, generated by academe, seemed all the less likely. In the face of increasing balkanization, Fichte's *Concept* pushed the holistic logic of *Wissenschaft* to radical consequences in two senses. The self-containment of his system was not simply a matter of all the parts forming an integrated whole; the first principle was the ground from which all of the system's statements derived their certainty and to which they all returned in a dialectical circle. And, if the first principle made philosophy itself a systematic *Wissenschaft*, it also promised to order the expanding field of knowledge into a new hierarchy. Philosophy would be foundational not only as a system based on a self-evident truth, but also as *the* system on which the truth value of all other systems rested.[56]

Fichte's vaulting ambitions for philosophy as a *Wissenschaft* attest to the strength of his conviction, but they are also a measure of his frustrated expectations. To young Kantians in the early 1790s, philosophy seemed poised at last to shed its second-class academic citizenship and to ascend to preeminence as, in Fichte's phrase, "the science of science as such."

---

[54] Hans Erich Bödeker, "Von der 'Magd der Theologie' zur 'Leitwissenschaft,'" in *Popularphilosophie im 18. Jahrhundert: Das achtzehnte Jahrhundert* 14:9 (1990): 19–57, is especially informative on the changing definition and institutional status of philosophy. On the evolution of the concept of *Wissenschaft*, see, e.g., Alwin Diemer, ed., *Der Wissenschaftsbegriff. Historische und systematische Untersuchungen* (Meisenheim am Glan, 1970); Horst Dreitzel, "Die Entwicklung der Historie zur Wissenschaft," *Zeitschrift für historische Forschung* 8:3 (1981): 257–84; Wolfgang Hardtwig, "Die Verwissenschaftlichung der Geschichtsschreibung zwischen Aufklärung und Historismus," in R. Koselleck, H. Lutz, and J. Rüsen, eds., *Formen der Geschichtsschreibung* (Munich, 1982), pp. 147–81; Hardtwig, *Geschichtskultur und Wissenschaft* (Munich, 1990); Rudolf Vierhaus, ed., *Wissenschaften im Zeitalter der Aufklärung* (Göttingen, 1985); Anthony J. La Vopa, "The Politics of Enlightenment: Friedrich Gedike and German Professional Ideology," *The Journal of Modern History* 62:1 (March, 1990): 34–56. Especially valuable on the expansion of academic knowledge and the accompanying conceptual shifts is Reill, *The German Enlightenment and the Rise of Historicism*.

[55] Gedike's lecture was published in the *Berlinische Monatsschrift* 15 (January–June, 1790): 219–30. On Gedike's concept of *Wissenschaft*, see La Vopa, "The Politics of Enlightenment."

[56] See esp. Emil Kraus, *Der Systemgedanke bei Kant und Fichte* (Berlin, 1916); Wolfgang Schrader, "Philosophie als System – Reinhold und Fichte," in K. Hammacher and A. Mues, eds., *Erneuerung der Transzendentalphilosophie im Anschluss an Kant und Fichte* (Stuttgart-Bad Cannstatt, 1979), pp. 331–44.

Kant's *Critiques* had opened the prospect that as a rigorously constructed system, philosophy would settle once and for all arguments about epistemology and ethics that had seemed hopelessly irresolvable.[57] The sheer cogency of transcendental Reason would make the Critical Philosophy an authoritative voice – the indisputable source of moral absolutes and the arbiter defining the possibilities and limits of knowledge as a whole. Rather than seizing this opportune moment, Fichte's generation of Kantians seemed to be letting it slip through their fingers. Fichte's initial expectation was that the urgently needed consensus among Kantians would form around his own system. Instead, he witnessed, and himself contributed to, a descent into disarray as Kantians squabbled about the true significance of the master's achievement and the steps needed to systematize it.

The German philosophical scene posed another obstacle to the establishment of a foundational discipline. Kant and his disciples faced formidable opposition from a loosely affiliated group who became known as the "popular philosophers" (*Popularphilosophen*). Centered in Berlin and Göttingen, the group included Christian Garve, J. F. Feder, and several other widely read authors. To them the obsession with systematizing philosophy in the late seventeenth and early eighteenth centuries had burdened Germany with the arid and esoteric "scholasticism" of the Leibniz-Wolff school. Philosophy would now become "popular" in the sense that it would break out of its academic ghettos, though it would not seek direct access to the great mass of the population. The *Popularphilosophen* agreed with David Hume that philosophy, having become a "moping recluse method of study . . . as chimerical in her conclusions, as she was unintelligible in her style and manner of delivery," should now bridge "the separation of the learned from the conversable world."[58] In the German states, as in England and Scotland, the conversable world meant the educated and polite reading public. To reach this audience, philosophy had to be a genre of belles lettres, at once "useful" and "entertaining." This in turn required that philosophy appeal to its readers' "healthy human understanding," or common sense; that it be eclectic, both in blending the best ingredients from a variety of systems and in merging with other modes of inquiry; and that it be presented in

---

[57] Reinhold, "Ueber die Möglichkeit," also articulates these expectations and frustrations among Kantians.

[58] David Hume, "Of Essay Writing," in *David Hume. Selected Essays*, ed. Stephen Copley and Andrew Edgar (Oxford, 1993), pp. 1–2. On the *Popularphilosophen* see Beiser, *The Fate of Reason*, pp. 165–92; Helmut Holzhey, "Der Philosoph für die Welt – eine Chimäre der deutschen Aufklärung?", in Helmut Holzhey and Walther Ch. Zimmerli, *Esoterik und Exoterik der Philosophie: Beiträge zu Geschichte und Sinn philosophischer Selbstbestimmung* (Basel and Stuttgart, 1977), pp. 117–38; Claus Altmayer, *Aufklärung als Popularphilosophie. Bürgerliches Individuum und Öffentlichkeit bei Christian Garve* (St. Ingbert, 1992); Gert Ueding, "Rhetorik und Popularphilosophie," *Rhetorik. Ein internationales Jahrbuch* 1 (1980): 122–34.

a polished but accessible language, free of intimidating abstractions and technical terms.

"Popular philosophy" became one of the main targets of Fichte's polemical wrath. His attacks were testy reactions to the charge that Kantians were returning philosophy to obscurantism and that his own writings were a particularly egregious case in point; but they also addessed fundamental questions about how philosophy ought to contribute to the formation of a modern public culture. Garve and others eschewed systematic analysis in favor of a kind of discursive cultural criticism. Their strategy was to win over the educated bourgeois reading public by satisfying its desire for respite from work demands as well as its need for moral guidance. Having tried but failed to popularize Kantianism in the *Contribution*, Fichte now preferred to make philosophy rigorous, even if that meant making it, at least for a while, incomprehensible to the educated public as well as to the uneducated masses. At the very moment when philosophy might earn its right to preside over a new field of *Wissenschaften*, it was in danger of being trivialized as a hobby or a drawing room amusement.

By satisfying the demands of "healthy human understanding," the popular philosophers hoped to rescue philosophy from academic self-absorption and irrelevancy. To Fichte this was tantamount to rationalizing the imprisonment of philosophy in the ideological distorting mirrors of mere "experience." One rose above ideological distortions and subjected them to rational criticism not by addressing a polite public in its own language, but by cleansing philosophy of the semantic imprecision inherent in any language of sociability. Whoever succeeds in establishing philosophy as a "genuine *Wissenschaft*," Fichte had observed to a correspondent in January 1794, will have earned the right "to create a philosophical language." It would be "a more flexible and especially a German idiom," but that would require "creating new words" and "determining existing words exclusively for a particular purpose." He had no regrets that the new language would not at first be "generally intelligible" (*gemeinfasslich*), though he expected that people would soon get used to its precision.[59]

Popular philosophy aimed to effect a new symbiosis between university scholarship and the public formed by educated and polite society. Fichte was now convinced that, if philosophy was eventually to shape the consciousness of a new public, it would first have to establish itself as the foundational *Wissenschaft* in the detached setting of the universities. The *Concept* was meant to lay out the criteria for "system" that such a *Wissenschaft* had to meet and to explain the position it would assume in

---

[59] Fichte to Anna Henriette Schutz (Jan. 15, 1794), in GA, III, 2: 50. See also Reinhold, "Ueber die Möglichkeit," p. 348.

the university's field of knowledge. Fichte was well aware that the imperative to systematize was double-edged. Rather than yielding an all-encompassing system or an integrated hierarchy, the new logic of *Wissenschaft* might simply pattern knowledge into an aggregate of separate but equal disciplines, each standing on its own first principle. Even as it promised to save philosophy from dissolution in an eclectic public discourse, the principle of "system" raised the prospect of disciplinary atomization. He used a revealing mix of metaphors to describe this possibility:

> If our minds originally contain several threads which have no point of connection and which cannot be so connected, then once again we are in no position to struggle against our own nature. Our knowledge . . . would constitute *many* sciences. . . . our dwelling . . . [would] be a conglomeration of separate chambers, and we would be unable to pass from one to the other. It would be a building in which we would always be lost and would never feel at home. . . . Every day we would have to expect that a new innate truth might express itself within us, or that experience might present us with a new simple element. We would always have to be ready to pitch a new hut somewhere.[60]

The passage recalls Fichte's dictum that "[the] sort of philosophy one chooses depends . . . on [the] sort of man one is" and resonates with his need for cognitive and moral certainty in a changing culture. Clearly an overarching system was not simply an impersonal cognitive structure. It was the indispensable framework for Fichte's ethic of self-mastery, the source of certainty needed to conduct the inner struggle against nature. The struggle could not be waged – the self would not have the needed ground, or "home," for waging it – unless the basic issues were settled beyond doubt.

In Fichte's alternative to cognitive and moral homelessness, the Doctrine of Knowledge would make philosophy the center of gravity of an intellectual universe. In a sense he was offering the other disciplines separate but equal status. The first principle would communicate its certainty to every planet in its gravitational field, and hence all knowledge would be of equal truth value. At the same time, though, the *Concept* left no doubt that the center was the source of authority, and that the derivatives were, as such, dependent subjects. As the "the science of science as such," philosophy was also the "the supreme science."[61] It was the arbiter of Truth, demarcating the realm of certainty, fixing the outer limits of inquiry, and determining the division of labor within the intellectual field as a whole. "The various sciences do not assign a place to the Doctrine of Knowledge," Fichte observed; "it assigns them to their places within and through itself."[62]

---

[60] Fichte. *Early Philosophical Writings*, p. 112.   [61] Ibid., p. 95, 106.   [62] Ibid., pp. 114–15.

In Fichte's argument, philosophy merited this authority because it was systematic in a unique way. Whereas other *Wissenschaften* were "infinite," the Doctrine of Knowledge would make philosophy "closed." His choice of terms can be misleading. Fichte was not conceding that philosophy had limitations with which other disciplines were not burdened. Philosophy was the only discipline that constituted an "absolute totality"; and hence, like the self-positing self from which it proceeded, it was unconditionally autonomous. As the *Wissenschaftslehre* would soon demonstrate, Fichte's system was closed – or, perhaps better, completely self-contained – because its systematic reasoning always returned it to the first principle from which it started. In so doing, the system proved that it yielded the only possible way of conceptualizing the possibility of any kind of knowledge. In contrast, all other disciplines proceeded out from philosophy in "a specific direction," into the virtually "infinite" world of particularity. It was the difference between conceiving the universal a priori laws of consciousness and applying their corollaries to "particular" sense objects.[63]

As one would expect, in the *Concept* Fichte applied this fundamental distinction to position transcendental philosophy over against the natural sciences. In the academic world of the 1790s, after all, the inductive procedures of natural science were often regarded as the epitome of system. In the first *Critique* Kant had cited their "revolution" as the inspiration for his own efforts. Kant's ultimate aim, of course, was to fix the jurisdictional boundaries of natural science at the same time that he secured its autonomy within those boundaries. Now Fichte proclaimed the epistemological and moral preeminence of philosophy with a new militancy, calculated to put natural science in its subordinate place. To assume a specific direction in the sense world, he argued, was to relinquish the freedom of judgment that was unique to philosophical inquiry. Precisely because philosophy as a system self-consciously eschewed empiricism, it ought to ascend from the lower ranks to the pinnacle of the knowledge hierarchy. Fichte's implicit claim was that an instrumental reason – a reason that simply applied cognitive laws to nature – had no claim to moral authority in a modern public. It should not be confused with or, worse, substituted for normative reason, which alone involves the moral freedom to choose human ends. Hence the *Concept* assigned the "natural" sciences to the status of "particular" sciences. The Doctrine of Knowledge furnishes us with "the laws according to which nature should and must be observed," but "the power of judgment" remains free "to apply these laws or not to apply them at all." Once the power of judgment "has been given the task of observing a particular object according to a particular law," it "is no longer free, but is subject to a rule."[64]

---

[63] Ibid.   [64] Ibid., pp. 120–1.

It will become apparent, however, that Fichte was not simply claiming precedence over the natural sciences. He used their case to assert the authority of philosophy, both as the route to the freedom of the self and as the source of norms for a public culture over the entire field of knowledge, including the humanistic disciplines. This had a dual implication for all other "disciplines." They need not be limited to instrumental rationality, so long as they recognized that philosophy was their only authoritative source of moral direction. That meant that they were integral parts of the larger "system" in which the pure self exercised its freedom. It also meant, however, that they could not presume to define, from within themselves, the meaning or the end of moral freedom.

3. THE HUMAN VOCATION

In his public lectures Fichte made the exercise of moral freedom virtually synonymous with the striving for wholeness. To be free was to be fully "human," and to be fully human was to form the self into a unitary personality.

It was in the development of this theme that Fichte began to lay out the full social and political implications of his theory. The injustice of old-regime corporate privilege receded into the background, as though it were for the most part too obvious to dwell on. Now Fichte's subject was the new society in the making as the corporate hierarchy acceded to a functional hierarchy of specialized work roles. Fichte was clearly ambivalent about the new order. He welcomed the fact that increasing technical mastery would advance mankind's struggle against Nature, but he nonetheless shared with many of his contemporaries the concern that material progress would be accompanied by a new moral blight. The demands of specialized work threatened to fragment the individual personality – to alienate the social persona of the *Bürger* from the purely human self of the *Mensch* – and to deprive individuals of any sense of vital connection with the collectivity. The public culture, like the individual consciousness, would have no normative center, no authoritative source of moral norms.

Fichte's expectation was that under the transformative impact of his system, *Wissenschaft* would cease to be a symptom of this impoverishment of personal and public life and instead would become the antidote to it. The Doctrine of Knowledge – the systematic "ground" on which the entire array of *Wissenschaften* formed into an integrated system – would provide the urgently needed vision of what the personality as a human whole and the culture as a collective personality ought to be.

Fichte developed this theme in his public lectures in part because it was immediately relevant to his audience. With rare exceptions, the students who thronged into his lecture hall were devoting most of their time to the "bread learning" in law and theology that would qualify them for careers in the administrative and judicial bureaucracies of the German states, in the clergy, and in academic teaching and scholarship. To one degree or another, specialized work was their destiny. Since the *Sturm und Drang* protests of the early 1770s there had been recurrent signs of youthful discontent with the social conformity and the intellectual tunnelvisioning that such work seemed to entail.[65]

But Fichte was also adding his voice to an issue that had engaged eighteenth-century thinkers throughout Europe. It was a truism of the era that modern societies were distinguished from their predecessors in the ancient world by their far greater specialization of labor. The modern division of labor had brought progress in the form of unprecedented levels of material prosperity, with a seemingly endless variety of goods produced and consumed. It had also brought, at least in a limited sense, political improvement; thanks to the expansion of legal and adminstrative structures, there was a new security of life and property. But what had been the effect on moral and civic life? In the transition from the simple to the complex had morals improved or had they been corrupted? Had civic life been enriched or impoverished?

The period from the spring of 1794 to the summer of 1795 – roughly the first year of Fichte's university teaching – might be called the Jena moment in the formulation of a distinctly German discourse on the modern division of labor and related issues. It was a moment formed by the intellectual chemistry of three men – Friedrich Schiller, Wilhelm von Humboldt, and Fichte – who had brought vastly different experiences to Jena but nonetheless had a certain generational affinity. All three were in their thirties; Schiller, the oldest and the most accomplished, was only three years older than Fichte and eight years older than Humboldt.

The distinctly German quality of their contribution is not surprising. In the late eighteenth century, the terms of the argument about the modern division of labor varied with the national frame of reference. In England and Scotland, to take a particularly instructive contrast to the German scene, the increasing complexity of the social and occupational order was attributed primarily to the expansion of commerce. Observers like Adam Ferguson, the Scottish moral philosopher and historian, warned that commercialization was exacting a high moral price for its benefits. Their model was the civic life of the ancient republics, where landowning citizens, free from the demands of physical labor and profit seeking, had placed patriotic duty over narrow self-interest and had defended their fatherland as citizen-soldiers. In recent centuries both patriotism and the martial virtues had declined as professional armies replaced

[65] La Vopa, *Grace, Talent, and Merit*, pp. 249–86.

citizen-militias; as the subjects of modern states were enervated by commercial "luxury"; and as they retreated from public life into a selfish privatism, marked by an exclusive concern with profit and the status that
wealth could buy.

There was a counterpoint to this moral indictment, perhaps best developed in the writings of Adam Smith and David Hume. Commercialization was credited with producing its own species of humanism,
appropriate to the urban culture of a great metropolis like London and
the provincial cities in its orbit. The "politeness" of a modern urban, commercial culture was no replacement, to be sure, for the civic virtue of the
ancient republics; but it was, in its way, morally efficacious. Modern specialization had a "polishing" effect that encouraged the "enlightened"
pursuit of self-interest and that might yield an enlightened consensus on
public issues. As people entered a variety of contractual relationships and
as they engaged in the multifarious intellectual and social exchanges that
modern urban life offered, they became more tolerant and adaptable. If
politeness rendered them incapable of disinterested virtue, it also made
them immune to sectarian fanaticism (or "enthusiasm") in their political
as well as their religious behavior.[66]

German thought proved particularly receptive to Ferguson's censure of
modernity, though it also had echoes of the Anglo-Scottish defense of
commercial humanism. It is striking, however, that German pessimism was
informed by different perceptions of threat. In the modern "commercial
state," as Ferguson and others used that term, emerging government
bureaucracies were a kind of byproduct of the larger set of changes
accompanying commercial expansion. The state expanded by emulating
the commercial specialization of labor. In Germany the state loomed as
the engine of change, the driving force behind increasing specialization
in society as a whole.[67] This was the perspective of men looking out
from an exclusive world of academic education and public employment,
or at least from the margins of that world. They knew, of course, that
increasing specialization and its effects – what they saw as fragmentation
and alienation – were a much wider phenomenon. But the immediate
threat to themselves was the blinkered routinism of office work in the
state bureaucracies and their confessional and academic extensions. In his
essay on the "limits of state action" Humboldt evoked this threat from
bitter experience. In April 1790, in deference to his mother's wishes, he

[66] See, e.g., Istvan Hont and Michael Ignatieff, eds., *Wealth and Virtue. The Shaping of Political Economy
in the Scottish Enlightenment* (Cambridge, 1983); J. G. A. Pocock, *Virtue, Commerce, and History. Essays
on Political Thought and History, Chiefly in the Eighteenth Century* (Cambridge, 1985).

[67] For a different but related reading of the German variations on Anglo-Scottish civic humanism,
see Oz-Salzberger, *Translating the Enlightenment*. Still relevant is Roy Pascal, " 'Bildung' and the
Division of Labor," in *German Studies Presented to Walter Horace Bruford* (London and Toronto, 1962),
pp. 14–28.

had begun an apprenticeship in the Prussian judicial bureaucracy; but he had found the work unendurable and by May 1791 had requested permission to resign. He wrote scathingly of the ever-growing horde of functionaries whose work was "partly empty, partly narrow," and who in their preference for "things" over people "relapse[d] into machines" and mistook the "trivial" for the "momentous," the "contemptible" for the "dignified." The bureaucratic state dehumanized its agents as well as its subjects.[68]

To Humboldt and others, the German states asserted their dominating presence not only through their standing armies or their detailed oversight of commercial life, but also through the production and dissemination of increasingly specialized public knowledge. It was not simply that the development of the universities had been tightly linked to state-building since the late Middle Ages. Looking back from its vantage point in the 1790s, Humboldt's generation had reason to believe that the ideological priorities of the *Aufklärung* had confirmed and reinvigorated this institutional legacy. The reform thought of the German Enlightenment had been emphatically statist in two senses. It had looked to the state to promote and implement its agenda, and it had been guided by a utilitarian ethic that harnessed the modern division of labor to state-defined needs. What validated the individual as a social being was his fullfilment of his duties as a *Bürger* or, in modern parlance, his specialized role in a functional hierarchy of occupations. As much as that role might constrict the individual, its requirements had to take precedence over (though they could not entirely preclude) the multidimensional development of his potential as a "human being" (*Mensch*).

This was the setting for Schiller's famous historical diagnosis of modern fragmentation and alienation in the sixth of the letters on "the aesthetic education of man," published in early 1795. The original blame lay with "culture itself," but the modern state had taken up culture's work with a vengeance:

> As soon as, on the one side, enlarged experience and more specific thought made necessary a sharper division of the *Wissenschaften*, and on the other side the more intricate clockwork of the states necessitated a stricter separation of estates and tasks, the inner unity of human nature was torn and a pernicious conflict corrupted its harmonious powers. Each regarding the other with hostility, the intuitive and the speculative understanding now diverged to their different fields, whose borders they now began to guard with mistrust and envy, and with the sphere to which one limited one's effectiveness one gave oneself a master within, who not seldom tried to

---

[68] Wilhelm von Humboldt, *The Limits of State Action*, ed. J. W. Burrow (Cambridge, 1969), pp. 34–5. On Humboldt's experience as a Prussian bureaucrat, see Paul R. Sweet, *Wilhelm von Humboldt. A Biography*, 2 vols. (Columbus, Ohio, 1978–80), 1, pp. 83–9.

terminate the other inclinations with opresssion. . . . The new spirit of government made complete and general this derangement that art and learning began in the inner human being. . . . Eternally fastened to only a single small fragment of the whole, the human being developed himself only as a fragment; with the monotonous noise of the wheel that he pushed around eternally in his ear, he never developed the harmony of his being, and, instead of stamping humanity in his nature, he became merely the copy of his official task, his *Wissenschaft.*[69]

Obviously Schiller, Humboldt, and Fichte shared an animosity toward the machine-state, but there was much more to their intellectual affinity. In his inaugural lecture at Jena in 1789 on "universal history," Schiller had to a degree anticipated Fichte's message to his student audience with an invidious contrast between the "bread scholar" and the "philosophical mind."[70] Humboldt had moved to Jena in early 1794, just a few months prior to Fichte's arrival, for the specific purpose of being near Schiller. He had already channeled his alarm about modern work roles into the essay on "the limits of state action." By 1794 Schiller had largely given up university lecturing. His illness left him with limited energy, and most of it was devoted to solitary study and writing. But he made an exception for Humboldt, who recalled seeing him "twice a day, preferably in the evenings alone and usually deep into the night."[71] Humboldt brought to their conversations his careful study of Kant's *Critiques* and his scholarly fascination with ancient Greece. As the *Aesthetic Education* attests, Humboldt's philosophical and historical speculations left a deep imprint on Schiller's thought.

In the summer of 1795, Schiller and Fichte broke off communications when Schiller rejected one of the philosopher's contributions to his new journal *Die Horen*. Even before then it was apparent that Fichte would not be admitted to the intimacy that bound Schiller and Humboldt. His arrogance grated on them, and his system was entirely too abstract and categorical for their taste. Nonetheless in the *Aesthetic Education* Schiller readily acknowledged his debt to his "friend" Fichte for the ideal of the "unchangeable unity" of each human personality and for the concept of interacting drives.[72] To Humboldt, Fichte, despite his egotism, was a "great speculative mind"; Humboldt found "extraordinarily good ideas" in the

---

[69] Friedrich Schiller, *Ueber die ästhetische Erziehung des Menschen*, ed. Wolfhart Henckmann (Munich, 1967), pp. 90–2. See also Lesley Sharpe, *Friedrich Schiller. Drama, Thought, and Politics* (Cambridge, 1991), pp. 146–55; La Vopa, *Grace, Talent, and Merit*, pp. 272–4; Josef Chytry, *The Aesthetic State. A Quest in Modern German Thought* (Berkeley, Calif., 1989), pp. 77–90.

[70] Friedrich Schiller, "Was heisst und zu welchem Ende studiert man Universalgeschichte?," in Schiller, *Sämtliche Werke*, vol. 4 (Munich, 1958), pp. 749–67.

[71] Wilhelm von Humboldt, "Ueber Schiller und den Gang seiner Geistesentwicklung," in Bernhard Zeller, ed., *Schillers Leben and Werk in Daten und Bildern* (Frankfurt am Main, 1966), p. 26.

[72] Schiller, *Ueber die ästhetische Erziehung*, pp. 84, 118.

published lectures, and the *Wissenschaftslehre* struck him as exceptionally penetrating, if also sophistic.[73]

It is not surprising, then, that Schiller's *Aesthetic Education* and Fichte's public lectures resonate with each other's language and insights, and that the influence of Humboldt's thought is evident in both texts. If Jena hosted a German moment of symbiosis, however, it also witnessed a sorting out within the larger German frame of reference. To an extent, to be sure, we can see parallel tracks in the Jena moment, all leading to the nineteenth-century concept of the *Geisteswissenschaften* (perhaps best translated as the humanistic disciplines). Within that larger rubric, however, we see the divergent pulls of, on the one hand, a radical philosophical reflexivity and, on the other, an ideal of self-realization through the hermeneutic recovery of meaning. The differences become quite audible when we listen closely to what Schiller, Humboldt, and Fichte had to say about the modern division of labor. Their shared language of inner spontaneity and wholeness can easily deceive. It tends to muffle their discordant views of the social meaning of specialized labor; of what constituted human wholeness; and of the kind of *Wissenschaft* that would counteract the fragmentation and self-alienation of the modern personality.

The three men were in agreement that in his evocation of man in the state of nature, Rousseau had indulged in a kind of primitivism that was blind to both the savagery of simpler ages and the benefits of modern civilization. There was a sense, however, in which Schiller and Humboldt nonetheless echoed Rousseauian antimodernism, particularly in the way they conceived a dichotomy between the natural and the artificial. To them, as to Rousseau, one of the most alarming symptoms of the artificiality of modern civilization was the fragmentation of the personality in the split between work and leisure, technical expertise and moral insight, socially defined duties and personal aspirations. The challenge was to allow the individual to cultivate to the full his unique configuration of energies and to integrate them into a unitary personality despite the modern division of labor. Restoring wholeness meant ending civilization's suppression of the natural instincts and energies, though with an education that would channel and refine them as it liberated them from a mechanical rationality.

In this view, modern labor was the source of the illness; it could not be the source of the cure. In the long run, work would become a humanizing agent only if our "inner" valuation of it underwent a fundamental change. Even the lowliest work could contribute to the development of fully human personalities if it was taken up for its own sake, as something inherently valuable as a medium for self-realization, rather than for the

[73] Humboldt to Brinkman, Nov. 3, 1794, in FG 1: 169–70.

utilitarian purpose that the state or society assigned it. The immediate task
was to create social spaces free of the state's tutelage and utilitarian priorities – spaces where the intimate exchanges of friendship and other
forms of association, outside the social organization of labor, could counteract the stultifying restrictions of work roles.[74]

Fichte's vision of human emancipation was suffused with his valuation
of work as the critical vehicle for self-realization. His ideal of human
wholeness – of the personality as a unitary self – was inseparable from
this ethic of work as struggle, and hence was not simply a variation on
Humboldt's and Schiller's ideal. To Fichte, in fact, there was a sense in
which the modern division of labor offered the cure to its own syndrome.
Though he too sought to counteract specialization, he blamed Nature,
and not modern society, for the constriction of human development.
Left to contend with nature in isolation, the individual unavoidably
pursued a "one-sided development" that realized some of his potentiali-
ties at the expense of others. In the society Fichte imagined, "Reason
. . . would see to it that every individual obtains indirectly from the hand
of society that complete education that he could not obtain directly from
nature."[75]

There were two ways in which a rational organization of the division
of labor would counteract the constricting pull of nature. With the elimination of arbitrary privilege, the individual, following his "social drive,"
would choose the work that best suited his talents, regardless of his family
origins. And, as specialized as it was, modern labor need not have a tunnel-
visioning effect. What struck Fichte was that at the same time that it
assigned individuals to narrow spheres, specialization created a society in
which knowledge flowed through intricate, multilayered networks of
communication. The crux of the matter was to make the terms of communication as open and as egalitarian – as free of introverted solidarities
and hierarchical dependencies – as possible. Then a new kind of personal
and collective wholeness could emerge from the specialized mutuality of
social relations. The individual would contribute to the multidimensional
development of others by communicating his specialized knowledge to
them; and he in turn, by being receptive to their knowledge, would
develop the full personality and broad vision that he could never achieve
in isolated engagement with nature.[76]

All three men had been inspired by Kant's *Critiques*; that was in fact
their strongest generational bond. But they had appropriated different
Kantian impulses, and they had different reasons for ambivalence about
the Critical Philosophy as a whole. Reacting against the dehumanizing
implications of utilitarian rationalism, Humboldt and Schiller fashioned

---

[74] Humboldt, *Limits*, pp. 16–19, 32–3. See also Burrow's comments in ibid., pp. xxxvi–xli.
[75] *Fichte. Early Philosophical Writings*, pp. 162–4.   [76] Ibid., pp. 165–9.

an aesthetic ideal of personality in which the rational and the sensory blended and nourished each other. In his holistic engagement with the people and objects around him, the individual formed himself into a work of art. This is not to imply that he retreated from moral demands to a merely formalistic aesthetic; sensory forms without intellectual content were empty, just as intellectual content without sensory form was lifeless. The commitment to moral self-discipline – the commitment to duty – flowed from a balanced integration of "powers"; left to struggle with each other, these would produce a personality enslaved either to "mechanical" rationality or to insatiable sensual appetites.

Kant's Categorical Imperative offered Humboldt and Schiller a seemingly unassailable philosophical justification for their ideal of self-determination. Kant had flatly rejected a utilitarian justification for moral choices; the individual personality was to be valued as an end-in-itself and not merely as the means to others' ends. What Humboldt and Schiller could not embrace was the rigorism of Kant's concept of duty. They sought a holistic antidote to the fragmentation of the modern personality, and instead Kant's ideal of virtue as the victory of abstract principles over the instincts, needs, and emotions of the sensual being seemed to make the self a mechanistic structure of domination and subordination. In late 1793 Humboldt couched his alternative in a political metaphor; "complete unity of the powers" must be achieved not through "the exclusive rule by one" but through "the equal participation of each in government."[77] He was convinced that the sensual core of the personality, and not its capacity for abstract reasoning, imparted creative life to human activity. The self-cultivation, or *Bildung*, he imagined was an organic process, with reason and sensuality fusing into a harmonious, well-balanced whole.

Informing Fichte's idea of wholeness, on the other hand, was a rigorism that may have been extreme even by Kantian standards. Wholeness meant "absolute unity, constant self-identity, complete agreement with oneself." The finite being sought to transcend its particularity by asserting its identity with the pure self. There could be no blending of reason and the natural; the self strove to subdue nature within and without, to free itself from the particularity of sense experience and re-attain the universality it had had as a pure act of self-positing. Life was, in this sense, a quest to recover spirituality, a ceaseless effort to liberate the

---

[77] Humboldt to Körner, Nov. 19, 1793, in *Wilhelm von Humboldts Briefe an Christian Gottfried Körner*, ed. Albert Leitzmann (1940: Berlin, 1965), p. 8. On Humboldt's ambivalence toward Kant's ethics, see also Burrow's comments in *Limits*, pp. xliii–xlviii; Christiana M. Sauter, *Wilhelm von Humboldt und die deutsche Aufklärung* (Berlin, 1989), pp. 294–309. On Humboldt's ideal of wholeness through *Bildung*, see esp. W. H. Bruford, *The German Tradition of Self-Cultivation: "Bildung" from Humboldt to Thomas Mann* (New York and London, 1975), pp. 1–28; Clemens Menze, *Das Bildungsreform Wilhelm von Humboldts* (Hanover, 1975), pp. 118–58.

Practical Reason within us from the constrictions of Theoretical Reason. As one "traverse[s] the world of appearance . . . one's sensibility must wither away."[78]

What Humboldt and Schiller advocated was an ideal of "individuality" (*Individualität*) — an ideal that Fichte's language sometimes echoed, but that he did not embrace.[79] In Humboldt's essay and Schiller's *Aesthetic Education*, state-guided specialization has a leveling effect. It reduces the great mass of people to the sameness of passive things at the same time that it isolates them from each other. In the process of self-cultivation (*Bildung*), each person would actively fashion himself into a unique whole. By itself, reason produced the abstractions that dictated sameness; in its proper symbiosis with natural sensuality, it generated myriad unique configurations — and it had efficacy only as it was refracted through them. In the logic of Fichte's system, by contrast, there was something morally dubious about a society in which everyone cultivated a unique sensibility. To be unique in this sense was to remain imprisoned within the particularity of sense experience. As people freed themselves from their sensibility, they would all approximate a universal ideal of the moral personality. In that sense, as selves shedding their particularity as they converged toward the universal, human beings would be more "equal."

It is a measure of the new expectations invested in *Wissenschaft* that in the thought of all three men, it promised to restore wholeness to the individual and the society. But what kind of *Wissenschaft* would fulfill this awesome therapeutic mission? On this issue the contrast between Humboldt and Fichte is particularly striking. In a sense, both men were pursuing the same paradox: they were looking for a scholarly vocation which, by the very nature of its specialization, would make whole its practitioner and ultimately the larger society. But they had different solutions to the paradox. They were spinning two of the threads — in Humboldt's case, the hermeneutic thread of historicism, and in Fichte's, the transcendental thread of philosophy — that would run through German academic culture in the nineteenth century.

Humboldt's fragment on the "theory of the cultivation (*Bildung*) of the human being" tells us a great deal about why personal wholeness was so appealing to him, and about how he conceived the path to it. A leisured young aristocrat in search of a vocation, he was intent on avoiding the

---

[78] Fichte. *Early Philosphical Writings*, p. 195.

[79] See esp. Clemens Menze, "Die Individualität als Ausgangs-und Endpunkt des Humboldtschen Denkens," in Klaus Hammacher, ed., *Universalismus und Wissenschaft im Werk und Wirken der Brüder Humboldt* (Frankfurt am Main, 1976), pp. 145–63; Gerald N. Izenberg, *Impossible Individuality. Romanticism, Revolution, and the Origins of Modern Selfhood, 1787–1802* (Princeton, N.J., 1992), pp. 27–35. Like Izenberg, I keep "individuality" distinct from "individualism," which has a related but different set of meanings. Cf. Louis Dumont, *German Ideology. From France to Germany and Back* (Chicago, 1994), esp. pp. 10, 82–144.

dilettantism of the gentleman-scholar but was hardly less put off by the tunnel-visioning of the scholarly "fields," including philosophy. He sought the kind of expertise about an "external" world that would be uniquely suited to revealing the myriad "energies" (*Kräfte*) of humanity in their inner unity. He thought he had found his vocation in the German renewal of classical studies, and particularly in its exploration of the Hellenic world. As a student of Heyne at Göttingen and as a friend and correspondent of Wolf at Halle, he had been introduced to the philological and historical expertise of this emerging *Wissenschaft*.[80]

In the new Hellenism Humboldt found a personal and public antidote to modern fragmentation. Ancient Greece, and particularly Athens, offered the purest historical testimony that the human personality and human culture could give form to an innate integrative energy. The culture of classical Greece seemed a perfect marriage of the sensual and the intellectual, natural simplicity and aesthetic refinement, and the Greek language had blended these dualities to a unique degree. Here was a historical particularity that, more than any other, refracted the universal qualities of "humanity" (*Humanität*). If the refraction was to yield its universal significance, the culture had to be understood on its own terms.

Humboldt expected the Hellenic ideal to counteract modern alienation and fragmentation by its example, but he was especially fascinated by the formative process of grasping the ideal, which seemed to have "healing" power of its own. The effort to recover the unity of a many-sided nation in the remote past – the hermeneutic engagement with its artifacts, and particularly with surviving texts, in their historical contexts – had a "therapeutic" effect in that it involved the "strain[ing] [of] all powers symmetrically."[81] The scholar absorbed the wholeness of personality and the breadth of vision that his specialized research opened to him.

The point is not simply that Humboldt and Fichte had different interests; their concepts of *Wissenschaft* entailed entirely different relationships between the scholar and the text. Here again the shared language can be deceptive. To both men the text was an object of active appropriation, a source of nourishment for a spontaneous development of the inner self;

---

[80] Wilhelm von Humboldt, "Theorie der Bildung des Menschen," in *Werke*, 2, esp. pp. 23–35. On the influence of Heyne, see Clemens Menze, *Wilhlem von Humboldt und Christian Gottlob Heyne* (Ratingen, 1966). On Humboldt's relationship to Wolf, see La Vopa, "Specialists against Specialization," esp. pp. 29–37.

[81] "Ueber das Studium des Alterthums, und des Griechischen insbesondere," in Humboldt, *Werke*, 2, pp. 7–8. Hans-Georg Gadamer, *Truth and Method* (2d rev. ed.: New York, 1994) is a sweeping exploration of the German hermeneutic tradition, including Humboldt's contributions. There is an insightful précis of the tradition in Ringer, *Fields*, pp. 94–108. See also George G. Iggers, *The German Concept of History. The National Tradition of Historical Thought from Herder to the Present* (rev. ed.: Middletown, Conn., 1983), pp. 44–62.

and that meant the ultimate aim of reading a text was to grasp its immanent meaning, its essential "spirit." The difference lies in the forms of
engagement. In Humboldt's hermeneutic engagement, the self realized a
preexisting entelechy through an empathic recovery of textual meaning
in context, with thorough and precise attention to the detail of language
and form. Fichte saw no reason to read a philosophical text, or indeed
any other kind of text, in this way. He was an uncompromising anti-
empiricist, indifferent to the mere particularity and contingency of historical facts. Texts were not artifacts to be interpreted historically but
physical occasions for exercises in philosophical reflexivity. Grasping the
"spirit" immanent in the text was a matter not of distilling its author's
meaning but of understanding the implications of the author's thought
better than he understood them himself (as Fichte claimed to have done
with Kant's *Critiques*). Where Humboldt sought to recover a historically
specific spirit through an exacting study of the "letter," Fichte wanted
to extract the timeless insight that the letter often obscured. Evocations
of *Bildung* notwithstanding, radical reflexivity committed philosophy to
a kind of antihermeneutic. The commitment was heightened as Fichte
became aware of how difficult it was to communicate a first principle
that was not self-evident in the rationalist sense, and whose validity would
only be demonstrated as the multiple parts of the system materialized.
Increasingly disillusioned with texts, and indeed with language itself, he
insisted that his published writings, like his lectures, were tentative formulations. What mattered was that the text occasion the "self-thought"
of readers and listeners.

In this radically contingent sense, texts were points of departure on the
route to wholeness. It is the "happy fate" of the philosopher, Fichte
explained to his student audience at the close of the fourth lecture, "to
have a particular calling which requires one to do just that which one
has to do for the sake of one's general calling as a human being."[82] Philosophy "must be our entire being . . . the whole education of our spirit
and heart." Most of his listeners would not, of course, be philosophers;
but, "no matter how trivial or subtle a particular inquiry appears to be,
we should at least retain within ourselves a feeling for the whole." Fichte
was trying at once to break the universities out of their historical (and
political) mold and to accommodate the new *Wissenschaft* to the universities' institutional mission. The future specialists of German educated
culture – the young men who would become bureaucrats, scholars, professors, teachers, clergyman, physicians – were not being told to abandon
these careers for a life of philosophical speculation. While Fichte challenged them to avoid tunnel-visioning, he also assured them that they
could maintain a vision of the purely "human" as they assumed the nec-

---

[82] *Fichte. Early Philosophical Writings*, p. 176.

essarily restricted viewpoints of *Bürger*. If the person had "philosophized with spirit," he "always remains whole, and whenever he acts he acts as a whole."[83]

For Fichte, as for Humboldt, it was the experience of the process that really mattered; but in philosophy as a genuine *Wissenschaft*, the process was one of self-reflecting abstraction. The point was not to cultivate oneself through hermeneutic engagement with the particular substance of a text. One used the text, or indeed the lecture, as the occasion to begin disengaging the self from particularity in all its guises. This was the rigorously transcendental version of *Wissenschaft* as moral therapy. It sought the essence of "humanity" not by recovering the historical meaning of objects outside the self but by becoming conscious of the pure self behind the accidents of historical (and textual) detail.

4. THE CLERISY

When Fichte decided to devote his fifth public lecture to Jean-Jacques Rousseau, he could hardly have chosen a more provocative figure. In the several decades before the Revolution a veritable cult had developed around the author of the *Confessions* and other soul-baring writings. In the early 1790s a younger generation of revolutionaries identified with Rousseau as a martyr to Virtue, crushed by the hypocrisy of the old-regime establishment; as the prophet whose jeremiads had gone unheeded; as the tribune who had championed the natural virtue of the People as the only legitimate ground for government.[84] Canonized as a revolutionary saint in Paris, Rousseau occupied center stage in the antirevolutionary demonology that developed throughout Europe as the revolution grew more radical and more frightening. Robespierre and his followers seemed bent on realizing the utopian chimeras of a paranoid misfit; and they were conducting bloodbaths in the effort. Could there be a more damning instance of the perverse marriage of "philosophy" and the spirit of revolution?

In the *Contribution*, Fichte had spoken as a young radical who revered Rousseau, though his reverence was filtered through the lens of Kantianism. Reacting against Rehberg's portrait of Rousseau as an impractical "dreamer," he had hailed Jean-Jacques as a heroic proto-Idealist whose only mistake was to have been too "kindly" toward the "empiricists" and their ideological self-delusions.[85] His renewed

---

[83] Ibid., pp. 213–15.
[84] See esp. Carol Blum, *Rousseau and the Republic of Virtue: The Language of Politics in the French Revolution* (Ithaca, N.Y., 1986).
[85] See Chapter 3.

engagement with Rousseau in the fifth public lecture reflected his effort
to redefine his posture toward his own society. The more attentive listeners in his audience were probably struck by the delicate balancing act
that this effort occasioned.

Fichte identified with Rousseau's disgust for a thoroughly corrupt age;
that was his way of asserting his right to retain the critical posture of the
alienated outsider, despite his new status as a university professor. But the
main point of the fifth lecture was to refute Rousseau's notorious contention that the advancement of the arts and sciences had contributed to
the corruption rather than to the improvement of human morals. Now
Fichte was speaking as a university professor, highly critical of academe,
to be sure, but committed to a "cultural advancement" that would radiate
out from the universites to regenerate the entire society. From this standpoint, Rousseau *was* a dreamer. When Rousseau imagined a return to the
"state of nature," he indulged his own "passive sensibility." It was precisely
that self-indulgent tendency that Fichte sought to counteract with his
appeals for "action" and "struggle" in a life of "exertion, effort, and labor."
His lectures aimed to inspire a new breed of scholars to assume "their
honorable place," and indeed their leading role, in the march of both
material and moral progress.[86]

Fichte brought a certain insight to his assessment of Rousseau's personality. If he exaggerated Rousseau's primitivism, he nonetheless clarified what separated his own view of the past and the future from the
Rousseauian perspective. But the assessment of Rousseau is also notable
for what it does not say; its very silences throw into sharp relief a tension
in Fichte's vision that he was not prepared to confront.

In the corrupt society that Rousseau found so alienating, the pursuit
of artificial needs locked people into dissimulating behavior – the relentless suppression of the real self behind social masks – in relationships of
domination and dependence. Permeating Rousseau's writing is an ideal
of truly egalitarian intersubjectivity, the longing for an emotionally
grounded communication in which human beings discarded their social
shells and became mutually transparent. It was something like this ideal,
recast in a Kantian vision of shared a priori insight, that Fichte had aspired
to realize through print communication in the *Contribution*. His rhetoric
had echoed Rousseau's conviction that it was the common people, and
not the self-deluded elite of learned men, who still had the capacity for
authentic moral feeling. When in the lectures, on the other hand, Fichte
portrayed his new breed of scholars as the exemplars of a new era of egalitarian communication, it was without any trace of Rousseauian populism,
even in suitably German philosophical translation. The community of
scholars he envisioned is perhaps best characterized as a modern clerisy,

[86] *Fichte. Early Philosophical Writings*, pp. 178–84.

detached from its society and guiding it from a position of privileged moral insight.[87]

In the public lectures Fichte developed the theory of intersubjectivity he had introduced in the *Wissenschaftslehre*.[88] It was only in "interaction" (*Wechselwirkung*) with others that the subject became conscious of himself and his own freedom as a finite consciousness. With the concept of interaction Fichte aimed to prescribe the terms of communication in a truly rational social order. Such an order would be built on Kant's Categorical Imperative, which, in one of its several formulations, forbade the reduction of any human being to a mere "means." Here again there was a radical distinction between selves and things; mechanical power – the causal force that governed relationships between things – had no place in communication among rational selves. The self must be accorded its dignity as an end in itself, and that meant that its inner spontaneity must be respected. Hence interaction was a reciprocal exercise in freedom; each communicant provided the other with "an occasion for developing through his own efforts those spiritual ideas which dwell within him."[89] To communicate as a human being was not to assert one's own power but to bring to life the dormant moral and cognitive freedom of the other.

With the concept of "interaction through freedom" Fichte, following Kant, formulated an eighteenth-century ideal of power-free communication as an a priori norm. He imagined a world of egalitarian social exchange, posed squarely against the obeisances and the false presentations of self that relationships of inequality required in eighteenth-century society. Paradoxically, a purely spiritual form of communication could be effected through the physical medium of sound and words. In "interaction," words, as physical phenomena, remained things; but they were neither active instruments nor passive objects of power:

> I set before you a product, into which I believe I have breathed a few ideas. But I do not give you the ideas themselves, nor can I do so. I give you the mere body. The words which you hear constitute this body. Taken in themselves, my words are no more than an empty noise, a movement in the air which surrounds us. I do not give them whatever meaning they have *for you* (assuming that they make rational sense to you). You place a meaning in these words *for yourself*, just as I place a meaning in them *for myself*.[90]

[87] On the concept of a modern clerisy and its origins in German Idealism, see esp. Ben Knights, *The Idea of the Clerisy in the Nineteenth Century* (Cambridge, 1978).

[88] See esp. R. Lauth, "Le problème de l'interpersonnalité chez Fichte," *Archives de Philosophie* 25, Cahier II–IV (July–Dec., 1962): 325–44.

[89] *Fichte. Early Philosophical Writings*, pp. 207–8, 212.   [90] Ibid., pp. 196–7, 207.

In principle, if not always in practice, this ideal defined Fichte's strategy as a university lecturer. As in the printed words of the *Contribution*,
but now in an oral performance at the lectern, he aimed to think "before"
and "with" his audience rather than thinking for it. This was not simply
a preference in rhetorical style; the rhetorical community of the lecture
hall, by its very commitment to communicative rationality, would form
the microcosm of a new order of freedom. If the listener was to make
the Doctrine of Knowledge his "entire being," he had to enter it and
penetrate to its first principle by his own route, through the creative exercise of his own "intuition." The lecturer's purpose was not to persuade in
the conventional sense, but to occasion "self-thought."

But who would have the spiritual fortitude to follow this invitation to
self-thought? How inclusive would this purified zone of communication
be? The public projected in the *Contribution* had been a radically inclusive enlargement of Kant's "republic of scholars." Something of that projection survived in the lectures, particularly in Fichte's expectation that in
their interaction with the society at large, as in their communion with
each other, the new breed of scholar-philosophers would replace patronizing tutelage with egalitarian reciprocity.[91] But the *Contribution* was a
failed experiment, and in its wake Fichte was struck by the abyss that
divided the great mass of the population, including most educated people,
from the tiny cohort of the truly philosophical. In a corrupt age, very
few could ascend to the ranks of the "ethically best."[92] The ascent required
a rigorous initiation, a relentless exercise in self-discipline to "think away"
sensual particularity and achieve awareness of the moral self through unal-
loyed abstraction. The chosen few would constitute a kind of vanguard,
a clerisy with a superior normative vision. Having grasped the universal
truths of a priori Reason, they could see beyond the limited horizons of
their time and place; and for that very reason they alone could give their
societies moral direction. They would, to be sure, interact with their
contemporaries in a spirit of mutual respect; but their mission nonetheless was to guide from above, from their zone of privileged moral insight.
As masters of the art of "giving" and "receiving," they would be able to
communicate through the modern division of labor; but as the exceptional few whose vocation was to be purely human, they would not be
part of that division.

There was something arrogantly exclusive, even cultish, about this
vision of a modern clerisy.[93] It went hand in hand with Fichte's resort to
rhetorical brutality in his dealings with intellectual adversaries. He could
be a sympathetic friend, but his public persona was often painfully lacking

---

[91] Ibid., esp. pp. 174–5.   [92] Ibid., p. 176.
[93] George Armstrong Kelly has aptly characterized Fichte as "a Jacobin of the elect"; *Idealism, Politics, and History. Sources of Hegelian Thought* (Cambridge, 1969), p. 188.

in the spirit of toleration and the openness to criticism that had defined Kant's "enlightened" public. Faced with complaints that his system was incomprehensible, he in effect absolved himself of any obligation to take them seriously. In his eyes his critics were not simply cognitively deficient. They could not understand his thought – and would never understand it – because they embodied the moral corruption of their age. In a moral as well as an intellectual sense, they were blind men who lacked the requisite "freedom of inner intuition." Trapped in a state of "protracted spiritual slavery," they had "lost themselves and with themselves their sense of private conviction." Such rhetoric dismissed further argument as futile; the opponent was deemed deficient in selfhood and hence morally unworthy of being engaged.

★ ★ ★

Toward the end of his fourth public lecture, in an effort to inspire his listeners to embrace their proper mission, Fichte evoked the language of the Word. Christ's words to his disciples applied in a unique way to scholars: "Ye are the salt of the earth, but if the salt has lost its savor wherewith shall it be salted" (Matt. 5:13). There was no hope of finding "ethical goodness" if "the elect among men have been corrupted." Hence each of them must realize that he was "called to testify to the truth"; that he was "a priest of the truth"; that "in its service" he might have to endure persecution and hatred, perhaps even death.[94]

Fichte was not simply trying to make himself understood in the familiar language of his audience's religious heritage. His rhetoric acknowledged that as he detached basic concepts of German Lutheranism from their theological framework, he gave them a new lease on life in the more secular culture in the making. In Fichte's version of radical reflexivity, freedom still had its "inner" source in a kind of spontaneity; and it still found "external" expression in self-control. Embodying this ancient paradox in a singular way, the philosophically educated elite constituted a modern clerisy, a vanguard by virtue of its cognitively and morally superior vision. The individual qualified for this clerisy by an act of Will, a purely human exercise of moral autonomy, and not by the gift of Grace. But the members constituted an Elect. Their spiritual calling – which was also their unique social calling – was to bear witness to the a priori truths of the Doctrine of Knowledge.

The road to the calling still lay through a spiritual rebirth, though now the struggle against the natural self and the World took the form of a daunting ascent to self-understanding through transcendental abstractions. And the calling itself was still a cross, though the terms of redemption had changed. In a degenerate age, bearing witness might require

---

[94] Fichte. *Early Philosophical Writings*, pp. 175–6

enormous personal sacrifice. It certainly demanded unrelenting dedication to the scholar's regenerative mission. The new Elect stood above the World's divison of labor; but, like dutiful Lutherans, its members embodied the principle that moral self-validation – what might be called this-worldly sanctification – lay through disciplined work.

Chapter 8

The Politics of Celebrity

Fichte gave his first public lecture on May 23, 1794, and it was by all accounts a stunning triumph. He reported to his wife that the largest auditorium in Jena had been too small to accommodate the throng. Students had filled the building, spilled out into the courtyard, and "stood on each other's heads on tables and benches." "My *Celebrität*," he confided to Johanna with palpable self-satisfaction, "is really far greater than I thought."[1] For a thirty-one-year-old who had craved an opportunity to "have an effect" on German public life but had had to endure a period of youthful obscurity longer than most, the change of status was exhilarating.

The word *Celebrität*, like the French *celebrité*, was a vernacular descendent of the Latin for fame or renown. By the late eighteenth century the German descendent had distinct institutional and social resonances. In prerevolutionary France the concern with celebrity marked the ascendancy of "public opinion," which formed as the ideas circulating in a rapidly expanding print market became the subjects of polite conversation in *le monde*. The court society at Versailles was somewhat peripheral to this world, and so were the universities. The magnetic center of *le monde* was the salons in Paris, where aristocrats and bourgeois men of letters gathered regularly under the guidance of prominent hostesses. Its emblematic figure was Voltaire, who had had to flee Paris as a brash young wit but returned there in 1775 to be feted as the national sage. The German territories of the Holy Roman Empire had no equivalent of this Paris-centered, socially mixed world. Instead there were two public audiences – socially and institutionally separate, though by no means unbridgeable – that might confer celebrity. One had its scattered centers in the court residences, where "the world" (*die Welt*) – the exclusive world formed by the ruling dynasties and their constellations of aristocratic families – displayed itself at the pinnacle of old-regime corporate hierarchies. The other audience was the university-educated intelligentsia, which was predominantly bourgeois. Thirty-odd universities formed the nodal points for a German-wide network of the "learned," including the many university graduates who pursued careers in government, the law courts, and the clergy. While some of the universities were provincial backwaters, and a

---

[1] GA, III, 2: 116.

few had declined to the point of near extinction, others were the thriving entrepôts for a German-speaking *Publikum* that had an expanding
appetite for vernacular scholarship and its more or less "popular" offshoots. Only in this emphatically academic world could Kant, an aging
professor who had spent his entire life in a Baltic town on the eastern
edge of German-speaking Europe, and who in 1781 had published the
first of three monumentally forbidding treatises, ascend to the ranks of
celebrity as the Sage of Königsberg.

Fichte came to Jena with a certain renown as one of Kant's disciples
and as a precocious author, but it was his feats in the lecture hall that
sealed his celebrity status. Long after their initial curiosity had been satisfied, the students kept coming. As many as three hundred regularly
attended his public lectures on the mission of the scholar. He had at
last the opportunity to devote his oratorical gifts to the regeneration of
his age, though his audience was a crowd of students rather than the
assembly at Sunday services he had once imagined. Fichte's success was
all the more gratifying because it came as something of a relief. He had
been somewhat intimidated by the prospect of filling the shoes of Karl
Leonhard Reinhold, and with good reason. It was Reinhold who had
made Jena the mecca for the new "Kantian Gospel" that was winning
disciples among educated German youth. Since the late 1780s his lectures
had been the main attraction at Jena. On the evening of his final performance, a huge crowd of students had demonstrated their appreciation
with a torchlight procession, complete with orchestra and three resound-
ing "Vivats."

Fearing that he would be Reinhold's epigone, Fichte very quickly
eclipsed his predecessor. At least for some students, the message itself was
compelling. Fichte's diagnosis of the moral ills of the era confirmed and
clarified their alienation from the status quo, and his appeals to "action"
offered a needed sense of mission. But the philosophy also acquired persuasive force in the very way the philosopher exhibited himself. This
short, stocky figure, flaunting his lack of elegance, seemed to embody the
combative ethos he preached. Friedrich Karl Forberg, a former admirer
of Reinhold and a colleague of Fichte, described how the two men
differed:

> [Fichte's] normal tone of voice is sharp and offensive; his speech is not
> beautiful, but all of his words have gravity and weight. He entirely lacks
> Reinhold's affectionate and devoted nature. His principles are strict and
> scarcely tempered with humanity. All the same he is able to bear being
> contradicted – which Reinhold never could. And unlike Reinhold, he
> appreciates jokes. When challenged, he is fearsome, though he does not
> convey the mortifying sense of his own superiority that Reinhold did. His
> is a restless spirit; he thirsts for some opportunity to act in this world.

Fichte's public lectures do not flow as smoothly and pleasantly as Reinhold's; instead, he roars like a storm and discharges his lightning in individual bolts. . . . It was obvious that Reinhold wished to make good men; Fichte wants to make them great. Reinhold had a gentle gaze and was a majestic figure; Fichte's gaze is withering, and his bearing defiant. . . . He penetrates his subject to its inmost depths and roams through the conceptual realm with an ease which shows that in this invisible territory he is not merely at home: he rules it.[2]

The appeal of Fichte's arguments was inseparable from the power, both visual and verbal, with which he asserted a public persona. And yet Fichte also took pains to put himself on an "equal footing" with students by being willing to engage his audience in argument and by putting them at ease in personal relations.[3] In an academic setting in which the lecture was often little more than a reading from a textbook and in which professors treated students with a distancing consciousness of rank, Fichte offered an unprecedented combination of commanding, even intimidating stage presence and egalitarian accessibility. By mid-June 1794, with his first month of teaching behind him, he could confide to Johanna that "very probably" he was "presently the most loved of all the professors here, and that already they would not trade [him] for Reinhold."[4]

But Fichte's first year at Jena, the year of his triumphs in the lecture hall, also brought tribulations and disillusionment. To a large degree, in fact, his troubles flowed from his popularity and from the aggressive egotism with which he tried to exploit it. To a young professor with Fichte's principles and ambitions, academe turned out to be more a political minefield than an oasis of intellectual freedom. Even as he launched what promised to be a brilliant academic career, he antagonized a professoriate that resented upstarts, particularly when they seduced away fee-paying customers; a clerical elite that saw Throne and Altar tottering; a student body that was appreciative of academic virtuosi but notoriously jealous of its right to be unruly; and a ducal government that wanted its professors to spotlight the university with their celebrity, perhaps even with a certain aura of controversy, but without casting doubt on its commitment to upholding the established order.

Fichte had entered a world rich in ironic juxtapositions. Jena lies roughly twelve miles to the southeast of Weimar, in one of the river valleys of Thuringia. In its political organization in the eighteeenth century, the region seemed intent on caricaturing *Kleinstaaterei*, the crazy quilt of petty principalities that had remained intact under the labyrinthine constitu-

---

[2] FG 1: 235–6. See also the description of Fichte's lectures in Johann Georg Rist, *Lebenserinnerungen* (Gotha, 1880), p. 70, and Johann Wilhelm Camerer's account, reprinted in FG 6.1: 56–8.
[3] See esp. Fichte's description of his way of dealing with students in GA, III, 2: 115.
[4] GA, III, 2: 134.

tional structure of the Holy Roman Empire. The four Ernestine duchies –
Sachsen-Weimar-Eisenach, Gotha-Altenberg, Meiningen, and Coburg-
Saalfeld – were jointly responsible for administering and financing the university. None of the four formed an integral territorial whole. Their
scattered parts were interspersed with the pieces of several other principalities, lilliputian in scale, as well as with outlying territories of larger (though
still quite modest) states, notably the electorates of Mainz, Hanover, and
Saxony and the bishoprics of Würzburg and Bamberg.

Though one of the larger states in the region, the Duchy of Sachsen-
Weimar-Eisenach was a small fry in the politics of the Empire and a negligible quantity in the European international arena. Its first census in 1785
counted roughly 106,000 souls – which meant that in population the
duchy was hardly more than one-twentieth the size of Saxony, the electorate immediately to the north, and roughly one one-hundredth the size
of the Kingdom of Prussia. The ducal residence, the town of Weimar, had
6,265 inhabitants, most of them tradesmen and domestics serving a small
circle of court dignitaries and government officials. Weimar had nothing
of the monumental splendor of a great court town like Dresden or
Munich; and its isolation from Germany's major trade routes, exacerbated
by Thuringia's notoriously poor roads, had deprived it of any commercial importance. When Madame de Staël visited there on her tour of literary Germany in 1803, the place struck her as completely removed from
urban life. Weimar was not even "a small town," she reported; just a "large
chateau."[5]

And yet Madame de Staël's visit is in itself testimony to the fact that
Weimar, despite its political and commercial insignificance, had come to
exercise an extraordinary magnetic attraction. Weimar was reputed to be
"the Athens of Germany," "the only place in which the interest in the
fine arts would be, so to speak, national," thanks to a "liberal court [that]
habitually sought the acquaintance of men of letters."[6] This marriage of
government and Kultur had begun under the regency of the Duchess
Anna Amalia, who combined a determination to restore the state finances
in the wake of the Seven Years War with a strong interest in belles lettres
and theater. In 1772 the Duchess had brought the poet, novelist, and
publicist Christoph Martin Wieland to court to tutor her son Karl

[5] Germaine De Staël, De L'Allemagne, 2 vols., introd. Simone Balayé (Paris, 1967), 1, p. 124. On the
population and social structure of Weimar (both the duchy and the town), see Hans Eberhard,
Goethes Umwelt. Forschungen zur gesellschaftlichen Struktur Thüringens (Weimar, 1951), esp. pp. 12–25.
[6] De Staël, De L'Allemagne, 1, p. 125. Still informative on intellectual life in Weimar is Walter H.
Bruford, Culture and Society in Classical Weimar, 1775–1806 (Cambridge, 1962). Another good introduction is T. J. Reed, The Classical Center: Goethe and Weimar, 1775–1832 ((New York, 1980). Now
indispensable for its wealth of detail on Weimar culture and politics, and for its richly informed
judgments on its leading figures, is Nicholas Boyle, Goethe. The Poet and the Age, 2 vols. (Oxford,
1991–2000).

August. It was Wieland who first made Weimar a presence on the new literary landscape; his *Der Teutsche Merkur*, launched in 1773, was one of the most wide-ranging and widely read periodicals in German-speaking Europe.

In 1775 Karl August had ascended the throne and Goethe, combining the roles of boon companion and judicious mentor, had joined him at the Weimar court. While Wieland's rationalist skepticism and courtly air opened him to ridicule as a "Frenchified" figure, Goethe – twenty-six years old when he arrived in Weimar and known as something of a literary *Wunderkind* since the appearance of *Götz von Berlichingen* and *Die Leiden des jungen Werthers* – represented the protean force of an indigenous literary renaissance. It was above all Goethe's presence that gave the town its German-wide éclat and drew other luminaries into its orbit. Through his initiative his friend Herder, already renowned as a literary critic and essayist, was called to Weimar as General Superintendant of the Lutheran Church in 1776.

Under Karl August's patronage and Goethe's guiding hand, new kinds of intellectual engagement in print, in polite conversation, and in the theater had modified, but had not displaced, the aristocratic formalism of Weimar's court culture. The university at Jena presents a more awkward pairing of old-regime immobility and the academic avant-garde. Jena was one of several universities – the others included Wittenberg, Erfurt, and Leipzig – clustered in central Germany. Established or overhauled during the Lutheran Reformation, they bore witness to the strength of the Lutheran bonding of church and state. While their law faculties supplied the state governments with God-fearing officials, their theology faculties guarded Orthodoxy and trained the ministers who kept watch over pious, obedient subjects.

In the sixteenth century these institutions had been dynamic centers of reform, but in the closing decades of the eighteenth century, with the standards of the *Aufklärung* in ascendancy, they were coming to seem so moribund that some critics considered them beyond resuscitation. The tenacious preference for a crude textbook Latin in scholarship; the professorial obsession with distinctions of rank; the elaborate ritual surrounding examinations and promotions: all this came to seem hopelessly anachronistic as the standards of utilitarian rationalism gained ascendancy. Likewise, theologians preoccupied with guarding confessional Orthodoxy seemed out of tune with the new spirit of religious toleration. Much of the ferment in academic scholarship was in classical studies, history, and philosophy; but these were relegated to the "philosophy" faculty, which was the poor cousin of the professoriate in law and theology. Emblematic of this status were its merely propaedeutic role, its subordination to theological authority, and its skimpy incomes. To the faculties, corporate self-government was the crux of "academic freedom"; to critics, it spelled entrenched resistance to change, particularly since it made for inbreeding and outright nepotism in the recruitment of new faculty.

Since the middle decades of the century, the Georg-August University in Göttingen had pointed the way toward a modernization of academic life. Established in 1737 and generously financed by the Hanoverian government, the Georg-Augusta broke the mold by giving preference in recruitment to scholars who were likely to eschew theological feuds and who sought to make scholarship accessible to a broad educated public; by giving a new prestige and autonomy to disciplines forming or reorienting themselves within the philosophy faculty; and by attracting aristocratic and wealthy bourgeois students with a curriculum that combined the expertise required in government careers with the cultivation expected of the gentleman. Neighboring universities, including Jena, seemed thoroughly outmoded by comparison; partly for that reason, they suffered a steep decline in student enrollments. The average yearly attendance at Jena in the period 1731–35 had been 1,344; in the period 1776–80 the yearly average reached a nadir of 408.[7]

But for a tumultuous decade and a half – roughly from the mid-1780s to the end of the century – Jena experienced a spectacular rebirth. The university had the advantage, of course, of its unique connection with Weimar and especially with Goethe, who found respite from court routine among the Jena professors who shared his interests. More important, though, was the intervention of the ducal government in university affairs. In the case of Jena, to be sure, breathing new life into academe was a particularly cumbersome and precarious process. Any change required the approval of all four co-administrating states, and the two smaller ones, Meiningen and Coburg-Saalfeld, were instinctively hostile to new ideas. But since the smaller courts contributed a pittance to the university's financial support and sometimes failed to pay at all, they had little choice but to concede a predominant role in university administration to Weimar.[8]

From the late 1780s onward, the two Weimar officials responsible for the university were Goethe himself and Christian Gottlob Voigt, who ascended the bureaucratic ranks with Goethe's support and joined him

---

[7] Eberhard, *Goethes Umwelt*, pp. 87–9. Comparative enrollment figures for Göttingen, Jena, and the other German universities in the late eighteenth century are in Franz Eulenberg, *Die Frequenz der deutschen Universitäten von Ihrer Gründung bis zur Gegenwart* (Leipzig, 1904). See also the adjusted figures on enrollment trends in W. Frijhoff, "Surplus ou déficit? Hypothèses sur le nombre des Étudiants en Allemagne à l'époque moderne (1576–1815)," *Francia: Forschungen zur westeuropäischen Geschichte* 7 (1980): 173–218.

[8] An informative account of Jena in the 1790s, with attention to the politics of court-university relations and useful references to archival sources, is Max Steinmetz, ed., *Geschichte der Universität Jena 1548/58–1958. Festgabe zur 400jährigen Universitätsjubiläum*, vol. 1 (Jena, 1958).

on the Privy Council, the duchy's executive body, in January 1794. These two men – one a literary prodigy who had been coaxed to Weimar by an impetuous young duke, the other a legal official carrying on a family tradition of service to the dynasty – formed a close working partnership. Goethe took a keen interest in university affairs despite his recurrent frustration with the demands of office.[9] Voigt combined the legal and political savvy of a career bureaucrat with an active interest in the literary and scholarly movements of his era.

In 1785 the philologist Christian Gottlob Schütz, with the help of Wieland and the encouragement of the Weimar government, launched the *Allgemeine Literatur-Zeitung.* Quick to broadcast new trends in literature, classical studies, and philosophy, the journal did much to make credible Jena's claim to be an intellectual entrepôt of German-wide and indeed European-wide importance. By the late 1780s it had become the chief organ for the group of young Kantians who had joined the faculty in recent years. One of these was Gottlieb Hufeland (a distant relation of Voigt), who in 1785 published one of the first systematic attempts to apply Kant's a priori principles to the field of natural law. The most distinguished of the young Kantians was Reinhold, Wieland's son-in-law. As Kant himself realized, it is unlikely that his philosophy would have commanded attention among the educated public in the late 1780s without Reinhold's popularizing efforts. In 1788 Reinhold drew a large student audience with a series of public lectures on Wieland's verse epic *Oberon.* He built on this promising start to become Jena's resident Kant-interpreter.[10] Thanks especially to its concentration of Kantians, Jena shed its stodgy image and became one of the trendsetters among German universities. The change helps explain why the university, having watched its student enrollments decline relentlessly for several decades, suddenly entered a boom. The average yearly enrollment climbed from 561 in

---

[9] Still informative on Goethe's official role are Hans Tümmler, *Goethe in Staat und Politik. Gesammelte Aufsätze* (Cologne, 1964); Tümmler, *Goethe der Kollege: Sein Leben und Wirken mit Christian Gottlob Voigt* (Cologne, 1970); Tümmler, *Goethe als Staatsmann* (Göttingen, 1976). But Tümmler's scholarship leans toward the apologetic when it comes to Goethe's politics and his role in dealing with Fichte and other problematic scholars at Jena. Healthy correctives are W. Daniel Wilson, *Geheimräte gegen Geheimbünde: Ein unbekanntes Kapitel der klassisch-romantischen Geschichte Weimars* (Stuttgart, 1991); Wilson, *Das Goethe Tabu: Protest und Menschenrechte im Klassischen Weimar* (Munich, 1999). See also Karl-Heinz Hahn, "Im Schatten der Revolution – Goethe und Jena im letzten Jahrzehnt des 18. Jahrhunderts," *Jahrbuch des Wiener Goethe-Vereins* 81–83 (1977–79): 35–58; Thomas P. Saine, "Revolution und Reform in Goethes politisch-geschichtlichem Denken und in seiner amtlichen Tätigkeit zwischen 1790 und 1800," *Goethe-Jahrbuch* 110 (1993): 147–62.

[10] Norbert Hinske, Erhard Lange, and Horst Schröpfer, eds., *Der Aufbruch in den Kantianismus. Der Frühkantianismus an der Universität Jena von 1785–1800 und seine Vorgeschichte* (Stuttgart-Bad Cannstaat. 1995); Dieter Henrich, *Konstellationen: Probleme und Debatten am Ursprung der idealistischen Philosophie* (Stuttgart, 1991).

238 The Jena Years

1781–85 to 867 in 1791–95. With the latter figure Jena surpassed Göttingen as well as Halle and Leipzig and became the largest German-speaking university.[11]

It is striking, however, that this rebirth was accomplished without any serious overhaul of the institutional structure of the university. Pursuing a strategy typical of Germany's reform-minded absolutist governments, Karl August and his officials bypassed corporate privilege with ad hoc maneuvers rather than forcing a head-on collision with corporatism itself. The locus of faculty self-government was the Senate, which was limited to the eighteen "ordinary" professors. The Senate was a jealous guardian of tradition, particularly when its own prerogatives and those of its members were at issue. Karl August and Goethe regarded the body with a large measure of contempt. Voigt shared their view; in 1795 he would dub the Senate "a quite useless *Corpus mysticum*, ready to hinder the good, but not to promote it."[12] Goethe and Voigt preferred to get their information and their advice from individual trusted professors. As for the new faculty of the late 1780s and early 1790s, most of them, including Hufeland and Reinhold, were appointed without consultation of the Senate and in some cases without acknowledgment of its opposition. The ducal government simply monopolized the power to appoint by creating "extraordinary" professorships, positions outside the Senate ranks, with court pensions rather than salaries from the university's own funds. Fichte's appointment was a refinement on this strategy; he was given the rank of "ordinary" but "supernumerary" professor of philosophy, which meant that, titular dignity aside, he too was a court appointee without Senate membership.[13]

Aside from allowing the ducal government to avoid Senate obstructionism, the resort to extraordinary professorships had the advantage of securing new talent on the cheap. The pensions were minimal; for the most part, these young scholars had to earn their living from student fees for individual courses. That meant that even with the rise in enrollments, the competition for students was intense. The salaries of ordinary professors at Jena were notoriously low; they too depended on student fees if they wanted to make a decent living from teaching alone. To make matters worse, the "poor students," who were particularly numerous in the the-

[11] Eberhard, *Goethes Umwelt*, p. 87.
[12] Voigt to Goethe, April 9, 1795, in *Goethes Briefwechsel mit Christian Gottlob Voigt*, vol. 1, ed. Hans Tümmler (Weimar, 1949), p. 169. On the extension of state authority into university affairs, see Thomas Pester, "Zwischen Autonomie und Staatsräson. Zur Institutionalisierung staatlicher Kontrolle an der Universität Jena im Übergang vom 18. zum 19. Jahrhundert," in Pester, *Zwischen Autonomie und Staatsräson. Studien und Beiträge zur allgemeinen deutschen und Jenaer Universitätsgeschichte im Übergang vom 18. zum 19. Jahrhundert* (Erlangen, 1992), pp. 87–98.
[13] As early as July 17, 1793, Voigt had reported to Goethe that Fichte could "probably be had as *Professor extraordinarius* for a moderate subsidy (*Zuschussquantum*)." *Goethes Briefwechsel mit Christian Gottlob Voigt*, 1, p. 104.

ology and philosophy faculties, customarily had their fees waived or at least reduced. If the university was a corporate enclave, it was also a kind of free market. Not surprisingly, the corporate establishment's principled objections to new intellectual fashions were inseparable from its resentment of market competition. Fichte was quick to size up the situation. In July 1794 he reported to a friend that the faculty was segregated into two camps, the "young, current" professors and the "old, reduced" ones.

Under these circumstances Fichte's instant popularity was bound to raise the hackles of some of his colleagues. One might expect that with the French Revolution sending shock waves across central Europe, the usual professorial squabbles about fees and perquisites would come to seem too trivial to be sustained. Instead, the squabbles continued, perhaps with renewed intensity. Rather than making the usual internecine rivalries irrelevant, the clash of moral and political principles occasioned by the Revolution offered new ways to camouflage and perhaps to rationalize them.

Driven by the Parisian popular movement and its allies among the Clubs, and provoked by an Austro-Prussian invasion to restore the authority of the monarchy in the spring of 1792, the Revolution had taken a radical turn that few German observers had expected in 1789. The abolition of the monarchy in September 1792 was soon followed by the trial and public beheading of "Citizen Louis." By May of 1794, when Fichte arrived in Jena, the Committee of Public Safety had been in power for eight months and the Terror was in progress. Meanwhile France's reorganized armies had begun exporting the revolution to its neighbors. In the fall of 1792 Custine's army had invaded the Rhineland, where, to the consternation of German rulers and their officials, it encountered little resistance. When the invaders occupied Electoral Mainz, a group of intellectuals, guided by their French sponsors, formed a Jacobin Club in support of democratic elections and union with the French Republic. One of the Club's spokesmen was Georg Forster, the Elector's librarian, the son-in-law of Germany's most renowned classicist, and a young scholar with numerous contacts in Jena and Weimar. To the German dynastic states, Forster and his colleagues stood as a warning that if countermeasures were not taken, central Europe would be plagued with its own breed of "Jacobin" radicals.

As the Revolution threatened to spread eastward and the German states reacted with counterrevolutionary vigilance, the ducal government in Weimar found itself in a ticklish situation. There was a certain tension between, on the one hand, its eagerness to promote Jena as a showcase for new intellectual fashions and, on the other, its need to keep in step with its larger and far more powerful dynastic neighbors to the north. Prussia had led the way in a crackdown on deviations from confessional and political orthodoxy, and Electoral Saxony, jolted by a peasant

insurrection in 1790, was following the Prussian example. The Weimar
government shared their fear of being engulfed by the Revolution, though
it was dubious of the inclination toward zealotry in their antirevolutionary posture and suspected that shortsighted *Staatsräson* might lie behind
it. In any case, the sheer geographic proximity of Saxony and Prussia,
reinforced by marital alliances with the Hohenzollerns, dictated that Duke
Karl August join in repulsing the revolutionary threat. At the siege of
Mainz in October 1792, Karl August served as a general in the Prussian
forces. Goethe, curious to see the face of a new age, was with him.

In the early 1790s the delicacies of the international situation made
Karl August nervous about what was being taught at Jena. The university
might bring Weimar recognition in the academic world as a "liberal" state,
but it threatened to make the duchy a reckless renegade in the eyes of
its powerful neighbors. In 1792 Gottlieb Hufeland, the Kantian jurist,
began a series of lectures on the new French constitution. Electoral
Saxony protested this intrusion of politics into the lecture hall, and Prussia
turned up the pressure by banning the *Allgemeine-Literatur-Zeitung* from
its territory. From his military encampment, where he had heard conflicting rumors about the lectures, Karl August fired off two testy letters
to Voigt. The Duke assured Voigt that he was not threatening to introduce "despotism" or to restrict "freedom of thought." But he had no
patience with scholars who presumed to lecture governments and stir up
popular discontent. Voigt relayed this messsage along with the Duke's wish
that Hufeland publish the lectures to prove his innocence, and saw to it
that the printed version contained nothing objectionable.[14] That Hufeland had been planning a confession of revolutionary faith is most
unlikely, but in any case he clearly took this warning to heart.

If the duchy's reputation for political reliability was at stake, so was the
university's financial health. Of the 892 students matriculated at Jena for
the winter semester 1793–94, 669 (75%) were listed as "foreigners" from
outside the Ernestine duchies. Many of these, perhaps most, were subjects
of the Elector of Saxony. If the electoral government forbade their attendance at Jena, as it sometimes threatened to do, the university's boom
would come to an abrupt end.

Nonetheless Voigt and Goethe opted for Fichte as Reinhold's successor. They took the precaution of sending Karl August a copy of one of
the philosopher's writings (either the *Contribution* or the *Attempt at a Critique of All Revelation*), but he returned it, perhaps unread, with the
comment that this "*Fichtiade*" was "extremely boring."[15] Had the Duke

[14] See esp. Voigt's letters to Hufeland in Sept., 1792, in August Diezmann, ed., *Aus Weimars Glanzzeit.*
Ungedruckte Briefe von und über Goethe und Schiller, nebst einer Auswahl ungedruckter vertraulicher
Schreiben von Goethes Collegen, Geh. Rat v. Voigt (Leipzig, 1855), pp. 59–61. On the intimidation of
Hufeland, see also Wilson, *Geheimräte und Geheimbünde*, pp. 227–30.
[15] FG 6.1: 22.

not been away at war, his councillors might have had more trouble getting the appointment through. While Goethe and Voigt considered it essential that Jena maintain its reputation as a Kantian mecca, they knew full well that they were playing with fire. Despite his efforts to remain anonymous, it was common knowledge that Fichte was the author of the *Contribution*. The substance of its argument aside, the essay had been calculated to antagonize with its radically egalitarian rhetoric and its fierce contempt for the "experience" of the political establishment. It was Fichte's notoriety as a radical, reinforced by Reinhold's recommendation, that made the Jena students impatient to hear what he had to say. In March 1794, Carl August Böttiger – a former schoolmate from the Schulpforta days, and one of Voigt's go-betweens in arranging the appointment – wrote to Fichte from Weimar that of the "triumvirate" of scholars about to join the university, the students regarded him as "the bravest defender of the rights of man." This impression, he added, "will soon be corrected."[16]

Böttiger had reason to be confident about this expectation. Voigt and Goethe had appointed Fichte because they assumed that under their quiet but firm tutelage, he could be expected to keep a low profile on volatile political issues. They used Hufeland, who had learned his lesson well, to secure advance assurances in that regard. In a letter at the end of December 1793, Hufeland had given Fichte the same advice he himself had received. Weimar stood "in the first row" among governments that favored freedom of teaching and writing, but in the current strained atmosphere it was necessary to avoid all steps "that are too loudly compromising" or could "draw criticisms" from other governments. To those who objected to Fichte's "democratism," Hufeland had responded that he [Fichte] defended "the democratic party only with regard to law and only in the abstract," and that he had "enough moderation, prudence (*Klugheit*), and coolheadedness (*Kälte*)" to avoid "useless statements offered at the wrong place."[17] In a letter to Böttiger, Fichte did not hesitate to subscribe to what he called Voigt's "*Professor Politik*," though he could not resist a note of arrogance in his very assurance of compliance. He was well aware that he had become a "gaped-at man" whose "every word" would now, through correspondence and travelers, enter the rumor mill "in all corners where the German language is spoken." Hence he would maintain "the greatest circumspection" and perhaps even "the appearance of some frivolity" toward people he did not know well.[18]

---

[16] GA, III, 2: 85. The youth of the other two new appointees is also striking. The theologian and orientalist Karl David Ilgen, at thirty-one, was one year younger than Fichte. The historian Karl Ludwig Woltmann was only twenty-four.

[17] GA, III, 2: 31.

[18] Fichte to Böttiger, April 2, 1994, in GA, III, 2: 90–1. See also Wilson, *Geheimräte gegen Geheimbünde*, pp. 232–8.

Fichte overestimated his capacity to be circumspect, much less frivolous; and his sponsors failed to realize how provocative his very presence
in Jena would be. In Jena itself and in the world impinging on it, the
loyalties and emnities, claims and counterclaims, of old-regime conflicts
were being sucked into the ideological maelstrom of the Revolution. The
Ernestine courts were still wedded, to be sure, to corporatist politics, and
indeed to the baroque corporatism of the German heartlands. But in the
arena formed by the courts and the university, the players were learning
to cut and thrust in a new language of political contestation.

★ ★ ★

The very act of giving public lectures was bound to irk some of Fichte's
colleagues. For the past several decades Jena professors had neglected
public lecturing, which was free to all comers. Their efforts were devoted
to the "private" courses that brought in fees. Even when public lectures
were announced, in fact, they were rarely given. But Fichte, like Reinhold before him, understood that newcomers could use the public lecture
as a self-advertisement to gain a piece of the student market. Of the hundreds of Fichte's listeners who were asked to embrace the mission of
scholars and who were told that the road to moral rebirth lay through
the new philosophy, some found their way into his private Collegium on
the Doctrine of Knowledge.

"Financial envy" (*Brotneid*) was a powerful motive in professorial feuds,
and it surely played a role in the initial attacks on Fichte. What gave the
attacks their bite, however, was the new language of ideologically inspired indictment. The increasingly radical course of the Revolution had
imparted a new momentum to the indigenous German conservatism that
had begun to shape government policy in Prussia and several other states
in the late 1780s. To Wöllner's clique in Prussia, and to like-minded government officials and clergymen in neighboring states, the rationalist critique of revealed religion threatened to spread both spiritual decay and
political subversion. The two were in fact inseparable, since ultimately the
legitimacy of thrones rested on the inviolability of confessional Orthodoxy. To replace the masses' unquestioned biblical faith with an "enlightened" veneration for the moral autonomy of the individual conscience
was to invite social and political chaos. Revolutionary France seemed to
confirm this view. The mobilization of the masses, culminating in the
destruction of the monarchy, went hand in hand with dechristianization
campaigns and the Jacobin sponsorship of a deistic cult of the Supreme
Being. As educated Germans followed these events, their perception of an
intimate connection between the Revolution and "philosophy," a catch-
all term that evoked figures as disparate as Voltaire and Rousseau, underwent a radical change. In 1789 it had been common to hail philosophy
as the inspiration behind a moderate legal revolution; and the frequent

assumption was that in Germany the new departure in philosophy could produce a similar transformation without any revolution at all. Now arrogant philosophical abstractions, sometimes labeled "metaphysics," loomed as the demonic force behind a mob rule that sought the complete annihilation of church and state.

Goethe and Voigt were not entirely immune to the logic of this demonology, and in any case they could not keep Weimar and Jena insulated from it. While the ducal government could tactfully deflect the cries of alarm issued by the smaller Ernestine courts, it could not simply ignore the conservative pressures emanating from Berlin and Dresden. Nor could it keep a lid on the guardians of Throne and Altar at home, especially in the higher ranks of the clergy. That became evident in January 1794, as Fichte's appointment was being finalized. The Superior Consistory (*Oberkonsistorium*) in Eisenach, supported by the court at Meiningen, launched an attack on the rationalist proclivities of the Jena theology faculty. Their main target was Heinrich Eberhard Gottlob Paulus, a thirty-two-year-old biblical scholar who had advanced from the philosophy to the theology faculty in 1793 despite considerable clerical opposition. Echoing the language of Wöllner's edicts in Prussia, the Superior Consistory sought to protect "the pure evangelical doctrine according to the symbolic books." The "speculation" of teachers like Paulus, President Herr von Berchtolsheim pointedly reminded the ducal government, was particularly inappropriate in the university's law and theology faculties, which had the task of training state servants for "actually existing states" and not for "a state on the moon." But even the "speculative disciplines" – and philosophy was obviously the chief culprit here – had to be stopped from undermining or obstructing positive religion and the state constitution.

Berchtolsheim and his consistorial colleagues wanted a crackdown along Prussian lines. A university curator would be installed to monitor teaching, and henceforth there would be general censorship for all publications except scholarly treatises in Latin. This was precisely the kind of blatant intrusion into academic life that the Weimar Privy Council, and particularly Goethe and Voigt, preferred to avoid. They regarded the clerical watchdogs as hysterical, if not malevolent, and their strategy was to head off their attacks by impressing on prospective victims the need to steer clear of explosive religious and political issues. But in an era when public discourse about religion and a host of other subjects was being politicized in an unprecedented way, that strategy was precarious.

Though careful not to comment on the course of events in France in his public lectures, Fichte proved unable to keep the low profile the strategy required. When he invoked the future to which a new breed of scholars would point mankind, he could not refrain from controversial evocations of the rational society and polity that would replace the current order. In the second lecture Fichte pronounced that "the goal of all government is to make government superfluous" – though he added that "the time has certainly not yet come" and that he "[did] not know how many myriads or myriads of myriads of years it [might] take." Plucked out of context and suitably reworked, the statement became a prediction that universal revolution was impending. On June 15, 1794, Voigt reported to Goethe that two officials from Jena – Bürgermeister Georg Wilhelm Vogel and Consistorial Councillor Christoph Heinrich Krüger – had "very obligingly" carried the rumor to the Weimar Privy Council that "Fichte [was] a terrible Jacobin who [had] said in a Collegium that in ten to twenty years there would no longer be any king or princes."[19]

Voigt had little patience with "people who smelled Jacobins everywhere" (*Jacobiner-Riecher*), particularly when professors became their victims. The pragmatist in him found it "too silly" that "the scholars are blamed for *Sansculotismus*, under which they would be the first to fall if such a misfortune were to break over our culture."[20] At the same time, though, Voigt feared the poisonous effect of rumor on Karl August's already jaundiced view of his professoriate.Voigt let it be known to Fichte that the Duke was being persuaded by a "formal alliance" against him, and that he ought to eschew "politics" for at least his first semester.

Fichte was being asked to make good on his promise to be "prudent." The issue was what professorial "prudence" (*Klugheit*) might mean and whether it was compatible with the philosopher's convictions. In one of its connotations – one that had its origins in Aristotle's discussion of *phronesis* – *Klugheit* meant the art of forming judgments and making decisions by applying general principles to the concrete circumstances of particular situations. This might be lauded as the practice of political wisdom – or it might be condemned as the rationale for a moral relativism that was, by Kantian standards, indefensible. At what point did the virtue of prudence shade into the mere "cleverness" or "cunning" of the political opportunist?

In his letter to Goethe on June 24, Fichte's righteous tone barely concealed his inability to resolve these questions. Having feared false accusations, he had written down word for word the lectures given to date – and would publish them unchanged. As for the future, he was indignant at the thought that he might be expected to alternate between a "summer-ethics" and a "winter-ethics," or that he might practice a "Jesuit-ethics" by hiding himself. He would have to quit Jena if academic teaching required that he foresake "the duties of a human being," which

---

[19] Quoted in GA, III, 2: 146, N. 4.
[20] GA, III, 2: 146, N. 4.Voigt used the term *Jakobiner-Riecher* in a letter to Goethe, March 16, 1796, in *Goethes Briefwechsel mit Christian Gottlob Voigt*, 1, p. 240.

included the duty to state one's conviction before a public audience. If he were to stay, he needed hard-and-fast assurances from the Duke, especially since his wife and his aged, infirm father-in-law would soon be joining him in Jena. If only for their sake, however, he was willing to qualify his equation of duty with complete openness. Though he could not agree to change anything in his lectures, he could promise, for example, not to write a continuation of the *Contribution* and indeed not to produce any anonymous writing about political subjects for a certain time. Likewise the Duke could rest assured that in due time he would give emphasis in his lectures to the duties of "*respect toward established order*, etc."[21]

Fichte was at once standing firm on principle and suggesting the price he might be willing to pay for government protection against calumnists. It is likely that at their meeting with him in Weimar a few days later, Goethe and Voigt also resorted to equivocation. In any case, both sides came away satisfied. The privy councillors felt reassured that they were after all dealing with a sensible fellow who understood the need for self-restraint. He found it "quite pleasant," Fichte wrote to his wife, that "fantastic rumors about [him] were going around everywhere"; it proved that he was "not entirely unworthy of notice." He assured her that the Weimar government had "unlimited confidence in [his] uprightness and prudence" and had "explicitly mandated [him] to teach entirely according to [his] conviction."[22] The underlying issue – whether he was really in a position to be both upright by his own standards and prudent in the sense his official superiors expected – seems to have been dodged.

Within a few months, Fichte was once again appealing to the ducal government for help. For the winter semester he had to transfer his public lectures from a hall in the home of one of his colleagues to the public auditorium of the philosophy faculty. Finding that all the weekday hours were taken with important courses, he scheduled the lectures from 9 to 10 on Sunday mornings, the same hour as the service in the large *Stadtkirche*. On Sunday, November 9, when Fichte and a large crowd of students gathered for the first lecture, they discovered that the auditorium was locked. The Dekan of the philosophy faculty, who kept the key, was out of town. It was perhaps no accident that the Dekan was Professor Ulrich, who had devoted all his lectures to refuting Kant and made no secret of his resentment at being much "reduced" by younger colleagues. After much commotion, Fichte led the crowd to his house and gave the lecture there.

Fichte had probably not intended to interfere with the *Stadtkirche's* service. Once he had become aware of the conflict, he had put back the remaining lectures an hour. But to clergymen eager to pounce, there was

[21] GA, III, 2: 146–50.   [22] Fichte to Johanna, June 30, 1794, in GA, III, 2: 161.

something sacrilegious about a notorious radical lecturing on the Lord's Day, and the noise generated by a moblike following of students made it all the more alarming. On November 16, the Sunday immediately following this incident, the Consistory in Jena protested to the Duke that Fichte was violating a university prohibition against Sunday lectures. The Weimar Superior Consistory promptly supported its clerical colleagues, and on its recommendation Fichte's lectures were temporarily suspended.[23]

Behind this sensitivity about the Lord's Day, Fichte spied entrenched corporate self-interest. In his letter of defense to Voigt, he spoke as one of the "poor non-senators." He dismissed the stated objection to his lectures as an obvious pretext. "My true crime," he informed Voigt, "is that I have influence and respect among the students, and that I have listeners." His enemies were becoming "old-orthodox Christians out of mere *odio academico*." Denying the legitimacy of corporate privilege and power, Fichte refused to submit to a "command of the senate." He would only comply with a law to which all university teachers were subject.[24] Voigt fully concurred, and in January 1795, in accordance with a compromise reluctantly accepted by the Senate, Fichte continued his lectures on Sundays from 3 to 4.[25] The Consistories had to suffice with this Pyrrhic victory.

It is striking, though, that they were proving adept at learning the new rules of the game. They too could appeal to the imperatives of "publicity" in a politically volatile era, though their logic was very different from Fichte's. The Weimar Superior Consistory argued that even if Fichte's Sunday lectures were not "an intended step against the public divine service of the land," they would make a most unfortunate impression "with Jena and the neighboring public as well as outside the duchy (*auswärts*)." It was this theme that the Senate elaborated in its report to the Duke in early January. The report began by exonerating Fichte of charges of violating the law and corrupting students. Fichte's Sunday lectures, however, could open the university and indeed the ducal government to the charge of being indifferent to the religious education of students. "Precisely at the present moment," the Senate warned, any publicly approved event that might seem to indicate "lack of respect for the usual celebration of Sunday among Christians" could be used "to draw highly hateful parallels, if also undeserved."[26]

The Senate's not-too-subtle allusion was calculated to warn the ducal government that it risked being branded a fifth column in the Revolu-

[23] GA, III, 2: 209, N. 2.   [24] Fichte to Voigt, Nov. 18–19, 1794, in GA, III, 2: 211–15.
[25] See Voigt's letter to Goethe, Nov. 19, 1794, in GA, III, 2: 216, N. 2.
[26] GA, III, 2: 217, N. 1, and 251–2, N. 3. The key phrasing was from the theologian Johann Jakob Griesbach; see the votes of Senate members, ca. Dec. 9–10, 1794, in FG 6.1: 89–101.

tion's war on Christianity. The warning took a relatively judicious and benign form; Fichte was to be faulted not for his intentions, but for actions that might damage the university's public image. In the more outlandish rumors making the rounds among his enemies in the university, in the clerical ranks, and in court circles, Fichte was charged with the worst of intentions. The charges surfaced in mid-March of 1796 in an article published in *Eudämonia*, a rabidly antirevolutionary journal in which several Weimar clergymen and officials were heavily involved.

Eudämonia was typically conservative in its coupling of the decline of religious authority and the onset of political anarchy, but its special obsession was with conspiracy. The key to it all was the secret Order of Illuminati, a hyperrationalist and anticlerical offshoot of freemasonry. The exposure and apparent suppression of the Illuminati by the Bavarian government in the mid-1780s had caused quite a stir, particularly as it became evident that the great bulk of the 600-odd members had been recruited from the ranks of academe, the clergy, and government officialdom. New details about this scandal among Germany's educated and official elite had continued to surface in the early 1790s. If the Order's surreptitious leaders can be said to have had a political strategy, it was to gain control secretly of masonic lodges and occupy the highest levels of government with the Order's recruits. That agenda, as vague as it was, smacked of conspiratorial subversion, and the very cult of secrecy encouraged the attribution of far more alarming ambitions to the Illuminati.

Readers of *Eudämonia* learned that the Order had not been suppressed at all. It had gone underground and become all the more effective, first joining with French freemasons to precipitate the Revolution, and now working hand in glove with the Jacobins to spread the revolutionary gospel throughout Europe. In fact the distinction between Jacobins and Illuminati was merely nominal; in mentality the two formed a single demonic force. The article on Fichte assigned him a strategic role in this conspiratorial plot. It did so with *Eudämonia*'s usual mix of arbitrary associations and brutally simplistic conflations. Fichte, it claimed, had had close ties with Jacobins and Illuminati since his stay in Zürich in 1789. That such a "philosophical hothead" received an appointment at Jena might very well be explained by the manipulations of a Jacobin "on the spot." Fichte's task at Jena was "to destroy the foundation of the Christian religion and the state constitution, and to introduce among the students instead of the Christian religious service a strange Divine Service of Reason, and, instead of order in the state, anarchy." Hence it was no accident that his failed attempt to use a university auditorium for lectures on Sunday mornings was reminiscent of recent events in revolutionary Paris. His plan had been "to dedicate the auditorium as the Temple of Reason."

In the ensuing controversy he had been supported by several professors connected with the Illuminati, including Paulus.[27]

Eudämonia's conspiracy theories were a far cry from the measured conservatism of a Rehberg. The journal represented the paranoid fringe of antirevolutionary ideologues. Voigt regarded the attack on Fichte as "disgraceful," all the more so since a theologian at Jena had probably supplied the "data." If rumors about Fichte's Illuminatism seemed absurd, however, they nonetheless reminded the ducal government of its vulnerability. In the mid-1780s, before its suppression, the Order had had considerable success recruiting in Weimar and Jena, as at several other court towns and university towns. For a short time the Duke himself and Goethe had been members, and other recruits had included Voigt, Herder, Reinhold, and Hufeland. In the early 1790s the ducal government had taken pains to demonstrate its anti-Illuminist policy, partly because it was genuinely shocked by the revelations of the leadership's conspiratorial agenda and partly because it wished to head off scandals about its own earlier complicity.[28]

As hysterical and unscrupulous as Eudämonia's journalism was, it shared certain basic perceptions with the more moderate strains of conservative ideology. Indeed the conspiracy theory, even as it played fast and loose with fact, threw those perceptions into bold relief. Like the more paranoid observers, the moderates assumed that the undermining of revealed religion had brought Europe the plague of revolution. They too assigned the ultimate responsibility for mob violence to the philosophical fantasies that the Aufklärung had begun to "popularize." Other conservatives might not agree with Eudämonia that "broader circles" of writers and academics were being used by an Illuminatist core, but the claim that the carriers of the revolutionary plague were to be found among the university-educated intelligentsia seemed more plausible. Hence in the conservative perspective, freedom of expression in university lecture halls and in the press, and not social injustice or arbitrary government, was the cause of revolution. The state of the universities was especially alarming. The university faculties were turning out disaffected intellectuals who, as office holders in church and state, formed a kind of revolutionary ferment within the very precincts of public authority; and since universities like Jena drew their students from a fairly wide area, the damage could not be confined to one state.

---

[27] "Verunglückter Versuch, im christlichen Deutschlande eine Art von öffentlicher Vernunft-Religions-Uebung anzustellen," Eudämonia oder Deutsches Volksglück 2 (1796): 28–30, 54–5. See also FG 1: 181–94. On Eudämonia and its contributors, see Klaus Epstein, The Genesis of German Conservatism (Princeton, N.J., 1966), pp. 535–46.

[28] See esp. Wilson, Geheimräte gegen Geheimbünde, which uses a wealth of archival souces to demonstrate the complex relationship between the Weimar government and Illuminatism and is an important corrective to the received image of classical Weimar.

Seen through these lenses, Fichte's celebrity did not bring credit to either Jena or Weimar. It was a glaring reminder that in the heartland of Lutheran Germany, "fantasies of freedom" (*Freiheitsschwärmerey*) were corrupting the young men who ought to form the pillars of Throne and Altar.

★ ★ ★

In the early 1790s Jena presented two faces to the German public, and the contrast between them was startling. The university's younger generation of scholars basked in and enhanced the radiance of Goethe's Weimar. They saw themselves as spearheading a philosophical revolution whose ultimate aim was nothing less than the moral regeneration of mankind. The Jena students, on the other hand, struck many observers as a thoroughly unregenerate lot. At the close of the century, as in earlier decades, Jena had a strong claim to be the locus classicus for a student subculture that was notorious for its crudity and for the tenacity of its commitment to boozing and brawling. Some of the students who flocked to Jena aspired to a Kantian awareness of "freedom," but others simply wanted to partake of the traditional freedom to carouse and flaunt conventions before entering the roles circumscribed by careers and marriage.[29]

Some of the latter were surely among the hundreds of students who attended Fichte's public lectures. While the student subculture mocked the pretensions of academic life, it did not preclude intellectual curiosity. Where Fichte ran into trouble was in provoking the secret Orders, which exercised an informal but imposing leadership over the student population as a whole. The Orders were a fairly new presence in university life. Three of them – the Constatisten, the Schwarzen, and the Unitisten – had entrenched themselves at Jena and several other universities since the 1760s. They exhibit, in a particularly concentrated form, the intermingling of traditional forms of youthful self-assertion and new "enlightened" values among new generations of students.[30]

---

[29] For a description of both types of students, see Rist, *Lebenserinnerungen*, esp. pp. 51–66. The contrast between Jena's student life and its intellectual revival is well illustrated in Theodore Zielkowski, *German Romanticism and Its Institutions* (Princeton, N.J., 1990), esp. pp. 228–46.

[30] See esp. Otto Götze, *Die Jenaer akademischen Logen und Studentenorden des XVIII. Jahrhunderts* (Jena, 1932), which is now dated but includes a wealth of detail on the Orders, and Jens Riederer, "Die Jenaer Konstantisten und andere Studentenorden an der Universität Jena im letzten Drittel des 18. Jahrhunderts. Eine statistische Untersuchung," in Joachim Bauer and Jens Riederer, ed, *Zwischen Geheimnis und Öffentlichkeit. Jenaer Freimaurerei und studentische Geheimgesellschaften* (Jena and Erlangen, 1991), pp. 42–109. The latter work provides a balanced analysis of the relationship between the Orders and freemasonry. Also rich on the details of eighteenth-century student life are Richard Keil and Robert Keil, *Geschichte des Jenaischen Studentenlebens von der Gründung der Universität bis zur Gegenwart (1558–1858)* (Leipzig, 1858), pp. 134–213. On the larger issue of continuity and change in the consciousness of German students in the late eighteenth century, see esp. Wolfgang Hardtwig, "Krise der Universität, studentische Reformbewegung (1750–1819) und die Sozialisation der

To a degree the Orders emulated freemasonry, which had won an impressive following in the German aristocracy and the educated and propertied *Bürgertum* in the middle decades of the century. The echoes of masonic culture are unmistakable in their rhetorical commitment to the Enlightenment's ideals of friendship, virtue, and moral self-improvement. To judge by such language, the Orders aspired to be the nuclei of a new moral order. Like freemasonry, however, they were in fact deeply rooted in the old-regime corporate culture from which they in some ways aspired to distance themselves. It was not simply that their internal hierarchies and their cult of secret rites and symbols were reminiscent of corporate practices. The Orders had grown out of the regional fraternities on which students traditionally had relied for fellowship and aid in coping with the hazards of university life. They are perhaps best characterized as the fraternities' elite inner circles. It was above all in that guise – as the guardians of the exclusive rights enjoyed by students as a corporate body – that they claimed preeminence and set the example. The defense of "academic freedom" in this corporate sense rested on the claim to an exclusive solidarity and code of "honor." As in freemasonry, the internal bonding in friendship and the contempt for "profane" outsiders went hand in hand.

The assertion of solidarity and the cult of honor took many forms, most of which perpetuated an image of student barbarism. The sacred bonds of friendship were regularly reconsecrated in evenings of beer or wine guzzling at the local tavern that the Order used as a kind of lodge. Mock disputations ended with the awarding of the degree of *doctor cerevisiae et vini* (doctor of beer and wine) to candidates who had downed the requisite quantity. Order members (and other students who imitated them) swaggered about the streets wearing swords, and these were used (or at least brandished) in recurrent clashes with local "philistines" (above all, municipal gendarmes and military personnel) who had encroached on student honor. The sword also announced that like the aristocracy, the Orders claimed the privilege of settling disputes with dueling. The exchange of insults between members of different Orders was highly formalized and carefully graded. If it went far enough, the duel became unavoidable, and Order members were bound to defend their offended brother. Less formalized, and usually less dangerous, were the actions taken against professors. The Orders led crowds of students in cheers and serenades outside the homes of popular professors, but they also subjected the unpopular to charivari. Since university policing was woefully inadequate,

jugendlichen deutschen Bildungsschicht," *Geschichte und Gesellschaft* 11:2 (1985): 155–76; Hardtwig, "Studentenschaft und Aufklärung: Landsmannschaften und Studentenorden in Deutschland im 18. Jahrhundert," in Etienne François, ed., *Geselligkeit, Vereinswesen and bürgerliche Gesellschaft in Frankreich, Deutschland und der Schweiz (1750–1850)* (Paris, 1986), pp. 239–59.

the victim usually had no choice but to stand by helplessly as his windows were smashed; and the violence occasionally extended to other property, including the furniture, particularly if the perpetrators were drunk. There was a thin line between token violence and wanton destruction.

Since the late seventeenth century the student subculture had been a thorn in the side of church and state. Even if one granted that young men needed a breathing space between childhood and the demands of adulthood, it seemed intolerable that future clergymen and government officials were dissipating their precious years at the university with boozing and brawling. And yet student life was largely impervious to admonitions by the authorities, and the occasional disciplinary measures had no long-term effects.

The ascendancy of the Orders from the 1760s onward posed a more direct challenge to the authority of absolutist states. The Orders' secrecy was not simply a matter of hermetic rituals and symbolism; the very names of their members were carefully concealed. At least to outsiders, peering into the student subculture, the Orders were invisible and hence inaccessible to discipline from above. Their secrecy formed a wall that the authority of the absolutist state found almost impossible to breach. When breaches did occur, they were necessarily temporary, since each government acted in isolation from the others and competed with the others for students. Even when an Order's leaders at one university were expelled, its branches at neighboring universities remained intact – and eventually it revived where it had been suppressed.

As early as 1765 newly matriculating students at Jena had been required to take an oath not to join Orders, on pain of being expelled and excluded from employment in the Ernestine territories. This proved to be one of many futile gestures of suppression. The only oath that mattered – the only one that corporate "honor" made sacred – was the oath not to reveal the Order's secrets, including the names of fellow members. Prospective members were assured that the promise required at matriculation could be given and then blithely ignored, since it was coerced. Betrayal by other students was unlikely; in the eyes of many, the Orders' members assumed heroic stature, and in any case an informer risked severe retaliation. As for the professors, they too were reluctant to cross the Orders. Aside from the risk of smashed windows and other forms of harassment, there was the danger that students would go elsewhere to study if the Orders were seriously combated.

The Jena professoriate's worst fears almost materialized in the summer of 1792, when roughly two-thirds of the students left en masse to protest the sending of troops to the university and waited at an outlying village, threatening to transfer to Erfurt, until the ducal government coaxed them back. As the government realized, the professors could not be counted on in disciplinary investigations of the Orders. Accepting the Orders as an unavoidable fact of university life, professors regarded their pranks with bemused indulgence and turned a blind eye to their excesses.

Again the events of the 1780s and early 1790s heightened a sense of alarm in government circles. The exposure of the Illuminati in the mid-1780s seemed to vindicate worries that secrecy could be the vehicle for conspiratorial opposition. And then there was the lesson of the Jacobins' rise to power in France. Conspiracy need not take the form of penetrating the inner workings of government, as some of the Illuminati leaders had planned; behind the rhetoric of liberty, equality, and fraternity, conspirators could make the masses their instrument and rule the streets. If the students at Jena were not already infected with the revolutionary plague, the Orders might very well serve as the carriers – and their invisibility would make them all the more lethal. Karl August had confronted this specter as early as July 1792, when he attributed a central role to the Orders in the student disturbances that had culminated in a mass withdrawal from the university. "The Orders must be rooted out in every possible way," the Duke had written to Voigt: "Your observation is quite correct that the students pour out democratic delusions (*Schwärmerei*) from the same dispositions, and also that they wait to step forward with it after their university years in the fatherland have ended. I can assure you that the fear of new-French principles being transplanted onto German soil was in no way a chimera."[31]

The Orders remained impervious to government intervention, but they were not without challenges from within the student ranks. In 1791 Heinrich Stephani, a thirty-year-old private tutor who had accompanied a young count to Jena, launched a campaign to replace dueling with a student court of honor. Opponents contemptuously dismissed Stephani and his supporters as "*Schokoladisten*" who were foolish enough to think that students could settle all their disputes over a cup of chocolate. If Stephani was naïve, it was the naïveté of the Kantian moralist. In a letter seeking support at other universities, he welcomed the arrival of the "golden" day when "human beings have been awakened by the light of philosophy from animal slumber." He challenged students "to raise Reason to its deserved throne of legislation." Clearly Reinhold's lectures on Kant were having an impact. In Stephani's eyes, and in the eyes of at least some of the nearly 300 students who signed his petition, dueling perpetuated an atavistic concept of "honor" as a corporate privilege. It was an affront to the Kantian vision of the moral equality of rationally autonomous individuals.[32]

---

[31] Quoted in Wilson, *Geheimräte gegen Geheimbünde*, p. 149.
[32] Paul Ssymank, "Die Jenaer Duellgegner des Jahres 1792 und Karl Augusts Kampf gegen die geheimen Studentenverbindungen," *Quellen und Darstellungen zur Geschichte der Burschenschaft und der deutschen Einheitsbewegung*, ed. Hermann Haupt (Heidelberg, 1913), pp. 6–7, 17.

At first the Senate and the ducal government welcomed the anti-dueling movement, since they saw it as a golden opportunity to launch a campaign against the very existence of the Orders. In reaction, the Orders were quick to portray themselves as victims of "arbitrary power" riding roughshod over academic freedom, and student sentiment began to turn in their favor. Ironically the government was not entirely unhappy to see the anti-dueling sentiment lose its momentum. As eager as it was to eliminate dueling, it was ambivalent about Stephani's proposal to establish a student-run honor court that would in turn be rooted in a reorganization of the entire student population into voluntary associations. Duke Karl August did not share Goethe's view that the proposed student court and associations would serve as badly needed training grounds for the exercise of civic responsibilities. While the Orders seemed to open the way to Jacobin conspiracy, these institutions smacked of French constitutionalism in their implication that students had a right to codetermination in university governance. The Duke preferred to rid the university of dueling "without sanctioning publicly a dubious confederation and without having the students themselves interfere in the academic judicial office."[33]

Hence, little had changed by the time Fichte arrived in Jena. His initial efforts to counteract the prevailing "rawness" and "wildness" of student life were limited to encouraging a new association that styled itself the "Society of Free Men." Founded by ten of Fichte's students in June 1794, the Society aimed to embody a concept of freedom diametrically opposed to that of the Orders. It was to be a kind of moral and intellectual meritocracy, open in principle to any student who met its rigorous standards. The "Act of Constitution" which it sought permission to print in early 1795 bore the clear imprint of Fichte's thought. The Society's aims were to "promote the purpose of humanity" and to achieve "universal validation" of the "laws" of Truth. It would spread its teachings through the "reciprocal communication" that Fichte extolled in his lectures. In pointed contrast to the Orders, members united "freely and publicly" so that "every eye" could recognize them – though, in recognition of their vulnerability to scandalmongers, lectures and essays were to be burned after being presented to the group. Likewise, in an obvious rejection of the Orders' exclusive cult of honor, they declared that their union separated them from "no one whose visage is human and whose heart is noble."[34]

[33] Ibid., pp. 3, 10–11.
[34] On the Society and Fichte's relationship to it, see Wilhelm Flitner, *August Ludwig Hülsen und der Bund der freien Männer* (Jena, 1913), esp. pp. 10–24; Paul Raabe, "Das Protokollbuch der Gesellschaft der Freien Männer in Jena 1794–1799," in *Festgabe für Eduard Berend zum 75. Geburtstag am 5. Dezember 1958*, ed. Hans Weiner Seiffert and Bernhard Zeller (Weimar, 1959), pp. 336–83; Walter Asmus, *Johann Friedrich Herbart. Eine pädagogische Biographie*, vol. 1 (*Der Denker 1776–1809*)

The Society eventually won the courts' permission to print its act of constitution, but not before promising that in committing itself to spread the truth, it had no intention of sowing disorder. Membership never exceeded twenty students, and at the meetings (at least one of which Fichte attended) the explicit engagement with current political issues, with strong leanings toward French revolutionary ideals, quickly acceded to a preoccupation with pedagogy, belles lettres, and aesthetics. It was obvious that the Orders, though also quite limited in membership, retained a commanding presence at Jena and that a serious reform of student life was inconceivable so long as they continued to set the tone.

Seen against this backdrop, the possibility that suddenly presented itself to Fichte and the ducal government in early December of 1794 was momentous. As Fichte later recalled it, representatives from the Orders appeared at his room and asked him "to accept their oath of renunciation on that very day." It was hard to know whether they had been persuaded by his condemnations of the Orders on "rational" grounds or by his warning that the "great courts" and the Imperial Reichstag would soon undertake an investigation throughout the Empire. In any case, since he had no authority to accept the students' oath and since they would not deal with Prorector Johann Wilhelm Schmid (the university officer in charge of student discipline), Fichte obtained their permission to consult with Schmid's predecessor. On his advice, Fichte informed Voigt by letter that at least two of the Orders – the Schwarzen and the Constatisten – were ready to dissolve themselves if an investigating commission were sent quickly. He offered himself as the honest broker in arranging this delicate business.

Since the Orders had successfully resisted government efforts to suppress them for nearly three decades, it is hardly surprising that colleagues who had been at Jena far longer than Fichte had washed their hands of the matter. Fichte was at least vaguely aware that he was being asked to negotiate a minefield. Nonetheless he found the prospect of pulling it off irresistible, and that was in part because his popularity over the previous seven months had given him an intoxicating sense of power. He felt that, thanks to the extraordinary impact of his lectures and to his unusually accessible manner, he held unique sway over the students; and he was eager to demonstrate to his colleagues and to the ducal government that he could succeed where they had failed. Voigt knew how to play on this ambition. He responded to Fichte's initial report by suggesting that the

(Heidelberg, 1968), pp. 75–80; Klaus Rek, "Die Jenaer Gesellschaft der freien Männer 1794–1799," *Wissenschaftliche Zeitschrift der Karl-Marx-Universität Leipzig, Gesellschaftliche- und Sprachwissenschaftliche Reihe* 32:6 (1983): 577–83; Felicitas Marwinski, *"Wahrlich, das Unternehmen is kühn . . ." Aus der Geschichte der Literarischen Gesellschaft der freien Männer von 1794/99 zu Jena* (Jena and Erlangen, 1992). Marwinski's study, based on recent archival research as well as published sources, is particularly informative. It includes a facsimile of the Society's published "Constitution" of 1795.

professor might manage "this significant service" by himself, without government intervention, and thereby "earn the great approval of the courts." "Take it to heart," Voigt concluded, that "I trust *you* more than I trust ordinary human beings."[35]

Even without Voigt's well-aimed flattery, Fichte would probably have assumed the role of mediator. In his lectures the universities figured as the centers of an intellectual and moral revolution. There was no more frustrating obstacle to the realization of that vision than the Orders. They were wallowing in bacchanalian sensuality, when future generations of scholars ought to be purifying themselves in a process of ascetic self-discipline. Their practice of secrecy flew in the face of the principle of openness that ought to govern a truly "public" culture, and their defense of the practice as a right of academic freedom blatantly contradicted the university's public mission. The unconditional subordination of members to the Orders' seniors; the collective sense of "honor," with its contempt for outsiders; the resort to violence in various forms: all mocked the ethic of individual self-determination and egalitarian communication that shaped Fichte's ideal of a regenerated university.

Voigt also decided to defy the odds, but not without trying to preclude the embarrassment that would accompany another failure by the ducal government. In his initial response to Fichte, he argued that an investigating commission was simply not feasible.[36] His stated reason was practical: all four courts would have to approve the commission's mandate and hence it could not possibly begin its work as quickly as Fichte felt necessary. Voigt left unsaid that if Fichte handled the matter without a commission, the ducal government could avoid putting its prestige on the line. When Fichte insisted that a commission was essential to instill fear in the Orders, Voigt relented. As Fichte reminded him, there was no other professor at Jena in a position to do the "impossible." The government would have to proceed on his terms or forfeit the opportunity.[37]

Fichte's terms, spelled out in mid-December in a memorial to Karl August, were deceptively simple. The Orders' members would appear before the commission and take an oath of renunciation, and the commission, speaking for the courts, would guarantee them amnesty. Fichte would already have received and would bring to this same meeting the Orders' sealed books containing membership lists and records of secret rites and symbols; and these would be burned, still sealed, on the spot.[38] Voigt was understandably dubious about the degree of trust this procedure entailed. Weren't the Orders notorious for their willingness to take "false oaths"? Why should they be trusted to hand over the real books?

---

[35] Voigt to Fichte, Dec. 2, 1794, in GA, III, 2: 222–3.   [36] GA, III, 2: 222.
[37] Fichte to Voigt, Dec., 1794, in GA, III, 2: 224–5; Fichte to Voigt, Dec.16–17, 1794, in GA, III, 2: 232–5.
[38] GA, III, 2: 237–8.

If the books could not be handed over to the Duke "in confidence," Voigt
wrote to Fichte, then the commission should at least look through them
to verify their contents.[39]

Secure in his own indispensability, Fichte now spoke as someone who
had broken through the Orders' facade to confront their humanity. The
simple fact, he informed Voigt, was that "the student does not trust the
Ministry and trusts the princes – least of all." He himself had learned that
if one treated students "as men of honor," they would act as such. Fichte
was using this opportunity to censure the political culture of the princely
state not only for its distrustful paternalism but also for its bureaucratic
legalism. "Could we sometimes depart a bit from the legal forms," he
asked Voigt, "and approach each other as human beings to human
beings?"[40]

Voigt found this lecture on trust, honor, and humanity hard to take,
but once again he had no choice but to follow Fichte's lead. On December 24 he informed Fichte that the senior member of the two-man commission was State Councillor Johann Karl von der Becke from Gotha,
who was "a great friend of [his]." Voigt was confident that "everything
[would] go very softly and *honnett*." Indeed he suggested that Fichte consider moving on to persuade the students, "without conspicuous scenes,"
to abandon their New Years bacchanals.[41] For all his arrogance, it would
seem, this young philosopher promised to be an effective agent on the
spot.

Voigt's optimism was premature. It was not until January 8, 1795, over
a month after the Orders' representatives had first approached Fichte,
that the commission finally arrived in Jena. Over the next two days the
Constatisten and the Schwarzen appeared before it and the stipulated
exchanges of oaths and guarantees and burning of books were carried
out. But the problem that had dogged Fichte's plan from the start was
that the third Order, the Unitisten, had refused to cooperate. Fichte had
hoped that the commission would make an example of the Unitisten with
swift and appropriately severe punishments. Instead, for several months
after the commission's departure on January 14, 1795, the authorities
persisted in the hope that threats would suffice to achieve the Order's
dissolution.[42]

Blamed for all the Orders' troubles and suspected of having been in
collusion with the government all along, Fichte now found himself the
target of a "frightful" hatred. On the evening of February 14 his wife was
insulted on the street, and that night his windows were broken. The
window-breaking was an unexceptional gesture – indeed colleagues
advised him to consider it "an honorable testimonial for a professor" –

---

[39] GA, III, 2: 231.   [40] GA, III, 2: 233.   [41] GA, III, 2: 240–2.
[42] The commission's reports are in FG 6.1: 110–22, 124–6, 130–1.

but Fichte took it as a challenge to stay the course in the "entirely valid mission" he had undertaken. On February 21, fearing that another attack was imminent, he notified Prorector Voigt that if he was not assured reliable protection, he would defend himself. As in the imbroglio over Sunday lectures, Fichte posed the issue whether the rule of law or arbitrary corporate tradition would prevail. He warned the Prorector that if the physical harassment of professors was "an old right," then any professor who found it intolerable had the right to leave.

The Unitisten's fight for survival was not limited to traditional forms of harassment. They too were aware that the Revolution had generated a new language of indictment, and they were quick to wield it. A few days before coming to Jena, the commission had received a letter from August Tiede, the Order Senior, denying that the Unitisten had any Jacobin leanings. Tiede went on to charge that Fichte, who had made himself "highly suspicious" through his "principles" and "statements" as well as through his close contact with a French revolutionary named Brechtel, was planning to replace the Orders with a "secret association" of his own. The Unitisten would disband voluntarily, Tiede informed the Duke of Gotha, if Fichte was privately warned not to found or promote another secret society and if the masonic lodge in Jena was also required to cease assembling.[43]

Even before the investigating commission's arrival Fichte had had to contend with these rumors. Their subtexts were clear enough. Pointing to his involvement with the Society of Free Men, the Unitisten were accusing Fichte of trying to found another branch of the notorious Illuminati. The reference to a masonic lodge at Jena was meant to suggest that in suppressing the Orders, the students' academic elders were guilty of hypocrisy. At the same time it evoked a fear of political conspiracy that conflated freemasons, Illuminati, and Jacobins into a single revolutionary force.

Fichte had become the victim of a smear campaign, and it was so transparently malicious that neither the commission nor Goethe and Voigt took it seriously. Nonetheless, in the atmosphere of ideologically charged suspicions that prevailed in the mid-1790s, the accusations against him carried some force, particularly in court circles. They encouraged the suspicions of, among others, the Duke of Gotha, who instructed von der Becke confidentially to include in his investigation at Jena "the way of thinking of the academic teachers there as well as private instructors (*Docenten*) in general, and their behavior toward the students." Without his being aware of it, Fichte was being investigated by the very commission that had been sent to the university on his insistence. Von der Becke's

---

[43] Götze, *Die Jenaer akademischen Logen und Studentenorden*, pp. 96–8; FG 1: 224–5. On Johann Franz Brechtel, see GA, III, 1: 302, 374.

report to the Duke on February 4 exonerated Fichte of the Unitisten's specific allegations but in a way that was not entirely reassuring about the professor's intentions. Von der Becke's main point was that Jena had built-in inhibitions against the kind of demagoguery Fichte might wish to exercise. Given the enemies surrounding him there, he would be a fool not to realize that he was being scrutinized "from several sides." In any case, he had rivals who would surely prevent him from exercising a monopoly over the student audience in philosophy.[44]

In early July 1795, six of seventeen Unitisten finally took the oath of renunciation, but Karl August had good reason to be skeptical about the commission's claim that the Order had been dissolved. Well before then Fichte had realized that he was losing the war. The failure to act quickly and decisively against the Unitisten not only encouraged most of them to persist in their resistance; it also sent a message to the other two Orders that their dissolution had been unnecessary. As early as February 16, the day after the first attack on his house, Fichte reported to Voigt that the Constatisten Order was being revived by a veteran emissary from its Göttingen branch.[45] By the end of the year all three Orders once again had their Jena branches, though, as it turned out, the heyday of student Orders was coming to an end.

The Orders had survived in part because they proved as wiley and intractable as they were reputed to be. Fichte was surely correct, however, in thinking that the success of their resistance also hinged on a supportive, or at least tolerant, environment. Fichte's efforts had collided with what he called the "punishable indifference" of the faculty.[46] Even among the professors who saw the Orders as a serious danger – and many simply laughed them off – there was an understandable reluctance to risk losing students and their fees. In the corporate faculty this indulgent instinct was reinforced by the inclination to settle accounts with an insufferably arrogant young upstart. When Fichte turned to the Senate and its Prorector for protection against harassment, he faced a body that nursed several grievances against him. As maddening as his popularity was his presumption in leaping into a quagmire that was best left undisturbed. Was Fichte's behavior not proof of the ducal government's folly in once again foisting an unwanted appointment on the university? In the affair of the Orders had not Fichte been willing and indeed eager to collaborate with the government in ignoring the Senate's authority? On what basis did he now press a claim on the university for protection?

The Senate responded to Fichte's request for protection on February 21 by implying that he himself was responsible for the curent "embitter-

---

[44] Götze, *Die Jenaer akademischen Logen und Studentenorden*, pp. 132–4.   [45] GA, III, 2: 255, 316.
[46] Fichte to Heinrich Theodor von Schön, (September?), 1795, in GA, III, 2: 405.

ment" and referring him to the Duke for any protection the university was not in a position to provide.[47] The Unitisten's second attack gave the Senate an occasion to twist the knife. During the night of April 8–9 several drunk Unitisten broke Fichte's windows once again. When he refused to come down to face them, they moved on to his landlord's windows. Were it not for the landlord's presence, they might have broken into the house. The next morning Fichte traveled to Weimar to protest in person to the Duke. Karl August fired off a letter to the Senate, rebuking it for "negligence" and "indifference" in the face of public disorders and raising the possibility of "connivance" in "excesses." Prorector Voigt, speaking for the Senate, countered by laying the blame for the entire mess squarely on Fichte's shoulders. This newcomer had taken on the Orders, after all, without consulting his senior colleagues and with "little experience of circumstances here." He ought to have heeded the Senate's earlier warning not to antagonize the Orders. Above all he ought to have refrained from misusing his lectures for that purpose.[48]

Fichte had in fact brought his campaign against the Orders into the lecture hall. His larger strategy had been to combine the threat of government coercion represented by the investigating commission with "arguments from reason" (*Vernunftgründen*). He had begun by condemning secret societies in general in his public lecture series – a provocation that probably occasioned the first attack on his house. His hope was that the lectures would "determine public opinion," particularly by strengthening "the vacillating." He was not at all surprised by the recalcitrance of some Order members, but the reaction of other students to his effort to mobilize public opinion was bitterly disillusioning. Fichte later recalled that by the early spring "the spirit of the whole had visibly become out of tune." He had underestimated students' attachment to the traditional concept of academic freedom. The best students, he reported to Reinhold in retrospect, "do not wish to use their right to storm houses, to plunder, and to rob, but that must depend on their good will; to prevent them with force is an outrageous injustice."[49] A *Publikum* of 800-odd students was not as receptive to "reason" as Fichte, exhilarated by the popularity of his lectures, had thought. His "celebrity" had encouraged him to take on the impossible; but celebrity was evanescent, and there was something illusory about the power it conferred.

Following the attack on April 8 Fichte, finding himself isolated with a small band of disciples and determined to protest publicly the Senate's neglect of his safety, received permission from the duke to withdraw temporarily to the country. He spent the summer of 1795 in a rented castle in Osmannstädt, a village about two hours riding distance from Weimar.

[47] GA, III, 2: 259–62.   [48] GA, III, 2: 287, N. 14.   [49] GA, III, 2: 387.

One of his first projects there was an "Accounting to the Public," explaining the events that had required his departure from the university.[50] What impact the "Accounting" would have had if it had been published (it was not) is hard to say. Fichte's denial of Illuminati connections was not likely to appease the paranoid, and his claim that he had not arbitrarily bypassed the Senate required some obviously tortuous logic.[51] And yet the "Accounting" is an impressive document on two counts. Though he had blinders, Fichte had in fact learned a good deal about the Orders. His effort to set the record straight about them brought out his acuity as a social observer, which is rarely evident in his philosophical writings. And his social observations had an uncharacteristically well-honed political edge. Where his opponents used the new language of political indictment as a blunt weapon, he counterattacked with more subtle associations between Jena and revolutionary Paris.

In the "Accounting," Fichte had to contend with the objection that attacking the Orders did more harm than good. Since their "enthusiastic" spirit, like that of earlier "religious sects," was only intensified by persecution, was it not best to let them die out in the "darkness" of their secrecy? His response was that within the boundaries of the university, the Orders were "nothing less than secret." To other students, in fact, their members were heroic figures; and that was because they played a prominent role in the public life and the sociability of the university. They recruited young men of "good birth," wealth, and outstanding talent; they "visit[ed] the best circles," including the homes of professors unaware of their "secret associations"; they organized "the public festivities in which the entire good society takes part, the balls, the picnics, the comedies, the sledding expeditions." "It is not unheard of," Fichte observed, "that he who smashed your windows yesterday night invites you and yours to the ball today with all possible politeness."[52]

This kind of detail was not only meant to expose the complicity of town and gown. Fichte was calling the professoriate to account for legitimizing the Orders, if only unwittingly. By describing how the Orders exercised a secret, indeed conspiratorial, control over student life, he made the "Accounting" a cautionary tale about the excessive solidarity of corporate bodies, which encouraged the public display of "crudeness and vice" and combative exclusiveness. It was this corporate solidarity, he argued, that allowed the Orders to replant the student traditions of disorder "from generation to generation." If the Orders represented corporate culture at its archaic worst, however, they also were symptomatic of a new danger. When they instigated and orchestrated disturbances, the

---

[50] "Rechenschaft an das Publikum über seine Entfernung von Jena in dem Sommerhalbjahre 1795. (Geschrieben zu Osmannstädt im Juli 1795.)," GA, II, 3: 413–47.
[51] "Rechenschaft," pp. 421–2, 426.   [52] "Rechenschaft," pp. 434–5.

Orders' corporatism took on the character of *modern* conspiratorial politics. Only the Orders could produce "reliable crowds of respectable size." It was their "main policy" (*Hauptpolitik*) to use other students as "entirely unknowing tools." To that end they spread false rumors against the authorities and "electrified young heads" by claiming to champion all sorts of causes, including the "elimination of supposed oppressions," the "defenses of defenseless groups (*Stände*)," and even the "defense of freedom of thought and all human rights." Since Order members lied flagrantly about the events in question, it was virtually impossible to convict them in investigations.[53]

The "Accounting" was a surprisingly deft exercise in the new rhetoric of political indictment. Rather than positing explicit analogies, Fichte's language insinuated affinities between the student subculture at Jena and the Parisian world of conspiratorial manipulation and mob violence. German readers of the mid-1790s would hardly have missed the point.

★ ★ ★

In December of 1793, several months before Fichte arrived in Jena, Voigt had wondered whether he was "prudent (*klug*) enough to moderate his democratic fantasy (or fantasizing)."[54] Fichte in turn was not at all confident that he would receive a friendly welcome from the Weimar court. Did their mutual distrust accede to mutual understanding in the course of Fichte's crisis-ridden first year at Jena?

From the distance of Osmannstädt, Fichte had reason to be satisfied with his relationship with the ducal government. In Voigt, the ducal official with whom he had had the most contact, he faced a legalist. But Fichte found that if one could penetrate to the "human being" behind the bureaucrat, as he thought he had done in arranging the dissolution of the Orders, the Privy Councillor was one of "the few upright men who still exist."[55] As for the Duke, he had responded to Fichte's calls for help with unequivocal rebukes of the Senate, though they had been without practical effect. Precisely because Fichte felt secure in the support of the Duke and his officials, he could take the unusual step of suspending his teaching duties at Jena.

In his role as mediator in Fichte's appointment, Hufeland assured him that Weimar stood "in the first row" of governments committed to "freedom in teaching and writing." Hufeland was surely echoing Voigt and Goethe, who prided themselves on the fact that their university remained a progressive enclave, allowing an unusually generous measure of intellectual freedom in an era of mounting repression. Undoubtedly

[53] "Rechenschaft," pp. 435–40.
[54] Voigt to Hufeland, Dec. 20, 1793, in Diezmann, ed., *Aus Weimars Glanzzeit*, p. 68.
[55] Fichte to Johann Kaspar Lavater, May 8, 1795, in GA, III, 2: 319.

there was an element of self-delusion in this view of what Jena represented. In July of 1791, when Hufeland had had the prospect of a more
lucrative appointment at Halle, Goethe (through Voigt) had warned him
to exact a high price, since he would, after all, be giving up the "intellectual freedom" that Jena afforded and would have to endure being
"schoolmastered" at a Prussian university. But several months later Hufeland was being schoolmastered at Jena, and by none other than Voigt. The
Privy Councillor had not hesitated to censor the printed version of Hufeland's lectures on the French constitution. One of the changes on which
he insisted was the elimination of anything that might be construed as
approval of the French "uprising."[56]

Still, there is a sense in which Jena's progressive image was justified.
Despite its unmistakably repressive impulses, the Weimar government was,
in the context of the era, quite restrained. As Voigt explained to Hufeland, the duchy faced the hazardous task of treading its way through a
polarized ideological terrain. Like many other German observers, Voigt
saw the Revolution chiefly as the product of a philosophical radicalism
that had ignored the masses' capacity for savagery. He was aware that this
"democratism" had its enthusiasts in Germany, but he saw no immediate
danger of a French-style revolution in his little corner of the world. The
immediate threat was posed by the "royalists" or "friends of monarchy."
The tragedy of the Revolution was that it had provoked their "intolerance" and their inclination to repression (rather than prudent accommodation), and hence it was "setting back many years our freedom of thought
and of the press in Germany."[57] For all its efforts to keep a lid on Jena,
the Weimar government did not follow the lead of Prussia and other
dynastic states. If it had followed them, Jena would not have remained an
entrepôt for Kantianism in the early 1790s, and Fichte, the most outspoken Kantian radical, would not have received an appointment there in the
panicky atmosphere of 1794.

And yet in that first year the makings of a collision between Fichte's
sense of mission and the ducal government's priorities were already
evident. Voigt and Goethe had not arranged Fichte's appointment because
they shared his philosophical convictions or even because they had intellectual leanings in that direction. Their concern was that Jena keep itself
and the duchy in the limelight by continuing to cut a progressive, even
daring, figure on the German academic stage. If they were intrigued by
the "Kantian Gospel," they also regarded it with a certain bemused detachment. To them its appeal lay less in what it preached than in the soaring
value of its preachments in the academic marketplace. Voigt observed to
Goethe with a mix of relief and irony that by securing Fichte as Rein-

[56] Diezmann, ed., *Aus Weimars Glanzzeit*, pp. 53, 60.
[57] Voigt to Hufeland, July 28, 1792, in ibid., p. 58.

hold's successor, "we will remain in possession of the new philosophy and the capacity to conceptualize will reach still higher levels of abstraction."[58] More cynical about the prospect of losing Reinhold, Goethe predicted that Kantianism would follow the same trajectory as "fashionable goods from the factory," which "at first are purchased at great expense" but "later are imitated everywhere and are easier to buy."[59] Fichte required a modest salary; obviously he represented the stage of cheap availability.

Fichte was too desirable a commodity, at too good a price, to be sacrificed to political witch-hunters or to venomous but obscure professorial rivals. While Voigt and Goethe knew they had found a bargain, however, they also were at least vaguely aware that they were playing a dangerous game. Would Fichte provide the academic celebrity that the university and the duchy needed, or would he burden them with precisely the notoriety they could not afford? As the duchy was drawn into the ideological arena formed by the Revolution and its opponents, the line between celebrity and notoriety became ever thinner, and it was not clear that Fichte was the sort of person who could avoid crossing it. He was, to be sure, aware that the "circumspection" demanded in his new position would require a special effort. Though his public lectures, unlike his seminar on the Doctrine of Knowledge, demonstrated the relevance of his philosophy to the immediate concerns of his student audience, they were, at least in the public version, notably free of reference to the political events and issues of the day. And yet it is not surprising that behind its public mask of serenity, the ducal government looked on the latest addition to its Kantian stable with alarm and occasional exasperation. Fichte was testing the limits of the permissible, and in a way that was bound to feed the paranoia about his political radicalism. In the year 1794 it was a provocative act to state that government was destined to make itself superfluous, even if one took pains to stress how distant that prospect was. It was perhaps even more provocative to identify publicly with Rousseau's alienation from a thoroughly corrupt age, even if one concluded that Jean-Jacques's diagnosis of the age had been wrongheaded.

Voigt and Goethe liked to think of themselves as standing above the new ideological arena, and that self-estimation is not entirely misleading. Deeply attached to a hierarchical order and its protocols of deference, they regarded "democratism" as a kind of collective frenzy, reminiscent of earlier eruptions of religious "enthusiasm." On the other hand, though, the marriage of religious orthodoxy and reactionary politics was an offense to their "enlightened," skeptical tolerance. While they had to demonstrate vigilance in the face of possible conspiracies, they attributed

---

[58] Ibid., p. 68.
[59] Goethe to Voigt, July 27, 1793, in *Goethes Briefwechsel mit Christian Gottlob Voigt*, vol. 1, p. 108.

the more outlandish conspiracy theories to paranoia or outright maliciousness.[60]

Nonetheless, in their dealings with Jena professors, Voigt and Goethe applied one of the operating assumptions of an emerging conservatism. Like their prince, they drew a line between philosophical theory and the practical experience needed in political decision making. In his response to rumors about Hufeland's lectures, Karl August had written to Voigt that it was time for scholars to stop regarding themselves as "future teachers of the people and of the governors" and to stop assuming that "every thought that indigestion suggests to them" was "a divine calling to rouse the people against apparent oppressions." Each scholar should stick to his particular area of achievement (*leisten*) and leave "the art of administration" to men who had mastered it through "practical experience."[61] Though interested in scholarship, Voigt was by heritage and by profession a master of the administrative art. His prince's view of the proper division of labor made eminent sense to him. It was an abuse of freedom of the press, he informed Hufeland, "to present all abstractions of human rights and equality to the people as imprescriptable authorizations that it can reclaim immediately."[62]

When Rehberg (and Burke) championed the weighty concreteness of "experience" over the free-floating abstractions of "theory" in politics, they spoke for men like Voigt. In the French Revolution the abstractions of eighteenth-century philosophy seemed to reveal their capacity to become "fantasies" about a "democracy" that neither should nor could exist in the real world of politics. As impractical as they were, the fantasies were anything but harmless. They had a way of raising popular expectations to absurd levels and of turning the masses into fanatical and violent mobs. As Voigt put it to Hufeland in September 1792, "metaphysics in France has turned into bloodthirstiness."[63] The solution was not to rid the world of metaphysics but to confine it to university textbooks and lecture halls, where an appropriately "academic" level of abstraction would keep it safely suspended above the "practical" affairs with which statesmen and bureaucrats were properly entrusted.

To Voigt and Goethe the denouement of the Orders affair was disappointing, but they nonetheless derived a certain bemused satisfaction from Fichte's tribulations. Fichte's "metaphysical demagogery has received a nasty kick," Voigt reported to Goethe in the wake of the Unitistens' second attack. "He thanks God if the Monarchy can maintain his windows."[64] Goethe's comments to Voigt were, as usual, more caustic and

[60] See esp. Diezmann, ed., *Aus Weimars Glanzzeit*, pp. 60–1.
[61] Quoted in Wilson, *Geheimräte gegen Geheimbünde*, pp. 227–8.
[62] Diezmann, ed., *Aus Weimars Glanzzeit*, pp. 59–60.   [63] Ibid., p. 60.
[64] *Goethes Briefwechsel mit Christian Gottlob Voigt*, 1: 170–1.

more specific about the links between metaphysical arrogance and violent disorder:

> You have seen the Absolute I in a great predicament, and of course it is very impolite of the Not-I, which has been subject to law, to fly through the window panes. It goes with [Fichte], however, as it goes with the Creator and Maintainer of all things, who, as the theologians tell us, also cannot manage his creatures.[65]

This was a logic that made it incumbent on Fichte, as on any other scholar, to restrict himself to his academic bailiwick. Confined to metaphysics, Flighte's flights of pure theory might burden the academic world with a new obscurantism, but they were at least safe. Though Fichte at first seemed cooperative enough, it was precisely on this issue that the philosopher's principles and his official superiors' expectations were in irreconcilable, though still muted, tension. Ironically, the tension was obscured by the preoccupation with Fichte's reputed "democratism." A careful reading of the *Contribution* (which neither Voigt nor Goethe was likely to undertake) would have revealed that its rhetorical projection of a radically egalitarian community bore no apparent relationship to the constitutional and political democracy of the French Republic. In any case, in his public lectures at Jena, the ones in which he was suspected of preaching Jacobinism, Fichte clearly abandoned that vision as he sought to make his philosophy the property of an intellectual and moral elect.

If Fichte was to remain a "philosopher" in his professorial office, however, he could not put aside the Kantian conception of a priori reason as the instrument of public criticism. Nor could he abandon his growing conviction that the universities had to be privileged forums for the exercise of criticism. In that sense, in fact, his lectures inevitably had political resonances and implications precisely because they *were* abstract and despite their inattention to political specifics. When others appealed to "experience" as the source of political wisdom, Fichte saw their very appeal as proof they they were in the grip of ideology and hence blinded to the truth. To construct a normative vision of a truly rational order from a priori principles – an order that would have no need for a coercive state, for example, and that would make the distribution of life chances hinge on talent rather than "birth" – was to censure the status quo and question the legitimacy of its configurations of power. At this level the Kantian Gospel, at least as Fichte conceived it, could not be confined to a sealed container of purely academic "abstractions." It had a normative authority and a critical thrust that made it inherently political.

[65] Ibid., p. 170.

There is also a sense in which standing under the critical gaze of the larger German "public" meant very different things to Fichte and the ducal government. A negligible factor in the international arena, the duchy could enhance its presence by exhibiting its academic celebrities. In an era when the small German states were maneuvering for their survival, however, Weimar was highly vulnerable to suspicions that it was sponsoring or at least tolerating subversives. Whenever Jena seemed to be exhausting the Duke's limited patience with academe, Voigt and Goethe practiced a politics of discretion. Their strategy was to subject potentially embarrassing professors to preemptive restraint, usually privately, beyond the public gaze, and preferably with a minimum of blatant intimidation. Well before he arrived in Jena, Fichte had undergone this treatment at the hands of Voigt's proxies Hufeland and Böttiger. Even the early rumors of Fichte's Jacobinism in the lecture hall – rumors that Voigt found "impossible" to believe – required a resort to preemptive restraint. Would it not be advisable, Voigt asked Goethe, to give Fichte "a reproach about this in confidence but where there are witnesses?"[66]

In the logic of the politics of discretion, the Weimar court had a dual profile. It was the locus of an absolutist public will, embodied in the dynastic ruler, and at the same time the progressive emblem of a public culture in which the decisive authority lay with the cogency of ideas. The difficulty lay in placating two German publics at once – the old-regime public formed by the other princely courts, which cast a suspicious eye on Jena and the ideas emanating from it, and a public of "scholars" who looked to Jena to gauge the outer limits of academic freedom. If the ducal government was to retain its aura of unimpeachable authority without damaging its progressive image, it had to work behind the scenes to rein in potentially indiscreet professors and thereby protect them, and the university, from attack. Precisely because this preemptive intervention kept the other courts at bay, it could be justified to indignant professors as a minimalist policy, sparing Jena the crackdown being conducted in other states.

Fichte threatened to sabotage this strategy with his capacity to be politically controversial and, more important, with his conviction that controversy ought to be conducted and resolved publicly. He too, of course, engaged in behind-the-scenes maneuverings and negotiations. But in principle he rejected the politics of discretion for a politics of candor. He had retreated from the egalitarian vision of the *Contribution*, but he still saw himself as the philosophical conscience of a new era of openness in which the *Publikum* constituted the highest tribunal, the court of final appeal. It was in the terms of this familiar eighteenth-century metaphor that Fichte reacted to warnings to keep a low profile as rumors of his

[66] GA, III, 2: 146, N. 4.

Jacobinism spread. He wanted to smoke out the slanderers and force them to state their charges before "the entire public," which he was confident would rule in his favor. Though he was turning to the Duke as his protector, he also wanted to prove that Karl August merited "reverence" (*Verehrung*) before "the entire public" for the "the human being in him."[67] If the Duke was to be judged by the same standards as any other human being, then neither he nor his officials had unimpeachable authority; they were accountable to a higher public conscience. The practical implication was that if they were going to restrict academic feedom, it would have to be with public acts open to public scrutiny. If the ducal government found fault with the published version of Fichte's lectures, it would have to ban them publicly. If Fichte was to be forbidden to give the lectures on Sundays, it would have to be with a "*universally valid, publicly promulgated* command, a *princely* command."[68]

In practice, both the politics of discretion and the politics of candor required blinders. The insistence on professorial discretion could very well render academic freedom meaningless in the very effort to protect it from a worse fate. When the government screened the written version of a professor's lectures before publication to make sure they were not incriminating, or merely opened the possibility of doing so, it might be said to be quietly intimidating him into self-censorship. Was that better or worse than having him bow to open coercion?[69] Neither Voigt nor Goethe confronted these issues, though Fichte certainly raised them when he protested that he was being asked to give up "the duties of a human being" as the condition for remaining an academic teacher. The issue Fichte could not face squarely, on the other hand, was whether his commitment to a politics of candor was compatible with his position at Jena. The tension between principles and circumstances was painfully evident in his letter to Goethe protesting efforts to muzzle him. This was the letter in which Fichte tried to demonstrate unshakeable defiance and offer a measure of prudence at the same time. The tension permeates the opening lines, where Fichte addressed Goethe as his "patron" as well as his "friend" and sought protection in the great man's "political prestige."[70] The use of "friend" was a futile gesture, calculated to remove their relationship from the instrumental alliances and dependencies of court politics. With "patron," on the other hand, Fichte acknowedged that as a professor, he was a creature of the state and a client of its officials. It was not simply that, like all other professors (including the Senate elite), he was a "state servant" under government authority. Fichte owed his appointment and his salary to the ducal government, not to the university's corporate faculty. When the Orders' representatives turned to him,

[67] GA, III, 2: 148. [68] GA, III, 2: 211.
[69] Wilson, *Geheimräte gegen Geheimbünde*, raises this issue very effectively. [70] GA, III, 2: 146.

he seized the opportunity to win court "approval." He had joined several of his colleagues as a trusted agent of the government, enabling it to steer the university behind its corporate facade. Exulting in his celebrity and in the indispensable role it seemed to give him, he ignored the hardening resentment of the Senate as his position became all the more dependent on the approval of the government.

Fichte's "Accounting" of his dealings with the Orders was an exercise in the politics of candor, but its fate is another reminder that he, too, was subject to the imperatives of the politics of discretion. His rhetorical strategy was to place himself before the "judgment seat" of the public, like a defendant arguing his own case, and to refute, point by point, the false charges brought against him. He appealed to his own sense of "duty," which required him as a "rational being" to help realize the "exclusive rule of reason" and to speak the truth without "an indefinite, ambivalent word." Though his "honor" lay in his judgment of himself and not in others' judgment of him, the test of honor (or "integrity") was "whether I am willing to acknowledge publicly before the entire world what I say and do, and to lay before the eyes of everyone all motives of my actions, as I myself, to the best of my knowledge, observe them in me."[71] Echoing the eighteenth-century ideal of an enlightened *Publikum* and informing that ideal with eminently Kantian logic, Fichte had placed himself and his audience in a new bonding of individual conscience and collective judgment. The author demonstrated the authenticity of his unflinching self-scrutiny – the honesty of his private examination of conscience – by committing himself to unconditional candor before the public's gaze.

It is a measure of Fichte's sense of isolation that he was remarkably conciliatory toward the Senate in the "Accounting," though he lambasted it in his private correspondence. His main concern in the summer of 1795 was to maintain the confidence of the ducal government. As he explained in a letter to Voigt on August 28, he wanted to avoid further "public censure" by announcing that his "Accounting" was appearing in print with the Duke's permission. To that end he was willing to accept any changes that Voigt advised. Voigt proposed only a few revisions concerning his own role in the Orders affair. But he also submitted the "Accounting" for approval to the court, which decided that it was best left unpublished.

Fichte had wanted public vindication, but in this case the politics of discretion dictated silence.

[71] Fichte, "Rechenschaft," pp. 413–18.

Chapter 9

Philosophy and the Graces

In December 1794, Friedrich Schiller announced the publication *Die Horen*, a new monthly journal to be devoted to literature, history, and philosophy. His choice of title signaled – to an audience with a shared patrimony of classical learning – the kind of cultural rebirth he aspired to effect. In classical mythology the *Horae* had been the goddesses who presided over life and growth in the changing of the seasons. Closely associated with them – and this kinship was crucial to Schiller's project – were the Graces, the goddesses who personified the grace and beauty expressed in supreme works of art. Schiller's hope was that the journal would fuse nature and art by rising above "the influence of the times" and devoting its pages to "what is purely human." In so doing, it would "reunite the politically divided world under the banners of truth and freedom" and would "remove the partition" between polite society and learning.[1]

The first issue of *Die Horen* appeared in January 1795. It marked the beginning of a mutually beneficial collaboration between Schiller and Johann Friedrich Cotta, a shrewd young publisher in Tübingen. Cotta would have preferred to launch a political newspaper, but eager to link a celebrated man of letters to his firm, he had agreed to Schiller's alternative. As the publisher had probably anticipated, the journal had a short life. The last issue appeared belatedly in March, 1798.[2]

In June 1794, shortly after his arrival in Jena, Fichte had been drawn into the planning of *Die Horen*. Schiller chose him, along with Wilhelm von Humboldt and Karl Ludwig Woltmann, a recently appointed historian at Jena, to join him on the editorial board. The first issue included Fichte's essay "On Stimulating and Increasing the Pure Interest in Truth," which he had managed to condense from two of his public lectures in the midst of his imbroglio with the student Orders.[3] Fichte's next

---

[1] Schiller's announcements are reprinted in Günter Schulz, *Schillers Horen: Politik und Erziehung* (Heidelberg, 1960), pp. 211–16. They are also available in *Schillers sämmtliche Schriften*, Th. 10 (Aesthetische Schriften), ed. Reinhold Köhler (Stuttgart, 1871), pp. 233–5, 267–73.

[2] Schulz, *Schillers Horen*, pp. 8–11; Daniel Moran, *Toward the Century of Words. Johann Cotta and the Politics of the Public Realm in Germany, 1795–1832* (Berkeley, Calif, 1990), pp. 30–5.

[3] Reprinted in *Fichte. Early Philosophical Writings*, trans. and ed. Daniel Breazeale (Ithaca and London, 1988), pp. 217–31. Fichte had joined Schiller, Woltmann, and Humboldt in the "first conference" about the new journal on June 7, 1794; Schulz, *Schillers Horen*, p. 10.

contribution, submitted to Schiller in late June of 1795, had been composed in the relative tranquillity of his self-imposed exile in Osmannstädt.
His accompanying note had a defensive tone and was obviously meant
to head off editorial meddling. He assured Schiller that he had worked
hard on the essay and, though it might be a bit longer than expected, he
did not think it could be broken up or changed in any other way. Schiller
in effect agreed; rather than suggest cuts or revisions, he rejected the essay
in toto. In a long letter to Fichte, rewritten twice in an effort to achieve
a measured tone but still dripping with exasperation, he explained that
the essay was shapeless, inconsistent and jarring in style, and "arbitrary"
and "murky" in its conceptualization. When Fichte protested that he had
been done an "injustice," Schiller responded that they could never settle
their argument, since their clash of "principles" reflected the incontro-
vertible fact that they were "extremely different natures."[4] They broke off
contact, though it must have been hard to avoid each other in the close
confines of Jena.

Schiller was right about their incompatible natures. He might have
added that each in his way had a penchant for provocation, was quick to
take offense, and was not above enlisting principles in the service of petty
retaliation. That Schiller's reaction to the essay took Fichte by surprise is
a measure of the latter's arrogance. Schiller was using *Die Horen* to publish
his *Letters on the Aesthetic Education of Man.* Though titled "On the Spirit
and the Letter in Philosophy," Fichte's essay was also devoted to aesthetic
issues and included an obvious refutation of Schiller's main argument. This
was a blatant incursion into Schiller's domain; to make matters worse, the
philosopher had had the effrontery to imitate his use of the epistolary
form. If there was a sure way to enrage Fichte, on the other hand, it was
to submit him to a condescending lecture on his fuzzy-headedness. He
had made the mistake, he informed Schiller, of assuming that he was
dealing with a "friend," only to find himself treated as a "disciple" and a
"pupil."[5] That was a reduction in status he could not accept.

It remains ironic, though, that Fichte and Schiller collided. As different as their personalities were, they had much in common. They were
contemporaries, separated by only three years, and formed in the intellectual crucible of the 1780s. They both retained something of the ardent
affinity with Rousseau that they had felt as young men. It found expression in their shared alienation from their age, and above all in their moralistic contempt for the artificiality and the falseness of courtly culture. Each

---

[4] There is a useful translation of the essay, as it appeared in *PJ* 9 (1798), in David Simpson,
ed., *German Aesthetic and Literary Criticism: Kant, Fichte, Schelling, Schopenhauer, Hegel* (Cambridge,
1984), pp. 75–93. GA I, 6: 333–61, includes an important opening to the Third Letter that was
omitted in the published version. The relevant correspondence is in GA, III, 2: 325–6, 329–40,
360–8.

[5] GA, III, 2: 338, 340.

saw himself championing intellectual freedom in the struggle against religious orthodoxy and state authoritarianism, and each feared being morally compromised by any accommodation with the established order.

In early 1791, just a few months after Fichte had discovered Kant, Schiller had begun a serious study of the *Critiques* that would extend over the next several years and would divert him from drama and poetry to an effort to construct a philosophy of aesthetics. He reported to his friend Körner on July 4, 1794, that Fichte's new view of the Kantian system contributed "not a little" to his penetrating "deeper into this material."[6] He found something absurdly egotistical, to be sure, about what he saw as Fichte's extreme Idealism. Schiller observed to Goethe in late October 1794 that by conceiving the world as "a ball that the I has thrown and that it receives again in reflection," Fichte "has really declared his divinity, as we recently expected." But Schiller remained fascinated by the new philosopher's bold originality. In November 1794, he judged Fichte "after Kant . . . certainly the greatest speculative mind in this century."[7]

Fichte and Schiller might also be expected to have shared a resentment of Goethe, the older man who had shed his youthful rebelliousness to become a courtier and Privy Councillor at Weimar and who regarded philosophy with a certain bemused skepticism. Instead, each saw Goethe as his ally in their dispute in 1795. Fichte went so far as to request that Goethe be brought in to adjudicate the dispute. His request proved naïve, but it was not as misguided as it might at first appear to be. Aware that he needed Goethe's support to survive at Jena and eager to win the approval of a figure of such eminence, Fichte had taken pains to cultivate the Privy Councillor. Goethe in turn had made it clear that he welcomed Fichte's presence in Jena, since he needed someone to "reconcile me with the philosophers, whom I cannot dispense with and with whom I can never unite."[8] It was probably with the prospect of this reconciliation in mind that Goethe had initially agreed to contribute to *Die Horen*.

Fichte found Goethe far more at home in the philosophical realm than Schiller, who "actually lives in two worlds, in the poetic and now and then in the Kantian-philosophical."[9] That was a false impression, based largely on Goethe's casual assurances of interest and reflecting the fact that, for all his celebrity, Fichte remained on the fringe of Weimar's literary and artistic inner circle. What had escaped Fichte's notice was that, in the wake of a meeting of the Society for Investigating Nature in Weimar on July 20, 1794, the relationship between Goethe and Schiller had entered an entirely new phase. For several years their encounters in the social circles of Weimar had done nothing to diminish their mutual guarded hostility. In the summer of 1794, however, mutual need made for a new bonding. Schiller had buried himself in work in Jena and felt

[6] FG 1: 129.   [7] FG 1: 60–1, 196   [8] GA, III, 2: 144.   [9] GA, III, 2: 182.

crimped by the lack of a public field of action for his literary talents. Since his return from Italy, Goethe had found his creativity atrophying under the pressure of social conventions and official obligations at Weimar. Now each found in the other escape from his alienating circumstances and an antidote to sterile "one-sidedness."[10] It was more than a friendship; self-consciously, and with a remarkably clear sense of purpose, Goethe and Schiller used their "Commercium" to form a united front in the intellectual and literary wars of the 1790s. Their strategy – their plan to win the wars by soaring above them into an aesthetic realm of "pure humanity" – would come to be known as Weimar Classicism. Its instrument – the voice of what Schiller would call their "ecclesia militans" – was *Die Horen*.[11]

Hence Fichte's request for Goethe's adjudication in the summer of 1795 could not have been more ill-timed. In the draft of his response (the letter may never have been sent), Schiller seized the opportunity to give him a stinging comeuppance. He found it amazing that Fichte rejected his judgment on matters of taste, since Goethe was now following that same judgment. And Fichte could rest assured that Goethe "is much too alien in the philosophical region to forgive [him] for what he would regard as aesthetic trespasses."[12]

Though the rivalry was petty enough and the tone supercilious, the dispute was much more than a barbed exchange between two prickly personalities. The immediate subject in dispute – the appropriate style for philosophical contributions to *Die Horen* – radiated out to a much larger set of issues. Under Goethe's influence, Schiller was withdrawing from his prolonged engagement with philosophical "speculation." The two artists saw themselves as guardians of the autonomy and indeed the preeminence of an aesthetic realm. With his second contribution to *Die Horen*, Fichte – unwittingly, but with characteristic arrogance – made himself a target for their war on the pretensions and the dangers of philosophical abstraction, particularly in its Kantian varieties.

In the exchange over Fichte's essay, the latent tensions between philosophical Idealism and an emerging classical aesthetic became manifest. The philosophical and the aesthetic agendas remained linked, to be sure, in

---

[10] See esp. Michael Böhler, "Die Freundschaft von Schiller und Goethe als literatursoziologisches Paradigma," *Internationales Archiv für Sozialgeschichte der deutschen Literatur* 5 (1980): 61–3.

[11] There is an enormous literature on this friendship and its literary ramifications. Most useful for my purposes were Böhler, "Die Freundschaft von Schiller und Goethe"; Friedrich Wilhelm Wentzlaff-Eggebert, *Schillers Weg zu Goethe* (2nd ed.: Berlin, 1963); Wilfried Barner, Eberhard Lämmert, and Norbert Oellers, eds., *Unser Commercium: Goethes und Schillers Literaturpolitik* (Stuttgart, 1984). See also the discussion of Goethe's changing view of the *Publikum* in Karl Robert Mandelkow, *Goethe in Deutschland. Rezeptionsgeschichte eines Klassikers*, vol. 1 (1773–1918), (Munich, 1980), pp. 27–34.

[12] GA, III, 2: 361.

their defiance of a commercially and politically corrupted age. But they parted ways on two questions: how philosophical knowledge and aesthetic awareness ought to be related in a modern public culture, and how a new rhetoric could be harnessed to print, the preeminently modern form of communication, to generate the normative authority for a public consensus.

★ ★ ★

In 1795 Fichte and Schiller faulted each other's writing for failing to be effectively "popular." Their use of the term "popular" is likely to strike the modern reader as curious, if not perverse. In fact, as their argument escalated they vied with each other to demonstrate their contempt for popularity. It was not simply that they eschewed any effort to communicate philosophical truths to the great mass of the population. Even in their commitment to making the results of scholarship accessible to educated and polite society, they distinguished sharply between legitimate "popularity" and commercial success. Fichte's claim that Schiller's philosophical writings were "bought" but "little read" and "not at all understood" was calculated to wound. The insinuation was that rather than earning a reputation in philosophy, Schiller was cashing in on the accomplishments in drama, poetry, and popular history that had made him a brand name. Schiller's response was to profess complete indifference to the reaction of the present "German *Publikum*," with its "crudity on one side" and its "contemptible slackness on the other." The course he considered honorable was to write in open defiance of such an audience, to "surprise, shock, and strain" it.[13]

A decade earlier, at age twenty-five, Schiller had assumed a markedly different posture toward the *Publikum* in his announcement for the *Rheinische Thalia*, the first of his several short-lived literary journals. In the wake of the popular success of his first play, *Die Räuber*, Duke Karl Eugen, the ruler of his native Württemberg, had forbidden him to continue writing and publishing. Schiller chose to exile himself from his fatherland to pursue a career as an independent writer. Having explained this decision in the announcement, he continued:

> From now on all my ties are dissolved. The *Publikum* is now everything to me, my object of study, my sovereign, my confidante. Now I obey it alone. Before this tribunal and no other I place myself. This tribunal alone do I

---

[13] GA, III, 2: 339, 364. Schiller had already called for a kind of "popularity" that would not cater to mass tastes in his critique of Bürger's poetry in 1791. See his "Ueber Bürgers Gedichte," in *Schillers sämmtliche Schriften*, Pt. 6, ed. Karl Goedeke (Stuttgart, 1869), pp. 314–21. See also Klaus L. Berghahn, "Volkstümlichkeit ohne Volk. Kritische Ueberlegungen zu einem Kulturkonzept Schillers," in Berghahn, *Schiller. Ansichten eines Idealisten* (Frankfurt am Main, 1986), pp. 97–124.

fear and revere. Something great impels me with the idea to endure no other fetter than the verdict (*Ausspruch*) of the world – to appeal to no other throne but that of the human soul.[14]

There was no contradiction between Schiller's indictment of the "crudity" and "slackness" of the German *Publikum* in 1794 and his paean to the sovereignty of the public ten years earlier. The paean is a *locus classicus* for a familiar normative concept, the one into which the Enlightenment had poured so much of its optimism about the efficacy of Reason and the educative potential of print. In the new world Schiller imagined, political authority, including that of the dynastic state, would no longer channel and obstruct the communication between author and reader. In its apotheosis as a "public" in this sense, the population ceased to be a collection of more or less "mediated" subjects; it became a collective moral will, formed somehow directly out of the judgments of myriad scattered human souls. Since this will was grounded in the individual reader's capacity as a purely human (i.e., rational) being, its compass was potentially the entire world.[15] What made possible this communion between the author and a far-flung, scattered audience was the market distribution of print.

When Schiller castigated the German public in 1794, however, he had in mind a print market that seemed to be expanding at the expense of his ideal public and the authors who revered its judgments. He had special reason to be bitter. In 1791 he had suffered the first attack of a lung inflammation that would disable him for the rest of his life, and he blamed the illness on his exhausting, futile efforts to earn a decent living with his pen. But even among authors who had enjoyed more financial security, a sense of disillusionment and alienation in the face of the real public, the actual buyers of print, was not uncommon by the 1790s. When observers complained of a "reading fury," a rapidly spreading addiction, they meant in part that the "half-educated" masses – artisans, shopkeepers, domestic servants, and even peasants – were being drawn into the print market. The number of such readers was probably exaggerated (though the literacy rate among adult Germans had increased to about 25 percent by the end of the century). Behind the perception of a popular "reading fury" lay a mounting fear, particularly in the wake of the popular violence of the French Revolution, that reading raised unrealistic expectations among the laboring classes and led to social upheaval. While the reading masses gave special cause for alarm, however, the typical educated reader was no less disappointing. The assumption had been that the

[14] Quoted in Todd Curtis Kontje, *Constructing Reality. A Rhetorical Analysis of Friedrich Schiller's Letters on the Aesthetic Education of Man* (New York and Berne, 1987), p. 39.

[15] See esp. Roger Chartier, *The Cultural Origins of the French Revolution*, trans. Lydia G. Cochrane (Durham and London, 1991), esp. pp. 20–66.

"enlightened" public – the tribunal to which authors would hold themselves accountable – would be a homogeneous community of the well-educated. But educated readers seemed to be dividing into two types, the tiny minority of serious readers who welcomed the intellectual challenges posed by a Schiller or a Fichte, and the large and ever-expanding majority of readers who preferred lighter fare. Schiller was one of many authors who characterized the majority as incorrigibly lazy (or "slack") and hopelessly fickle (or "frivolous").[16]

This stereotype marked the undermining of vaulting expectations in the last three decades of the century, when the print market underwent radical changes in scale and structure and a new kind of reading made its presence felt. The total number of titles listed in the Easter Catalogue of the Leipzig Book Fair grew from 1,144 in 1770 to 2,569 in 1800. The number of new journals leapt from 410 in 1761–70 to 1,225 in 1781–90. In 1795 *Die Horen* was one of twenty-five new journals devoted to literary and historical subjects.[17] As the supply of print mushroomed and as literacy expanded (albeit more slowly), cash transactions replaced bartering among publishers, and bookselling began to separate out from publishing as a growing branch of retail trade. At the same time, the distribution of reading interests shifted; the percentage of German titles devoted to theology dropped from 24.8 in 1770 to 13.5 in 1800, while the percentage devoted to "Schöne Künste und Wissenschaften" (the category that included poetry, drama, and novels) grew from 16 to 21.5.[18] Particularly striking was the growth industry in novel writing. The average yearly publication of German-language novels (including translations, new editions, and repeated editions) climbed from 38.2 in 1771–75 to 172 in 1791–95.[19]

These figures are dwarfed, of course, by the output of pulp fiction and other kinds of print in contemporary western societies. Nonetheless there was something to the frequent observation that the German print world

[16] See esp. Helmuth Kiesel and Paul Münch, *Gesellschaft und Literatur im 18. Jahrhundert. Voraussetzungen und Entstehung des literarischen Markts in Deutschland* (Munich, 1977), esp. pp. 154–79; Christa Bürger, "Literarischer Markt und Öffentlichkeit am Ausgang des 18. Jahrhunderts in Deutschland," in Christa Bürger, Peter Bürger, and Jochen Schulte-Sasse, eds., *Aufklärung und literarische Öffentlichkeit* (Frankfurt am Main, 1980), pp. 163–213; Jochen Schulte-Sasse, "Das Konzept bürgerlich-literarischer Öffentlichkeit und die historische Gründe seines Zerfalls," in Bürger, ed., *Aufklärung und literarische Öffentlichkeit*, pp. 83–115; Jochen Schulte-Sasse, *Die Kritik an der Trivialliteratur seit der Aufklärung* (Munich, 1971), esp. pp. 45–51, 73–101.

[17] Hans Erich Bödeker, "Journals and Public Opinion. The Politicization of the German Enlightenment in the Second Half of the Eighteenth Century," in Eckhart Hellmuth, ed., *The Transformation of Political Culture. England and Germany in the Late Eighteenth Century* (New York and London, 1990), pp. 428–9.

[18] See the figures in Kiesel and Münch, *Gesellschaft und Literatur*, pp. 186–93, 199–203.

[19] Albert Ward, *Book Production, Fiction, and the German Reading Public, 1740–1800* (Oxford, 1974), pp. 166–7.

of the late eighteenth century was taking on a "factory-like" organization. Like the textile industries, though on a much smaller scale, it was
entering a new era of mass production. In 1798, in an open letter to the
Berlin publisher Friedrich Nicolai, Kant spelled out the implications of
the factory analogy. As books became "commodities" (*Waren*), writing was
reduced to a more or less skilled form of wage labor. Concerned with
the profitability of the commodity and not with its "inner content and
value," publishers moved from fashion to fashion in response to ever-
changing demand.[20]

The image of the lazy, fickle reader registered the emergence of a recognizably modern form of print consumption. Authors like Schiller hoped
to form intimate connections with active, totally engaged readers, who
would labor over their writing in an unceasing effort to enlighten and
cultivate themselves. The expansion of the print market confronted them
with a growing body of educated men and women who consumed books
and journal articles as a form of leisure activity. They read as much for
entertainment and for respite from the demands of work as for moral
guidance and other kinds of instruction. The recipe for a popular novel
included a brimming cup of "enlightened" bourgeois moralism, several
spoonfuls of domestic sentimentality and romantic adventure, and perhaps a pinch of oblique eroticism. In 1795, the year *Die Horen* was launched and Goethe's *Wilhelm Meisters Lehrjahre* began to appear, Karoline
von Wobeser published a novel with the fetching title *Elisa, or Woman as
She Ought to Be*. The heroine of this tearful narrative is a dutiful young
woman who is forced to marry a rake but in the end converts him to
her virtuous way of life. *Elisa* was the greatest commercial success of the
decade.[21]

Serious writers saw themselves faced with an unenviable choice. If they
tried to adapt to popular demand, they ran the risk of being reduced to
the hirelings of greedy publishers and consumers seeking mere amusement. If they defied market demand, they risked becoming marginal
figures, looking on helplessly as the mainstream of literature was trivialized. Though the market did allow serious writers small pockets of readers,
it made a mockery of their aspiration to establish the ethical and aesthetic
norms for a public culture. On September 7, 1794, Schiller had written
to Goethe that in the "anarchy" presently reigning in "poetical criticism,"
the critic was hamstrung by "a complete lack of objective laws of taste."[22]

[20] Immanuel Kant, "Ueber die Buchmacherei. Zwei Briefe an Herrn Friedrich Nicolai," in *Kant's
gesammelte Schriften*, vol. 8, Abteilung 1, ed. Königlich Preussischen Akademie der Wissenschaften
(Berlin and Leipzig, 1923), pp. 436–37. See also the observations of Georg Friedrich Rebmann,
quoted in Kiesel and Münch, *Gesellschaft und Literatur*, pp. 154–5.
[21] Ward, *Book Production*, 137–40.
[22] *Der Briefwechsel zwischen Schiller und Goethe in drei Bänden*, ed. Hans Gerhard Gräf and Albert
Leitzmann (Lepzig, 1912), I, p. 15.

Eight months later he set this dilemma in a long-term historical perspective: the German *Publikum* was "in the middle" between "the unity of children's taste" and "the unity of a complete development (*Bildung*)." Hence the era was "wonderful . . . for bad authors" but "all the worse for those who don't want merely to earn money."[23] What another observer might have welcomed as the openness of market pluralism Schiller saw as a kind of leveling chaos, a cacophony where there ought to be an authoritative consensus.

The problem was not simply that commercialization had produced a consumer potpourri. In 1773, in the foreword to his new journal *Der Teutscher Merkur*, Christoph Martin Wieland had noted that German-speaking Europe lacked a capital city that could serve as "the general academy of the virtuosos of the nation" and "the legislator of taste."[24] Wieland had in mind Paris (the home of the original *Mercure*), which concentrated intellectual talent from throughout the nation and, by virtue of that concentration, generated national standards. Friedrich Nicolai had hoped that in German-speaking Europe, journals would compensate for the lack of such a center, but by the 1790s it was an open question whether the proliferation of journals was an antidote to chaos or one of its most telling symptoms.[25] Rather than generating a consensus, journals might be erecting barriers among a profusion of submarkets.

It was this combination of commercial popularization and political and regional fragmentation that *Die Horen* was meant to counteract. Schiller was not planning to add one more journal to the crowd. Through *Die Horen* he hoped to institutionalize for the first time a "society" of the nation's outstanding authors. He explained to prospective members that if the journal won the lasting approval of the public with its "inner value" and if it was not priced too high, it would consolidate an audience that was now parceled out among too many journals. Through *Die Horen*, in other words, a "literary association" would unite a splintered *Publikum*. In counteracting the centrifugal and leveling forces of the market, the journal would quietly build "the better concepts, purer principles and nobler mores on which ultimately all true improvement of the social situation

---

[23] Schiller to Goethe, May 15, 1795, in ibid., p. 104. See also Hans J. Haferkorn, "Zur Entstehung der bürgerlichen-literarischen Intelligenz in Deutschland zwischen 1750 und 1800," in Ulrich Dzwonek et al., eds., *Deutsches Bürgertum und literarische Intelligenz, 1750–1800* (Stuttgart, 1974); Wolfgang von Ungern-Sternberg, "Schriftsteller und literarischer Markt," in *Hansers Sozialgeschichte der deutschen Literatur vom 16. Jahrhundert bis zur Gegenwart*, ed. Rolf Grimminger (Munich and Vienna), 3, pp. 133–85. On the aesthetic theory developed in reaction to a commercializing literary market, see esp. Martha Woodmansee, "The Interests in Disinterestedness. Karl Philip Moritz and the Emergence of the Theory of Aesthetic Autonomy in Eighteenth-Century Germany," *Modern Language Quarterly* 45:1 (March, 1984): 23–47.

[24] Quoted in Ward, *Book Production*, p. 115. The excerpt from the *Vorrede* in *Wieland Lesebuch*, ed. Heinrich Bock (Frankfurt am Main, 1983), pp. 216–20, includes the relevant passage.

[25] Bödeker, "Journals and Public Opinion," p. 424.

depends."[26] To help insure this quiet ascendancy, Schiller arranged for Cotta to compensate the *Allgemeine Literatur-Zeitung* for the extra costs involved in singling out his journal for monthly (rather than the usual yearly) reviews. In the long run, *Die Horen*'s concentration of literary talent would insure it something like a monopoly, which would in turn make it the arbiter of public standards.[27]

This was not a scheme calculated to win over the German literary establishment. Editors were not pleased to learn that their own journals were slated for extinction. Behind the newcomer's lofty agenda they heard the petulance of men spurned by the reading public they had aspired to lead. Critics found it ironic that a journal committed to avoiding exclusively "learned" material was in fact filled with esoteric essays in obscurantist prose, often crowded with the technical jargon of Kantianism.[28] Schiller's own contribution, the "Aesthetic Letters," was a striking case in point. Even to serious readers such fare seemed uninviting, if not forbidding; subscriptions plunged from about 2,000 by the end of 1795 to half that number in 1797.[29] W. F. A. Mackensen, a Kantian with a very different notion of "popularity," saw the journal's very title as a solipsistic coterie's expression of contempt for the German public. "Precisely in this journal that should actually be dedicated to the German People (*Volke*)," MacKensen observed in an overwhelmingly negative review of the first volume, "a little crowd of idiosyncratic authors runs around in their narrow circle, to which none but the initiated have entry, and with which the people can have so little in common that it would rather tremble and fall before a magician's circle."[30]

Fichte was no more likely to be unsettled by this kind of criticism than were Schiller and Goethe. It would be hard to find a more dramatic case, or a more telescoped one, of the descent from the Enlightenment's optimism about print to disillusionment and alienation. Having tried in the *Contribution* to bypass the "learned" and bond with the masses in an egalitarian rhetorical community, Fichte had been faulted for "obscurity." He had responded by attacking the new consumerism; serious philosophy could not adapt itself to the "flightiness and distractedness" of readers who preferred "modish novels, or travel accounts." His antagonism toward

[26] Schulz, *Schillers Horen*, pp. 211–14.

[27] Ibid., pp. 34–6, 79–81. On the larger agenda that Schiller and Goethe were pursuing with *Die Horen*, see also Böhler, "Die Freundschaft von Schiller und Goethe," esp. pp. 47–53; Helmut Brandt, "Die 'hochgesinnte' Verschwörung gegen das Publikum," in Barner, ed., *Unser Commercium*, pp. 19–35; T. J. Reed, "Ecclesia Militans: Weimarer Klassik als Opposition," in Barner, ed., *Unser Commercium*, pp. 37–49.

[28] For samplings of the reactions to *Die Horen*, see Schulz, *Schillers Horen*, pp. 64–79; Oscar Fambach, *Schiller und sein Kreis in der Kritik ihrer Zeit* (Berlin, 1957).

[29] Moran, *Toward the Century of Words*, p. 34.

[30] Mackensen's review has been reprinted in Fambach, *Schiller und sein Kreis*, pp. 150–67. Quotation on p. 152.

the reading public at large intensified as critics savaged, ridiculed, and often misrepresented his efforts to explain his new philosophy and as his hopes of leading the way to a philosophical consensus proved illusory. There was no point, he explained in the preface to his public lectures, in trying to win over those blinded by "ordinary experience"; but they in turn should not "pull down to their own level everything which they cannot themselves reach" by demanding "that everything which is published should be as easy to use as a cookbook or an arithmetic book or a book of rules and regulations."[31] Those who opposed him – the "dogmatists" of various sorts – were consigned to the familiar category of lazy consumers, morally as well as intellectually trapped in ideological self-deceptions. Most of his contemporaries, whether educated or uneducated, could not rise above this "slavery," and the academic philosophers who published in journals were no exception.

Fichte had nothing more to do with *Die Horen*. A few months after his clash with Schiller, he presented Cotta with his own publishing scheme. He hoped to present the results of his recent investigations into natural law and state law with "a high elegance and warmth." The presentation would also be distinguished by its "popularity," though it would be "nothing less than democratic." Could he and Cotta not use their contacts to prearrange a subscription for the book, with his honorarium to be determined by the number of subscribers? This strategy would work only if the subscribers knew beforehand what they could expect, and for that purpose he would publish substantial samples in a journal.[32] Fichte's scheme relied on demand, but of a special sort. The point was to legitimate the publication by listing the subscribers by name – not to attempt to satisfy the whims of an anonymous mass of consumers. If this example were followed, the "bunglers among authors and bookdealers," those who could not justify their products with such lists, would decrease and "the upright bookdealers" would "gain more and more space." Hence, in the process of organizing a viable business venture, Fichte and Cotta would "at least prepare the way for an order and justice (*Rechtlichkeit*) in the German book trade that has not existed to this point."[33]

Nothing came of this proposal, but it is revealing of Fichte's outlook. Like Schiller, he saw an urgent need to impose order on an open print market. Neither author thought of the market, in its present state, as enriching German public culture with a healthy pluralism of discourses. They saw the voice of intelligence being submerged in a great flood of the trivial, the ephemeral, and the morally dishonorable.

★ ★ ★

---

[31] *Fichte. Early Philosophical Writings*, pp. 144–5.
[32] Fichte to Johann Friedrich Cotta, Nov. 15, 1795, in GA, III, 2: 433–5.   [33] GA, III, 2: 434–5.

Alienated from the actual public of print consumers, Fichte and Schiller
had all the more reason to project an ideal *Publikum*. There was, of course,
something visionary, even utopian, about their projections.[34] The ideal
public could only be approximated in the world of empirical constraints,
and even an approximation would require a process of regeneration that
might extend over centuries. And yet their attachment to the ideal cannot
be characterized simply as an apolitical retreat into abstraction. There is a
sense in which both men assumed an inherently political role, even as
they rejected the politicization of public discourse in the 1790s. Evoking
an ideal *Publikum* was an act of radical critique, a way of indicting what
was there by demonstrating what ought to be. Existing social and political arrangements need not be criticized in detail; they stood condemned
in the light of an imagined order of alternative possibilities, a world of
rational moral freedom that brought into sharp relief the crippling of
human potential in the present.

Fichte and Schiller saw themselves creating the nucleus of a modern
clerisy, positioned somehow above the commercially and politically driven
trivialization of ideas. This was Fichte's elect of the "ethically best," who
would realize their potential for freedom in a rigorous philosophical
initiation. Schiller likewise saw citizenship in his "State of Beauty in
Appearance" as a kind of election. At the close of the "Aesthetic Letters"
he compared this state to "the pure Church and the pure Republic." If
it was to be found at all in the present era, it was "only in a few
select circles."[35]

And yet, despite this common ground, Fichte and Schiller faced each
other across a fissure in the Kantian movement of the 1790s. Each was
convinced that he had grasped the true "spirit" of Kant's ideal of freedom,
which lay hidden behind the "letter" of his notoriously technical presentation. Each saw himself "popularizing" that ideal not by spreading it to
the masses, or even to the educated public at large, but by making Kant's
esoteric formulations communicable to the few who were ready to
embrace their truth. But as their notions of the spirit of Kant's philosophy differed, so did their strategies for communicating it.

Kant himself had evoked an ideal *Publikum* – he called it the "republic of the learned" – in his essay on "Enlightenment" in 1784. When
someone adressed "the entire reading public" in his capacity as a "man of
learning," Kant argued, he made "public use of [his] reason." The same
person made "private use of reason," however, when he addressed his con-

---

[34] On the utopian dimensions of Schiller's aesthetic theory, see esp. Klaus Berghahn, "Aesthetische
Reflexion als Utopie des Aesthetischen," in Berghahn, *Schiller*, pp. 125–55.

[35] Friedrich Schiller, *Ueber die ästhetische Erziehung des Menschen*, ed. Wolfhart Henckmann (Munich,
1967), pp. 187–8. See also Schiller's evocation of a new "class of human beings" in "Ueber naive
und sentimentalische Dichtung," in Schiller, *Ueber das Schöne und die Kunst. Schriften zur Aesthetik*
(Munich, 1984), pp. 296–7.

gregation as a clergyman.[36] Kant's example of the "private" may seem puzzling today (did not the clergyman occupy a "public" office?), but it made sense in context. He was offering a German variation on the distinction between universality and particularity. The distinction was as old as western philosophy, but in the eighteenth century it had taken on new dimensions and significances in discourse about the public and "public opinion." Public communication was universal in the objective validity of its content, in the unbounded scope of its enquiry, and at least potentially, in the inclusiveness of its audience; as such it was not restricted or distorted by the mediation of the particular in any form. The print market seemed to have the potential to approximate this ideal; it allowed author and reader to communicate not as members of particular communities but as morally autonomous human beings to whom universal truths would be self-evident. In contrast the clergyman, like any other official, was constrained by particularity; he could not contradict the authority, whether it be institutional or social, or symbolic, that bound a particular community when he was actually performing his duties within it.

In 1784 Kant had good reason to use the institutions of church and state as his examples of restrictive particularity. Momentum was building for a state-enforced reimposition of confessional orthodoxy, and it threatened to deprive enlightened men of learning in the clergy and the universities of the public use of their reason. By the mid-1790s the lines of tension between the universal and the particular seemed more complex. Over the previous decade the exposure of the Illuminati had raised the specter of conspiratorial opposition within the academic and official elite. The religious fanaticism of "sect" or "party" – the fanaticism that had produced so much popular disorder and civil war – seemed to be assuming secular political forms. In the German states, alarm about this development escalated in the early 1790s as the Jacobins and other parties radicalized Revolutionary France and spawned a new partisan press. In their blinkered pursuit of social and political "interests" and in their ideological and rhetorical manipulation of their followers, parties represented the particular with a vengeance. They stood between the individual reader and the universal truths to which print was supposed to give him access. Pointing to Revolutionary France, and speaking for many German observers, Christian Garve declared that a truly "public" consensus was incompatible with the very existence of parties.[37]

---

[36] Immanuel Kant, "An Answer to the Question: 'What Is Enlightenment'?," in *Kant. Political Writings*, ed. Hans Reiss and trans. H. B. Nisbet (2d, enl. ed.: Cambridge, 1991), pp. 55–7. On the meaning of "public" and "private" in Kant's essay, see also Chartier, *Cultural Origins*, pp. 23–7; Onora O'Neill, "The Public Use of Reason," in *Constructions of Reason. Explorations of Kant's Practical Philosophy* (Cambridge, 1989), pp. 28–50.

[37] Christian Garve, "Ueber die öffentliche Meinung," in Garve, *Popularphilosophische Schriften über literarische, ästhetische und gesellschaftliche Gegenstände*, vol. 2 (1796: Metzler, 1974), pp. 296–9. For a

Against this backdrop, it becomes understandable that in the announcement for *Die Horen*, the immediate grievance was that a commercializing
print market was heightening the splintering effect of politics. Thanks in
part to the proliferation of journals, German culture was being engulfed by a "battle of political opinions and interests." The mission of *Die
Horen* was to rise above the deafening "political tumult" to disinterested
contemplation of the "purely human"; and that meant that everything
"stamped with an impure spirit of party" must be "banned." There would
be no room in its pages for the "all persecuting demon of state critique"
and indeed for anything dealing with "state religion" and "political organization (*Verfassung*)."[38]

Fichte was an appropriate choice for the editorial board of this kind
of journal. He subscribed to Schiller's negative view of political partisanship, and he too wanted to assert a public voice above the ideological
melee. But there was a large gray area between the positive political thrust
of critique and the fractious partisanship of party conflict. It was an area
Schiller himself felt sure he was avoiding. In the first installment of the
Aesthetic Letters he did argue that in the French Revolution an "apathetic
generation" had failed to provide the moral grounding to make "true
freedom the basis of political association." But this was his way of dismissing politics, he assured Goethe; now he need say "nothing more of
[the political misery] for all eternity."[39] He was not satisfied that Goethe
had steered clear of the political misery in his first contribution, the
"Unterhaltungen deutscher Ausgewanderten," which included a bitter
argument about the Revolution among a group of aristocratic émigrés.
The argument, to be sure, prompts a return to the self-disciplined avoid-
ance of political partisanship that polite society requires, but Schiller
nonetheless worried that Goethe's piece opened *Die Horen* to the charge
of admitting onto its pages the "political judgments" it opposed in
principle.[40]

Fichte's violation of the ban on politics struck Schiller as far more egregious, though the philosopher had nothing explicit to say about the
Revolution. In "On the Spirit and the Letter," Fichte questioned Schiller's
argument that the road to freedom lay through aesthetics. Such an idea,
he argued, "will get us into a vicious circle if we do not find beforehand

similar view of the dichotomy between "public" universals and parties, see Christoph Martin
Wieland, "Das Geheimnis des Kosmopolitenordens," in Wieland, *Werke*, vol. 3 (Munich, 1964), pp.
550–75.

[38] Schulz, *Schillers Horen*, pp. 211–14.
[39] Schiller, *Ueber die ästhetische Erziehung*, pp. 87–9; Schiller to Goethe, Oct. 20, 1794, in *Briefwechsel*,
p. 57.
[40] Schulz, *Schillers Horen*, p. 69; Goethe, "Unterhaltungen deutscher Ausgewanderten," in Goethe,
Sämtliche Werke, Briefe, Tagebücher und Gespräche, 1. Abteilung, vol. 9, ed. Wilhelm Vosskamp and
Herbert Jaumann (Frankfurt am Main, 1992), pp. 993–1081.

a means of arousing the courage of the individual amongst the throng to be neither master nor slave of anyone." Pointing to earlier periods of "serfdom," he described masters and slaves as locked in a relationship that deprived both of the opportunity to develop aesthetic taste. The oppressed were preoccupied with surviving under the oppressor's boot, while the oppressor struggled "not to lose his balance during the twistings and turnings of the victim." "More repugnant and disturbing for art," though, was that in modern times, "under freer skies and milder men of power," those allowed to be free bowed and scraped before their rulers and reduced "all forms of culture" to utilitarian value.[41]

Fichte knew very well that he was testing the limits of the permissible with observations that "could appear democratic." In the note accompanying the essay, he directed Schiller to the opening of the third Letter, which was designed to prevent "dangerous infusions into [his] words." The opening claimed that in the Germanic regions "a fortunate middle estate (*Mittelstand*)" had been formed from individuals who had detached themselves from both the oppressors and the oppressed. It was from this middle estate that "all salvation must and will develop." The mission of its members was to free themselves by looking inside themselves. It would be left to "almighty Nature, to which millenia are like a day," to "develop" and "ripen" the seeds they scattered. Anyone who tries to "free others" without "making himself free," Fichte warned, merely wants to "bring down the powerful in order to take their places" and to change "the manner of his own servitude."[42]

Fichte obviously sought to dispel any suspicion that he was advocating revolutionary activism. Salvation lay in gradual reform, not in revolutionary upheaval; and emancipation was a matter of individual self-renewal, not collective action. But Schiller was not reassured. He complained that the essay leapt directly from "the most abstruse abstractions" to "tirades." Fichte was repeating, on a larger scale, the "mistake" that had given offense in his earlier writings.[43] Even Fichte's effort to prevent "dangerous infusions" had a political bite that Schiller probably found regrettable. While his apotheosis of the middle estate was clearly not "democratic," it carried the politically charged implication that an oppressive aristocracy had forfeited its moral right to rule. Perhaps more disturbing was Fichte's extension of critique to the issue of the social distribution of power. He may have thought that he was supplementing Schiller's observations in the *Aesthetic Letters*, but in fact he was plunging into a subject that Schiller had taken pains to avoid.

In the fifth of the *Aesthetic Letters*, Schiller had argued that there could be no moral basis for political freedom so long as "the lower and more

---

[41] Fichte, "On the Spirit and the Letter," pp. 85–6.
[42] GA, III, 2: 325; GA, I, 6: 353.   [43] GA, III, 2: 335.

numerous classes" followed "crude, lawless impulses," and so long as "the civilized classes" exhibited "a depravity of character that is all the more shocking since culture itself is the source of it."[44] To Schiller the lower classes' lawlessness was more understandable than their social superiors' decadence; the have-nots at least had the excuse of being trapped in the grinding effort to satisfy basic needs. His sympathy for their plight makes it all the more striking that he did not ask whether the social distribution of power and material resources was unjust, or whether lower-class "savagery" and civilized "barbarism" reinforced each other within a structure of class relations. These were the questions Fichte tried to raise, however obliquely, with his discussion of masters and slaves, the exploiters and the exploited. While he acknowledged that coercion had softened in modern times, he could not resist censuring intellectuals and artists for their failure to assume the responsibilities of freedom, and indeed for their complicity in the abuse of power. At all levels of a class hierarchy, Fichte suggested, the psychological dynamics of power foreclosed the possibility of disinterested aesthetic pleasure.

In what sense were these observations "political"? Had Fichte added his voice to the deafening "noise" of partisan politics, or had he simply made the point that a rational critique had to confront the issue of power? Schiller's objection to the philosopher's "tirades" conflated these choices; and that was a measure of how broad *Die Horen's* ban on politics was intended to be.

★ ★ ★

The larger issue was how to make the presentation of philosophy "popular," so that it could contribute to the formation of a new public. Both Fichte and Schiller imagined a new rhetorical community, but they had markedly different ideas about what the relationship between the philosophical author and his reading audience ought to be. In the spring of 1795, just a few months before he submitted his second essay to *Die Horen*, Fichte had formulated his "principles" in a letter to Reinhold. Accused of attacking Reinhold in his lectures, Fichte countered that Reinhold's philosophy, unlike his own, betrayed his "passions" as an "individual" (*Individuum*):

> The pure friend of truth never mixes it up with his Individuum; he considers it [truth] too sacred to expose it to the influences of such an infirm being as the latter is. He brings to light what he considers the truth, and how it has been produced from his inner self he has himself forgotten, and he considers the result as a common property that belongs to him no more and no less than it does to anyone among the people who can and want to possess it. . . . If I [were] to present philosophy as a *Wissenschaft*, as I of

---

[44] Schiller, *Ueber die ästhetische Erziehung*, pp. 88–9.

course believe I can do, I would not think that *thereby* I had achieved the slightest value. I am in this only an instrument of Nature, and what is mine is only what I am through freedom.[45]

Fichte's view of the philosopher's mission is rich in paradoxes. The philosopher's purpose in scrutinizing his "inner self" is not to explore the unique authenticity of his personality. Quite the contrary; he takes his self as representative of the species and finds truths about being human that are latent in everyone. The reflexive turn, in other words, is not an exercise in subjectivity, if by the subjective we mean the private, limited standpoint of a particular consciousness. It yields a "common property," public in the sense that it is universally valid, or objective. When Fichte calls himself an "instrument of Nature," he means that he is the instrument of the universal Reason that is the ethical core of human nature. His empirical self, his being as an *Individuum*, is the obstacle he must rise above.

Schiller had good reason to conclude that Fichte's essay for *Die Horen* subsumed the "spirit" and the "letter" of aesthetics under this philosophical claim to universality. Fichte derived the impulse to aesthetic representation from the self's unconditional act of self-positing, which he called "the one indivisible primary force" in human consciousness. It was the "practical drive," he argued, that translated the aesthetic impulse into sense imagery. This was to imply that artistic creation was an expression of Practical Reason, and hence that it was a capacity to which only the a priori insights of the new philosophy held the key. The conflation of art into philosophy is especially striking in Fichte's depictions of the artistic genius. The artist uses "his own inner experience" to awaken and engage human beings' awareness of their "common characteristics" and to "silence individuality for as long as he has us under his influence." As in philosophical inquiry, "the spirit raises him as an intelligent being over the whole sensible world, and removes him from its influence." The "true illusion" of "art" is "our elevation to a wholly other mood . . . in which we forget our individuality." Hence art affects "momentarily" what philosophical reflexivity achieves in a relentless struggle with the empirical self. To achieve the effect, of course, artistic inspiration must be embodied in images; but these are merely the "letter," the "contingent" particulars that "dead matter" contributes.[46]

To Fichte, "individuality" was a product of the blind forces of nature; it threatened to reduce the moral personality to a thing among things, determined rather than self-determining. To exercise moral freedom was to strive constantly to liberate oneself from this form of particularity. For Schiller, "individuality" had acquired a different meaning, and that was in

---

[45] GA, III, 2: 279. See also the earlier draft, in GA, III, 2: 272.
[46] Fichte, "On the Spirit and the Letter," pp. 78, 88–90.

part because he had a radically different vision of nature. Where Fichte saw natural objects as things in a force field of mechanical coercion, Schiller, drawing on a scientific vitalism that rejected this mechanistic model, saw self-generating organisms, each giving unique expression to a vital inner energy. In the metaphors of vitalism, the myriad particulars of nature appeared to be free, and that was why they were morally inspiring. To Fichte, the realization of human potential was a kind of transcendence, a victorious struggle of the conscience, the locus of Reason's universal principles, over the constraining particularity of sense experience and mere appearances. Schiller struggled to elaborate the Kantian ideal of self-determination without accepting this dualistic view of conflict and subordination. The truly human lay in a harmonious integration, a blending of the rational and the sensual, abstract universals and sense particulars, within an organic totality.[47]

By 1795 Schiller had spent several years trying to articulate this ideal by adapting Kant's ethics and aesthetic theory to his purposes. He devoted far more serious study to Kant's thought than Fichte gave him credit for – and that despite the fact that, as he was drawn deeper and deeper into the *Critiques*, he was repelled by their "cold" and "dry" abstractions. During his early years in Weimar and Jena, Schiller persisted in entertaining the possibility that artistic creativity was governed by "objective" theoretical principles. Exploring that route seemed preferable to joining Goethe at the other extreme. On a social visit to Weimar in August 1787, Goethe had struck him as having an exaggerated contempt for "all speculation and research" and an "attachment to nature carried to affectation and a resignation in his five senses."[48] In 1791, when Schiller was beginning his systematic study of Kant's thought, he complained that Goethe's philosophy was too "subjective" to allow for real commitment or dispute, and in any case drew "too much from the sense world."[49]

In the summer of 1794, however, it was these very same characteristics that drew Schiller into friendship with Goethe. By then he had spent three years trying to develop a philosophy of aesthetics, and he was beginning to wonder whether the philosopher in him was killing the artist.

---

[47] On Schiller's appropriation of vitalism see esp. Peter Hanns Reill, "Anthropology, Nature and History in the Late Enlightenment: The Case of Friedrich Schiller," in *Schiller als Historiker*, ed. Otto Dann, Norbert Oellers, and Ernst Osterkamp (Stuttgart, 1995), pp. 243–65. Recent reexaminations of the cultural and political dimensions of Schiller's aesthetic ideal are Josef Chytry, *The Aesthetic State. A Quest in Modern German Thought* (Berkeley, Calif., 1989), pp. 70–105; Deric Regin, *Freedom and Dignity. The Historical and Philosophical Thought of Schiller* (The Hague, 1965), esp. p. 35. See also the insightful discussion of concepts of "individuality" in Gerald N. Izenberg, *Impossible Individuality. Romanticism, Revolution, and the Origins of Modern Selfhood* (Princeton, N.J., 1992).

[48] Schiller to Körner, Aug. 12, 1787, in *Briefwechsel zwischen Schiller und Körner*, ed. Klaus L. Berghahn (Munich, 1973), p. 58.

[49] Quoted in Wentzlaff-Eggebert, *Schillers Weg zu Goethe*, p. 39.

He saw himself as a kind of "hermaphrodite," suspended "between the concept and the intuition, between the rule and the sensation, between the technical mind and the genius." What he found wondrous about Goethe was his capacity to incorporate selected bits of philosophy to enliven and strengthen his "intuiting nature" – always remembering that the "object before [him]" was "a more solid authority" than any philosophical idea. Against philosophy's impulse to subordinate everything to its "absolute demand," Schiller now posed Goethe's "observing gaze," the disinterested intuitive imagination that, resting "quietly" and "purely" on things, prevented him from losing his way in either "speculation" or in "an arbitrary power of imagination, merely obeying itself."[50]

The friendship with Goethe would eventually lead Schiller back to poetry and drama, but its initial effect was to refuel his effort to formulate a philosophy of aesthetics. His ideal of beauty blended the extremes of his own and Goethe's natures in the paradox of the "extended middle," where apparent opposites were reconciled.[51] Reason and sensuality fused to form an "individuality," a unique organic whole. The paradox was that the universal was knowable only as it was refracted through the particular and indeed through the unique – or, to come at it the other way, that the particular, as a self-generated and unique configuration of the totality of forms, embodied the universal. In its spontaneous and self-contained particularity and in its manifestation of rational harmony, "appearance" – the world of sense experience – ceased to be Kant's force field of instrumental relations and became the sense analogue to moral freedom. If the artist was to create "freedom in appearance," he had to embody this same paradox of totality in individuality.

This was the theme Schiller wanted his friend Körner to develop in a contribution to *Die Horen*. He acknowledged that a written presentation necessarily differed from face-to-face "intercourse," where "the entire *Individuum* speaks" and "effects an *Individuum*." Writing required an effect on the genus (*Gattung*) through the genus. But the author could also communicate through individuality and thus achieve a "generalized individuality." Schiller reiterated this point to Christian Garve in a letter urging him to devote an essay to the same theme. The writer could find a way "not to abandon the objective topic (*Sache*) and yet to inspire through the communication of his individuality."[52]

The *Aesthetic Letters* was not simply a philosophical essay, its argument constructed to demonstrate that in a corrupt era aesthetic "play" offered the only route to moral and ultimately to political freedom. Schiller

---

[50] Ibid., pp. 45–6, 273; Schiller to Goethe, Aug. 23, 1794, in *Der Briefwechsel zwischen Schiller und Goethe*, 1, p. 33.

[51] The phrase "extended middle" is from Reill, "Anthropology, Nature and History."

[52] Quoted in Herman Meyer, "Schillers philosophische Rhetorik," in Meyer, *Zarte Empire: Studien zur Literaturgeschichte* (Stuttgart, 1963), pp. 373–5.

wanted to demonstrate that in the very beauty of its lucid but richly metaphorical prose, a philosophical essay could achieve totality in individuality and freedom in appearance. By the time he collided with Fichte, he was already facing complaints that the *Letters* were too esoteric and abstract. But Fichte cut especially deep with the criticism that in his philosophical writing, Schiller relied on an "immeasurable stock of images" that the reader had to "translate." Schiller responded by reasserting his ideal, and in a way calculated to put the philosopher in his place. Unlike "a merely didactic writer," he strove to engage "the ensemble of the powers of temperament" and "so far as possible to affect all of them at once." He offered the reader "a description of his entire nature," even when his subject was the human being "as genus"; and that required that he "affect [the reader's] sensual as well as his intellectual powers." In a century or two, he predicted, a philosopher like Fichte would be remembered for advancing his discipline but would be too dated to be read. But writings in which "a living *Individuum* imprints itself" were irreplaceable.[53]

★ ★ ★

Bruised egos aside, Fichte and Schiller were arguing about the form philosophy ought to take as a public discourse. Both men were acutely aware that in the transition from the ancient world to modern civilization, print had replaced oratory as the dominant form of public communication. The question was whether philosophy could be "popularized" with a new rhetoric in print – a rhetoric that would exploit the communicative potential of the medium while avoiding its pitfalls. At issue, it should be stressed, was far more than stylistic preference. The collective judgment of a "public" would derive its unimpeachable moral authority from the moral and intellectual autonomy of the individuals who contributed to it. Could a philosophical rhetoric in print respect and develop that autonomy? Could it preclude, or at least limit, the potentially coercive effects of language?

Fichte and Schiller clashed over this issue within a larger field of discourse about rhetoric and print in the late eighteenth century. In its strict sense, as it was practiced in the ancient polis, rhetoric was an oral performance, made possible by the physical proximity of a circumscribed audience. As commercialization gave print communication an open-ended reach and made it increasingly impersonal, there seemed to be something appealingly bounded and personal about this oratorical event. Like the participant in a conversation, the orator brought his entire person to the effort to persuade. His words were sounds, not written signs; and they

[53] GA, III, 2: 338–9, 360–1, 368.

were given a contextually specific meaning by the speaker's inflections, by his dress and carriage, by his facial expressions and physical gestures. It was in that sense that Schiller saw an "entire *Individuum*" manifesting himself in face-to-face communication.

In late eighteenth-century Germany, regret about the decline of oratory since antiquity was balanced by a certain relief at its absence from modern public life. There was an ingrained suspicion of the orator, heightened in the closing decade of the century. The suspicion was rooted in a philosophical tradition that went back to Plato's attack on the Sophists.[54] In an oratorical performance, after all, rhetoric was the art of expressing thought in sense images and pitching thought to the symbolic universe of a particular audience; on both counts it seemed incompatible with the philosopher's aspiration to communicate in the pure realm of universals. The pernicious effects of this art – effects abundantly illustrated in the history of the classical polis – seemed to be confirmed by the revolutionary demagoguery in Paris in the early 1790s. Particularly in the form of political oratory, rhetoric was not a vehicle of clarity but an art of obfuscation, designed to manipulate the listeners' volatile "passions." It made language a cunning instrument of power, camouflaging the selfish pursuit of particular "interests."

Just how emphatically Kant confirmed the philosophical hostility to rhetoric becomes apparent when his view is contrasted with Herder's. Herder shared the age's suspicion of political oratory, but he idealized the sermon as the exception, its uplifting effect sharply distinguished from the political use of oratorical manipulation. In Kant's censure of rhetoric, on the other hand, the sermon figured prominently. In "What Is Enlightenment?," Kant made the rhetoric of the pulpit, as such, an instance of the constricting and therefore distorting mediation of the particular. In the *Critique of Judgment* he went much further. The preacher was lumped together with the "Roman forensic orator" and the "modern parliamentary debater"; all three practiced an "insidious art," calculated to "rob [the listener's] verdict of its freedom." If oratory was to be morally legitimate, it had to be an "oratory without art" that would be so "lucid" as to grant the audience the same "freedom" and "calm reflection" that print allowed the reader. Kant hoped, to be sure, that other writers, combining "thoroughness of insight" with the "talent for lucid expression" that he lacked, would make his thought accessible to the reading public; but he

[54] Samuel IJsseling, *Rhetoric and Philosophy in Conflict: An Historical Survey* (The Hague, 1976). See also the insightful discussion of the relationship between rhetoric and power in Jill Anne Kowalik, "Kleist's Essay on Rhetoric," *Monatshefte* 81:4 (Winter, 1989): 434–46. On the revival of political rhetoric in the late eighteenth century, particularly among German "Jacobins," see Franz Hubert Robling, "Political Rhetoric in the German Enlightenment," in Hellmuth, ed., *Transformation*, pp. 409–21.

gave no indication as to how that might be done while at the same time keeping philosophical discourse uncontaminated by rhetoric.[55]

In the thought of Kant and Herder we see a parallel ambivalence about the implications of an ascendant print culture. It was no accident that Kant equated the "republic of scholars" with the "reading public" in his essay on "enlightenment." In a sense, oratory's disadvantage was print's advantage. Precisely because print communication occurred at a distance – because it insulated author and reader from the effects of each other's physical presence – it could be said to be especially suited to transcending the restrictive mediation of the particular. From that standpoint, market expansion was a positive development: the resulting impersonality seemed to heighten print's capacity to negate differences in status and power and create a usable fiction of equality between author and reader. Unlike the listener in an audience, the reader, as consumer, had the freedom to form his own reasoned judgment. To Herder, this new kind of autonomy was inseparable from the impersonality of print consumption; while "the orator blinds me with his form, with his following and his prestige, the writer speaks invisibly, and it is my fault if I let myself be deceived by his word pomp or be robbed of time by his prattle; I should test him, I can throw him away."[56]

And yet it was also Herder who yearned to see print reimbedded in a vital oral culture. Since the 1760s he had observed that print, as a system of visual signs, had an inherent tendency to make language more abstract and hence more likely to rely on philosophical "universals" at the expense of the concrete imagery, metaphors, and idiomatic expressions formed within the life cells of a particular culture. If print had the potential to remove communication from the distortions of power relations, it also abstracted communication from the rich density of context. Print and philosophy reinforced each other in dissolving the particular in an inflexible hierarchy of concepts and categories.[57]

In their efforts to resolve these tensions, Fichte and Schiller followed their respective strengths. Fichte's public triumphs were at the lectern. His lectures were written down, but he spoke without a text, sensing the reaction of his audience and elaborating when necessary on his prepared remarks. He openly admitted that he found it frustrating to explain his philosophy in print, where such interaction was not possible. His strategy

---

[55] Kant to Christian Garve, Aug. 7, 1783, in *Kant's Briefwechsel*, vol. 1 (Berlin and Leipzig, 1922) (*Kant's gesammelte Schriften*, ed. Königlich Preussischen Akademie der Wissenschaften, vol. 10, Pt. 2), pp. 338–41; Immanuel Kant, *Critique of Pure Reason*, trans. Norman Kemp Smith (New York, 1965), p. 36.

[56] See esp. Chartier, *Cultural Origins*, pp. 23–34; Johann Gottfried Herder, "Haben wir noch das Publikum und Vaterland der Alten?," in *Herders Werke in Fünf Bänden*, 5 (1978): 129–30.

[57] Anthony J. La Vopa, 'Herder's *Publikum*: Language, Print, and Sociability in Eighteenth-Century Germany," *Eighteenth-Century Studies* 29:1 (1995): 5–24.

was in part to transfer to the printed page what he saw himself doing in his lectures. The reader, like the listener, could activate his own reasoning capacity by witnessing a philosopher in the "process" of thought. To the extent that he employed traditional rhetoric to make his essay "popular" – to give the esoteric an exoteric direction – it was by reinforcing the strictly philosophical exposition with metaphoric illustrations from common experience. But this was a concession to particularity, a recourse to sense imagery as an unavoidable but limited and treacherous medium. The concession was legitimate precisely because, as he explained to Schiller, "the image stands not in the place of the concept, but rather before and after the concept, as comparison (*Gleichnis*)."[58]

In his critique of Fichte's essay, Schiller dismissed this procedure as a mere "alternation" between image and concept, lacking the required "interaction" and "evenness of tone." His strategy for a new print rhetoric was at once more traditional and more radically innovative than Fichte's.[59] His career as a lecturer at Jena had been frustrating and short-lived. He had read his lectures in a rasping voice, and despite his literary stature student attendance had soon dwindled.[60] His illness gave him a much-needed reason to abandon lecturing entirely. Print was his medium of preference, and he sought to demonstrate that on the printed page the aesthetic techniques of traditional rhetoric could form a seamless web with the new kind of philosophical reasoning Kant had developed.

Here lay the other paradox of Schiller's ideal: philosophical abstractions could and indeed must be "objectified" (i.e., represented or embodied in particular sensual forms) without sacrificing their objectivity (i.e., their universal validity). As an expression of the author's individuality, the philosophical essay could communicate universal truths through the symbolic universe of a particular rhetorical community, rather than being abstracted out of any particular context. Schiller's use of "*Gemeinsinn*" to evoke that community stood in marked contrast to Fichte's use of the same term to designate the shared characteristics of human beings as moral agents. To Schiller, the sense image, "ennobled" within a rhetorical aesthetic, was itself an expression of freedom in appearance; and as such it effected an emancipatory mediation. He was not denying that sense imagery, undisciplined by reason, was open to tyrannical manipulation; his point was that the purely abstract reason of philosophy also had the power to coerce. Like Fichte in his sermon drafts a decade or so earlier, he regarded rational abstraction by itself as "insult[ing]" the "freedom" of the individual. In a letter to the Duke of Augustenberg in November 1793, he drew a distinction between "the dogmatic teacher," who "forces his concepts on

[58] GA, III, 2: 339.
[59] GA, III, 2: 335. My discussion of Schiller's agenda for a new rhetoric is indebted especially to Meyer, "Schillers philosophische Rhetorik"; Kontje, *Constructing Reality*.
[60] Regin, *Freedom and Dignity*, pp. 50–2.

us," and the "rhetorician" (*Redner*) and the poet, who "give us the opportunity to generate [concepts] out of ourselves with freedom in appearance." While the "dogmatic" presentation advanced in "straight lines" and
"sharp corners," the "beautiful" presentation was a "free wave movement,"
returning "unnoticed" into itself.[61]

Schiller conceived of freedom as the reconciliation of apparent opposites. His philosophical rhetoric was meant to remove two threats to the
individual autonomy on which public judgments were to be grounded:
the unyielding abstraction that print imparted to language, and the oral
exploitation of sensual and emotional volatility. He wanted to counter
the tendency of print communication to encourage abstraction but at
the same time sought to exploit its advantage over face-to-face oral
exchanges. The fact that a writer affects a reader "at once invisibly and
from afar," he observed to Garve, had mixed implications. Since the writer
cannot "[affect] the temperament with living expression of speech" and
with "gestures," he could address feeling only through "abstract signs." For
that very reason, however, he could "[leave] his reader a greater freedom
of temperament than is possible in living intercourse."[62] In Schiller's ideal
of "beautiful" prose, rational abstraction and sense imagery were in a state
of constant "interaction" (*Wechselwirkung*), negating each other's potential
to coerce and reinforcing each other's emancipatory effect. Conceived in
this way, a rhetorical aesthetic both represented and activated freedom.
As the reader absorbed the individuality of the author through the
metaphoric lucidity of his prose, he became aware of his own individuality. The very form of the *Aesthetic Letters*, the use of an epistolary dialogue between the author and an interlocutor, was meant to dramatize
this interaction in freedom.

There was an element of self-delusion in both men's leap from practice to theory. To judge by listeners' recollections of Fichte's lectures, it
was more his dynamic physical presence – what one might call his stage
manner – than the rigorous exhibition of his mind at work that mesmerized audiences. His effort to reinforce logic with metaphor in the
essay on "the spirit and the letter" was indeed, as Schiller complained,
jarring. He asked the reader to think of the individual's aesthetic and practical drives as a magnetic force attracting iron – a puzzling choice for an
antideterminist and made all the odder by his having to attribute to the
magnet feelings of pleasure and displeasure to make the metaphor workable.[63] In the *Aesthetic Letters*, on the other hand, Schiller found that he
could not sustain his commitment to a fusion of philosophical reasoning
and imagistic evocation. At the close of the tenth *Letter* (roughly halfway
through the entire text), he warned readers that to grasp the "pure ratio-

[61] Meyer, "Schillers philosophische Rhetorik," pp. 368–71.
[62] Ibid., p. 375.   [63] Fichte, "On the Spirit and the Letter," p. 82.

nal concept of beauty," they would have to abandon "for a while" the "intimate circle of appearances" and the "living presence of things" and enter "the road of abstraction."[64] On the whole, the *Letters* were as vulnerable to the charge of obscurantism as was Fichte's essay. If Fichte's display of "process" was often tortuous, Schiller's rhetorical aesthetic often achieved elegant paradoxes at the cost of logical coherence.[65]

In his essay, Fichte had in effect anticipated one weakness in Schiller's claims for a rhetorical aesthetic. What did it mean to say that the reader enjoyed "freedom in appearance"? Schiller meant to suggest that appearances, far from being obstacles to moral freedom, could inspire us to exercise it through the analogous freedom of aesthetic play. But why not conclude, as Fichte did, that the "inspired artist" did not address our "freedom" at all but instead, like the rhetorician, worked a "magic" that "begins only when we have given [freedom] up"? Schiller's concept of *Bildung* posited an analogic relationship between the cultivation of aesthetic sensibility and the development of moral character. This view was extraordinarily suggestive; but in explaining how *Bildung* advanced from the aesthetic to the moral, it was also maddeningly elusive. By comparison Fichte's view was simplistic but consistent. The poetic Art, he argued, does not make us "any better"; it simply "momentarily raises us, through no agency of our own, to a higher sphere." Only in that sense could art be said to prepare us to "decide in freedom," but "for other reasons," to "take possession" of "the unploughed field of our minds (*Gemüths*)."[66]

Committed to an uncompromising Kantian dichotomy between ethical truth and sense knowledge, Fichte saw a potentially dangerous illusion in Schiller's attempt to fuse sense imagery and abstraction, imagination and reason. It was this objection that lay behind his complaint that Schiller's philosophical writing was unprecedented in its reliance on an "immeasurable stock of images." The effort to understand such writings was "exhausting," he wrote, because the imagination, which cannot "think," was being forced to think. Far from enlisting the "power of imagination" in the cause of freedom, Schiller was "chaining" it.[67] It was Schiller, in other words, who was guilty of trespassing. The explanation of art was philosophy's prerogative; but when art insinuated itself into philosophy's business, each endeavor lost the communicative "freedom" peculiar to it.

---

[64] Schiller, *Ueber die ästhetische Erziehung*, p. 110. Cf. the discussion of this shift in strategy in Kontje, *Constructing Reality*, p. 63.

[65] See esp. the critique of Schiller's aesthetic theory in Dieter Henrich, "Beauty and Freedom. Schiller's Struggle with Kant's Aesthetics," in Ted Cohen and Paul Guyer, eds., *Essays in Kant's Aesthetics* (Chicago and London), pp. 237–57.

[66] Fichte, "On the Spirit and the Letter," p. 93. "Gemüth" might also be translated as "temperament."

[67] GA, III, 2: 339.

Perhaps without entirely realizing it, Fichte had targeted the point of severe strain in Schiller's thought. Schiller's dilemma was that he continued to think in terms of the very dualism of reason and imagination, concept and image, that he wanted to see dissolved in art and rhetoric. Hence he could not simply dismiss Fichte's countercritique. In fact, passages in his essay "On the Necessary Limits in the Use of Beautiful Forms," published in *Die Horen*, suggest that Fichte had forced him to rethink his position. Now Schiller distinguished cleanly between "philosophical" writing and "beautiful" writing. The former was a teaching vehicle that aimed for a "strict persuasion from principles," so that the recipient became a "complete proprietor" of knowledge. Hence, the presentation had to conform to the laws of strict logical necessity, without interference from the imagination's tendency to break down the universal into individual cases and to "give the abstraction a body." Beautiful writing, on the other hand, was of limited philosophical efficacy. Its purpose was to evoke a "possibility" rather than to persuade. It lent the reader knowledge "only for momentary enjoyment and use," and it relied on the senses to satisfy "a present need" of a scattered, anonymous *Publikum* as quickly as possible.[68]

If Schiller granted the force of Fichte's critique, however, he also deflected it. He was merely conceding that his own ideal of a philosophical rhetoric had no place in teaching. Though he seemed at times to admit that the ideal was ethically limited, he nonetheless clung to it as the norm for truly human communication. There was, or at least could be, a kind of rhetoric in which "concepts develop according to the laws of necessity" but at the same time "migrate into the power of imagination according to the law of freedom." This was the realm of the "truly beautiful," which "speaks as pure unity to the harmonizing wholeness of the human being." Echoing the most stinging of Fichte's criticisms, Schiller acknowledged that "the common judge," whether he was fixated on the particular or on "naked understanding," would have to "translate" to understand the "beautiful and harmonious." But the writer who "thinks in describing" could not take his law from "the limitedness and need of his readers"; he had to "approach the ideal that he carried in himself."[69] The implied payback was subtle but barbed, particularly when one recalls Fichte's remark about Schiller's "bought" but "little read" writings. Practicing a heavy-handed didacticism, the philosopher consigned himself to the mass of print consumers who demanded crude fare.

---

[68] Schiller, "Ueber die nothwendigen Grenzen beim Gebrauch schöner Formen," in *Schillers Werke. Nationalausgabe*, vol. 21, Pt. 2 (Weimar, 1963), pp. 4–10. The elusiveness of this essay, I should stress, has left room for considerable disagreement about Schiller's intended emphasis. Cf. Meyer, "Schillers philosophische Rhetorik," pp. 381–7; Kontje, *Constructing Reality*, pp. 54–60.

[69] Schiller, "Ueber die nothwendigen Grenzen," pp. 13–15.

Schiller's "On Naive and Sentimental Poetry" was composed largely in the fall and winter of 1795, just a few months after his argument with Fichte. The essay was Schiller's parting contribution to aesthetic theory, and it displays his genius for drawing larger significances – insights about the complementarities and polarities he found to be inherent in the culture – from his relationships with contemporaries. The debt to his friendship with Goethe is obvious. Goethe was the modern reincarnation of the ancient world's "naïve" poet, who grasped the particulars of his natural environment intuitively and represented them with spontaneous, innocent immediacy. By contrast, Schiller defined the modern poet – and he included himself – as "sentimental," in that his vision of nature was self-conscious, intellectualized. Once again the road to cultural regeneration, like the friendship with Goethe, lay in the paradoxical blending of qualities which, by themselves, produced "one-sidedness."

Schiller concluded the essay with a lengthy discussion of the "antithesis" between the "realist" and the "idealist." He saw these as modern types, reminiscent of the näive and sentimental characters but drained of their "poetic" sensibility. The pathology of modern civilization, Schiller argued, lay in a "psychological antagonism" between these "inner mental dispositions" – an antagonism so radical that the artist and the philosopher prevented each other from achieving a universal effect.[70] Schiller may very well have been thinking of his clash with Fichte when he conceived this antithesis, and in any case their argument had certainly inspired his profile of the idealist.

The final word in the argument, it is fair to say, was Schiller's. He brought to his diagnosis of idealism the rhetorical mastery of the printed word that Fichte did not have. The diagnosis was all the more devastating because it was so evenhanded. Schiller took pains to itemize the virtues as well as the pitfalls of both "dispositions." In doing so, however, he put the idealist and the realist on the same level; he deflated the claims of both by reducing them to truncated psychological types. Idealism was not a philosophical route to wholeness, as Fichte claimed; it was an extreme, a symptom of modern fragmentation. When idealism claimed to command a superior vision, and when it sought to be the moral arbiter for the culture, it only revealed its blindness to its own limitations.

Schiller conceded a certain moral efficacy to both psychological types, but his overriding point was that both posed moral and ultimately political threats. As early as 1791, Georg Forster had articulated a growing sense of alarm that Kantians were effacing the integrity of the particular, its

[70] Schiller, "Ueber naive und sentimentalische Dichtung," pp. 298–9.

vital, spontaneous *Individualität*, in a new "despotism" of abstract universals.[71] Now Schiller issued a similar warning about the soaring vision of
the philosophical idealist:

> [The idealist] is indeed generous because in his relations with others he
> does not remember his own individuality so much; but he is often unfair
> because he as easily overlooks the individuality of others. . . . [T]he ideal-
> ist is the sworn enemy of everything petty and jejune and will reconcile
> himself even with the extravagant and monstrous if it only testifies to a
> great potentiality. [The realist] shows himself to be a philanthropist, but
> simply without entertaining any very high idea of humanity; [the idealist]
> thinks so highly of humanity that he thereby falls into the danger of despis-
> ing man. . . . The striving of the idealist too far surpasses the sensuous life
> and the present moment; only for the whole, for eternity, does he want to
> sow and plant, and thereby forgets that the whole is only the consummated
> cycle of the individual, that eternity is only a totality of moments.[72]

It is a cautionary typology, suggesting the potential for inhumanity in
Fichte's vision of a regenerated humanity. If Idealism was as consequential as Fichte wanted it to be, the Kantian promise of liberation from
"mechanical" coercion might make philosophy itself a coercive machine.
The Moral Law – the law that promised to make individuals free – might
become the iron law of conformity.

★ ★ ★

To Schiller, Fichte came to represent a philosophical way of thinking to
which he was strongly attracted, but which he found ultimately blinkered
and sterile. In 1801 he recalled that even he had been "gripped by the
metaphysical-critical era" in Jena. He dismissed his efforts as "a perhaps
necessary unburdening of metaphysical material, which, like the smallpox
infection, sticks in us and must be gotten out."[73]

It was friendship with Goethe that drew Schiller back to art, but the
pull of Goethe's sensibility was powerfully reinforced by the recoil from
Fichte's rigorism. By declaring Fichte a thoroughly incompatible nature,
Schiller exorcised the Fichtean tendencies in himself. The exorcism was
complete by the time Fichte paid him an unexpected visit in August of
1798. Schiller reported to Goethe that since the philosopher had been
"extremely obliging," he would try to make their relationship lively and
pleasing; but a "fruitful" rapprochement was out of the question, since
"our natures do not harmonize." Goethe encouraged his friend to make

---

[71] Georg Forster, "Ueber lokale und allgemeine Bildung," in Forster, *Werke in vier Bände*, ed. Gerhard
Steiner (Frankfurt am Main, 1967–70), 3, pp. 281–4.

[72] Schiller, "Ueber naive und sentimentalische Dichtung," pp. 303–4.

[73] From Schiller's letter to Rochlitz, April 16, 1801, quoted in Wentzlaff-Eggebert, *Schillers Weg zu
Goethe*, p. 275.

the renewed contact mutually beneficial, but he agreed that "a closer bonding with [Fichte] is unthinkable," though "it is always very interesting to have him in the vicinity."[74]

Fichte had recoiled as well – from an aesthetic vision of public culture, and from an aestheticized philosophy for which he had neither talent nor sympathy. Having returned to Jena and to the lecture hall, he was rethinking the relationship between culture and power, symbol and truth.

[74] *Der Briefwechsel zwischen Schiller und Goethe*, 1, pp. 668, 671.

Chapter 10

Law, Freedom, and Authority

In early April, 1793, when he was en route from Poland to Zürich, Fichte sent Kant a letter explaining how he planned to use the "leisure without care" that his upcoming marriage would provide. Once his theory of revelation was solidly grounded, he would undertake the great task Kant had laid out in the *Critique of Pure Reason*.[1] His reference was to Kant's spirited defense of Plato's *Republic*. To dismiss the *Republic* as a "useless" exercise in "visionary perfection," Kant had argued, was to indulge in a "vulgar appeal to so-called adverse experience." Rather than rejecting abstract ideas on the pretext of their "impracticality," the philospher's task was to formulate an archetype by "abstract[ing] from the actually existing hindrances." The archetypal "constitution" would allow "*the greatest possible human freedom* in accordance with laws by which *the freedom of each is made to be consistent with that of all others*." This was not an idle dream, but a "necessary idea, which must be taken as fundamental not only in first projecting a constitution but in all its laws."[2]

Kant's defense of Plato was an argument for theory as the indispensable instrument of critique. In the early 1790s, as it became commonplace to blame the excesses of the French Revolution on political "metaphysics," Kant became all the more determined to defend his own version of rational criticism. If a priori theory had to pass the test of "experience," there would be no cognitive space in which to posit rational alternatives to the status quo. That was the larger point of the essay "On the Common Saying: 'This May Be True in Theory, but It Does Not Apply in Practice,'" published in 1793. Fichte had already made the same point, more elaborately and with considerably more venom, in his *Contribution*.

Fichte had written the second installment of the *Contribution* in the summer of 1793 but had then abandoned the project. He did not return to his "great idea" until the summer of 1795, when his self-exile in Osmannstädt freed him from the day-to-day demands of lecturing and allowed him to devote several months to preparing a new course on natural law. By then his standpoint had shifted. He was no longer the reverent disciple, aspiring to "popularize" the master's principles by apply-

---

[1] GA, III, 2: 389–90.
[2] Immanuel Kant, *Critique of Pure Reason*, trans. Norman Kemp Smith (New York, 1965), pp. 311–12.

ing them to the great public issues of the day. Having entered Kantian philosophy with a vague admiration for its systematic structure, Fichte was now convinced that as the grounding for an all-encompassing "system" of knowledge, a priori philosophy could claim unassailable normative authority. When he began to formulate his principles for law and related subjects, it was with the intention of proving the systematicity of his project by demonstrating that the parts (the *Wissenschaften*), though autonomous vis-à-vis each other, did indeed form a coherent whole.

Fichte was engaged in a thorough intellectual repositioning, remarkable both for its creative leaps and for the new tensions it generated within his thought. In 1796 and 1797 he published in two parts a revised version of the lecture series he had begun to prepare at Osmannstädt. Entitled *Grundlage des Naturrechts*, it attracted considerable attention at the time and has become a key text in the renewed interest in Fichte's contribution to legal and political theory.[3] Still another lecture series produced *Das System der Sittenlehre* in 1798.[4] This text had hardly appeared when Fichte unintentionally triggered the Atheism Conflict, which ended his academic career at Jena. In the public melee about Fichte's alleged atheism, the *Sittenlehre* was largely ignored. From a strictly philosophical standpoint it is of secondary importance, but it has considerable historical significance, particularly for what it tells us about Fichte's efforts to position the German universities at the center of a new public culture.

[3] Johann Gottlieb Fichte, *Grundlage des Naturrechts nach Prinzipien der Wissenschaftslehre*, ed. and introd. Manfred Zahn (Hamburg, 1967). All references are to this edition. There is a more fully annotated edition, with an informative editorial preface, in GA, 1, 3: 291–460, and GA, 1, 4: 1–165.

The *Naturrecht* has been declared "surely the greatest expression of the power of a certain critique of reason in grounding a 'non-naïve' idea of juridical values (without lapsing into a naïve metaphysics of subjectivity)." Luc Ferry and Alain Renaut, "How to Think about Rights," in Mark Lilla, ed., *New French Thought: Political Philosophy* (Princeton, N.J., 1994), p. 152. Several recent contributions were particularly helpful: Alain Renaut, *Le système du droit: Philosophie et droit dans la pensée de Fichte* (Paris, 1986); Johann Braun, *Freiheit, Gleichheit, Eigentum. Grundfragen des Rechts im Licht der Philosophie J. G. Fichtes* (Tübingen, 1991); Susan Shell, "'A Determined Stand': Freedom and Security in Fichte's *Science of Right*," *Polity* 25:1 (Fall, 1992): 95–121; Frederick Neuhouser, "Fichte and the Relationship between Right and Morality," in Daniel Breazeale and Tom Rockmore, eds., *Fichte. Historical Contexts/Contemporary Controversies* (Atlantic Highlands, N.J., 1994), pp. 158–80; Richard Schottky, *Untersuchungen zur Geschichte der staatsphilosophischen Vertragstheorie im 17. und 18. Jahrhundert (Hobbes-Locke-Rousseau-Fichte) mit einem Beitrag zum Problem der Gewaltenteilung bei Rousseau und Fichte* (Amsterdam, 1995); Jean-Christophe Merle, *Justice et progrès. Contribution à une doctrine du droit économique et social* (Paris, 1997); Gary B. Herbert, "Fichte's Deduction of Rights from Self-Consciousness," *Interpretation* 25:2 (Winter, 1998): 201–22. Dated but still useful are Georges Vlachos, "Dialectique de la liberté et le dépérissement de la contrainte chez Fichte," *Archives de philosophie du droit*, Nouv. Ser. 8 (1963): 75–114; Hansjürgen Verweyen, *Recht und Sittlichkeit in J. G. Fichtes Gesellschaftslehre* (Freiburg and Munich, 1975).

[4] Johann Gottlieb Fichte, *Das System der Sittenlehre nach den Prinzipien der Wissenschaftslehre (1798)*, ed. Manfred Zahn, Philosophisches Bibliothek, vol. 257 (Hamburg, 1963). All references are to this text. See also GA, I, 5: 1–317.

Our third text – *The Closed Commercial State (Der geschlossene Handelsstaat)*
– was written in Berlin in 1800; but as its subtitle makes clear, it was a
"supplement," elaborating the economic principles Fichte had adumbrated
in the *Naturrecht*.[5]

Fichte left no doubt that with these steps in system building he was
leaving the youthful naïveté of the *Contribution* behind him. But how
did his thinking about law, government, economic life, and culture actually change? There has been considerable disagreement about where he
started and about the new direction he took. The *Contribution* is generally read as a "liberal" statement, but does its liberalism lie in its Lockean
view of property and labor or in its virtually "anarchic" individualism?
Did Fichte move on to a kind of democratic vision, or to authoritarian
socialism, or to incipient totalitarianism, or to an eccentric blend of
all three?[6]

In the *Contribution* a belief in the emancipatory potential of the free
market goes hand in hand with a marked anticommercial animus. There
is no concern whatsoever with the principles of representative government or with the division of powers that was at the heart of the constitutional agenda of political liberalism. Hence, if the *Contribution* has a place
in modern liberalism, it is only as a very awkward fit. And that in turn
is symptomatic of a larger problem. There is nothing inherently misguided, to be sure, about efforts to locate Fichte – or, more precisely,
the Fichte of the *Contribution* and the Fichte of the second half of the
1790s – on the spectrum of modern political ideologies. But that is not
the issue that ought to guide a contextual recovery of Fichte's meaning.
Clearly nineteenth- and twentieth-century ideologies did have roots in
eighteenth-century thought. If they supply the questions and the distinctions brought to the eighteenth-century's profusion of discourses,
however, they become so many distorting lenses. Ideological labels are at
once too rigid and too elastic; their denotations impose a grid of dis-

---

[5] The full title is *Der Geschlossene Handelsstaat. Ein philosophischer Entwurf als Anhang zur Rechtslehre
und Probe einer künftig zu liefernden Politik*. Citations (GH) are to the edition in Zwi Batscha and
Richard Saage, eds., *Johann Gottlieb Fichte. Ausgewählte Politische Schriften* (Frankfurt am Main, 1977),
pp. 69–167. See also GA, I, 7: 37–141. The book was dedicated to the Prussian State Minister von
Struensee.

[6] See, e.g., Nico Wallner, *Fichte als politischer Denker. Werden und Wesen seiner Gedanken über den Staat*
(Halle, 1926); Zwi Batscha, *Gesellschaft und Staat in der politischen Philosophie Fichtes* (Frankfurt am
Main, 1970), Georges Vlachos, "L'état et l'économie dans l'oeuvre du jeune Fichte," *Revue internationale d'histoire politique et constitutionnelle*, Nouv. Série 7 (1957): 226–61. Bernard Willms, *Die totale
Freiheit. Fichtes politische Philosophie* (Cologne and Opladen, 1967). Willms concludes that "the goal
of the rational state of the '*Grundlage*' is . . . to elevate humanity to absolute freedom by enslaving
it as empirical *Bürger*." He exaggerates the "totalitarian" impulse in Fichte's thought, in part because
he conflates Fichte's distinction between law and morality and in part because he reads twentieth-
century preoccupations back into an eighteenth-century text.

tinctions on fluid ground, while their sprawling ranges of connotation obscure the historical specificity of texts. In Fichte's case, the effect is to oversimplify, sometimes brutally, the field of argument he entered and his perceptions of choice within it. We read back into his texts fissures that are all too familar, rather than becoming attentive to the tensions that actually resonate through them.

If Fichte's intellectual repositioning is to be taken seriously as a philosophical endeavor, we need to retrace the steps he took as a philosopher. That in itself is an intriguing story, complete with false starts, dead ends, breakthroughs, and at least apparent resolutions of intellectual dilemmas confronting German thinkers of his generation. The story – and this will be a recurrent theme – has an ironic denouement. Committed to allowing, in Kant's phrase, "the greatest possible human freedom" within a framework of legal constraint, Fichte provided a new philosophical justification for a formidable state machinery. The freedom of the individual required a state of vast scope and unprecedented power. Why did Fichte conclude that statism on such a large scale was necessary, and why was he so confident that it would be emancipatory rather than oppressive? A historical answer requires that we eschew ideological labels and understand how Fichte interlaced the threads of several eighteenth-century discourses.

We seek a contextual answer, but that is not to imply that Fichte's repositioning was in reaction to changes in his life at Jena or to the course of public events, whether in the German states or elsewhere. For this phase of his intellectual career the salient context is the field of argument he was addressing. In the second half of the 1790s the field was shifting on two levels at once. Fichte looked out at the world from a distinctly German philosophical core, and in that sense there was still something provincial about his commitment to universalism. But he could no longer claim to be speaking for the Kantian camp; he was conducting arguments within it, both against a Kantian orthodoxy and against other mavericks. At the same time, from this more complicated philosophical standpoint, his awareness of a larger European set of arguments was widening. He was now searching for an alternative to Rousseau's ideal of direct democracy and to competing theories of representative government as well. His sharpest turn – the change in his economic thought – was taken with a clear awareness that Anglo-Scottish political economy was beginning its ascendancy.

★ ★ ★

In the 1790s German-speaking Europe produced a flood of books and articles on the subject of natural law. An ancient discourse, extending from pagan antiquity through nearly eight centuries of Christian thought, was being recast under the combined impact of the French Revolution and Kantian philosophy.[7] By the time Fichte's *Naturrecht* appeared in print, Jena had established itself as the most productive center of this process. The years 1795–96 witnessed the publication of a revised second edition of the *Lehrsätze des Naturrechts* by Gottlieb Hufeland, the Jena professor who had been instrumental in Fichte's appointment; the *Grundriss des Naturrechts* (1795) by Christian Erhard Schmid, another Jena professor and the opponent who provoked Fichte's notorious "act of annihilation"; and no less than six articles on natural law in the *Philosophisches Journal einer Gesellschaft Teutscher Gelehrten*, a Kantian journal edited by Friedrich Immanuel Niethammer, still another of Fichte's colleagues in the Jena philosophy faculty.[8]

The arguments among Kantians about natural law had seemingly infinite variations, but they all turned on how to define the relationship between law and morality. This was a familiar issue, as old as philosophy itself; but it acquired a new urgency as the moderate constitutionalism of revolutionary France in 1789 acceded to the Jacobin agenda for a Republic of Virtue. In Jacobin ideology, old-regime law had served privilege and cloaked abuses of power; henceforth law would embody the universal moral principles evoked by the phrase "the rights of man." Though Fichte's rational order was quite distinct from the Republic of Virtue, he had entered the political arena in 1793 in passionate agreement with the Jacobins that the existing states had to be judged by moral standards of universal validity – standards that, in the advance to a just society and polity, would make no exceptions for particular historical circumstances. It was precisely that belief that Rehberg and like-minded opponents of the Revolution found alarmingly wrongheaded. To them a particular juridical community was legitimate not because it applied abstract (or "metaphysical") universals but because it had evolved organically, in symbiosis with its particular contexts. As revolutionary France was demonstrating, efforts to erase historical particularity in the name of purely "human" or "natural" rights produced a dialectic between anarchy and a new, terror-driven despotism.

---

[7] Diethelm Klippel, *Politische Freiheit und Freiheitsrechte im deutschen Naturrecht des 18. Jahrhunderts* (Paderborn, 1976), esp. pp. 178–84.

[8] The importance of the "Kantian juridical school" is noted in Ferry and Renaut, "How to Think about Rights," p. 152. See also Schottky, *Untersuchungen*, pp. 270–316; Wolfgang Kersting, "Sittengesetz und Rechtsgesetz – Die Begründung des Rechts bei Kant und den frühen Kantianern," in Reinhard Brandt, ed., *Rechtsphilosophie der Aufklärung: Symposium Wolfenbüttel 1981* (Berlin, 1982), pp. 148–77; Horst Schröpfer, "Carl Christian Erhard Schmid – der 'bedeutendste Kantianer' an der Universität Jena im 18. Jahrhundert," in Norbert Hinske, Erhard Lange, and Horst Schröpfer, eds., *Der Aufbruch in den Kantianismus. Der Frühkantianismus an der Universität Jena von 1785–1800 und seine Vorgeschichte* (Stuttgart-Bad Cannstatt, 1995), pp. 37–56; Gerhard Lingelbach, "Vernunft-Wahrheit-Freiheit. Zur frühen Kantrezeption in der Rechtswissenschaft an der Jenaer Universität," in Hinske, ed., *Aufbruch*, pp. 191–201.

Kantians had a special reason to ask what the spectacle of the Revolution might reveal about the relationship between law and morality. From the mid-1780s to the mid-1790s, Kant himself had sought to define that relationship from several angles, mostly in densely packed and more or less polemical essays. It was not entirely clear whether his approach was a priori or historical, or some hybrid of the two. His effort to dispel the confusion did not appear until 1797.

Since the late 1780s, Kant's disciples had rushed to fill this gaping hole in his system. At stake was nothing less than whether the fundamental dualism that cut through Kantian philosophy could be bridged. By distinguishing so sharply between moral knowledge ("practical") and knowledge of the physical world ("theoretical"), Kant had in effect dissolved the conjunction between the "is" and "ought" that natural law discourse had maintained for centuries.[9] From a Kantian standpoint it was simply not clear how the ought – the purity of "inner" intention that Kant ascribed to the moral will – could be efficacious in a world of appearances, governed by causation; or how the actions of the person as a sense being, subject to the law of causation, could lead to morality. What the concept of law, suitably reshaped, might offer was a way of reconjoining, a mediation, perhaps the crucial mediation, between practical reason and theoretical reason, morality and natural causation, "inner" freedom (autonomy) and coercion from without (heteronomy).

To appreciate the momentous implications for both law and morality, we need only consider the extreme alternatives to finding a point of mediation. Suppose the Moral Law were declared completely irrelevant to law. Would not that solution confirm, and indeed confirm with a vengeance, that the Kantian dualism was unbridgeable? It would not matter whether we complied with the law because we honored it or because we feared its coercive force; in either case, our external behavior as sense beings in relation to others would have no grounding in the conscience and would play no role in forming the conscience. And yet from a Kantian standpoint the other extreme, the complete subsumption of law under morality, might be worse. Wheareas law clearly involved a kind of coercion, morality, as Kantians defined it, could not become coercive without falling into self-contradiction. A morality relying on legal coercion to acquire causative force in the sense world would be a perversion of itself.

To add still another dilemma: if law had to conform invariably to universal moral principles, was it not stripped of any historical agency? Was it not denied a role in shaping historical particularity? The other side of

[9] Still essential on this subject is Leonard Krieger, "Kant and the Crisis of Natural Law," *Journal of the History of Ideas* 26:2 (1965): 191–210. An important analysis of Kant's efforts to resolve the crisis is Steven Lestition, "Kant and the End of the Enlightenment in Prussia," *Journal of Modern History* 65 (1993): 57–112.

the same coin, however, was that morality might find in law points of entry into historical change, but only by denying its essence. It could make concessions to historical contingency only at the cost of its categorical authority.

These were, in stark outline, the pitfalls Fichte knew he had to avoid when he began developing his own theory of law in the summer of 1795. He had attempted to define the relationship between law and morality once before, in the *Contribution*; but the attempt had drawn him into a maze of conflations and distinctions, and that was one reason he looked back on the *Contribution* as an embarrassing exercise.[10] The *Contribution* had distinguished between "alienable" rights, which the Moral Law merely permitted, and the "inalienable" rights without which the individual could not fulfill his duty and hence could not be a moral person. Even as the concept of alienable rights seemed to circumscribe a distinct sphere, a contractual arena for social and economic exchanges, it made that sphere a function of ethics. The Moral Law, after all, determined what was and was not permitted, what could and could not be alienated; and ultimately the legitimacy of legal contracts rested on the same postulate of moral autonomy (or self-legislation) that made the fulfillment of duty an act of freedom.[11]

It was with the concept of inalienable rights, however, that Fichte effected a radical conflation of law and morality. Law in this sense – he called it "natural law" – meant the rights grounded in "the rational nature of man." Such rights defined the moral relationships among "human beings," which were conceptually anterior to their legal relationships as *Bürger* in a state and which obtained without need of legal guarantees. There was a certain recklessness to this position. Fichte was not simply arguing that the state ought to regard certain rights, including the right to property, as inviolable; by implication those same rights need not be protected in positive law.

If Fichte ignored the dangers lurking in this implication, that was because he was so intent on refuting his opponents. To Rehberg, the right to property was the lynchpin of the social order, and there could be no *right* to property without a historical continuity of state authority. A people that arrogated a "right" to "change" its constitution would plunge back into the state of nature, the war of all against all to which state-imposed order had put an end. Fichte redefined the state of nature to mean the moral community that rational beings ought to form. Such a community – a society whose members respected each other's inalienable right to be a moral person – did not depend on the state and would

[10] See esp. Georges Vlachos, "Le droit, la morale et l'expérience dans les écrits révolutionnaires de Fichte," *Cahiers de philosophie du droit*, Nouv. Série 7 (1962): 211–45.
[11] Neuhouser, "Fichte," pp. 160–1.

survive the transition from one state to another. In this scheme of things, state authority derived from a contract about alienable rights, one among many, which the *Bürger* could repudiate for the simple reason that it failed to satisfy their needs.

In the summer of 1795 Fichte knew that he would have to rethink the meaning of natural law, and indeed the entire issue of law and its relationship to morality, from the ground up. It was not simply that his first principle – the definition of the I as self-positing activity in the *Wissenschaftslehre* – had given him a new point of departure. Fichte was now committed to proving that the first principle overcame Kantian dualism by yielding an all-encompassing, completely coherent "system." The system would in turn be mapped into subsystems, or "particular" *Wissenschaften*, all deriving their certainty from the same first principle, but each autonomous vis-à-vis the others. He may have approached law simply as the first test case, but he soon came to regard it as the crucial case, the mediating *Wissenschaft* that the system urgently needed. Looking back on the *Naturrecht* in 1798, he explained the mediation that law effected. The study of ethics, or "how the law of reason commands IN ABSTRACTO," can be conducted "from a higher standpoint . . . where particularity or individuality disappears." With the concept of law we descend from the universal to the individual, from rational abstraction to the particularity of the sense world:

> If the goal of Reason is to be achieved through {the unification of the individual goals of} these individuals, then their physical force must be restrained {and limited}, and everyone's freedom must be restricted {so that they will not hinder one another and} so that one person will not inter-fere with the goal of another and {thereby} thwart {the overall goal of reason}. The theory of right or natural law is what arises {from an inquiry into how this can be accomplished}. The nature of this science has been misunderstood for a very long time. It occupies the middle ground between theoretical and practical philosophy; it is theoretical and practical philoso-phy at the same time.
>
> {It is theoretical, because it speaks of a world – namely of the world as it ought to be found. If the goal of reason is to be achieved in a moral world, then a juridical world, thanks to which the struggle between effi-caciously acting forces is restrained and limited, must already exist.} The juridical world must precede the moral world.
>
> Furthermore, the theory of right is practical as well. {Unlike nature,} a just constitution of this sort does not come into being by itself; it must be produced. But unlike morality, this cannot be accomplished by means of self-limitation; external means are required.[12]

---

[12] Fichte. *Foundations of Transcendental Philosophy (Wissenschaftslehre) nova methodo (1796/99)*, trans. and ed. Daniel Breazeale (Ithaca and London, 1992), pp. 469–71. The text combines two student

How had Fichte come to assign this mediating role to law? The erstwhile disciple now claimed to understand Kant's philosophy better than Kant himself understood it, and he castigated less daring disciples for perpetuating dogmatism in the guise of Critical Philosophy. In his letters and unpublished papers we see him plotting his way through a new field of argument. In the early 1790s the conventional wisdom among Kantians – the position represented by Hufeland and Schmidt – was that the Moral Law was the foundation of law and determined its sphere of action. Salomon Maimon's article "On the First Principles of Natural Law," published in the *Philosophisches Journal*, seemed to promise a new point of departure. Maimon's purpose was to treat natural law "purely," separated from morality on the one hand and from positive law on the other.[13] While morality took as its subject the rationality common to all human beings, natural law considered "the sense individual." In the end, however, Maimon kept law "subsumed" under morality. Natural law was the sphere of "apparent exceptions" to the Moral Law. Rather than yielding "external rights of coercion" that were incompatible with the inner freedom of morality, it simply established "the conditions for the possible use of the Moral Law."[14] In another article in the journal, Anselm Feuerbach, a law student at Jena, crossed the Rubicon by arguing that the law could not be deduced from the Moral Law. And yet there was a sense in which he too turned back; in "the systematic unity of reason," the grounding of law lay in the "sanctioning of certain conditions" for "the sake of the Moral Law," including the use of coercion against rational beings.[15]

Fichte found "hints" in these articles; but where Maimon retreated and Feuerbach hedged, Fichte was ruthlessly consequential. In the *Naturrecht* he argued that law (*Recht*) and the Moral Law were incompatible concepts on several counts and hence that there was no way to derive the one from the other. Having a good will was an "inner" act of self-legislation, an assertion of freedom from any form of "external" constraint. Precisely because law relied on external constraint, it did not require a good will. Whereas the Moral Law was universally valid, a *Recht* was merely "permissive" and "conditional." Its validity was always "limited" to the "specific sphere" in which its conditionality obtained.[16]

---

transcripts of Fichte's lectures, which Breazeale designates H and K. Passages from transcript "H" are enclosed within the scrolled brackets. Text is also available in "Wissenschaftslehre nova methodo," GA, IV, 2: 262–3.

[13] Maimon, "Ueber die ersten Gründe des Naturrechts," in Maimon, *Gesammelte Werke*, ed. Valerio Verra, vol. 6 (Hildesheim, 1971), p. 328.

[14] Ibid., esp. pp. 328–33.

[15] Anselm Feuerbach, "Versuch über den Begriff des Rechts," PJ 2:2 (1795): 138–62. See also Schottky, *Untersuchungen*, esp. pp. 314–15.

[16] NR, pp. 7–11. See also Renaut, *Le système du droit*, p. 239.

If law was not grounded in the Moral Law, however, what legitimated its reliance on coercive power? Was there a way of conceiving justice that did not require a moral premise and yet distinguished legal coercion from arbitrary force? In Fichte's notes for a never-completed review of recent literature on natural law in the *Philosophisches Journal*, written sometime in the late spring or the summer of 1795, we find him circling this issue in search of a point of entry. As he reminded himself in a marginal note, he had already concluded that he had to extrude from "this entire investigation" what was "morally good." His dilemma, then, was to explain the fact that law, though it had "something of *power* (*Macht*), *force* (*Gewalt*)," was nonetheless "also opposed to it." The question was why "the sphere of the concept of *Rechte*" was at once "larger" and "smaller" than that of the concept of force.[17]

It is a measure of the quandary Fichte and other Kantians faced that his initial strategy in the review notes pointed him right back to the conflation he was intent on avoiding. He entertained the possibility of conceiving of law as an "inner" self-constraint, a "counterweight" to the inner assertion of power. To define law in that way, however, was to make it a kind of duty. Then one would have to choose between two equally absurd implications: that law could not be coercive, or that duty was coercion internalized. In another marginal note, Fichte had to remind himself that "law has to do with something *exterior*," whereas duty was an inner "*drive*" that "comes (purely) from the *heart*."[18]

It may have been in the face of this impasse that Fichte decided to return to the beginning. "I have taken this opportunity to review K.'s *Grundlegung* z. M.d.S.," he reported to Reinhold in a letter of August 29, 1795, "and found that *here*, if anywhere, the inadequacy of the Kantian principles, and the assumption he makes of higher principles without noticing it, can be palpably demonstrated."[19] The text in question was the *Fundamental Principles of the Metaphysics of Morals* (1785), where Kant first formulated the Moral Law as the Categorical Imperative. All duties, Kant argued, could be derived from the imperative to "act only on that maxim whereby thou canst at the same time will that it should become a universal law."[20] Kant's failure, Fichte explained to Reinhold, lay in not explaining "why I should make maxims from a certain sphere mine only on the condition that they can be considered generally valid." The underlying task was to account for the "I" or, in Fichte's terms, to explain what made rational self-consciousness possible; and that was inseparable from asking how "the mere I" accepted other "rational beings" outside itself.[21]

[17] "Zur Recension der NaturRechte für das Niethammersche Journal," in GA, II, 3: 395–406.
[18] GA, II, 3: 398.   [19] GA, III, 2: 385.
[20] Immanuel Kant, *Fundamental Principles of the Metaphysics of Morals*, trans. T. K. Abbott (Buffalo, 1987), p. 49.
[21] GA, III, 2: 385.

Fichte was not simply saying that the self-positing I, and not the Moral Law, was the first principle from which the concept of law had to be derived. His critical move – the one that grounded his concept of law – was to set the self-positing I within a process of intersubjectivity. Again Kant's formula seemed inadequate. Implicit to the Categorical Imperative was the assumption that the individual's maxim was moral only if it could be accepted as a principle of action by all other rational beings. But what does universality mean here? When I seek the agreement of others in the sense world, Fichte asked Reinhold, how do I distinguish rational beings from mere objects? If "the general opinion" supports me in both cases, what is the difference between my riding a horse and "the Russian noble-man [who] . . . gives away and sells his serfs and knouts them for fun"? Why are these not both examples of "injustice"? Why must I regard some of the "appearances" to which I am related as "inviolable," while others are "things" that "are completely subjected to me"?[22]

Fichte's point was that the concept of *Recht* derives not from Kant's rational test for the morality of an action, but from the very condition for subjectivity – that is, from what makes it possible for the moral per-son to be an individual among individuals, one rational but finite being among others in the world of appearances. It was in this sense that the *Wissenschaftslehre* pointed the way:

> There is found in the synthetic process of the W. L. the principle: I must think myself *as Individuum*, that is, as *determining* in a sphere of things that cannot begin (first of all, my body) . . . determined in a sphere of rational beings outside me: I cannot do this without positing such a sphere and each object in this sphere likewise as Individuum . . . *The conditions of indi-viduality* are called *Rechte*. It is absolutely impossible that I ascribe a Recht to myself without also ascribing one to a being outside me; since it is absolutely impossible that I posit myself as Individuum without positing a being outside me as Individuum.[23]

Fichte was drawing a clear line between two kinds of rational freedom, two ways of restraining oneself on the basis of concepts. The "freedom" that needed explanation was the I's self-positing as an *Individuum* – that is, the individuation of the self in the sense world. Clearly it was not adherence to the Moral Law that effected that individuation. Moral freedom meant the freedom to perform duty or, in negative terms, freedom from the conditions of sense being that inhibited the fulfillment of duty. To the extent that individuals were moral, they transcended their differences in sense being in a shared adherence to a universal principle. Law, on the other hand, allowed the I to make itself a "determinate indi-vidual" in relationships with others. Individuation required the freedom

---

[22] GA, III, 2: 386.   [23] GA, III, 2: 387.

to choose among ends as a sense being and to act efficaciously on that choice. It was through law that the rational subject made itself a causal agent in the world of causality.[24]

The *Naturrecht* begins with what Fichte considers an a priori deduction of the concept of law as a necessary condition of individuation. Searching for the fundamental distinction between persons (or subjects) and things – the distinction the Categorical Imperative seemed to assume but lack – Fichte completed a move he had begun to make in the *Wissenschaftslehre* and had continued, still within the framework of an inquiry into the conditions of moral freedom, in his lectures on "the mission of scholars." When the Not-I took the form of objects in consciousness, it was a "resistance" (*Anstoss*) that provoked the self-positing I to reassert (through moral concepts) its capacity for infinite expansion. But in the sense world a free being can posit itself as such only at a "summons," and that necessarily implies a free being outside it (as the cause of the summons). One cannot assume other free beings without positing oneself as being in a relationship with them. This is the "relationship of law," "the relationship of an interaction through intelligence and freedom." The concept of law is that "I must in all cases . . . limit my freedom through the concept of the possibility of [the other's] freedom." Without this self-limitation – this mutual giving up of some freedom – each would risk the complete negation of his freedom.

The logic of the deduction, then, was that freedom was grounded in self-positing, the coming to self-consciousness. That in turn required the intersubjectivity Fichte called "free interaction though concepts," and since the concept of law made intersubjectivity possible, it was the condition of self-consciousness and hence of freedom.[25] But what did rational freedom mean in this context? Somewhere in the transition from the review notes to the writing of the *Naturrecht*, Fichte had come to to realize that if he was to arrive at a truly independent concept of law, he would have to conceive of "free interaction" in natural rather than moral terms. Since the concept could not rely on "good wills," it had to take human beings exclusively as they existed in the world of appearances, strictly as sense beings. It had to assume a world with no good wills, no capacity to act on disinterested reverence for the Moral Law. In such a world the only motivation was "self-love." Or, as Fichte put it in the *Naturrecht*, law as coercion must be based on the assumption of universal egotism. This was the limiting case, the worst-case scenario. If one could assume universal egotism, but in a way that justified, rather than

---

[24] See esp. Neuhouser, "Fichte," pp. 162–71. Neuhouser argues persuasively that in the shift from the *Contribution* to the *Naturrecht*, Fichte's view of individuality changes from that of the "substantive self-determination" of a "morally autonomous subject" to that of the "formal freedom" of the "causally efficacious" person.

[25] The deduction and its implications are elucidated in Herbert, "Fichte's Deduction," esp. pp. 203–8.

precluded, legal coercion, there was clearly no need for a moral justification. If, on the other hand, the experiment was not taken to this extreme,
law would be reabsorbed, however surreptitiously, into morality.

The "hint" in this direction had been provided by Johann Benjamin
Erhard, another maverick Kantian. In an article entitled "Apology of the
Devil," published in the same issue of the *Philosophisches Journal* as
Maimon's piece, Erhard took precisely the step Maimon was unwilling to
take. The law derived "not from morality" but "from the possibility of
reciprocal sociability (*Verträglichkeit*) of the selfish impulse in human
beings." Hence, a "*Wissenschaft* of *Rechte*" could "precede ethics."[26] As a
response to conventional Kantianism, Erhard's move was provocative; but
it proceeded from a commonplace of European thought. Since the seventeenth century, in several rich veins of literature, European thinkers had
explored the possibility that there was something inherently self-limiting
about the motive force of self-interest, and they had suggested the forms
self-limitation might take. If most people could not be expected to practice virtue (or if most people in modern societies could not be expected
to do so), could a rational order nonetheless arise out of the pursuit
of self-interest?[27] The text that most obviously influenced Fichte – the
one Erhard surely pointed him back to, if he had not already returned to
it – was Cesare Beccaria's *An Essay on Crimes and Punishments* (1764).
Beccaria made self-interest the psychological equivalent of gravity, a
motive force that "acts incessantly, unless it meets with an obstacle to
oppose it." The "legislator," he wrote, acts like "a skillful architect"; he
"erects his edifice on the foundation of self-love, and contrives, that the
interest of the public shall be the interest of each individual." Building
an entire system of penal justice on that principle, Beccaria assigned the
state the role of maintaining a mechanical equilibrium between, on the
one hand, myriad self-interests and, on the other, the legal coercion that
constrained them.[28]

Particularly in the discussion of penal law, the *Naturrecht* is heavily
indebted to Beccaria's book. Fichte was clearly entranced by the prospect
of a legal system operating with mechanical predictability and precision,
so that the "power" of the laws would "follow every subject, as the shadow
follows the body."[29] What remained in question, however, was how such
a system could be justified. An a priori deduction from "the pure form
of Reason" could not be grounded, as Becarria's argument was, in a def-

---

[26] Johann Benjamin Erhard, "Apologie des Teufels," *PJ* 1: 2 (1795): 136–9.

[27] See, e.g., Nannerl O. Keohane, *Philosophy and the State in France. The Renaissance to the Enlightenment* (Princeton, N.J., 1980); Albert O. Hirschman, *The Passions and the Interests. Political Arguments
for Capitalism before its Triumph* (Princeton, N.J., 1977).

[28] Cesare Beccaria, *An Essay on Crimes and Punishments* (4th ed.: Brookline Village, Mass., 1983), esp.
pp. 8, 77. On Fichte's debt to Beccaria, see also Renaut, *Le système du droit*, pp. 252, 352–3.

[29] Beccaria, *Essay*, p. 64.

inition of "public utility," since the grounding would then unavoidably be empirical. At the same time, though, Fichte could not find a justification for legal coercion *simply* in his a priori deduction of the concept of law from intersubjectivity. As Fichte had deduced it, the concept of law was the condition of the very possibility of intersubjectivity. It posited the need for mutual self-limitation, but by itself, it did not justify external coercion in the event that self-limitation broke down. Suppose I failed to limit my freedom, or the other failed to limit his. Suppose one of us needed protection from a third party. What was needed was a deduction of why and how the concept of law was institutionalized in the form of a state with coercive authority.

We return to the paradox with which Fichte had begun his notes: law had to be conceived at once as "power," or constraining force, and as something more and less than power. In his effort to resolve the paradox, Fichte returned to Rousseau's concept of the General Will, which had received perfunctory attention in the *Contribution,* and reworked it. If law was to partake of power without being reduced to it, he argued, it had to depend on a will that was "determined necessarily and unalterably by the law" but "would have power only where the law wished it." Only a collective will, and not the will of an individual, met that requirement. If law was the product and the instrument of such a will, its coercive force would be applied predictably, without exceptions, just as power followed the laws of nature in the world of causation. But the crux of the paradox was that this machinelike necessity could arise only from a union of free beings. It was that union that made law "the moderation of power through concepts" and in doing so, legitimated it.

Ultimately the power of the law was distinguished from arbitrary natural power because the individual remained "free" even as his will was integrated into a General Will. The law's exclusive concern with externality meant that the individual retained his "inner" freedom, including his freedom to fulfill his duty. If the law did not require a good will, it also did not seek to force one into being. At the same time, the General Will was the product of its members' active exercise of freedom. Law, after all, was conditional. It was not "necessary" that "all coexist beside each other as *free beings*" – although if they chose to do so, they had to form a General Will. Even if that Will was formed, the individual did not have to enter it; he might choose to live in isolation.

The critical point was that in entering a General Will, the individual made a rational choice; unless and until he withdrew, that voluntary act continued. The rational freedom of the act was grounded in the very logic of self-interest. Because I want to secure myself as much freedom to pursue ends as possible – or, to put it negatively, because I do not want my freedom restricted any more than it has to be – I choose to join others in a commitment to mutual self-restriction. In this sense Fichte could write that "every member of society allows his own external freedom to be limited through inner freedom." Whatever its "material" (and that will vary from state to state), the individual makes the law of the state "his law acording to *form*, through his consent." It is as the sum of these individual acts of self-determination that the General Will has legitimacy as a public will, a collective exercise of rationality.

There are two crucial steps, then, in Fichte's transcendental deduction: making the concept of law the condition of intersubjectivity and grounding the concept of a General Will (and hence of a state) in reciprocal acts of self-determination. The implication was not simply that a "science" of law could *not* be built on the Categorical Imperative, Kant's rational test for the morality of an intention. The rational freedom that grounded law could not be conceived as the autonomy of the individual conscience. It could not be a matter of the I judging itself as though it were abstracted from the sense conditions of its being. For purposes of a theory of law, Fichte's strategy was to conceive of the subject as "a discrete unit of free causal efficacy," an individuated sense being freely choosing ends and able to realize them; and to demonstrate that rational freedom in this sense, precisely because it was self-interested, necessarily entailed an intersubjective relationship with other free beings. Only in that way could the concept of law take the *Individuum* as its subject and, in so doing, mediate between freedom and natural causality. And only in that way could the concept set individuals within a social world, at once guaranteeing their freedom and legitimating their collective use of coercion.

As a product of the General Will, the state organized a uniquely human kind of interaction – one in which individuation and integration were the conditions for each other. To capture this duality, Fichte compared "the state as a whole" to "an organized product of Nature," an "organic union" in which the parts and the whole sustained each other and kept themselves "mutually in balance." The *Bürger* "receives the whole in his part," while the whole, by maintaining each part, "turns back into itself and maintains itself."[30] Fichte's metaphor echoes the discourse of scientific vitalism that was gaining currency in Germany in the 1790s, but it did not, it should be stressed, signal his abandonment of a mechanistic view of Nature. When Fichte compared the state to an organism, it was to improve on, not to reject, Beccaria's image of a precise and efficient machine. The texts surrounding the *Naturrecht* make it clear that Fichte equated "organism" with "organization" and "articulation." All three terms signified that Nature, in the very operation of its mechanical laws, formed integrated wholes or "products." Nature "produces itself" in the sense that

[30] NR, p. 203.

its products form "in conformity with mechanical laws," not through freedom of the will.[31] For that reason, vitalism had a very different meaning in Fichte's usage from its meaning, for example, in Humboldt's. Humboldt's ideal of *Bildung* pitted a vitalistic ideal against mechanistic coercion, to define individual autonomy as spontaneous self-generation and the realization of an unique "inner" teleology. Fichte needed a metaphor for a kind of interdependence, a reciprocal guarantee of space to pursue free choices, that was inconceivable without the threat of machinelike coercion.

With the image of an "organized product of Nature" Fichte conveyed what his original language of mechanism – evoking as it did a world in which objects attracted and repelled each other, but could not sustain each other – could not convey. The point was that the General Will formed a genuine community, and not just a force field in which self-interested wills coupled and collided. Ultimately, however, even the articulation of Nature's power into organic wholes did not suffice for Fichte's purpose. Nature's creative power – its capacity to form integrated wholes – offered "an analogue of freedom"; but "it is not real freedom, since it is a creating according to definite fixed rules." The distinction was crucial to Fichte's concept of freedom in intersubjectivity. In the sense world, free beings could recognize each other – could distinguish each other from things – only through their physical signs, or through their bodies. The human body had to be conceived as freedom in appearance, which meant that it was qualitatively different from even the highest form of organic life. It was the difference between the organism's bounded freedom of movement, operating within causally determined parameters, and the embodied human being's unbounded capacity to individuate itself by conceptualizing ends and choices.

Likewise the "union" effected in the juridical world only "appears to be a product of Nature":

> The task of the doctrine (of law) is: free beings should be brought into a certain mechanism, under the rules of being subjected in a connection and a reciprocity. Now there is no such mechanism in itself, it depends in part on freedom. The effectiveness with which this legal structure (*Verfassung*) is produced by human beings is an effect of Nature and freedom in their union.[32]

---

[31] See, e.g., *Fichte. Foundations of Transcendental Philosophy*, pp. 469–71. On Fichte's view of physical nature, see Peter Ruben, "Natur und Freiheit. Zum Naturverständnis Johann Gottlieb Fichtes," in Karen Gloy and Paul Burger, eds., *Die Naturphilosophie im Deutschen Idealismus* (Stuttgart-Bad Cannstatt, 1993), pp. 24–49. But cf. Claude Piché, "Le Concept de Natur chez Fichte," in Daniel Schulthess, ed., *La Nature. Thèmes philosophiques. Thèmes d'Actualité*, pp. 553–6.

[32] GA, IV, 2: 264.

The concept of law, then, took the I as an embodied subject, at once sensually caused and rationally causing. At the same time, it posited the union of such subjects as a collective will, legitimately coercing the sense being because it was grounded in the rational being's freedom of choice. Conceived in this way, the science of law promised Fichte the point of mediation, the bridge across Kantian dualism, that his system needed.

It was a bridge, though, that threatened to land Fichte's thought in another dilemma. Could one make the concept of law truly independent of the Moral Law without allowing it to be drawn inexorably into the contingent particularity of history? Fichte was acutely aware of this danger. He knew that in detaching law from the Moral Law, he was abandoning his unconditional denial of Rehberg's historicism. He could no longer conceive of a rational legal order purely and simply as an overcoming of historical contingency, a liberation from the blind accidents of experience. Even as he retreated from the principle of universality in this strong sense, however, he sought to subordinate the relativistic pull of history to a universal principle in the weak sense. For a collective will to be truly "general," every *Bürger* – every member of the juridical community – had to have a precisely equal quantum of freedom and restraint. But the General Will could exist only as a *particular variation* on this formal principle of legal equality, differing from other variations in the degree of equally distributed freedom (and equally distributed restraint). This was to say that the positive law yielded by Fichte's principle would vary from context to context, depending on the specific community and its circumstances. To put it another way, the form of the principle of law made no concession to differences in context, but the application of the principle, its realization by a particular aggregate of people, was necessarily contextual.

With this distinction between form and content Fichte sought to acknowledge historical relativism without surrendering to it. And yet, by the very fact that his concept of law assumed a world of "universal selfishness," it was also in danger of being pulled into the teleology of another kind of eighteenth-century historicism. Why was it that a myriad of self-interested pursuits – pursuits that blinded people to the common welfare – seemed to propel European societies as a whole along a path to prosperity and enlightenment? Was there not a natural teleology at work behind the apparent chaos, a set of natural laws of human behavior that harnessed self-interest to a rational dynamic of progress? It was this view of progress as an unintended consequence, an ironic product of the cunning of history, that the Scottish Enlightenment had explored to such effect in its theories of historical stages.

Fichte was, at best, only vaguely familiar with the Scottish contribution, but he faced a formidable variation on it much closer to home, in Kant's essays on history and politics. In his "Idea for a Universal History with a Cosmopolitan Purpose," published in 1784, Kant had sought to "formulate in terms of a definite plan of nature a history of creatures who act without a plan of their own."[33] In the natural teleology he outlined, the species developed its moral capacities through "*unsocial sociability*," the interactions through which individuals competed to satisfy their "insatiable desires" for "honour, power, or property." Kant found the same irony of unintended consequences in the modern competition among nations. The very pursuit of national power required the states to promote "internal culture." Likewise the states were aware that if commerce and industry, the key ingredients of national power, were to flourish, the realm of private freedoms had to be expanded. As a result enlightenment would gradually spread; war would come to be considered too risky a venture; and a cosmoplitan federation would become possible.[34]

Kant returned to this theme in his "Perpetual Peace. A Philosophical Sketch," published in 1795. "How," he asked, "does nature guarantee that what man *ought* to do by laws of his freedom (but does not do) will in fact be done through nature's compulsion, without prejudice to the free agency of man?" Ultimately, he argued, peace would be guaranteed when states acquired "republican" constitutions, guaranteeing their citizens freedom and legal equality. In this state of justice, the citizens, mindful of their self-interest, would be very unlikely to give their consent to a declaration of war. In any event, however, the modern "*spirit of commerce . . .* cannot exist side by side with war."; and hence "states find themselves compelled to promote the noble cause of peace, though not exactly from motives of morality."[35] Fichte wrote an anonymous review of "Perpetual Peace" in 1795, soon after it appeared, and as he was developing his thoughts on law. He took pains to summarize Kant's appeal to the "mechanisms" of "Nature itself" as the guarantor of eternal peace, and then sketched out an alternative scenario. He began by puncturing Kant's optimism; the fact was, he observed, that to this point in history self-interest had not driven people to establish a just constitution. The hard reality behind the apparently benign spirit of commerce was that a "considerable part of people" still had "more to gain than to lose" from "the general disorder." Given the flexibility of the hierarchical structure and the availability of resources, everyone still hoped to enrich himself by robbing others. And in any case, "the oppression of foreign peoples and territories in commerce opens up an ever flowing, rich source of help."[36] People would prefer the secure maintenance of what they had to the insecure seizure of others' posessions only when intense competition, population increase, and the development of all branches of production

[33] *Kant. Political Writings*, ed. Hans Reiss and trans. H. B. Nisbet (2d, enl. ed.: Cambridge, 1991), p. 42.
[34] Ibid., pp. 44–53.   [35] Ibid., pp. 112–14.   [36] GA, I, 3: 227.

(*Nahrungszweige*) produced a general "balance" in wealth. Under those circumstances, the exploitation of foreign peoples could continue only on
condition that they be reduced to slavery. But hope lay in "two new phenomena in world history": the creation of the American Republic, from
which "enlightenment and freedom necessarily must spread to the parts
of the world oppressed to this point," and "the great European republic
of states, which opposes a dam that did not exist in the old world to the
invasion of barbarian peoples into the workshops of Culture." From these
developments it could be expected that "finally a People will set up in
reality the single just state constitution . . . and by observing their happiness other peoples will be stimulated to imitation. "In this way," Fichte
concluded, "the process of Nature is designed (*angelegt*) for the production of a good state constitution."[37]

As a comment on global developments in the eighteenth century, this
is a puzzling blend; a certain heavy cynicism about European colonial-
ism, a censure of the exploitation of less developed peoples, operates
within a pronounced Eurocentrism. Fichte's economic prognostications
are equally curious, and their details need not detain us. What is striking
is the unresolved tension in his effort to improve on Kant's view of self-
interest as the motive force in a "natural" historical teleology. On the one
hand, having decided that only self-interest could generate a rational legal
order, he sought to be more consequentially teleological than Kant about
the momentum inherent in historical change. What made the establishment and spread of a rational legal order an inevitable product of historical change? Commercial culture would, to be sure, play a vital role in
creating such an order, but not simply because it "grounds a security on
selfishness." The turning point – the point of inevitability – would come
when the expansion of commerce, by effecting specific changes in the
economic and social structures of nations and in the global economy,
made "the majority" directly aware that a rational legal system was to their
advantage.

Fichte offered his own version of the historical realization of unintended consequences. And yet he also stopped short of conceding a determining role to history in the form of a natural process. Kant's paradox –
the working out of "nature's compulsion, without prejudice to the free
agency of man" – had in effect been heightened. The compulsion of
history opened the way to a new era of historical agency; natural processes
brought a particular "people" to the point of making a rational choice
for justice and thus yielded an example that other peoples could choose
to follow. It is a measure of Fichte's commitment to the deduction of
the *Naturrecht* that, in sharp contrast to his vision of moral rebirth in the
Contribution, he was now more than willing to envision a leap forward

[37] GA, I, 3: 228.

that did not require the exercise of moral freedom. Equally striking, however, is that the leap forward could not mean that the "natural" course of history obviated the need for an exercise in *rational* freedom. If the French Revolution was not the revelatory moment he had expected, there would still be a pivotal moment of collective self-determination.

★ ★ ★

The *Naturrecht* had many admirers, including Reinhold and, oddly, Humboldt. But there was an undercurrent of unease about Fichte's theory, particularly among students at Jena who had witnessed him developing it in lectures and seminars. The "state" projected in the *Naturrecht*, Johann Erich von Berger wrote to a friend in February 1796, "will not please people here" – and I myself, he added, consider this state "very severe" (*Streng*).[38] Johann Georg Rist recalled years later that he had been struck by "the ruthlessness and imperative of [Fichte's] deductions and principles" but "could not submit against [his] free sense" to the "iron force that [Fichte] wanted to impose on all conditions for the sake of consistency."[39]

There is a certain puzzlement behind these reactions. Having entered the public arena as the tribune of a new era of freedom, Fichte seemed to have become the advocate of an authoritarian statism. The full scale of his statism would not become apparent until the appearance of *The Closed Commercial State* in 1800, but its basic features were already evident. Fichte envisioned an executive power that in normal times would have exclusive control over the interpretation as well as the enforcement of the law, without the counterweight of a judicial branch of government and without regard for popular opinion or indeed for public opinion in any form. In the eyes of this state, civil society would be nothing more than an aggregate of subjects. The law itself had to operate with the complete and invariable efficiency of a machine; if a single perpetrator went unpunished, the legitimacy of the entire system would be thrown into question. Hence every *Bürger* had to be recognizable wherever he or she went, and that required that the police maintain a system of passes, each with a precise description of the person or, in the case of the more affluent, a portrait. The police could demand to see a pass, Fichte noted, only for "the legitimation of the person"– and not out of "mere mischief or curiosity."

Fichte, it should be stressed, had not brought a statist vision to his initial effort to develop a philosophy of law. As he pursued the project, he *became* preoccupied with guaranteeing individual "freedom" by constructing a

[38] *Briefe von und an J.F. Herbert*, ed. Theodor Fritzsch, vol. 1 (Langensalza, 1912), p. 17. Quoted in FG 1: 334.
[39] Johann Georg Rist, *Lebenserinnerungen (1775–1847)*, ed. G. Pöbel, 3 vols. (Gotha, 1880–1888), 2: 69ff. Quoted in FG 1: 335–6.

statist form of order. He had not begun by dismissing the alternative: a civil society that constituted itself and regulated itself with minimal state tutelage. In fact, it would be hard to imagine a more promising philosophical grounding for such a society than Fichte's deduction of reciprocal freedom in the intersubjectivity constituted by the concept of law. He remained concerned to guarantee a sphere of privacy, particularly in the home, into which the state could not peer. Why, then, did he see the need for such a self-sufficient and pervasive executive authority?

If we attempt to frame the answer in terms of Isaiah Berlin's celebrated distinction between "positive" and "negative" freedom, we confront an irony. It will become apparent that, to an extent, Berlin's diagnosis of the authoritarian, if not totalitarian, logic of positive freedom applies. There is a sense in which Fichte resorted to coercion to realize an ideal of justice, and ultimately he saw the state and law as conditions for the realization of the "real" – that is, rational – self.[40] His immediate project, however, was premised on a "negative" concept of freedom. The point was to focus on and proceed from what Berlin calls "poor empirical [selves] in space and time" and to keep their interference with each other's freedom to a minimum. What is striking about the *Naturrecht* is that his statism also grew out of that strategy.

To appreciate how the strategy played out in Fichte's hands, we need only compare his philosophy of law with what has aptly been described as the discourse of "commercial humanism" in the Anglo-Scottish Enlightenment. Adam Smith and others not only questioned whether the ancient republican ideal of virtue, with its emphasis on self-sacrificing devotion to the public good, could realistically be expected to guide the increasingly affluent commercial societies of the late eighteeenth century; they also doubted that such an ideal was necessary. Though the motive force of self-interest was rooted in the passions and the appetites, it nonetheless could assume civilized and indeed "enlightened" forms. What tamed it – what made it reliably self-limiting – was the myriad kinds of social interaction in a complex division of labor and in the forms of sociability (or "politeness") that complexity made possible. Hence the search for an alternative to virtue entailed an exploration of the intricate social psychology of modern civilization.[41]

In Anglo-Scottish discourse, social psychology served as the middle term between nature and morality. It was precisely that middle term that

---

[40] Isaiah Berlin, "Two Concepts of Liberty," in Michael J. Sandel, ed., *Liberalism and Its Critics* (New York, 1984), esp. pp. 22–5.

[41] See esp. J. G. A. Pocock, "Virtues, rights, and manners: A model for historians of political thought," in Pocock, *Virtue, Commerce, and History. Essays on Political Thought and History, Chiefly in the Eighteenth Century* (Cambridge, 1985), pp. 49–50; Pocock, "The mobility of property and the rise of eighteenth-century sociology," in ibid., pp. 103–23; Istvan Hont and Michael Ignatieff, eds., *Wealth and Virtue: The Shaping of Political Economy in the Scottish Enlightenment* (Cambridge, 1983).

Fichte's thought about law lacked and could not accommodate. This is not to deny that with his theory of intersubjectivity Fichte took a major step toward providing transcendental philosophy with the social dimension it badly needed.[42] But – all the more ironic – even as his "deduction" posited the social in the abstract, it precluded engagement with the psychological substance of social life in the concrete. In Fichte's logic, the concept of law mediated between morality and nature but not in a way that dismantled the Kantian dualism. In the absence of the Anglo-Scottish middle term, law had to be justified by analogy both with moral reasoning and with the mechanical force of nature – and, in *both* directions, the implication was a kind of statism. The general will represented a collective act of rational freedom, though not a moral act. Because it was rational in that analogous sense, it was also sacrosanct. Rather than reflecting the empirical state of opinion at a particular moment, it embodied a kind of "ought." To Fichte, there was perfect sense in the executive authority – the institutional state – interpreting the same laws it was charged with enforcing. Above the mere reflection of interests in opinion, there had to be a single authority that determined what the ought, in this nonmoral but nonetheless rational form, meant.

At the other end of the dualism, where positive laws were enforced, Fichte's deduction consigned society to the realm of nature. When he imagined a world that made self-interest the only motive force, he made law, as the necessary counterforce, analogous to a mechanical cause. Ultimately the analogy was between self-interest and physical motion. The one, like the other, was assumed to operate on the principle of inertia, though Fichte did not use that term. This was to imply that modern sociability could *not* be relied on to constrain the motionlike force of self-interest – the force on which Fichte premised his deduction. Every member of the juridical community, as a rational calculator, had to be absolutely certain that, if he did not himself restrain the force of his self-interest, it would collide with a counterforce. That counterforce was the state, which dealt with the human will "insofar as it is at the same time a part in the chain of the mechanism of Nature."[43] The state had to be strong enough to prevail in all collisions with its subjects; extensive enough to counter the threat to freedom posed by any subject; and informed enough to respond effectively to even the smallest threat anywhere in the force field of social relations.

★ ★ ★

---

[42] See esp. Robert R. Williams, "The Question of the Other in Fichte's Thought," in Breazeale and Rockmore, eds., *Fichte*, pp. 142–57; Herbert, "Fichte's Deduction," pp. 208–13.
[43] The quotation is from "Ascetik als Anhang zur Moral," a lecture Fichte gave sometime in the period from the beginning of 1798 to the beginning of 1799. GA, II, 5: 61.

If readers were alarmed by the statist implications of the *Naturrecht*, their fears were surely confirmed by its supplement. The purpose of *The Closed Commercial State* was to specify the set of economic policies that would produce a "pure state law." It was quite possible, Fichte admitted in the introductory dedication, that his theory would "remain without effect in the real world."[44] His mood of resignation was a measure of his awareness that he was contradicting not only the policies of the status quo but also the new wisdom in political economy.

In Fichte's rational commercial state, every member would have the right to develop his or her human potential in work and to make a decent living through work. The state would guarantee that right with constant and detailed regulatory intervention, aimed at maintaining a just "balance" (*Gleichgewicht*) between production and consumption and, on the production side, between agricultural products and manufactured goods. The state would also assume a host of other regulatory responsibilities to keep each branch of the economy at its proper size (closing it when overcrowding threatened; attracting new recruits with subventions when it threatened to become too small). Within each branch, guilds would serve as vehicles for state monitoring of the supply and the quality of goods. The state would set a fair price for goods and would assure against a deterioration of both producers' real incomes and consumers' buying power by making necessary adjustments in the monetary supply. All these internal regulations would be in vain if the state did not at the same time prevent intrusions from destroying the balance. Hence the commercial state had to be "closed" in the literal sense that there could be neither export nor import of goods. A just balance required a completely autarchic economy, its walls formed by state law and guarded by state officialdom

The *Handelsstaat* at once echoes the regulatory mania of eighteenth-century German cameralism and points ahead to the centrally planned economies of twentieth-century socialist regimes. And yet Fichte's economic thought cannot be reduced to a link between these two species of dirigismus; that would blind us to both the distinctly Fichtean logic that gives the text its internal coherence and to the values that informed it. Fichte's ambivalent relationship to the cameralist legacy will become apparent in due course. If his thought is to be labeled socialist, it can only be in a limited sense. Obviously he no longer posed a free market in land against the "agrarian law," as he had done in the *Contribution*. But in turning away from his earlier faith in market freedom, he stopped well short of Babeuf's communitarian alternative, which had no room for private property. Juxtaposed to the realm of public regulation, where the

[44] GH, p. 64.

individual's right to dispose of his property as he pleased was severely restricted, was a sphere of property that *was* private in a real sense. The private was what remained after the individual gave the state part of his surplus, as his contribution to the welfare of the whole. In the one sphere, the state's presence left "property" with hardly any private status. In the other, the state could have no presence; the privacy of property was inviolable.

In the overall structure of Fichte's statist economy, however, the principle of private property was so restricted as to be left with hardly any breathing space. This denouement, like the others, had its source in the *Wissenschaftslehre* and in the theory of intersubjectivity to which Fichte's new concept of freedom had led him. According to the principle of *Recht*, in the interaction of free beings, each retained as much freedom as possible by restraining himself from violating the freedom of others. Freedom here meant the rational self's capacity to individuate itself in relation to other selves and to the natural world, to interact with others under reciprocal self-restraint and to assert itself as an embodied intelligence by dominating, or at least by modifying, the resistant materiality of things. To put it more simply, freedom was exercised in and through participation in the division of labor. Self-consciousness and hence freedom were inconceivable without intersubjectivity, and in the face of nature, labor was the crucial medium of intersubjectivity.

In a just society, every member would have the right to modify things within his exclusive sphere of labor. Precisely because that sphere was inviolable in law, it gave the individual the autonomy he needed to interact freely with other free sense beings. "Property," as Fichte now defined it, was an exclusive right to a free activity, an entitlement that could only be guaranteed if each labored securely within his "specific part of the sense world." Justice was a condition of "rough equality" in the social distribution of spheres of activity. It could not be produced by the "blind chance" of individual decisions and the relationships of unequal power to which they gave rise. Fichte's new vision of rational order required the collective authority of the state "to *install* [each person] in his property" and to maintain him there or provide him with a viable replacement.[45]

Though Fichte's definition of property in terms of labor is to some degree indebted to Locke's, the logic of his transcendental deduction carried him well beyond the Lockean tradition. In the Lockean view, property is an extension of the personality in the sense that the person makes his own what he invests with his labor. The investment of labor and the resulting modification of nature justify a claim to exclusive control

---

[45] GH, pp. 71, 106–8.

over a thing.[46] Fichte sought a way to define property in terms of the "activity" (or labor) invested *without* equating it with exclusive control over things. The exclusivity guaranteed by a *Recht*, or a right, had to do not with control over the modified object but with the act of modification itself, the labor performed. The right to property was a right to free activity, the exercise of the free being's capacity to appropriate nature, and to the decent living such activity ought to provide. To the extent that an individual's control over things violated others' spheres of free activity, it had to be curtailed.

The difference between the Lockean view and Fichte's may be regarded as one of emphasis, but it had momentous implications. To over-simplify the issue, but in a way that underlines its significance: should the terms of human relationships be defined through the legal status of things, or should the legal status of things serve the overriding requirements of human relationships?[47] Since the seventeenth century the discourse of natural law, including the Lockean tradition, had leaned heavily toward the former conclusion. That, of course, carried the danger that in the legal structuring of relationships among persons through the things they owned or did not own, some persons would be reduced to things. The right to property would become the right to make others the instruments of one's control, things in the service of other things, with no causal efficacy of their own, merely transmitting the force of things and their owners through nature's mechanical chain of causes and effects. Fichte's point was that people's power or lack of power over things ought *not* to define their relationships. It was the right to individuate the self in work, and not the right to assert the self in the use of objects modified by work, that was inviolable.

To appreciate the full import of this difference, we need only consider the issue of how property rights are to be reconciled with the satisfaction of basic human needs. Since Aquinas, natural law theorists had sought rationales for satisfying the needs of the poor in times of scarcity without resorting to a distributive theory of justice, which would subordinate property rights to the need to redistribute wealth. In the seventeenth and eighteenth centuries, this was still a pressing issue; recurrent harvest failures raised the specter of famine, with grain and bread prices soaring well

---

[46] There is an immense literature on Locke's theory of property. For a brief and judicious analysis, see Alan Ryan, *Property and Political Theory* (Oxford and New York, 1984), esp. pp. 31–44. Ryan identifies one of the "hostages to egalitarianism" in Locke's theory: "If the title to propety is labor, naïve common sense will be sure to wonder why the natural title of the worker is so much weaker than the legal title of the owner at any given time" (ibid., p. 44).

[47] Pocock, "Mobility of property," p. 104. In natural law jurisprudence, Pocock argues, "property became a system of legally defined relations between persons and things, or between persons through things." See also Jay Lampert, "Locke, Fichte, and Hegel on the Right to Property," in Michael Baur and John Russon, eds., *Hegel and the Tradition: Essays in Honour of H. S. Harris* (Toronto, 1997), pp. 40–73.

beyond the means of large numbers of people living on the edge of poverty. Though not unsympathetic to the plight of the poor, Locke and Pufendorf were convinced that private property provided the essential motivation for increasing resources; and hence that the surest way to limit scarcity, if not to overcome it entirely, was to leave property rights unrestricted. The economic implication was that the market – the laws of supply and demand – should be left to determine the "just" price for a good. Relief of the needy was a moral rather than a legal obligation, a matter of charity rather than of "strict justice."[48]

In *The Wealth of Nations*, Adam Smith pushed this logic to a startling conclusion. Smith did not deny that modern commercial civilization exhibited a great deal of "oppressive inequality." What required explanation was "the superior affluence and abundance commonly possessed even by [the] lowest and most despised member of civilized society, compared with what the most respected and active savage can attain to." Yawning inequalites were tolerable precisely because the laboring masses could enjoy levels of prosperity unimaginable in "savage" societies. The explanation for this paradox lay in the complexity of the modern division of labor, which so vastly increased productivity, and in the fact that private property provided such a powerful incentive to increase productivity. Hence there was no need to overcome an antinomy between property rights and basic human needs; it was by giving the exercise of property rights maximum play that the basic needs of all were best served. The legal order provided only the minimal framework for justice in this sense. A just distribution of wealth – one that did not require a legally imposed redistribution – was a product of the free market, the operation of a natural order discernible behind the apparent chaos of individual choices and actions.[49]

Even in the *Contribution*, Fichte's economic prognosis had little to do with this Smithian optimism. He did not share Smith's view that modern commercial growth was eliminating the antinomy between property rights and the satisfaction of basic needs even as it created unprecedented degrees of inequality. Instead he condemned rampant commercialization for creating mass hunger at the base of modern societies. And hunger, he stressed, was an absolute deprivation, not to be confused with the mere inability to continue a socially acquired consumer habit.

And yet in the *Contribution* Fichte saw no need to justify a substantial limitation of property rights to relieve hunger. He had begun to define property in terms of labor, it should be recalled, as part of an effort to make property a vehicle of freedom that did not require the existing

---

[48] Istvan Hont and Michale Ignatieff, "Needs and Justice in the *Wealth of Nations*: An Introductory Essay," in Hont and Ignatieff, eds., *Wealth and Virtue*, pp. 1–44.
[49] Ibid.

political and legal order for its legitimation. In one sense, property was an inalienable right. Through it the "pure I," the rational self of the conscience, sought to bring its sense being into agreement with itself. It was this moral self-mastery that became invested in things through labor and, by way of that investment, justified a right to exclusive use of things. Precisely because in this definition the right to property was a necessary condition of moral freedom, it did not require the state's coercive power and ought to lie beyond it. In the pursuit of self-interest through contracts, on the other hand, property (including control over one's labor) could be alienated. But Fichte's expectation was that under market forces the agrarian order would vastly increase its productivity at the same time it became more egalitarian. Those two changes, in fact, seemed reciprocal. No longer stifled by patrimonial restrictions, the rural laboring masses would apply their natural "powers" to becoming landed proprietors in their own right. As they did so, their labor would vastly increase in productivity.

The new departure in the *Naturrecht*, then, lay less in Fichte's diagnosis of modern social pathology than in his remedy for it. What is striking is how decisively the thrust of the transcendental deduction had turned Fichte's egalitarianism from promarket assumptions to a categorically antimarket vision. The first step had been to define the free self-positing of the "I," for purposes of the concept of law, as a process of individuation in interaction with other free sense beings. The effect was to deprive legal relationships of the categorical authority of moral imperatives but also to liberate them, one might say, from the need to meet the moral standard of pure autonomy. At the same time Fichte had had to think through what it meant, within his new transcendental deduction, to conceive of property in terms of labor. The result was a way of overcoming the antinomy of rights and needs that was fundamentally at odds with Smith's. Redefined as the universal right to work, the right to property guaranteed the satisfaction of basic human needs.

Again the full significance of Fichte's turn becomes clear against the backdrop of natural law discourse and its way of dealing with the issues raised by harvest shortages and the threat of famine. In such exceptional circumstances, should the local magistrates impose a maximum price on grain and bread, to keep them within reach of the laboring poor? Did theft become permissible if there was no other way to survive? The rights of the needy were defined in terms of consumption, not labor. In Fichte's *Naturrecht*, need and right fused in the concept of labor. As the means to satisfy the basic needs of consumption and as the medium for the reciprocal interaction without which individual freedom was inconceivable, work was the essential condition of self-formation. To guarantee everyone "property" in this sense was to respect a human right and fulfill a human need. Self-formation through labor became an entitlement that was just only if it was universal. The universal provision of labor was now the critical test of the justice of a legal order.

Fichte had not simply abandoned his earlier conviction that a free market in land and labor would realize the potential of the agricultural order. He had arrived at a categorical denial of Smith's contention that modern commercial societies reconciled gross inequality with the demands of justice. Where Smith saw the free market generating commercial growth through a spontaneous equilibrium of natural forces, Fichte consigned the market to the "blind" realm of mechanical laws operating without "concepts" (or, to put it another way, without rational volition). Ultimately, of course, self-interested market choices were blind because they were at the opposite pole from moral willing. For purposes of Fichte's theory of law, however, their immorality was, in a sense, secondary; what mattered was that reliance on the market left self-interest to operate without the mutual guarantees of freedom through self-restraint. The result was a force field, a play of power, without a legitimizing context. Just as the stronger had no reason to restrain themselves from taking advantage of the weaker, the weaker had no reason to respect the property rights of others. In the *Naturrecht* Fichte went so far as to argue that any "poor person" included in the civil contract had "an absolute right of coercion for support." If the civil contract could not secure him that right, it could not legitimately constrain him; he was "no longer legally bound to recognize anyone's property." It was in this sense that need grounded an "inalienable" right: "from the moment when someone suffers need, no one still owns that part of his property that is required as the contribution to pull someone out of need, but rather it belongs to the needy."[50]

Rather than expecting the modern division of labor to yield a just order, Fichte asked how, under his transcendental concept of law, the distribution of labor could be made just. The answer was that the state must secure viable work for all with a structural redistribution of wealth, on a limited but still significant scale. It was this argument, more than any other, that demonstrated how far Fichte's theory of justice had diverged from Kant's. One of Kant's formulations of the Categorical Imperative – the one that pointed most explicitly to its social implications – was this: "Act in such a way that you always treat humanity, whether in your own person or in the person of any other, never simply as a means, but always at the same time as an end."[51] The words "simply" and "at the same time" left ample room for interpretation, as became evident in Kant's argument for equality before the law in the essay on "theory and practice." Kant

observed that the "uniform equality of human beings as subjects of a state
is . . . perfectly consistent with the utmost inequality of the mass in the
degree of its possessions, whether these take the form of physical or
mental superiority over others, or of fortuitous external property and of
particular rights (of which there may be many) with respect to others."
Kant's tolerance for extremes of inequality may seem callous, but it
becomes more understandable when we recall that his target was the old-
regime corporate order, where the inherited legal privileges attached to
"birth" (or to rank) excluded others from rising in society. Here injustice
was defined in terms of the actions of individual wills. Kant's implicit
logic was that the person enjoying a legal privilege *was* morally responsible for an injustice; he in effect consented to enjoy privilege at the
expense of others, and hence used the law as a coercive instrument of his
own will. The material advantages of property, on the other hand, were
"fortuitous" or accidental and hence did not implicate the individuals
who enjoyed them. For the person lacking such advantages, the explanation lay "with circumstances for which he cannot blame others."
There was no "fault" to be attributed to "the irresistible will of any
outside party."[52]

Fichte's very different conclusions about the relationship between property and justice in the *Naturrecht* flowed from his reconception of selfhood and the rights attached to it. Having set out with the conviction
that the Categorical Imperative could not ground a concept of law, he
ended by expanding the concept of the rational freedom of the I to
include its empirical efficacy, its right to appropriate Nature through work
as a form of self-activity. A just order was one in which "*even in commerce*
each would remain a purpose, and no one would become the means of
another in any way." Or as he put it with only slightly more qualification, if a "dam" was to be set against "*blind nature*," each person would
have to be used "as co-purpose (*MitZweck*), in no way merely as a means
for the purpose of another."[53] Behind the apparently minor variations in
wording, Fichte was pursuing a logic that Kant's preoccupation with individual moral responsibility precluded.[54] There was a sense in which injustice was inherent in the very structure of inequality in economic and
social life. Even if the individual did not will to reduce others to things,
he was implicated in the structural injustice that had that effect – and
hence he shared in the collective responsibility to correct it. The corol-

[52] *Kant. Political Writings*, pp. 75–7.   [53] GA, II, 6: 5, 7.
[54] On this aspect of Kant's thought, see esp. Howard Williams, *Kant's Political Philosophy* (New York,
1983), pp. 69–94; Victor J. Seidler, *Kant, Respect and Injustice. The Limits of Liberal Moral Theory*
(London, 1986), pp. 68–116. Seidler argues that for the most part Kant did not consider that "social
relations of inequality" could be "proper objects of moral assessment without questioning the
autonomy of morality" (Ibid., p. 82).

lary of his own right to property – that is, of his own right to an autonomous share of work – was his legal obligation to redistribute wealth to the extent necessary to secure viable work to all.

★ ★ ★

If the *Naturrecht* revealed Fichte's capacity for stubborn eccentricity, the *Handelsstaat* made him seen downright quixotic. He was as opposed to reform sentiments gaining currency in the 1790s as he was to defenses of the old order. In 1796, when the *Naturrecht* appeared, *The Wealth of Nations* was finally beginning to have an impact on the mainstream of economic thought in German universities. Fichte was not, to be sure, bucking a German tide of wholesale conversions to Smith's free-market principles. In their German reception, the new rationales for market freedom were diluted as they were incorporated into a Kantian conception of civil society and as they were accommodated to the long-standing statist assumptions of cameralist theory.[55]

Where other German thinkers domesticated the new political economy, however, Fichte rejected it categorically. It was not simply that he conceived of a national economy as the object of minute state regulation. He opened the second book of the *Handelsstaat* by relegating the advocates of free international trade to the category of "non-thinker[s]." That was his way of saying that, like his other opponents, they could not rise above the ideological assumptions of their own era. Unable to imagine rational alternatives to the present situation, their "incurable disease" was to "take the *accidental* for the *necessary*."[56] In an unusually detailed indictment of modern economic life, Fichte sketched out an alarming scenario, calculated to demolish the assumption that in relationships of interdependence in a global division of labor, each nation would be serving its own interests. Free trade created relationships of mutually exploitative dependence. With a common currency in gold and silver, the international market was turning the European states and their colonial empires into the modern equivalent of Hobbes's state of nature, "an endless war of all against all in the trading *Publikum*." Under anarchic competition, the national wealth of each state was actually dwindling. The "war between sellers and buyers" intensified as global population increased, as the states grew in territory through colonial acquisitions, and as production increased. The resulting overproduction brought mass pauperization and emigration. Ultimately there would be severe labor shortages, which would cause a collapse in the production of manufactured goods.[57]

---

[55] Keith Tribe, *Governing Economy. The Reformation of German Economic Discourse, 1750–1840* (Cambridge, 1988), esp. pp. 133–82.
[56] GH, p. 113.   [57] GH, pp. 114–22.

Fichte accompanied this dire prognosis with an exercise in conjectural history very different from Smith's. Setting his argument within the Scottish Enlightenment's theory of historical stages, Smith expected free international trade to complete Europe's transition from the oppressive localism of feudalism to the material affluence and the civil freedom of commercial civilization. To Fichte the same openness, far from being a vehicle of progress, was an "accidental" relic from a bygone era of European unity under Christianity and Roman law. Free trade had once been tolerable only because under primitive economic conditions there had been little danger that manufacturing would enter crises of overproduction or would fail to meet consumer expectations. It was the modern states that were, or at least could be, the carriers of progress; and with their emergence free trade had become a destructive anachronism. Having already formed a self-enclosed political and legal whole, the state must now complete its maturation with an economic policy aimed at autarchy.

If Fichte left no doubt about his opposition to the new political economy, his relationship to mercantilism and its German cameralist variant is not so easily defined. In an unpublished set of reflections on "state economy," he himself took exception to being "misunderstood" as an advocate of cameralist policies. In a sense, "the postulation of general freedom of trade" was the lesser of two evils; it at least "aims at placing (physical) necessity at the rudder, instead of the reigning *arbitrariness* (*Willkühr*) in the usual restrictions." His purpose was to replace *Willkühr* (as well as physical necessity) with a system "aimed at moral necessity, and well-considered art."[58]

What struck Fichte about the status quo was that cameralist policies merely overlay anarchic competition, rather than replacing it; and the result was the worst of both worlds. The existing states were still oppressive machines, as they had been in the *Contribution*. But whereas earlier Fichte had condemned the existing governments for preserving and feeding off a multitiered hierarchy of corporate privilege, he now indicted them for maintaining great wealth in the midst of growing poverty. The state used the law "to maintain the *Bürger* in the state of possession in which one finds him." Even if one accepted that "one-sided" objective, the means were obviously inadequate. National economies were trapped in mutually destructive wars of protectionism and underselling. The irony was that even as they imposed "incomplete measures," the states left intact the assumption that "each individual has claim to all advantages that his power (*Kraft*) can secure him in the immense republic of trade, of which he is an independent and free member." Hence governments faced wide-

---

[58] "Ueber Staatswirtschaft," GA, II, 6 (1983): 7. The editors advise "a certain caution" about concluding that this manuscript was written sometime in the summer of 1800 (when Fichte was writing *Handelsstaat*); it could also have been written in connection with Fichte's *Rechtslehre* of 1812. The internal evidence suggests strongly, however, that the earlier date is correct.

spread resentment for imposing taxes and trade restrictions at the same time they tolerated exploitative wealth; and in reaction to popular efforts at deception, a parasitic "army of top-level and petty officials" came into being.[59]

Fichte's ultimate point, of course, was that the objective *was* "one-sided" and the measures taken *were* incomplete. A just state was one that accepted its "deeper-lying duty," which was "to install each in the property owed to him." That required a state-maintained equilibrium in the division of labor, which would not be possible until perfunctory efforts at closure acceded to a thoroughgoing policy of autarchy.

In the second book of the *Handelsstaat*, the object of Fichte's wrath was the current practice of mercantilism throughout Europe. Was he nonetheless engaged in a reformulation of the assumptions and values that had informed the specifically German discourse of cameralism? In one fundamental sense, he clearly was not. When Kant attacked the paternalism of eighteenth-century governments, cameralism was one of his prime targets. In the *Naturrrecht* and the *Handelsstaat*, as in the *Contribution*, Fichte saw himself following through on this campaign, with the difference now, of course, that his view of justice, unlike Kant's, necessitated a more equitable distribution of wealth. The irony is that this vision of justice – pitted as it was in principle against paternalist tutelage and designed as it was to maximize freedom through the provision of work – produced a blueprint for statism that went far beyond cameralist ambitions.

It is an irony that points to underlying continuities. As Fichte in effect admitted with the phrase "incomplete measures," the cameralist legacy had shaped his vision in some ways. It was no accident that he echoed cameralist language, particularly with his use of the term "equilibrium." Though his social contract theory was designed to transform radically the legitimation of state authority, he too looked to a machinelike state as the creator of social and economic order, and indeed as the only source of coercive force that could mediate tensions and redress imbalances. There can be no doubt that his key ideas – the definition of justice in terms of the distribution of freedom and constraint, and the concept of property as labor – had a radically egalitarian thrust. Unlike Kant, he did not stop at eliminating inherited legal rights; he wanted a "relative" equality in living standards. But "relative" allowed for considerable differences; Fichte considered it obvious that in his more egalitarian order, people who did intellectual work would need (and deserve) a more refined lifestyle than farmers.[60] He was not simply betraying the snobbery of the academic. If his egalitarianism was reinforced by a moral disapproval of superfluous consumerism, it was also counterbalanced by a quasi-corporate logic that had pervaded cameralist discourse. To replace "birth" with function as the

[59] GH, pp. 133–5.   [60] GH, p. 87.

decisive criterion for social rewards was to reduce hierarchy to a considerable degree but also to modernize it. Differences in the public importance of occupations, and in their corresponding work cultures, would be
marked by differences in lifestyles. If some legitimate needs were purely
human, others were status-specific.

The concern with production brings us to the final continuity between
cameralism and Fichte's theories of law and political economy. In the long
view, they were two moments in the secularization of the Lutheran ethic
of calling. Arguably neither moment would have occurred if work, in the
form of the calling, had not been sanctified in the Lutheran economy
of salvation. But now the sanctification took a secular form; work was
revalued as the self-disciplined use of human energy to increase productivity in a rational division of labor. In the modern economy's increasingly complex intermeshing of roles, people validated themselves, socially
and ultimately morally, through their work. The corollary to the right to
work was that the human being could not validate himself without
working. In the *Naturrecht* and the *Handelsstaat*, Fichte spelled out
categorically what cameralist discourse had already implied: in the new
order, unlike the status hierarchy of the old regime, there could be no
parasitism. Just as there could be "no poor" in the rational state, there
could be no "slackers." The right to work and the duty to work were
inseparable.[61]

★ ★ ★

"There is nothing higher on earth than the People," Fichte declared in
his discussion of state laws in the *Naturrecht*. In a letter to Reinhold, who
objected to this view, Fichte insisted that only the "nation" (or the *Volk*)
"has the right to equate *its* decision with the decision of pure Reason."[62]
This position was not as incompatible with his statism as it might at first
seem. Though he had put the *Contribution* behind him, Fichte was still,
in his way, a radical Kantian supporter of the French Revolution. In
recasting the concept of the General Will to serve his deduction of the
concept of law, he had formulated a transcendental rationale for the
principle that the only legitimate government was one resting on, and
accountable to, the sovereignty of the People.

But how could the People exercise its right to speak as the voice of
pure Reason if all its members were completely subject to a formidable
machinery of law? Fichte recognized the potential contradiction but
sought to avoid it with another system of forces in equipoise. Under
normal circumstances, the nation would transfer (or alienate) its sovereignty to an "administrator of the executive power." This was the state, a

[61] NR, pp. 206–9; GH, pp. 91–2.   [62] GA, III, 3: 72: NR, p. 179.

"higher seat of judgment" to which the nation, dissolved into an aggregate of individual subjects, subordinated itself. Fichte envisioned a single, unitary corps, fusing administration of the law with judicial interpretation, with no legislative body juxtaposed to it. In the event that this corps made itself suspect of abusing the People's trust, its authority would be suspended; the supreme judge would suddenly become the defendant in a national trial. In such cases a second institution – Fichte called it the ephorat, a term evoking both classical and Protestant precedents – would announce a "state interdict" (Staatsinterdikt), which suspended public force and called the nation together in local communities. Before this national audience the ephorat would assume the role of plaintiff. The executive corps had to defend itself against formal charges, and the reconstituted nation, serving as a jury, rendered a verdict. The stakes were high; whatever the nation-as-jury decided would become "constitutional law," and whoever lost – the executives or the ephors – would be guilty of high treason.[63]

Fichte offered this dualistic structure as a necessary deduction, entirely within the pure theory of law. How the deduction would be applied in an actual set of constitutional arrangements, adapted to the contingent particularities of time and place, was a subject for the separate Wissenschaft of politics.[64] Depending on the particular circumstances of the community, the executive corps might be filled by election, or by cooption, or even by heredity. Whatever the constitutional arrangement, the critical element, the guarantee against an "Asiatic despotism," was the accountability of the executive to the ephorat. As Fichte explained in his review of Kant's essay on "eternal peace," the executive could safely function as an "absolute positive power" precisely because an "absolute negative power" was juxtaposed to it:

> [The executive corps] is unappealable; all private persons are subject to it without restriction, and any opposition to it is rebellion. Only the People (Volk) is the judge of how it administers the law, and it must necessarily reserve its judgment on that issue. But as long as that corps is in possession of its power, there is no People, but rather only a crowd of subjects; and no individual can say, the People should declare itself as the People, without making himself guilty of rebellion; and the executive power will never say that: only the People could constitute itself, but it cannot constitute itself if it does not exist. Hence alongside the executive power there must be another magistrate, an ephorat, which – it would not judge

---

[63] NR, pp. 149–78.
[64] See Fichte's comments on the Wissenschaft of Politik in "Ascetik als Anhang zur Moral," in GA, II, 5: 59–61, and Ives Radrizzani, "Fichte's Transcendental Philosophy and Political Praxis," in Rockmore and Breazeale, eds., New Perspectives, pp. 193–212.

– but, where it believes freedom and right to be in danger, always on its own responsibility, calls the People to be a court over [the executive authority].[65]

The passage is typical of the logic and the language of Fichte's effort to institutionalize the exercise of popular sovereignty as a resort in extremis, without making the state directly and continually accountable to it. Except for those rare moments when they assemble as a court, individuals are a collection of private persons, a "crowd of subjects" who would be "guilty of rebellion" if they confronted the state with public, collective opposition. The authority to which they are subject is their collective free will, and in that sense the state embodies their ongoing act of self-legisation; but rather than exercise their sovereignty in a legislative process, they have entrusted it to a "higher seat of judgment." When they do assume a public role, it is merely as jurors; they become an audience whose strictly circumscribed juridical assignment is to listen to a debate, weigh the evidence, and render a verdict.

Conspicuously absent from Fichte's rational polity is the eighteenth-century republican discourse of active citizenship. His commitment to freedom had little in common with Adam Ferguson's conviction that "the agitations of a free people, are the principles of political life." Like most of his German contemporaries, Fichte was intent on avoiding the kind of intensely participatory, conflictual political culture Ferguson had in mind.[66] His debt to the eighteenth century lay elsewhere, as the recurrent use of judicial metaphors – the language of trials, of plaintiffs and defendants, of jury verdicts – makes abundantly clear. With the ephorat he attempted to incorporate into his system the eighteenth-century trope of the *Publikum* as the highest court of appeal, the tribunal to which all, including the state, were accountable.

At least since the middle decades of the century, the expectations invested in the public-as-tribunal had rested on two inseparable assumptions. One was that if the public was to constitute a unitary will with unimpeachable authority, its individual members had to form their judgments independently, without being influenced by partial communities pursuing particular "interests." The other was that once the evidence was fully open to the public gaze, once the secrecy of court cabales and bureaucratic manipulations acceded to "publicity," public opinion could be expected to form into a rational consensus. Hence the public-as-tribunal promised to make government accountable but without encouraging the "agitations" and the endemic conflicts that a participatory political culture seemed to portend. It represented the unmediated formation

---

[65] GA, I, 3: 225–6.
[66] This reaction to Ferguson is emphasized in Fania Oz-Salzberger, *Translating the Enlightenment. Scottish Civic Discourse in Eighteenth-Century Germany* (Oxford, 1995).

of a collective will from individual judgments, bypassing the danger of chronic political contestation among interests blind to the public welfare.[67]

It was this discourse, so pervasive in the *Aufklärung*, that Fichte had imbibed as a young man and had brought to his efforts to mediate between the student orders at Jena and the Weimar court. For Fichte, as for many of his contemporaries, the appeal of the guiding trope was tenacious. Even as he saw himself completing the liberation of philosophy from eighteenth-century rationalism, he continued to equate the sovereignty of the People with the verdict of the public-as-tribunal. To the extent that he sought to advance beyond the received trope, it was by giving the public an institutional locus in the ephorat and in its constitution of the nation as a jury. He pointed out to a skeptical protégé that this was no small step. It did not suffice to require "publicity of public affairs." Publicity provided the People with knowledge, which was only "the condition of reaching the goal." What was needed was a "link"(*Mittelglied*) that would "lead to the goal," and that was the ephorat.[68] The ephorat gave public opinion what it had conspicuously lacked in the eighteenth-century metaphor of the tribunal: an actual legal recourse, a procedure in law for turning criticism into a reform of public life. The point – the purpose of the "state interdiction" and the subsequent trial – was to remedy injustices and not merely to expose them.

More striking, though, is that Fichte's faith in the ephorat allowed him to reject other ways of insuring the sovereignty of the People. Since the People could be assured of rendering its verdict and finding redress in a national trial, a revolution from below – a spontaneous popular revolt against injustice – would be virtually unthinkable. Fichte realized, of course, that there had to be ways for the subjects to take the initiative legitimately, to constitute themselves as a community of juror-citizens, even in the event that the ephorat failed to call an unjust government to account. He allowed for two exceptions, two scenarios in which a revolution from below might justify itself, though he clearly considered neither of them to be desirable or likely. One was a unanimous uprising, a people acting "as one man"; but that had never happened, and it would happen only if injustice had "risen to the highest level." The subjects might still constitute themselves as a People in response to the appeal of one or more "private persons." If this People, assembled as "judge,"

---

[67] See esp. Keith Michael Baker, "Public Opinion as Political Invention," in Baker, *Inventing the French Revolution* (Cambridge, 1990), pp. 167–99; Mona Ozouf, "L'opinion publique," in *The Political Culture of the Old Regime*, ed. Keith Michael Baker, *The French Revolution and the Creation of Modern Political Culture*, vol. 1 (Oxford, 1987), pp. 419–34; Roger Chartier, *The Cultural Origins of the French Revolution*, trans. Lydia G. Cochrane (Durham and London, 1991), esp. pp. 20–37; Anthony J. La Vopa, "Conceiving a Public: Ideas and Society in Eighteenth-Century Europe," *The Journal of Modern History* 64:1 (March, 1992): 79–116.

[68] Fichte to Johann Jakob Wagner, Sept. 9, 1797, in GA, III, 3: 79.

rendered its verdict against the executive authority, the "summoners" (*Auf-förderer*) became "preservers of the nation through their heart and their virtue, and, without being called, natural ephors." If the summoners' appeal went unheeded, however, they had made themselves rebels and the executive could punish them accordingly.[69]

On the issue of revolution from below Fichte was entirely in agreement with contemporaries who were quick to brand him an extremist. The course of events in France in the early 1790s seemed to confirm that a popular revolution brought violent disorder and the tyranny of the mob. Fichte's fear of the mob found expression in the very way he sought to justify a popular revolt. In a sense, the revolt was no revolt at all; it acquired legitimacy only because popular mobilization was channeled into the ordered process of a trial. The exercise of popular sovereignty was limited to an exceptional, clearly bounded moment of judgment. By its very definitiveness, the verdict guaranteed closure; and the result was less a change in the structure of the state than a renewal of its personnel.

Even this form of legal "revolution" would be unnecessary, of course, so long as the ephorat played its proper role. Like "public opinion" as a normative ideal, but now in an exceptional and concentrated moment, the national trial offered a rational alternative to the kind of political contestation that fractured the polity into partial, blindly self-interested solidarities and brought disorder and violence. There would be none of the murky controversy, none of the restricted vision that fractured communities. Granted a full view of the evidence – a clear description of the *Faktum* of the executive's behavior – the citizens as jury would find it "very easy" to choose with virtual unanimity between a decisive "Yes" and "No."[70] And the very form of the event insured against its spinning out of control. Fichte assured readers who might be horrified at the prospect of "[an] assembling of the People into a court" that "the lawless mob commits excesses, not the People assembled according to and under a law, and deliberating in a certain form." "Formulas," he added, require people "to go to work with care."[71]

By giving the metaphor of the tribunal a literal application, Fichte at once institutionalized popular sovereignty and severely contained it. The logic of juridical form not only dispelled the specter of revolution; it also made direct democracy a "completely illegal constitution." In a direct democracy, the People would be both party and judge in its own case; and from a legal standpoint – or, more precisely, from the standpoint of Fichte's deduction of the concept of law – that meant that the state would embody an intolerable contradiction. This argument made explicit what Fichte had left implicit in the *Contribution*: that for all his sympathy with

---

[69] NR, pp. 179–81.   [70] NR, p. 176.   [71] NR, p. 183.

Rousseauian populism, he regarded the direct, unmediated democracy advocated in *Of the Social Contract* as incompatible with both law and reason. He had given a Kantian spin to Rousseau's famous distinction between the General Will and the will of all. In its pure form, as a unanimous commitment to the Categorical Imperative, the General Will represented what ought to be. Fichte was more than willing to concede that the nation as jury might not express that will; his point was simply that in exceptional moments, when the People had to judge whether the state had been unjust, its verdict had to be respected *as though* it were the voice of Reason. But this was the exceptional moment of judgment; in the ongoing administration of the law, the People could not judge itself precisely because it was not in a position to be rational. To submit the clarification and interpretation of the law to direct popular approval was to subject it to "the crowd," which could yield "the true, common will" only "very impurely." Only an executive, perched on its legal platform above the mass of subjects, could "oversee the whole and all its needs" and see "that the strictest law reigns unbroken."[72]

More puzzling, at least at first glance, is Fichte's rejection of a "system of representation," by which he meant a nondemocratic but nonetheless representative legislature, sharing government authority with the executive in a constitutional "division of powers." He was probably familiar with the views of the Abbé Sieyès, the French politician and constitutional theorist who argued cogently for a representative legislature in the debates of the early 1790s. Sieyès saw the modern division of labor as an intricate network of "representation," with groups of experts delegating responsibilities to each other to maximize their freedom to engage in productive labor and to minimize personal (as opposed to structural) dependence. A national legislature was an integral part of such a society, the group of experts in government.[73]

Fichte shared Sieyès's positive estimation of the modern division of labor and his insistence on universal productivity. When he characterized the executive as an "estate (*Stand*) in the state" with its assigned property, he might be understood to be incorporating Sieyès's thought into his own theory of property-as-labor.[74] Hence it is all the more striking that he did not share Sieyès's enthusiasm for a representative legislature. If the whole could not judge itself, it also could not delegate its judgment to a part. Again we are reminded that Fichte was still plotting his way through

---

[72] NR, pp. 14–16. On the differences between the Fichte of the *Naturrecht* and Rousseau, see Schottky, *Untersuchungen*, pp. 348–62.
[73] Keith Baker, "Representation Redefined," in Baker, *Inventing the French Revolution*, pp. 244–51; William H. Sewell, Jr., *A Rhetoric of Bourgeois Revolution. The Abbé Sieyès and What Is the Third Estate?* (Durham and London, 1994), esp. pp. 80–108. In the summer of 1794, Fichte tried to arrange the publication of a German translation of a work by or about Sieyès; see GA, III, 2: 131, 183.
[74] NR, p. 64.

an eminently Kantian dichotomy between morality and nature. The effect was to reinforce the assumption, central to the eighteenth vision of the public as tribunal, that no partial community could transcend "interest" to provide disinterested judgment. From one standpoint, the issue was a moral one. To delegate one's judgment to a representative was to sacrifice autonomy for heteronomy, to surrender the personal freedom of conscience from which the public derived its moral authority. At the same time, in the force field of politics, power could not be divided; one force would eventually dominate. Either the nation would cease to be a counterweight to the executive as it tired of giving laws, or it would reduce the executive to a "will-less machine."[75]

Fichte's alternative division – the equipoise between an executive and an ephorat – left no space for organized political opposition; and in that, too, it was faithful to the eighteenth-century trope that guided it. In fact, it is fair to say that if in eighteenth-century French discourse "public opinion" promised "a politics without politics," Fichte's way of institutionalizing public opinion implied a polity without politics.[76] He himself would find this judgment surprising. His concern in the *Naturrecht* was with the pure theory of law, which could only establish the framework for the separate discipline of politics. But if politics means organized conflict and ceaseless negotiation, it was in effect precluded by Fichte's preoccupation with deducing a legal order that would make choices self-evident and would insure definitive resolutions.

The impulse to preclude politics explains some of the most striking details of Fichte's order. There would be no social context for negotiation between the executive and the ephorat; they could be connected neither by kin ties nor by friendly relationships, nor indeed by "intercourse (*Umgang*)."[77] Even if it was an elected body, the executive would represent the principle of legal detachment; it was not a form of political leadership with a constituency. Again it seemed imperative to prevent a social context from yielding a political culture, a bonding of leaders and constituents. In addition to enjoying the independence afforded by secure incomes, the executive must have "as few *Freundschaften*, connections, dependencies, and private persons as at all possible."[78] Only then would they have no "interest" but the common interest. In decisions about the form of government, and in the exceptional moment of a national trial, Fichte expected the People to yield complete unanimity or something very close to it. But he took care to make provision for a dissenting minority, however small it might be. If they did not choose to embrace the majority view, they would have to leave the territory of the state.[79]

---

[75] GA, III, 3: 80.
[76] The phrase "a politics without politics" is from Baker, "Public Opinion," p. 196.
[77] NR, pp. 177–8.   [78] NR, p. 164.   [79] NR, p. 177.

Hence no collective opposition could form; if unanimity did not emerge from below, it was legally guaranteed from above.

By the very nature of his vision, Fichte could not entertain the possibility that a political culture of negotiated contestation could be a viable alternative to a chaos of "interests." There were only two choices: complete consensus, or compulsory secession.

★ ★ ★

To say that Fichte's vision of a rational order had no room for "politics" is not to say that he had no political agenda. The course of events in France had posed fundamental political quandaries to his generation. Did the kind and degree of individual freedom proclaimed by the Revolution fatally undermine political authority? Was it possible to restore stability to a polity without imposing new contraints on the freedom of its individual members – constraints perhaps more severe than the ones that prerevolutionary regimes had enforced? With his experiment in a priori deduction in the *Naturrecht* Fichte sought to remove the resolution of these issues from the ideological maelstrom of the 1790s. In the way it reconfigured the relationship between the state and society, his new order would avoid what he saw as the despotism of both a democratic left and a neo-absolutist right.

It is typical of Fichte's preoccupations, however, that he did not advance from his pure theory of law to the *Wissenschaft* of politics and hence did not spell out the constitutional provisions for his new order. Instead he devoted his next lecture series to constructing a *Sittenlehre*, or a "system of moral doctrine." In the third part of the published version of the *Sittenlehre*, where he applies his moral theory to the social division of labor, the pivotal assumption in his strategy for reconciling freedom and authority becomes apparent. What mattered ultimately was not the details of constitution making but the functional and jurisdictional relationship between the state and the intelligentsia. Fichte's expectation was that the university-educated professions – the professoriate, the clergy, and state officialdom – would constitute a modern clerisy. It would be a strikingly dualistic clerisy, at once fused with the state and juxtaposed to it. The key institution – the one that made a legislative body superfluous – was the university, the site of both fusion and juxtaposition.[80]

The relevant sections of the *Sittenlehre* are brief and are distinguished by a kind of specificity that was largely absent from Fichte's lectures on "the mission of the scholar" in 1794. Where he had earlier evoked the rigors and exultations of initiation into a philosophical elect, he now

---

[80] On the concept of a "clerisy," see Ben Knights, *The Idea of the Clerisy in the Nineteenth Century* (Cambridge, 1978). On Fichte's view of the relationship between academic knowledge and the state, cf. Karl Hahn, *Staat, Erziehung, und Wissenschaft bei J.G. Fichte* (Munich, 1969).

offered a sober schematic breakdown of the clerisy into its subgroups, with emphasis on the precise way in which each group ought to be positioned between the state and the larger society.[81] This new concern was in itself a measure of the distance that separated the professor at Jena from the young man who had aspired to dispel academic ideology by popularizing Kant's self-evident truths. The outsider had become an academic insider, albeit one prone to bold departures from conventional wisdom. What now distinguished Fichte was his willingness to acknowledge a potentially paralyzing conflict to which most university-educated men were blind or indifferent. His recent experiences at Jena had heightened his awareness that the mission of the universities had become all the more problematic in the new era of philosophical critique. Was it possible for an intelligentsia to be "public" in two senses at once – as the voice of rational criticism, recognizing no limits in that capacity, and as the voice of public authority, contributing to the legitimation of state-enforced constraints?

Over the previous decade, as enlightened reform from above had acceded to religiously obscurantist and politically reactionary state policies, these questions had acquired a new urgency. Through the prism of confessionally driven politics and politically driven confessionalism, the German intelligentsia had had to confront the larger tensions inherent in its social and institutional situation. Conceived as the institutional loci of the "republic of scholars" – as the centers for free inquiry and unrestrained public expression – the universities assumed a key role in constituting a new civil society. In the German states, perhaps more than anywhere else in Europe, their presence made it conceivable that as the civil society in the making formed a new public culture, church and state would become increasingly accountable to public criticism. But the universities were also an integral part of the apparatus of church and state. As training centers for the clergy and government officialdom, they were the instruments of the very institutions which, in their other role, they were expected to judge with critical detachment. Could they really play both roles at once? Could they critique the institutional power of church and state even as they remained deeply complicit in its exercise?

Fichte's stormy debut at Jena – the charge of Jacobinism, the conflicts with theologians and clerical officials, the efforts of the Weimar court to keep him in line – had made him acutely aware of this conundrum. It was the same conundrum that Kant had been puzzling over for more than a decade, and a comparison of their attempts to solve it is instructive. Kant's best-known attempt – the one with which Fichte was surely familiar – was his essay on "enlightenment" in 1784. Intent on demonstrating that freedom of thought and expression was compatible with the

[81] SL, pp. 341–62.

imperatives of the Frederician bureaucratic state, Kant had drawn a clean distinction between the scholar's "public" freedom to reason without constriction before the entire "*reading public*" and his "private" obligation to conform in office. To illustrate how this duality might work, Kant used the examples of the pastor and the army officer. He did not apply his distinction to university professors, perhaps because he realized that it was especially problematic in their case.[82]

In the mid-1790s, reacting at least in part to his own experience of professorial vulnerability, Kant had to abandon his scholar/official dichotomy for a more intricate "division of labor" *among* the university faculties. By then *Religion within the Limits of Reason Alone* had made him a target of the Prussian censorship, and he had had to promise his sovereign that he would cease publishing and lecturing on religious subjects. In the autumn of 1798, in the immediate aftermath of the King's death, Kant published a set of essays he had written during his enforced silence. Entitled *The Conflict of the Faculties*, they began with a general consideration of the universities' division into faculties and proceeded to detailed analyses of the philosophy faculty's proper relationship to theology, law, and medicine.

Conspicuously absent from the *Conflict* was Kant's earlier distinction between the "public" and the "private" (i.e, official) roles of the educated man. Now he drew a sharp line between "scholars proper," most of whom were "incorporated" in the universities, and the university-educated men who, as "technicians of learning," were "instruments of the government."[83] It was by delineating the proper jurisdictions of the incorporated faculties of the universities, in their relationships with each other and with the state, that he sought to insure progressive change within a political order of unshakeable stability.

Kant retained the traditional nomenclature, which distinguished the philosophy faculty, as the "lower" corporation, from the "higher" faculties of theology, law, and medicine. But that was an ironic gesture; in his transcendental revaluation of their division of labor, the lower faculty ascended to the position of epistemological and moral preeminence. The responsibility of the higher faculties was to transmit public authority under direct government sanction, and for that purpose they "base the teachings which the government entrusts to them on *writings*" rather than on reason. The biblical theologian "draws his teaching not from reason

---

[82] "An Answer to the Question: 'What is Enlightenment?,'" in *Kant. Political Writings*, pp. 55–7.

[83] Immanuel Kant, *The Conflict of the Faculties*, trans. Mary J. Gregor (New York, 1992), p. 25. Gregor's introduction is informative on the circumstances in which Kant wrote the various pieces of *Conflict*. Gregor suggests that Kant added the introduction, on the "division of labor" among the faculties, in an unsuccessful effort to pull three disparate essays into a coherent framework. She may well be correct, but as a general statement on the universities and their role in the public sphere, the introduction is important in its own right. Ibid., p. xxv.

but from the *Bible*," and likewise the professor of law works not from "natural law" but from "the *law of the land*."[84] The reference to "writings" was Kant's way of saying that the higher faculties dealt with repositories of recorded traditions, procedures, and rules. Acting as trustees of the state, they communicated publicly the historically contingent formulations with which a community ordered itself. While they confined themselves to that role, to the exclusion of speculative reasoning, the lower faculty offered the needed counterpoint of rational critique – and the result was a via media between immobilism and destabilizing skepticism. It was in this capacity, as the voice of critique, that the lower faculty was really the higher. "It is absolutely essential," Kant argued, "that the learned community at the university also contain a faculty that is independent of the government's command with regard to its teachings, one that, having no commands to give, is free to evaluate everything, and concerns itself with the interests of the sciences, that is, with truth: one in which reason is authorized to speak out publicly."[85]

There was something deeply paradoxical if not blatantly self-contradictory about Kant's ideal university. Pure *Wissenschaft* would be an integral part of a state institution, but it would operate entirely free of state authority and hence would not be even indirectly complicit in the exercise of political power. Its power took the purely moral form of truth; and that was why, in the face of the political knowledge that Kant consigned to the realm of mere "utility," it was the final arbiter.

In the *Conflict*, Kant reaffirmed his conviction that progressive change need not threaten public authority, but he no longer saw that change as the product of an unmediated interaction between the state and an educated public. The officials and clergymen who figured so prominently in the larger German public were no longer free to speak publicly in the arena of print. They had become mere instruments of government, technicians who could *not* contradict the "teachings" of church and state publicly. The source of orderly change was the interfaculty contestation within the university, which, precisely because it was a kind of corporate enclave, served as a micropublic. Within the segregated "public" space of the university, the lower faculty could not presume to deny the text-based expertise of the higher faculties; but it must judge them from a higher vantage point, by subjecting their teachings to the rational critique that it alone, as the disinterested practitioner of *Wissenschaft*, could provide. The technicians changed their teaching only if and when the higher faculties, persuaded by the lower faculty's voice of reason, commanded them to do so.

Even as he claimed that radical independence was the right and indeed the duty of scholars like himself, Kant sought to demonstrate that it was

[84] Ibid., p. 33–5.   [85] Ibid., pp. 27–9.

in the interest of the state to sponsor this division of labor. The beauty of his schema was that it provided a kind of unlimited freedom to criticize but without in any way throwing the authority of the state into question, and indeed without making the state immediately accountable to any form of public will. The contestation was not between the community of scholars in the looser sense (university-educated men) and the government, but among university-based scholars. From the state's standpoint, Kant argued, this arrangement had several advantages. It meant that the public critique of government was deflected into the intra-university critique of one faculty by another. It excluded "the people," who were simply "incompetent," from the process of critique and insured that the instruments of government would not exploit the people's incompetence to become a power unto themselves. If the state did not allow the philosophy faculty to exercise critique within the closed space of the university's walls, Kant warned, it might pay a high price. It exposed itself to the danger that in a wider public debate, the higher faculties and their bureaucratic extensions would usurp power with demagogic appeals to the population at large.[86]

Here again, as in several other essays, Kant asserted the authority of "theory" over "practice," of normative universals over the blinkered "practical" vision that mistook the historically given for the sacrosanct. His politically cast argument was designed to vest the role of public conscience in the humanistic disciplines, and particularly in philosophy itself. If the *Conflict* was a bold counteroffensive, however, it was also a striking retreat, marking the degree to which Kant had been chastened by both obscurantist government policies and popular disorders over the previous decade. It was not simply that, in his effort to secure unconditional autonomy for the philosophy faculty, he denied the considerable body of officials and clergymen the public freedom of expression he had wanted them to enjoy in 1784. That reversal marked a larger shift from the eighteenth-century ideal of the public as an open arena, an alternative to the corporate fragmentation of old-regime society, to a kind of corporate closure. Kant's assurances that "the people" were "incompetent" and that they were in any case uninterested in academic disputes, spoke volumes.[87] It was the corporate segregation of the universities from the society at large that made them safe forums for the exercise of critique. If the mission of the universities was to mediate between the state and society, it was in a way that treated the latter as a body of subjects rather than as a civil society in the making. Rather than being drawn into the process of critique, society received its results in the form of "commands."

What is immediately striking about Fichte's schema in the *Sittenlehre* is that he wanted clergymen and officials to remain participating members

<hr />

[86] Ibid., pp. 51, 57.   [87] Ibid., p. 25.

of the "learned republic," with the public freedom of expression that Kant had extended to them in 1784 but was now denying them. That in turn marked the larger difference in their visions. Fichte did not share Kant's conclusion that if reason and the state were to be protected from each other, they had to confine themselves to the separate spheres of pure *Wissenschaft* and political power. He was intent on connecting the university to the sociey and the polity, on identifying the medium that would allow mutual engagement without undermining their proper (and safe) division of labor. Fichte called that medium the "symbol" (*Symbol*), and he distinguished between the "invisible church" that grasped timeless truths and the "visible church" that subscribed to the symbolic representation of those truths in a historically specific community.

It was Luther, of course, who had originally posited the distinction between an invisible church and a visible church. Here again Fichte wanted his voice to sound within the Lutheran tradition, indeed, to resonate through it, though he imagined a community that was far removed from Lutheran fideism. His choice of the term "symbol" reminds us how deeply his vision of a new political order had been shaped by the politics of religious contestation in the late German Enlightenment. The most obvious allusion was to the Symbolic Books, the repository of the formulas of confessional orthodoxy to which Woellner and his king had wanted university professors as well as clergymen to conform. But attentive readers might also have heard echoes of the Neologists' rational theism, and indeed of Kant's moral theology in *Religion within the Limits of Reason Alone*. In these alternatives to Orthodoxy, the pure moral truth of religion had been distinguished from its more or less opaque representations in the symbols specific to a historical community at a particular stage of development. The "enlightened" few – the members of the invisible community – did not reject the symbols that bound the majority in a visible church, much less deny them publicly. They simply pierced through them, to their rational core of truth.

In the *Sittenlehre*, Fichte put the concept of the symbol to a related but different use, so that it kept the "learned" public safely detached from the "unlearned" mass; at the same time it offered a way to integrate the two gradually into something like a unitary community, where "the will of each is really universal law." The paradox of the symbol was that it expressed universal truths, but only by embodying them in a historically contingent "shell" of sense images. The "essence of any possible symbol" was a moral belief in the supersensible. While the shell of Protestant representations still left that belief partially obscured, it also served as the vital condition of communication between the public community, bound by creedal unity, and the "learned public" that "sees farther." The symbol was the shared assumption that the enlightened few, though not accepting its impurities "inwardly," could accept publicly as the culture's moral point of departure. As such it was also the medium of connection; working through the symbol in public communication, the learned public had the opportunity to "elevate" its audience gradually, so that public culture as a whole would approach, though it could never reach, a state of pure universality in which the historically contingent has been shed. Thus "the spirit of Protestantism," which lay in continual "elevation of the symbol," worked through history, and in the process, the conflict between "the absolute freedom of conscience of individuals" and "a stable church and state" was resolved.[88]

From this vision of moral progress, Fichte drew several implications about the proper division of labor between the universities, the state, and the larger society. As a preserve of the "learned republic," the university – and that meant all its faculties – had to be allowed to practice internally an "absolute democracy." There the "chains of the church symbol" have been cast off; everything is open to doubt; and "nothing is valid there but the right of the intellectually stronger." The state granted this exceptional freedom to its professors, including those in law and theology, though they lived off its salaries and trained its officials. And since the officials (including clergymen) were trained as true "scholars," they would live in the split world Kant had called for in 1784 – forbidden to question the creedal unity of the symbol in their official capacities, but free to express their "dissenting convictions" in learned journals. Only under these conditions could reason work through the symbol, "indirectly" but effectively, without either rejecting it or becoming paralyzed in conforming to it.[89]

Fichte's variation on the concept of the symbol confirmed what his lectures and publications over the previous few years had made clear. He no longer assumed that self-evident truth, broadcast in a new philosophical rhetoric, would simply lift the veil of ideology; hence, he had abandoned his earlier tendency to conceive of mass enlightenment as a spiritual revolution, the communal regeneration effected in a revelatory moment. The concept of the symbol marked his need for a middle term between truth and ideology, a kind of ideological medium, opaque but malleable, through which to advance gradually toward a rational community. Though he had stepped back from his youthful philosophical radicalism, he was clearly trying to avoid Kant's retreat to corporate closure. The freedom that Kant wanted confined to the philosophy faculty Fichte extended to the university as a whole. In Kant's schema, the professional faculties form the zone of mediation, where pure scholarship, the free inquiry of pure reason, and the historically contingent ideology imposed by church and state must adjust to each other. For Fichte, the zone of mediation is the representation of public consensus outside the university.

[88] SL, pp. 238–42, 343–50.   [89] SL, pp. 246–50.

While the symbol is a representation of authority, and hence something the scholar must reject inwardly, it is also the stock of words and images through which he gradually removes the need for authority. Communication through the symbol necessarily keeps knowledge veiled to a degree, but it also rescues knowledge from corporate ghettoization.

Neither Kant's nor Fichte's division of labor is likely to strike us as viable. Each in its way seems naïve in its exemption of "pure" scholarship from the dangers of ideological distortion, and each in its way restricts public discourse to a degree that has become unacceptable in modern western societies. They remain significant, however, because they register an awareness of the German intelligentsia's structural dilemmas and because they give us a sense of the range of perceived choices.

The distinguishing features of Fichte's schema can be explained in part by the epistemological ambitions of his quest for "system." Determined to demonstrate that, as derivatives of the same primal insight, all genuine *Wissenschaften* had separate but equal truth status, he could not go Kant's route and distinguish between the rationality of the philosophy faculty and the mere utility of the other faculties. But Fichte was also trying to resolve, from his new position and in this reformulation, the dilemma he had confronted as a young man in search of a public voice. He still wanted to combine the freedom of a kind of spiritual elect with the emotional sustenance that only membership in a larger community could provide and with the capacity to "have an effect" on that community. Hence, his university-educated men formed a clerisy that segregated itself from the larger society but at the same time connected with it, and indeed connected on its terms. The clerisy would be an intellectual and moral vanguard that saw farther, beyond the limited horizons of its historical situs; but it would also be able and willing to put on blinders when a self-enforced restriction of vision was a requirement of public efficacy.

Within a few months of the appearance of the *Sittenlehre*, Fichte himself would inadvertently put this way of situating the universities between state and society, reason and ideology, to a severe test.

Chapter 11

Men and Women

A fatally flawed "philosophical adventure," one reviewer concluded. Another extolled a brilliant exercise in a priori reasoning – one that distilled the "essence" of marriage and saved "the dignity of the female nature."[1] The text in question was Fichte's deduction of "the concept of marriage," which appeared as a supplement to the *Naturrecht* entitled "Outline (*Grundriss*) of Family Law." With characteristic aggressiveness, Fichte had added the voice of Transcendental Idealism to an increasingly polarized discussion of a cluster of issues: the nature of human sexuality; the differences between males and females in physiology, temperament, and intellectual capacity; marriage and the family as moral communities and as legal institutions; and the proper division between the public and the private, or domestic, spheres. He returned to the same themes, in a shorter treatment, in the *Sittenlehre*. Both texts have been largely ignored in the recent renewal of interest in Fichte's philosophy of law, but in feminist scholarship they have become notorious.[2]

Virtually every conclusion Fichte drew was likely to displease, or at least to unsettle, some of his readers. Spouses learned, for example, that their marriage was morally legitimate only if it bonded them in reciprocal "love"; legal details aside, a divorce occurred as soon as one spouse stopped loving the other. Confirmed bachelors were told that they had forfeited their chance to become fully human; that was possible only in marriage. But it was women, and especially women sympathetic to an incipient feminism, who were most likely to take issue with Fichte. The female reader was told that when she married, she ceased to be a "juridical person" and entered an exclusively "domestic" life, where her "love" for her husband took the form of complete and exclusive subjection to his will and unlimited willingness to sacrifice herself to his needs.

---

[1] FR 2: 91, 120–2.

[2] The major exception to the neglect of the supplement in the history of philosophy and political theory is Susan Shell, "'A Determined Stand': Freedom and Security in Fichte's *Science of Right*," *Polity* 25:1 (Fall, 1992): 95–121, which provides an insightful explication of Fichte's view of marriage within the framework of his deduction of the concept of law. See also Daniel Morrison, "Women, Family, and the State in Fichte's Philosophy of Freedom," in Tom Rockmore and Daniel Breazeale, eds., *New Perspectives on Fichte* (Atlantic Highlands, N.J., 1996), pp. 179–91. Morrison faults Fichte for failing to offer reasons for "his claim that the man and not the woman ought to be the family's representative in the public domain" but leaves us wondering what "prejudice of [Fichte's] era" this failure represents.

Within the privacy of the household, the husband exercised unlimited sovereignty, and that included control over the property his wife had brought to the marriage. In the public sphere of law (including property) and politics, he was the sole representative of the family.

It is not hard to see why contemporary feminist scholars have singled out Fichte as the "chief ideologue of bourgeois patriarchalism."[3] They may be underestimating the competition for that title, but Fichte is certainly a leading contender. If patriarchalism means the subordination of women to male authority, his thinking was patriarchal with a vengeance. It was also bourgeois, though in a loose sense, not to be confused with more precise (and more rigid) ideological meanings of "bourgeois." To the extent that his ideal of marriage had a social correlative in the late eighteenth century, it was the kind of conjugal relationship and culture of domesticity to be found in, among other social circles, the educated and propertied *Bürgertum* of German-speaking Europe.

And yet Fichte's patriarchalism, as uncompromising as it seems, is not without its idiosyncrasies, and some of them give his deduction a quite progressive coloration in the context of its era. One of his conclusions was that women outside marriage – the unmarried, the divorced, and the widowed – ought to have the same civic rights as men, with the exception of the right to hold public office. Equally contrarian was his position on divorce. In 1804 the Napoleonic Civil Code, retreating from the new French divorce laws of 1792, would allow divorce only on grounds of ill-treatment, criminal conviction, or adultery; and on adultery it discriminated blatantly against women. In Fichte's view, the wife, unlike the husband, should make every effort to forgive her partner's infidelity, but she was not obliged to do so. Morally, a divorce occurred at the moment when *either* spouse stopped loving the other, and adultery by either spouse was a sure marker of that moment. Divorce law simply confirmed the end of the marriage and protected the legal rights on both sides.[4]

Or consider Fichte's view of arranged marriages, which were still common in the late eighteenth century, particularly in the upper reaches of the social hierarchy, where inherited titles and substantial wealth were at stake. Fichte's opposition to this practice could not have been more emphatic, and it was the violation of the woman's freedom of choice that he found most inexcusable. "Marriage," Fichte argued, "must be concluded with absolute freedom." Parents who "forced" a daughter to marry someone against her will committed a punishable offense – an offense that was in a sense more "harmful" than rape, since it was calculated to

---

[3] Ute Gerhard, *Verhältnisse und Verhinderungen. Menschen Rechte haben (k)ein Geschlecht* (Frankfurt am Main, 1981), pp. 142–4.

[4] NR, pp. 322–7. On the divorce provisions of the Napoleonic Code, see Martyn Lyons, *Napoleon Bonaparte and the Legacy of the French Revolution* (New York, 1994), pp. 98–102.

make the woman the unwilling "instrument" of a man for the rest of her life. To claim that the girl had been "persuaded" to comply with her parents' will was nonsense; persuasion under these circumstances was simply another form of coercion. As soon as she left her parent's home to enter such a marriage, the daughter could go to law to reclaim her right to freedom of choice. The parents would forfeit not only authority over their daughter but also control over the property coming to her. If the daughter did not press a charge, the state could do so on her behalf.[5]

Fichte's deduction was pitted against tradition in another sense: he did not make state law on marriage the instrument of church policy. If he had done so, of course, he would have flatly contradicted the axiomatic principle of his theory of law: that law, because it was an instrument of coercion, should not intrude on the inner freedom of the moral agent. Instead he applied rigorously the principle of the separation of church and state – a principle that had a long pedigree in the Enlightenment and that had led the French National Assembly to remove marriage from clerical authority by declaring it a civil contract in 1791. While Fichte had no objection to clergymen admonishing members of their confessional community on matters of sexual and marital behavior, he allowed them no role in the state's legal regulation in these areas. He went remarkably far, in fact, in tolerating legally behavior that was immoral from a confessional standpoint, and indeed morally repugnant from his own standpoint. Adultery – whether by the husband or by the wife – was not punishable by law, though it automatically ended the marriage as a moral union. Neither was "public" concubinage, so long as the woman had entered it voluntarily. Fichte denied prostitution the status of a legitimate trade (*Gewerbe*) on the grounds that there would be no need for people to resort to it in his state-regulated economy. But if prostitution was not the woman's "fixed station" – if it was practiced alongside another trade – it must be tolerated. Fichte's rational state would take no notice of such "irregularities."[6]

★ ★ ★

These unconventional features of Fichte's thinking about sexuality and marriage may be characterized as "liberal," but that does not imply that his thinking was progressive. In recent feminist literature, in fact, we find a brief for the opposite verdict: that as a "liberal" ideologue, Fichte articulated, or at least anticipated, an approach to marriage that, far from being progressive, aimed to replace old-regime patriarchy with a new and in some ways more discriminatory regime. The issue is complicated by the fact that the relationship between the formation of liberal ideology in the

[5] NR, pp. 314–17. [6] NR, pp. 329–31.

late eighteenth and early nineteenth centuries and the articulation of modern marriage laws during the same period has been conceived in different ways. In one view, the reconception of marriage and marriage law was integral to the process in which liberalism imposed a new "sexual system." Marriage, in the ideal, was emblematic of the civic morality of a self-regulating civil society. Once civil society entrenched itself in law, its "practitioners" demanded that "the state reenter the moral sphere to uphold its [gendered] values" of individual self-determination and productivity, with legitimate "willed desire" attributed only to males.[7] To construe Fichte's thinking on marriage as liberal in this sense, we would have to ignore the fact that in the *Naturrecht* he purposely chose not to conceive of civil society as a norm-generating community and instead sought to structure a civil society whose members could not be expected to follow moral rules. Marriage, however, was another matter entirely. Fichte insisted that marriage was essentially a moral association, and that was precisely why it had to be dealt with in a supplement, as an exception to the contractual logic of reciprocal self-interest at the heart of Fichte's concept of law.

The alternative approach is to make contractualism the defining feature of liberalism. In that case, "the internal order of the marriage association" becomes the glaring exception to the rule in a new liberal order, a throwback to feudal terms of rule and subordination in a society otherwise ordered by "the logic of private autonomy" in civil contracts. The dilemma of nineteenth-century liberals was to find "an argumentative strategy that would shelter the husband's prerogatives against the logic of equal liberty without, however, jeopardizing the credibility of liberal principles in general."[8] Again the framework of the *Naturrecht* makes Fichte's contribution at best an eccentric variation. Certainly his point of departure – his aim to maximize individual freedom in a field of contractual relationships – fits this definition of liberalism. But if Fichte grounded civil society, in principle, in a "logic of private autonomy," he also subsumed it under a tutelary and interventionist state to such a degree that by liberal standards, it was hardly a civil society at all. There is no doubt that his conception of marriage was meant to give traditional gendered terms of rule and subordination a new lease on life; and yet, in contrast

[7] Isabel V. Hull, *Sexuality, State, and Civil Society in Germany, 1700–1815* (Ithaca and London, 1996), esp. pp. 1–7, 314–23, 407–11. Hull argues that whereas in Kant's thought the "sexual assumptions" of early liberals were "implicit," Fichte's "sexual theories" were explicitly "representative of the assumptions of liberal-progressives of his day" (ibid., p. 314).

[8] Ursula Vogel, "The Fear of Public Disorder: Marriage between Revolution and Reaction," in Dario Castiglione and Lesley Sharpe, eds., *Shifting the Boundaries. Transformation of the Languages of Public and Private in the Eighteenth Century* (Exeter, 1995), pp. 74–75. Vogel does not cite Fichte as an example of the liberalism she has in mind. See also Shell, "'A Determined Stand,'" p. 103, on Fichte's concern with "liberal self-preservation," which he struggles to reconcile with "Rousseauian submergence of self within the greater community."

to the larger argument of the *Naturrecht*, he kept the state's enforcement of legal hierarchy in marriage (as opposed to the moral sanctification of hierarchy in marriage) to a minimum. This too explains why the discussion of marriage had to be relegated to a supplement.

★ ★ ★

If we simply make Fichte a voice of liberalism in his thinking about gender, marriage, and the public and private spheres, we glide blindly by the contextually most salient dimension of his relationship to an incipient liberal ideology – and miss an opportunity to clarify both the structural coherence of his argument and its severe internal strains. It was primarily in reaction against recent efforts to secure equality of rights for women – efforts proceeding from principles of the Enlightenment that would become axiomatic in modern liberalism – that Fichte framed his argument. In July 1790, Condorcet had published his essay on "the admission of women to the rights of citizenship." "Now the rights of men follow only from the fact that they are feeling beings, capable of acquiring moral ideas and of reasoning about these ideas," Condorcet argued. "Since women have the same qualities, they necessarily have equal rights."[9] It would be hard to imagine a more succinct refusal to allow contingent circumstances to limit the extension of the rationalist logic of rights to women. In September 1791, in reaction to the National Assembly's omission of all women from active citizenship, Olympe de Gouges submitted a sweeping demand for female emancipation in her pamphlet *The Declaration of the Rights of Women and the Citizen.*[10] In 1792

---

[9] Condorcet, "On the Admission of Women to the Rights of Citizenship," in Lynn Hunt, ed., *The French Revolution and Human Rights. A Brief Documentary History* (Boston and New York, 1996), p. 120. Cf. the translation in Keith Michael Baker, ed., *Condorcet. Selected Writings* (Indianapolis, 1976), p. 9. See also Keith Michael Baker, "Defining the Public Sphere in Eighteenth-Century France: Variations on a Theme by Habermas," in Craig Calhoun, ed., *Habermas and the Public Sphere* (Cambridge, Mass., 1992), pp. 198–208. The "rationalist discourse of the social," Baker argues, "was contingently masculinist to the extent that it admitted contingent grounds for denying women (and others) full and immediate participation in the exercise of universal individual rights, but it was not essentially masculinist in the sense that women were excluded from the exercise of such rights by definition of their very nature." I agree with Baker that Condorcet's defense of women's political rights demonstrates that in the late eighteenth century this rationalist discourse could avoid being even contingently masculinist (ibid., p. 202). On the larger issue of the relationship between liberalism and feminism, see also Martha C. Nussbaum, "The Feminist Critique of Liberalism," in Nussbaum, *Sex and Social Justice* (New York, 1991), pp. 55–80, and the concluding remarks in Lynn Hunt, *The Family Romance of the French Revolution* (London, 1992), pp. 199–204.

[10] See William H. Sewell, Jr., "Le citoyen/la citoyenne: Activity, Passivity and the Revolutionary Concept of Citizenship," in Colin Lucas, ed., *The Political Culture of the French Revolution, The French Revolution and the Creation of Modern Political Culture*, vol. 2 (Oxford, 1988), pp. 113–20. Joan Wallach Scott, *Only Paradoxes to Offer. French Feminists and the Rights of Man* (Cambridge, Mass., 1996), includes a fascinating chapter on Olympe de Gouges. Scott emphasizes "an enduring conflictual relationship" between feminism and "the discourse of liberal individualism" from which it derived (p. 18). On Wollstonecraft, see Baker, "Defining the Public Sphere," pp. 203–8.

Mary Wollstonecraft, also outraged by the National Assembly's omission, published the most famous feminist tract from the period, her *A Vindication of the Rights of Woman*.

Like most educated German men, Fichte was at best vaguely aware of these French and British developments; he was not likely to have read the texts. But he knew that a new sentiment for female emancipation was in the air, and one of its voices was much closer to home. In 1792, the same year in which Wollstonecraft's book appeared, a book with the provocative title *On Improving the Civic Status of Women* (*Über die bürgerliche Verbesserung der Weiber*) had been published anonymously in Berlin.[11] Its author was Theodor Gottlieb von Hippel, one of Kant's fellow bachelors and dining companions in Königsberg and a jurist who had risen from humble origins to the office of Director of Police and then Governing Mayor of the city. Hippel's argument was more diffuse than Condorcet's but no less radical, both in its rejection of the standard wisdom supporting gender hierarchy and in its unqualified vision of gender equality. In an age when "scientific" efforts to identify the "natural" differences between the sexes were multiplying rapidly, Hippel took a refreshingly skeptical stance toward any claims to scientific authority on these subjects. "Nature," he observed, is "a document which has in common with all documents the quality of allowing everyone who searches therein to find what he is looking for." What males sought in their reading of Nature were reasons to allay their insecurity and "fear"; if women were made their "equals," they would often be forced to "exert [themselves] trying to keep step . . . to a greater extent than [they] can either imagine or are capable of." The physical differences between the sexes were undeniable, but there was no reason to conclude from them that women were inferior to men in intellectual or moral capacity.[12] If many women were intellectually shallow, incapable of acting on moral principles, and helpless, that was because they had been socialized to be so. Physiology aside, women's social orientation did give them distinctive traits of temperament; but far from disqualifying them, these traits promised to humanize the practice of law, medicine, and other professions in emerging civil societies. Hence both the public good and justice required that women be made equal to men in their education; in their access to occupations, including the uni-

---

[11] Theodor Gottlieb von Hippel, *On Improving the Status of Women*, trans. and ed. Timothy F. Sellner (Detroit, 1979).

[12] Ibid., esp. pp. 72–73, 111. See also Claudia Honegger, *Die Ordnung der Geschlechter. Die Wissenschaften vom Menschen und das Weib, 1750–1850* (Frankfurt am Main, 1991), pp. 85–93; Hull, *Sexuality, State, and Civil Society*, pp. 323–32. Hull argues that Hippel's "basic assumptions were the same liberal, progressive, Enlightened views as those of his contemporaries," but two other "sources" – his "religious conviction" and his "legal-bureaucratic principle" – account for his "universalism" in applying those assumptions. I find very little evidence for these "sources" in the text, and do not see why it is necessary to emphasize them to explain Hippel's consequential liberalism.

versity-educated professions; in their right to occupy state offices; and in their rights of citizenship (including the right to vote and be elected to office).

Much of the rhetorical energy of Hippel's book derives from a deep sense of disappointment. Like Wollstonecraft, he found it absurd that the French Constitution of 1791 had blithely denied rights of active citizenship to "an entire half of a nation," particularly in view of the fact that it had extended those same rights to the minority of French Protestants.[13] Ultimately his disappointment was with the Enlightenment itself, which he saw as having inspired the Revolution and from which he drew his arguments for emancipation. Until females were as enabled as males to develop the human capacity for intellectual and moral autonomy, and until they could exercise that capacity without restrictions on their occupational and civic activity, the Enlightenment would be a movement in contradiction with itself.

As early as the spring of 1795 Fichte had planned to publish a response to Hippel and other proponents of women's rights. What was needed, he wrote to the publisher Friedrich Cotta, was a "basic investigation," perhaps in the tone of his essay on the Revolution.[14] His supplement to the *Naturrecht* was not the book-length treatment he had intended, but, in its polemical nastiness it was quite reminiscent of the *Contribution*. With obvious reference to Hippel's bachelorhood, he dismissed the male advocates of women's rights as "some lost heads" who "for the most part honored no particular woman by making her a life's companion" and who "in compensation wished to see the entire sex immortalized in history in the lump." As for women who published in the same cause, they were merely seeking "celebrity" as "a new means to ensnare men's hearts." Indeed for any woman who wrote for publication, whatever the subject, writing was nothing more than "a tool of coquetry."[15]

Fichte's venom was a measure of the depth of his conviction on the issue of women's rights. It hardly comes as a surprise in view of his admonishments to his wife in 1795. But to Johanna he had simply preached the standard wisdom of patriarchy, in the language he felt she was most likely to take to heart. In the supplement to the *Naturrecht* he faced a different task: developing a theory of marriage that would take its place in his larger philosophical system. To be understood contextually, the theory has to be read as one of a range of more or less direct refutations of the advocates of female emancipation. Fichte's refutation does stand out in the crowd; but that is because it carries to new heights the self-contradiction that Hippel had found in the Enlightenment. His dilemma – the lurking contradiction that made him resort to strained

---

[13] Hippel, *On Improving the Status of Women*, esp. pp. 56–8.
[14] GA, III, 2: 295.   [15] NR, pp. 342–3, 349.

efforts at paradox – was that he had to justify the exclusion of women from Enlightenment principles without throwing the universal validity of the principles into question.

It was a dilemma Fichte shared with Kant. In *Improving the Status of Women*, Hippel had already challenged Kant to draw feminist implications from his own philosophy. The challenge was largely oblique and was often hidden within the profuse eclecticism of Hippel's rhetoric; but there were moments of specificity that his readers were not likely to miss. Hippel did not restrict himself to arguing that women had the same rational capacity as men. Thanks to their distinctive bonding of rationality and sensibility, he claimed, women were more inclined than men to grasp Kant's insight that the existence of God was a "postulate of practical reason" and not a fact to be proved by theoretical reason. Indeed, it was women above all who could mediate the dualisms that Kantians found troubling. Precisely because head and heart, reason and sense experience, were so intimately bound in their temperaments, they could turn Kant's formal universals into virtuous habits of the heart. Hippel's point was not that in women's temperaments reason had less authority but that it received more nourishment from lived experience. And that made all the more outrageous that in the age of enlightenment, women's minds were left to stagnate while men's minds advanced:

> Without wishing at this point to incur the displeasure of any particular philosophical school, may I be permitted, in the interest of convincing justice just how much she is at odds with herself, to note that the perfection of all men appears to me the ultimate purpose of moral law? And what does mankind desire more than this highest development? Should not for this very reason the law be extended to all men? Can a rational being be considered merely as a means to higher goals?[16]

The Enlightenment was contradicting itself by violating the Categorical Imperative, the purest statement of its ethical ideal.

Kant certainly was aware that his philosophy had strongly influenced Hippel. In a curious notice published in 1797, shortly after Hippel had died and his authorship had been revealed, Kant claimed that his friend's writings had appropriated, sometimes literally, "his own thoughts" as they had been formulated in his lectures and his publications since the *Critique of Pure Reason*.[17] But in his published thoughts in the 1790s on gender relations and marriage – in *The Metaphysics of Morals* (1797–98) and *Anthropology from a Pragmatic Point of View* (1796–97) – Kant did not take the direction Hippel had urged him to take. In his views on the dis-

---

[16] Hippel, *On Improving the Status of Women*, p. 159. See also Ursula Pia Jauch, *Immanuel Kant zur Geschlechterdifferenz. Aufklärerische Vorurteilskritik und bürgerliche Geschlechtsvormundschaft* (Vienna, 1988), pp. 209–36; Honegger, *Die Ordnung der Geschlechter*, pp. 78–93.

[17] Jauch, *Immanuel Kant zur Geschlechterdifferenz*, pp. 203–9.

tribution of authority and power, both at home and in the public sphere, he largely accepted the standard wisdom of patriarchy.

Kant did, to be sure, assign women a critical role in the moral progress of the species, particularly in his university lectures on anthropology, given periodically from 1772–73 onward and published in 1796–97. In the long view, Nature worked with ironic design to create the social and cultural conditions for the moral ascent of mankind, and one of its instruments was modern marriage. Marriage – precisely because it subjected men to female manipulation – "brought [men], if not quite to morality itself, then at least to that which cloaks it, moral behavior, which is the preparation and introduction to morality."[18] But even when Kant conceded this ethical mission to women, it should be stressed, he did not credit them with acting as virtuous persons or even as rational moral agents. Women were by nature morally as well as physically weaker than men. They acted on their physical and emotional inclinations as unwitting instruments of Nature. They reigned over "social life," where the "chief perfection" is not "the truth," but "beautiful appearance." Their distinctive "virtue" was of the social kind – which is to say that in Kant's scheme of things, they were incapable of the uncompromising autonomy in the face of social pressures and the commitment to truth over mere appearance that constituted true (male) virtue.

To define women's civilizing role in this way was, in Kant's view, to make it entirely compatible with patriarchal authority. While the wife should "reign" at home through "inclination," like a self-indulgent monarch, the husband should "rule" through "reason," like a prudent cabinet minister.[19] In *The Metaphysics of Morals*, Kant's phrasing was less politic. Even as he defined the conjugal relationship as one of "equality of possession," he insisted that the definition left intact the husband's right to legal sovereignty over the household. The husband's legal right to command at home was in recognition of "[his] natural superiority . . . to the wife in his capacity to promote the common interest of the household." In Kant's ideal republic, gendered subordination extended to the public or "civic" sphere. He simply took it for granted that women, like other "dependents," could not enjoy active rights of citizenship, including the right to vote.[20]

These views point to the deeper sense in which Kant, like Fichte, can be said to have fallen well short of realizing the critical mission he claimed for philosophy. On the issues of sexuality and marriage, both philosophers

[18] Immanuel Kant, *Anthropology from a Pragmatic Point of View*, trans. Victor Lyle Dowdell and ed. Hans H. Rudnick (Carbondale and Edwardsville, 1978), pp. 219–20.

[19] Kant, *Anthropology*, pp. 216–25.

[20] Immanuel Kant, *The Metaphysics of Morals*, trans. Mary Gregor and intro. Roger J. Sullivan (Cambridge, 1996), p. 63; *Kant. Political Writings*, ed. Hans Reiss and trans. H. B. Nisbet (2d, enl. ed.: Cambridge, 1991), p. 78.

simply failed to honor their commitment to undercutting the putative authority of "experience" and "tradition" by constructing an alternative, built on the universally valid principles of reason. Rather than taking the axioms of their culture on gender and sexuality to be historically contingent and therefore subject to critique, they followed most of their followed most of their contemporaries in taking them to reflect unchangeable natural givens. Neither thinker, to be sure, simply accepted the status quo in gender relations; but the radical skepticism one might expect is conspicuous by its absence. It simply did not occur to them that in any given historical and cultural context, both sexuality and gender were constructs, not realities anterior to discursive construction, and that they served to legitimate specific inequalities and exclusions that were, by rational standards, arbitrary. Observable (and in some cases merely imagined) characteristics of male and female cognition, psychology, and social behavior were assumed to be grounded ultimately in sexual physiology; and that was taken to mean that basic inequalities between men and women in rights and obligations were, by the command of Nature, sacrosanct.

This essentialism went hand in hand with a view of sexuality that echoed centuries of disdain for the body and its appetites in Christian asceticism and philosophical mind-body dualism. If sexuality had a certain authority as Nature's way of insuring the continuance of the species, sex itself – the act of intercourse – was nonetheless, by itself, an animal activity. To pursue sexual pleasure for its own sake was to enslave oneself to animal instinct and appetite in their most despotic forms and thereby to degrade the moral person in oneself.[21] A society that gave free reign to the sexual appetite would be a society in chaos, which is to say that it would be no society at all. Hence sexuality had to remain controlled, though with limits on legal coercion; and that meant that *morally* legitimate sexual satisfaction had to be contained within the institution of marriage. The question was how sexuality, despite itself, could be made compatible with morality.

The obvious cautionary tale here is that philosophical reasoning is not as detachable from its context as we might want it to be, particularly when it deals with concepts as saturated with normative social and cultural assumptions as sexuality and gender have been.[22] The tale does *not*, however, confirm the sweeping generalization, often unquestioned in current scholarship, that the very concept of rational moral agency in "the western philosophical tradition" has been inherently gendered (i.e.,

[21] See esp. Robin May Schott, *Cognition and Eros; A Critique of the Kantian Paradigm* (University Park, Penn., 1993).

[22] The point is made judiciously, and with due attention to Kant, in Genevieve Lloyd, *The Man of Reason. "Male" and "Female" in Western Philosophy* (2d ed: Minneapolis, 1993).

inherently male-biased). To judge by the cases of Kant and Fichte, even within an obviously essentialist tradition there are differences, both in what is essentialized and in what essentialism entails.

It is not at all surprising that Kantianism plays a major role in contemporary feminism. Feminists who draw on Kant proceed from a critical distinction between the concept of rational moral agency and applications of that concept. They are more than willing to admit that when it came to applications, Kant's thinking about rational moral agency was deeply gendered, and indeed, even by the standards of its era, sometimes struck a misogynist note. Nonetheless, Kantian feminists argue, quite persuasively, that Kant's ethical universalism offers a promising way of grounding claims to rights for women and that it may offer the only way of asserting those claims without making them vulnerable to the charge of being merely the rationale of one more interest group in the political arena.[23] Kant's statement of the Categorical Imperative as the duty to respect "humanity" as "an end in itself" in every other human being – or, as he also puts it, never to treat another human being only as a "means" to one's own ends – has emancipatory potential for women precisely because it is at a level of abstraction that, in principle, excludes gender differences as irrelevant to issues of justice. One clear implication is that the exploitation of women, sexual or otherwise, is immoral simply because they are human beings.

The formalism of Kant's rule may also, of course, be its disadvantage; if it cannot be used to justify the subordination of women's human rights to male interests without contradicting itself, it also resists application to the particular contexts and relationship in which the exploitation of women occurs. But Kant can also be read as offering a way around precisely "the impasse of particularism versus universalism [that has been] dogging" feminist theory. In this view, the advantage of Kant's "formal rule" is that it is "both strictly universalist (it applies to all people equally) and radically individualizing (it requires that one perceive and support the specific needs of others)." To value humanity as an end, one must fulfill what Kant called the "duties of love," which entails supporting others in their pursuit of their freely chosen ideas of happiness. The implication is that supposed differences in gender cannot be used to determine what are and are not legitimate needs of women.[24]

---

[23] See, e.g., Herta Nagl-Docekal, "Feminist Ethics: How It Could Benefit from Kant's Moral Philosophy," in Robin May Schott, ed., *Feminist Interpretations of Immanuel Kant* (University Park, Penn., 1997), p. 120. Also relevant is Onora O'Neill, "Justice, Gender, and International Boundaries," in Martha Nussbaum and Amartya Sen, eds., *The Quality of Life* (Oxford, 1993), pp. 303–35.

[24] Nagl-Docekal, "Feminist Ethics," p. 118. But cf. Hannelore Schröder, "Kant's Patriarchal Order," in Schott, ed., *Feminist Interpretations*, pp. 275–96; Robin May Schott, "The Gender of Enlightenment," in ibid., pp. 319–37; and Hull, *Sexuality, State, and Civil Society*, pp. 301–13, which emphasizes Kant's "lack of critical self-awareness" on issues of sexuality and gender.

When we compare Fichte with Kant in this regard, we encounter an irony. Arguably Fichte's theory of self-positing in intersubjectivity suggests a way to combine a universalist ethics with the relational orientation that critics find lacking in Kantianism. The I becomes self-conscious – that is, individuates itself as a person, as opposed to a thing – *only* in the intersubjective encounter with another person in which each, to have his own moral freedom confirmed, must recognize the moral freedom of the other. The concept of law does not simply, as in Kant, ground a framework of legitimate "external" coercion in which the individual can pursue his or her self-development; it becomes the very condition for the finite existence of human selfhood. This is, to be sure, a highly abstract opening to a relational ethic, but it is one not without radical implications. In the *Naturrecht*, after all, Fichte's conception of property as labor justifies an agenda for distributive justice that is far more radically egalitarian than Kant's principle of procedural justice. His blueprint for a planned economy did not extend that right to women as mothers and in the household, though he considered the "free activity" of work to be essential to the development of the capacities that women, as human beings, obviously possess. That is a measure of his commitment to gendered hierarchy. But something like his rationale for the right to work would seem to be essential to a revaluation of women's reproductive and domestic labor, particularly for the millions of women who suffer greater physical and material deprivation than the male members of their own families.

These are routes that Fichte himself – had he not been Fichte – might have taken. In fact, however, it would require a certain obtuseness to attempt to build a feminist theory on Fichte's thought. Fichte's thinking about marriage differed from Kant's in several critical ways, and the differences are essential to understanding why his argument is so much more blatantly patriarchal and so much more tension-ridden. To clarify the first difference, we need only apply a recent useful distinction between genuine abstraction and "idealization masquerading as abstraction." Whereas genuine abstraction "hinges nothing on the satisfaction or non-satisfaction of the predicates from which it abstracts," idealization masquerading as abstraction "may privilege certain sorts of human agent and life and certain sorts of society by covertly presenting (enhanced versions of) their specific characteristics as the ideal for all human action and life."[25] This is a fair way of distinguishing between the exercise of Practical Reason, as Kant had conceived it, and Fichte's reconception of practical reasoning in the *Wissenschaftslehre* as an act of pure Will, the self-positing of the transcendental ego in its confrontation with the resistant world of

---

[25] O'Neill, "Justice, Gender, and International Boundaries," pp. 309–10. O'Neill does not apply this distinction to Kant and Fichte.

Nature. In Fichte's hands the very concept of rational moral agency – and not just the applications of that concept – resonated with the set of binary opposites that were central to discourses of gendered hierarchy. Independence versus dependence; self-assertion versus self-abnegation; domination of Nature versus subjection to it: these were the pervasive dichotomies of gender difference. In Fichte's concept of rational self-consciousness, as in the discourse of gender, they all rested on the basic dichotomy between the active and the passive.

Another thinker might somehow have extricated the transcendental concept of "activity" (*Handeln*) from this cultural thicket of affiliations and might have concluded that as embodied personalities, and not simply as reasoning subjects, women had the same capacity for willed activity as men. In the supplement on marriage, Fichte moved in precisely the opposite direction. Both Kant and Fichte, to be sure, subscribed to biological essentialism, but what matters here is that they did so in quite different ways. Kant's biological essentialism pertained to the species. Ignoring the possibility of social and cultural construction, he assumed that Nature had implanted the same sexual drive in men and women. Fichte's biological essentialism pertained to gender. He read "nature" in precisely the way Hippel found bogus. The supplement on marriage begins with the observation that in "organic Nature in its entirety" there is a sexual division between contrasting but complementary "halves," and the human species is no exception. "Male" sexuality is "only active," and "female" sexuality is "only passive."[26] With this distinction as his point of departure, Fichte had to confront a dilemma that an a priori deduction by itself could not resolve.

★ ★ ★

We come now to the most striking difference between Kant and Fichte on the subject of marriage: the ways in which their texts blend philosophical arguments with more obviously figurative language from other eighteenth-century discourses, each with its own posture toward the play of power in intimate relationships. From this angle it becomes apparent that on the issue of patriarchal authority, Kant's jaundiced view cut both ways; and that Fichte's idealized alternative provided a highly serviceable justification for a kind of hyperpatriarchy.

The ideal in question is the exalted view of marriage in the culture of *Empfindsamkeit*. Within the limits of social respectability, the febrile language of sensibility made the choice of a partner, for the woman as for the man, an act of individual freedom, the expression of an

---

[26] NR, p. 300. On Fichte's gendered view of reason and morality, see also Hull, *Sexuality, State, and Civil Society*, pp. 314–23; Karen Kenkel, "The Personal and the Philosophical in Fichte's Theory of Sexual Difference," in W. Daniel Wilson and Robert C. Holub, eds., *Impure Reason. Dialectic of Enlightenment in Germany* (Detroit, 1993), pp. 279–97.

358

The Jena Years

individualized personality, rather than an act of submission to parental
authority or to the requirements of corporate status. In the ideal, marriage became, to recall Fichte's term, a kind of "friendship," in an era when
the cult of friendship sometimes reached feverish heights. In the friendship formed by husband and wife, to be sure, egalitarianism had its limits,
if only because the wife, however well educated, could not and should
not match the husband in intellectual profundity. But there were also
senses in which marital love carried friendship to a new level of spiritual
communion. In the rhetoric of *Empfindsamkeit* marriage represented a
unique exclusivity. As the couple often realized in a kind of epiphany,
they had been assigned to each other, and only to each other, by Providence. The providential assignment was meant to insure a fusion of virtue
– a spiritual union in which the self-development (*Bildung*), or "ennoblement," of each soul throve on the nourishment that only the other
could provide. It was this moral, affective, and ultimately spiritual affinity
– and not the animal force of sexual attraction – that gave the experience of "falling in love" its rapturous quality.[27]

The process of reconceiving marriage as a species of friendship, and
indeed of making it a kind of spiritually heightened friendship, was not
without its tensions. As egalitarian as the new ideal of marriage was in
the context of old-regime society, it was less a rejection of patriarchal
authority than a recasting of it. The husband remained the public representative of the household, while the wife practiced virtue within the
confines of the domestic sphere. And the husband still ruled at home,
though the wife was now compliant spontaneously, out of "inner" devotion to a man deserving of her respect, rather than merely out of duty.
The language of *Empfindsamkeit* did not acknowledge, much less resolve,
the potential conflict between marriage as friendship and marriage as a
new form of patriarchy. Instead it had the rhetorical effect of extruding
power calculations from the relationship and hence of dispelling the very
possibility of conflict. Spiritualized in the new key of *Empfindsamkeit*, the
marital union transcended the world of power, just as it transcended the
physical force of sexual desire. The two kinds of transcendence were, in
fact, inseparable.

How did *Empfindsamkeit* figure in Kant's thinking about marriage? The
extensive notes Kant made to himself in his own copy of his *Observations
on the Feeling of the Beautiful and the Sublime* in 1765 – notes written on
the margins of the text and on slips of paper inserted between the pages
– include a great deal about marriage, sexuality, and gender differences.[28]

[27] See Chapter 6.
[28] Immanuel Kant, *Bemerkungen in den "Beobachtungen über das Gefühl des Schönen und Erhabenen,"* ed.
Marie Rischmüller (Hamburg, 1991). Susan Meld Shell, *The Embodiment of Reason. Kant on Spirit,
Generation, and Community* (Chicago and London, 1996), pp. 81–105, includes a perceptive reading
of the notes.

In his efforts to distill his thought into *aperçu*, he circled back to these subjects repeatedly. Aside from their Rousseauian provenance, the comments on marriage derive from Kant's observations of his own social world, the circles of the educated and propertied *Bürgertum* in Königsberg in which he mixed. We hear a forty-one-year-old, unmarried university scholar drawing conclusions from what he observes of the courtship rituals and the married lives of his friends and acquaintances, and perhaps from what he has endured at dinner parties designed to pry him away from his growing commitment to bachelorhood.

Kant's notes are anything but an endorsement of *Empfindsamkeit*. Their contextual meaning, in fact, lies precisely in the fact that the philosopher regarded the new ideal of marriage with a cold, often cynical eye. Kant distinguished between the "concord" (*Einigkeit*) of friendship and the "unity" (*Einheit*) of marriage. Friendship, he observed, was a harmony of sentiments in a relationship of equality; neither *needed* the other to be a whole person. Marriage, on the other hand, was a relationship of mutual dependence in which each needed the other to approach "completion" and in which inequality was the rule.[29] As Kant used it in this context, the term *Einheit* connoted an alliance for the mutual provision of needs and pleasures. If politics is a competition for power, Kant implied, then marriage is an eminently political institution. He was bent on dispelling the nimbus of sentimentality with which the rhetoric of *Empfindsamkeit* surrounded marriage, so that it could be seen for what it was: an economy of sexual forces vying with each other for domination, of attractions and repulsions that channeled raw sexual energy into a social dynamic.

To Kant it was above all marriage that effected the transmutation of raw animal life into modern sociability. He had no doubt that in modern civilized societies like his own, that process put real power in the hands of women. "Women are strong," Kant observed, "because they are weak."[30] That paradox rested on two apparently contradictory facts: that women are "closer to Nature" than men, and that they, and not men, are the masters of artificiality and delusion, the active agents of modern social corruption.[31] Women are not closer to nature in the sense that their sexual drive is stronger or more vital. The critical difference is, rather, that the woman's desire for sexual pleasure is inseparable from her need for the physical and mental strength of a male to insure her survival, while for the male sexual pleasure is a superfluity. Nature compensates – indeed, overcompensates – for this dependency by making the woman adept at the art of deceiving, at appearing more virtuous than she is or can be. In courtship it is the man who is truly tender and amorous; the woman,

---

[29] Kant, *Bemerkungen*, pp. 9, 57–9, 121, 129.
[30] Ibid., pp. 8, 17, 54, 92.   [31] Ibid., pp. 17, 42, 49, 78.

in keeping with the dictates of the power game, maintains a calculating detachment from these feelings even as she seems to embody them.[32]

Hence the man is a willing and eager dupe; his sex drive, operating as it does in a world of superfluity, takes the form of an indulgence in "fantasy" that makes him the easy prey of female dissimulation. The apparent virtue of the young woman – the nobility of soul revered in the rhetoric of *Empfindsamkeit* – is a delusion that she spins to trap her man. So many marriages inevitably turn sour because in the transition from courtship fantasy to marital reality, the woman, constituted as she is to overcome her weakness, cannot possibly be the virtuous friend her lover expects her to be. With marriage "novels cease and history begins."[33] If the wife is to consolidate her power despite this disillusionment, she not only has to make renewed efforts to hide her sexual desire behind a façade of virtue. She must coax the man away from his natural tendency to find his "honor" in his self-estimation and make him preoccupied, as she is, with the "estimation of others." The husband emulates his wife in becoming a slave of "opinion," and his penchant for fantasy finds its outlet in conspicuous consumption. Hence in modern societies, ever more in thrall to the artificial needs of "civilized" consumption, corruption takes the form of men becoming "soft and feminine." In this state of "luxury" (*Üppigkeit*), the human being does not demand "to be satisfied for himself or to be good," but merely to appear so. The female sex becomes "the greatest obstacle to the male sex's return to happy simplicity."[34]

Against the backdrop of the culture of *Empfindsamkeit*, it is fair to say that Kant was something of a misogynist. He was also a cynic. More precisely, his view of marriage as an unequal alliance, driven by the will to power and built on false appearances, exhibits a historically specific kind of cynicism, formed in aversion to what he saw as the naïve delusions of *Empfindsamsamkeit* as a culture of spiritualized affect. But Kant's cynicism, it turns out, was double-edged; if it licensed misogyny, it also cleared away the sentimentality that kept sexuality beyond the pale of legitimate discourse. He was in a position to make the conjugal relationship, and indeed intercourse itself, the quintessential site of contractual reciprocity and, in so doing, to extend to women a new measure of legal equality. This latter implication was made explicit in the discussion of marriage in *The Metaphysics of Morals*, the last of Kant's great treatises, published in 1797. We are still in a ruthlessly desentimentalized world of mutual dependencies; of competition for power; of instrumental relationships. Kant begins by defining "sexual union" (*commercium sexuale*) as "the reciprocal use that one human being makes of the sexual organs and capacities of another" (*usus membrorum et facultatum sexualium alterius*).[35] His phrasing struck some

---

[32] Ibid., pp. 55–9, 61, 68, 118, 125.   [33] Ibid., pp. 83, 99–100.
[34] Ibid., pp. 11, 61, 66, 82.   [35] Kant, *The Metaphysics of Morals*, pp. 61–2.

of his contemporaries as unnecessarily crude. To a recent scholar it typi-
fies Kant's "basically nonemotional and nonrelational understanding of
sexual relations" in terms of a model of "mutual objectification" and "cold
property exchange," and indeed of "masturbation in which one uses the
organs of another instead of one's own."[36] If the model posits "two solipsistic egotists," however, there was nonetheless a "relational" *legal* agenda
behind Kant's unadorned use of the language of property transactions and
mechanical control.[37]

The Kant in question now, of course, is the creator of the Critical Philosophy. Sexuality posed, in a particularly problematic way, the question
whether the Categorical Imperative could survive the transition from the
inner realm of individual conscience to the dense and intricate field of
human relations. If intercourse was the use of another's "sexual organs and
capacities," why were the sexual relations between husband and wife not
a blatant violation of Kant's stricture about ends and means? Was it not
the case that even in marriage sexual partners dehumanized themselves
by reducing themselves to mere instruments of each other's animal pleasure? And if that were so, was not marriage, by its very nature, an immoral
institution?

Kant avoided these conclusions with two moves. One was to abandon
his earlier Lockean argument that the person could dispose of his body
and its parts as forms of property, just as, in the physical world surrounding
him, he was free to dispose of the objects he had appropriated as property. The body, he now argued, is an integral part of the person; it cannot
be detached and put at another's disposal. Kant applied this logic not only
to deny moral legitimacy to prostitution, but also to endow the sexual
act *in* marriage with a unique legal sanctity. If the latter move was to have
purchase in a philosophy of law, marriage had to be understood as the
locus for a "new phenomenon in the juristic sky," "a strange type of right
which has recently been added to the doctrine of natural law, although
it has always been tacitly in use." This was the paradoxical category of
"rights to persons akin to rights to things," with "right" here meaning "possession of an external object *as a thing*" but "use of it *as a person*."[38] Sexual
intercourse could embody this paradox only in the contractual relationship of marriage; that was the only way intercourse could be compatible
with morality despite the fact that it was "in itself a mere animal act." In
the sexual act, Kant reasoned,

---

[36] Hull, *Sexuality, State, and Civil Society*, p. 308. See also Martha C. Nussbaum, "Objectification," in
Nussbaum, *Sex and Social Justice*, pp. 213–39.

[37] For a particularly interesting explication of this point, see Barbara Herman, "Could It Be Worth
Thinking about Kant on Sex and Marriage?" in Louise M. Antony and Charlotte Witt, eds., *A
Mind of One's Own. Feminist Essays on Reason and Objectivity* (Boulder, 1993), pp. 49–67.

[38] Kant, *The Metaphysics of Morals*, pp. 127–8.

A human being makes himself into a thing, which conflicts with the right to humanity in his own person. There is only one condition under which this is possible: that while one person is acquired by the other *as if it were a thing*, the one who is acquired acquires the other in turn; for in this way each reclaims itself and restores its personality. But acquiring a member of a human being is at the same time acquiring the whole person, since a person is an absolute unity. Hence it is not only admissable for the sexes to surrender and to accept each other for enjoyment under the condition of marriage, but it is possible for them to do so *only* under this condition.[39]

The logic of this passage is admittedly tortuous, but its intent is clear enough. Defined to exemplify Kant's new category of "rights," the sexual relation – an act that, in itself, entailed an assault on autonomy – became the expression of mutual respect for personhood in marriage. Kant leaves no doubt that the respect must be mutual; that the law must protect the wife as well as the husband from dehumanizing objectification. And the contractual reciprocity in sex necessarily implied a broader equality in ownership; "nothing can belong to the one that does not also, *aequo jure* [by equal right], belong to the other."[40]

In the *Naturrecht* and the *Sittenlehre*, Fichte also sought to explain why husband and wife could have sex without degrading each other to the status of mere things. His task was made more difficult, of course, by the fact that even as he regarded human reason as a capacity common to both sexes, he posited a strict sexual division between male activity and female passivity. That gendered distinction meant that for the husband, sexual intercourse was not dehumanizing. Since reason was "absolute self-activity," Fichte argued, the active character of the male sex drive was not incompatible with it. (He could as well have argued, of course, that they *were* incompatible. If rational self-activity is a struggle against a resistant Nature, why is it not at odds with a male's pursuit of sexual satisfaction as a natural being?) It was women who posed a seemingly intractable dilemma. If they followed their natural inclination to sexual passivity, they would be acting against the active rationality that made them human. Their sexuality would stand in blatant contradiction to their humanity. But how could it be otherwise? Women obviously could not forgo sex; that would be a way of preserving their human dignity at the absurd cost of bringing the species to an end. There had to be a way to give female sexuality an active turn.

It was in the face of this dilemma that Fichte folded the rhetoric of *Empfindsamkeit* into his a priori deduction of marriage. I do not mean to imply that Fichte drew conclusions that were intrinsic to the logic of

[39] Ibid., p. 62.   [40] Ibid., pp. 63, 379.

Empfindsamkeit or that were typical of the way it recast, and relegitimated, patriarchal authority. The culture of sensibility was quite labile, and there is increasing evidence that in actual marital relations it made for greater equality between the sexes than its formulation as a public ideology would imply. What is striking about Fichte's texts, however, is not simply that they are sodden with the conventional language of sensibility that had inspired him as a young man. The ethos of *Empfindsamkeit* informs the very logic of a hyperpatriarchal argument and indeed is crucial to its effort to dissolve an apparent contradiction into a moral paradox.[41] The entire deduction proceeded from the contention that marriage was not "merely a juridical society"; its essential uniqueness lay in the fact that it was both a "natural" and a "moral" society. There were ways in which law had to protect the rights of the partners, but the existence (or termination) of the marriage did not depend on law. Through "love," marriage became what the culture of *Empfindsamkeit* had implicitly made it: "the innermost point of union of Nature and Reason." Only in marriage was "true friendship" possible. The "sexual union" became "a total fusion of two rational individuals into one." Uniting male and female in a relationship of mutual "tenderness of feeling," marriage was the institution par excellence for moral "ennoblement." To put it another way, marriage was the institution in which the elemental forces of Kant's (and Fichte's) contractual world, the pursuit of self-interest and the competition for power, had no place.

Like the culture of *Empfindsamkeit* itself, Fichte's formulation kept marriage solidly patriarchal when it came to private and public authority. To appropriate the ethos of *Empfindsamkeit*, however, was also to admit into the discussion, at least obliquely, a disturbing set of questions that Kant had been able to ignore. If marriage was a kind of friendship, why did it not exemplify the equality that was considered essential to friendship? If marriage was a moral union, why was the moral equality of the partners not reflected in the legal and institutional structure of authority? Fichte had to get past two potential contradictions, and they pulled against each other. He needed a rationale for keeping women human despite their sexuality. But he also had to find a way to keep marriage patriarchal despite the new ethos with which his own theory was saturated.

He found the solution to both problems in his concept of "love." The female sex drive can assume another "form," as a kind of "activity" peculiar to females and hence can become compatible with human rationality while fulfilling its function in the reproduction of the species. The drive cannot take the form of using sex simply to have children or to

[41] Shell's point that Fichte rejects Rousseau's reliance on "inner virtue" is well taken, but her discussion ignores the discourse of *Empfindsamkeit*, in which Rousseau was a key figure. "'A Determined Stand,'" pp. 104–5.

secure financial security or any other self-interested goal. A woman pursuing such motives would still be degrading herself to a thing. There has to be a "step" that raises her from her naturally inferior position, as an "object of [the male's] power," to a position of moral equality. The woman takes that step — and here is the paradox on which the entire argument pivots — by *freely* sacrificing herself in her devotion to satisfying one man exclusively. The commitment is to unlimited self-sacrifice, but it preserves and indeed completes the human "dignity" of the woman because it is freely made. Only if the woman's satisfaction is "of the heart" (i.e., the emotional satisfaction she derives from satisfying her husband's sexual desire) and not a sexual pleasure does the female sex drive receive "the character of freedom and activity." If the woman acts freely, however, she nonetheless gives her entire "personality." And that in turn means that she ceases to be a person in the eyes of the law; the one man to whom she has devoted her capacity for self-sacrifice — the one man she loves — serves as her legal guardian.[42]

It is this argument that allows Fichte to insist that marriage is not in its essence a "juridical society" and indeed that it does not require legal recognition to exist (or to cease to exist). While law forms the zone of mediation between the universality of the Moral Law and the particularity of individualized sense being, marriage has a different place. It is the unique point of fusion between Nature and Reason, the one instance in which an "external impulse" (sexuality as a natural appetite) promotes "virtue." The framework of coercive law simply insures that the right to unrestricted moral freedom on both sides — to the freedom without which Nature could not become the medium of Reason in marriage — is respected, and to regulate the dissolution of marriage when mutual love ceases to be its binding agent. What marriage effects is mutual moral "ennoblement," though the male and female routes to it are different. Unlike the woman, the man enters marriage as the sexually active agent, but the woman's love transforms that activity into a kind of love as well. As the ruler of the household, to be sure, the husband cannot offer his wife the same unlimited devotion (and obedience) that she offers him; his love takes the form of a "benevolence," a learned willingness to sacrifice all for the "companion" who has devoted herself to him. But the result is a "marital tenderness of feeling" in which "each side wants to give up his personality, so that the other part rules." "The exchange of hearts and wills becomes complete," and "the union becomes deeper with every day of the marriage."[43] In the *Sittenlehre*, Fichte described the relationship this way:

[42] NR, pp. 301–7. Shell puts it well: "In woman, man sees a being who is simultaneously beneath him and above him — a peculiarly ambiguous being whose dignity paradoxically lies in her capacity to renounce her own personality." "'A Determined Stand,'" p. 117.
[43] NR, pp. 307–8.

In marriage the sexual union, which in itself carries the imprint of animal rawness (*Roheit*), receives an entirely different character, worthy of the rational being. It becomes a total fusion of two rational individuals into one; unconditional devotion on the female's side, vows of the most inner tenderness and benevolence (*Grossmut*) on the man's side . . . even in the man the natural drive, which he can otherwise admit to himself, receives another form; it becomes love reciprocated (*Gegenliebe*).[44]

We are now in a position to understand the apparently odd juxtaposition of elements in Fichte's texts. His deduction has two pivotal moments: its metamorphosis of the conjugal relationship from its physical status, as the most obvious example in human relationships of instrumental power in raw nature, into the spiritualized union of affects under rational control; and within that "ennoblement," the attribution of freedom to the woman's sacrifice of her juridical self in marriage, and only in marriage. This logic allowed Fichte, in contrast to Kant, to place the property the woman brought into the marriage under her husband's exclusive authority (though she, like her husband, received back her property in the event of divorce). But Fichte was acutely aware that if the argument was to have any claim to credibility, he had to be rigorously consistent on the subject of women's freedom. Precisely because the legal erasure of the woman was justifiable only on one condition – the completely voluntary sacrifice of freedom that made possible her moral ennoblement in marriage and that could occur only in marriage – it could not extend to unmarried women. Likewise the woman had to have the right to terminate a forced marriage, since it was really no marriage at all; if the woman did not sacrifice herself freely, the moral union simply did not occur. And there could be no marriage from the moment the wife's (or the husband's) love ceased. Morally, one might say, divorce occurred as soon as the wife, by no longer loving her husband, ceased to be committed freely to the union – and the law had to guarantee her right to regain her freedom.[45]

These provisions notwithstanding, Fichte's ideal of marriage rationalized gendered injustice. That it perpetuated a view of sexuality that denigrated women, even as it purported to save them from dehumanization, is obvious. More to the point, in his effort to build a new justification for patriarchy, Fichte had to wreak havoc with some (though not all) of the principles of his own system. His deduction was really two deductions: the transcendental one, which took as self-evident a "fact" about human consciousness that implied no distinction between men and women, and the biologically essentialist one, which made that fact deeply problematic in the case of women. Unable to reconcile his two points of

---

[44] SL, p. 329.   [45] NR, esp. pp. 334–6.

departure, either logically or rhetorically, he singularly failed to make marriage the exceptional case within the overarching framework of the *Naturrecht*.

That was not, to be sure, the verdict rendered by the reviewer of the *Naturrecht* in the *Allgemeine Literatur-Zeitung*. To him, it was Kant who had opened himself to the charge of inconsistency. Contrary to his intention, Kant's view of marriage as an exchange of property in the form of sexual characteristics implied the destruction of personality "*on both* sides." Fichte had succeeded where Kant had failed because he had grounded "the *essence* of marriage" not in "mere *reciprocity*," but "*deeper in human nature in an original relationship between both sexes*"; and hence he had saved "the dignity of the female nature."[46] This was to say, as Fichte had indeed argued, that the only solution to the enigma posed by marriage lay in gender essentialism. It was precisely that essentialist premise that led the reviewer in the *Annalen der Philosophie* to dismiss Fichte's deduction as a thoroughly misconceived "philosophical adventure." Even he, to be sure, saw "great difficulties" in conceiving of sex as a drive to be satisfied but at the same time preserving "its value in a *moral* regard." But Fichte had not removed the difficulties. The philosopher could not have it both ways. If "love" was "something *Natural*," as Fichte argued, then it could not occur "through freedom." If, on the other hand, the natural drive is "governed by freedom," then satisfaction of the drive for its own sake was permissible so long as it did not destroy the "morally conceivable purpose." Particularly when it came to the issue of property ownership, the reviewer found Fichte's view of the relationship between morality and power in marriage unconvincing. If the woman retained her moral personhood in marriage, as Fichte maintained despite his insistence on her sacrifice of her juridical personality, why was she required to entrust her property to her husband?[47]

★ ★ ★

Arguably the inner world of marital intimacy offered the most fully human example of what Fichte meant by intersubjectivity. And yet it had to be exempted from the contractual structure of egalitarian reciprocity that ordered intersubjectivity in the surrounding society. Here was the bitter irony behind Fichte's attempt at paradox: by placing marriage in a uniquely privileged position as an intersubjective union – by making it so deeply essential to both natural life and moral freedom as not to depend on law for its essence – Fichte had made married women, by his own logic, morally inviolable, but at the cost of making them legally right-

---

[46] FR 2: 120–25.

[47] FR 2: 91–95. The review posed another unsettling question. What about cases in which the woman had social or political power over the man? In what sense was she giving up her "personality" by having sex with him?

less. The problem was not simply that they could not speak or act for themselves in the public sphere. So long as the woman chose to be married, she was, in the domestic sphere, a subject of male rule. No appeal to the keywords of the discourse of sensibility – no rhetorical recourse to the "tenderness" and the emotional and spiritual depth of marital union – could dispel the fact that the husband owed the wife respect not as a legal obligation but as a matter of "benevolence." She had duties; he offered promises out of his "tenderness."

Like Kant, Fichte had sought to protect married women from reification without allowing them to share in the exercise of private and public authority. For modern readers concerned with eliminating gender inequality, the choice between them is not likely to seem enviable. But it is not, as it might at first appear to be, a toss-up. To be sure, Kant and Fichte shared a visceral disgust of sexual pleasure, and in that sense they both retained a Christian and especially Protestant impulse, even as they sought to justify marriage in strictly secular terms. But there is a difference. It did not occur to the cynic in Kant that in marriage women could or should strive to avoid experiencing physical pleasure in sex; it was just that, for reasons of sexual politics, they had to hide their sexual desire and appear indifferent to its satisfaction. To Fichte, on the other hand, the woman's "free" commitment to marriage had to expunge the very desire for sexual pleasure if she was to retain her human dignity.

And what of the role of language, in the expression of intimacy and in the normative construal of intimacy? It would be silly, of course, to conclude that to make marriage a relationship between equals, we must extrude from it the language of love and tenderness that the culture of sensibility has bequeathed to us. We cannot dispense with such language; even in our efforts to communicate an exclusive intimacy, we cannot but resort to the conventional, if only in the hope that it will inflect somehow the uniqueness of *this* relationship. Thanks in part to feminism, however, we now have a heightened sense of just how powerfully, and how insidiously, the modern rhetoric of affect can sanction and enforce gendered terms of inequality. The rhetoric often plays this role latently, but in Fichte's deduction of marriage the latent becomes blatantly manifest. That is why the text stands as a warning. If there was something icily, even eerily, impersonal about Kant's effort to retain the woman's moral dignity without resort to sentimentality, it at least opened a way to make marriage, as a sexual union, a locus for legal reciprocity. Fichte fashioned the reigning sentimentality into a philosophical idyll of moral union that made women the recipients of a kind of marital noblesse oblige. Measured by Fichte's own standards, that was a very odd way to make love an exercise in moral freedom. The rhetoric of affect and the apparent logic of paradox cloaked contradiction.

Chapter 12

The Atheism Conflict:
Reason and the Absolute

On May 19, 1798, Fichte turned thirty-six. His wife was devoted, if occasionally contrary, and his son was nearing the age of two. He had, at last, the family nest he had lacked since his abrupt removal from his own home over a quarter-century earlier. Still stigmatized as a Jacobin in conservative circles at the German courts and in the clergy, he was in fact settling into a fairly conventional life of work and family in the academic *Bürgertum*. He saw himself pursuing a life in *Wissenschaft*, or pure scholarship. Once he had spun out the implications of his philosophical system, he planned to move on to other "discoveries." He devoted his prodigious energy to preparing lectures and revising them for publication. It was the kind of work, he would explain a few months later, that left him with neither interest in nor time for political activism.

The bitter feuding of the mid-1790s seemed to have receded. Fichte had learned his lesson about meddling in the student subculture; in any case, as fashions changed, the Orders were losing their grip on student life. Spared the harassments that had driven him out of Jena four years earlier, he could enjoy his unrivaled popularity as a lecturer. He was ready to make peace with Friedrich Schiller, in part because he now had his own forum. He had joined Immanuel Niethammer, a younger colleague at Jena, as coeditor of the *Philosophical Journal of a Society of German Scholars*, a periodical unencumbered by the aesthetic concerns Schiller had wanted to bring to philosophy.

And yet Fichte was uneasy about his future at Jena, particularly when he considered the international situation. The Habsburg military disasters of 1797 had left the French Republic in undisputed possession of a string of territories along the Rhine, including Mainz. Unable to remove this French presence, the surviving German states were likely to become all the more vigilant about insulating their subjects from the spirit of revolution. In a letter in early September 1798, probably with this prospect in mind, Fichte alluded to the "impending political changes" that might "[shrink] the pleasant sphere of activity that I have had in Jena until now." He was apprehensive enough to consider the possibility of an appointment at a new French university being organized in Mainz, but nothing materialized.[1]

---

[1] Fichte to Franz Wilhelm Jung in Mainz, Sept (5?), 1798, in GA, III, 3: 140. As Bureau Chief of the French Central Administration in Mainz, Jung hoped to recruit Fichte for a new *Zentralschule*.

Events over the next several months seemed to confirm his pessimism. The issue of the *Philosophical Journal* that appeared in November 1798 included an essay entitled "Development of the Concept of Religion" by Friedrich Karl Forberg. Fichte later recalled that he had advised Forberg to withdraw the piece. But Forberg demurred and understandably took exception to Fichte's plan to correct his argument with notes under the text. Unwilling to violate his own commitment to freedom of the press but not wanting to leave the impression that Forberg was speaking for him, Fichte preceded Forberg's contribution with one of his own on "the basis of our belief in a divine world government."[2] Discussion of the two essays might have been confined to scholarly circles had it not been for the appearance of a pamphlet entitled the *Writing of a Father to a Son Studying at the University.* The pamphlet accused both Fichte and Forberg of preaching a "crude atheism" which "tears away from inexperienced young people the primary support of virtue, the belief in God, immortality and retribution." Signed by "G.," it was published in Nürnberg but circulated in Leipzig and in Dresden, the court residence and capital city of Electoral Saxony.[3]

And so began the controvery that would become known as the Atheism Conflict. On October 29, 1798, shortly after the articles appeared, the High Consistory of the Saxon Lutheran Church brought Forberg's essay to the attention of the Elector. On November 19 the government of Electoral Saxony ordered the issue confiscated within its borders on the grounds that both essays contained "atheistic statements." A week later the confiscation order was read publicly in the town hall of Leipzig, the center of German publishing, before the assembled members of the bookdealers' guild.[4]

The confiscation was not a step taken lightly. If the Saxon government was eager to wall off its subjects from the flow of dangerous publications, it was also reluctant to sacrifice revenue by scaring off bookdealers from the highly profitable Leipzig fairs. As a scholarly journal, the *Philosophical Journal* was an unusual though not unique target. Most of the forty-one publications confiscated from 1794 to 1798 were in the categories of revolutionary propaganda, attacks on Christianity for popular consumption, and pornography.[5]

---

[2] Forberg, "Entwicklung des Begriffs der Religion," in Frank Böckelmann, ed., *Die Schriften zu J. G. Fichtes Atheismus-Streit* (Munich, 1969), pp. 42–58; Fichte, "Uber den Grund unsers Glaubens an eine göttliche Weltregierung," in ibid., pp. 25–38. The latter text is also in GA, I, 5: 347–57. On Fichte's decision to publish Forberg's essay and his own, see GA, III, 3: 328.

[3] *Schreiben eines Vaters an seinen studierenden Sohn über den Fichteschen und Forbergschen Atheismus,* reprinted in GA, I, 6: 121–38.

[4] The relevant documents are in GA, III, 3: 168, 174–5.

[5] Johann Goldfriedrich, *Geschichte des Deutschen Buchhandels,* vol. 3 (Leipzig, 1909), pp. 420–2.

A month later the Saxon government protested to the Weimar court that the "principles" expressed in the essays were "incompatible" not only with Christianity but also with "natural religion." It was intolerable that "teachers of youth" were spreading "the inclination to unbelief," which threatened the "security of states" by eradicating "the concepts of God and religion" from the human heart. Duke Karl August and his ministers would have to choose: if they did not punish the authors and take measures to end "this kind of disorder" at Jena and in their schools, Saxon subjects would be forbidden to attend the university.[6]

Four years earlier, following the publication of *Religion within the Limits of Reason Alone*, Kant had faced the prospect of being officially censored and disciplined. Speaking for the Prussian king, Minister von Woellner had charged the philosopher with acting "irresponsibly" by "denigrat[ing] many important and basic teachings of Holy Scripture and Christianity" and had threatened him with "unpleasant measures." Kant had flatly denied the charge but nonetheless had promised to refrain henceforth from "all public presentations concerning religion, be it natural or revealed, in lectures as well as in writings." Only with the king's death in 1798 did Kant consider himself freed from the promise. He sought to discredit the "obscurantists" by publishing Woellner's letter and his own response in the preface to *The Contest of the Faculties*.[7]

Fichte identified with Kant as a fellow victim of repression but could not emulate his decision to weather the storm in circumspect silence. Aside from the differences in their personalities and in their views of their professorial obligations, they faced quite different situations. In 1794 Kant had been an aging and frail professor, intent on sparing his waning energies to complete his life's work. In 1798 Fichte was still a young philosophical talent, just four years into his academic career. He had only begun to realize his vaulting ambition to make philosophy an unshakeable system. He had good reason to fear that if the charge of atheism stuck, he would lose credibility as an author and would find himself, once again, marginalized and without a public voice.

And so Fichte undertook an uncompromising public self-vindication – one that he hoped would save his reputation as well as his university position and might also put a halt to the political reaction that seemed to be sweeping across the German states and the rest of Europe. In early 1799, he issued a 114-page pamphlet under the title *J. G. Fichte's Appeal to the Public about the Atheistic Statements Attributed to Him by the Electoral Saxon Confiscation Order*. In the subtitle he requested that the pamphlet "first be read before being confiscated." Also published were the lengthy

[6] GA, III, 3: 174–5.
[7] The documents, both in German and in English translation, are in Immanuel Kant, *The Conflict of the Faculties. Der Streit der Fakultäten*, trans. Mary J. Gregor (Lincoln and London, 1992), pp. 8–21.

Justifications (*Verantwortungschriften*) that he and Niethammer had submitted to the Weimar government. Fichte used the occasion to range well beyond a legal defense of his editorial judgment into the larger moral and political issues at stake in the case.[8] His parting gesture, in May of 1799, was an admission – or perhaps better, a defense – of the mistakes he had made in his dealings with the Weimar government. It took the form of a circular letter to Reinhold, complete with full texts of his communications to Privy Councillor Voigt, that he hoped would be passed on to his "friends."[9]

The Atheism Conflict may be said to have returned Fichte to his point of departure as an author, his "oration" to Europe's rulers in 1793 (the first of his writings to be confiscated in Saxony). Once again freedom of thought was being violated. But the author of the oration had been an obscure theology candidate, still unburdened by the responsibilities of office and profession and only recently converted to Kantian moral rigorism. Now, even as he insisted on the moral rigor of his own philosophy, Fichte had to shake off the potentially damning charge that by preaching atheism from the lectern, he was corrupting the young. He was still a "freethinker," no less critical of authority than he had been; but he was also a public figure, a highly visible university professor in the employ of a German court with unique prestige. The politics of his relationship to government and to the German academic community had become far more complicated.

With the possible exception of Fichte's initial article in the *Philosophical Journal*, the writings occasioned by the Atheism Conflict are not of major philosophical significance. Even in 1798–99 much of Fichte's philosophical argument was familiar and unexceptional; it was his timing and the polemical casting of his self-defense that caused the commotion. The Conflict has pivotal significance, however, as an episode in Fichte's career. It forms a natural endpoint to the Jena years and not simply because its upshot was that Fichte lost his university position. There was, most obviously, his seemingly inevitable collision with confessional Orthodoxy and counterrevolutionary politics. Less predictable but more noteworthy, even to many of his contemporaries, were his maneuvers on several other fronts. Within a multivalent field of argument, we hear a mature philosopher spelling out his relationship to the three cultural legacies to which he was, in more or less qualified ways, indebted: Lutheranism, the Enlightenment, and Kant's Critical Philosophy.

As he counterattacked and sought allies within this discursive configuration, Fichte had to justify his decisions and his motives, both rhetor-

---

[8] *Appellation an das Publikum über die durch ein Kurf. Sächs. Confiscationsrescript ihm beigemessenen Atheistischen Aeusserungen*, in GA, I, 5: 413–53; "Die Herausgeber des philosophischen Journals gerichtliche Verantwortungsschriften gegen die Anklage des Atheismus," in GA, I, 6: 25–144.

[9] GA, III, 3: 363–75.

ically, before a public audience, and to himself. In defending himself –
as a philosopher, as an author, and as a moral person – he stood on his
principle of transcendental reflexivity, which made the awareness of an
essential moral self categorically different from psychological introspection. As we follow the Conflict, we see the connections and the disjunc-
tions between this philosophically constructed self – the transcendental
"I" of the *Wissenschaftslehre* – and his public persona. We also catch
glimpses of a psychological interior, partially obsured by both the philosophical self-construction and the public self-representation. In Fichte's
dilemmas we come to understand the full ambivalence of his presence in
an official intelligentsia. Fichte was at once a prominent member of the
intelligentsia and one of its mavericks. In some ways he called into question its efforts to position itself between the state and the larger society
– and in some ways he exemplified them.

★ ★ ★

"With my article," Fichte acknowledged in December 1798, "I fell right
into their hands, as though called."[10] It was an irony (one that may not
have escaped him) that the instrument of this calling had been Friedrich
Karl Forberg, the twenty-eight-year-old author of "Development of the
Concept of Religion."

Forberg had been teaching at Jena for two years when Fichte arrived,
and he had not left the university until 1797. The two men knew each
other fairly well, but critics grossly oversimplified their relationship when
they assumed Forberg to be Fichte's disciple. To judge by Forberg's
Fragments on the philosophical scene at Jena, published in 1796, he was
no less in awe of Fichte's Promethean presence than the students who
crowded into his lecture hall. But he kept the great man at arm's length
with a skepticism bordering on cynicism. If "Kantian philosophy has been
criticized for obscurity," Forberg quipped, then "Fichte's must be faulted
for pitch darkness." Fichte was carrying to new extremes the current
philosophical obsession with the "chimeras" of "system." Listening to him
philosophizing was like watching a juggler. "Since he has made me mistrustful of the insights I had before him, should I be any less mistrustful
of those I had through him?"[11]

If Forberg saw Fichte as a man obsessed, Fichte had doubts about his
former colleague's seriousness of purpose. Forberg had a "clever" and
"lively" mind, he had reported to a protégé in Göttingen in early 1798,
but his lack of "steadiness" and "industry" lay so deep that he was "entirely
lacking in character."[12] Though he never said so publicly, Fichte probably

[10] Fichte, *Appellation*, p. 420.
[11] Friedrich Karl Forberg, *Fragmente aus meinen Papieren* (Jena, 1796), esp. pp. 71–8. There is a biography of Forberg in the *Allgemeine Deutsche Biographie* 7 (1877: Berlin, 1968): 153–4.
[12] Fichte to Johann Jakob Wagner in Göttingen, January 2, 1798, in GA, III, 3: 111.

found this judgment confirmed by Forberg's contribution to the *Philosophical Journal*. The essay seemed to offer a badly needed dose of plain speaking – an elucidation of Kant's distinction between theoretical and practical reason that spelled out its implications for religious belief without indulging in the new obscurantism of system builders like Fichte. Whether there is a God, Forberg concluded, "is and remains uncertain." His point was that the theoretical understanding could know neither whether God existed nor what his attributes were. It was superstition to feel "reverence for Divinity," and "whoever fears the Godhead has not yet found it." True "religion" was "nothing other than a *practical belief in a moral world government*," grounded in the "wish of the good heart that the good in the world maintain the upper hand over the evil."[13]

Was this atheism? In a sense it was; "righteousness" did not require a belief in God. But the other side of Forberg's argument was that, having been denied ontological status, God remained a necessary "practical" inference. One had a "duty" to "*act as if one believed*" in "a God as a world ruler." In an effort to avoid the "style of system" and perhaps to minimize the risks he was taking, Forberg offered these conclusions tentatively, as a set of "insidious questions." In the final paragraph he came close to disowning his own text. Was "the *concept of a practical belief more a matter of playing than a seriously philosophical concept?*" The reader would have to decide – and would have to judge "whether the author of the present essay in the end has only wanted to play with him!"[14] This was precisely the kind of flippancy that had led Fichte to conclude that Forberg's cleverness was in lieu of character.

Forberg's tentativeness did little to distract from the radical thrust of his essay. In France or England his argument might have been too commonplace to raise eyebrows, but in northern Germany, where the Enlightenment had such a marked Protestant coloration, it was bound to cause a stir. To be sure, one of the central goals of the German Enlightenment had been to clear away doctrinal clutter, so that the moral core of Protestantism would shine forth in its rational purity; but that effort had stopped well short of Forberg's simple equation of religion with a moral disposition. Its slippery ending aside, the clear import of Forberg's essay was that true morality and true religion were incompatible not only with evangelical fideism but also with the rational theism of several generations of German Protestant theologians.

The essay had a more immediate framework – one in which most German readers inevitably placed it. A little more than a decade earlier, Moses Mendelssohn and Friedrich Jacobi had waged their "Spinoza Controversy" before the educated public. In the wake of that controversy, questions about "atheism" – what intellectual routes led to it, how it might

[13] Forberg, "Entwicklung," pp. 56–8.   [14] Forberg, "Entwicklung," esp. pp. 43–4, 55–8.

be shown to be tenable or untenable, what its ethical implications were – took their place in a larger set of arguments about the epistemological configuration of philosophy, natural science, and religious belief in modern culture. Mendelssohn not only denied that his friend Lessing had been a Spinozist; he also insisted that philosophical reason, by itself, made the existence of God a certainty. In Jacobi, however, he faced a new kind of fideist. Rather than appeal to the authority of tradition or revelation, Jacobi bore witness to his existential need to embrace the irrational, to make an unmediated commitment to God with a "leap of faith."

Even those unwilling to make such a leap could not ignore Jacobi's brief against modern philosophy. If philosophy was consequential, Jacobi argued, it ended inevitably in "Spinozism." Its logic was the logic of natural science, the world of abstract relations among objects, governed by the all-encompassing law of sufficient cause. There could be no God distinct from the self-sufficient totality of this world, no independent presence that caused without being caused. Indeed modern philosophical rationality ultimately threw into doubt the existence of any objective reality, independent of the representations in consciousness. Aspiring to subsume everything under its abstractions, it ended with nothingness, a formalistic set of laws emptied of the concrete particularity of life, including the very existence of the personality.[15]

Fichte's stated agenda was to explain why Forberg's essay fell short of his own convictions, but his larger purpose was to offer a resolution to the issues with which Jacobi had confronted the German philosophical community. Where Forberg had applied Kant's distinction between theoretical understanding and practical reason, Fichte linked his essay more explicitly with Jacobi's position by distinguishing between the standpoint of "natural science" (or "common awareness") and the "transcendental" standpoint. If natural science remained within its cognitive limits, the world itself was an "absolute existence," an "organized and organizing whole"; in that case it became "total nonsense" to explain such a world by appeal to "the purposes of an Intelligence." If, on the other hand, natural science transgressed its limits in an effort to understand God, it produced an anthropomorphic concept, "full of contradictions" and hence "wavering." It was this road that led to "true atheism, actual unbelief, and Godlessness."[16]

[15] On the Spinoza (or "Pantheism") Controversy, see esp. Frederick C. Beiser, *The Fate of Reason. German Philosophy from Kant to Fichte* (Cambridge, Mass., 1987), pp. 44–108; Hermann Timm, *Gott und die Freiheit: Studien zur Religionsphilosophie der Goethezeit*, vol. 1: *Die Spinozarenaissance* (Frankfurt am Main, 1974); John H. Zammito, *The Genesis of Kant's Critique of Judgment* (Chicago and London, 1992), pp. 228–60. There is also a lucid précis in George di Giovanni, "The Early Fichte as Disciple of Jacobi," FS 9: 257–73. On Jacobi's thought see also Klaus Hammacher, *Kritik und Leben II. Die Philosophie F. H. Jacobis* (Munich, 1969); Karl Homann, *F. H. Jacobis Philosophie der Freiheit* (Munich, 1973).

[16] Fichte, "Über den Grund," pp. 29, 34–5.

All this implied that in his sweeping attack on pre-Kantian metaphysics Jacobi had hit the mark. But Fichte's larger point, of course, was that conceiving the "world" transcendentally, as "merely the reflection of our own inner activity," closed *both* roads to atheism. Though he claimed to be simply pushing beyond Forberg's essay, Fichte was in fact providing what he saw as a needed corrective to it. "Acting as if one believed" in God was, in Forberg's logic, a "*duty*"; but his choice of words might very well leave the impression that such a belief was closer to a self-conscious game, a kind of strategy of illusion, than to the grasp of truth, and the concluding coyness suggested that the "duty" was really a matter of subjective inclination. Hence Forberg made his position vulnerable to the charge that had been leveled against atheism for centuries: that it provided a rationale for the evasion of moral duty.

Fichte would later observe that Forberg had adopted the "currently fashionable" but "false" view that "belief" was "no more than an aid to lazy and despairing reason."[17] His own purpose was to demonstrate that transcendental idealism, properly conceived, justified a truly rational belief, which was the *only* grounding of true morality. The assumption that a good purpose could be realized was not, contra Forberg, "a wish, a hope, a consideration and speculation about reasons for and against, a free decision to accept something whose opposite one could also consider possible." Rather, that assumption "is simply necessary under the presupposition of the decision to obey the law in its inner essence; it is directly contained in that decision; it is itself that decision." To the extent that "God" could be said to exist "outside" the human conscience, it was not as a "being" in the usual sense but as the "ordering order" (*ordo ordinans*) of the Moral Law. God was in that sense the "moral world order" itself, the order of practical reason in which, despite the "immanent laws" of the sense world, the individual was free to follow his conscience and act dutifully.[18]

Fichte saw himself closing off the routes to evasion of duty that Forberg had inadvertently opened. Precisely because he was so confident of having

---

[17] Fichte, "From a Private Letter" (1800), in *Fichte. Introductions to the Wissenschaftslehre and Other Writings (1797–1800)*, trans. and ed. Daniel Breazeale (Indianapolis/Cambridge, 1994), p. 173. Originally published in PJ, 1800, and reprinted in GA, I, 6: 369–89. Cf. the contrast between Forberg's position and Fichte's in Hans Vaihinger, *The Philosophy of As If*, trans. C. K. Ogden (2d ed.: London, 1935), pp. 319–27.

[18] Fichte, "Über den Grund," pp. 33–5. Fichte later elaborated his defense against the charge of atheism by defining a "moral" order as "an order by means of which there arises a moral or intelligible *interconnectedness* or *system*," and by arguing: "a person who posits this moral order undoubtedly does not posit it within the finite, moral being, but posits it outside of the latter. Accordingly, he undoubtedly assumes something else in addition to and outside of this finite being." Fichte, "From a Private Letter," pp. 171–2. On Fichte's notion of an "*ordo ordinans*," see also Heinrich Rickert, "Fichtes Atheismusstreit und die Kantische Philosophie," *Kant-Studien* 4: 2 (1899): 154–60.

done so, he did not hesitate to push beyond Forberg's equivocations. Here is the key passage, the one that would soon be notorious:

> It is, accordingly, a misunderstanding to claim that it is doubtful whether a God exists or does not exist. What is by no means doubtful but is, rather, the most certain thing of all, and indeed, the ground of all other certainty and the sole absolutely valid objective [truth], is this: that there is a moral world order; that every rational individual is assigned his own specific place in this order and has a contribution to make to it through his own labor. . . . On the other hand, it can remain as little doubtful to anyone who reflects upon this, even for a moment, and who is willing to admit honestly to himself the results of his reflections, that the concept of God as a particular substance is impossible and contradictory.[19]

There is a certain irony in the fact that Fichte's rejection of "the concept of God as a particular substance" outraged many of his contemporaries. In the long view it was an unexceptional conclusion. If the human mind aspired to conceptualize the Divinity, it could do so only by imagining a particular substance – that is, by attributing to transcendent Being qualities derived from the finite world of sense experience. It had been widely recognized for centuries in western metaphysics, and indeed in theology as well, that this cognitive leap from finite particularity to infinite universality was inherently contradictory. One could avoid the leap, of course, and still posit the *existence* of a Supreme Being. But what if the Supreme Being could be said to exist only in the form of the pure rationality of the Moral Law? Was that a way of avoiding atheism or a way of embracing it?

This was the crux of the issue posed by Fichte's essay. He later claimed to have said exactly what Kant had said and professed to be puzzled that he, but not Kant, had been accused of atheism. To appreciate the full historical significance of his essay, however, we need to see how Fichte moved beyond the Critical Philosophy even as his thought developed out of it. Kant sought to develop a moral theology, grounded in practical reason. He saw this strategy as an alternative both to a theological morality and to the ontological proof of God's existence that traditional metaphysics claimed to offer. If a moral end is to be rational, one must believe that it is possible of attainment through one's actions and that one will be granted happiness in accord with one's moral desert. Both possibilities depend on the existence of an omniscient, omnipotent, just, and benevolent being.[20] In 1788, in an essay entitled "What It Means to Orient

---

[19] Fichte, "Uber den Grund," p. 37.

[20] Kant's thinking about "religion" and "God" is something of a conceptual minefield. I have relied heavily on the exceptionally lucid and balanced explications by Allen W. Wood. See esp. *Kant's Moral Religion* (Ithaca, N.Y., 1970); *Kant's Rational Theology* (Ithaca, N.Y., 1978); "Rational Theology, Moral Faith, and Religion," in Paul Guyer, ed., *The Cambridge Companion to Kant* (Cambridge,

Oneself in Thought," Kant had elaborated this moral (or practical) argument. The essay was a delicate, not to say excruciating, exercise in mediation, designed to counter Jacobi's irrational fideism without repeating what Kant considered to be Mendelssohn's violation of reason's self-imposed limits. The concept of God as the "highest independent good," Kant argued, was a "belief of reason" (*Vernunftglaube*). He had chosen a term rich in paradox. It made belief in God a "subjective" maxim of practical reason and not, as Mendelssohn would have it, an "objective principle" of theoretical reason. But this was not the irrational subjectivity in which Jacobi took refuge; it did not imply a blind "leap of faith." Rather, the assumption that God exists was a "postulate," produced by a felt "need" of practical reason, and grounded only in the "data" of "pure reason." Unlike theoretical knowledge of the natural world, it could not be demonstrated; but it was different in kind from such knowledge, not inferior to it in degree of certainty.[21]

Kant made it clear in other contexts that he did not consider belief in God to be *necessary* for morality. What did it mean, then, to characterize belief in God as a postulate? That such a belief was "rationally justified," in the sense that Practical Reason made God's existence a certainty? That the only rationally justifiable belief was in the *possibility* of God's existence – in which case the postulate really was an if/then proposition, a hypothesis (neither provable nor unprovable) serving what has been called a "hopeful agnosticism"? Or was Kant simply stating, in a roundabout way, Forberg's "as if" argument, and indeed in a more radical version? Was he saying that acting as if God existed could be morally efficacious, but without implying that, as Forberg would argue so tentatively, it was morally obligatory? Kant's varying emphases seemed to allow for all these alternatives, probably because he was intent on making his position compatible with as wide a spectrum of belief (and nonbelief) as possible. But his preference was clearly for the kind of "moral theism" (his term) to be found in *Religion within the Limits of Reason Alone*, and that was precisely what Fichte's approach precluded.[22]

Kant had begun the "orientation" essay by observing that no matter how much we abstract our concepts from sense experience, "imagistic representations" are still attached to them. Thanks to those representations, the concepts, though not derived from experience, are made usable in experience. With this concession to sense experience he developed what he called a "symbolic" anthropomorphism, an "analogical predication" of

---

1992), pp. 394–416. On atheism and Kant's position, see also Michael J. Buckley, S. J., *At the Origins of Modern Atheism* (New Haven and London, 1987), pp. 326–31. On the larger issue of the origins of atheism, see Alan Charles Kors, *Atheism in France, 1650–1729* (Princeton, N.J., 1990).

[21] There is a translation of the essay in *Kant. Political Writings*, ed. Hans Reiss (2d, enl. ed.: Cambridge, 1991), pp. 237–49.

[22] Wood, "Rational Theology," esp. pp. 401–4.

moral perfections to the Deity. As the moral theology of *Religion* demonstrated, it was an approach that accommodated a great deal of Protestant
doctrine. The mission of critical reason was not to disprove the essential
tenets of Protestantism, but to penetrate behind their historical shells to
their pure rationality. Reason confirmed what the imagistic narratives of
Scripture had revealed in historically specific terms: that the Supreme
Being is a "living God," a moral Person and a moral Legislator.[23]

When Fichte's essay is set against this approach, it becomes understandable that he alarmed even "enlightened" believers in a way that Kant
had not. Jolted by Forberg's mix of recklessness and timidity, Fichte completed the line of reasoning he had begun in *An Attempt at a Critique of
all Revelation*, roughly two years before he had worked out the first version
of his system. In the *Attempt*, belief in God was neither a postulate in
Kant's strong sense nor an illusion in Forberg's (and perhaps Kant's) weak
sense. Instead, "the idea of God, as lawgiver through the moral law in us,
is based on an alienation of what is ours, on translating something subjective into a being outside us." The projection was necessary for individuals and peoples who could only be influenced through sensibility, but
from the standpoint of pure reason it was a regrettable resort to anthropomorphism. To project a God was to alienate oneself from the inner
voice of conscience, and thus to create a potential instrument for the
oppression of conscience.[24]

In the 1798 essay Fichte, having sketched out his own theory of consciousness, was in a position to pursue another implication of this argument – one that put the emphasis on the danger of a kind of moral
escapism rather than on the threat of oppression. There was no way of
conceiving of God as a Being distinct from the moral order without
assuming a "particular being . . . capable of having a personality and consciousness." With such a concept, one has not "thought God" but has
merely "multiplied [oneself] in thinking." Precisely because the concept
mediates between the self and the moral law, it eliminates the "absolute
certainty" that reverence for the moral law, by itself, entails and opens the
way to all sorts of duty-evading "cleverness" (*Klügelei*).[25] *Any* projection,
in other words, was a dangerous illusion; behind the apparent awe in the
face of the Absolute, it offered a subjective escape from the categorical
demands of duty.

Even as Fichte's move precluded the "as if," it argued for the immorality of belief in an Absolute Other. His article denied that the practical
reason of transcendental philosophy could be expressed, even by analogy,

---

[23] Wood, *Kant's Moral Religion*, pp. 132–98.
[24] Fichte, *Attempt at a Critique of All Revelation*, trans. Garrett Green (Cambridge, 1978), p. 73.
[25] Fichte, "Über den Grund," pp. 35–6.

in Christian images of God. It shut the door on any effort to salvage moral theism, including Kant's.

★ ★ ★

How could the governments of six German states give credence to a pamphlet as scurrilous as the *Writing of a Father*? In his *Justification* to the Weimar government Fichte wrote that, since no one had dared print the obvious answer, he would have to supply it himself:

> To them I am a democrat, a Jacobin; that is it. Of such a person one believes any abomination without further examination. . . . It is not my atheism that they persecute legally, it is my democratism. The former has only given them the occasion. If I defend myself only against what is allowed to be heard, the process against me is merely put off; they continue to hate me and to execrate me, and will seize the next opportunity to get an even tighter grip on me.[26]

Fichte went on to exonerate himself from the charge of "democratism" by citing the relevant pasages from his *Naturrecht*. That "more maturely thought-through writing," and not the *Contribution*, was the proper "measure of [his] political principles." Determined to shake off the albatross at last, he dismissed the *Contribution* as an understandable, though regrettable, indiscretion of his youth, a one-sided fragment by a young man "who had given up his fatherland and was attached to no state."[27]

As Fichte saw it, the articles in the *Philosophical Journal* had provided an excuse for a political witch-hunt. This view was not entirely off the mark; the alarm about his "godlessness" often did serve an unspoken political agenda. That he distinguished between a religious excuse for persecution and the real political motive behind it, however, was a measure of his näivete about the ideological climate of the late 1790s. In the recoil from the excesses of the Revolution – the nationalization of church property, the persecution of the clergy, the spasms of mob violence, the Reign of Terror – atheism and Jacobinism, irreligion and democracy, had become virtually coterminous. The lesson of the Revolution was that "democratism," the political corollary of "atheism," licensed anarchic violence from below; and if there was any doubt that democrats were atheists, it was dispelled by the Jacobins' merciless war on Christianity.

But who were "they"? Intent on proving that he was the victim of a concerted movement, Fichte saw the Saxon government as the instrument of "a numerous, clever, politically weighty party" pursuing "a long-considered and slowly and intentionally executed plan."[28] And yet, as his

---

[26] Fichte, *Verantwortungsschrift*, pp. 72–3.   [27] Ibid., pp. 73–4.
[28] Fichte, *Appellation*, p. 422. See also GA, III, 3: 354–5.

efforts to defend himself implicitly acknowledged, he was facing a broad
spectrum of hostile opinion, far more varied than the word "party" would
suggest. Even as he tried to lump all his "enemies" into one camp, he had
to wage several wars at once.

At one end of the spectrum Fichte placed those who believed that
only the repression of "free inquiry" and the imposition of certain "confessional beliefs" would insure "the security of states." He predicted that
if they were allowed to include him in that rare event, the "theatrical
exhibit (*Schauspiel*) of some deniers of God," there would be within a
decade "no smaller fuss" about "the slightest deviation from the slightest
phrase in the *Concordien* formular."[29] Here Fichte was pointing to the
species of modern conservatism that had its normative source in Lutheran
Orthodoxy. The mounting hostility to the Enlightenment's efforts to
rationalize Protestantism from within, already apparent in the 1780s, had
become a full-blown antirevolutionary ideology over the next decade. In
this view the deification of Reason bore the blame for the horrors of the
revolutionary decade. By spreading unbelief, the Enlightenment had cor-
roded political as well as ecclesiastical authority, and the result was "democratic" anarchy. The indictment rode roughshod over the fundamental
differences among eighteenth-century philosophes, and then simply added
the German transcendentalists and idealists of the 1790s to its cast of vil-
lains, despite their open disdain for French rationalism. In one of its many
versions, Fichte had joined a "crowd of spirits of revolution (*Revolu-
tionsgeistern*)" who had been inspired by the "systems" of Diderot,
Helvetius, Rousseau, and Mably to commit and indeed sanctify all sorts
of crimes against nature, humanity, justice, and property.[30]

Fichte's public commitment to "atheism" was a moment of vindication
in the counteroffensive by Orthodox conservatism against the Enlightenment and its revolutionary offspring. The horrors of the Revolution stood
as a condemnation of modern "philosophy," and philosophy was so
broadly defined as to represent secular rationalism in all its forms. It was
above all this strain of antirevolutionary sentiment that fed on the grossly
exaggerated danger of German "Jacobinism" and that targeted Fichte, from
his debut as a philosopher with the writings of 1792 and 1793, as a prime
exhibit. As he well knew, his fiercest opponents in Weimar and neighboring states were a number of well-placed Orthodox clergymen. They
had spearheaded the attacks on his teaching at Jena and had supplied the
rumors for the rabid exposés of his Jacobinism in *Eudämonia*.

Forberg wrote Fichte in late January 1794 that in the face of this reactionary force there was virtually nothing to fear. On their side was "the

---

[29] Fichte, *Appellation*, pp. 419–20.
[30] The author was Johann Gottfried Dyck, whom Fichte had known in Leipzig. Fichte appended
Dyck's brief pamphlet to the published version of his *Justification*. GA, I, 6: 138–43.

Enlightenment," and in Germany the Enlightenment was a "power" to be reckoned with.[31] It is hard to know whether Forberg was displaying a naïvete that sat oddly with his cynicism or was simply feigning courage (he also asked Fichte to help him find another position). His remark would have made some sense fifteen or twenty years earlier, though even then the concept of a single, unitary "Enlightenment" papered over numerous fissures. By 1799 the German Enlightenment had lost whatever unity of purpose it might have had; the movement had generated severe internal strains and was fracturing beyond repair. With the Atheism Conflict some of the deepest sources of stress became visible. For that very reason, the Orthodox, though they surely used their influence behind the scenes, particularly at the courts, did not figure prominently in the Conflict's war of printed words. They could afford to sit back and watch as the Conflict activated fault lines between different kinds of rationalism within the Enlightenment broadly defined.

Fichte was well aware of this situation, though he could not refrain from exacerbating it. In the *Appellation* he complained that "theologians known as enlightened and benevolent" were pressing for his removal from office. Perhaps uppermost in his mind was Franz Volkmar Reinhard, the High Court Chaplain in Dresden and a member of the Saxon High Consistory since 1792. Reinhard's philosophical theology, recorded in volume upon volume of his renowned sermons, represents an ambitious variation on the German Enlightenment's commitment to reconciling faith and reason. His unshakeable belief in biblical revelation was balanced by qualified admiration for Kant's moral philosophy. He also admired Fichte's *Attempt at a Critique of all Revelation*, which he, like so many others, originally attributed to Kant. Indeed Reinhard had gone so far as to encourage Fichte to seek an appointment in Saxony. In a letter in February 1793, Fichte had tried to turn Reinhard's reservations about the Critical Philosophy to his own advantage. Only his systematic advance beyond Kant, he had confided to the Court Chaplain, would repel "the most unholy skepticism," far worse than Hume's, that threatened to destroy "all of philosophy."[32] Still without an office and hoping to secure a potential patron in his fatherland, he added an effusive dedication to Reinhard to the second edition of the *Attempt*.

But the articles in the *Philosophical Journal* were a far more serious affront to Reinhard's fideism than anything he had found in Kant. He was one of the three signators of the notice about Forberg's article; and though rumors may have exaggerated his role, he probably supported the Saxon government's subsequent actions against the journal and Fichte.

---

[31] Friedrich Karl Forberg to Fichte, Jan. 24, 1799, in GA, III, 3: 182.
[32] GA, III, 1: 374. On Reinhard, see the *Allgemeine Deutsche Bibliothek* 28 (1889: Berlin, 1970), pp. 32–5.

More typical of Ficht's "enlightened" opponents was the author of the initial attack, the *Writing of a Father*, a vitriolic pamphlet in the form of a letter to a son studying for the clergy. This paternal warning clearly was not in the voice of Orthodoxy, but it also had none of Reinhard's openness toward the new philosophy. The authors recommended as correctives to Kant and Fichte were Reimarus, the German Deist made famous in Lessing's *Fragmenten*; Spalding, the most widely read of the group of enlightened theologians that the Orthodox called the Neologists; Jerusalem, another popular neologist; and Friedrich Nicolai, a prominent publisher and a doyen of the Berlin Enlightenment. The signature "G . . ." was probably meant to suggest that the author was J. P. Gabler, another enlightened theologian.[33]

The antagonists Fichte faced in this direction were veterans of the pre-Kantian Enlightenment. That label, to be sure, crowds into one camp a varied assortment of philosophers, theologians, government officials, publicists, and men of letters. While some leaned toward Wollfian metaphysics, others preferred Lockean empiricism or Scottish "common sense" philosophy. Their religious beliefs ranged from a Deism largely stripped of Christian trappings to an "enlightened" but still emphatically theistic (and Protestant) theology. What nonetheless bound them was a sense of frustration and disappointment that had been mounting since Kant's *Critiques* had begun to command attention in the late 1780s and that now found a splendid target in Fichte. The new philosophy was not simply one more academic novelty; it seemed to shatter assumptions that underlay the veterans' very belief in enlightened progress. As much as they disagreed on epistemological issues, they shared a trust in what they called a "healthy human reason." They were convinced that theory, so long as it was derived from the concrete empirical data of "experience," could be publicly accessible. From this standpoint Kantian transcendentalism was a regression to the metaphysical system building of the seventeenth century and worse, to *Schwärmerei*, the German counterpart to "enthusiasm," the mistaking of chimeras for a spirituality of privileged insight, as had happened so often in radical Protestant sectarianism. The veterans had expected philosophy to play a key role in building the consensus that would endow the reading public with moral authority; and that required a new clarity that would make philosophy far more accessible to the educated public at large. Kant seemed to have introduced a new obscurantism, hyperabstract, jargonish, disdaining even to make the effort to be accessible. Progress required public openness, but this philosophical variation on religious enthusiasm offered instead a new scholastic introversion, the paradox of sectarian closure within the apparent promise of universality.

---

[33] *Schreiben eines Vaters*, pp. 137–8.

The polemical outpourings of Friedrich Nicolai record this reaction profusely, perhaps to the point of unintended caricature; and they register the disappointment that lay behind it. Nicolai's generation of rationalists had fought for decades to free German public life from the grip of confessional Orthodoxy. It came as a shock to them that the upcoming generations – the generations of young men who ought to have represented the enlightenment come of age – were so susceptible to new forms of irrationalist obscurantism. By the 1790s Fichte was an all-too-familiar type, one more *enfant terrible*, his popularity among students reminiscent of the Werther-cult of the late 1770s. Having taken root in literature, the new subjectivism had spread, via Kant, to philosophy. In Kant's "unphilosophical consequence," Nicolai charged, lay the basis for Fichte's "unphilosophical *Schwärmerey.*" Like earlier outbreaks of *Schwärmerei*, this one was marked by the translation of emotional self-indulgence into a vaulting presumption of "inner" wisdom; by an extreme intolerance that demonized opponents; by the perversion of public language into esoteric nonsense; by the abuse of words as verbal instruments of violence. Nicolai saw a direct line of descent from Kant's "dictatorial" Reason to Fichte's way of "elevating the heart over the head." Under the guise of a priori knowledge, bottomless subjectivism had produced a sectarian claim to the monopoly of objective truth.[34]

In view of the recent Orthodox crackdown in Prussia and several other North German states, there was something ironic about the Orthodox conservatives and pre-Kantian *Aufklärer* overlapping, albeit only partially, in their shared animus toward an Idealist philosopher. By 1798 the Orthodox campaign to purge the clergy and academe of "enlightened" subversives was largely spent, but even the provocations of a Fichte could not bridge the underlying disagreement between Orthodoxy and Enlightenment. Orthodox conservatives envisioned the restoration of a public community of belief, an adherence to articles of faith that would preclude social conflict and political contestation. To them, Fichte's public advocacy of atheism confirmed that freedom of the press, like other "freedoms" that licensed all sorts of abuse, had to be severely curtailed. Rationalists sought a public community of inquiry, moving toward consensus by the force and counterforce of criticism. They saw gradual reform from above as the only alternative to revolutionary upheavals, and the moral force exercised through "publicity" – through the public openness

---

[34] Friedrich Nicolai, *Ueber meine gelehrte Bildung, über meine Kenntniss der kritischen Philosophie und meine Schriften dieselbe betreffend, und über die Herren Kant, J. B. Erhard, und Fichte* (1798), in *Sämtliche Werke*, vol. 6 (1995), esp. pp. 542–78. For a similar view see J. A. Eberhard, *Ueber den Gott des Herrn Professor Fichte und den Götzen seiner Gegner* (Halle, 1799), esp. pp. 4–7. On Nicolai and the Enlightenment, see Horst Möller, *Aufklärung in Preussen: Der Verleger, Publizist, und Geschichtsschreiber Friedrich Nicolai* (Berlin, 1974).

of a free press – as the sine qua non for reform. Fichte's recklessness deserved censure precisely because it might provide an excuse for a new wave of repression. With this danger in mind, Nicolai took pains to assure the reading public and the German governments that there was nothing immoral or even morally slack about Fichte's alleged atheism. Quite the contrary; it derived from an uncompromising moral rigorism. As wrong-headed as it was, it posed no danger to public order.[35]

On that issue, however, other rationalists were closer to the Orthodox position than they might at first appear to be. A prominent case in point was Fichte's sovereign, Duke Karl August of Weimar, who took seriously his responsibilities as titular head of his duchy's Lutheran Church but who was a freethinker behind the closed doors of his masonic lodge. Fichte's "theoretical" equation of God with "virtue" struck the Duke as no more "absurd" than "theoretical religion." The problem was that the equation made no sense to anyone who "cannot let himself plunge into the bombast of incomprehensible words"; hence, from the standpoint of the public utility of religion, it was hopelessly inadequate.[36] Georg Christoph Lichtenberg, the mathematician and natural scientist at Göttingen, applied much the same logic, though his rationalist skepticism was of a different shade:

> We more sophisticated Christians have contempt for image worship, that is, our dear God does not consist of wood and gold froth, but He remains always an image that is only another piece in the series, finer, but always an image. If the spirit wants to tear itself from this image worship, it falls finally into the Kantian Idea. But it is presumption to think that a being as mixed as the human being will recognize the All so *purely*. All that the truly wise person can do is to guide everything to a good purpose, and yet take human beings as they are. Herr Fichte seems to understand nothing of this, and in this respect he is a rash fool.[37]

Rationalists like Lichtenberg agreed with Fichte that "God" need not be depicted as "an old man, a young man, and a dove."[38] But Fichte's position brought to the surface a social logic they shared with Ortho-doxy. For the great mass of the population, and perhaps for most edu-cated people as well, moral self-discipline – ultimately the only guarantor of public order – had to be grounded in reverence for a transcendent authority; and only a sense image – whether it was the Persons of the Trinity, or the figure of the wise Legislator, or the wondrous design of nature – could command that reverence. Lichtenberg and like-minded contemporaries were well aware that the Orthodox brandished images of a stern but benevolent God the Father to justify their own abuses

[35] Nicolai, *Ueber meine gelehrte Bildung*, p. 544–5.
[36] FG 2: 31. [37] FG 2: pp. 56–7. [38] Fichte, *Appellation*, p. 435.

of authority; but they were also convinced that *some* image of the Divine was the symbolic lynchpin of order and stability in a public culture. Fichte's atheism was dangerous not because it advocated immorality and disregard for public authority but because it licensed them unintentionally. Subjectivity, even in the form of an ardent embrace of virtue and duty, could not be left to itself; without an authority objectified in some form – without some sort of public object of reverence – subjectivity could not be trusted.

In its simplest variation, this argument harked back to Voltaire's rationalism, which was as skeptical about the possibilities of human nature as it was about Christian dogma. However superfluous the belief in God might be for the enlightened few, it was their only guarantor that the masses would not descend into savagery. Fichte's old adversary August Wilhelm Rehberg, a conservative in politics but a religious skeptic, put the case clearly in his contribution to the Atheism Conflict. Thanks to his ethical commitments, Fichte was not "personally" an atheist; but his philosophy would produce "frightful atheists" if it penetrated "the people and the most mindless part of people." Fichte's fault lay in being "the strictest purist." By "mistak[ing] the possibilities of human nature" and advocating a "superhuman" ideal, he threatened to license barbarism.[39]

In the *Appellation* Fichte took a swipe at the Orthodox agenda for a politically imposed dogmatism, but his main purpose was to refute the *Writing of a Father* and the broad spectrum of rationalist opinion it represented. In an attempt to throw the rationalists into the same pot with the Orthodox, he accused all his opponents of subscribing to a "doctrine of happiness" that amounted to "idolatry" and, in substance if not in intention, was atheistic. Whether one performed one's duty to enjoy happiness in an afterlife or to achieve self-fulfillment in this life, the result was the same: spiritual growth was reduced to daily progress in becoming "more reasonable and clever about your true advantage." But the rationalist version of this "enervating" strategy was clearly more pernicious, and that was precisely because in rejecting the Orthodox doctrine of Original Sin, it licensed the natural man to pursue a false freedom. There lay the real threat to "civil order"; the individual was being told that "he himself undoubtedly is the best judge of what constitutes happiness for his person," and the result was rampant materialism and social climbing.[40]

Fichte was arguing that an apparently irreconcilable disagreement between Orthodoxy and rationalism (including the Neologists) camouflaged a shared logic of motivation. So long as the motive for virtue was

---

[39] August Wilhelm Rehberg, *Appellation an den gesunden Menschenverstand, in einigen Aphorismen über des Herrn Professor Fichtes Appellation an das Publikum wegen ihm beygemessener atheistischen Aeusserungen* (Hanover, 1799).

[40] Fichte, *Appellation*, pp. 436–44.

the pursuit of happiness (or personal "advantage"), it hardly mattered whether human nature was considered to be inherently corrupt or inclined to good. Eudaemonism in all its forms licensed arbitrary subjectivism, the self-serving calculation that Fichte called "cleverness." He, on the other hand, was, as Rehberg would put it, "the strictest purist." True freedom was the freedom to perform one's duty despite the pull of natural desires. Through the rational commitment to duty for its own sake we "attain a higher existence, which is independent of all nature and is grounded only in us." The concept of God – what he called the "holy order" – was "posited directly in [our] inner life (*Innern*)," which was to say that the moral feeling derived not from the concept of a Supreme Being meting out rewards and retribution, but from "the absolute self-sufficiency of Reason."[41]

Fichte aimed to convince his readers that his philosophy, and *only* his philosophy, distilled the essence of Protestant spirituality; and to that end he employed language resonant with the metaphors of the evangelical tradition. Was he not affirming the message of the New Testament: that salvation lay in the death of the flesh, the denial of the "natural being" in a "total rebirth"? The human being could acquire "power" only "through struggle with himself and overcoming of himself." To those who objected that he expected too much of people, Fichte could offer no compromise. People could not be lifted gradually to morality through the "allurements and fear tactics of superstition," and then through "legality." This was "the language of weakness and half-measures." It failed to recognize that "there is no steady transition from sensuality to morality that proceeds, for example, through external honorable behavior; [that] the transformation must occur through a leap, and must be not merely improvement, but an entire re-creation; [that] it must be a rebirth (*Wiedergeburt*)."[42]

In this defense of his contention that "God" was to be found in the true self, the moral person, Fichte had to lay bare the foundation of his own construction of selfhood. That the alleged atheist chose to speak in the idiom of Lutheranism was not simply a tactical decision; in his irreducible moral vision, he *was* a Protestant. The language of rebirth was more than a rhetorical allusion. Fichte was grounding his public self-defense in the new conviction of selfhood – the transcendental centering in conscience – that he owed to his reading of Kant. He preached the same ethic of freedom through self-denial that had rescued him from fatalism nearly a decade earlier. It was the essentially Protestant moral rigorism of the *Critique of Practical Reason*, though now formulated as an asceticism that even Kant might have found excessively grim.

There was a sense, then, in which the rhetorical strategy of the *Appellation* was a cry from the heart. It was also, however, a tactically dubious

---

[41] Ibid., pp. 426–7.   [42] Ibid., pp. 432–3, 445–7.

move. Even to readers who found the attacks on Fichte's essay intolerant, there was something shocking about his response. The victim was hurling the same irresponsible charge of atheism against his persecutors. Indeed he was leveling the charge at the only people who might be expected to come to his defense, despite their disagreements with him. The Protestant rationalists of the German Enlightenment – the veterans who had taken such pains to reconcile faith and reason – were infuriated to find themselves lumped together with godless British and French materialists at one extreme and with Orthodox zealots at the other.[43] Was this not a reckless abuse of the term "idolatry?" In his attempt to tar all his opponents with the same brush, Fichte seemed to isolate himself.

Taking the moral high ground had another disadvantage, rich in irony. The controversy had begun with familiar cries of alarm that atheism licensed immorality and hence threatened to undermine public order. In the wake of the *Appellation*, the more common complaint about Fichte's position was that it was morally rigorous to a fault. Within the larger context of his philosophy, of course, it was clear enough that Fichte was not calling for a complete withdrawal from worldly comforts to a life devoted to mortifications of the flesh; but that was the impression left by his rhetorical contrasts between his own ethic and his opponent's moral flaccidity. Rationalist critics like Nicolai were quick to charge that Fichte's philosophy, for all its claims to be pointing humanity to perfectibility, was in fact regressive. While the Enlightenment had sought to make the world a better place by inculcating a civic ethic of "usefulness" and service, Fichte seemed to be preaching a "monkish" other-worldliness, all too reminiscent of the dark side of Christianity.[44]

Fichte had put himself in a double bind. If his view of human nature was open to the charge of being hopelessly utopian, it could also seem depressingly negative. From the latter standpoint, whether he denied the existence of God was of secondary importance. Veterans of the Enlightenment found his kind of rigorism *in itself* offensive, even if it did not entail a commitment to "atheism."

★ ★ ★

Toward the end of the *Appellation*, in a belated effort to effect a truce, Fichte asked his antagonists to consider two possibilities. One was that the process of public debate would leave him standing "entirely alone," and in that case they could dismiss him as a mere *Schwärmer*. But was it not also possible that some of the most esteemed thinkers of the age agreed with him? He appealed for confirmation to two widely read theologians, Reinhard and Spalding, and "among the philosophers" to the

---

[43] Perhaps the best example of this reaction is Eberhard, *Ueber den Gott des Herrn Professor Fichte.*
[44] Nicolai, *Ueber meine gelehrte Bildung*, pp. 550–7.

"noble Jacobi," whose differences with him were surely over "mere theory."[45]

That Spalding and Reinhard remained silent came as no surprise to Fichte. His purpose in naming them had been to expose their timidity or, worse, their hypocrisy. But Jacobi was another matter. To Fichte, Jacobi was a kindred spirit, a man who had used his literary gifts, the "power" and "warmth" of his prose, to convey the same core truth that he himself struggled to demonstrate philosophically.

Jacobi's response to Fichte's appeal took the form of a long letter, composed over the first three weeks of March, and published, with a preface, an expanded conclusion, and appendices from his earlier writings, shortly thereafter. Fichte's initial impression was that the letter had vindicated him, and in a sense he was right. Only later, when the smoke was beginning to clear, did he realize that Jacobi had questioned his thought far more radically than had his opponents among the Aufklärer. It was Jacobi, more than any other contributor to the Atheism Conflict, who challenged Fichte's position at its philosophical core. Even as he defended Fichte's moral integrity, Jacobi charged him with "nihilism" – a conceptual expunction of God that made the very notions of moral freedom and responsibility meaningless and that evaporated the self into abstract "nothingness."[46] Though the charge did not do justice to Fichte's philosophy, it was incisive. Jacobi made clear what the intensity of Fichte's spiritual and ethical commitments easily obscures: that Transcendental Idealism was as much a rejection of German Protestantism as it was a reformulation of it, since it precluded Protestant fideism in any form.

This is not to imply that Fichte had deluded himself about Jacobi; he had good reasons to expect his support. As young men, both had initially found the logic of materialist philosophy irrefutable and had escaped its grasp still shuddering at the possibility that man's will was subject to the same "mechanical" laws as physical nature. Confronted with the mechanistic determinism of natural science, they seemed to

[45] Fichte, Appellation, pp. 447–81.
[46] Particularly important for my analysis of Jacobi and his argument with Fichte is the recent work of George Di Giovanni; see esp. his "The First Twenty Years of Critique: The Spinoza Connection," in Guyer, ed., The Cambridge Companion to Kant, pp. 417–48; "From Jacobi's Philosophical Novel to Fichte's Idealism: Some Comments on the 1789–99 'Atheism Dispute,'" Journal of the History of Philosophy 27 (1989): 75–100; "Fichte's Rhetoric of Deception: Reflections on the Early Fichte in the Spirit of Jacobi," Revue International de Philosophie 49, No. 191 (February, 1995): 59–78; "The Early Fichte as Disciple of Jacobi." Also relevant are Reinhard Lauth, "Fichtes Verhältnis zu Jacobi unter besonderer Berücksichtigung der Role Friedrich Schlegels in dieser Sache," in Klaus Hammacher, ed., Friedrich Heinrich Jacobi. Philosoph und Literat der Goethezeit (Frankfurt am Main, 1971), pp. 165–97; Hans-Jürgen Gawoll, Nihilismus und Metaphysik (Stuttgart, 1989), esp. pp. 22–71. The essays in F-S 14 (1998) ("Fichte and Jacobi") provide a broad reexamination of the affinities and disagreements between Fichte and Jacobi, particularly in the years following the Atheism Conflict.

share an urgent need to vindicate the inner, unconditioned spontaneity of the self as a moral being. Each in his way a moral rigorist, they also shared a repugnance for the materialism and the sensuality of their age and for the Enlightenment principles – the appeals to eudaemonism, to utilitarianism, to rational self-interest, and so on – that seemed to license them.[47]

Even Jacobi's sweeping rejection of "philosophy" seemed to make him Fichte's natural ally, particularly when it became apparent that he made no exception for Kant's Critical Philosophy. In early 1786, at the height of his controversy with Mendelssohn about Lessing's alleged Spinozism, Jacobi had assumed that Kant's critique of traditional metaphysics was parallel to his own. Kant's "orientation" essay disabused him of that view. The concept of a "belief of reason" was meant to correct, not to repudiate, Mendelssohn's effort to provide a rational alternative to the emotional intuitionism, the "pretended secret sense of truth," that Jacobi's famous "salto mortale" entailed. Dismissed by the Sage of Königsberg as a kind of *Schwärmer*, Jacobi proceeded to apply to Kant's Critical Philosophy the same method of immanent critique to which he had subjected Spinoza. What mattered was not the manifest content of a philosophical text but its latent implication. The philosopher might not acknowledge that implication, and indeed might not be aware of it, but it was unavoidable; without it the logic of his thought impelled him into hopeless contradiction.

To Jacobi, Spinoza, though claiming to achieve a knowledge of God, in fact conceived of material "substance" monistically, as an absolute totality, thus precluding the existence of God as "an absolute otherness." Likewise Kant argued that we had to assume the existence of "things in-themselves," but his epistemology could not make that assumption without destroying the very transcendentalism to which it was committed. This was the thrust of Jacobi's initial public criticism of "Transcendental Idealism," which appeared as the supplement to his *David Hume on Faith* in 1787. He issued a challenge to Kant's "supporters," who were intent on avoiding the charge of "idealism." Refusing to abandon the presupposition that objects "bring about representations," they continued to posit "objects outside us as things in themselves," even as they made them "mere determinations of our own self." Jacobi described the double bind he had entered in trying to grasp Kant's *Critique of Pure Reason*. Without the presupposition of things-in-themselves he "could not enter the system," but with it he "could not stay within it." Kantians must "have the courage" to go the full route, to "disavow" the presupposition and "assert the strongest idealism that was ever professed." If Kantian philosophy "distance[d] itself even by a hairsbreadth from the transcendental

---

[47] Cf. di Giovanni, "The Early Fichte as Disciple of Jacobi."

ignorance that transcendental idealism professes," it could not claim to have set reason "to rest."[48]

Seven years later, when Fichte set out on the path that ended in the *Foundations*, it was from precisely this point of departure. He had seen the same epistemological contradiction that Jacobi had targeted. He agreed with Jacobi that the only way to avoid the contradiction – and hence to avoid reducing the self to a thing among things – was to embrace transcendental idealism as an unconditional principle, disallowing the very thought of a thing-in-itself. Having taken this radical turn, Fichte had reason to believe that he and Jacobi, sharing the same moral vision, had arrived at the same truth, albeit by different routes. On August 30, 1795, in the tranquillity of his self-imposed exile in Osmannstädt, he wrote Jacobi a letter that was obviously designed to enlist him as an ally but was also a gesture of sincere admiration. Over the summer he had reread again and again Jacobi's writings and especially the philosophical novel *Allwill*. He was well aware that they differed in their philosophical approaches; Jacobi was a known "realist" while he himself was a "transcendental idealist and an even stricter one than *Kant*." Hence he was all the more "astonished by the striking similarity of [their] philosophical convictions." By demonstrating that idealists "are content to protect their own boundaries," he (Fichte) had met the "condition" for the "peace" and even for the "sort of alliance" with realists that *Allwill* allowed.[49] In his response on December 24, 1795, Jacobi pleaded lack of time, but promised to "say something more definite" at a later date about "[his] feeling of [their] harmony."[50]

In late April 1796, in response to a complimentary letter from Jacobi, Fichte returned to this theme:

We are in complete agreement, and this agreement with you proves to me more than anything else that I am on the right track. You too seek all truth where I seek it: in the innermost sanctuary of our own being. But whereas you promote the revelation of the spirit *as spirit*, insofar as human speech allows, my task is to construe this spirit in the form of a system . . . You go directly to the heart of the matter . . . Thus it is quite possible that no one but you could see my agreement with you as clearly as I see it. For you have shown in dealing with Spinoza that you are able to divest a system of its artificial trappings in order to present its spirit in its purity and are able to extrapolate from the parts to the whole to which they belong.[51]

[48] George di Giovanni, trans. and ed., *Friedrich Heinrich Jacobi. The Main Philosophical Writings and the Novel Allwill* (Montreal, 1995), pp. 331–8. See also Beiser, *The Fate of Reason*, pp. 108–26; Timm, *Gott und die Freiheit*, pp. 440–65.
[49] GA, III, 2: 391–3.   [50] GA, III, 2: 436.
[51] *Fichte. Early Philosophical Writings*, p. 413 (GA, III, 3: 17–18).

Jacobi's published letter of 1799 would make it painfully obvious that they were not in agreement. As Fichte conceived of their prospective alliance, Jacobi deserved the credit for intuiting, in the immediate experience of "real life," what the transcendental philosopher demonstrated from the detached (and hence admittedly artificial) standpoint of speculation. That was a division of labor Jacobi found unacceptable, and not simply because it patronized him as someone unable to ascend to the true philosopher's speculative heights. Jacobi, like Fichte, conceived of selfhood as an inner sanctuary, the sacred space in which the moral person formed himself despite the pushes and pulls of power. Jacobi did not, however, share Fichte's conviction that philosophical reasoning, properly recast, would delineate that space and inculcate the self-consciousness needed to make it inviolable. Quite the contrary; it was Fichte's thought that prompted Jacobi to extend to the new philosophy – not only to Kantianism but to the "idealist" variations on it – the same verdict he had passed on pre-Kantian species of rationalism. Philosophy *as such* threatened to annihilate the sacred core of selfhood.

The Atheism Conflict provoked Jacobi to give full expression to this categorically antiphilosophical animus, but the animus itself had already been a driving force in his instigation of the Spinoza controversy fifteen years earlier. There was a distinctly German quality to Jacobi's discontent; it echoed with the hostility to philosophical reasoning that had characterized Lutheranism from its inception. In the 1770s and 1780s, several German thinkers, dissenting from the German Enlightenment's often facile efforts to reconcile faith with reason, had contributed to the reformulation of this Lutheran tradition. Chief among them was the cryptic but compelling Johann Georg Hamann, who played the mentor to Jacobi as well as to Herder. It was above all Hamann who had rescued Jacobi from the relentless reductionism of French materialism and who had nourished his instinctive skepticism about Kant's claim to have legitimated Reason by defining its proper jurisdiction.

As thoroughly unorthodox as they were, Hamann and Jacobi thought of moral freedom in fundamentally Lutheran terms. Freedom was grounded in the mystery of a "living knowledge," a faith experienced as a spontaneous (i.e., self-generated) response, and not as a submission to "external" power. Their thought remained structured around Luther's binary opposition between the "inner" spontaneity of faith and "external" observance of the Law, the blind observance of rules. Luther had condemned medieval scholasticism as the philosophical equivalent of Jewish legalism, and Hamann and Jacobi took a similar view of the modern varieties of philosophical rationalism. As different as they might appear to be, they all aspired to exercise a power of annihilation, the relentless erasure of individual moral choice, and indeed of individuality itself, by a cognitive regime claiming universal validity. Priding itself on its immunity to the plague of *Schwärmerei*, "cold" philosophy was blind to the fact that it was a particularly insidious strain of the disease. The purism of reason – no less than the hyperemotionalism of the religous *Schwärmer* – was a self-delusion, a flight into chimeras that ended in the obliteration of the individual moral will.[52]

This despotism of "rational" or "metaphysical" *Schwärmerei* was especially evident in the materialist rationality that Spinoza had come to represent. The principle of sufficient cause was all-encompassing; it left no room for the individual moral person, as a unique being, to assume responsibility for his actions and give them meaning. The root of the danger, however, lay in the process of abstraction with which *any* philosophy articulated itself. In philosophy the despotism of the Law took the form of a coercion inherent in logical deduction, an absorption of all particularities into universal categories, a positing of categorical ethical rules, entirely detached from the emotional textures and the specific contexts of lived experience. Seen through this lens, Kant's Critical Philosophy was a particularly imposing threat to the spirituality of the inner self.

It was this view of philosophy that pervaded Jacobi's letter "To Erhard O★★," added to *Allwill* in the 1792 edition. The letter would become a key text in the Atheism Conflict; Jacobi appended it to the published version of his letter to Fichte, explaining that it made apparent the philosophical "antipathy" as well as the "sympathy" between them. In the late summer of 1795, Fichte had reread the first edition of *Allwill*, without "To Erhard O★★"; but by late April of 1796, when he wrote of their "complete agreement," he had read the new edition.[53] His reading was predictably selective, though not entirely willful. He still assumed that he and Jacobi were using different idioms to bear witness to the same truth. And in a sense they were. The "Erhard O" letter included a spirited indictment of the "egoism" of Lockean empiricism, with its idolization of "happiness," utility, and self-interest. Like Kant and Fichte, Jacobi refused to equate "reason" with "a *mechanistic* representation of creation." He even seemed to have anticipated Fichte's *Wissenschaftslehre* by characterizing true "*inwardness*" as the "joy in striving."[54]

---

[52] Oswald Bayer, "Die Geschichten der Venunft sind die Kritik ihrer Reinheit. Hamanns Weg zur Metakritik Kants," in Bernhard Gajek, ed., *Hamann-Kant-Herder. Acta des vierten Internationalen Hamann-Kolloquiums im Herder-Institut zu Marburg/Lahn 1985* (Frankfurt am Main, 1987), pp. 19–22; Isaiah Berlin, *The Magus of the North. J. G. Hamann and the Origins of Modern Irrationalism*, ed. Henry Hardy (New York, 1993), esp. pp. 14, 42–5. On the theme of philosophy (including Kantianism) as *Schwärmerei*, see also Anthony J. La Vopa, "The Philosopher and the *Schwärmer*: On the Career of a German Epithet from Luther to Kant," in Lawrence E. Klein and Anthony J. La Vopa, eds., *Enthusiasm and Enlightenment in Europe, 1650–1850* (San Marino, Calif, 1998), pp. 85–115.

[53] Fichte had probably read the 1796 edition, which Jacobi had sent him. *Fichte. Early Philosophical Writings*, pp. 413–14.

[54] Di Giovanni, ed., *Jacobi*, pp. 485–7.

As the "Erhard O" letter progressed, however, it adumbrated the central themes of Jacobi's letter to Fichte in 1799. When Jacobi wrote of the "wretched pride" that "would trample under its feet all that it despises as affairs of fleeting feeling" in its search for "a *pure* reason," he was taking aim at Kantianism, not Lockean empiricism. Any attempt to define "*the idea of Something Unconditioned, Something Self-Sufficient*," inevitably was "distorted . . . into an unfounded non-thing," with the result that reason itself was "dreadfully shaken." The only escape was to accept "the riddle of [one's] incurable non-knowledge," and to anchor one's "worth" in the "capacity for intimation and faith," the irreducible experience of a "rapturous non-light." And that in turn required "an obstinate anthropomorphism," a belief in a "*living* God," intimated as a "*discerning* personal being."[55] At stake was not only the "worth" of the self but also its moral integrity:

> As little as infinite space can determine the particular nature of any one body, so little can the *pure* reason *of man* constitute with its will (which is evenly good everywhere since it is *one and the same* in all men) the foundation of a particular, *differentiated* life, or impart to the *actual person* its proper individual value. . . . If I rely on the word of a man who goes by such and such a name, I don't take his pure reason into account thereby, any more than I do the movement of his lips or the sound from his mouth. I trust the word for the sake of the man, and the man for *his own sake*. . . . I believe in the *invisible* word which is deeply hidden in his heart, and which he wills to give and can give. I put my trust in a secret force in him which is stronger than death.[56]

Jacobi was beginning to spell out the irreconcilable difference between the philosophical distillation of a purely rational (i.e., abstracted) self – the process Fichte would pursue so systematically in the *Wissenschaftslehre* – and his own conviction that the only ground for the selfhood of the moral person was the immediate experience of individuated being. By 1799 Fichte had given him added incentive to pursue this line of thought. In his second introduction to the *Wissenschaftslehre*, published in 1797, Fichte had elaborated his point that the commitment to a philosophy was a matter of "character." His opponents' moral failing lay in conceiving of the "self" as "their individual person" and reason as its "mere accident." In truth, it was "individuality" that was "merely accidental"; the "personality" was a "means" of reason and "must increasingly merge into the general form thereof."[57] Fichte had in mind "dogmatic" realists and probably did not intend to draw Jacobi's "realism" into that category. But as Jacobi made quite clear in his letter in 1799, he took the remarks as a contemptuous dismissal of his own thought. He understood, of course,

---

[55] Ibid., pp. 491–6.   [56] Ibid., pp. 488–9.   [57] Ibid., pp. 499–503.

that "even when we have a *particular* person in mind," such attacks were not "personal"; and he asked Fichte to read his own letter with the same distinction in mind.

In the letter Jacobi took pains to avoid impugning Fichte's character. Even if he "were obliged to call [Fichte's] doctrine atheist, like that of Spinoza," he would not "consider [him], *personally*, an atheist for that reason; nor a godless man." He gave Fichte's extended hand a "friendly squeeze," in fact, because he felt for a fellow victim of a materialist age. "The great crowd of those who call themselves philosophers and teachers of religion" always hurl the charge of "*Schwärmerei*," whether in the form of "atheism" or "mysticism," at "any philosophy . . . that invites the human being to raise himself with the spirit above nature and above himself insofar as he is nature." What made Fichte unique was his "*unprecedented* thought power." Jacobi was more than willing to pay homage to that power. Indeed he used the occasion to "proclaim" Fichte, "ever more zealously and loudly," the "true Messiah" among "the Jews of speculative reason," the Messiah for whom Kant had served as John the Baptist. Like Christ, Fichte was being rejected by "the obdurates."[58]

It would be hard to imagine a tribute more pleasing to Fichte's ears. Jacobi was not simply comforting a battered ego; as inflated as it was, his rhetoric conveyed a substantive point. It seemed obvious to him that in a "true reason–system," "everything must be given in and through reason, in the I as I, in the *selfhood of the I* alone." Fichte's thought had realized the full potential of that insight, after centuries of philosophical groping. He had pushed on where Kant had stopped short – to the conclusion that "by fashioning concepts the human spirit only seeks, in all things and from all things, to retrieve itself." That was the "*element of unity*" that constituted "the science of knowledge."[59]

With all this Jacobi declared himself to be in complete agreement. If Fichte was the true Messiah of philosophy, however, he was, in the larger scheme of things, a false Messiah of a particularly dangerous sort. Even as he acknowledged the cognitive power of *Wissenschaft*, Jacobi stood guard before a sacred space that he called "Non-Knowing" or "Un-philosophy," where the rational construction of "truth" gives way to the immediate intimation of "the true" or, in simpler terms, reason accedes to faith. Kant's timidity from a philosophical standpoint had been a kind of wisdom; he had "preferred to sin against the system" rather than against the "majesty" of "the place of *the true* inaccessible to science." Fichte, on the other hand, "sins against this majesty *whenever* he wills to include the place within the domain of science, allowing it to be looked down upon from the standpoint of *speculation*, allegedly the *highest* of all, or the standpoint of *truth itself*."[60] As the preface to the published version of the letter made clear,

---

[58] Ibid., pp. 498–503, 520.   [59] Ibid., pp. 507.   [60] Ibid., p. 499.

Fichte's most flagrant transgression – the one that had turned Jacobi's letter into a cry of outrage, despite his admiration for Fichte's speculative genius and sympathy with his plight – had been the *Appellation*, where the philosopher had couched his defense in the Lutheran language of rebirth. In Jacobi's reading, Fichte had tried to justify his philosophy as "a new, *unique* theism." He should have simply acknowledged that transcendental idealism had nothing to say about God. Instead, by making belief in God conceptual, he had in effect denied His existence. With that move the false Messiah was misleading the people into atheism.[61]

Jacobi's evocation of modern philosophy as a reenactment of the New Testament turned out to be double-edged. Within the philosophers' jurisdiction, Fichte-as-Messiah had defied a "Jewish" obstinacy, and with good reason; but as an arrogant violator of "the true," he provided the ultimate proof for the charge, recently revived in the discourse of *Schwärmerei*, that philosophical rationalism was the successor to Jewish legalism. That Jacobi characterized Fichte's thought as "*naked logical enthusiasm*," and not as logical *Schwärmerei* is a measure of the delicate balance he sought to maintain. He had too much respect for Fichte's speculative boldness and felt too strong an affinity with his moral zeal to consign his thought publicly to the category of philosophical *Schwärmerei*. If he avoided the usual name-calling, however, the underlying point was clear: Fichte differed from all the "rational" *Schwärmer* who had preceded him not in escaping self-deluding logic, but in embracing "the pure and essential *truth of the deceit*."[62]

Fichte had expected Jacobi to hail his philosophy as the breakthrough to a new order of spiritual self-awareness, the radical alternative to the mechanistic totalism whose essential logic Jacobi had found in Spinozism. Instead, Jacobi claimed that he had been able to grasp the *Wissenschaftslehre* only by conceiving of it as an "*inverted* Spinozism." Idealism was simply Spinozism turned inward, thus marking the culmination of the entire reflexive turn in modern philosophy. The essential feature of both systems was the process of abstraction, "an action of dissolving all *being* into *knowledge*, a progressive annihilation through ever more universal concepts leading up to science."[63] Fichte had replaced Nature with the "I" as the abstracted totality, the concept that allowed nothing to exist outside itself. That was the move that brought philosophy to its point of culmination; it was now apparent that Spinoza's "absolute substance" was really only "the expression in objective shape of our subjective power for reflective abstraction."[64] Fichte's delusion lay in his conviction that in making this move, he had established practical reason as the epistemological

---

[61] Ibid., p. 500. See also Hammacher, "Jacobis Brief an Fichte," pp. 79–82.
[62] Di Giovanni, ed., *Jacobi*, p. 511.   [63] Ibid., p. 227.
[64] Di Giovanni, "From Jacobi's Philosophical Novel," p. 97.

alternative to scientific rationality, thus rescuing the I as a moral being from the "mechanical" world of power. In fact he had simply redirected "mechanical" abstraction inward, positing a *"mathesis pura* in which a pure and empty consciousness counts for mathematical space" and, like pure mathematics, can create "mathematical *bodies* in thought out of nothingness."[65] Subjectivity does to itself what it has already done to Nature.

Claiming to have realized Kant's goal of establishing the complete autonomy of moral reasoning, Fichte had instead completed Kant's project of creating "the higher *Meckanik* of the human spirit." His achievement was to have "fully expounded a system of intellect, *the theory of motions in resisting media*."[66] To Jacobi, the conceptual power of the system was precisely what made it so repugnant morally. His outrage peaked in an intensely personal profession of faith, echoing with the long-standing conflict between Lutheran fideism and secular knowledge:

> If a universally valid and rigorously scientific system of morality is to be established, one *must* necessarily lay at its foundation that *will that wills nothing*, that *impersonal personality*, that naked *selfhood* of the I without any *self* – in a word, *pure and barren inessentialities*. For the love of the secure progress of science you *must*, yea you cannot but, subject conscience (*spirit most certain*) to a living-death of *rationality*, make it *blindly* legalistic, deaf, dumb, and unfeeling . . . For only so are *unconditionally* universal laws, rules *without exceptions*, and is *unswerving* obedience possible. . . . The moral principle of reason, the *accord of a man with himself, a fixed unity*, is the highest principle *within the concept* . . . But this unity is not itself the *essence*, it is not the *true*. Its self, in itself alone, is barren, desolate and empty. So its law can never become the *heart* of man and truly elevate him above himself . . . Transcendental philosophy shall not wrest this heart from my breast and put a pure drive for *selfhood alone* in its place.[67]

Jacobi's critique denied the raison d'être of Fichte's philosophical project. The freedom of the self could not be posited in and through *Wissenschaft*; the ontological self could not be reconceived with an a priori concept of striving. To Fichte, objective "being," independent of our representations in consciousness, was philosophically inadmissable. To admit objectivity in that sense was to sacrifice freedom as he defined it – that is, the freedom from the contingent particularity of Nature, the freedom in striving against Nature. To Jacobi it was precisely the denial of objective being that sacrificed the freedom of the self, defined as freedom *through* the contingent particularity of Nature, as freedom from the annihilating power of ratiocination. To assume that "we conceive of a thing [*Sache*] only in so far as we construe it" was to make reason truly systematic, but only by making the self the substance into which everything else was dissolved. And therein lay the nihilistic deception; this totalizing self was not a substance, in the ontological sense, at all. Fichtean subjectivity precluded God by declaring itself God, the creator of everything, and in so doing "attain[ed] only to the *nothing-in-itself*."[68] Aspiring to generate all things at once, it was in fact "none of them in particular." The self escaped reduction to thing-ness only by dissolving into an empty – and lifeless – universal.

The escape from this conceptual void – the true grounding of selfhood, and hence of moral meaning – lay in the immediate experience of individuated being. And that in turn was possible only through the belief in God as "Someone entirely outside me." "Either God is, and is outside me, a living being existing for itself, or I am God," and in the latter case the self is annihilated by the very conceptual structure with which it aspires to make itself the totalizing power. And yet there is also a sense in which Jacobi's God was "inside" the self. The paradox of his leap of faith was that in keeping with Christian tradition, it made God at once transcendent and immanent, absolutely alien and palpably human.[69] The individual is truly aware of his being only as a finite and hence individuated being – that is, as an individuality embodied in space and time, without which the freedom of the will is a chimera. That awareness comes only through the intuition of an absolute Otherness, a totality that cannot be subsumed within one's particularity and that makes the ontological fact of that particularity a felt experience. And yet the Otherness must also be experienced anthropomorphically, as a living Person "*immediately* present through his image in our innermost *self*." Otherwise God could not "announce" Himself, since He would be limited to "sounds" and "signs" that "give us to know what is already understood." Thus the ground of selfhood is also its irreducible mystery, beyond the nihilistic grasp of reason. "God lives in us, and our life is *hidden* in God. . . . Man finds God because he can find himself only in God."[70]

Fichte formed his initial impression of Jacobi's critique from the unpublished letter. In need of encouragement in this moment of crisis and obviously flattered by the tribute to his philosophical prowess, he found himself almost entirely in agreement with the letter and wondered why Jacobi thought of it as a critique. He still thought of their differences in terms of a division of labor. What puzzled him was that Jacobi felt compelled to choose between, on the one hand, being imprisoned in "the standpoint of speculation" and, on the other, shunning speculation

---

[68] Ibid., p. 519.

[69] See George J. Seidel, "Fichte and Secular Christianity," *Antigonish Review* 1 (1970): 108–9, which makes this point about "the God of both Judaism and Christianity" but does not apply it to Jacobi's faith.

[70] Di Giovanni, ed., *Jacobi*, pp. 522–4.

derisively from "the standpoint of life." The answer must lie in the very "individuality" Jacobi held so sacred. In the 1789 edition of his *Ueber die Lehre des Spinozas*, Jacobi had recalled that as a child he had found the prospect of "annihilation" and the thought of "eternal duration" equally terrifying. He had come away from this trauma, Fichte conjectured, with a fierce "enthusiasm of life" that made the very effort to "abstract from real life" seem horrifying. This "psychological phenomenon" must explain why Jacobi, the age's most profound thinker, could not acknowledge what the transcendental idealist knew very well: that there was a clean difference between the "natural" and "common" standpoint, where "one thinks objects directly," and the "artificial" standpoint of speculation, where "one intentionally and consciously thinks one's thinking itself." There was no need to choose between these two spheres of consciousness, since they need not touch on each other. The speculator did not presume to expand the sphere of immediate knowledge, the "active surrender" to the "mechanism of thought." He understood that "without speculating one can live, and perhaps live entirely according to reason," though "one cannot know life."[71] To paraphrase: one did not have to be a transcendental philosopher to be a virtuous person; one could act morally from intuition, without conceptualizing abstractly the rational grounding of intuition. This was a point Fichte had long acknowledged, though it sat oddly with his celebrations of his own version of the reflexive turn as a kind of moral rebirth. He had avoided attributing Jacobi's incomprehension to moral weakness, but his psychological diagnosis was in its way no less patronizing.

On January 8, 1800, shortly before leaving Jena, Fichte returned to Jacobi's critique in a letter to Reinhold. By then he had pondered the published version of the letter, and he was no longer in a conciliatory frame of mind. His view of Jacobi as a seer, albeit one with a blind spot, had acceded to the more sinister image of a despotic "mystic" hiding his true colors. He had been stung by the reference in the preface to his "*unique* theism," and he was chagrined that Jacobi, willfully ignoring his "practical" philosophy, seemed to be confusing him with a Mendelssohn (or worse, a Nicolai) who "wants to reason a religion into people."[72]

[71] GA, III, 3: 326–7, 330–3. For lucid explications of Fichte's distinction between the "standpoint of life" and the "standpoint of philosophy," see Daniel Breazeale, "The 'Standpoint of Life' and the Standpoint of Philosophy' in the Context of the *Jena Wissenschaftslehre* (1794–1801)," in Albert Mues, ed., *Transzendentalphilosophie als System. Die Auseinandersetzung zwischen 1794 und 1806* (Hamburg, 1989), pp. 81–104; Wolfgang Müller-Lauter, "Uber die Standpunkte des Lebens und der Spekulation: Ein Beitrag zur Auseinandersetzung zwischen Fichte und Jacobi unter besonderer Berücksichtigung ihren Briefe, " in Hans-Jürgen Gawoll and Christoph Jamme, eds., *Idealismus mit Folgen. Die Epochenschwelle um 1800 in Kunst und Geisteswissenschaften* (Munich, 1994), pp. 47–67.
[72] GA, III, 4: 181.

The published letter had jolted Fichte into reconsidering Jacobi's curious statements from the past and particularly his insistence on "a personality of God." Now Fichte suspected that behind Jacobi's eloquence lurked "a very harmful error":

> What does he want to start, then, with his Non-Knowledge (*Nichtwissen*)? To implant something in the empty place, following the craving of the heart – we others call it grotesqueries and chimeras – in accord with his individuality – and – if it retires gracefully – to allow every other person to place in it what he wishes – also following his individuality? – Now that is in no way my calculation. I think that from the One outward, what we really know – our duty through common laws of reason, downward – to the sense world – and upward – to the supersensual, in that way is determined precisely what we can further posit; and that there, of course, no one can require another to posit this (since the impulse must come from himself), but if he posits it against the laws of reason and beyond them, it can be said to him: You are a *Schwärmer* . . . If this is my single possible theism, I admit to everything, but in no way as a fault.[73]

Fichte was giving Jacobi a dose of his own medicine, though not in print. It was Jacobi, he charged, who "denied the actual personal freedom of the finite being, in order to transfer all activity in this being to the Infinite, the ultimate ground of it."

★ ★ ★

And so these two thinkers, so close in their shared contempt for the conventional wisdom of the German Enlightenment, accused each other of threatening to sacrifice individual freedom to the compulsion of a totalistic vision. Each had reason to fault the other for not listening, or at least for not hearing. Once again Jacobi's immanent critique yielded insights, but at the cost of brutal oversimplification. Jacobi had not seriously contended with Fichte's reworking of Kant's concept of Practical Reason. Fichte's purpose in reconceptualizing the moral self as pure "striving," after all, had been to avoid the reification that mechanistic thinking entailed. Fichte's thought was certainly vulnerable to the charge of hyperrationalist solipsism, but a fair judgment of the issue would have had to take into account his theory of intersubjectivity, a theory in which the self could become self-conscious only by recognizing the otherness of other selves.

By characterizing the standpoint of "life" as an "active surrendering in the mechanism," Fichte had misconstrued the vitalistic element in Jacobi's sense of selfhood. Hence their radically different valuations of "individuality." To Jacobi, individuality was the irreducible site of moral freedom;

[73] GA, III, 4: 181–2.

and to Fichte, that view licensed a self-indulgent transgression of the laws
that formed the sanctuary of moral freedom. The published letter had
made Fichte confront features of Jacobi's thought he had preferred to
ignore. When he concluded (in the January 8 letter) that Jacobi was one
of those people closed to persuasion, he was consigning him, finally, to
the category of morally blind dogmatists. But he was also confirming what
Jacobi had been saying all along: that the choice was not between kinds
of philosophy, as Fichte would have it, but between philosophy and a fundamentally different way of being conscious of selfhood. Jacobi did tend
to take refuge in overheated prose, substituting rhapsodic evocation for
argument, but that did not suffice to explain the chasm between them.
His disclaimers about the relevance of philosophy to "life" notwithstanding, Fichte was committed to systematic knowledge – to *Wissenschaft* as
the vehicle of human emancipation from the blind laws of power. He
could not seriously consider the possibility that reason, particularly as he
had systematized it, was itself a form of power, subjecting the individual
to a relentless cognitive regime.

The impasse between Jacobi and Fichte, it should be stressed, does not
mark the difference between Orthodoxy and heterodoxy. Jacobi was no
more likely to pass the litmus tests of Orthodoxy than was Fichte. His
rhetoric resonated with the language of Scripture, but he did not regard
Scripture as the source of a divine revelation. For all his emphasis on
the historical nature of religious truth, he could not accept the doctrine
of the Incarnation; his fideism did not extend to a belief in the divinity
of Christ. Nor did he conceive of God's indwelling presence as an
infusion of Grace, though his language often testified to his yearning for
the experience of rebirth that Grace, in the evangelical tradition,
promised.[74]

Fichte and Jacobi may have had more common ground than they realized. What gives their argument its larger historical significance, however,
is their impasse. It throws into sharp relief two quite different impulses in
the German secularization of the Lutheran legacy. And the contrast
between them yields a larger lesson: if we are to continue to posit a historical lineage from Protestantism to modern "individualism," we will have
to make more precise distinctions both within the Protestant legacy and
among different conceptions of the freedom of the individual.

Both Fichte and Jacobi made vital contributions to modern discourses
of selfhood. But if we define secularization as the reformulation of religious ideas within a more secular framework, then Fichte's thought is
clearly a better example of the process than Jacobi's. What is most sub-

---

[74] On Jacobi's relationship to Lutheran Orthodoxy, see Homann, *F. H. Jacobis Philosophie der Freiheit*,
esp. pp. 160–79; Theobald Süss, "Der Nihilismus bei F. H. Jacobi," in Dieter Arendt, ed., *Der Nihilismus als Phänomen der Geistesgeschichte in der wissenschaftlichen Diskussion unseres Jahhrhunderts*
(Darmstadt, 1974), pp. 65–78.

stantively Protestant about Fichte's concept of the self is its ethical rigorism – its view of the ascent to philosophical insight as a process of
rebirth, a struggle against natural corruption, and its channeling of that
"inner" struggle into a social ethic through a recasting of the Lutheran
doctrine of calling. But devotion to the calling could not flow from faith
in the evangelical sense. Fichte's philosophical assimilation and reinterpretation of his religious heritage, as substantive as it was, precluded the
abjection before a transcendent Being that was essential to Protestant
fideism. Selfhood-in-work now served Reason, not the Lord. A life
devoted to Reason was sanctified, figuratively, through work discipline, to
the exclusion of worship.

For all its oversimplification, Jacobi's critique underscored what Fichte
had made quite clear in the article that triggered the Atheism Conflict:
that the uncompromising equation of God with the Moral Law, though
couched in the language of sin and rebirth, could not accept even heterodox reassertions of fideism. Fichte had replaced the majesty of the
Absolute Other with the categorical authority of the completely immanent, the Law within. Jacobi, to be sure, had also replaced Orthodox
fideism with something else. But the something else was a kind of fideism,
an unabashedly "blind" impulse of the heart, unmediated by the head's
capacity for abstraction, that made his conception of individual freedom
radically different from Fichte's.

To Fichte the compulsion of reason was emancipatory. The transcendental self – the self-positing I – discovered within itself the categorical
authority needed to conduct a relentless struggle against the constraints
of its empirical particularity. Having become aware of universal truth in
a reflexive act, a turn back into the sacred interior of selfhood, the individual remained morally autonomous in the face of external authority,
including the authority attributed to "God" (whether the otherness of
God was conceived as transcendent or personal). To put it another way,
the individual could not evade moral responsibility by making "God" the
external source of moral authority. Jacobi's leap of faith was, by contrast,
a variation on the Christian mystery of freedom in slavery, moral autonomy in spiritual abjection. To him, reason compelled in another sense.
The compulsion to abstract – the power on which reason based its claim
to universality – erased, in Jacobi's words, the "proper individual value"
of "the *actual person*"; and indeed, in Fichte's transcendental idealism, the
ultimate form of this compulsion, individuated selfhood dissolved conceptually into nothingness. It did so, in fact, in the very effort to recover
the totalizing freedom of the "I." Abstracting an empty concept of selfhood from the dense particularity of lived experience, reason stripped the
individual of the worth with which it claimed to endow him.

Chapter 13

The Atheism Conflict:
Selfhood, Character, and the Public

By the spring of 1799, the focus of the Atheism Conflict had shifted. A few months earlier, thanks to the *Writing from a Father* and the subsequent confiscation order in Electoral Saxony, two scholarly articles – pieces that otherwise would have remained in obscurity, like everything else published in the *Philosophical Journal* – had become the objects of a wider public controversy. But now the controversy was fixed on the *Appellation*, which Fichte had published in January 1799 in an explicit effort to win over the broad educated public to his cause.

Most of the *Appellation* was written in mid-December 1798, roughly a month after the confiscation order but before Fichte knew of Electoral Saxony's official complaint to Weimar. For a man renowned for his egotism, the pamphlet was, in passages, disarmingly contrite. Fichte admitted that his article had been ill-timed. As free of atheism as it was, it had given the enemies of freedom of thought precisely what they needed, the "seldom experienced spectacle" of a "God-denier." In language that recalled his youthful aspiration to "have an effect" – the aspiration that had led him into philosophy – he acknowledged that he was now in danger of losing his "entire sphere of effectiveness."[1]

To be sure, Fichte's sense of victimization freed him to indulge a penchant for inflated self-dramatization. Contemporaries found particularly preposterous his claim that as one of the "martyrs to truth," he faced the prospect of being removed from "human society" and burned at the stake.[2] If "pyres" were not in the works, however, there was nonetheless a real sense in which Fichte's person was in danger and his fate hung in the balance. Even if he did not lose his academic position, and indeed even if he received only a mild public reprimand from his own government, the Conflict might cost him his "honor" as a "scholar." He valued that precious commodity no less jealously now than he had valued it as a young man. The difference was that now his honor was grounded in his philosophical conception of the "I" as pure activity; for him, the critical act of willed agency, the objectification of the I, was unrestricted philosophical engagement. To put it another way, Fichte's public voice was the

---

[1] Fichte, *Appellation an das Publikum über die durch ein kürf. Sächs. Confiscationsrescript ihm beigemessenen atheistischen Aeusserungen*, GA, I, 5: 416.

[2] Ibid., pp. 418–19.

necessary extension of his "inner" selfhood, the vehicle of his self-validation; now, if the charge of atheism stuck, he would be stripped of his credibility and condemned to silence.

Hence Fichte's defense had to vindicate his concept of selfhood, as it was embodied in his own person, with an uncompromisingly public act of rhetorical engagement. His "judge" would be "the impartial readers" who constituted the public, and he would argue his case directly before them, "as loudly, as warmly [and] as powerfully" as he could.[3] The immediate issue was whether Electoral Saxony, a government that had stigmatized an innocent man and arbitrarily confiscated his journal, could be made to honor the principle of the rule of law. But the confrontation with the Saxon government was the site for a much larger conflict between justice and arbitrary power. Would "force" (*Gewalt*) be allowed to violate the public realm of scholarly discourse, where "reasons" alone should decide? Would the state refrain from "reasoning" and confine itself to its proper domain, "the administration of external power"?[4]

Fichte and Niethammer addressed their *Justifications* directly to Duke Karl August of Weimar, in response to his order that they submit a written response to the charge of "atheism" to the Rector. They were subjects pleading their case before their ruler, but their rhetoric was calculated to impress on the Duke and his officials that the reputation of Saxe-Weimar and its university was also on the line. Even if the articles in question had been atheistic, Fichte argued, there was no German imperial law requiring one German state to punish its own officials at the request of another. Surely Weimar would not assume the onus of confirming that the Germans were ruled by "blind arbitrariness." Fichte's strategy was not simply to drive a wedge between enlightened Weimar and reactionary Dresden; he was also playing on the ducal government's awareness that its small principality owed its prestige in Germany and indeed its international presence largely to the progressive image of its university. It was the "friends of light" who had put Jena in the limelight. Only by protecting that party could the duchy retain the gratitude of the public as "almost the last refuge of free inquiry." If the university was surrendered to the "obscurantists," Fichte warned, it would sink into the "obscurity" to which other German universities had long since descended.[5]

Fichte accompanied this appeal to ducal vanity and self-interest with assurances that German rulers had nothing to fear from scholars like himself. Even in principle he was no democrat, and in any case he was too wrapped up in his purely "speculative" scholarship to support a

[3] Ibid., p. 449.
[4] J. G. Fichtes als Verfassers des ersten angeklagten Aufstazes, und Mitherausgebers des phil. Journals Verantwortungsschrift, GA, I, 6: 41.
[5] Ibid., pp. 34–6, 58–60.

"political revolution," much less to "[place] himself at the head" of one.[6] And yet, though Fichte could honestly abjure political radicalism, he did cast himself in an openly oppositional role, and he did confront the Weimar government as a political antagonist. His very decision to publish the *Appellation* had been a calculated gesture of defiance, a declaration of independence from the cautious paternalism of the court. He remembered the last time he had sought to argue his case before the public, in the wake of his embroglio with the student Orders in 1795, when he had bowed to the court's wish to avoid further publicity. That episode had taught him a lesson, as he explained in the circular letter to Reinhold in May of 1799. In such cases the court expected its client to negotiate behind the scenes with one of its councillors, who would make clear "what steps one should and should not take." In return for protection, he would have to make "this or that sacrifice" – defending himself with as little fuss as possible, avoiding the substance of the issue, admitting some carelessness, promising improvement. There would be no "purely legal judgment" of his guilt or innocence. He might be "injured as little as possible," but "this forebearance must appear as mercy."[7]

This was a fair description of the politics of discretion, the mix of onstage feints and backstage maneuvers with which Weimar exercised its "enlightened" paternalism and eluded public accountability. Fichte knew that behind the court's commitment to academic freedom, the price for its protection was a certain willingness to play the game; this in turn required from its professors a measure of self-censorship. This time he would have none of it. He had "long since" grown "thoroughly tired of [the court's] secret process," he explained a few months later, and he would not submit himself once again to their "*Politik*."[8] Determined to avoid another round of compromising negotiations, he had purposely not sought the court's permission to publish the *Appellation*. In defending himself publicly, he was exercising his "juridical right" as a scholar and as a professor exempt from censorship. The court would have to make a public choice; it must either lend its authority to Fichte's cause or reveal itself as one more arbitrary power.

The article had been poorly timed, but the *Appellation* was calculated to seize an extraordinary opportunity. Fichte warned his readers that the suppression of freedom of inquiry and expression was no longer a matter of random acts. It had become a "systematic" application of "principles." As he explained a few months later, the actions of Electoral Saxony signaled that a European-wide alliance was forming "to eradicate intellectual freedom."[9] Hence the attempt to brand him an atheist offered all learned men a rare, if not unique, occasion to rally around the principle

---

[6] Ibid., pp. 73–9.   [7] GA, III, 3: 364–6.   [8] GA, III, 3: 364, 366.
[9] Fichte, *Appellation*, p. 417; GA, III, 3: 354.

of freedom of thought and expression, perhaps the only principle on which they could all agree. "This has least to do with individuals," he explained in the announcement about the *Appellation*, "but rather with all." His expectation was that "putting aside all other controversies, the honorable German republic of scholars and everything that in any way belongs to it will unite on this matter into one mind and will have only one voice."[10] For once the public would suspend its internal squabbling and become the collective moral force, the unitary will, it was supposed to be.

In need of a counterforce to state power, Fichte took unusual steps to harness the print market to his cause. What is striking, in fact, is the deliberateness with which he pursued a German-wide marketing strategy. In early 1799 the announcement appeared in seven literary and scholarly journals, including two published out of Nürnberg, one out of Würzburg, and one out of Hamburg. The announcement ended with an appeal to all "learned journals" to notify the public of the *Appellation*, so that "every upright man could disseminate [it] in his circle."[11] For the *Appellation* itself, Fichte made arrangements with two publishers: J. G. Cotta in Tübingen, and C. E. Gabler in Jena and Leipzig. Gabler was to be responsible for Saxony and North Germany, Cotta for South Germany, the left bank of the Rhine, Switzerland, and the rest of the Reich. Altogether the two publishers printed 10,000 copies of the pamphlet. Fichte had them send roughly 150 copies gratis to individual scholars throughout Germany. His acompanying letter urged the recipients to exercise their "right" as members of the learned public by distributing the text to others. He foreswore an honorarium so that booksellers could retail the pamphlet at the very low price of six Saxon Groschen. Depending on the size of the order, individuals who purchased multiple copies would receive anywhere from two to forty free copies.[12]

★ ★ ★

Fichte was not the first German academic to defend himself publicly against official calumny. What made his defense so unusual, and perhaps unique, was his use of the print market to orchestrate and, to a limited but significant degree, to organize a public campaign. In the space of six months, however, his vaulting expectations acceded to bitter disillusionment. By the time he published the *Justification* in May 1799, he was already aware that his "relationship to the public" had been "changed or, to speak more precisely, destroyed." He would soon lose his position at Jena and face the prospect of being hounded from refuge to refuge, like

---

[10] "Ankündigung der Appellation an das Publikum," GA, I, 5: 364.

[11] "Ankündigung," pp. 361, 365.

[12] See, e.g., the printed letter to August Wilhelm Schlegel, Jan. 16, 1799, in GA, III, 3: 174–5. For the details of the publication arrangements and the resulting complications, see GA, I, 5: 385–92.

Rousseau. Though he would continue to "*act* as if [he] really believed [human beings] had some worth," he confided to Reinhold, the "present mood of [his] heart and head" was "inner aversion to the so-called learned public and its entire being."[13]

What had happened? To a degree, Fichte's alienation was his own doing. While some readers applauded his uncompromising self-defense, others shook their heads in dismay or rubbed their hands in glee over the shrillness and the recklessness of his counterattacks. The initial question – whether Fichte was in fact an atheist – was eclipsed by the issue of his character. That issue became all the more pressing, and all the more puzzling, as the public learned of Fichte's dealings with the Weimar government in late March and early April.

But Fichte's defeat was not simply personal. It marked a moment of crisis in the moral authority and in the political viability of one of the Enlightenment's central normative metaphors. The Conflict had put to the test the very expectation that the *Publikum* could act as a court of appeal, a collective moral tribunal. Its denouement exposed what the rhetoric of publicity usually ignored: that the Publikum's capacity to mediate between state and society was severely limited by inhibitions and strains in the very way it conceived itself, and by the social and institutional realities on which it rested.

In "From a Private Letter," published in the *Philosophical Journal* in early January 1800, Fichte responded to the many complaints about his style of philosophizing. His admission that he lacked the talent to anticipate misconstruals of his writings by "our half-wits" was hardly an act of self-criticism. As an original thinker, he insisted, he had "a right to demand" that people become acquainted with his novel use of language. And how could he not claim to possess "one-sole-philosophy"? Did authors not expose themselves as "ridiculous idiots" when they "rush to market with [their] haphazardly ventured bright ideas," or when they "behave outwardly as if [they] intended to *offer as an opinion* something that [they] really think that they *know*"? Before a public audience the philosopher could not speak merely for his "person"; "you must intend to put forward a pronouncement of universal reason and not simply your own pronouncement; and you must be able to vouch for this with your entire inner dignity and morality." Hence philosophy, and indeed any science (*Wissenschaft*), "is in its very essence, 'one-sole science,' and every philosopher is a 'one-sole-philosopher'."[14]

To Dietrich Tiedemann, a veteran opponent of Kantianism and its offshoots, Fichte's response only confirmed "the ever more prevalent arro-

---

[13] Fichte, *Verantwortungsschrift*, p. 26; GA, III, 3: 353–4.
[14] "From a Private Letter (January 1800)," in *J. G. Fichte. Introductions to the Wissenschaftslehre and Other Writings (1797–1800)*, ed. and trans. Daniel Breazeale (Indianapolis and Cambridge, 1994), pp. 158–64. Original version reprinted in GA, I, 6: 369–89.

gant tone of *the most recent* philosophers." Writing in 1801, when he could no longer be accused of attacking a persecuted man, Tiedemann called Fichte to account for his *"monstrous arrogance"* or worse, his *"Charlatanerie."* In matters of broad significance for humanity as a whole, Tiedemann argued, "each *Individuum* has his voice." It was permissible to appeal to one's "importance" by impressing on readers how "long and hard" one has thought about something – so long, of course, as one admitted, at least implicitly, that one might still be wrong. No philosopher could say (as Fichte said): "*I alone know the matter, all you others know nothing*, you are all struck with blindness" – hence claiming "that the *entire human reason has united in its greatest purity in his person.*"[15]

The collision here was between irreconcilably different approaches to philosophy itself and to its public communication. Tiedemann spoke for the German Enlightenment's generation of philosophical latitudinarians, leaning now toward Wolffian metaphysics, now toward Lockean empiricism, and in any case preferring what they saw as a judicious eclecticism to the single-mindedness that systematicity required. Committed to eclecticism as a matter of principle, they imagined the public debate of philosophical issues as a multivocal exercise in mutual respect, open-mindedness, and inclusiveness. Arguably there was nothing new about the "arrogance" they found in the writings of "the most recent philosophers." Philosophical prose had long been characterized by an antirhetorical rhetoric, a strategy designed to position the philosophical text above the manipulative arts of rhetorical persuasion. The unique role of the philosopher was to make universal and therefore quintessentially "public" truth claims, disengaged from the particularity of his personal agency and interest as a writer in a given context and situation.[16] At least implicitly, there was something necessarily exclusionary about the polemical defense of such claims. One might admit one's personal fallibility in principle, but the point of the posture of impersonality was to brand the opponent an imposter, trying to pass off private opinions as public truths.

In the late eighteenth century this rhetorical strategy was facilitated, and perhaps even encouraged, by the quickening commercialization of print. The more the printed text became a market commodity, the more it could be idealized as the medium for conveying the pure cogency of ideas, detached from the personality of the author and undistorted by physically proximate personal (and social) relationships in which power was at play. This effect had, of course, an ironic corollary. By lending credence to the philosopher's posture of disengaged universality, the impersonality of the market served his exclusionary polemicism quite nicely.

---

[15] FR 2: 349–50. Tiedemann's review appeared in the *Neue Allgemeine Deutsche Bibliothek* 57, St. 2, Heft 6 (1801): 359–408.

[16] See, e.g., Tobia Bezzola, *Die Rhetorik bei Kant, Fichte und Hegel. Ein Beitrag zur Philosophiegeschichte der Rhetorik* (Tübingen, 1993).

Arguably, in fact, the more impersonal the print market became, the more the practitioner of exclusionary polemics could indulge in personal attack with impunity.

There was another sense in which market impersonality encouraged a kind of personalism. As the market expanded, bridging physical distances and breaking down corporate barriers, the effect was not simply that ideas seemed to acquire a new potential for "universal" acceptance. Texts, including philosophical texts, entered the public arena as emblems of individualized personalities, floating free of traditional corporate moorings. The implication for philosophical writing was paradoxical: even as the impersonality of print made it more possible to conceal the "person" behind the ideas, it also promoted a new way of asserting a personality, or at least a persona, before a scattered and largely anonymous audience. That meant that the judgment of ideas was inseparable from the reputation of the individual as such – or, to be more precise, from the image of "character" (or lack of such) that print, often aided by the oral circulation of rumor, could shape without face-to-face encounters in specific social circles of a corporate hierarchy. In the widening arena of the market the fate of an idea hinged at least in part on whether the author, as an individualized personality open to public scrutiny, earned or forfeited credibility. He was held responsible for the public persona that print allowed him to broadcast and became vulnerable to a polemical strategy that made his persona – or, in moral discourse, his character – the real issue. The opponent could be dismissed not simply because he was wrong by impersonal standards, but also because, as a particular moral person, he was incapable of being right.

These structural changes form the backdrop for the increasing concern in the 1790s that the "tone" of German philosophical debate was degenerating to a shameful degree. With the ideological polarization occasioned by the French Revolution, personal attack often took the form of political stigmatization. One discredited the philosophy by making its advocate a threat to order or, from the other side of the spectrum, a conspirator against progress. Even before the Revolution, however, the rise of a new quest for system in the form of Kant's Critical Philosophy had heated up the arena. Kant was a principled and self-conscious practitioner of the philosopher's antirhetorical rhetoric. In philosophical scholarship he saw no place for the devious techniques of "eloquence" (*Beredsamkeit*). He distinguished between the traditional rhetorician's use of words as instruments of power, wielded to "talk someone into something" (*überreden*), and his own effort at rational persuasion (*Uberzeugung*) through a simple, natural use of language (*Wohlredenheit*). This was in itself a rhetorical move. By the very fact that Kant claimed to have determined what was and what was not a legitimate use of reason, he provided a new rationale for an exclusionary polemics that was at once impersonal and fiercely personal.[17] As the efforts to systematize transcendental idealism multiplied, so did the exclusionary claims.

Kant himself wielded this kind of polemic with a unique combination of finesse and ruthlessness. He thought of himself, to be sure, not as resorting to *ad hominem* tactics but as applying what he called "the polemical use of reason." Having demonstrated that the critical use of reason, properly limited, had objective validity, he had to expose counterfeit philosophies, the merely subjective products of private wills. Kant justified these exposés as necessary defenses of objectivity from the threat of obliteration by merely subjective forms of exclusiveness. But they were inherently exclusive themselves; the objective was to annihilate the opponent's credibility and thus leave him with no choice but to fall silent. Since the opponent had dared to claim public status for personal impulses, he could be, indeed had to be, discredited as a person. Kant's use of irony for this purpose sometimes degenerated into slashing sarcasm. He pilloried Johann August Eberhard, his most dogged opponent among academic philosophers, as a malicious fake, "a metaphysical sleight-of-hand artist"; in turn he was charged with resorting to the "violent means" of "literary despotism." Others Kant dismissed not simply as rank amateurs but as intellectually lazy and morally self-indulgent imposters. His final target was Fichte, in the repudiation notice he published in 1800. Fichte's claim to have completed Kant's system was not simply wrongheaded; it represented the treachery of "so-called friends," "deceitful, cunning, plotting our ruin but doing it in the language of benevolence."[18] Schelling protested that given Fichte's circumstances, this was an act of calculated malice.

There is a sense, then, in which the fierceness and the arrogance of Fichte's polemicism was typical. And yet, even in this context, Fichte *did* raise, or lower, philosophical polemic to a new order of brutality. To be sure, he had been an emphatically combative personality when he turned to philosophy nearly a decade earlier. What is striking is the way the abstract justification for his combativeness – his philosophical construction of selfhood – licensed an unrestrained exhibition of personal egotism and gave free rein to a transparent urge to compel. There was a certain logic to it all. He could claim to stand above any particular identity, whether it be as a member of group or simply as an individual, because he assigned himself the role of Reason's instrument, the transmitter of

---

[17] On Kant's dichotomy between "rhetoric" and philosophical persuasion, see esp. Bezzola, *Die Rhetorik*, pp. 20–63. The indispensable study of Kant's polemical rationale and strategy is Hans Saner, *Kant's Political Thought. Its Origins and Development* (1967: Chicago and London, 1973). The English title does not do justice to the richness of Saner's monograph. For a similar tension between civility and aggression in French public discourse, see Daniel Gordon, *Citizens without Sovereignty. Equality and Sociability in French Thought, 1670–1789* (Princeton, N.J., 1994), pp. 177–208.

[18] Kant's notice is in FG 2: 217–19. See also Saner, *Kant's Political Thought*, esp. pp. 104–65.

universal truths. Hence, as he explained in response to Reinhold's reservations about his polemical excesses, his "individuality" was irrelevant and there was no question of "vanity." In his own eyes, his public assertion of selfhood was a kind of self-effacement; he could not take credit as an individual for his philosophical achievement.[19] The logic of his self-construction left him blind to his lack of self-restraint.

Whatever its philosophical merits, Fichte's concept of selfhood had the effect of exempting him from shared rules of public civility, tolerance, and modesty. His conviction of his own modesty was reinforced by his outrage in the face of reviews that seemed willfully to misrepresent his views and for good measure, smeared him with the charge of Jacobinism. He saw himself as the victim of a "scholarly establishment" that rendered deference to persons of status in "prestigious" institutions and periodicals, rather than respecting "reasons," and that felt justified in dismissing philosophical arguments simply because it could not understand them. He would not, he declared in February 1797, "request permission to be right" by displaying the requisite "politeness and humility." He wanted to force the "literary aristocracy" to engage in real argument, and so he had to provoke them and indeed mock them "outrageously." He claimed to be mercilessly derisive in the cause of open, straightforward debate, though his tone left little doubt that he would be very pleased to have intimidated people into silence.[20]

The result was a persona that seemed alarmingly self-contradictory. Here was a man who brought a higher order of purism to the philosophical ideal of power-free communication and to the ideal of the autonomous reader in a rational *Publikum*. He saw his own texts not as acts of intrusion into the reader's mind, but as occasions for the reader, in a free creative act, to discover the truths latent in his inner self. He went so far as to claim that his own choice of words was incidental; there might be as many verbal "representations" of transcendental truth as there were people who succeeded in grasping it. And yet, even as Fichte imagined this autonomous reception in the public space reserved for pure intellect, where the only legitimate "force" was the sheer cogency of ideas, he profiled himself in print as a reckless and overbearing egotist, quick to resort to verbal brutality.[21]

---

[19] GA, III, 2: 279.

[20] Fichte, "Annalen des philosophischen Tons," in PJ 5: 1 (Feb., 1797). The article has been reprinted in GA, I, 4: 293–321. I have quoted the translated excerpt in *Fichte. Early Philosophical Writings*, trans. and ed. Daniel Breazeale (Ithaca and London, 1988), pp. 341–54. Fichte's article was occasioned by an anonymous review of the *Naturrecht* in the *Göttingische Anzeigen*, Dec. 1796.

[21] For a defense of Fichte's species of *ad hominem* arguments (but not of his expressions of "scorn" and "derision") as a philosophically justifiable extension of his Idealist premises, see Peter Suber, "A Case Study in *Ad Hominem* Arguments: Fichte's *Science of Knowledge*," *Philosophy and Rhetoric* 23:1 (1990): 12–42.

The most notorious instance was Fichte's settling of accounts with Christian Erhard Schmid, his Kantian rival at Jena, with whom he had been feuding since 1793. In an article published in 1796, Schmid had contrasted Fichte's philosophy invidiously with his own. Fichte retaliated by trying to demonstrate that Schmid's "system" was not a philosophy at all but a simplistic exercise in natural science that "denies all philosophy, abolishes it altogether, and leaves us with nothing but science."[22] One can imagine Kant making the same point with a considerably more oblique irony and letting the matter rest there. Fichte felt "perfectly entitled" to conclude his counterattack with an "act of annihilation":

> I hereby declare that everything that Professor Schmid henceforth has to say concerning any of my philosophical assertions – whether he says it straightforwardly or obliquely, and wherever he says it, whether in philosophical journals and annals, in reviews, in his lectures, or in any other respectable or unrespectable place – I hereby declare *to be something which does not exist at all as far as I am concerned*. And I declare Professor Schmid himself to be *nonexistent as a philosopher* so far as I am concerned.[23]

Reinhold was one of many people shocked by this gesture. Kantian philosophy, he wrote to a colleague, seemed to be undergoing a "hideous change"; "more and more [it] seems to be turning into a shameless display of practical egoism."[24] Reinhold was blind to the fact that the new philosophy's tone of dismissal could be found in Kant's polemics and indeed in his own explications of the Critical Philosophy. Still, he had reason to be alarmed. Fichte's exclusionary polemics crossed a line that Kant, even at his most supercilious, had not crossed. Kant distinguished carefully between opponents he found fatally flawed in character and those (like Garve) he continued to respect and even admire. Fichte left the impression that anyone who disagreed with him – anyone who did not embrace his system without reservation – was hopelessly deficient morally as well as intellectually. He stated bluntly what Kant's irony left implicit: that since the opponent was too blinkered to ascend to his heights, futher debate would be futile. Kant had channeled his urge to destroy into an apparently detached (though still venomous) irony; Fichte trumpeted his rage to annihilate. Where Kant slashed, Fichte bludgeoned.

One of the ironies of the Atheism Conflict was that the article in the *Philosophical Journal* – the article that launched the controversy – was a lucid and measured piece, in keeping with the seriousness of the subject.

---

[22] "A Comparison between Prof. Schmid's System and the *Wissenschaftslehre* [Excerpt]," in *Fichte. Early Philosophical Writings*, p. 319. The full text is in GA, I, 3: 235–71.

[23] *Fichte. Early Philosphical Writings*, p. 335.

[24] Reinhold to Erhard, Aug. 2, 1796, quoted in ibid., p. 312. In his brief reply in the *Reichs-Anzeiger* (June 13, 1796), Schmid announced that, Fichte's "act of annihilation notwithstanding," he continued to exist. Ibid., p. 312.

But the article was soon eclipsed by the *Appellation*, a very different performance before a much wider audience. Here was an impassioned defense of scholarly freedom, often cogent and indeed eloquent, and yet disturbingly unrestrained. There was the virtual embrace of martyrdom as the heretic's "pyre" drew ever closer; the contention that all opponents of Transcendental Idealism, including "enlightened" theologians and Kantians, were "idolators" and "atheists"; the insistence that the only road to morality lay through a severely ascetic and emphatically willful assertion of selfhood.

Friedrich Gentz concluded from the *Appellation* that Fichte was "an extraordinary phenomenon," a rare union of "greatness of thought" and "human commonness" in one person.[25] By commonness Gentz meant coarseness, the lack of elementary civility. The performance offered Fichte's detractors – those who had been waiting for an opportunity to give him his comeuppance – precisely what they needed. To them Fichte's complaints about his reader's incomprehension were a lame excuse for willful obscurantism. In its resort to an all-too-familiar language of spiritual rebirth and "inner" wisdom and in the aggressive self-righteousness of its claim to exclusive occupation of the moral high ground, the *Appellation* seemed to exhibit the new plague of philosophical *Schwärmerei* at its most solipsistic and its most intolerant. Aiming for "the domination of opinion," Tiedemann concluded, Fichte had claimed the "*privilege of infallibility*."[26] He had gotten what he deserved. Reinhold, who had recently declared himself won over to Fichte's philosophy, was more sympathetic. But even to him the talk about witch-hunts and stakes seemed a bit ridiculous, and there was something self-destructive about including one's only potential allies among the vast crowd of atheists.

The Atheism Conflict confronted Reinhold and many others with a dilemma. Was this a case in which intellectual freedom had to be defended against political force, despite the troubling persona of the victim? Or did the victim's flaws of character make this the wrong case on which to take a stand? With Fichte's actions in the early spring of 1799 the waters became still muddier. Rumors had spread from Weimar to Jena that a public reprimand was forthcoming. On March 22, hoping to forestall this blow to his honor, Fichte suddenly abandoned his principled resolve to avoid any communication with the court "outside official channels" (*extra acta*). He wrote privately to Privy Councillor Voigt, explicitly permitting him to make further use of the letter.

It was an altogether curious letter. If he received a public reprimand, Fichte informed Voigt, he would have no choice but to resign. "Several like-minded" colleagues had promised to do likewise; there was a "plan" to found a new institute somewhere. To justify his resignation, he would

[25] FG 2: 69.   [26] FR 2: 350.

have to publish the letter. And he would also allow "another" (probably Schelling) to raise publicly the issue of the court's inconsistency. It was common knowledge, after all, that "the General-Superintendant of this Duchy" had published a book about God that "looks as similar to atheism as one egg to another." Why was he [Fichte] facing a reprimand, despite his position as a "censure-free" professor, when the court had turned a blind eye on a more questionable publication by its most prominent ecclesiastical official?[27] The reference was to Herder and his *God. Some Conversations*. Though Fichte surely exaggerated Herder's proximity to a purely atheistic position, he had a point. Unlike Fichte, Herder was an insider, one of the literary celebrities whose presence gave Weimar its unique glitter as a court residence. The government allowed him considerable latitude as an author because it knew it could count on his discretion. Now Fichte – the troublemaker, never welcomed into the Weimar coterie – was threatening to subject Herder to the same public scrutiny he himself had to endure and to cause the court a great deal of embarrassment.

Fichte knew that Voigt and Goethe wanted to negotiate a compromise as they had done in the controversy over the student Orders, a "byway" that would "[placate] both interested parties, Electoral Saxony and the great Publikum."[28] His message was that this time they would not be able to appease their neighbors at the expense of his reputation and that they would have to risk serious damage to Weimar's own reputation as an "enlightened" haven. If his letter marks his awareness of the court's vulnerability, however, it was nonetheless tactically maladroit. Voigt and Goethe knew that Fichte's supporters at Jena would not resign; hence, the "plan" to found a new institute was an empty threat. As for Fichte himself, they were aware that his renown still drew students to Jena, but they were more willing to see him leave in 1799 than they had been in 1795. In the intervening four years their estimation of his value to the university had declined. He had crossed the line between celebrity and notoriety once too often; in any case, he was no longer the rising star. He had become one more voice in the philosophical cacophony. Their main regret was that they might lose younger stars like Niethammer and Schelling.

The other difference was that the privy councillors now faced a thoroughly exasperated prince. In a letter to Voigt on December 26, 1798, Duke Karl August had reacted to the complaint from Dresden by venting

[27] GA, III, 3: 283–6. Cf. the account of Goethe's and Voigt's role in the Atheism Conflict in Nicholas Boyle, *Goethe. The Poet and the Age*, vol. 2: *Revolution and Renunciation (1790–1803)* (Oxford, 2000), pp. 625–31. Boyle concludes that Goethe "must have been aware" that his role in the Conflict had been "a shabby act," and suggests that that was why he "asked Voigt to return to him all his papers relating to the Fichte case and destroyed them" (p. 631).

[28] GA, III, 3: 354–5, 364–7.

his "gall" about professors whose indiscretion made them "extremely useless and dangerous." Had he not been away at war, he lamented, Fichte's appointment would not have been approved. Now they faced the prospect of "ruin[ing] [their] entire university to accommodate the tasteless silliness of an ephemeral intellectual illness." Later on the same day the Duke sent Voigt a second letter. His fury had fixed on Goethe, who spent much time in Jena and could have used his influence with its "shakers" to prevent this crisis. Seeking in Jena the intellectual amusement he could not find at court, Goethe was eager to amuse Jena in turn. Now the government was paying for his "frivolity." All the Duke had been able to elicit from Goethe were "words and sophisms" about Jena. Voigt would have to impress on him "the political aspect of the matter."[29]

Goethe did use Jena to escape the relentless formalities of court life, but he did not react to the crisis of 1799 as a sophistic defender of academe. Having witnessed nearly a decade of revolutionary upheavals and blindly reactionary responses, he still hoped that Weimar – and he himself – could somehow remain serenely poised above the muck of politics and religious controversy. "In these days," he wrote to Voigt, we can only "apply some barrels of oil to soften the waves around the ship"; "we may never see the high sea in peace again for our entire lives."[30] Goethe and Voigt were in agreement that the safest way to placate Dresden without alienating the enlightened public was to issue "the briefest, driest, most unpartisan rescript," opening "the broadest and roomiest path." They would require the university Senate to submit a report on the atheism charge, thus signaling Saxony that they took the matter seriously, but without violating official procedure and without being dragged into the substance of the controversy. In late December, despite the Duke's outburst, they were still willing to contemplate the possibility that Fichte would remain at Jena. But they were sick of "crazy philosophers" and their hopelessly murky "*Logomachie*," and Fichte had made himself expendable. What mattered was that the university not forfeit its good reputation and that the government do what it must do, but no more, to appease its powerful neighbor.[31]

On December 26, the very day of the Duke's explosion, Voigt and Goethe sent Fichte a mixed message through Schiller. The court, Fichte learned, was unhappy that he had chosen to appeal to the public rather than letting the government settle the matter; but he was also assured that his fears of persecution were completely misplaced.[32] Three months later, with Fichte's *Justification* in hand, the two councillors prepared a reprimand that he might be able to swallow and that in any case would satisfy

[29] FG 2: 29–32.   [30] FG 2: 32.   [31] FG 2: 27–9.
[32] Schiller to Fichte, Jan. 26, 1799, in GA, III, 3: 183–4.

Saxony. Then Fichte's letter of March 22 opened a new "byway." Voigt and Goethe were quick to realize that they could now be "entirely free of and finished with Herr Fichte" without endangering their main objectives. As Voigt explained to Councillor Frankenberg in Gotha, no government with any "energy" could tolerate "such arrogance"; in any case the university would surely survive the loss of Fichte. In the letter, Fichte had threatened to resign if he received a public reprimand. Since he had also made explicit his intention to publish the letter if resignation became unavoidable, Voigt felt justified in using it publicly. And so the public reprimand of Fichte (as well as Niethammer) included a postscript, accepting Fichte's resignation on the grounds that his stated conditions had been fulfilled. The message to the public was clear. The government was not sacking its controversial professor; it was simply honoring his wishes.[33]

Even with this step the Weimar councillors continued their tightrope walk. It was at the Duke's insistence that the threat about Herder had been kept in the copy of Fichte's letter sent to the university and the other courts. Voigt and Goethe had hoped to keep a lid on that subject, to spare Herder and probably themselves public embarrassment. Likewise it was the Duke, following a suggestion from Frankenberg, who had included in the reprimand a warning to professors to avoid anything that conflicted with the generally accepted church doctrine. Voigt would have preferred a less explicit departure from procedural terrain – one that would not imply that Weimar had entered Saxony's ideological camp. The actual censure of Fichte (and Niethammer) was in Voigt's phrasing; it upbraided them not for atheism "in the actual sense," but for "carelessness" in the use of philosophical terms that could be misunderstood by the public. Voigt had purposely avoided the word "errors" since that would have linked Weimar to Saxony as one of "two parties" in the dispute.[34]

Aside from being very late, Fichte's resort to behind-the-scenes politics was stunningly indiscreet. To a government that expected its professors to defer to its judgment on politically delicate issues, his letter was a crude provocation. Voigt and Goethe, two seasoned practitioners of the art of shaping public perceptions, had simply seized the opportunity he had so rashly handed them. Their victory was sealed by Fichte's next blunder. Fichte allowed himself to be persuaded by the theologian H. E. G. Paulus, one of his few professorial allies and the Prorector of the university, that he was duty-bound to keep his position. On April 3, 1799, he wrote to Voigt that he "never want[ed] to have the impression – neither before [himself] nor before the public – that he had *voluntarily laid down* his position" because his "freedom to teach" had been violated. In fact

---

[33] FG 2: 78–94   [34] FG 2: 93.

the reprimand had merely blamed him for using a potentially misleading terminology and had "expressly recognized that philosophical speculations cannot be the subject of a judicial decision."[35]

Fichte had a point; the government had stopped short of censuring his teaching. But now he wanted the government to honor a distinction he had not bothered to make in the letter of March 22, and his effort was bound to be read as an undignified resort to sophistry. Paulus carried the second letter to Weimar in the hope of persuading the Duke to withdraw the acceptance of Fichte's resignation, but Voigt told him that this last-minute retreat changed nothing. Determined to stay the course, Voigt was now practicing without inhibition, and indeed with a certain zest, the political cunning that so disgusted and unnerved Fichte. While he waited impatiently for the other courts to approve Weimar's decision, Voigt feigned a willingness to help Fichte and his allies. If they did not consider their cause "hopeless," he wrote to Goethe on April 8, they would behave "all the more cautiously."[36] The Duke's reaction to Fichte's second letter was predictable: "What a wretched character! . . . The matter takes its course, and adieu, Fichte!"[37]

Over the next few months, as Fichte prepared to leave Jena, the court used print as well as the informal circuitries of rumor to supply the academic world with its own account of his resignation. It knew that to most onlookers Fichte's letters would reveal a man trying to squirm out of the consequences of his own reckless arrogance, and so it did not hesitate to reveal their content. It was "small" enough, Tiedemann concluded, "first to speak in high tone of submitting his resignation, and then to declare that one would rather accept a reprimand than have his position disappear." Worse still was the transparently "sophistic" argument of the second letter. It left no doubt that the claim to speak for Reason veiled a deeply flawed character.[38]

Fichte's circular letter to Reinhold on May 22 was designed to repair some of the damage, at least among the people whose judgment he valued. In an accompanying letter he explained to Reinhold that in his contempt for the "so-called learned public," he had resolved to fall silent for some years. But now he felt compelled to speak. Otherwise he would forfeit all credibility and the cause of philosophy might be totally lost. The letter itself included the full texts of both letters to Voigt. Fichte admitted that through his own fault he had given Weimar "an appearance of right." He should never have abandoned his initial decision "not to diverge in any way from the path of open judicial process, and to let the government act entirely at its own risk." He hoped that with this "candid admission" he would "atone sufficiently" for his "mistake."[39]

[35] GA, III, 3: 291–2.   [36] FG 2: 111–13.   [37] FG 2: 108.   [38] FR 2: 327.   [39] GA, III, 3: 367–8.

This was a blatantly confessional performance, a plea for forgiveness. It would have been a remarkable step for any public figure, and it was in a sense a total inversion of the defiantly self-righteous posture Fichte usually assumed. And yet, for all his candor, Fichte could not confront squarely the moral implications of his actions. Even as he admitted to having failed himself and to having let down the public that mattered, he counted himself among the righteous few. He would not consider the possibility that he had turned to Voigt at least in part to survive, to keep his academic position. Instead he explained his mistake as an act of self-delusion, a "fantasy" that he was acting not for his own advantage but for the good of scholarship. And it was others, "the really clever people" among his colleagues at Jena, who had led him from "strictly upright" behavior down the path of self-delusion. Though he mentioned no names, his readers would know that the chief culprit, the "political" seducer behind both letters, had been Paulus (who much later admitted to having persuaded Fichte to write the second letter but denied responsibility for the first one).[40]

The subtext of Fichte's confession was a claim to innocence. His admitted fault lay in falling prey to the "clever" political types, not in becoming one of them. The letters had marked a moment of weakness, "an unfortunate departure from [his] character," and not a fatal character flaw. Fichte claimed to draw this conclusion from "[his] entire knowledge of [himself]," and he asked his readers to do likewise.[41] In the end, he was convinced that his character – his self-presentation as a moral agent – remained grounded in his philosophical construction of selfhood. That very conviction marked the limitations of transcendental reflexivity, at least as he defined and practiced it. This is not to say that we are now in a position to fathom the real motives behind his actions. For the most part his psychological interior lies beyond our view. The point is that by the nature of his philosophical self-construction, Fichte saw no need to fathom his motives himself. Indeed he would have regarded any advice to engage in pyschological introspection as an invitation to self-corruption. In the absence of reflexivity of that kind, he was relieved of the need to ask how an uncompromising moralist, so insistent on the freedom and hence the responsibility of the inner self, could excuse himself as the victim of external manipulation – and how he could be so willing to shunt onto others the moral responsibility for his own decisions.[42]

[40] GA, III, 3: 367–70. Paulus's version (from his memoirs) is in FG 2: 160–7.
[41] GA, III, 3: 367.
[42] George di Giovanni, "Fichte's Rhetoric of Deception: Reflections on the Early Fichte in the Spirit of Jacobi," *Revue Internationale de Philosophie* 49: 191 (February, 1995), 57–78, does not examine Fichte's behavior during the Atheism Conflict but does reach the general conclusion that "Fichtean

The Jena Years

Fichte suggested to Reinhold that the circular letter appear to be edited by "friends," including Jacobi. But Jacobi's response to it was anything but supportive. He had already judged that Fichte's first letter to Voigt would make him "appear everywhere as a fool (*Unsinniger*), and a fool of a bad sort." It seemed to him that it was Fichte, and not Voigt, who had embarrassed himself. Jacobi expected many to sympathize nonetheless with Fichte as "someone persecuted," but he doubted whether anyone would "really help" him.[43]

Jacobi wrote to Reinhold again on June 25. He found Fichte's rationale in the second letter to Voigt "laughable." He had spent the entire day with the circular letter, reading it again and again, and he was not moved by Fichte's confession. He could add nothing to the text, though he hoped that for Fichte's sake Reinhold would be able to put together "something bearable" from his comments (and then erase them). Fichte had to be told "directly and purely" that "he must be silent or he is a lost man." Only "time" and "intellectual works that have nothing in common with this unholy business" could "bring it into forgetfullness."[44]

★ ★ ★

Even among those who supported Fichte's cause, there was nothing like the collective expression of will he had expected. In April, 1799, the Weimar government did receive (and summarily rejected) two petitions from students at Jena, the first one with 280 signatures. The petitioners predicted that Fichte would "one day be the pride of our century" and assured the government that "we all revere and love in him a teacher in whose leadership we can trust with complete assurance"; but they avoided the question of whether he had been leading them into atheism.[45] No equivalent support came from the faculty (or the students) at any of the thirty-odd German universities. There were, of course, pamphlets and reviews in Fichte's defense, but most of them were qualified. And these were scattered voices, not a concerted protest.

Hence, despite his awareness of his own blunders, Fichte had reason to be disappointed with the "so-called educated public." He had been quite

man" is "one who, through abstractive powers on the one hand and social manipulation on the other, will hide from himself the natural and unconscious forces that influence his existence, in fact giving them free play over his motive and actions." In that sense, the "self" of the *Wissenschaftslehre* was not simply a "fake," as Jacobi charged; it "provided . . . a whole strategy of self-deception" (p. 76). See also George J. Seidel, "Fichte and Secular Christianity," *Antigonish Review* 1 (1970): 105–6. In Fichte's concept of the self, Seidel observes, "there is no way in which the self, which in its freedom is essentially practical, might theoretically reflect upon itself to know how it is actually doing in its process of self-making."

[43] FG 2: 179.   [44] FG 2: 196–8.

[45] The petitions were published in *Der Verkündiger*, 37. Stück, May 10, 1799, and have been reprinted in GA, III, 3: 339–40. For background on the petitions, including the possible treachery of Gottlieb Hufeland, see the account by Henrik Steffens, reprinted in FG 2: 133–5.

right to assume that even among scholars and men of letters who scoffed at his philosophy, there was widespread agreement on the principle at stake. The realm of scholarship and literature must be exempt from "political" interference. Otherwise the moral authority of an "enlightened" public was an illusion, a product of collective self-deception. That the public defense of this axiomatic principle was quite muted cannot be explained simply by the fact that Fichte's character made the case problematic. If Fichte failed the public, there was also a sense in which his blunders let the public off the hook. Were it not for the increasing focus on the issue of his character, the German intelligentsia might have had to take a hard look at the strains and inhibitions inherent in its relationship to the state and to the larger society. It might have had to confront an uncomfortable reality: that its vision of itself as a self-governing "republic," with all that term implied about a body of citizens occupying an autonomous zone of intellectual freedom, sat oddly with its dependence on the resources, the approval, and indeed the protection of dynastic states. And behind that fact lay another: that the intelligentsia's aspiration to constitute a public conscience – to exercise moral authority as the voice of criticism – was undercut by its complicity with power.

In the discourse of publicity, the fact of dependence was all too easily occluded. It becomes obvious when certain institutional and political realities are brought back into view. The broad center of the educated public was formed by an official intelligentsia, an elite of university graduates who entered offices that made them, to one degree or another, state servants. Even occupants of offices not financed by the state – most notably, the broad ranks of the clergy – acted increasingly as extensions of government authority. They knew very well that they could not step publicly outside the fairly narrow parameters of officially tolerated dissent without endangering their careers if not their livelihoods. In the university faculties, traditions of corporate self-government were by no means dead, but they were acceding to direct forms of state intervention and control. In the face of state oppression a professor could, of course, resign in protest; but for most, that was virtually unthinkable. One could not make a living simply as a man of letters, and there would be virtually no prospect of finding refuge in another German university. Nicolai's proposal for dealing with professors like Fichte speaks volumes about this situation. They should be removed from teaching but should keep every penny of their incomes.[46]

Appointed and salaried directly by the Weimar government, without the approval of the university Senate, Fichte was beyond the reach of spiteful rivals in the professoriate; but that also meant he was not shielded by corporate solidarity. Not surprisingly, he and Niethammer sent their

---

[46] Nicolai, *Uber meine gelehrte Bildung*, p. 564.

Justifications directly to Weimar, though the court, intent on following proper legal procedure, had instructed the Senate to report on their case. The regular procedure, they argued, would take too long. Fichte left unmentioned (but Voigt knew very well) that he could not expect sympathy, much less public support, from most Senate members, who regarded him as a state-imposed intruder on their turf.

The universities were at once islands of relatively free inquiry and training centers, responsible for replenishing the ranks of government bureaucracies and the state churches. Even in states like Weimar, which allowed "academic freedom" unusual latitude, it was in a sense beside the point to defend Fichte's freedom of expression as a publishing scholar. The immediate legal and political issue – the one raised by, among others, Nicolai and the author of the *Writing of a Father* – was whether scholarly freedom ought to extend to the lecture halls. "Can the state," one of Fichte's critics asked, "be indifferent to what philosophical theorems its future teachers of religion and judicial officials imbibe at the university?"[47]

It was not simply Fichte's persona in print that cost him support. His position on "freedom to teach" (*Lehrfreiheit*) was radical, and perhaps uniquely so. The readers of his article in the *Philosophical Journal* had learned in the very first sentence that his students had already heard the argument he was about to expound.[48] This admission was a measure of Fichte's unwitting capacity to provoke, but it also reflected a conviction to which he held fast throughout the Conflict. Since his arrival at Jena he had insisted on treating students as young citizens of the scholarly republic, owed the same freedom and candor as their elders. Fichte informed the Weimar government in the *Justification* that whether the professoriate liked it or not, the "thinking heads" among students brought a "most determined and free spirit of examination" to fundamental religious questions. He had been "driven" to his own conclusions about religion by his students' "well founded objections" to "the usual deductions." It was a new age – one tired of "knockdowns (*Niederschlagen*) by authority, shallowness, or intentional cloaking (*Bemäntelung*)," and satisfied only by "thoroughness and openness."[49]

If Fichte hoped to reassure the Weimar government with these comments, he was mistaken. In his tirade of December 26, Karl August told Voigt that he regarded Fichte's published article as harmless. It contained "nothing new," after all, and in any case most people were not likely to read it. What infuriated him – and what he could not justify to Electoral Saxony – was that one of his professors had been so "careless" as to try to inculcate "young, immature, for the most part very weak and unformed

---

[47] GA, I, 6: 143.   [48] Fichte, "Über den Grund," p. 27.
[49] Fichte, *Verantwortungsschrift*, pp. 54–5.

souls" with "skeptical sophistries."[50] Perhaps understandably in view of the raucousness of the student subculture, the Duke shared a traditional view of students as overgrown children, without worldly experience, still lacking a moral compass, and easily impressed and manipulated. Such childish vulnerability was particularly alarming in the young men destined to be the instruments of ducal authority. In the case of students, in other words, the moral logic of paternalism reinforced the power considerations of *Staatsräson*. To be sure, professors did not necessarily have to dispense a state-approved orthodoxy on questions of religious belief and moral obligation (though Electoral Saxony, in contrast to Weimar, seemed to be leaning in that direction). It would be more accurate to say that in the eyes of an "enlightened" state the dualism Kant had advocated in "What Is Enlightenment?" – the split between one's freedom as a scholar and one's obligation to conform in office – applied to professors as well as to clergymen and government officials, though not to the same degree. The split ran through the university itself, assigning scholarly exchange and the dissemination of knowledge in the lecture halls to two separate compartments.

That Karl August and his fellow rulers took this view of the universities is hardly surprising. More striking is that the same view, with its potent blend of paternalism and pragmatic statism, was common and indeed probably typical in the ranks of the intelligentsia. In his attacks on Fichte, Nicolai took pains to balance two convictions: that students, most of them destined to be "useful" servants of the state, had to be protected from their professors' abuse of academic freedom; and in the interests of progress, scholarly freedom of expression in print must be unlimited. Professors like Fichte were turning lecture halls into the equivalents of Pietist conventicles – breeding grounds for "blind *Schwärmer*" who "are usually as lost for the state as if they were castrated."[51] To Nicolai, Fichte's recklessness, precisely because it threatened to undermine the state, also posed a danger to the republic of scholars. The publisher's commitment to freedom of the press went hand in hand with his view of the bureaucratic state as a tutelary authority, at once guaranteeing stability and promoting reform. Others – including defenders of Fichte who did not share Nicolai's rationalist utilitarianism – took the same paternalistic view of students and were careful to observe the same distinction between scholarship and teaching. "The greatest part of young students," one professor acknowledged, were nearly as childish, and hence nearly as vulnerable to misguidance, as "the greater part of the public."[52]

[50] Duke Karl August to Voigt, Dec. 26, 1798, in FG 2: 29.
[51] Nicolai, *Über meine gelehrte Bildung*, pp. 556–62.
[52] Karl Friedrich Ernst Ludwig, *Freymüthige Gedanken über Fichte's Appellation gegen die Anklage des Atheismus und deren Veranlassung* (1968: Gotha, 1799), pp. 18–21.

As such language reminds us, students were not the only objects of paternalism. In the eyes of scholars and men of letters, most readers were immature, stuck in a childhood of the species that the enlightened few had long since put behind them. In the 1790s the accelerating commercialization of print had combined with the spectacle of revolutionary violence to heighten the Enlightenment's sense of threat from an ignorant or at best "half-educated" mass, still in the iron grip of confessional orthoxody or, worse, highly susceptible to the lure of *Schwärmerei* in one form or another. Where Fichte differed from mainstrean opinion was in exempting students from this view. To him the university as a whole, as an institution for teaching as well as for research, ought to be a preserve of privileged freedom of inquiry and expression.

As for the reading public at large, however, Fichte had written off most of it (including most university graduates) well before 1799. Niethammer's *Justification*, written separately, but published with Fichte's explicit endorsement, drew a sharp line between two "classes" of publications, the scholarly and the popular. If exchange in print was truly scholarly (as Fichte's and Forberg's articles had been), the state need not bother with it at all; to the larger reading public scholarship was and should remain a "closed book," a "fully separated territory." The audience for "popular" writings, on the other hand, blindly followed mere "authority" or its own passions. There the state must exercise strict censorship, rejecting anything that might threaten "the true civil order." The state should punish its censors if they allowed something dangerous to slip into the popular realm or if they intruded on the scholarly sphere.[53]

The Atheism Conflict had not occasioned this dualism. It had simply forced to the surface the fear of mass disorder and engulfment, so easily turned into a retreat behind the academic walls, that had underlain broader appeals to the *Publikum* throughout the century. The problem was not simply that this perspective made it virtually unthinkable for the "republic of scholars" to break out of its isolation, to seek in the wider society a political counterforce to an oppressive state. If the state embodied a political logic in a negative sense – a logic of potentially arbitrary power, as opposed to rational law – it was also the refuge of Reason, the only source of protection from a benighted and volatile mass. Implicitly acknowledging this form of dependence, defenders of scholarly freedom in 1799 resorted to the quid pro quo that had long reconciled it with the imperatives of state power. The universities' exceptional status as enclaves of free inquiry was conditional on their remaining strictly segregated in that capacity from the larger society, including its relatively well-educated minority. To put it another way, the right to scholarly freedom hinged on, and indeed was predicated on, the obligation not to

---

[53] GA, I, 6: 94–107.

seek a hearing in a broader audience. What the scholar could not do, or at least could not do without risking his privileged status, was to draw the larger society into the process of critical rationality.

That Fichte subscribed to this view in 1799 is a measure of the distance he had traveled since his entry into public life in the early 1790s. He was a renegade *in* the ranks of the official intelligentsia, which is to say that he was more daring than most of its members but was no longer the marginal young intellectual who had claimed to speak for the People. Having once sought to bond with the mass, he now feared that the charge of atheism would make him another martyr to popular savagery. As the Conflict ran its course, the specter of a fanatical mob – the kind of mob that might have been turned on Rousseau – loomed all the larger. If he stopped publishing, Fichte wrote to Reinhold, the courts might leave him alone; but would not the clergy "stir up the the rabble against me, to have me stoned by them, and then – request the governments to remove me as a man who incited disturbances?"[54]

To Fichte, the Atheism Conflict confirmed that the forces of religious obscurantism and political reaction were poised to snuff out intellectual freedom. How else could one explain the concerted vilification of a purely "speculative" denial of the "objective" existence of God, so solidly grounded in moral rigorism? His view of the larger political scene was tinged with paranoia, but he was not misreading the implications for his own future. He knew that in the political climate of 1799 he could not hope to find state protection at another German university; that was why he had tried, belatedly and ineptly, to keep his position at Jena.

By the time he wrote to Reinhold in late May, he was once again entertaining the possibility of finding refuge in France. But that would be a last resort. He knew very well that the *"practice"* of the French (and of "republicanized Germans") stood in sharp contrast to their *"principles."*[55] He preferred to secure the protection of a benevolent and enlightened German prince. His reasoning marks a bitterly ironic turn, a repudiation of the vision with which he had first appeared in print seven years earlier. The axiomatic assumption of the eighteenth-century discourse of publicity – that the public could judge competing ideas purely on their merit, in an arena free of external "authority" – now seemed naïve to him. "The great crowd," he confided to Reinhold, "is impressed by the authority that has decided against me"; "I would like it to be impressed by the same authority, so that it would at least listen to me." Ludwig-Friedrich II of Schwarzburg-Rudolstadt at first seemed willing to grant him refuge, but then he bowed to pressure from the neighboring courts. Fichte asked Reinhold to intercede with Duke Friedrich Christian of Schleswig-Holstein-Augustenberg, Schiller's benefactor. He was willing to promise

---

[54] GA, III, 3: 355.   [55] GA, III, 3: 358.

that as the Duke's guest he would write nothing more about the events of the Atheism Conflict.[56]

Nothing came of the request. In the spring of 1800, Fichte, Johanna, and their son moved to Berlin, where the philosopher would pursue his calling in a very different setting.

[56] GA, III, 3: 357–8.

Conclusion

The twentieth century closed as it opened, with acts of inhumanity on a scale and often on a level of efficiency that would have been unimaginable to Enlightenment humanists. Viscerally we have no doubt that such acts violate rights owed to every human being. When we condemn them publicly, however, it is with the sense that the resources of western cultures – linguistic, cognitive, ultimately moral – no longer empower us to speak authoritatively. We have entered a crisis of judgment and of speech that may have no precedent, and at its core is the issue of human selfhood. It has become questionable whether we can conceive of the self in a way that endows it with undeniable moral value and efficacy. We have to entertain the possibility that the very notion of a moral self is one of those delusions of western philosophy that intellectual honesty now requires us to put behind us. If we cannot speak compellingly about moral selfhood, then grounding the freedoms and obligations that we evoke with the term "rights" becomes deeply problematic. Even claims to the most basic rights – the rights to satisfy elementary physical and emotional needs – seem to lose their moorings.

To Fichte, it was the capacity to conceptualize the inner sanctum of selfhood and to build an ethics of rights and needs on that act of reflexivity that gave transcendental philosophy its purely human voice. This was his mission, his calling in a world in which the value and dignity of the human being could no longer be demonstrated by reference to the revealed truths of a sacred text, or to any knowledge of the transcendent. Is his a voice that we ought to be listening to now? What, if anything, might it tell us about our current choices? The questions were not uppermost in my thoughts as I wrote this book. My agenda was emphatically historicist: to recover the historical meaning of Fichte's life and thought by coming at them through their eighteenth-century contexts, and to use contextual biography, with the multiple angles of vision it affords, to advance our understanding of German culture, society, and politics in the last third of the century. I have contextualized a thinker who rested his claim to a calling, and indeed his claim to selfhood, on his own and his discipline's capacity to defy the constraints of historical context. Fichte would not be pleased, but hard-nosed historicists, who now come in many varieties within and outside the discipline of history, are not likely to sympathize with him. To them, historicism means relativism without exception; they welcome that implication, and some find in it liberation from the futility of the search for Truth and from the threat of oppression that lurks behind it. Fichte's claim to have discovered in transcendental idealism *the* foundational Truth about selfhood – the one which all other disciplines must accept as the legitimating source of their knowledge claims and to which the society at large must turn for normative guidance – will have struck them as an absurdly arrogant gesture, another moment of empyrean fantasy in the history of western philosophy.

My own preference is for what Thomas L. Haskell has called "the moderate variety of historicism" – a way of historicizing Fichte that would *not* make him, from the philosopher's standpoint, a figure of merely antiquarian interest, his thought too densely entangled in the contingent particularities of its historical location to be pulled forward into our fields of argument, to enter current philosophical conversations as a position worth engaging. Haskell has observed that despite the unqualified commitment to relativism that characterizes our post-Nietzschean "age of interpretation," we find ourselves unable to do without "rights talk"; and that having recognized that we can no longer ground claims to human rights in objective and universal truths, we must nonetheless understand rights as "conventions" that "need to be open to rational criticism" and that are "capable of commanding rational allegiance." From a moderate historicist point of view, Haskell argues, "mankind's persistent effort to achieve impersonal and intersubjective knowledge about morality, even in the face of perpetual and predictable disappointment . . . deserves the respect of all who claim to appreciate in a balanced way both the strengths and the limitations of theoretical reason."[1]

This is the kind of respect I hope to have brought to the study of Fichte. It assumes that, even if we find his militant universalism untenable, his effort to pose questions and formulate answers in a distinctly philosophical way remains relevant to our own task of conducting "rights talk" as rational argumentation. To read Fichte historically is to understand his texts contextually, as rhetorical moments, and hence to see how his efforts to argue rationally were *refracted* historically through specific discourses. It is to listen to those of his contemporaries who found his philosophy wrongheaded, even dangerous, and who found fault with his behavior, and to weigh his reponses to them. The result is that we expand, complicate, and ultimately make more efficacious our possible conversations with him. This is not, I should stress, a simple matter of finding in Fichte's thought credible ways to justify and protect human rights today. In some of its refractions, Fichte's devotion to Reason confronts us with glaring danger signals. If he is to serve us well as an interlocutor, he *ought*

[1] Thomas L. Haskell, "The Curious Persistence of Rights Talk in the 'Age of Interpretation,'" *American Historical Review* 74:3 (1987): 984–6, 1005–12.

to be an ambiguous figure, at once calling us to account and disappointing us, attracting us and alarming us.

★ ★ ★

In this volume, the historical Fichte has meant, quite literally, the eighteenth-century figure, the man who was thirty-eight when the century closed and who would live another fourteen years.[2] Contextual biography counters any temptation we might have to think of the eighteenth-century Fichte as a fixed point on the historical map. Even in the brief period from 1792, when he first made his mark as a thinker and writer, to 1799, when his career at Jena ended, Fichte's life circumstances and thought underwent radical changes. The marginal figure – seemingly condemned to obscurity by his plebeian origins and outside the patronage networks through which careers were made – became an academic celebrity, and the celebrity crossed the line into a kind of notoriety that cost him his academic employment. The aspiring preacher, content to make his mark as a disciple popularizing Kantian moral truth, became the philosopher intent on revolutionizing philosophy as *Wissenschaft* by giving it the unassailable systematicity that Kant had failed to provide. The ambivalent suitor, shunning domesticity even as he sought refuge in it, settled into a conventional, though not typical, bourgeois marriage.

Fichte's thought was no less in flux. As he found his calling as a philosopher and matured in that role, his thought became, by our standards, in some ways more daring, in some ways less radical. In the late 1780s he had been a fairly typical specimen of the cautiously enlightened German Protestant, seeking ways to reconcile evangelical faith with reason. In 1798 he made it clear that if by "God" we mean a transcendent Being, he was an atheist. In 1793 he looked to a free market in property and labor to advance moral as well as material progress, but within a few years he was challenging head-on the very notion that a free market was rationally

---

[2] It has become increasingly apparent that Fichte's thought took significant new turns in the last fourteen years of his life, from 1800 to 1814. The themes pursued here may alert us to an undertow of continuity beneath a changing surface. As late as 1799, Fichte was not on the road to a nationalist reconception of community. And yet, in the light of his social and intellectual odyssey to that point, the nationalism of the *Addresses to the German Nation* in 1807–8 is not surprising. In his apotheosis of the German nation as an ethical community constituted by its language, Fichte found still another way to bond a clerisy with a larger public culture, to justify the creation of a spiritual elect that would hover above the masses and yet communicate with them through a shared medium of emotionally charged symbols. Nor is it surprising, when we recall his disillusionment with the print market, that that vision gave a marked preference to oral communication. But there is, of course, much more to the intellectual career of the post-Jena Fichte. Even if we limited ourselves to tracing his route to the nationalism of the *Addresses* (and there are many other themes worth pursuing), we would need to consider, in the intellectual and political setting of the Prussian capital, his reengagement with the evangelical tradition; his renewed interest in language and pedagogy; his new efforts to come to terms with political power; his reevaluation of historical knowledge.

defensible and was subordinating the right to property, as conventionaly defined, to the right to labor. His aspiration to constitute a radically egalitarian rhetorical community had acceded to a cultish vision of a spiritual elect. Having entered the public arena as a tribune of "the people" constituted as a *Publikum*, he had become skeptical of the very notion that the modern *Publikum* could serve as the collective conscience of a society and polity. He came away from Jena and the Atheism Conflict a disillusioned man, confirmed in his alienation from what he (and many others) saw as the commercial trivialization of print communication and regarding the real public as hopelessly in thrall to confessional and political authority.

Through all these shifts and turns, however, we see permanent imprints, the recurrent markers of conflicting pulls and perceptions of choice. They are already discernible in the university graduate trying to justify himself – to validate himself in his own eyes and in the eyes of others – in the late 1780s as he sought a foothold on the precarious climb into a career. Like many other educated young Germans of the late eighteenth century, but to an extreme degree, Fichte faced the dilemmas of the uprooted and the marginalized. There was no turning back, no retreat to the world from which he had been removed, but he had good reason to wonder whether he would ever advance to a secure position in the learned estate. He was distinguished by the depth and breadth of his alienation. That is not to imply that because he came at issues from an odd angle, his thought lacks the wider resonances that philosophy ought to have. Quite the contrary; his alienation propelled him down a philosophical road of enormous significance in modern culture. If his "pride" was, by his own admission, excessive, it also marked his sensitivity to the arbitrary play of power behind the exercise of social as well as political authority in old-regime society and his awareness that the myriad asymmetries of power left little space for undistorted, or "purely human," communication. The task he assigned himself was to ground the human right to freedom in a new way of conceiving the essentially human – a way that, by the self-evident status of its truth, would draw a line of defense for the moral self that the differentiating and the distorting effects of power could not violate.

As the young Fichte endured obscurity on the bottom edge of a bourgeois intelligentsia and as he sought to validate the social ascent he had yet to achieve, he developed a heightened awareness of a profound discordance in his world. The intimacy he found in friendship – the emotional as well as intellectual sustenance it offered to a young man uprooted from his own family – was not simply a private compensation for the lack of a public voice. In Fichte's aspiration to "have an effect" by asserting a public voice, we see with unusual clarity the eighteenth-century ideal of friendship – its insistence on moral equality and intellectual and emotional openness – being transmuted into the norms for an imagined public sphere. What confronted him was the rude disjuncture between that imagined world and the realities of power in the corporate hierarchies of eighteenth-century Germany. In the face of arbitrary treatment and the indignities inflicted on the dependent, he sought to preserve an inner sanctum of autonomy and dignity. He had no choice but to practice the dissimulation that the intricate rules of deference required, and that made the principle of openness all the more sacred to him.

What led Fichte to embrace philosophy as his calling in 1790 was his newly won Kantian conviction that there *was* an inviolable moral self and that he had found a public voice for it. The severe constraints of his situation notwithstanding, he was a free moral agent. Over the next decade he labored to demonstrate how philosophy, as the most human of callings, could determine what the relationship between morality and power ought to be. In 1795 he described his "system" as "the *first system of freedom*" and attributed the inspiration for it to the French nation's "struggle for its freedom" in the Great Revolution. Just as the French Revolution had "broken the political fetters of human beings," his revolution "[tore them] from the chains of the thing in itself."[3]

Fichte was drawing an analogy between his philosophy and the emancipatory dynamic of the Revolution; he was not conflating the two. In the course of his ascent into academe, he embraced the bourgeois ethos that permeated so much of public discourse in eighteenth-century France as well as Germany and that was central to the revolutionary agenda of 1789. We find its core values in his censorious stereotypes of a parasitical, frivolous, and false aristocratic culture; in his fierce pride in his own hard-won learning and sober work ethic; in his conviction that the individual's talent and merit should define his life chances; in his need for a haven of intimacy and innocence, and for an emblem of respectability, in family life. The "bourgeois" label becomes misleading, however, if it carries the implication that Fichte has to be assigned to one of the ideologically loaded categories that trace their lineage, at least indirectly, to the Revolution. Whatever move he made, he took with him the tensions that were intrinsic to his social sense of self. It makes some sense to think of him as a bourgeois radical, but his radicalism did not take the form of Jacobinism. He was, in George Armstrong Kelly's phrase, "a Jacobin of the elect."[4] With the failure of his attempt in the *Contribution* to bond with "the great crowd," he turned his attention to using the universities to create the new spiritual elite that I have called a clerisy. To characterize his vision as elitist, however, would be to miss the egalitarian impulse that pervaded it. That

---

[3] GA, III, 2: 300.
[4] George Armstrong Kelly, *Idealism, Politics, and History. Sources of Hegelian Thought* (Cambridge, 1969), p. 188.

impulse found expression in his yearning to reproduce somehow, in philosophical reflexivity, the emotional spontaneity and certainty of the simple Christian believer and in his expectation that the new clerisy, in the way it generated and disseminated knowledge, would set the example for power-free communication at all social levels. Labels like "populist" and "democrat," on the other hand, occlude Fichte's need to demonstrate to others and to convince himself that he had cleansed himself of popular superstitions and crudities. The "populism" of the *Contribution*, if the term applies at all, was of a peculiarly philosophical (i.e., Kantian) sort, and that was soon extinguished by his disillusionment with print culture. Obviously he was no political democrat, though he sought, ever so cautiously, to anchor his rational state in a principle of popular sovereignty.

If Fichte was not a political democrat, he also was not a political liberal. And yet there is a real sense in which, from the outset of his career, he found in the calling of philosophy a way to pursue an emancipatory agenda with radically egalitarian implications about rights and needs. In his philosophical grounding of that agenda, and in his working out of its implications as he built his system, he gave the political cultures of modern democratic liberalism much to ponder. It was precisely because he was so intent on securing freedom in the face of power that Fichte became, arguably, the foundationalist and essentialist philosopher par excellence. That is not to say, however, that his transcendental idealism belongs in the dustbin of empty abstractions and false universalisms cloaking hegemonic impulses. Foundationalism has taken many forms, and Fichte's variety is less out of tune with current philosophical orientations than might at first appear to be the case. Kant had been content to entertain the prospect that we would one day discover the "transcendental unity of apperception," the unitary ground of consciousness beneath his architectonic division between theoretical and practical reason. In the *Wissenschaftslehre*, Fichte claimed to have discovered that irreducible unity in an originary act of self-consciousness, absorbing cognition into a unitary act of will. It was an audacious, perhaps reckless move, and Fichte justified it with unabashed arrogance. And yet his attempt to ground the right to freedom in an unassailable first principle had a certain epistemological modesty. He was more than willing to acknowledge that our knowledge of an originary act of self-positing could be no more than inferential; and indeed he remained so aware of the circular reflexivity of consciousness that one scholar has argued, with some plausibility, that behind his manifest commitment to foundationalism we find a subtext of nascent antifoundationalism.[5]

---

[5] Tom Rockmore, "Antifoundationalism, Circularity, and the Spirit of Fichte," in Daniel Breazeale and Tom Rockmore, eds., *Fichte. Historical Contexts/ Contemporary Controversies* (Atlantic Highlands, N.J., 1994): 96–112.

Fichte's essentialism was also in a new key. Like Kant, he sought to ground human value in what distinguished human beings from things and hence to place strict moral limits on people's use of each other as things. Here again, though, collapsing Kant's distinction between theoretical and practical reason had radical implications. Fichte's definition of the essential self as a self-positing moral will carried the emancipatory thrust of Kant's transcendentalism in several new directions at once. He labored to preclude the danger of the self, even with the moral autonomy Kant attributed to it, finding itself "only in the presentation of things," and being "lost" when its image was not reflected back at it by things. He sought to eradicate the objectification of moral subjectivity at its source, in the propensity of consciousness to objectify itself. Human beings, he argued, were distinguished from things because their selfhood was not a kind of being, or a set of capacities, but a unitary process of becoming, a continuous act of self-constitution; because they could only become selves – they could only acquire the self-consciousness that was uniquely human – by recognizing each other's moral freedom in inter-subjective encounters; because they could appropriate things for moral purposes in the act of labor. These are arguments worth listening to, if only as cues for recasting rational argumentation about rights in our own idioms.

The arguments are especially deserving of our attention because they extended the critical reach of transcendental philosophy into areas where Kant chose not to carry it. To put it another way, Fichte enlarged the space for normative critique that Kant had opened. He expanded philos-ophy's self-authorization as the voice of criticism, enabling us to judge the moral legitimacy of the existent by imagining rational alternatives to it and asserting the authority of the "ought" in the face of objections that what "is" has been sanctioned by "experience" and hence ought to be, or that, from a "practical" standpoint, what is simply cannot be otherwise. The two shifts in Fichte's thinking in the mid-1790s, now receiving renewed attention, spell out the truly radical implications of this com-mitment to transcendental critique. There is, first, his philosophy of law. Against the backdrop of the Enlightenment, to be sure, Fichte's strict seg-regation of the concept of law from morality seems quite derivative, though it distinguished him from more cautious Kantians of his genera-tion. And if the point of his a priori deduction of the concept of law was simply that legal equality is necessary for the protection of human dignity, that too would lack originality. But the deduction cut much deeper through conventional thinking. Fichte sought to make the concept of law, its core concept of reciprocity, the necessary condition for ground-ing self-consciousness and hence for constituting selfhood, or, to put it more simply, for acquiring the moral value that we recognize when we speak of human dignity. The result was a radically new justification for a rational legal system – one that, as the condition of selfhood, had to guarantee complete reciprocity in rights and restrictions.

Of equally lasting importance is Fichte's argument, from his concepts of selfhood and freedom, that the right to "property" must be understood as the universal right to fulfill one's material needs and to develop one's capacities in labor, and that the provision of the right to labor required a more egalitarian distribution of wealth. This was not a move to full-blown socialism, but to judge it from that teleological standpoint is to miss its larger historical significance. What makes the move pivotal is its abandonment of Kantian formalism for a conception of morality with explicitly social import, one that made social justice a condition of individual freedom. To Kant, the Categorical Imperative not to reduce human beings to mere means implied the need for a legal system that would guarantee procedural justice. In contrast, in the *Naturrecht* Fichte's imagined community of labor was constituted on the principle of distributive justice. What he identified – and he was certainly not alone in this regard – was a kind of injustice that I have called structural, a kind that was immoral despite the fact that it could not be explained simply, or even primarily, as the product of individual moral choices. The logic is open to abuse; it can easily lead to the conclusion that individuals, simply because they belong to certain (ideologically constructed) groups, are guilty and subject to punishment. Without a concept of structural injustice, however, it is hard to imagine how we can credibly argue for a significant redistribution of resources in societies where the differences in people's life chances and capacity to satisfy needs are immense.

All this is not meant to imply that on the issue of selfhood, or freedom, or human dignity, Fichte has more to say to us than do Schiller, Humboldt, Jacobi, and some of his other critics in the 1790s. The stereotyping of his philosophy as a hyperrationalist inversion of religious *Schwärmerei*, a tyranny of implacable abstraction over the concrete particularity of life, was not without justification. Like so many other German thinkers of his era, Fichte sought to explain individuation, the process in which the universality of the rational conjoined with the particularity of the empirical in embodied human beings. One thinks of his dramatic narrative of the struggle between the "I" and the "Not-I"; of his concern to find moral meaning in the specialized roles of the modern division of labor; and of his attempt to make the concept of law the point of mediation between the Moral Law and the empirical reality of the *Individuum*. To the moral rigorist in Fichte, the question was how the self could remain aware of, and bound by, an unconditionally universal moral law *despite* its individuation. In collective moral progress, individuals would become more and more alike as they all drew closer to a universal norm.

This obviously was not a brief for Rousseauian (or Romantic) authenticity, or indeed for individualism in the modern relativistic sense. More troubling is that individuation as Fichte conceived it leaves no moral space for, and no way of attributing moral value to, *individuality*, if by the latter term we mean the unreproducible form that the totality of human attributes assumes in a particular person, the wholeness in particularity that makes an individual qualitatively unique and irreplaceable. It was individuality that Schiller and Humboldt sought to nourish. Even if we do not share their aesthetic ideal of personality, we can understand why they were repelled by Fichte's alternative. Friedich Jacobi, though he misread Fichte in some ways, saw the same danger when he spoke of him reducing the personality to a "means" of reason. A secure sense of self may not require, as Jacobi contended, a belief in the Absolute Other, but we cannot dismiss his claim that Fichte's construal of selfhood, having no place for "the proper individual value" of "the *actual* person," posits "that naked *selfhood* of the I without any *self.*" Jacobi's language – his image of the living self facing annihilation, needing to experience itself immediately in its unique particularity but stripped down instead to the nakedness of a purely abstract concept – confronts us with a danger that has become all too familiar: that abstract universals, promising emancipation in the name of "humanity," can dehumanize.

Fichte's philosophy represents, in heightened form, the trade-off that a universalist concept of selfhood and rights entails. Even as it posits, with compelling logic, the value intrinsic to any human being, it devalues one's need to experience oneself as unique in one's mode of being human. It does so because it is so insistent on detaching an essential self from the tangle of needs, motives, and emotions that constitute the physical and psychological self. To Fichte, as to Kant, it was imperative to conceive the moral self in this way; otherwise the moral will would lose its unique value, its capacity to be disinterested. The result is what Michael Walzer calls the "critical" self in its philosophical guise, as a moral superagent "in touch with universal values." Walzer identifies a certain analogous relationship between this concept of moral superagency and its opposite, the critical self of psychoanalysis, which pits the universality of instincts against "the standards of a particular culture." He is surely right that at both of these extremes we find "a simple linear and hierarchical arrangement of the self" and that we need instead "thick, divided selves," more suited to "the thick, differentiated, and pluralist society" of a modern democracy.[6] If the univocal voice of the internal critic gives the self the advantage of

---

[6] Michael Walzer, "The Divided Self," in Walzer, *Thick and Thin. Moral Arguments at Home and Abroad* (Notre Dame and London, 1994), esp. pp. 88–91, 98–104. See also Jürgen Habermas, "Individuation through Socialization: On George Herbert Meade's Theory of Subjectivity," in Habermas, *Postmetaphysical Thinking: Philosophical Essays*, trans. William Mark Hohengarten (Cambridge, Mass.,

a kind of certainty, it is also open to abuse. In the psychoanalytical variation, the very concept of morality can be dismissed as nothing more than a rationale for repression. In the philosophical variation – the one Fichte advocated with such conviction – the concept of morality threatens to subvert itself. The subversion flows from the refusal to make psychological introspection integral to the development of moral self-knowledge. We risk becoming hardened to the emotional needs of others in the name of morality. At the same time – and here Fichte's way of acting on his conception of selfhood provides an exemplary warning – we are in danger of impoverishing the self's internal dialogue. We license ourselves to remove from our moral self-examination precisely those impulses – dark, brutal, or just petty – that we ought to be confronting.

In a sense, then, what makes Fichte's philosophy of freedom problematic is its very insistence on the universality of moral knowledge. We are apt to find his rationale for the dignity of the human being as such so categorically abstract as to be dehumanizing. But there is also a sense in which Fichte's universalist discourse disappoints, and indeed exasperates, because it is not universal at all. We first encounter this irony of universalist exclusion in the antisemitic outburst of the *Contribution*. The outburst was fueled by Fichte's alienation from his own community of belief and not by some deep psychic energy in the German national character. Again, though, the young Fichte's angle of vision as a marginal man makes his thought a heightened example of a larger phenomenon. Even as he acknowledged that Jews ought to have "human" (as opposed to civic) rights, he wrote them out of the Kantian moral community that he insisted lay, latent but ready to be constituted, beneath the ideologically sanctioned corruption of eighteenth-century societies and cultures. And he did so on the grounds that Jews, by the very nature of their commercial and religious culture, were incapable of moral universalism. There is a cautionary tale here about the dangers lurking behind the promise of emancipation in universalist discourse. It may be obvious, but it bears repeating, if only because so much of the scholarship on Fichte, including recent work, has ignored his antisemitism or explained it away as a merely accidental blemish on his thought. The point is not simply that in Fichte's case an ancient religious prejudice survived the commitment to Kantian universalism. In the new form of universalism the prejudice found precisely the kind of imprimatur it needed in a secularizing world.

Fichte's thinking about sexuality, gender, and marriage is no less sobering in this regard, despite the flights of logic and rhetoric with which he

1992): 149–204, which includes an interesting discussion of Fichte's concept of individuation, and the discussion of Habermas's alternative concept in John Doody, "Fichte, Habermas, and Luc Ferry," in Lenore Langsdorf and Stephen H. Watson (with Karen A. Smith), eds., *Reinterpreting the Political. Continental Philosophy and Political Theory* (Albany, N.Y., 1998): 141–54.

tried to prove that a woman's sacrifice of her will in her love for her husband was a quintessentially rational act of human freedom. The question of sexual gratification aside, Fichte's ultrapatriarchal view of marriage made married women legally rightless and publicly selfless. It is a classic example of exclusion under cover of universality. Here above all we see the tension in Fichte's quest for self-justification; in marriage to Johanna he sought a safe haven from the corrupting influences of polite society but also a way to appease an anxious need for social respectability. In his marriage, and in his philosophy, he found some resolution of this tension in the rhetoric of *Empfindsamkeit*, which offered a powerfully appealing reformulation of the ancient binary division between male activity and female passivity. I do not conclude that Fichte's thought exemplifies what some scholars see as the inherently gendered concept of rational agency in western philosophy. The contrast with Kant is instructive on the need to confront that kind of generalization with informed historical analysis. Nor do I think that Fichte's gendered logic represents the false univerality of "liberalism." If we classify Fichte as a liberal, the category becomes so capacious as to lose all meaning. The fact remains, though, that in recent efforts to demonstrate that Fichte's thought still has emancipatory potential at the close of the twentieth century, philosophers have practiced a "rational reconstruction" (to recall Rorty's phrase) that has largely evaded the question of gender. Whether Fichte's concept of selfhood can ground a truly universal claim to human rights hinges in part on whether it can be detached from a gendered distinction between the activity of moral persons and the passivity of things. The very concept of "will" has a gendered historical baggage that is difficult to shed. If we get past that problem, there is another. If we are to speak of and to ground rights in the affective terms of intimacy, then we must somehow avoid reinserting the terms of inequality that the language, and indeed the rhetoric, of affect can so insidiously sanction. The lacing of transcendental deduction with affect-laden rhetoric in Fichte's ideal of marriage stands as a warning in that regard.

★ ★ ★

Fichte's patriarchalism is symptomatic of an authoritarian impulse in his thought. The impulse is inescapably there in the historical Fichte, in several refractions; and it must be confronted, even if, and especially if, we wish to enlist him for antiauthoritarian purposes. Can we find guidance in Fichte's emancipatory agenda without at the same time becoming complicit in his authoritarianism? A study of this sort cannot answer the question. It can only suggest how a historical understanding of Fichte can help us clarify it.

Fichte was an outspoken member of a generation of German intellectuals who rejected old-regime states as machines, arbitrary instruments of morally blind power hiding behind the rhetoric of paternalism. It is all the more ironic, then, that in its machinelike enforcement of the conditions for rational behavior, Fichte's rational state promised to be no less coercive than its predecessors, and perhaps more so. Efforts to give Fichte's legal and political philosophy a new hearing have tended to simply bracket off this ominous side, when the question is whether what we see as his positive contribution can be separated from what we find ominous. The question is pressing; what many scholars (including myself) see as Fichte's two key breakthroughs in the *Naturrecht* and related writings – his theory of labor as property, and his philosophy of law – are precisely the points at which his authoritarianism becomes prominent and functions, it would seem, as an integral part of his transcendental argument.

The superregulatory machine that Fichte called a "closed commercial state" had a distinctly eighteenth-century German lineage. For all his disdain for eighteenth-century cameralism, he remained deeply wedded to the cameralist vision of modernity, with corporatelike cultures and ways of life assigned their places in an intricately graded functional hierarchy. But his hyperstatism also reflected his commitment to distributive justice, and any effort to add his voice to current debates about justice has to contend with that fact. In the course of the 1790s, he reversed direction in his effort to imagine a legal order that would recognize and enforce the universal right to satisfy basic physical needs. What is striking is that, in both directions, he came up with solutions that were radical in their context and that are likely to strike readers today as naïvely radical. In the *Contribution* he opted for an extreme version of free market contractualism, with private property figuring as both a vehicle of moral self-realization and an instrument of self-interest. A legal order that universalized the right to property, he assumed, would tap vast human capacities for productivity and hence eliminate poverty. By the time he wrote *The Closed Commercial State* he had concluded that the free market abandoned people to the blind power of Nature; and that autarchic statism – a system that not only controlled the supply of labor and the distribution of goods in minute detail but also walled off the economic life of the community from the rest of the world – was the only way to rescue people from that fate.

As we leave behind the ideological pieties of the Cold War, we are in a better position to understand these positions historically. Even in his free market phase, Fichte was anything but an apologist for the commercial world of capitalism as we know it. At the other extreme, his closed commercial state differed significantly from the former Soviet Union and its clones. And yet, on the basic issue of how to secure freedom by constraining it, Fichte's alternatives are all too similar to the ones that the Cold War asked us to accept. On one side, within an overarching framework of moral rights and obligations, constraint will be intrinsic in the relationships of mutual advantage and vulnerability in free market contracts. The public authority of the state, we are told, will be largely superfluous. On the other side, constraint will be imposed by a bureaucratic Leviathan. The Leviathan will wither away, we are assured, as people become more and more virtuous. In the meanwhile there will be no need for either representative institutions or an independent judiciary; for the most part, the state can be expected to restrain itself. We would do well not to frame our choices in these terms.

We find a similar either/or in Fichte's deduction of the concept of law. It suggests that a historically specific feature of the Kantian philosophical revolution – the dualism between morality, the sphere of choice without coercion, and the blind coercion that reigns in physical nature – severely narrowed the parameters for imagining a civil society that would be capable of generating its own political culture. While Fichte strove to overcome the dualism at the epistemological level, in his concept of the self striving for unity, his thinking about society and politics continued to be structured by it. Throughout the 1790s he subsumed the social and the political under the eighteenth-century construct of Nature as a field of mechanical power, the world of externally observable things, blindly imparting and receiving force. That he persisted in this view – that he remained largely oblivious to the alternative view that has been called "enlightenment vitalism" – is hardly surprising; abandoning mechanism would have required a fundamental rethinking of what distinguished morality from power.

His persistence meant, however, that when he set out to detach the principle of law from morality in 1795, he could do so only by conceiving of people, for purposes of law, as carriers and recipients of mechanical force. He did, to be sure, rework Rousseau's concept of the General Will to demonstrate that even when the freedom at stake was the mechanical pursuit of self-interest, human beings could ground the right to freedom in an exercise of collective rationality. But this a priori deduction, designed to maximize freedom in principle, yielded a vision of a legally constituted society that was inexorably authoritarian in its workings. While the moral self was capable of disinterested devotion to duty, the natural self had to be conceived as impelled by self-interest. Since in the act of choice there was no middle ground, no zone for negotiation between the authority of moral principles and the force of natural impulses, only a mammoth state could prevent individuals from invading each other's spheres of freedom. And whereas moral selves were transparent to each other in their mutual recognition of their freedom, natural selves, like other natural objects, were observable only in their externality. The motives they brought to relationships were mutually impenetrable. That is why Fichte's theory of intersubjectivity, for all its emphasis on reciprocity as the very ground of selfhood, had no place for the development of what might be called social trust and for the building of social solidarities on some measure of mutual trust in everyday life. The absence of trust as a motive force meant that Fichte's rational order was, in social terms, grimly atomistic at any level beyond that of the family. And that in turn meant that even in its zones of autonomy from the bureaucratic state, "civil society" remained largely a passive aggregate of subjects. There was no space for the participatory politics of an active citizenry, no way for civil society to constitute itself as an actively autonomous set of collectivities.

What we see here, I should stress, is only one eighteenth-century way of thinking about the motive force of self-interest – a way that, premised on a transcendental principle of social interaction, was markedly blind to actual processes of sociability. Consequential in his trancendental deduction, Fichte had to reject categorically Anglo-Scotttish efforts to understand, in the dense complexity of their modern social contexts, kinds of intersubjectivity that are driven neither by naked self-interest nor by pure virtue. That was, in political terms, a high price to pay.

The fact that Fichte persisted in his thought experiment about law – that he imagined a rational legal order peopled with "devils" – is not as puzzling as it might at first appear to be. That was the only way he could be sure of keeping morality pure, beyond contaminating complicity with power and coercion. The experiment reminds us, paradoxically, that Fichte's vision was first and foremost a vision of moral regeneration.

It is here, in his moral rigorism, that we find the most powerful and pervasive refraction in Fichte's philosophy. If we wish to know how the core values of the Protestant ethos survived the rejection of Protestant fideism, Fichte is a striking case in point. We see the shaping presence of the Lutheran tradition in his recurrent efforts to give "inner" freedom an element of emotional spontaneity, despite the commanding role assigned to Reason; in his awareness that demonstrative reason could be an instrument of coercion; in his various distinctions between, on the one side, the Spirit and, on the other, the Letter and the Law, including the Judaic Law; in his view of a modern clerisy as a kind of spiritual elect; in his ideal of work as a secular calling.

Fichte was one of many thinkers involved in translating the moral ideal of calling from the Protestant discourse of the sacred to a secular language of labor. His thought reveals with unusual clarity how the translation was effected and what it signifies. Perhaps more than any of his German contemporaries, he was intent on grounding the dignity of the human in the dignity of work. We find in his ideal of calling, in fact, the key themes in one of the most pronounced normative commitments of modern secular cultures: the commitment to work as the critical source of self-validation. Work validates by allowing the inner self to find expression in forms of externality; by demonstrating the self-mastery of the rational moral agent; by providing the forms of communication and exchange in which, in the intricate grid of the modern division of labor, each enhances the other's freedom; by making the human engagement with Nature productive.

As the philosopher who, perhaps more than any other, endowed the calling with a kind of sacred meaning in the very process of desacralizing it, Fichte speaks to us with uncommon immediacy. His thought becomes a revealing moment in the long-term cultural process that has endowed work-discipline with such respect, and indeed has made it a secular object of reverence, in advanced capitalist societies. And yet, on this theme, we also look back on Fichte across a distance that may be unbridgeable. It was because work embodied the spirit of Protestant inner-worldly asceticism that it had a kind of secular sacredness in his thought. In a sense, to be sure, Fichte fused moral right and physical need in his concept of labor; he argued cogently that the exercise of moral freedom is contingent on the satisfaction of basic physical wants. But this dimension of Fichte's moral rigorism coexists uneasily with another: his view of the needs of the natural self as resistances, or indeed as temptations, to be overcome in the moral self's struggle to realize itself. He was confident that a more rational economic order would also be a vastly more productive one, but that expectation sat oddly with his view of work as the vehicle of the moral self's struggle against the natural creature, the spirit's route to victory over the flesh, the site of a relentless practice of self-denial in devotion to duty. Even the older generation of *Aufklärer*, who were no slouches when it came to extolling work as a sacred duty, found something grim and harsh about Fichte's preachments to embrace a life of relentless toil. Something like his ascetic strain still lurks in the interstices of modern consumer cultures, despite their apparently heedless embrace of materialism; but it is hard to square with an increasingly dominant message in the modern commercial celebration of work – the reassuring message that work validates us by making us deserving of the luxury car, or the Carribbean vacation, or the early and comfortable retirement. While we may recognize something of Fichte's inner-worldly asceticism in ourselves, we have to acknowledge that the values of modern consumer culture have weakened its authority considerably. It is not likely that the moral rigorism of Fichte's ethos of calling can be reinvigorated, or indeed that it should be. Without it, however, we face the challenge of rethinking the very notion that labor endows people with human dignity – so that, in some sense, the notion still has a credible moral logic but also has a purchase on our culture.

Fichte's thought is not amenable to a neat distinction between the religious and the secular; it represents, and invites further inquiry into, the historical continuum from the one to the other. Likewise Fichte can be

understood neither as a "political" thinker *tout court* nor as a classic
example of the "unpolitical" German intellectual. The reason is that, in
still another refraction, Fichte approached the political through the normative concepts of a "public" and "publicity" that the Enlightenment had
bequeathed to him. Indeed he made those concepts central not only to
his vision of progress but to his own assertion of selfhood. Hence we find
writ large in his thought the simultaneous commitment to a kind of political action and recoil from politics that characterized the eighteenth-
century discourse of publicity.

To appreciate the nature of Fichte's political engagement, we have to
set aside our own complacency about the discourse of publicity – and
perhaps our own disillusionment with it in an age when so much commercially driven invasion of privacy is justified by "the people's right to
know." In the eighteenth century, the appeal to the judgment of "the
public" was a new and emphatically secular way of grounding the legitimacy of authority, including the authority of government. That government ought to be morally accountable to a public, and hence ought to
be fully open to its scrutiny, was a profoundly political principle. Fichte's
commitment to the principle was in response to an intense need; it offered
the vital connection between his inner sense of freedom and his determination to *practice* freedom by living a public life of candor. He saw the
right to be candid in public – to bear witness to one's convictions – as
the sine qua non of philosophy's critical mission. Modernity seemed to
offer the unprecedented possibility of societies, cultures, and polities
becoming self-critical without self-destructing. The possibility would be
realized, however, only if intellectuals, and especially philosophers, could
criticize established authority without restraint.

Understood as political in this sense, the principle of publicity is of
course axiomatic in the political culture of liberal democracy; and when
we trace it back to its origins in the Enlightenment, Fichte – though he
came at the tail end of the Enlightenment and in many ways rejected
it – deserves a prominent place. At the same time, though, Fichte's
commitment to the principle of publicity also demonstrates why its
eighteenth-century formulation now seems so incompatible with politics
as practice and as process in modern liberal democracies. The problem is
not simply that having failed in his effort to imagine an egalitarian public,
Fichte joined most of his contemporaries in the German intelligentsia in
limiting the exercise of public criticism to a micropublic of university-
educated men. There is a deeper incompatibility. Even if his vision of the
public had remained inclusive, it would represent an aspiration to *avoid*
the politics of modern democracy. Fichte shared with many other
eighteenth-century thinkers the expectation that publicity would produce
a unitary moral consensus, or something very close to it. The consensus
would arise not from a process of political contestation but from the exer-

cise of autonomous judgment by myriad individuals in what has aptly been called "a discourse of reason outside power, which nevertheless is normative for power."[7]

And so, once again, Fichte ought to make us ambivalent. The principle of publicity, in the classic eighteenth-century version that we find in his thought and action, is constitutive of modern democratic politics. It is also, however, at odds with our current efforts to conceive the democratic political process as one of rational deliberation. If we are to speak credibly of a public culture of rational deliberation now, it has to be in the weak sense that a position of moderate historicism, confronting the politics of pluralism and competing interest groups at the beginning of this century, allows. How can we maintain some sense of an encompassing public community while at the same time recognizing that if we are to have a deliberative democracy, it will have to take the form of "a multiplicity of public spheres nested within each other"?[8] How can such a democracy be organized so that rational argumentation operates not outside power but through it, in communication among the social collectivities that give individuals a public voice and among the organizations that mobilize people for political contestation? Reading Fichte for answers to these questions may be a futile exercise.

In a sense, Fichte saw no reason to pose the questions. In what is perhaps the most distinctively German orientation of his thought, he placed his hopes in the universities and in the public knowledge they would generate. Absolutist and corporatist paternalism; a commercializing world of print that seemed to trivialize ideas; an emerging arena of modern ideological politics: in the face of all these symptoms of corruption, the universities would be the havens of free and pure thought, the source of the criticism that would insure the eventual triumph of Reason. We cannot appraise this vision without asking how it was refracted through the historicity of his life. And when I ask that question, I become especially aware that, the appeal of historicism aside, biography lures by offering occasions for autobiographical reflection. My conflicted response to Fichte marks my own sense of self and my own doubts about whether a university-based scholar and teacher can still be said to have a calling.

Even a public university like my own is, of course, far less subject to state tutelage than was Fichte's Jena. And there are other huge differences between German universities in the late eighteenth century and contemporary western universities – in their kinds and degrees of specialization, in their internal organization, and in their relationships to the larger

---

[7] Charles Taylor, "Liberal Politics and the Public Sphere," in Taylor, *Moral Arguments* (Cambridge, Mass., 1995): 266.

[8] Ibid., p. 280.

society, economy, and culture. And yet, across this great distance, I find something familiar about the aspirations, the strains, and the flaws in Fichte's life and thought, and I suspect that academic readers of this book will have a similar reaction. I cannot help thinking that the university ought to have something like the moral mission that Fichte assigned to it, though the visceral democrat in me has no patience with self-appointed clerisies and is skeptical of any claim to privileged moral insight. I admire the depth and the scope of his commitment to academic freedom, and for that very reason I find myself regretting his abuses of that commitment in practice. In Fichte, public candor shaded into a polemical brutality that worked to foreclose deliberation. His construal of himself as the instrument of Reason was not a harmless display of vanity; it licensed him to depersonalize his public self in a way that exempted him from the civic rules of tolerance. It was a posture that threatened to negate the very ideal of publicity in an open society that it was supposed to assert. The same posture would be no less threatening to the rational argumentation of a deliberative democracy in our own times. Fichte was, in that sense, all too faithful to his guiding principle.

It must also be said that, in certain moments of crisis, he was not faithful enough. He abandoned principle for the practice of political prudence and thus became, ineptly and without admitting it to himself or to others, complicit with the power he was committed to defying. There is another warning here: as he practiced it, philosophical reflexivity precluded the self-knowledge that would have required him to face up to this failure. And yet, even as I indulge the impulse to be judgmental, I find it hard to condemn him. In his academic world, after all, complicity with power, and especially with the power of the state, was a condition of survival. Both in principle and in practice, Fichte was far more resistant to the imperatives of complicity than were most of his contemporaries in German academe.

Is the difference between Fichte and us that two centuries later, we enjoy the kind of academic freedom – the *right* to submit power in all its forms to relentless critical scrutiny – that he championed but sometimes fell short of practicing? Or is it simply that in the intricately self-justifying conventions of our professional lives, we have accepted a more accommodating notion of what the scholar's calling entails? The question cannot be answered historically. It is still worth asking.

Index

Abrams, M. H., 13
academic freedom, 377–44, 441–2
    and corporate self-government, 235–6
    and secret Orders, 250–9
    position of Weimar government on, 266–7,
        420–1
    See also censorship; universities, German;
        Wissenschaft
Academy of Sciences, Berlin, 137
Achelis, Henrich Nikolaus, 33
agrarian law, 120, 320
alienation, 98, 100, 378, 428
Anabaptism, 106, 203
Anna Amalia, Duchess, 234
antisemitism, 12, 192
    and capitalism, 141
    and commercialization, 146
    and the Enlightenment, 137–45, 147–9
    and Fichte, 3, 20, 131–49, 434
    German, 134–5
    in Kant's thought, 134–5, 148
    See also Judaism
aristocracy:
    and Countess Luise von Krockow, 169
    culture of, 55
    ethos of, 35–6
    Fichte's disapproval of, 31, 42, 283
    and French Revolution, 282
    ideal of personality of, 52–3
    interest of, 109
    and lineage, 33
    marriage in, 174
    patronage of, 57
    and privilege, 84
    Rahn family's view of, 153
    Rehberg's relationship to, 102, 107
    role in salons, 231
    and social hierarchy, 29–31
    sociability of, 39, 165
    wealth of, 49
    and universities, 236, 250
asceticism:
    and the calling, 203
    in Fichte's courtship of Johanna, 157
    in Fichte's Kantianism, 77, 386
    in Fichte's personality, 51
    and sexuality, 354

in Transcendental Philosophy, 205
    and work, 145, 439
    See also calling; self, selfhood
Ascher, Saul, 132–8, 148
atheism:
    and Fichte, 71, 299, 370–1, 374–6, 379–80,
        383–7, 394–5, 402–6, 413–15, 423, 427
    and Forberg, 373
    and students, 418
    See also Atheism Conflict
Atheism Conflict, 2, 14, 15, 299, 428
    and censorship, 422
    Fichte's role in, 368–424
    Jacobi's contribution to, 388–401
    Orthodox reaction to, 381
    Rehberg's contribution to, 385
    Reinhold's reaction to, 412
Aufklärung, see Enlightenment, German
authenticity, 164, 166, 168, 268

Babeuf, Gracchus, 120, 320
Bastholm, Christian, 157
Beccaria, Cesare, 310–11
Becke, Johann Karl von der, 256–8
Bekehrung, see conversion
Berchtolsheim, President von, 243
Berlin, Isaiah, 318
Bildung, 108, 224, 277
    in Fichte's courtship of Johanna Rahn,
        158
    in Fichte's sermon drafts, 68–9
    and Herder, 31–2, 42–3
    and Humboldt, 221–5, 313
    in ideal of marriage, 358
    and Schiller, 221, 293
    See also Humboldt, Wilhelm von; Schiller,
        Friedrich
Böttiger, Carl August, 241, 266
Bright, Capitaine von, 31
Burgsdoff, Christoph Gottlob von, 54, 56–8
Bürgertum, 52, 165
    bourgeois ethos of, 153, 429
    and freemasonry, 250
    and friendship, 32
    Fichte's relationship to, 9, 38–42, 55, 150
    and Jews, 133, 138, 141–5
    marriage in, 72–6, 346, 359, 368